THE COLONIAL AMERICAN JEW 1492-1776

THE
COLONIAL
AMERICAN
JEW
1492–1776

JACOB R. MARCUS

Hebrew Union College

Jewish Institute

of Religion

VOLUME II

WAYNE STATE

UNIVERSITY PRESS

DETROIT

1970

CONTENTS

[*v*]

Contents

Contents

Contents

[viii]

Contents

Contents

[x]

ILLUSTRATIONS

[*xi*]

PART VI

THE ECONOMIC ACTIVITY OF THE JEW

IN BRITISH NORTH AMERICA

CHAPTER 26

BACKGROUND FOR THE NORTH

AMERICAN ECONOMY

The Economic Background of the Jew
in Europe

With exceedingly few exceptions, Jewish immigrants to these shores in the seventeenth and eighteenth centuries were Europeans. Asians were practically unknown. Most of the immigrants were Central Europeans who had been businessmen or had come from regions where Jews were engaged in some form of commerce and trade. In Eastern Europe, it is true, the pattern of occupational distribution differed somewhat from that in Central Europe. The Jews of the lands beyond the Vistula were frequently innkeepers, leaseholders, and stewards of estates, but few Russian, Lithuanian, or Polish Jews came as far west as America prior to the nineteenth century. The typical Jewish immigrant to eighteenth century America was a German who had been raised in a village or small town where Jews were characteristically peddlers, cattle dealers, shopkeepers, petty moneylenders and pawnbrokers, traders and brokers. To be sure, craftsmen were not uncommon, and Jews who lived near the Polish border were often enough, like their Polish brethren, petty distillers and innkeepers.

Eighteenth century German Jewry also included in its ranks merchants who participated in the overland export and import trade and traveled to the large fairs to buy and sell. A few Jews of Spanish-Portuguese origin, living in German territory on the Baltic and North Sea shores, were merchant-shippers like their fellow Sephardim on the Atlantic littoral and the Mediterranean. The mercantile aristocrats among the Jews of the German lands were the *Hofjuden*, the rich and competent court Jews who enjoyed close relations with the rulers at various German courts and served them as army purveyors, jewelers, merchants, and bankers. As the century moved forward a few enterprising individuals moved on with it into industry, textile manufacturing, finance, and banking. The Rothschilds, for instance, typified the rise of large-scale Jewish businessmen in Europe. Thus, though the German and East European Jews who came to America were not themselves men of affairs, they had been trained to think in large terms. They had grown up in a century of vast economic expansion in which Jews had played no insignificant part. The Jewish Simsons of New York had come from the money markets of Holland and Frankfort on the Main, while the Gratzes hailed from Upper Silesia, a core trading area linking together Eastern and Central Europe.[1]

In both an economic and a political sense, Europe was moving forward. Jews could hope for a future on that continent; there was no compulsion to leave. France and England had come to entertain national and imperialistic hopes and were extending themselves to build worldwide self-sufficient empires. Both kingdoms were rapidly developing socioeconomic structures which were basically opposed to the medieval limitations of the craft and merchant guilds and which sought in varying degrees to circumscribe the privileges of the clergy and nobility and to undermine the last bastions of feudalism. A number of Central European states also nourished dynastic ambitions. In need of money to strengthen their armies and their civil services, and eager for taxable industry and taxable industrialists, even the Jew-baiting states of German-speaking Central Europe were like France, her monolithic Catholicism notwithstanding, content to encourage a measure of Jewish entrepreneurial activity. The young Jewish businessman without capital, looking for larger opportunity and cherishing some lust for adventure, might turn his face to the Far West, to America, but the typical European Jew either remained at home, moved into the larger cities, or crossed the channel to industrial England.

Because they found Jewish economic capacity useful, forward-looking statesmen both on the continent and in England made it possible for Jews to participate in the commercial and industrial revolutions. But of all the lands that tolerated Jews, England was the most liberal. England's toleration of industrious foreigners, including Jews, was conditioned, as we have already indicated, by her economic-political philosophy of protectionist or exclusionist mercantilism. In the final analysis the aspiring London merchant and the landed aristocrat who often joined forces with him craved power and wealth; they understood that in the world of the 1700's wealth was to be achieved primarily through manufacturing and foreign trade. If industry was to be furthered at home, the state had to have easy and unlimited access to cheap raw materials. If England was not to be at the mercy of her rivals, in particular the Dutch, the French, and the Spaniards, she had to have timber, naval stores, sugar, potash, tobacco, rice, indigo, furs, hides, oils, flax, hemp, silk, and wines. Colonies able to supply her with these commodities would render her nearly self-sufficient and capable of competing successfully in foreign markets. The ideal system was to barter the raw materials of the colonies against English manufactures. The colonies would then have a market for their products, while in its turn the mother country would pay for colonial imports with finished goods.

This mutually advantageous system would work, of course, only if the colonies were barred from engaging in manufacturing, except in primary stages like the production of pig and bar iron. In order to effectuate this master plan, in the mid-1600's England had begun issuing a series of acts of trade and navigation serving to control foreign trade with her empire. Goods of foreign manufacture bound for markets in British America had to be channeled through England, while aliens were kept out of the carrying trade by laws limiting shipping to British and colonial vessels. It became mandatory for certain raw materials from the English colonies to be shipped to the mother country. The colonies were very important in this scheme, but to produce they needed reliable, industrious, and loyal immigrants. Along with Protestant groups from the continent, Jews were deemed such and were encouraged to participate in the economic life of the transatlantic colonies. It was England's severely realistic approach that helped develop her empire in the eighteenth century.[2]

A man could not play his part in the colonies unless he fitted into the scheme of productivity. He had to produce goods as a farm or craft laborer, or he had to become a link in the chain whereby colonial commodities were transmitted to the commercial and industrial mother country. The Jews of North America were not primarily farmers or craftsmen, and very few of them were active in the professions. They functioned in the colonial economy as shopkeepers, merchants, and shippers, bringing in foreign wares, selling them, and shipping out the raw materials they had secured in exchange.

North American Commerce during the Eighteenth Century

The Jewish part in the colonial economy is to be understood only against the eighteenth century background of North American commercial and mercantile life. American Jews numbered two or three thousand souls during the 1700's, in marked contrast to the preceding century when there had been but two or three hundred.

We have already indicated the extent to which imperial legislation—directed unerringly toward the aggrandizement of the mother country—limited commerce, trade, and industry in British North America. But this does not tell the whole story, for America was a pioneer country on the frontier of a far more highly developed Europe. Apart from and in addition to the transatlantic flow, trade was carried on in every American town and village, although in many instances, to be sure, the capital involved was pitifully small. Farmers were visited by foot and horse peddlers, but most of the yeomen went to the nearest town to make their purchases. The villages harbored shopkeepers and merchants of different degrees, so that a small town might shelter a large merchant, while petty shopkeepers abounded in the largest cities. The most important merchants, those who imported their goods from abroad—often in their own ships—lived in the coastal towns on the tidewater rivers. Nearly all who kept stores dealt in goods of three types: soft, hard, and wet. The soft or dry goods were textiles of English manufacture or transmission; the hard goods were English iron, steel, copper, and brass products; the wet goods were rum, wines, and brandies.

Country storekeepers and even urban businessmen bartered their wares for produce, provisions, livestock, or any manufacture the farmer and his family had produced in their leisure hours. Frequently the country shopkeeper shipped or carted his produce to a larger town and credited it to his account with the city merchant to whom he was indebted. The wars which proliferated during the century before the Revolution made army supply and purveying important elements on the economic scene, and privateering was another war-inspired enterprise of promise. With an eye on the sea, ambitious and energetic merchants speculated in buying shares in privateers —when they had any hazard capital left over after buying lottery tickets.

With the French defeat in 1763 and English assumption of hegemony in Canada and the transallegheny west, the fur trade—the Indian trade—beckoned to a host of venturesome businessmen who tapped the fur resources of the entire Mississippi basin. Punitive land payments assessed on marauding Indians and purchases, often enough of dubious legality, of large tracts of wilderness paved the way for land speculation and for grandiose colonization schemes, primarily in the Ohio valley.

Even though the colonists were primarily agricultural—or because they were—commerce and trade were important. No small proportion of the capital needed for new enterprises and much of the wealth in the country were developed through commerce or made possible by it. Farmers and planters were as dependant on maritime commerce and the merchant marine as were shopkeepers and merchants. Trade and shipping helped build the wharves and warehouses of the coastal cities which came to rank among the largest English-speaking towns in the British Empire. Even during the seventeenth century the growth of colonial commerce was simply tremendous.[3]

"Language," said Coleridge, "is the armory of the human mind; and . . . contains the trophies of its past." Some hint of the difficulties of colonial life still lingers on in the fact that Americans refer even today to the overland transportation of goods as "shipping." Because of the bad roads or the absence of passable roads in many areas, shipping or receiving commodities in the narrow coastal strip which was seventeenth and eighteenth century America depended to a very large extent on creeks, rivers, and the Atlantic Ocean. The ocean was the great highway for commerce, and interprovincial scarcely less than overseas trade was carried on by boat in bottoms owned by the British or by the colonials themselves. This coastwise interprovincial trade bulked large in American commerce, though to be sure, not as large as the combined overseas and West Indian trade.[4]

The holds and decks of coastal sloops were loaded with European manufactures, West Indian staples, and American products transported from the major American ports to other American harbors, to smaller river towns, or even to the wharves of tidewater farms and plantations. Purchasers—shopkeepers and planters—who had no vessels of their own relied on the coastal trade for their supplies. There was much regional trade. Boston, Newport, and Salem provided for the needs of central and northern New England; New York City, for her own hinterland as well as Canada and neighboring Connecticut and eastern New Jersey. Below New York, Philadelphia supplied Delaware, western New Jersey, and the Pennsylvania backcountry. The Chesapeake Bay area, characterized in colonial times by the absence of good-sized towns—and of Jews—was another region involved in the coastal trade of Philadelphia. Farther south, Charleston saw to the needs of South Carolina and neighboring North Carolina, Georgia, and after 1763, the Floridas. The coastal and interprovincial trade was of least importance in the relatively isolated South. There the British merchants traded with the plantation owners either directly or through factors who carried stocks of goods, and the merchants or their agents supplied European wares in exchange for the tobacco, rice, or indigo of the southern farmers.

While the Southerners secured a living from their plantations, many New Englanders sustained themselves on the ocean, and for them the coastal and interprovincial trade of the New England and Middle Atlantic provinces was crucially important. The different merchant-shippers from Boston south to Philadelphia were competitive, often selling and shipping the same European wares and even the same local commodities. What on occasion prompted merchant buyers to seek goods from a distant rather than a local supplier was that particular items were in short supply locally or more attractive credit terms were offered in more remote towns. Northern shippers peddled out of their ports up the various rivers and bays of the South, selling, bartering, and trading. They supplied farmers and planters with textiles and hardware from Europe and with American or West Indian rum and staples in exchange for lumber, naval stores, tobacco, rice, and indigo from the local shopkeepers and plantation owners. The cargoes thus accumulated were either used in the colonies, traded in the West Indies, or sent over to England.[5]

Though the great bulk of their trading was with England, the West Indies, and the lands of the Caribbean and the Spanish Main, the American colonists, eager to advance their own ends, carried on a foreign and not infrequently extralegal commerce with a number of continental European lands, especially Holland, Portugal, and Spain. They were in constant touch, too, with the islands off the African coast, the Azores, the Canaries, and the Madeiras, and with the slave coasts of Africa herself. Such foreign commerce was essential, especially to the Middle Atlantic and northern provinces.

Under the protectionist system she had developed, England was determined to channel needed colonial raw materials into her own markets. Still, much that North America produced, such as cereals, meat, and fish, could find neither entrance nor acceptance in British ports, for the mother country was equally concerned to protect her own farmers, fisheries, and processors. The colonists were directed to supply England with timber, naval stores, furs, whale oil and fins, bar and pig iron, tobacco, sugar, molasses, rum, cocoa, hardwoods, and dyewoods. Such a system benefited some colonies far more than others.[6]

The arrangement to trade English manufactures for colonial staples was very acceptable to the plantation owner of the American South, and in consequence there were close ties between the southern farmer and his British supplier. Serving as an agent, the merchant in London sold the crops of his American planter client and in turn supplied him with all his needs. Accounts were kept open for years. Little scope was thus afforded for large American merchants in many parts of the South, where there were few large-sized towns, less coastal trade, and not much industry.

The arrangement was considerably less advantageous to the

Middle Atlantic provinces, primarily New York and Pennsylvania, which commonly found in England only the meagerest of markets for their foodstuffs. These colonies had perforce to engage actively in foreign trade to secure the means to pay for the finished wares the English sent them. Foreign commerce thus assumed sizeable proportions; in 1772 about 700 ships cleared the port of New York alone, many headed for foreign lands.

More so, however, even than the Middle Atlantic colonies, the New England provinces were involved in commerce. Ever since the middle 1600's Boston, Newport, and Salem had been engaged in shipping along the American coast, to the West Indies, and to various European ports, trading American provisions and raw materials for foreign staples. The better grades of New England fish found ready markets in southern Europe and in the West Indies, whose planters used them for their own tables; the poorer grades were sold to feed the slaves of the West Indies.[7]

MANUFACTURING AND SHIPPING IN NORTH AMERICA

The northern commercial provinces constantly faced the prospect of an adverse trade balance in relation to the British for, as has been noted, the New Englanders, New Yorkers, and Pennsylvanians had few native products which the English sought. One way the Americans might have escaped this impasse was to suspend purchases from the mother country and to develop their own manufacturing. Of course the British prohibited this; the Americans were not permitted to manufacture textiles, apparel, steel, and the like. But the Americans did manage to manufacture some commodities, either for their own needs or to augment their meager supply of currency and foreign exchange. They turned lumber into barrelheads, staves, and hoops to provide containers for tobacco and for a variety of food products and other native commodities. Surplus woods were turned into potash and pearl ash. They processed tobacco and indigo. The colonists also packed and shipped meat and fish, made candles out of whale head matter, and occupied themselves extensively with the manufacture of rum.

Ships were needed to distribute products of the soil and the sea, as well as domestic manufactures, to other American provinces, the West Indies, Europe, and Africa, and so the northern provinces began to develop a substantial shipbuilding industry of their own. As a result the share of the empire's carrying trade which fell to the lot of the colonies became rather considerable; about one-third of all British shipping was American-built. Ships that carried a cargo to England were often sold there, the captains and crews returning to America on other vessels or receiving compensation in lieu of transportation.[8]

Owing to the empire's trade and navigation acts, no problem offered greater difficulties than the problem of securing hard cash or good bills or foreign valuta. If obeyed, these acts limited shippers almost exclusively to the confines of the markets in England and her colonies, a hardship because of the congenitally adverse trade balance obtaining on this side of the Atlantic. Colonial shippers were thus impelled to disdain no expedient to secure specie or products acceptable to the English. They engaged in coastwise and interprovincial trading and shipping, carried freight to many parts of the Atlantic basin, built and sold ships, and were active in the industries tolerated by the empire. The most obvious method of solving their problem was to peddle off their northern cargoes in diverse regions and lands and to take in exchange specie or goods acceptable to the English. Thus they found it necessary to engage in various forms of roundabout or overseas commerce, following a series of routes to the West Indies, Africa, or Europe. It was only by this circuitous method—the "triangular trade"—that they were able to rid themselves of their surplus products and to pay the English merchants enough to keep them pacified.[9]

These are the reasons why colonial merchants sent their ships to southern Europe and the Wine Islands (the Azores, Canaries, and Madeiras) with rice, fish, and grains, bringing back wines which were in heavy demand on this side of the Atlantic. Trade with the Mediterranean continued to grow. Cereals, provisions, and lumber were exchanged in Europe for fruits, salt, spices, textiles, and wines. To the English, of course, the colonies continued shipping staples from the American South and the West Indies.[10]

Commerce with the west coast of Africa was typical of the circuitous trading pursued by American merchants. Molasses from the West Indies was manufactured into rum which in turn, along with New England provisions, was traded on the Guinea Coast for slaves, gold dust, and ivory. The slaves were then transported in specially constructed slave ships to the West Indies where they were sold for cash or bills, or for another cargo of molasses. The molasses was sold in the North, or if necessary, distilled into rum for another trip to Africa; the cash or bills ended up in the tills of English creditors. There were, however, few if any regularly scheduled runs in this triangular traffic.

Second only to trade with Great Britain was the West Indian market. This was most vital for the Americans. Whether English, French, Dutch, or Spanish, the islands welcomed the cereals, meat, fish, cattle, horses, lumber, casks, and prefabricated houses the North made available, for West Indian agricultural production focussed almost exclusively on sugar and its associated industries of molasses and rum. The islanders were rich enough to pay for what they bought, although they were often deplorably slow in meeting their obligations. There were other products of the islands and the Spanish Main in which the Americans trafficked: cocoa, mahogany, dyewoods, indigo, and even some cotton. The trade with the West Indies was important, for it enabled the American colonists to sell their supplies and products, helped spur on their shipping industry and carrying trade, built the rum industry, created towns, engendered wealth and prosperity, and made it possible for the North to repay its English creditors, thereby promoting the economic self-sufficiency of the empire.[11]

Bearing this in mind, we may proceed now to a detailed analysis of the Jewish involvement in colonial economic life.

CHAPTER 27

AGRICULTURE, RANCHING, CRAFTS,

AND PROFESSIONS

AGRICULTURE

Most of the people who came to the colonies expected to farm. Even in New England, America's most highly developed commercial and industrial area, over ninety percent of the people were engaged in agriculture. In that respect, however, the Jews were exceptional. As a group, as a people, they had not been farmers since their departure, over a millennium before, from the ancestral homeland in Palestine. In agrarian feudal Europe, Jews had never been farm-bred serfs tied to the land. As non-military city dwellers, they had lacked any desire to become manorial lords. As Jews, in any case, they had generally been denied agrarian functions in a politico-economic system closely intertwined with Christian religious tradition; in some parts of Europe landowning had been prohibited to them. By law, then, and by training, inclination, and the force of historic circumstance, Jews were divorced from the soil.[1]

This was the general situation but, to be sure, exceptions had obtained all through the Middle Ages and early modern centuries. Spanish Jewry had participated in agriculture, and many Jews settled in the villages of Central and Eastern Europe were exposed to the dominant rural economy. If Jews could not buy land, they could lease it, and some did become excellent farmers. Even village dwellers learned to garden in their backyards. In America there was nothing to prevent Jews from going back to the soil, but few in fact cared to settle down on a farmstead amidst non-Jews, some of whom cherished the weirdest attitudes toward them. Few Jews were drawn to the edge of America's primitive and hazardous frontier when they could remain in the towns and enjoy the urban amenities to which the preceding fifteen centuries had habituated them. Even when Jews could afford to buy plantations, they frequently declined to do so, in all probability believing they would be rejected by their more pretentious and aristocratically-inclined neighbors. The elder William Pitt, defending alien-born English Jews in 1753 against the charge that if naturalized they would buy too many estates, replied with some justice that "they are not likely to become great purchasers of land, for they love their money and can employ it to much better advantage in trade." What Pitt had overlooked was that other basic considerations of a social and religious character moved the Jews whom he championed. He had perhaps failed to appreciate the fact that as Jews they could not survive without a synagogue and schools and Jewish friendships.[2]

There was, in any event, no need for Jews to rusticate on a farmstead; they could nearly always manage to make a living of some sort in a town and at worst could move into a village that was not too far from a Jewish metropolis. With rare but some notable exceptions, then, the Jews who came to the American mainland colonies in the seventeenth and eighteenth centuries did not come seeking cheap land and the chance to build a new life as tillers of the soil.

Jewish immigrants, it is true, often bought farms and unimproved lands, but the fact that a man made such purchases is no proof that he was a farmer. Many bought acreage for purely speculative purposes, and when Samuel Judah acquired from Franklin and Underhill two rights of land in what is today Vermont, he certainly had no intention of settling down on the New Hampshire frontier. Mathias Bush may have been listed in the tax duplicate as an owner of 150 acres in Chestnut Hill Township near Philadelphia, but the land lay fallow. On occasion Jewish businessmen came into possession of farms when mortgages were foreclosed, and it happened in some of the colonies, especially in Maryland, South Carolina, and Georgia, that Jewish settlers received grants of land as headrights for themselves, their children, their servants, and their slaves. As we have seen, this was particularly true in Georgia where practically every settler received tillage lots and land grants upon application.[3]

Very few dirt farmers were found among the first Jewish settlers, certainly less than five percent. Yet it is fairly certain there were some wherever Jews settled. Following a pattern which characterized the generality of the settlers, Jews who farmed attempted to supplement the meager income derived from the soil by engaging in other activities. John (Jacob) Lumbrozo of seventeenth century Maryland was a tobacco planter, but also a physician, a merchant, an attorney, an appraiser, an innkeeper, and an Indian trader. In the next century John Franks of Quebec was both a farmer and a businessman.[4]

Newport merchant-shippers like Naphtali and Isaac Hart, Aaron Lopez, and Jacob R. Rivera bought and operated farms; the Harts at Tiverton and Scituate, Lopez and Rivera at Portsmouth not far from Newport. The Harts had tenants, and it is not known to what extent their holdings served their firm Naphtali Hart & Co., but Lopez and his father-in-law Rivera closely integrated their farm into their various economic enterprises, even though it had originally been purchased for purposes of recreation. The Lopez-Rivera farm was run by an overseer, and laborers along with an occasional Negro slave were employed. The property was managed rationally and scientifically, and was constantly improved by its owners, whom it served as a source for agricultural produce and as a stock and feeding lot, primarily for sheep which were raised for meat or sent on the hoof to the West Indies. As a typical merchant-shipper, Lopez reached out commercially and industrially in all directions to secure supplies, to cut down expenses, and to enhance profits.[5]

In the Middle Atlantic provinces, too, there were Jews interested in farming—members of the Hays clan for instance. David Hays farmed in New Jersey during the 1740's; his nephews Michael and David of Westchester County, New York, reversed the norm of occupational progression. Apparently beginning as shopkeepers and merchants, they ended up as yeomen. An interesting couple were Abraham and Feiga Cassell (Kasscle), possibly converts to Christianity, who lived among the Pennsylvania Dutch in Uppersalford Township near Philadelphia. One may assume that after their conversion, if indeed they were not birthright Christians, they came over with a group of fellow Germans and made their living as farmers.[6]

Where Jews were concerned, the occupational situation in Georgia was unique. The Jews who sailed up the Savannah River in 1733 came as colonists. Having purchased or more likely been given land, they were expected to farm, and most if not all of them did so at first. There can be no question that they were determined to go back to the soil and some, depending on their training, aptitude, and enterprise, were successful. But as the colony itself deteriorated due to the characteristic hardships of pioneer life, the Jewish settlers, like their non-Jewish fellows, stole away. The two families that remained, the Minises and the Sheftalls, supplemented their agricultural activities with business interests; they were farm owners, ranchers, and merchants.[7]

PLANTERS

Anxious to maintain religious and social relations with their co-religionists, as we indicated above Jews with means were commonly hesitant to invest their capital in farms where they would be isolated from their own group. There were exceptions, however. Isaac Miranda, an ambitious and well-to-do convert to Christianity, operated a sizeable farm in Lancaster County during the first quarter of the eighteenth century. Another landowner was the Canadian Jewish "seigneur" Aaron Hart of Three Rivers, ultimately to own several seigneuries in whole or part. Hart's lands and fiefs, however, came into his hands in postrevolutionary times during the late eighteenth century. They were investments for him, for prior to 1776 he was interested primarily in commerce, not farming, though he had begun to buy real estate as early as 1764.[8]

The word "plantation" is of frequent occurrence in records touching on Southern land grants, but where it appears it designates a farm, *not* an ante-bellum cotton latifundium with hundreds or thousands of acres and dozens of slaves. The Jewish farmers of mid-eighteenth century Georgia probably cultivated at most a few hundred acres with a handful of slaves. Typical was the farm of the convert Joseph Ottolenghe, the first owner of what was to become in later generations the famous Heritage Plantation. Though the grants that Ottolenghe received over the years amounted to hundreds if not thousands of acres, he started out with a 100-acre homestead which he called Exon or Exonia in memory of Exeter, England, where he had once lived. Still, while latifundia were exceedingly rare, there were some middle-sized plantations, if one may judge from the fact that Minises, Nunezes, and Lucenas farmed with from fifteen to twenty slaves.[9]

The Jews of South Carolina seem to have engaged sporadically in planting. It is impossible to determine whether Emanuel Marques ever farmed the thousand acres he received from the provincial proprietors in 1704, but four years later Moses Madina (Modina) owned and very probably farmed a plantation on Goosecreek. In 1714 Simon Valentine and Mordecai Nathan ran a 500-acre farm about twenty-two miles out of Charleston and were eager to make it pay. By 1758 Joseph Tobias, merchant and founding father of present-day South Carolina Jewry, owned a tract of 950 acres, but there is no indication that he ever turned to agriculture as a way of life. One Jewish planter who did engage in large-scale farming was the young South Carolina aristocrat Francis Salvador who grew indigo on his 6,000-acre plantation and worked some thirty slaves.

THE GEORGIA EXPERIMENT IN VINE GROWING

Viniculture had been a major consideration in the establishment of Georgia whose sponsors hoped that a colony able to grow grapes and produce wines would relieve mercantile-minded England of her reliance on the Wine Islands and the viniferous countries of southern Europe. The trustees of the colony thought themselves well on the way to achieving this goal when they secured the services of Abraham De Lyon, a Portuguese Jew who had been reared among the vineyards of Portugal. Apparently a competent vigneron, De Lyon brought over some choice cuttings from Portugal, began to plant in 1734 or 1735, simultaneously augmenting his income by some trading, and by 1737 had produced some beautiful translucent grapes as big as a man's thumb. De Lyon entertained great hopes for the industry. He expected in a few years to have 40,000 vines and to produce wine of the Porto or Malaga type for sale to the settlers at a modest price. Declaring that he had invested £400 sterling of his personal estate in this project and needed more money, De Lyon appealed for a grant to the trustees who, convinced that his experiment offered great promise, were quite willing to help him. But, even though he taught others to plant, nothing came of this attempt to create a new industry, except complaints that the aid promised by the trustees was withheld by Oglethorpe, that white help was too expensive, and that Negro slave labor was not tolerated. When the colony declined about 1741, De Lyon left with most of the others, and his vines were relinquished to one of the German Protestant newcomers.[10]

RANCHING

Cataloguing the various stages through which America passed before she achieved industrialization, historians of the economic scene list hunting, ranching, and farming. Actually, farming was always basic in the early days, while hunting and ranching were ancillary to tillage.

All along the Atlantic coast farmers ran cattle and raised horses in the backcountry adjacent to their holdings, but not as full-time ranchers in the sense that the American West of the nineteenth and twentieth centuries has imparted to the term. Asser Levy of New York was a partner in the goat business, but this may have been a dairy rather than a ranching enterprise. He traded his sheep for lumber, and there is no evidence that he was in any sense a rancher. Isaac Miranda of eastern Pennsylvania, who held thousands of acres of land in that province and in neighboring New Jersey, did have a few horses pastured in the woods, but it would be hyperbolic to call him a rancher.[11]

In the South, however, there were Jews who engaged in ranching systematically and on a relatively large scale. The many-sided Dr. Lumbrozo of Maryland raised hogs and cattle in 1658, and his brand was duly noted in the provincial archives, but it was Georgia in particular that produced Jewish ranchers. The hundreds of acres granted Jewish settlers in Georgia were used for ranching purposes; to judge from the fact that some of them sought and secured ad-

joining tracts, it may well be that they pooled their resources. Georgian Jews raised horses and cattle for the local markets and for export to the nearby West Indies. Mordecai Sheftall maintained a cowpen or ranch on Horsecreek in St. George's Parish near Augusta, and possibly one or two others. His cattle and that of his young children grazed on his lands and on the neighboring public land. Mordecai also cultivated hay or grain, probably for supplementary feeding, and raised some hogs and dairy cows. We know from the "Georgia Marks and Brands Book" that he employed the brand 5S on the ranch of his five children, a holding originally stocked with 264 head of black-horned cattle. Mordecai's brother Levi used the brand L diamond S for his own stock and S3 for his children's. Abraham and Abigail Minis employed the initials A.M. Abraham must have had extensive ranch holdings, for at his death he left his horses and mares to his sons and his cattle to his daughters, with his wife inheriting the rest of his estate.

Jewish businessmen generally looked with favor on ranch investments, because ranches required little labor in an economy where labor was scarce and expensive. Jewish cattlemen did not follow the frontier, however. They owned cowpens on the fringe of settlement, but they themselves lived in the larger cities, administering their holdings with hired hands and partners.[12]

CRAFTSMEN

Jewish craftsmen in colonial America, one does well to bear in mind, in most cases came from Europe where Jews had long been denied admittance to the craft and merchant guilds. This policy of exclusion was reflected in a letter the Dutch West India Company addressed to Peter Stuyvesant on June 14, 1656, instructing him that "Jews or Portuguese people however . . . shall not be permitted [in New Amsterdam] to establish themselves as mechanics which they are not allowed to do in this city [of Amsterdam]." Still, the Jews who came to these shores were not without skills or traditions in the crafts, since the fact was that in most parts of Europe, particularly Eastern Europe, the craft guilds were not strong enough to crush Jewish craftsmen, and at times Jews had their own guilds. Even in Central Europe, where the crafts had always been strong, there were trades and areas of manual skills which escaped a monopolistic organization, and these were the interstices into which Jews crawled.[13]

The ghetto always had its craftsmen in nearly every area of industrial activity. By the eighteenth century the craft guilds had begun to break down, and it was no longer so difficult for a Jew to learn a trade if he was sufficiently interested. Many did learn. Europe at that time had many skilled Jewish workingmen, and in the rising economy of that century they found their opportunity. A clever engraver like Aron Isak, for example, was one of the first Jews invited to settle in Sweden, which prior to that time had been closed to nearly all Jewish immigrants. On the whole Jewish craftsmen could do well in Europe, and yet some of them came to these shores. Perhaps they sought adventure, more opportunity, less competition, a land of wider tolerance. Then again, perhaps they were not highly skilled by European standards and believed that here in a less advanced country, which moreover lacked sufficient craftsmen, their work would be acceptable. Whatever the reasons, some did come, and from the 1680's on there were a number of men skilled in trades among the Jewish freemen listed in New York.[14]

Of course, not all craftsmen were immigrants. The most famous eighteenth century American Jewish craftsman, the silversmith Myer Myers, was a native New Yorker. Other natives, too, learned trades, for in New York at least a man could become a freeman if he practiced a craft. Once a freeman, he could open his own shop and thus become an artisan shopkeeper like his European prototype.[15]

Among the earliest craftsmen were the butchers, for Jews had to have kosher meat. Asser Levy, who came to New Amsterdam in 1654, was a butcher and probably served the small Jewish group in that capacity. All through the seventeenth and eighteenth centuries there were Jewish butchers, although the Jewish community frequently permitted Gentiles to cut and sell the meat slaughtered by the Jewish religious functionary qualified to do that job.[16]

Inasmuch as the names and careers of some men inevitably fail to crop up in the documents, one cannot know all the crafts in which Jews were represented. Among the best sources are the records of the city of New York where the avocations of freemen are listed. The Jewish craftsmen there included chandlers and soapmakers, sealing-wax makers and watchmakers, saddlers and shoemakers, wig-makers, bakers, and tailors. Levy Marks (*né* Lippman Schneider) of Lancaster and Philadelphia was a tailor well-known in Jewish circles. In 1777 he applied to the Continental Congress for the job of su-perintending the making of army uniforms. There were Jewish tailors in other colonies also. Maryland had at least two, perhaps three, during the 1750's in Annapolis and Anne Arundel County. A gen-eration later Isaac Nunez Cardozo, one of the first of his clan in the North American colonies, practicing his craft at Newport, ad-vertised himself as a New York tailor.[17]

Among the artisans in the country was Lazarus Isaacs of Lan-caster County, Pennsylvania, a glass cutter and engraver for Henry William Stiegel, the founder of the Stiegel glass factory. Some of Stiegel's products, which are now very much sought after by antique collectors, were handled in the Lancaster area by Jewish shopkeepers like Meyer Josephson, Barnard Jacobs, and Benjamin Nathan. Bos-ton, New York, and Maryland sheltered Jewish tobacconists, snuff-makers, and distillers. Abraham Isaac Abrahams of New York pur-sued two vocations at the same time, distilling and "tobacco manu-facture." [18]

During King George's War, when Oglethorpe made his head-quarters at Frederica, Georgia, as he advanced to attack the Spanish in Florida, a Jew reportedly showed his soldiers how to make temporary shelters. One of the Gomezes advertised that he was prepared to quicksilver old looking glasses and to take the stains out of them, though instead of doing this type of work himself, he may have relied on skilled workmen. Levy Simons, a New York crafts-man, advertised that he worked in gold and silver cloth and in silk, could clean gold and silver lace, and was prepared to remove spots from silk and other types of cloth. David Campanell of a seven-teenth-century Barbados family made his living as a weaver in Ipswich, Massachusetts, and several New Yorkers boasted that they were furriers from London. One of them, in his capacity as skin dresser, considered himself an authority on curing corns. There were, in addition, glaziers, menders of broken china, starchmakers, and a cleanser and grinder of surgical instruments. The cleanser of surgical instruments may also have been a surgeon or barber of sorts.[19]

Isaac Navarro, a humble Sephardic Jew, painted the New York synagogue and also served as its caretaker. In 1748 and 1749 he lived in Annapolis, Maryland, where he made a living as a tobacconist and manufacturer of chocolate. Navarro, who finished out his life as a pensioner of the congregation in New York, may not have been a skilled craftsman, but an incompetent unfortunate, nibbling at any business or job in order to eke out a living. Aaron Lopez of Newport was, in addition to much else as we shall see, a clothing manufacturer, employing seamstresses, among whom were Jewesses.[20]

A craftsman need not have been a poor and humble artisan. Some began very modestly and went on to achieve a measure of success—the skilled gold and silver refiner Isaac Moses from Hanover, for example. (This German immigrant is not to be confused with the far more distinguished New Yorker named Isaac Moses.) He was shipped to Georgia in 1758 and sold as an indentured servant for a period of three years in payment for his passage. Redeemed within a year by the well-known Savannah merchant Mordecai Sheftall, Moses probably remained in the South and made a good living. Chepman Ashers (Ahers) of New York was another smelter and refiner of gold, and like many metalworkers, had learned his trade in Germany.[21]

Silverware was important not only for its utility and beauty, but also for its intrinsic value as collateral, and it figured frequently in the wills of prosperous Jews. Goldsmiths and silversmiths thus generally did very well, and there were Jewish silversmiths in many of the colonies. By 1768 Jacob Moses was practicing this craft in the tiny Jewish community of Savannah, Georgia, and another silversmith, Isaiah Isaacs (so far as we know the first Jew to establish himself in Virginia), ultimately became a well-to-do merchant and a partner in the Richmond firm of Cohen & Isaacs. During the Revolutionary War, Cohen & Isaacs employed Daniel Boone to survey some of their lands on the Licking River in what is today Kentucky. A man named Jacob Cohen (not to be confused with

Jacob I. Cohen of Cohen & Isaacs), who served in the Virginia militia as a cavalry captain, was also a silversmith. Jeremiah Levi, very probably a Jew, worked as a jeweler, silversmith, and engraver in Charles County, Maryland, near Pickawaxon Church. Joseph Jacobs was both a silversmith and a shohet in Newport. Moses Isaacs also carried on the craft in that city and in nearby Swansea, Massachusetts. In the second half of the eighteenth century New York sheltered at least nine or ten such craftsmen.[22]

The Myers brothers of New York, both smiths, seem to have prospered. Asher, who was a brazier and a merchant as well as a coppersmith, soldered the flat copper roofs of the town hall and made or at least sold the bells that tolled on that official building, on the town jail, and in the Exchange Room.[23]

Asher's brother Myer was the best known of the Jewish smiths who worked in precious metals. There can be no question of his competence, for some of his fine pieces have survived to be prized by discriminating collectors, and Myer's customers included notables like Sir William Johnson of Johnson Hall, a superintendent of Indian affairs. At the beginning of the Revolution, Myer Myers had already been elected president of the Gold and Silver Smith's Society in New York. He fashioned alms basins for the First Presbyterian Church in his native New York and a baptismal bowl for the Brick Presbyterian Church of the same city. Sauce boats which Myer made were presented by the Earl of Loudon to Colonel Nathaniel Merserve of New Hampshire for the colonel's good services in the defense of Fort Edward against Montcalm and his Indians during the French and Indian War. Many other beautiful pieces of silver also bear one of Myer's several hallmarks: salvers, spoons, ladles, tea and coffeepots, sugar bowls, buckles, rings, and swords.[24]

Myer's fellow Jews employed him to make surgical appliances for circumcision and silver ornaments to decorate the Scrolls of the Law. Some of the beautiful *rimmonim* (pomegranates or Torah-stave ornaments) he created are still treasured by the old congregations in New York, Newport, and Philadelphia. Though Myers continued practicing his craft for many years, like many another smith he was engaged in a variety of occupations. He was interested in lead mining and land speculation; he was a jewelry jobber and retailer, in all probability buying ready-made some of the jewelry items he sold to retail customers and petty shopkeepers; and at least one occasion found him shipping pearls to London.[25]

In general it would seem, when apprenticing themselves to learn crafts, young Jews leaned toward those that were of a sedentary nature and did not entail hard manual labor. There are no records of Jewish carpenters and blacksmiths.

JEWS IN THE PROFESSIONS

Aside from physicians, surgeons, and congregational employees, there were few professionals among the Jews. It is, of course, a moot question as to whether eighteenth century performing artists were professionals, but such performers did appear occasionally on the American scene. Henry Hymes and Benjamin Abram, both presumably from London, were jugglers and balancers, giving public and private shows. Hymes was particularly skillful, for he was able to balance on his chin nineteen wine glasses—to a height of almost six feet. His fellow artist Abram could boast of having performed before the crowned heads of Europe and promised his audience a dexterity of hand in a manner altogether new, never yet exhibited in any part of America! [26]

Ever since the seventeenth century Jewish settlers had served as interpreters. It was only natural that they should, since many of them were of Spanish or Portuguese origin and had come to America via Holland and England or the English West Indies. Some command of the Iberian vernaculars, as well as Dutch and English, was common among them, and their services were valued. The proliferating commercial traffic between the mainland colonies and the Caribbean, not to mention the vice-admiralty court litigation which throve on privateers bringing in contested prizes, created a need for interpreters in Dutch, Spanish, and Portuguese.

The New York merchant Rodrigo Pacheco served the province as an interpreter in Spanish, and in 1735 Judah Monis, an instructor in Hebrew at Harvard College, was similarly employed when the Massachusetts authorities investigated the case of a vessel lost on the high seas. In a notable lawsuit in Connecticut during the early 1750's, when a Spanish ship laden with silver, gold, cochineal, indigo, wool, chocolate, and hides was salvaged, three Jews were employed as interpreters. Daniel Gomez served the governor and council of New York as a Spanish linguist from 1734 to 1751; and later during the early years of the Revolution, Hyam Solomon (Haym Salomon?) acted as interpreter for the French scientist Dr. Joseph Gerreau. The Newport Jews in particular were active as interpreters in the eighteenth century, especially during the French and Indian War when privateering flourished. In 1774 Aaron Lopez of Newport charged Henry Lloyd of Boston the substantial sum of ten guineas for translating some Portuguese papers to be sent to England. The work was probably done, if not by Aaron himself, then by some member of the numerous Lopez-Rivera clan.[27]

The first specific reference to a Jewish settler in the Carolinas involved the art of translation. In his *New Description of That Fertile and Pleasant Province of Carolina*, Governor John Archdale wrote he had employed a Jew as his interpreter in dealing with some Spanish-speaking Indians from Florida. A generation later during the wars with Spain, the South Carolina merchant Joseph Tobias was called on as a linguist and interpreter when a flag of truce ship arrived from St. Augustine. Tobias had earlier served the British and their fleet at Gibraltar, whence he hailed, in the same capacity. When Georgia collided with the Spanish on her southern frontier in Florida, one of the Portuguese-born Nunezes was asked to call upon his knowledge of Spanish. The Nunez brothers Daniel and Moses seem to have possessed linguistic ability and a taste for public service. Daniel served as a Spanish linguist, and both functioned as Indian interpreters. Actually, they were Indian agents to a considerable degree and as such exerted a great deal of influence on their forest friends. It was their job to pacify the Indians and to keep the borders quiet, which explains why both the Loyalist and Whig governments continued to employ them in negotiations with the Indians. Settlers of their educational background, however, did not limit themselves to one job, craft, or economic activity. A pioneer economy like America's led competent and ambitious men to explore any and every means to supplement their incomes.[28]

SYNAGOGAL AND COMMUNAL EMPLOYEES

Though it is a fact that throughout the prerevolutionary period, Jews were found in the three learned professions of theology, law, and medicine, the term "learned" should not be taken too literally. There were no rabbis or theologians in the country. The functions of such officiants were performed by the hazzan (the "Jew priest" as he was sometimes known to the Gentiles) who served the community as reader or cantor. The hierarchy of salaried Jewish communal officials also included the shohet (ritual slaughterer of cattle and fowl), the shammash or beadle, and the teacher, strictly speaking not an official of the Jewish community, although frequently the recipient of a congregational subsidy for teaching the children of the poor.[29]

In some of the towns, particularly in the hinterland (Northumberland and Lancaster Counties in Pennsylvania are good examples), well-established Jewish merchants would occasionally employ a coreligionist to serve as both shohet and teacher for their families. Such privately employed religious functionaries probably also worked as clerks for their employers, and like their communally employed colleagues, engaged in modest ventures of their own. Practically all communal religious employees devoted their spare time to business of one sort or another. This was true even of those who maintained themselves as congregational "rabbis." [30]

ATTORNEYS AND PHYSICIANS

In the absence of professional lawyers, laymen often served as attorneys during the colonial period. Trained lawyers were few in colonial America, particularly in the early days, due in no small part to the strong and bitter popular prejudice which held both the legal and the medical professions congenitally guilty of unethical practices. Gabriel Thomas expressed no eccentric bias in 1690 when he wrote: "Of lawyers and physicians, I shall say nothing, because this country is very peaceable and healthy. Long may it so continue and never have occasion for the tongue of the one [the lawyer] nor the pen of the other [the physician]—both equally destructive of men's estates and lives." In 1773 Cullen Pollok, a North Carolina planter, paid his compliments to the men of the legal profession in eulogizing a lawyer friend as "a gentleman of the law, possesed of every virtue and of a liberal education. He was the only one of that profession that I ever knew whose acquaintance with the most vilinous part of mankind had not deprived [him] of the feelings of humanity, for the better part, and whose sentiments were as delicate as possible." As late as 1786 the good citizens of Braintree, Massachusetts, recommended that lawyers be restrained in their practice; they tended, it was thought, to destroy rather than to preserve a town.[31]

Still, prejudice was not all that kept legal ranks spare in America. Profits and money were both scarce in the primitive colonial economy, so even in matters of law, thrifty men looked for savings and bargains. Given such conditions as prejudice added to economic scarcity, it is not surprising that knowledgeable amateurs assumed quasi-professional functions, or that litigants found themselves obliged to resort to lay arbitrators. The lay attorney would collect debts, represent his clients in the courts, and generally perform services now usually rendered by professional advocates.

As early as the 1660's the Marylander Lumbrozo served as attorney in a number of cases. One was a morals case in which he was personally involved and represented two of his indentured servants. Margaret Gould, the wife of one of his servants, had been defamed as a woman of ill repute. Dr. Lumbrozo defended her, pointing out that

> Shee lives for ever in eternall shame
> That lives to see the death of her good name.

In that same generation the forceful and able Asser Levy represented clients on more than one occasion. Levy's contemporary David Ferera appeared before the court in New Amsterdam as attorney for a non-Jew, although two years earlier, when Ferera himself had been a defendant, his ignorance of Dutch had compelled him to engage Joseph D'Acosta as his interpreter.[32]

During the following century it was quite common for Jewish businessmen in New York and Newport to serve as attorneys, particularly in admiralty court cases involving clients from the Antilles. In 1720, for instance, New York Jewish merchants represented a group of Curaçaon shippers whose sloop had been illegally seized by American privateers. Many years later Aaron Lopez handled an estate problem in Newport for a Jamaican client.[33]

When Jacob Gomez was sent to Barbados in 1718, his brother Mordecai gave him a general power of attorney "to ask . . . and receive all such . . . sums of money, debts, goods . . . belonging to me." Though in this instance we lack details of any specific action to be taken, we know that in general, whether one served as an attorney for others or authorized others to serve as attorneys, collecting a debt was the prime concern. Mordecai Gomez had designated Jacob as his "true and lawfull attorney," but not infrequently the one so empowered was a non-Jew, as when Isaac De Medina commissioned Joseph Bigelow of Hartford to sue and collect a debt for him in that city. Usually, however, Jews turned to Jews for such services because they knew each other. Thus David Gomez of New York was authorized by a London merchant to secure payment for a bill from a Kinderhook merchant, and Isaac Hart of Newport was empowered to sue a London Jewish merchant—who incidentally may have been his brother! Manuel Josephson of New York gave Samuel Jacobs of Quebec the authority to collect a debt for him in Canada, while in Philadelphia the Gratzes protected the legal interests of their Reading client Meyer Josephson. Abraham Minis of Savannah invested the well-known London merchant Simpson Levy with a power of attorney to collect a debt from the Georgia Trustees. Sometimes, moreover, Jews might be called upon to represent non-Jews, as when Joseph Spear of Carlisle appointed Isaac Adolphus of New York his attorney to collect a debt from an officer of the Royal American Regiment.

Most if not all of these services were undoubtedly rendered on a fee basis, and it is important to bear in mind also that Jews serving as attorneys were acting almost without exception as agents to achieve ends which the granter of the power might himself have properly and legally undertaken. In any event, such lay attorneys were never officers of the courts during the eighteenth century, though we find that in 1768 Eleazar Levy of Canada was a registered notary and had been properly certified such in London.[34]

Since many English legal and customary restrictions were applicable in the colonies, no professing Jew could become a lawyer in the full sense of the term. Such disabilities, however, did not affect the Jewish convert to Christianity, and therefore Isaac Miranda, an immigrant of Jewish birth, was able to serve as an admiralty officer or judge in Pennsylvania during the 1720's. Miranda is unlikely to have had any legal training, but was appointed to his judicial post despite the fact that he was a layman in the law. Shortly before the Revolution, Moses Franks of Philadelphia, a son of the prominent Jewish merchant David Franks, became an attorney. Reared as a Christian by his mother, Moses had studied at the University of Pennsylvania and had been admitted to the bar in England after completing his studies there. In later years he became attorney general and chief justice of the Bahamas, but probably never practiced his profession on the North American mainland.[35]

Jewish physicians and surgeons had been practicing in the colonies ever since the 1650's when Dr. Lumbrozo appeared on the scene in Maryland. Judging from the accounts Lumbrozo rendered patients in the 1660's, his fees were substantial. All through the eighteenth century Jewish medical practitioners cropped up in the different colonies, in Rhode Island, New York, South Carolina, Georgia, and even in Virginia, which lacked a Jewish settlement in prerevolutionary times. Dr. Jacob Isaac, a German immigrant, advertised himself in the *New-York Gazette* during 1752 as an expert in the cure of venereal diseases, while a Dr. Marks emerged into the records in 1756 from a New York debtors' prison. A Dr. Siccary, whose name may have represented the anglicized spelling and pronunciation of the common Anglo-Sephardic surname Sequeira, is mentioned in Dr. James Thacher's *American Medical Biography* (1828). Thacher described Dr. Siccary as "a Portuguese Jew" who had practiced medicine in eighteenth century Virginia. Citing

Thomas Jefferson as his source, Thacher reported that Siccary had been a great believer in the therapeutic value of "that admirable vegetable, the tomato"—such a believer indeed, that in Siccary's opinion, "a person who should eat a sufficient abundance of these apples would never die." [36]

Some of the Jewish physicians and surgeons apparently traveled about soliciting business in the different colonies where they had temporarily settled. Daniel Torres of Providence, for example, seems to have been an itinerant medical practitioner. Dr. Nathan Levy and Dr. Andrew Judah both practiced medicine in New York and Charleston; the year 1772 found Dr. Judah in Surinam. Philip Russell, who would appear as a surgeon's mate during the Revolution, was selling tooth-drops, tooth powders, cosmetics, eye-water, worm-powders, and the like, at New York in 1775. Dr. Isaac Cohen, a Hamburg Jew who settled for a while in the prosperous town of Lancaster, Pennsylvania, advertised he would cure the poor gratis if they brought a certificate from a clergyman certifying them as unable to pay for his services. [37]

Physicians, said Napoleon, would "have more lives to answer for in the other world than even . . . generals." Would such a remark have been merited by colonial America's Jewish physicians? Were these itinerant medical men quacks who cured people "of a consumption in their bodies and sending it into their purses"? It is not always easy to say. New York had a licensing law in 1760, and other provinces probably had such laws too, but the extent to which they were enforced is questionable. There were only two medical schools in colonial America—none at all before 1769— and even their instruction certainly left much to be desired. Most men acquainted themselves with medicine by serving an apprenticeship to a physician who had learned his craft in the hard school of experience. Bohemian-born Dr. Elias Woolin, for instance, informed the public through an advertisement in Zenger's *New-York Weekly Journal* of May 25, 1741, that he had served in the Hapsburg army "as chirurgeon four years." At most Dr. Woolin is likely to have been a skilled craftsman, though this is not to asperse his proficiency. [38]

Still, among the Jewish practitioners there undoubtedly were genuine physicians. Colonel Oglethorpe himself is authority for the statement that Dr. Samuel Nunez landed in Georgia in 1733 just in time to stop a dangerous epidemic. Nunez was certainly no quack and as a "Christian" may well have secured a professional medical education in Portugal. By 1738 he was already in the employ of the colony's trustees. Dr. Isaac Abrahams, son of the well-known New York Jewish functionary, circumciser, teacher, and petty merchant Abraham I. Abrahams, was the first Jewish graduate of King's College in New York City. In 1774 he received a bachelor of arts degree. His medical training undoubtedly came through an apprenticeship.

All things considered and bearing in mind the prominence of Jews in the medical annals of the Old World, one might well ask why there were so few Jewish physicians in the New World. Jewish practitioners faced no disabilities in America as Jews. There was no quota system to deny them entrance into medical school. The answer is probably that the practice of medicine was not then a very lucrative profession. The colonial American was simply not in the habit of consulting trained physicians, nor was he accustomed to spending money for doctoring. In fact he resented it, holding no doubt with Benjamin Franklin that "God heals and the doctor takes the fee." Socially, the successful merchant stood higher than the physician, and the typical American Jew looked for success to commerce and trade, not to the professions. The Jewish tradition of a doctor in the family lay far in the future. It was not until the second half of the nineteenth century that Jews turned in numbers to the professions of law and medicine.[39]

CHAPTER 28

JEWISH BUSINESSMEN

How Many Jews Were in Business?

The key man in American business life during the colonial period was the merchant. Craftsmen and industrialists were certainly not unimportant, but it was the merchant who dominated the economic scene. It is not surprising, therefore, to find that most of North America's gainfully employed Jews, including craftsmen and so-called professionals, were involved in some form of trade. A study of Book B of the Superior Court of Newport for the 1730's and 1740's indicates, for example, that every Jew mentioned in the records was a tradesman.

What percentage, we may ask, did Jews constitute among merchants and shopkeepers? How large did Jewish tradesmen loom in the general occupational pattern? What was the visibility of the Jewish merchant on Front Street?

In vastly underpopulated Canada, even in the larger towns of Montreal, Quebec, and Three Rivers, Jewish merchants, though few, were proportionately significant. Judging from the signatures of Jews on petitions presented to the British authorities, Jewish merchants may have numbered ten percent of Canada's substantial businessmen. A Jew was very probably the largest merchant in Three Rivers.

The thirteen British colonies south of Lake Champlain, however, afford insufficient data for definitive conclusions to be drawn. Though it is not difficult to determine the name and number of the Jewish merchants, similar data for non-Jewish merchants are not easy to muster. Even more imperative, in this connection, would be a comparison of the amount of business carried on by Jews and non-Jews, and it is doubtful that such data could ever be assembled except in very unusual instances.

A rough but safe guess is that from 1760 to 1775 the Jewish merchants of Newport constituted about ten percent of the town's substantial merchants. In a list of sixteen Newport molasses importers in 1769, two were Jews. Of the twenty-two merchants in Fairfield County, Connecticut, who petitioned the General Assembly for a customs rebate in 1749, three or approximately 14 percent were Jews, two of whom were still in the county in 1752.[1]

Five of New York City's sixty-seven leading merchants in 1705 were Jews, about 7.5 percent, although Jews formed less than one percent of the town's total population. Twenty-eight years later, two of the twenty-seven merchants engaged in New York City's flour trade were Jews, roughly seven percent, and yet Sampson Simson seems to have been the only New York Jewish merchant to be invited to become a member of the New York Chamber of Commerce in 1769. There may not have been any other substantial Jewish businessmen in the city at that time. The New York port records indicate that, though there were dozens of non-Jews, there were never more than six or seven New York Jewish shippers dispatching cargoes in any one year.[2]

The seventy-four Philadelphia merchants and notables who signed a petition in 1742 respecting the rate of exchange included two Jews, about three percent. Nineteen years later, at least two, that is perhaps eight percent, were Jewish of the twenty-four firms protesting a bill levying a duty on Negro slaves, and when the merchants of Philadelphia affixed their signatures to the nonimportation agreement in 1765, eight or two percent of the approximately 400 signers were Jews.[3]

In Charleston, it is interesting to note, four of the eleven merchants naturalized in 1697 were Jews. Two generations later, however, when the tradesmen, merchants, and planters of South Carolina petitioned the governor to appoint Moses Lindo inspector general of indigo, not a single Jewish name appeared among the forty-one merchant signatories. Charleston supported several Jewish businessmen at the time, but Jewish shopkeepers and merchants either were not invited to join the petition to the governor or refused to. In neighboring Savannah too, there were nearly always Jewish businessmen, but it is difficult to determine whether or not they constituted an appreciable percentage of those devoted to commerce and trade. What does strike the observer is that few colonies lacked Jewish businessmen: Jews were always doing business even in Virginia which was virtually without Jews during the colonial period. One of the Pintos, for instance, worked there in 1751 as a traveling salesman for the Scotch Snuff Manufactory, and during the 1770's Enoch Lyon, whose home base was in Rhode Island, sold cordials in the Old Dominion for Aaron Lopez.[4]

The Jews in the tidewater towns and backcountry villages always formed a higher percentage of the business than of the general community. The percentage of Jews in business—miniscule as it was, compared to the total number of American businessmen—was far out of proportion to the percentage of Jews in the country. But whether or not Jewish businessmen had high visibility depended on the attitude of the Christian who swept his glance up and down Front Street. If he had a jaundiced eye, if he disliked Jews, if he feared Jewish competition, if for him every Jewish shopkeeper was a Shylock or a Barabbas, then Jewish visibility was high! John Lees, a sturdy Quebec merchant who visited Newport in the late 1760's, reported a "vast number of Jews in this place." Actually, of course, there were fewer than 200 in a town of some 7,000.[5]

The "Jew Pedlar"

How did a man start out in business? Certainly no one became an Aaron Lopez overnight, and most mercantile beginnings were, for obvious reasons, very modest. Peddling, we might expect, would commonly have been an initial phase, but the fact is that not many colonial Jewish traders actually did begin as peddlers. Peddling as a form of commerce required fairly good roads, a large settled rural or village population, and peaceful highways, all of which were notably absent in colonial America.[6]

Another factor that surely deterred Jews from peddling was the opposition frequently offered the itinerant businessman by established merchants and shopkeepers. The sedentary trader of the 1760's had nothing but contempt for his peripatetic colleague and did what he could to embitter his life. In contemporary England, Jewish peddlers were constantly caricatured, attacked, and even murdered, but in North America too, the peddler's competition was resented, and as a class peddlers were deemed potential thieves, cheats, receivers of stolen goods, and carriers of disease. Merchants distrusted them and at best gave them short-term credits. As sedentary businessmen saw it, a peddler could serve no useful economic function, and they warned the consumer against him: caveat emptor! [7]

Influenced by the powerful mercantile class, most provinces passed laws either prohibiting peddlers from working at all, or severely restricting their activity by requiring bonds or heavy license fees. Samuel Naphtali, for example, secured permission to hawk and peddle in New York during the 1720's, but his license was limited to a period of six weeks. There is no indication, however, that any of the anti-peddling laws were motivated by Judeophobia. Jewish peddlers were simply too few to draw the ire of established businessmen in the colonies. Not a single Jew is known to have resided in New Hampshire and Maine in 1687–1688 when a law was passed to ban all peddling in the "Dominion of New England" which Sir Edmund Andros had organized by royal fiat a few years before.[8]

Its bitterness notwithstanding, the anti-hawking legislation the mercantile groups inspired seems more often than not to have been futile. The peddler would not be discouraged from making his contribution to colonial society. He stubbornly persisted in the face of legal impediments and social obloquy, and his crowded saddlebags and packhorse continued to bring amenities, basic necessities, and even an occasional luxury to the outlying farmers. The legislators, themselves at times unable to deny his worth and utility, saw fit now and then to lower the peddler's license fees. In some places laws to regulate peddling reappeared after it had been abolished, which testifies to the persistent character of the hawker and the perennial need for him.[9]

The heavy licensing fees, added to all the other difficulties peddlers encountered, certainly deterred sizeable numbers of Jews from engaging in this vocation, even though it had been a characteristic economic pursuit in the lands of Central and Eastern Europe from which so many of America's early Jews had come. After all, for what a license and a horse would have cost him in the colonies, a Jew could open a shop in a promising village or even in a large city, and this probably accounts for the fact that Jewish chapmen were not typical of the colonial scene.

Still, though few, there were always Jewish peddlers, even as early as the first decades of American Jewish settlement. By the 1660's Jewish peddlers were already to be found in Connecticut, going from house to house, buying, selling, and bartering cattle, horses, and local products, but the paucity of their numbers is striking when one considers that peddling has been regarded as a Jewish form of commerce. Did this paucity suggest that they were no match for the Yankee protopeddlers of New England? A greater probability is that the economic instability of Jewish peddlers caused them to be warned out of most New England towns. But the Jewish peddler was not confined to the rural or village scene. Some of the Jewish shopkeepers of early eighteenth century Boston were, for example, in reality city peddlers or canvassers who ran about soliciting patronage. The line of demarcation between the itinerant peddler, the sutler, the city canvasser, the traveling salesman, and the petty shopkeeper who frequently changed his base of operations, is simply not easy to determine.[10]

While Jewish peddlers were probably to be seen in every colony which had a Jewish settlement, their presence is documented primarily in New York and Pennsylvania. Joseph Brown (*né* Pardo), a relative of the early New York hazzan or "rabbi" Saul (Pardo) Brown, was peddling in Ulster County during the 1680's; a fellow hawker was Isaac Gabay Faro, who seems to have been Brown's partner. The following century found other Jewish hawkers and chapmen in New York Province. What those men carried in their packs is not known, but a safe guess would be that they offered for sale cloth patterns, notions, kitchen wares, and the like—what one of the Gomezes called "sundry merchandise." In the days before the Revolution, Levi Solomon lived and peddled in the neighborhood of Freehold, New Jersey, not too far from New York. Thrice married, Solomon was no doubt a firm believer in the resurrection, since he arranged for his wives to be buried one on either side of him and one at his feet.[11]

If the licensed Indian traders who roamed eastern Pennsylvania in the decade before the Revolution were also peddlers, and they may well have been, most of them were Germans and Scots. But a number of them were also Jews. The presence of Jewish peddlers is further documented by the occasional advertisements about Jewish hawkers who had absconded with unpaid goods. Benjamin Franklin's *Pennsylvania Gazette* of March 13, 1753, reprinted the story of a "Jew pedlar" who had exchanged a piece of calico for the charms of a farmer's wife—and then tried to regain the calico from the cuckolded husband. The *Gazette*'s "account . . . of the . . . comical affair" (further testimony to the disdain peddlers aroused) is probably pure fiction, but at the least it does reflect the fact, confirmed in other sources, that peddlers traveled the roads of eastern Pennsylvania to ply their trade. There is, however, every reason to believe they did not cross the mountains. Most of the suits involving Jews in seventeenth century Maryland concerned sums of ten pounds or less. The Jewish traders there used boats and small ships; they were maritime peddlers, rather like the nineteenth century boat peddlers who went up and down the Mississippi and its tributaries.[12]

APPRENTICES AND CLERKS

If a tiny minority of colonial Jews began their business careers as peddlers, an even tinier minority made commercial debuts as indentured mercantile apprentices. Solomon Marache of New York was one of these. His widowed and apparently illiterate mother signed for him in 1749 by making her mark, and taking him to Isaac Hays, a Jew of Dutch origin, apprenticed him to Hays for five years to learn the art, trade, and mystery of a merchant. Marache was to receive his food, lodging, wash, evening schooling every winter, and even a small sum of money. If he finished the five years to his master's satisfaction and then went to the West Indies, Hays was obligated to consign him ten tons of provisions. Hays, however, left New York before the five years had expired, and so Marache did not finish his period of apprenticeship. He did become a shop-keeper and merchant nonetheless, and by 1760 was a partner of Hayman Levy. During the 1780's Marache lived in Philadelphia where he dealt in groceries, pottery, and glass, and became a founder of the Mikveh Israel Synagogue. However, when Marache took his second wife, a non-Jewess, a few years later, he drifted away from Jews and Judaism.[13]

While peddlers and indentured apprentices were uncommon among the Jews, clerks were not. Many if not most Jews who came here as immigrants, it must be borne in mind, had cut their eyeteeth in Europe as peddlers, often as early as the age of thirteen. Whether abroad or here, they learned the rudiments of bookkeeping, mastered the Latin script, and taught themselves to write English at least phonetically. They knew a great deal about goods and the intricacies of buying, selling, finance, and banking, much or perhaps all of it learned through bitter experience. Not surprisingly, therefore, many on arrival here began to clerk and were ready to obey all lawful commands relating to "traffick, merchandising, and bookkeeping." [14]

Many of the clerks employed by Jews were Gentiles of course, but it was a common practice for Jewish businessmen to employ Jews also. Levy Andrew Levy, for example, clerked for his uncle Joseph Simon in Lancaster, and the outbreak of the Revolution found Alexander Abrahams working for the Gratz brothers in Philadelphia. When the indigo expert Moses Lindo arrived in South Carolina in 1756, he brought young Jonas Phillips over with him as a clerk. The twenty-year-old Phillips may have been a redemptioner who had bound himself out for the passage to America and subsequently redeemed himself as speedily as possible to begin his own business career. One of Phillips' grandsons, Major Mordecai Manuel Noah, would serve in later years as United States consul to Tunis and would enjoy considerable repute as an American playwright; another grandson, Uriah Phillips Levy, was to achieve the rank of commodore in the United States Navy.[15]

A man who started as a clerk often found it easier to get a job and to learn the ways of the new country by running a branch for a city merchant or by working for a country shopkeeper. Meyer Josephson was thus able to hire Jewish clerks for his business in the village of Reading on the Pennsylvania frontier. The fact that Josephson offered his employees low wages was no impediment, for they knew he would be willing to open branch stores for them on half-profits if they proved proficient. Only too often, however, clerks were incompetents who entered the service of others because they could not stand on their own feet. Samuel Jacobs of Quebec had such a schlemiel in Hart Aaron, from all indications an unsuccessful Long Island businessman who had wandered north into Canada. When Jacobs discharged Aaron, he wrote to him, "Ingenuity will shine in a man even if he is carrying a log of wood." Stay away from my house! Ultimately incompetents like Hart Aaron and Levy Moses, another Long Islander, were locked away in debtors' prisons.[16]

Though small towns and villages had Jewish clerks, most Jews who started their careers in that capacity preferred to stay in a good-sized town where there was a religious community. Typical of such city clerks was Enoch Lyon. An immigrant from London, Lyon went to work for Aaron Lopez of Newport under an indenture which bound him to serve four years as clerk and bookkeeper in return for board, lodging, and an annual salary of fifty Spanish milled dollars. Simultaneously, however, Lyon found it possible to engage in mercantile adventures, using shipments of goods consigned to him on his own account from England. He ordered some of these goods himself; others were sent to him by eager friends who had misjudged the American market. When Lyon fell into debt and was threatened with arrest in 1767, Lopez interceded for him. For a time at least, Lyons did achieve a degree of success; during the early 1770's he owned a vessel. Soon enough, however, he fell into debt again, this time to his erstwhile employer Lopez, who seized his ship. The former clerk threatened to litigate the matter, but before long the two had mended their differences, and in 1774 Lyon turned up in Virginia peddling cordials for the Newport shipper. Thus Lyon was at one time or another a clerk, a merchant, and an itinerant liquor salesman. He seems at length to have settled permanently in Virginia, for he is listed in the Old Dominion's published census of 1790.[17]

David Franks, the largest Jewish merchant in colonial Philadelphia, had a clerk in whom he reposed great confidence, Patrick Rice, his Irish name notwithstanding, a Jew. Much more, however, is known about another of Franks's clerks, a youngster named Barnard Gratz. Born at Langendorf, Silesia, Gratz was only a lad when he went to London to work for his cousin Solomon Henry, a successful merchant. Either cousin Solomon or the English branch of the Franks family sent him to Philadelphia where he entered the service of David Franks. Still in his teens, Gratz spent over four years in the employ of Franks, from whom he received board and wages.[18]

Like most competent clerks, young Gratz engaged in small business ventures on his own, and some of these were carried on conjointly with a partner, Benjamin Moses Clava. Almost from the very beginning, then, Barnard Gratz had several strings to his bow: he clerked for David Franks, ran a small business with a friend, and also probably had a little shop of his own. Importing goods from London—in small lots to be sure—he sold some at retail, sent some (women's stays!) to the fairs, bought flaxseed from one country merchant, credited another with a bale of furs, and shipped goods to one of the Frankses in Halifax as well as to another customer in Jamaica. By 1759 Gratz had acquired enough capital and experience to go out entirely on his own. That year he rented a shop or warehouse and secured a substantial stock of goods from Moses Franks of London, with David Franks, Moses' brother and Barnard's erstwhile boss, guaranteeing payment. Barnard had not been an independent businessman very long when he began cautiously exploring the possibility of bringing his brother Michael, two years his junior, to this country.[19]

Michael, like most young Jews, had wandered about rather prodigiously, working in Berlin and Amsterdam, clerking in London for cousin Solomon Henry, and even trying his luck briefly in India. He was still a teenager when he joined Barnard at Philadelphia in 1759. Barnard, of course, had Michael's career all planned. Michael was to find a clerking job in the countryside or take Barnard's place and work for David Franks, or perhaps even open a shop in Philadelphia. Barnard had already warned Michael that to achieve success in America, one had to be prepared to "do every thing pertaining to the business." Michael did not balk. On arrival in the New World he dropped his middle name Solomons and went out on his own at once, starting with the jewelry and trinkets he had been enterprising enough to bring with him from Europe. Gradually Michael expanded his business, dealing on a small scale with local and regional shopkeepers and sending small ventures from Philadelphia to Halifax, Georgia, London, and even the West Indies. Working closely with relatives like Solomon Henry of London and Isaac Adolphus of New York, as well as his own brother Barnard and the Philadelphia magnate David Franks, Michael made his way. By the early 1760's he already had a modest share in the fur trade and no later than 1768 formed the firm of B. & M. Gratz, Philadelphia merchants, in partnership with Barnard. The new firm's specialty was the western trade.[20]

Shopkeepers

Jews, it is clear from contemporary records, opened retail shops not long after their disembarkation at New Amsterdam during the mid-1600's. Undiscouraged by the refusal of Peter Stuyvesant and the Dutch West India Company to allow them "open retail shops," they were soon vending goods in improvised shops, often perhaps surreptitiously, so that by January 1657, little more than two years after their arrival, the New Amsterdam records could speak of "keeping open store and selling by retail practiced to the present time . . . by Jews."

About the same time Maryland too had a "Jewes store," though it may have been only a warehouse used by the trader Ferera. As we have already noted, the Jews of New York were officially forbidden to sell at retail even under the more enlightened British regime which succeeded the Dutch in 1664, but the prohibition had become a dead letter by the turn of the century, and throughout the 1700's Jews operated small stores. The fact that they freely participated in the retail trade did not escape the attention of the mid-eighteenth century Finnish traveler Peter Kalm who reported that Jews were "allowed to keep shops in town." Kalm was struck by this because he knew that in Sweden, a country very familiar to him, Jews were severely restricted in residence and mercantile activity.

New York was not unique, however, for by the middle of the century if not earlier, Jews had opened shops and stores in other coastal towns—Boston, Philadelphia, Charleston, Savannah—and in the backcountry as well. Few of these enterprises were notably lucrative. There were exceptions of course, but for the most part Jewish tradesmen in the towns and villages, especially in the backcountry, enjoyed only modest circumstances and were rarely more than petty shopkeepers. Though their establishments dotted the countryside, albeit sparsely, from Canada to Savannah, it was in New York and environs that they were most in evidence. In short, what we might call "Greater New York" was their mother community, and they waited on trade in at least five towns on Long Island as well as villages in Westchester County and neighboring Connecticut. Occasionally a shopkeeper settled in New Jersey—Spottswood, Bound Brook, and Mount Holly, for example. A number of the smaller towns west of Philadelphia sheltered at least one Jewish shopkeeper. By the 1770's Aaron Levy had established himself as far west as Northumberland, and from the 1760's on, there was nearly always a Jewish merchant in Pittsburgh.[21]

How small was a shopkeeper? Small enough sometimes for a man merely to leave his samples—assorted medicines for instance—with a local newspaper and then go out himself to peddle his wares. How big was a shopkeeper, and when was a shopkeeper a merchant? The line of demarcation was often a thin one. Aaron Hart of Canada and Joseph Simon of Lancaster were certainly not mere shopkeepers. Simon was in reality a merchant-capitalist. Hart too, and another Canadian, Samuel Jacobs of St. Denis, were inland merchants on a very substantial scale like Simon, wealthier by far than some coastal merchant-shippers.[22]

How did the colonial shopkeeper first set himself up in business? Some storekeepers like the Minises of Georgia, for instance, may have begun as agents; others took over the shops of coreligionists who had died or moved away. A few of course, but very few in the eighteenth century, may have come over to the colonies with means. For example, Moses Levy and Jacob Franks, both of whom had successful brothers in London, probably brought some capital with them to America. Others, native Americans like the second generation of the Hays family of New York and Westchester County, are likely to have secured some aid from their relatives when they went into business. David S. Franks, one of the lucky few with funds at their disposal, summed up his beginnings rather cryptically: "Early in the year 1774, I settled in Montreal with a small capital and a considerable credit as a merchant and was successful in business." [23]

As a rule, however, the shopkeeper had only meager means. The typical shopkeeper, provided with a small stock and very little in the way of capital, was dependent on the nearest merchant patient enough to extend him a line of credit and to replenish his scanty store of merchandise in exchange for local produce, furs, hides, and some cash. Some shopkeepers had the advantage of friends in England who would vouch for them and get them a cargo. Not much can be said of Jacob Henry's mercantile activity, for instance, but we do know that he secured a credit of £3,000 from Christian businessmen in England to engage in trade here, though it is obvious he was more than a shopkeeper. On the other hand, Michael Judah of Norwalk looked to his fellow colonials for help; he received a loan of five pounds from the New York congregation to open a business. Philip Moses started selling cordials for Aaron Lopez in Savannah and subsequently asked for other goods on credit. Commercial beginnings like those of Philip Moses were quite common, and it is very probable that most small businessmen got their start through a helping hand from some metropolitan merchant willing to aid a newcomer to establish himself. Aaron Lopez himself had depended on suppliers like Benjamin Gomez, Hayman Levy, and Solomon Marache. The merchant might even have allowed the beginner a stock at prime cost; if the beginner succeeded, he might prove a good customer! The pattern of dependence on a neighboring supplier, or on a more distant urban jobber or wholesaler, survived the colonial period by more than a century; it would, in fact, maintain itself on the American scene well into the twentieth century.[24]

A number of businessmen probably made debuts as country shopkeepers. There is evidence, for example, that Nathan Simson, ultimately to return to London in 1722 a wealthy merchant-shipper, had begun his career only seventeen years earlier in the Long Island hamlet of Brookhaven. But Simson was hardly typical, and by no means were all beginners able to survive in the villages or to move triumphantly to a big city. Abraham Pinto of Stratford, one of Simson's correspondents, wrote to ask for an extension of time in the payment of a debt; Pinto blamed his misfortunes on one of the New York Levys who had apparently dispatched him to the countryside. Another of Simson's correspondents, Nehemiah Marks of Stamford, piteously begged Simson not to push him to the wall.[25]

What did the shopkeeper handle? Actually, the very same type of goods as the much larger merchant. There were commercial staples of course—textiles, notions, hardware in all forms and shapes, liquors, groceries, and especially West Indian sugar and molasses. Country storekeepers carried, in addition, substantial supplies of saddlery. Some tradesmen, particularly in the larger cities, were specialists, dealing mainly in poultry, or tobacco and snuff, or tobacco and some hardware, or tobacco and groceries. The goldsmiths sold jewelry and cutlery. In general, however, even small shopkeepers offered their customers a surprising variety of goods. At his death in the late 1750's the inventory of the Fairfield shopkeeper Andris Trube included iron pots, axes, earthenware, dry goods, and notions of all types, papers, pens, ink, looking glasses, razors, fishhooks, and corkscrews. In 1745 the stock of shopkeeper Isaac Levy of New York included all types of yard goods and several pieces of ready-made apparel like cloaks for women and children. Though Levy's was substantially a dry-goods store, he also handled tea, beeswax, and indigo for dyeing garments, and had twenty-four dozen Jews' harps on his shelves. His merchandise amounted in value to over £1,000—not the stock of a small shopkeeper.[26]

Actually, it was essential for colonial shopkeepers to carry an assortment of goods. Even in the villages people wanted a variety to choose from, so that Samuel Jacobs of St. Denis, Quebec, could write in 1772: "A retail shopp in the countrey shoud be well assorted, as the inhabitants does not like to go from place to place to make their impleat." The shopkeeper's life was never an easy one in any event; some customers were captious, as Samuel Jacobs testified in the same letter: "To keep in favour with that old woman requires a courtier such as my past time never was master of, to cringe, dangle, flatter, laugh, and cry all of a breath." [27]

Almost every customer was carried on the books, both in the villages and in the cities. Currency was very scarce, and cash sales were consequently rare. Ultimately all accounts had to be balanced and the shopkeeper was paid, but not always in cash. Most business was done on a barter or commodity-exchange basis. Even in the towns customers often settled their debts through barter by supplying some form of commodity satisfactory to the shopkeeper. Thus Newport tradesman Samuel Moses sold John Wigfall a gold watch and seal, and the latter agreed to provide stock (cattle?) or lumber in exchange. Asher Etting of North Castle, Westchester, would take produce in exchange for his wares. He had about 300 customers on his books; most of the debts due him involved sums under five pounds. His debtors owed him over £2,000 all told, but he himself owed £1,000 to his own creditors. In 1662 Lumbrozo and Ferera of Maryland sold sugar and brandy in exchange for tobacco and mortgages on cattle or crops. As late as the second half of the eighteenth century, at Albany and Savannah furs served as a commodity to settle debts. Jacobs of St. Denis, eager to secure wheat for his principals in Montreal and Quebec, traded for it with salt and rum; he was ready to buy a farmer's tobacco if the farmer would sell him his grain as well. Meyer Josephson of Reading sold dry goods, blankets, harnesses, and an occasional piece of Stiegel glass from the Elizabeth furnace, in return for fodder, provisions, and hides. Levi & Jacobs of Lancaster County traded dry goods for furs, hides, rags, butter, tallow, wax, hemp, grain, and fruits. In 1744 a South Carolina tradesman paid for rice with cordials and sundries in addition to cash.[28]

JEWISH WOMEN AS SHOPKEEPERS

Central and East European Jewry was heir to a long tradition of distaff participation in trade. In fact it was not uncommon in the pious communities of Eastern Europe for the wife to make the living so her husband could devote himself entirely to his talmudic studies. The memoirs of Glueckel von Hameln should suffice to allay any doubts as to the commercial competence of European

Jewish women and their capacity for achieving success in trade. On this continent too, Jewish women proved their expertise on the economic scene. A less distinguished contemporary of Glueckel ran a grogshop in seventeenth century New York, and throughout the eighteenth century women were found in business as far south as Savannah, though some engaged merely in occasional ventures, as when Mrs. Aaron Lopez imported a Negress from South Carolina. Parents might also dispatch parcels of goods on the account of their small children, as the Gratzes did, sending jewelry to the Illinois country. Rachel Levy of New York imported rum from Boston and Rhode Island, and Rachel Luis brought in cocoa from Curaçao. Hetty Hays ran a boardinghouse and sold pickled vegetables, sweetmeats, and jellies. Not infrequently the female shopkeeper was a widow trying to continue her deceased husband's business. Thus for several years Frances Polock of Newport and her son Jacob carried on the apparently substantial establishment of the late Isaac Polock. No Jewish woman in colonial America, however, ever became or remained a merchant in the real sense of the term. Some of these distaff shopkeepers seem to have been incompetent, soon going out of business and sometimes, as in the case of Hannah Louzada, appearing subsequently on the charity rolls of a congregation. Mrs. Nathan Simson, it is true, carried on her husband's American business—a very large one—but that was in London after his death in that city.[29]

One widow who seems to have managed was Hannah Moses of Philadelphia, at whose home young Barnard Gratz boarded. Gratz sold her some if not most of her stock of goods, which included a host of small items: notions, trinkets, jewelry, cutlery, enameled fountain pens, razor strops, and the like. Miriam Gratz, Michael's wife, occasionally worked in the store when her husband was away on a trip. Miriam was no businesswoman, but as the daughter of Joseph Simon the Lancaster trader, she had grown up in an environment which could not have failed to impress on her the rudiments of commerce. No American Jewish woman was more reminiscent of Glueckel von Hameln than Abigail Minis whose husband, after a long illness, left her a widow with eight children. This matriarch took over ranches, a farm, a store, and a tavern, and seems to have prospered over the years. Like others who dispensed liquor in that generation, she may have considered herself a public benefactress:

> We pour the spirits down
> To keep the spirits up.

The tradition of the Jewish wife carrying on after her husband's death was, of course, only fortified in America by the example of many colonial Gentile women who engaged in trade.[30]

CHAPTER 29

TYPES OF MERCHANTS

WHAT IS A MERCHANT?

There was a great difference between the shopkeeper who bought from the nearest source which offered him credit, and the merchant who, as one contemporary source defined him, was "an exporter and importer . . . superior to . . . any other" class of traders. Of course the merchant was a shopkeeper in part, for he sold at retail, but he was also a wholesaler who sold in bulk and maintained a warehouse. The extent to which Dutch Jews like D'Acosta, De Lucena, Cohen Henriques, and Dandrada who came to New Amsterdam in 1655, probably directly from Amsterdam, deserved to be called merchants is perhaps questionable, though like Asser Levy and some of the other Jewish businessmen of that generation, they were undoubtedly wholesalers. In any case, as we have seen, it was not until about 1690 that Jews were permitted officially to sell at retail, though even before that, unofficial if not precisely extralegal retailing had been common enough among colonial Jews.[1]

The merchant was primarily, to be sure, a large-scale shopkeeper. In contradistinction, however, to the average shopkeeper, he was more than a retailer and wholesaler. He traded in bulk at a distance, and his business was regional, interprovincial, and if he was a merchant-shipper, transatlantic. Men like Aaron Hart of Three Rivers, Samuel Jacobs of St. Denis, and Joseph Simon of Lancaster were entitled to the rank of principal or large-scale merchants. Had these enterprising men lived on the coast, each would have inevitably become a merchant-shipper, as later generations of economic historians would designate that ne plus ultra of merchantry, and in fact Jacobs did buy goods on occasion from suppliers in London. Many, probably the majority, of the merchants as far south as Savannah dispatched goods by boat to their clients, but they were not necessarily merchant-shippers.[2]

Merchant-shippers were in fact a breed apart—what the prophet Isaiah had in mind when he spoke of "Tyre . . . whose merchants are princes, whose traffickers are the honorable of the earth." The merchant-shipper was to the merchant as the merchant to the shopkeeper. Merchant-shipping and big business were practically identical in colonial America. Most of America's important towns lay on the coast, by or on the tidewater rivers, which meant they were mercantile seats immensely attractive to merchants. Exporting and importing were major interests to such merchants, whose status was truly princely in a North America which was essentially an undeveloped continent and could boast of few manufacturers. The continent's local products, in the main raw materials and provisions, were shipped out to distant markets, or the entrepreneurial businessman might create an empire by trading in wares assembled from other colonies and from abroad, for home use, for reworking, or for reexport. Exchanging the raw materials, produce, and semi-finished industrial goods of the colonies, the merchant-shipper was enabled to import from the industrial Old World the finished goods so much in demand in the agrarian New.[3]

The American merchant-shipper was thus heavily involved in regional and overseas trade. He was a businessman who had fulfilled himself, who had followed natural and logical areas of expansion. For his time he had rationalized business to its utmost and permitted his ambition to extend his activities into nearly every known form of commerce and trade. If a Jew became a merchant-shipper—there were not many who did—it was not because the authorities had looked askance for a brief period at Jewish retailing. It was because geography and colonial need had made him sharply aware of how imperative merchant-shipping was, and how much it beckoned as the open road to success and wealth.[4]

Variety of Economic Interests

The Jewish merchant operated no differently from his non-Jewish compeer, and in America, unlike Europe, there was no distinctive or visible Jewish mercantile and industrial pattern—with one possible exception: Jews played no part in heavy industry, the production of iron. The variety of concerns which attracted the American merchant, Jew and Gentile alike, staggers the imagination of our own age, given over so relentlessly to specialization. The variety was such indeed that no two Jewish merchants were alike in their economic interests, pursuits, and specialties—a statement which would probably have applied with equal force and validity to American non-Jews engaged in trade of large proportions. The all but infinite diversity of economic concerns animating the colonial Jewish merchant is best grasped through a somewhat detailed survey of the commercial activities pursued by a number of them.

To begin with the Canadians, Aaron Hart of Three Rivers ranked high on the scale of diversification. Merchant, army supplier, fur entrepreneur, liquor dispenser, and postmaster (not a political appointment but an economic activity), Hart became, as we have noted, the wealthiest Jew north of Lake Champlain. Some fifty miles southwest of Three Rivers up the Richelieu River, was St. Denis whose outstanding businessman Samuel Jacobs served the British crown as a commissary and sutler at a number of army posts in North America. After the conquest of Canada he set himself up as a merchant-shipper with headquarters in Quebec and throughout the 1760's maintained a series of shops, warehouses, and branches in Montreal, Sorel, and several other towns, particularly in the Richelieu valley where he settled permanently at St. Denis around 1770.

Actually a merchant-capitalist in the guise of a large-scale country shopkeeper, Jacobs dabbled only a bit in the fur trade, but sold a great deal of liquor to the habitants, set up a distillery of his own, and also manufactured soap, potash, and pearl ash. His chief commercial activity, apart from his shops, was the purchase of grain, which on one occasion he proposed shipping directly to Spain. For the most part buying grain as an agent for Montreal and Quebec exporters, Jacobs in turn employed a number of runners or rovers as his own agents. The scope of his enterprise is reflected in the fact that some of the vessels he used in his intraprovincial shipping were his own and were quite large. There were times when Jacobs' speculations in wheat led him to attempt to manipulate prices and control the market. He was a banker too, in a small way, for he advanced money to the farmers for their wheat or for the rent they owed the seigneur.[5]

Aaron Lopez was the outstanding merchant-shipper in Newport, Rhode Island, during the years immediately preceding the Revolution. Lopez' far flung mercantile interests involved him in the ownership of a fleet of vessels, in the transportation of freight, in the importing and exporting of goods, in retailing and wholesaling, and in the outfitting of ships. He was, in addition, active in the fishing, whaling, and candlemaking industries, and as a large-scale entrepreneur, interested himself also in the production of rum, in the slave trade, in ship and house building, and in the delivery of prefabricated houses to Caribbean markets. Lopez supplemented his business by buying and selling lottery tickets, and as we have already said, ran a farm as an adjunct to his other commercial activities. Though he showed little interest in privateering and in maritime insurance, he came very close to embodying in his widespread concerns the classicity of eighteenth century American merchantry. Like other notable merchants in his part of the country, Lopez secured fish from New England and Newfoundland, collected livestock from neighboring farmers, and acquired lumber from the backcountry, iron from Providence, flour and wheat from New York and Pennsylvania, naval stores and rice from the Carolinas, sugar, molasses, and rum from the West Indies, and textiles, notions, and hardware from England.[6]

On Long Island one of East Hampton's leading businessmen— he may have been the most important one—was Aaron Isaacs who would attain a measure of posthumous distinction as the maternal grandfather of John Howard Payne, the composer of "Home Sweet Home." In his own time and in his own right, Isaacs was an aggressive merchant, buying and selling farms, land, and houses, owning a windmill and part of a wharf at Sag Harbor, and in his trade with

New England, exchanging beef for salt or cash. The beef sent to New Englanders very probably came from the ranchlands at Montauk.[7]

In New Jersey the Louzada brothers of Bound Brook owned land, a general store, and a gristmill. Across the Delaware in Philadelphia, David Franks operated on a grand scale as a merchant-capitalist, shipper, army purveyor, fur trader, and would-be colonizer. By the time Franks was fifteen he was already doing business in Boston. Myer Hart, one of the founders of the town of Easton, Pennsylvania, was its first shopkeeper. He was also a liquor dealer, innkeeper, landowner, and shipper of grain to the Philadelphia market. West of Easton, Joseph Simon owned the largest general store in Lancaster and a number of branch stores at Fort Pitt and other settlements. Simon was also an arms manufacturer, fur trader, and supplier and financier for Indian traders operating in the Ohio valley. Still farther west of Lancaster, in Northumberland, Aaron Levy sold goods to the farmers and took their products in exchange. Though he carried on Indian trading and army supply on a small scale, he was more a shopkeeper than a merchant.

In seventeenth century Maryland, Jacob Lumbrozo occupied himself as a physician, rancher, planter, tavern keeper, Indian trader, attorney, and appraiser. Lumbrozo had been first and foremost, however, a petty merchant, and his prime concern had been business. Isaac Da Costa maintained himself in Charleston, South Carolina, as a shopkeeper, merchant, dealer in Indian goods, and importer of slaves, while Mordecai Sheftall of Savannah, Georgia, who worked as a tanner and acquired ownership of a warehouse, a wharf, sawmills, ranches, and plantations (farms), was in addition always a shopkeeper or petty merchant.[8]

Selecting at random a few illustrations of trading from the hundreds if not thousands available, we find that when the pirate Joseph Bradish was arrested in 1699, a Jew was called in as an expert to appraise a bag of jewels seized from the buccaneers. Judah Monis supplemented his meager income as an instructor at Harvard College by selling pipes, tobacco, nails, and hinges. Moses Lopez of Newport made his living as a translator, potash and candle manufacturer, merchant, and as a supercargo for his more successful brother Aaron.

Isaac Pinto of New York, Charleston, and probably other towns as well, supported himself as a merchant, teacher, and interpreter, and also translated the Sephardic Hebrew prayer book into English. Clearly there was no normal pattern or standard in the routine of a trader's activity. On the contrary, a bewildering heterogeneity prevailed in the business of buying and selling.[9]

LIQUOR DEALERS, INNKEEPERS, AND OTHER SPECIALISTS

Benjamin Franklin's admonition in *Poor Richard's Almanac* of 1749 that "drink does not drown care, but waters it, and makes it grow faster," seems to have had scant effect. Liquor was and remained a principal commodity on the colonial scene. It was offered for sale virtually everywhere and by every shopkeeper, even though in most cases a special liquor-dispensing license was required. Rum, for instance, was one of the staples of American commerce. Used in the home, in the western trade, and for the fishing fleets, and rationed out to workmen on the job, it appeared together with molasses and sugar on almost every price list.

Jews were far from inactive in the sale of liquor, but whether any Jewish dealers limited themselves solely to the sale of strong drink is very difficult to ascertain. It would be no surprise to discover, for example, that Mrs. Aaron Isaacs, the grogshop mistress of 1680, sold notions and trinkets in the same shop. Aaron Hart of Canada, Lumbrozo of Maryland, Myer Hart of Easton, Israel Jacobs of Philadelphia, and the Minises of Georgia all owned taverns in addition to their other interests. On the king's birthday in 1772 Abigail Minis served over seventy notables in the Savannah courthouse, "and the day was spent with good humour." Samuel Jacobs is known to have sold goods surreptitiously at his Richelieu valley taverns in which, during the last years of the French and Indian War, he was licensed to sell spirits alone.[10]

Any attempt to sum up the types of business in which Jewish merchants were engaged would probably show that a majority operated as undifferentiated general merchants dealing, like Barnard Gratz, "in most all sorts." Within these admittedly almost limitless confines, however, there were a great many merchants who did specialize to some degree. Individual Jews emphasized the sale of snuff and tobacco, or grain, or candles, or groceries, or some other commodity. Nearly every merchant had a specialty of sorts, so that their other concerns notwithstanding, Samuel Jacobs stressed grain, Aaron Lopez cultivated a particular interest in candles, Jacob Abrahams was primarily a grocer, and Hayman Levy was known as a fur merchant. A number of businessmen were licensed auctioneers or vendue masters, although the typical merchant resented the price-cutting tactics of the men who sold job lots and goods at forced sales.[11]

Still, specialization never amounted to a very commanding proportion of Jewish mercantile enterprise. Jewish merchants were active as jobbers, retailers, and wholesalers, as coastal, regional, interprovincial, and transatlantic shippers, as importers and exporters, as freighters, warehousers, and passenger agents, as maritime brokers and insurers. In time of war they outfitted privateers, and in time of peace, to satisfy their urge for speculation and gambling, they bought and sold lotteries. They took part in the slave trade, in army supply, and in the western—Indian or fur—trade. Some, acting on behalf of the provincial authorities, supplied the Indians with presents of tobacco, beef, and the like.[12]

Jewish businessmen bought real estate, large tracts of undeveloped lands, and in a few instances, even attempted colonization on a large scale. Some distilled rum or brandies; others manufactured flour, or because of their special interest in the candle trade, engaged in whaling. Most of them were commission agents, while a few supplemented their incomes by offering their services as commercial brokers, or in a very limited sense, as bankers. Many served as attorneys, acted as credit agents, rating prospective customers for other businessmen, and functioned occasionally in effect as information agents, such as helping an anxious family when a husband disappeared.[13]

Everything we know testifies that the colonial Jewish businessman operated on a wide horizon—very little lay beyond his scope. Like other merchants of his day, he may have preferred to occupy himself with many types of business. Diversification may have appealed to him, not only because it would help minimize his losses, but also because it would tend to enlarge his area of opportunity. The colonial merchant knew his importance; he understood that he was the hub of a whole world of commerce and industry. In North America, with her lack of a rival hereditary aristocracy, the merchant was moreover politically powerful, though this last could not have played much part in the calculations of Jewish merchants whose religion relegated them at best to the fringes of political power.

THE MECHANICS OF DOING BUSINESS

Like all other merchants, the Jewish businessman maintained an office or countinghouse with separate pigeonholes for papers relating to each of his vessels on a voyage, as well as a warehouse or "store," a wharf or part of one, and a shop. A notable merchant-shipper like Aaron Lopez might house all these facilities together with his dwelling place under one roof, thereby conjoining office, home, warehouse, shop, stable, and sail loft. The Lopez home on Thames Street in Newport was commodious enough, in fact, for a British officer to estimate during the Revolution that he could pack 200 men into it. The extent of Lopez' activities was such, however, as frequently to render his own storage facilities inadequate, and he would rent additional space from his neighbors. There were times when he used at least four storehouses.[14]

Not all businessmen, of course, enjoyed the advantage of a large complex of buildings like those occupied by Aaron Lopez, and advertisements in the *Newport Mercury* indicate that Jewish businessmen in the Rhode Island port offered their wares for sale in their homes, in shops, in storehouses, at wharves, and often even on board ship. Unlike the case today, small purchasers were not limited to buying at the shop, nor were substantial purchasers always directed to the store or warehouse. The account book records leave no doubt that retail and wholesale purchasers alike did business at both types of establishment.[15]

By twentieth century standards even the largest of colonial firms had very few employees and usually consisted, in addition to the merchant and his partners, of a clerk, an apprentice or two, and a number of unskilled laborers. It seems to have been characteristic of many Jewish firms for owners to prefer coreligionists as clerks. At Lopez' countinghouse this preference is reflected in the firm's papers by the use of Jewish and Hebraic terms in both English and Hebrew, and in the account books by such clerkly doodles as "Israel," "Samuel Lopez," "Jacob Lopez," "David Lopez," "Moses Lopez," "Enoch Lyon," and "Joseph Jesu Pinto." Even when the Jewish clerk was not a relative, a close social relationship obtained between employer and employee, for the clerk frequently lived with his employer's family. Such a friendship is clearly evident in the personal letters Miriam Gratz addressed to her husband's clerk "Allick" (Alexander Abrahams)—"The dear children gives thare love to you." [16]

The manner in which colonial Jewish businessmen kept records of their affairs presents an interesting and ofttimes variable problem. Commonly enough the small shopkeeper kept a "waste book" for initial entries and probably a ledger as well. Important merchants like Lopez, however, maintained an extensive series of letter books, record books, and account books. Unfortunately, not all of Lopez' business books are extant, and the difficulties of understanding the method he employed in keeping records are exacerbated by the fact that his clerks appear to have eschewed any consistent terminology in characterizing the books they posted. In general it can be said there were books of initial entry—omnibus waste books and shop or store blotters. These rough jottings were then copied out in a fair hand and entered in what might be called journals, records of daily sales which were in turn entered into ledgers. Besides his ledgers, Lopez kept in ledger form a series of special account books, dealing variously with sailors, individual vessels, and carpenters who repaired his ships. There were, in addition, invoice books for outgoing cargoes, receipt books, books for bills of lading, files for letters received, books of memoranda dealing with warehouses and contracts, spinners' and tailors' books for the women who supplied Lopez with yarn and finished garments, and finally, a sedakah book, the record of his dealings with the synagogue in Newport. In all likelihood, however, this list does not exhaust the various types of record books employed by this merchant whose affairs reached out to at least three continents.[17]

Lopez' correspondence was, of course, crucially important to a businessman, and one of the chief jobs he assigned his clerk was the writing of letters. A competent clerk, one able to write English well, was a particularly valuable asset to a firm. Letterwriting was a prime form of maintaining communication with clients and agents, but Jewish merchants, many of them born abroad, were not always conversant with English. Since the colonial merchant possessed no more rapid means for the communication of market information than newspapers, personal statements, and letters, he and his agents were constantly exchanging prices current in order to take advantage of special situations of short supply and high demand. Aaron Lopez, for example, was in constant correspondence with Henry Lloyd of Boston, while Jacob Franks of New York, who carried on a heavy correspondence with his sons and relatives in business at Philadelphia, found it profitable to pay the postrider by the year to carry his mail between New York and Philadelphia. (In the twentieth century he would have had a direct telephone line or a teletypewriter.) During the 1750's Nathans & Hart of Halifax permitted themselves the luxury of printed forms for prices current. All they had to do was insert the price next to the nearly 100 commodities listed on the form.[18]

"Jews are linguistic amphibia," observed the Austrian bibliographer Moritz Steinschneider, and that was certainly true of early American Jewry. Sephardic Jewish merchants commonly wrote to their fellow Sephardim in Portuguese and sometimes in Spanish, while Ashkenazic Jews often addressed Yiddish letters to the relatives and friends with whom they did business. Even French and German were employed, albeit rarely. On at least one occasion the eminent New York merchant of German birth Jacob Franks addressed a Portuguese letter to Aaron Lopez, although Franks himself is unlikely to have known any Portuguese and his letter was probably the work of a clerk. The New Yorker intended his use of Portuguese as a courtesy to Lopez who had arrived in America less than four mouths before and was no doubt still somewhat uncomfortable with the American vernacular. In any case, English exceeded in frequency any other language used by American Jews; most letters, even those posted to foreign lands, were written in English.[19]

Substantial merchants like Aaron Lopez required a sizeable supply of workers for the manual labor their affairs involved. Lopez met this need in large part by employing unskilled workers on a per diem basis. He further assured himself of an adequate labor force by recourse to apprentices and indentured servants, some of whom he boarded out, paying for their maintenance with shop goods. Since white help was scarce and expensive, Lopez always retained a staff of Negro domestics and in addition often hired Negro slaves from their masters, though in his papers such laborers were always referred to as servants, never as slaves. At least half a dozen Negroes were usually employed at one time at the Lopez shop, storehouse, and wharf. For his own living quarters, Lopez supplemented his Negro domestics by hiring an Indian woman to wash and scrub and a white seamstress to sew and make garments for the family and the Negro household servants.[20]

CHAPTER 30

PHYSICAL MOBILITY AND RELOCATION

PHYSICAL MOBILITY

The colonial American merchant was constantly on the move. His business often made it necessary for him to travel, since correspondence was inadequate at best, and no more rapid form of communication was available to him. The American Jewish merchants, too, were characterized by a high degree of physical mobility, and like their eighteenth century Central European counterparts, rarely balked at traveling about a great deal to gain a living. "The cares of giting a liveing disperses them up and down the world," said Abigail Franks. Until the American Jewish trader finally settled down in a place where he could achieve a measure of happiness and economic sufficiency, mobility was the rule rather than the exception. Manuel Josephson, a keen observer of colonial Jewish life, testified to this in his emphasis on "the frequent mutability of the [congregation's] members from one place to another," while one of the standard blessings in the Sephardic synagogue of the preindustrial age, a blessing constantly recited in New York's Shearith Israel Congregation, invoked God's favor upon those who traveled by land or sea.[1]

In all probability, to be sure, the colonial merchant traveled no more extensively than the businessman of our own day, but an airborne journey to the market is scarcely comparable in time and discomfort to travel in eighteenth century America. Whether he went by land or sea, the colonial merchant constantly braved a host of hardships and dangers. Roads were frequently impassable, while travel by sea meant storms, disease, and occasionally even pirates. But travel was as essential as it was hazardous, and so the colonial businessman was more often than not an itinerant businessman. It was the quest for opportunity—primarily the opportunity to sell goods—that impelled American merchants of the 1600's and 1700's to move about as they did. Their main thoroughfare was the Atlantic Ocean which they were forever traversing to reach neighboring colonies in North America or the West Indies, or distant England and the continent. One of the reasons why Jewish communities were so slow to develop in America, and why they experienced so desultory a growth even after their establishment, was very likely that their members were so often away from home.

Certainly the first Jewish settlers were a mobile lot. Some, born on the Iberian Peninsula, had moved to France or Holland, and from there in many instances on to England, Dutch Brazil or the neighboring Guianese Wild Coast, or the Dutch West Indies. Some of the Sephardic Jews who had crossed the channel to England moved on to the English colonies in the West Indies or the North American mainland. During the 1670's, for instance, a number of Jews from Speightstown, Barbados, sailed for New England in search of opportunity. Some probably returned, but others remained or moved on to the miniscule Jewish community which had been established in New York a generation earlier. The Mesquitas of seventeenth century New York City were among those who had come there via the West Indies. Benjamin Mesquita had lived on the Iberian Peninsula and in Holland, Brazil, Barbados, Jamaica, and it is probable, in other places as well, before coming to New York where he died in 1683. Abraham De Sousa Mendes, a Jew of either Iberian or Dutch birth, was endenized on Jamaica, moved on to London, took ship from there to Barbados in the West Indies, proceeded then to New York, and returned to Barbados, but spent his last days on Curaçao where he died in 1709. Such prodigies of wandering, settlement, and resettlement were not at all uncommon.[2]

The fact that Jewish merchants traveled almost invariably with business in mind did not prevent them from enjoying the pleasures of social visits with Jewish suppliers, and not infrequently a traveler would avail himself of the opportunity to turn his trip into a vacation or to secure good medical advice. This was particularly true of the Charlestonians whose visits to Newport often combined business with the delights of a superior climate.

On occasion a businessman might accompany his own shipments or travel as a supercargo. During the seventeenth century in particular, many a merchant-shipper was really a sea-peddler setting out in a small ship with a modest load of goods.[3]

By the eighteenth century America had become more widely settled. The country had more towns, better roads, coach systems between some of the larger settlements, and especially, since journeys were still made most commonly by boat, more adequate coastal transportation. The interprovincial trade had burgeoned, and merchants were moving about as frequently as ever. New York Jews, for instance, often traveled to Connecticut where they did business and carried on litigation. A New York tobacconist in Stamford urged his Newport friend to buy Connecticut tobacco; another businessman settled in Connecticut to open a potash factory. The New York "rabbi" and businessman Abraham Haim De Lucena journeyed by boat to Philadelphia eight times in less than four years, while Aaron Lopez of Newport repeatedly took the overnight run to New York to make purchases.

Hyam Myers of New York frequently made the trip between New York and Canada. Taking the short route directly north up the Hudson and over Lake Champlain on his way to Montreal and Quebec, Myers was away from New York for months at a time. As Montreal increased in importance, especially as a fur center, he and other New York merchants decided to settle in Canada permanently.[4]

Though New York City was not the hub of American commerce during the mid-1700's, her metropolitan synagogue made her the center for Jewish businessmen, and she attracted Jewish buyers and visitors, not only from the surrounding region, but from virtually everywhere in North America. Jews were eager to see one another, and the congregational records of religious donations indicate that they journeyed to New York from as far south as Savannah. Philadelphia too was a regional center, and from Philadelphia, Jewish businessmen like David Franks, Joseph Simon, and the Gratz brothers constantly traveled westward as far as Pittsburgh and southward into Virginia to look after their interests in the western trade and army supply. Smaller businessmen, however, traveled about as much if not more. Benjamin Moses Clava, for example, lived at one time or another in Lancaster and Philadelphia, and across the Delaware in New Jersey.[5]

In the South, Charleston was the regional center from which Jewish merchants moved out in all directions into the hinterland. One of Isaac Da Costa's trips into Georgia took him away from his Charleston home for five months, but Da Costa also traveled north to Newport where he transacted business, visited with his friend Aaron Lopez, and discussed religion with Ezra Stiles. Aaron Lopez' brother Moses made several trips to Charleston over the years. On one in 1764 he sailed to Charleston as a supercargo for his brother. Mordecai Sheftall of Savannah traveled as far north as Boston to do business with Henry Lloyd, and other Savannah Jewish merchants too were constantly on the move, especially between Charleston and their home city.[6]

PERMANENT RELOCATION IN NORTH AMERICA

There were occasions when circumstances, primarily of an economic nature, induced American Jews to relocate themselves, often permanently, in another community. In the 1680's, for example, Saul Brown of Newport moved on to New York, and after the turn of the century Michael Asher of New York left for Boston to serve as an agent for a number of firms, although for a time he lived also in Charleston and on Jamaica. New York was often a colonial Jewish base. Newport, for instance, during the 1740's and 1750's witnessed a steady influx of New York Jews, undoubtedly drawn there to take advantage of the Rhode Island town's more attractive economic conditions. Again, most of the Jewish businessmen who settled in the villages of Long Island and Connecticut had originally come from the Jewish metropolis on the Hudson. Another New Yorker, Nathan Levy, made his home permanently in Philadelphia and brought in his nephew David Franks, who had been born and reared in New York, but had lived and done business in Boston and Charleston. Solomon Marache of New York set sail for England, no doubt to make credit arrangements with some of the London suppliers. During the French and Indian War, Marache did business for a time in Canada, later formed a partnership in New York, and following the dissolution of that company, moved to Rhode Island, and at length on to Philadelphia where, as we saw, he ultimately pursued his career with a Christian as his associate.[7]

Relocations, as the case of Solomon Marache indicates, could be very short-lived. Another example is afforded by Carvallo and Gutteres who were in business at Charleston by 1734. Two years later, however, they announced their intention to depart. They must have carried out their intention, for their names do not appear in the records after January 1736. Commercial disappointment may have been responsible for their departure, since it is hard to believe they had made their fortune at Charleston in so brief a period. Jacob I. Cohen, a German Jew who had come to Pennsylvania and had peddled or bought furs in and around Lancaster, later lived in Charleston, Richmond, and Philadelphia. A generation earlier, when the colony of Georgia had fallen apart in the 1740's due to economic difficulties, the original Jewish settlers, as already noted, for the most part permanently relocated in Charleston, Lancaster, and New York.[8]

TRAVELING ABROAD

The demands of business often made it necessary for merchants to travel great distances overseas, especially to London, their most important market. It was in London that a beginner might seek to establish his credit and bring back to his American home a cargo and sometimes, as Naphtali Hart Myers did in the 1750's, even a wife.[9]

There were always hazards associated with any long trip. In 1722 Jacob Gomez of New York was cut to pieces by pirates on Cuba while a cargo was being landed. His family memorialized him by naming a ship after him. The fearful perils which befell many a voyager were powerless, however, to inhibit travel. The same year that Jacob Gomez met his fate on Cuba, Jacob Franks was awaited in London, and a year later Ulloa & Maduro, his prime correspondents on Curaçao, were expecting his arrival on their island. Franks's brother-in-law Nathan Levy was in London in 1734, and David Franks, Levy's nephew and business associate, thought of going to India in 1743. Traveling on their own account or as agents for northern Jewish businessmen, Jews—especially in the South—made frequent trips to the West Indies.[10]

One much-traveled merchant was Abraham Sarzedas who was apparently of foreign birth and had come to New York where he married Caty Hays, daughter of a well-known and successful New York merchant. Sarzedas' father-in-law Judah Hays seems to have had no use for his son-in-law and tied up Caty's inheritance. Sarzedas was in Savannah during the 1750's and in Newport during the 1760's. In 1764 he returned to Georgia where he may have farmed for a while. That decade and the next found Sarzedas spending much time on Haiti where he carried on business and served intermittently as agent for the Newport merchants Lopez and Rivera. Sarzedas' "firm resolution of [n]ever more plowing the ocean and absent[ing] my self from my dear family" had had to give way before his eagerness "to provide . . . comfortably" for his children. In 1774 he was dead and his wife and children were living in Newport, comfortably enough if we can draw any conclusion from the fact that Mrs. Sarzedas included four Negro servants in her ménage.[11]

RELOCATION ABROAD

North American colonial history is replete with accounts of failures on the part of the oldest settlements—Jamestown, Virginia, Wessagusset, Massachusetts, and Popham Beach, Maine, to name but three. The experience of the earliest Jewish settlements was little different, and in general the first Jewish newcomers to a settlement did not remain long enough to become the nucleus of a community. Of the twenty-three original Jewish pioneers in New Amsterdam, for example, Asser Levy was one of the very few whose presence is documented after the Dutch ouster, and he too made at least one trip back to Holland. Though a number of Dutch Jewish businessmen arrived from Holland during the 1650's to do business in the fur station of New Amsterdam, none of them remained permanently. Asser Levy's kinsman Simon Valentine Van der Wilden quit New York for Jamaica; suffering heavy losses in the earthquake at Port Royal, however, he moved back to the North American mainland and settled at Charleston where he again engaged successfully in business. All this took place before the dawn of the eighteenth century, but Jewish settlement was often temporary even in later years.

Nathan Simson, who seems to have been the first of his family in New York, became a successful businessman there, but retired to England with a substantial competence in the early 1720's. Two more merchants who achieved success in America and then returned to Europe were Rodrigo Pacheco and Naphtali Hart Myers who continued their commercial careers in London. Pacheco maintained close relations with the colonies, however, even after his departure for London, while Myers became very active in London's Ashkenazic Jewish community. Closely associated with Myers in his communal work were the two sons of Jacob Franks of New York, Naphtali and Moses, who had been sent to England by their father. Remaining permanently in England, they became eminent businessmen there.

Benjamin Franks of New York, an uncle of Jacob Franks, was the first of the family in New York as far as the records show. By the time he came to New York, he had lived in Germany, England, Barbados, and the Danish West Indies. In 1696 he signed up with Captain William Kidd of the *Adventure* to go on a privateering voyage against pirates and King William III's enemies. In a deposition made at Bombay, India, in October 1697, Franks claimed to have lost a fortune of £12,000; he had signed for the voyage, he said, only to get to India where he hoped to establish himself as a jeweler. Franks swore that he had never had any part in Kidd's acts of piracy and that he had escaped from Kidd in India the preceding August.

Isaac Gomez, the son of Mordecai Gomez, was a native New Yorker who married at Curaçao where he died in 1764; he was a scion of the well-known mercantile family of that name. Isaac Levy, a member of the New York Levy-Franks clan, was active as a merchant and land speculator at New York, Boston, and Philadelphia, but also dwelt for many years in London. Jacob Henry, brother of a successful London merchant and a cousin of the Gratz brothers, spent some time in this country, made some money here, and then returned to Germany where he was robbed. Securing a large consignment of goods, Henry returned once more to the colonies and carried on trade successfully during the French and Indian War until sickness and death put an end to his career.

Many of the men described above had succeeded in making some money in the colonies and had only then returned home to larger communities to enjoy the fruits of their labor or to engage in more ambitious enterprises. There were, however, other and probably even more numerous Jews who, experiencing reverses, abandoned North America in the hope their luck would change elsewhere. Thus Naphtali Hart Jr. of Newport, after setbacks at home, gathered his family together and set sail for Barbados and St. Eustatius in the West Indies. Others fled the country because they were bankrupt and wished to avoid imprisonment for debt. Although their creditors, advertising for their whereabouts, said or implied their failures had been fraudulent, these unfortunates may simply have lost everything through circumstances beyond their control.

In brief, there were very few businessmen—even the wealthy and successful—who did not travel abroad to improve their affairs. Merchants were always searching for opportunities to make money, and a number relocated permanently or temporarily in other colonies and countries. Jews commonly traveled about, therefore, in all the mainland provinces and to the Caribbean, India, and Europe. They were already conversant with the cities of the Atlantic world in a generation when young Thomas Jefferson was yet to see a town of more than a hundred souls or to travel more than twenty miles from his home.[12]

CHAPTER 31

AGENTS, BROKERS, FACTORS, PARTNERS,

AND THE FAMILY IN BUSINESS

AGENTS AND CORRESPONDENTS

Much as a merchant needed to travel for the proper governance of his business, he could not hope to manage everything himself and often found it necessary to employ agents in distant ports. The papers of Nathan Simson, for example, indicate that he made use of agents in, among other places, Madeira, London, Jamaica, Barbados, Curaçao, Albany, Philadelphia, and Charleston. His trade with Jamaica and Curaçao was particularly heavy. These agents would buy and sell for Simson or any other merchant-shipper who engaged them, and in turn the merchant himself would commonly serve as a commission agent for goods consigned to him by his regional or foreign suppliers.[1]

In the North American colonies nearly every Jewish merchant served as an agent for his suppliers and his customers. It is not always easy, however, to determine the nature of the agency, for the possibilities of variation were rather numerous. A businessman, for instance, might receive a consignment to be sold on the joint account of the shipper and the agent, the recipient himself. The agent was thus a partner, but was he entitled to a commission? How merchants functioned as agents in less complicated, indeed typical, cases is seen in the fact that Lopez was requested to charter a vessel for a North Carolina client, while Samuel Jacobs of Canada bought huge quantities of grain for his Montreal and Quebec principals.[2]

The rather complex nature of agency is clearly exemplified in the Simson papers. In 1720 Nathan Simson sent provisions to his agent in Charleston, some on Simson's account and some on the agent's account, which meant that the South Carolinian was acting both as a commission agent for Simson and as one of Simson's purchasers. About the same time Simson dispatched North American food supplies to a Jewish agent at Curaçao on the account of two New York Jewish merchants and a similar cargo to a Gentile agent at Barbados on the account of two London Jewish merchants. In both of these instances, however, Simson was himself serving as an agent for the New Yorkers and the Londoners.[3]

One of the colonial merchant's chief problems was to keep in close touch with his agents at distant ports, for they not only supplied him with wares and staples, but also sold his cargoes and bought for him others to be returned home or forwarded to some other port for sale. It would be difficult to exaggerate the importance of a merchant's agents, for they did far more than send or receive goods. They helped their principal to determine the state of the market and the credit capacity of the purchasers. Consequently, it was imperative that they be men of integrity as well as of good judgment, for if they were not, their employer might well be undone. A responsible agent was, in short, an absolute necessity. If the goods a merchant sent to a far-off market were live or perishable, their sale had to be handled immediately by an able person. Frequently a merchant would use as his agent the captain of the vessel carrying his cargo, or he might employ a supercargo as his agent, or the merchant himself might act as his own salesman, accompanying a shipment and arranging for its sale or the purchase of a new cargo. In most cases, however, the merchant would secure the services of a trustworthy businessman in the port to which he was sending his goods. The agent to whom the cargo was consigned was usually himself a merchant, although there were some merchants who refused to serve as agents.

A commission agency could be a lucrative business. During the French and Indian War, Uriah Hendricks of New York charged 12.5 percent for his services: He received 5 percent on sales, 2.5 percent on storage, and 5 percent for collecting and remitting. A supercargo in the West Indies, for instance, would draw from 5 to 7.5 percent for sales; on cargoes purchased for return to his employer, however, he was entitled to no commission at all or at most, only a modest compensation.

The agent served his employer in another way as well. Whether he was a prominent New York merchant writing to his principal in Newport, or a West Indian writing to the North American mainland, he added prices current to almost every letter, for a businessman had to keep his finger on the pulse of the market at all times and cargoes in demand had to be dispatched without delay. On the whole, prices current told a merchant what he was best advised to send and assured agents of a load that would sell. Even so, trade being risky at best, the merchant could never be certain that some competitor would not anticipate his shipment or that some untoward event would not mar the voyage. All he could do was pray that these threats never rise to confront him.[4]

JEWS AS AGENTS FOR JEWS

For Gentile merchants to use Jews as agents was not at all uncommon. The Browns of Providence, for example, employed the services of a number of Jewish merchants. Jewish merchants, however, showed no preference for Jews as agents, and while one cannot generalize, the suspicion is not entirely unfounded that at times Jews went out of their way to use Christian rather than equally competent Jewish agencies. There was, after all, always the fear that Jewish suppliers and agents might communicate information to Jewish competitors which might impair a merchant's credit rating, a matter about which most Jewish businessmen were sensitive and apprehensive. As a young beginner, Aaron Lopez had been dependent on the Gomezes and on Levy & Marache as his New York correspondents; as he rose to eminence, however, he seems to have fixed upon Gentile firms of New York, the Crugers and the Ludlows among others.[5]

Firms employed in Spain and Portugal as agents by American Jewish merchants obviously could not have been in Jewish hands, though it is true some of their proprietors may have been crypto-Jews or Marranos, for Jews and Judaism were not tolerated as such in eighteenth century Iberia. In ports which lacked substantial Jewish

merchants—Bristol, England, for example—merchants like Lopez had
no choice but to employ a Gentile. Why, however, in London where
there were numerous Jewish suppliers, did Aaron Lopez and Samuel
Jacobs both bypass the American-born Frankses to deal almost exclusively with Gentiles? Lopez' correspondent in Amsterdam was
Daniel Crommelin, also a Gentile, and the Newporter had Gentile
agents in other countries as well where Jews were available. Was this
choice of correspondents fortuitous, or were Jewish merchants like
Lopez and Jacobs deliberately trying to avoid employing Jews? Jews
who did business in Boston, as was the case in Bristol too, had no
choice, for no Jewish merchants of substance were resident there.
In Boston, Henry Lloyd was the favorite agent of the Newport, New
York, and Charleston Jews. He bought and sold for them and showed
their friends around the city. Well-connected politically, he was
able with dispatch to shepherd his correspondent Aaron Lopez
through naturalization proceedings in Massachusetts.[6]

So much for Europe and North America, but conditions were
different in the West Indies. Jewish businessmen were very numerous
there and were employed as agents, but even so, not to the exclusion
of Gentiles. For years Lopez maintained as his factor in Jamaica a
New England sea captain named Benjamin Wright, a non-Jew of
whom more will be said below. He did business also with Isaac
Werden, another non-Jew who had been one of his correspondents
in Canada and who, on moving to the Caribbean, asked Lopez for
a cargo of candles, lumber, salt fish, and staves, and served him as an
agent in Dominica. Jews from practically all the North American
colonies made frequent trips to the islands, usually on business of
their own, and they were quick to proffer their services to their
fellow American Jewish merchants. Whether such voyagers planned
only temporary visits or were determined to remain in the islands,
they were eager for the additional income to be gained from serving
as correspondents.[7]

THE FAMILY AS AGENTS

For obvious reasons, members of a merchant's family seemed to
him ideally suited to serve as agents; they could be trusted, though as

we shall see, there were times when this trust was misplaced, and wherever possible, a merchant made extensive use of his relatives in this capacity.[8]

No later than 1712 Daniel Simson of London was shipping yard goods to his brother Nathan in New York, while from 1718 on, Jacob Gomez of the New York Gomezes worked in Barbados for his family. Isaac, another member of the Gomez clan, was on the same island in 1745, probably as an agent, and Benjamin Gomez, employed at Philadelphia in 1749 and at London the following year, was utilized to receive consignments from his relatives in North America. The Savannah firm of James Lucena & Son employed the "son" John as a purchasing agent in Newport where the Lucenas did business with cousin Aaron Lopez. Uriah Hendricks of New York served his London family as a commission agent, handling for them anything from watches to muskets.[9]

Working as agents for their Lancaster kinsman Joseph Simon, Michael Gratz's father-in-law, the Gratzes of Philadelphia sold country produce for him and shipped him English and West Indian staples. The cargoes the Gratzes sent Simon in return for his shipments to them may have been made up of goods purchased outright by the Gratzes on their own account or bought on commission for him—which, it is not always possible to determine. The Gratzes also shipped furs to the London markets for the Lancaster trader and imported textiles and other wares for him. The final proceeds from the sale of Simon's furs in England would be credited to his account with some London supplier to whom he was in debt. Seemingly, the Gratzes earned a double commission every time they sold something for their kinsman client and bought something on his account with the money received from the sale.[10]

The classical example of a family working closely together in business is afforded by the Frankses of London who had migrated to England from Germany during the seventeenth century. Sent by his family to North America in the early 1700's, Jacob Franks remained in close touch with his brothers in London. As Jacob expanded his business and became one of New York's most prominent merchant-shippers, he in turn sent two of his sons back to England where, while they acted as partners in special ventures, their primary and ongoing function in their earlier years was to serve their father as resident purchasing and sales agents.

Another of Jacob's sons, David, did not leave North America, but was sent on business missions to Boston, Charleston, and Savannah, as well as Philadelphia where David settled permanently. Jacob Franks appears also to have had commercial connections with his Charleston nephew Moses Solomons (Salomons), while the firm of Minis & Salomons (Abraham Minis & Co.?), which served the Frankses as agents in Savannah and Frederica during the days of Oglethorpe, may have included Calman (Coleman or Collman) Salomons, possibly a brother of Moses Solomons and thus another of Jacob Franks's nephews.[11]

BROKERS AND FACTORS

We lack conclusive evidence that there were any colonial Jewish businessmen whose careers were limited solely to brokerage. Most if not all commission agents were, as we have indicated, simultaneously merchants, selling at retail or wholesale on their own account. Jacob Isaacks of Newport may have been an exception, for after reverses in business, he seems to have confined himself to a straight brokerage business. Announcing in his advertisements that he would buy or sell for anyone, that he was a "broker in all branches," he offered for sale, among other things, houses, farms, lands, vessels, tea, coffee, rice, indigo, meat, and liquors.[12]

Perhaps even rarer than the Jewish broker was the Jewish factor, an agent who worked exclusively for one employer. In actuality, very few Jews on the North American mainland are known to have made a living solely as factors. Abraham Isaacks of New York, who was charged with Nathan Simson's American affairs after Simson's return to London, was more of a branch manager than a factor. It is doubtful whether Abraham Minis of Savannah was a factor for the Frankses. Minis was probably both partner and commission agent and at any rate is certain to have carried on business simultaneously on his own account. Members of the Franks family, David for example, traveled for the parental firm; they were certainly not factors.[13]

In ascertainable fact, Aaron Lopez is the only American Jewish merchant known to have employed factors, though the advantages of such agents were obvious. A factor expedited sales, thus permitting an arriving vessel to unload quickly and return or proceed to its destination without delay. Merchants employing factors avoided the costly procedure of having their captains peddle cargoes in neighboring ports. In the event a factor became incapacitated, the merchant-shipper made provision for one or two alternate agents to take over.[14]

Lopez' factor on Newfoundland during the early 1770's was George Sears. Captain Benjamin Wright served Lopez as his factor in the West Indies, primarily Jamaica, from the late 1760's and throughout the 1770's. This is not to say that Wright handled all of Lopez' business in the West Indies, for the Newport merchant, always one to have many strings to his bow, continued consigning cargoes to his captains. In certain transactions, moreover, Wright was "concerned with" (in partnership with) his employer, which was by no means an uncommon practice and which Lopez may have taken up to encourage Wright. Wright was not Lopez' first factor in the Caribbean; Lopez had originally employed his son-in-law Abraham Pereira Mendes in that capacity. However, when the young man gave unmistakable signs of his unsuitability for so delicate and responsible a position, Lopez turned to the older and more astute Wright who was not to disappoint him.[15]

Captain Wright once wrote to Lopez that success in the Jamaican trade required not only patience, but also "a stock of assurance." There is every evidence that Wright possessed both qualities in abundant measure. As Lopez' Jamaican factor, he tried with admirable energy to outstrip his employer's competitors in dispatching a return cargo to the North American mainland, and when sales were slow, he was not dilatory in peddling what he had from port to port. The captain was something of an original—clever as well as able. At times he would twit his employer, addressing him as "Dear Couzen" and calling himself "Poor Old Yankey Dodle." Referring to

America's increasingly precarious relations with Great Britain, Wright once observed ironically, "I must conclude with wishing you all may escape the gallows this time, notwithstanding you are all a parcell of rebells." Wright was as valuable a factor as a merchant could hope to employ, and Lopez was not exaggerating when during the Revolution and the ruin it visited on his affairs, he spoke of Wright's "zeallous wishes" on his behalf.[16]

Samson Mears, an American Jewish goldsmith who was to become Lopez' chief agent (in function if not name, his factor) in Connecticut during the Revolution, was closely supervising the Newport shipper's interests at St. Eustatius in 1775. Two years earlier Lopez and his father-in-law Jacob Rodriguez Rivera had sent Samuel Hart and Samuel Hart Jr. as factors, supercargoes, or special agents to Barbados where the Harts brought in a load of goods and were also authorized to collect outstanding debts. The Newporters instructed their agents to accept payment in rum and sugar if cash or bills were unavailable. One firm alone owed Lopez and Rivera nearly £2,000 sterling, a sum reflecting the magnitude of the operations carried on by the two Rhode Island shippers.[17]

PARTNERS

The multiplicity of problems faced by colonial businessmen— problems of communication, transportation, capital, credits, and collections—made them dependent on their colleagues. Doing business involved so many hazards that help and cooperation in the form of reliable agents, special acts of friendship, and courtesies of one sort or another from relatives and coreligionists were virtually indispensable. Since partnerships offered businessmen one means of relieving some of the difficulties and cutting down losses, Jewish as well as Gentile businessmen rarely disdained this method, and joint enterprise became a form of self-help, practically a necessity.

Many of the partnerships formed in colonial days were highly informal in character; they were commonly joint ventures for a single shipment. Thus in 1719, for instance, Joseph Isaacs the butcher joined Moses Michaels and Nathan Simson, merchant-shippers, just for the purpose of packing and selling 150 barrels of kosher beef. A generation later Lyon Lepmon (Lipman) combined with two Gomez brothers to prepare a shipment of pork, and it was very much to the advantage of the Gomezes to import a cargo of wine from the Madeiras in cooperation with the influential New York politician Paul Richard.[18]

There were also, to be sure, more formal partnerships to which individuals brought capital, strategic geographic location, political influence, or technical skills. Even formal partnerships, however, were usually of brief duration, seldom lasting for more than a few years, and the percentage of participation in them often varied from venture to venture. Partnerships in the family between relatives or in-laws tended to last longer, sometimes perhaps because younger partners expected to assume control of a business on the demise of their elders. Sons-in-law of the Lancaster merchant Joseph Simon, for instance, may have hoped to take over his business ultimately, but he lived to be a very old man.

Practically all Jewish businessmen at one time or another entered into some form of partnership. Aaron Lopez was exemplary in this respect, and Rabbi Carigal may have had him in mind when in the course of a sermon, he discussed what a merchant did in his counting-house—"drawing bills, settling accounts, adjusting companies [partnerships]." Lopez shared many ventures with others, especially with captains of his vessels, and it was not unusual for him or for the typical merchant to be involved in several brief partnerships at one time. One of Lopez' most remarkable, and as it happened most ill-fated, partnerships took shape in 1775 when he joined forces with Francis Rotch of Nantucket and Richard Smith of Boston and London, among others, to send a whaling expedition to the Falkland Islands off the Patagonian coast. This venture involved an overall investment of £40,000, and Lopez found it imperative to co-opt partners sturdy enough in the face of impending war to confront rigorous demands for capital, an urgent need for executive direction and guidance, and the intercontinental nature of the enterprise.[19]

JEWISH PARTNERS

Partnerships among Jews are documented frequently. In Boston during the 1720's Michael Asher and Isaac Solomon were partners in the snuff business, while some years later Newport's Jewish firms included Naphtali Hart & Co. (Naphtali's partners were Isaac, Samuel, and Abraham Hart) and Hays & Polock. Moses M. Hays was his company's resident partner in New York; Myer Polock attended to the firm's business in Newport. Another Newport partnership included Aaron Lopez and Jacob Rodriguez Rivera. Lopez enjoyed exceptionally close personal and commercial relations with his father-in-law Rivera, and the two joined together in many ventures, especially those involving the African slave trade. It is very probable that Rivera played a far more important part in his partnerships with Lopez than has hitherto been recognized, but the Rivera office records are unfortunately not extant.[20]

In New York there had been numerous Jewish partnerships since the early eighteenth century. They included not only commercial tycoons, but humble shopkeepers as well. The merchant-shipper Nathan Simson had established partnerships with his in-laws Isaac and Samuel Levy who lived in London and handled the English end of the firm's business. He set up another London partnership with his brother-in-law Joseph Levy. Simson, in fact, had at least three partnerships with London businessmen, two of them, as just noted, with members of the same Levy family. Around the same time in the early 1700's, Luis Gomez of New York worked closely with the De Pazes of London in shipping American provisions to Antigua. A generation later another New Yorker, Hayman Levy, a specialist in furs and army accoutrements, was the key figure in a series of partnerships. He was the Levy in some if not all of the following firms: Levy & Marache, Levy and Lyon & Co., Levy, Solomons & Co., and Blaggs (Boggs?) & Levey. Solomon Myers Cohen & Company supplied oil for the lamps of New York in the early 1770's. Cohen, a pillar of the Jewish community, was then president of its synagogue.[21]

The brothers Moses and Aaron Louzada were in business together at Bound Brook, New Jersey, and even paid their bills to the New York synagogue jointly! Levy Hart and Jonas Solomons were partners at Shrewsbury and Freehold, East Jersey, within easy sailing distance of New York. In neighboring Pennsylvania the wealthiest Jewish businessman was David Franks. When he first came to Philadelphia he was in partnership with his older brother Moses; later, in association with his uncle Nathan Levy, he became a member of the firm of Levy & Franks. Some years later, during the 1760's Franks was the senior partner of another firm with the same name, Levy & Franks or Franks & Levy, whose junior partner, Isaac Levy, was another uncle, the late Nathan Levy's brother, and thus also a brother of David Franks's mother Abigail Levy Franks. Other, though far less consequential, Pennsylvania Jewish firms were the partnerships of Michael Moses and Israel Josephs, and of Jacob Levi and Barnard Jacobs. The latter were running a country store on Muelbach Road in Lancaster County in 1759.[22]

Samuel Levy and Moses Solomons carried on a business in Charleston, South Carolina, in the early 1740's till they ran into severe financial difficulties. Philip Hart and Samuel Isaacs of South Carolina had a shop in Georgetown as early as 1761; the Sheftall brothers of Savannah, Levi and Mordecai, were also partners in buying large quantities of English wares—about £2,000 sterling—directly from London and paying for them in tobacco, indigo, and deerskins, while Abraham Minis and Coleman Salomons were among the first merchants in Georgia during the 1730's.[23]

It was not uncommon for Jewish merchants to take partners for the management of branch stores. Writing to his friends the Gratzes in 1764, for example, Meyer Josephson asked that a man be sent out to him as a clerk and added, "If the Jew shows ability in business, I shall give him a store on half-profits, if I think he will do." Samuel Jacobs maintained affiliates in a number of small Canadian towns, and the men who ran them were probably his partners. Myer Hart of Easton had set up branches in Oxford, New Jersey, and in Philadelphia; some or perhaps all of these Hart shops were operated by a Gentile partner, Peter Smith.[24]

GENTILE PARTNERS

Myer Hart was hardly unique in having a Gentile partner. Because there were so few of their coreligionists in the country, Jews formed partnerships very frequently with non-Jews. This practice was especially helpful when it came to acquiring additional capital for enterprises in an age which lacked stock exchanges, had little in the way of banking facilities, and was yet to accept corporations as business structures. It was usual for several merchants to pool their resources in order to buy a ship, and ever since the seventeenth century Jewish merchants had joined with their Christian and Jewish friends in such purchases.[25]

As early as the 1660's and 1670's American Jewish businessmen in Maryland and New York formed mercantile partnerships with non-Jewish associates. Asser Levy of New York set up his slaughterhouse with a Christian partner, and a group of five merchants, one of them a non-Jew, joined together to traffic between New York and Barbados. Nathan Simson had at least two Gentile associates with whom he did a great deal of business—the New York merchant William Walton and the London merchant Richard Jeneway (Janeway). It may seem curious that Simson, who traded so extensively with his own brother and with the Levys in England, should also have had a Gentile partner in London, but there were undoubtedly good economic reasons prompting Simson's division of his English trade. In any case, most of the cargoes dispatched by New York Jewish merchants during the first half of the eighteenth century were ventures with two or three or even four Gentile partners.[26]

The firm of Grant & Solomon is documented in Montreal for the year 1760, while in Quebec, as has already been noted, Samuel Jacobs formed numerous partnerships with Gentiles to manage his branch shops, to manufacture potash, to distill liquors, and to buy and sell wheat. In Rhode Island, Lopez' father-in-law Rivera manufactured candles in partnership with Henry Collins, one of Newport's outstanding merchants. Lopez himself was engaged in numerous business deals with Gentiles, particularly in the areas of shipping and whaling. We have already mentioned his joint whaling venture with Francis Rotch and Richard Smith, but he seems to have had no permanent partners in his career as a sedentary merchant.[27]

Sampson Simson, the merchant, and Myer Myers, the silversmith, had a Christian partner, George Trail, in some of their land speculations in Connecticut town lots. David Franks & Company represented a congeries of interests and partners extending from Philadelphia to the Illinois country. In addition to his membership in the firm of Franks & Plumsted, David Franks was one of the partners of Franks & Childs, Franks & Inglis, and Franks, Inglis & Barclay. Many of the Pennsylvania Jewish merchants who were heavily involved in land speculation took Gentile partners. The Gratzes, who were concerned in numerous land deals, nearly always had Gentile associates, and foremost among those with whom they did business was Colonel George Croghan. Joseph Simon too, as we shall see, engaged in numerous partnerships with Gentile businessmen.[28]

Isaac Da Costa and Thomas Farr of Charleston were partners as ship agents, merchants, and slave importers, and Abraham Minis—to his undoing as it happens—took his bookkeeper Samuel Clee as his partner. A partnership that documents the union of capital and technical skill was that of Levi Sheftall of Savannah and a German butcher.[29]

Partnerships between Jews and Christians were, clearly, common enough during the 1700's. Still, one cannot help suspecting that what motivated partnerships between the Gomezes and New York's Mayor Paul Richard, between Daniel and Isaac Gomez and Abraham Van Horne, between Sampson Simson and Theophylact Bache, between David Franks and William Plumsted, was at least to some degree a desire on the part of the Jewish partner to associate himself with a man of political influence. Such political patronage was, after all, not to be despised, especially in view of the second-class citizenship colonial America reserved for her Jewish settlers.[30]

JOSEPH SIMON AND HIS PARTNERSHIPS

Practically every form of partnership was reflected in the economic activities of the Lancaster merchant Joseph Simon. In 1750 he entered into partnership with the young mechanic and inventor William Henry. Their Lancaster store, known as Simon & Henry, occasionally advertised in the German-language press in order to secure the patronage of the neighborhood's numerous German Americans, the so-called Pennsylvania Dutch. In the nearby town of Heidelberg too, Simon and another partner Benjamin Nathan announced they had goods "suitable throughout for the Germans." In still another of Simon's partnerships, he was associated in Lancaster with his nephew and son-in-law Levy Andrew Levy as Simon & Levy. Levy was not the only one of Simon's sons-in-law to be taken into partnership; at various times several of his Jewish sons-in-law (he also had a Gentile son-in-law) were similarly involved.[31]

Simon's informal partnership with the Indian trader Alexander Lowrey was remarkable for both length and quality. It lasted for about forty years and apparently was maintained without the benefit of any extensive system of bookkeeping. The partners' accounts were finally settled with the aid of three arbitrators in a verbal discussion marked by a complete absence of acrimony, and no books or papers were presented by the contending partners.[32]

This notable merchant did not confine himself to Lancaster, but began no later than 1760 to conduct an extensive business at Fort Pitt as well. Most of the firms he established or associated with were engaged in the Indian or fur trade, and some of them operated as far west as the Illinois country and as far north as Detroit. Among the formally organized business concerns in which Simon held membership at Fort Pitt (Pittsburgh) during the 1760's and 1770's were Simon, Trent, Levy & Co., Simon & Mitchell, Simon & Milligan, Simon, Milligan & McClure, and Simon & Campbell.[33]

THE GRATZ PARTNERSHIPS

Two of Joseph Simon's kinsmen, Barnard and Michael Gratz, with whom the Lancaster merchant engaged in various enterprises, have appeared before in these pages. The Gratz brothers, as we have already said, had not always been partners. They had, in fact, set up no formal partnership with each other until several years after Michael's arrival in America to join his older brother. No later than

1768, however, they arranged a formal association, B. & M. Gratz, which lasted until about the turn of the century. Prior to the establishment of their partnership the brothers had a modest interest in merchant-shipping. In order to tap the West Indian market they established a working relationship of sorts with the Mirandas of Curaçao, and this partnership may also have included Isaac Adolphus of New York. The Gratzes would thus have had the advantage of agencies in three geographic areas for the import of West Indian products and the export of American provisions. Nevertheless, neither the merchant-shipping of the Gratzes nor the importance of their relationship with Isaac Adolphus should be exaggerated, for compared to notable merchants like the Frankses or Aaron Lopez, the Gratzes and the Adolphuses were of little consequence in the area of exporting and importing.[34]

THE FAMILY IN BUSINESS

We have had frequent occasion to mention the family in business, but what part did it actually play in a business undertaking? The relatives of a merchant—parents, in-laws, brothers, children, cousins—were assigned important roles in those precorporation days, for wherever possible, the merchant would attempt to keep the business in family hands. The reasons are obvious. The family had to be provided for, and so capital and profits were to be kept for the merchant's own kin. Then again, agents and factors were not always trustworthy; the family was—its loyalty was assured. Of course a kinsman's loyalty might far outstrip his competence, as Aaron Lopez discovered on granting a West Indian factorship to his son-in-law Abraham Pereira Mendes, a sickly neurotic youngster utterly inadequate to the job.[35]

Luis Gomez of New York had six sons, most if not all of them sharing to some extent in his business during his lifetime. The New York Levy brothers Samuel and Moses worked very closely with three members of their family in London. The Simson papers reveal indeed that the various members of the Levy clan on both sides of the ocean were partners in ventures or employed one another as agents. Every effort, it is clear, was made to keep the business in the family, so that

on one occasion which found him short of capital, Moses Levy
could write to Samuel: "Speak to brother Joseph and have him ask
his mother-in-law to lend her money to me. She will improve herself and you, too, through the commissions you will make on the
goods I buy from you." When one of the New York Gomezes seemed
to be overextending himself, seeking more credit than he merited,
Moses Levy hastened to warn one of the Levys in London. Years
later when one of Moses Levy's sons, then living in London, was
accused of evading his obligations, the family in New York rallied to
his support and denounced the scandalmonger through an advertisement in the *New York Gazette*.[36]

As long as Moses Levy lived, his sons appear to have remained
with him in his business, and after his death the business was carried
on for a time by the family with the help of his son-in-law Jacob
Franks. Later the Levys scattered, and at least two of them found
homes in Philadelphia. Some of the brothers apparently continued
to work together after their father's passing, for Nathan of Philadelphia consigned goods to his brother Isaac who had settled in London.
Another brother, Benjamin, lived at intervals in Maryland where he
served in 1752 as a resident tobacco buyer for Isaac of London.[37]

Of the several Lopez brothers who ultimately settled in Newport,
Moses and Aaron worked together, and when the elder brother
Moses fell upon hard times, Aaron and Jacob Rodriguez Rivera assumed responsibility for his debts to one of the Lloyds of Boston. A
third brother, Abraham, a latecomer to Newport, was probably supported by the wealthy Aaron. Lopez and his father-in-law Rivera
were not only associated for years as an economic team, but participated also in joint ventures with less fortunate members of the clan.
Abraham Lopez Sr., whose precise kinship to the Lopez-Rivera family
is unclear, seems to have ridden on Aaron's coattails, and Moses' son
David Lopez Jr. was enabled to gain a livelihood by making candle
boxes for his wealthy uncle. Judging from Aaron Lopez' various
account books, he employed several of the younger Lopezes as clerks
and maintained close and constant business relations with his cousins,
the Lucenas of Newport and Savannah.[38]

Three generations of Riveras appear to have participated in the
same business at Newport. During the late 1740's Abraham Rodri-

guez Rivera had moved to Newport where his son Jacob became a prominent merchant and was in turn succeeded by his own son, who bore the grandfather's name Abraham, but unlike his father, never amounted to much as a businessman. Of all the Riveras, then, only Jacob Rodriguez Rivera ever achieved commercial importance, and it was his misfortune, though he may not have thought it such, that his solidity, success, and mature wisdom were obscured by the brilliance, daring, and far-reaching ambition of his cousin and son-in-law Aaron Lopez.[39]

A generation earlier Nathan Simson of New York had probably been responsible for bringing over his nephew Joseph. Joseph Simson's two sons ultimately became very successful businessmen, and their father seems to have shared in their business and through them to have attained a competence. The two Gratz brothers, as we have seen, were constantly helping one another in business and finally became partners. In the South, Mordecai and Levi Sheftall occasionally engaged in common ventures, and at the outbreak of the Revolution, Sheftall Sheftall served as his father Mordecai's deputy in army supply. Before Aaron Lopez became the chief merchant-shipper in Newport, one of the town's most prominent business families was that of the four Hart brothers who on occasion were all in the same firm. One of the brothers of this family of merchants and candle manufacturers, Samuel, may have maintained a residence in New York; another, Abraham, seems to have lived for a time in London.[40]

The general tendency in nearly all these families was to keep the children at home in the parental business as they grew up, though occasionally they were employed as agents or sent out as supercargoes. Most of the Gomez brothers, for example, remained in New York, and Michael Gratz's sons worked with their elders in Philadelphia. The children of the Levys and the Frankses, however, scattered. During the lifetime of Jacob Franks his children were sent away or went off to different cities where they remained. This was in all likelihood deliberate on Jacob Franks's part. As we have already pointed out, after receiving their commercial training in America, Jacob's two older sons were resettled in England, Naphtali during the early 1730's, Moses several years later. London was the headquarters of the Franks clan and the city from which the Frankses had branched out to India and the Americas in the late seventeenth and early eighteenth centuries. The English Frankses, with whom Jacob's sons maintained constant economic and social contact, were exceedingly wealthy and powerful, well able to help their American-born kinsmen to establish themselves in London. Precisely what prompted fond parents like Jacob and Abigail Franks to send their children abroad cannot be said with certainty, but from all indications the boys were intended to serve their father's New York firm as purchasing and sales agents in England and also to make resplendent careers for themselves in one of eighteenth century Europe's great Jewish communities. That Naphtali and Moses were expected to contract Jewish marriages seems beyond doubt. If indeed these were Jacob's motivations, he succeeded in all that he sought for these two sons. It may be that Abigail had an additional reason for sending her beloved sons abroad. To her New York was a "degenerate place," and she deplored the heavy drinking which characterized the younger set there.[41]

Some of the correspondence of Jacob and Abigail Franks with their children in England has survived, but even so, it is difficult to determine the exact nature of the commercial relations between the American Frankses and the expatriates. What we do know is that the London sons were in business with their father at various times, that ever since King George's War both Jacob and his sons were engaged in army supply in North America and the West Indies, and that during the late 1760's and early 1770's the sons, the one here as well as those abroad, were members of large colonial enterprises like the Grand Ohio Company of 1769 and the Illinois Land Company of 1773. We know, too, that Jacob owned a vessel in partnership with his son Moses, and there can hardly be any doubt that when David, another of Jacob's sons, became a merchant in his own right, he requested his London brother Moses, with whom for a short time he had operated a partnership in Philadelphia, to serve him as a supplier.[42]

Retaining businesses under family control and working closely with relatives by blood or marriage were not characteristics peculiar to the Jews, for Gentile merchants too were moved by similar considerations. Opposed to intermarriage though they were, the older

PRAYERS

FOR

SHABBATH, ROSH-HASHANAH, AND KIPPUR,

OR

The SABBATH, the BEGINNING of the YEAR,

AND

The DAY of ATONEMENTS;

WITH

The *A*MIDAH and MUSAPH of the MO*A*DIM,

OR

SOLEMN SEASONS.

According to the Order of the Spanish and Portuguese Jews.

TRANSLATED BY *ISAAC PINTO.*

And for him printed by JOHN HOLT, in New-York.
A. M. 5526.

בשם הבחור הנחמד וכו' בר שלוה חבר פו...בעולם אם חוזר על הנכיר עד'
בר מרדכי חבר הנ"ל השולח לקפינה הנקרא

ושם הלאש · · · ההולכת נכק ברבאדוש ו חל חביות
בשר ב' קטני תביות שורי' קא בללע ואחד של שוחן בסימן זה · · · והג' עזה כשר
בדרך אחת וישר ואני נותן רשות לכל בר ישראל לאכול מכל אלה בשם הבחור הנחמד הנ"ל
שאני יודע שהוא יהודי · · בכל לבבו ובכל נפשו לבן כא━━━━━ ב' יורק יום עשק כ"ח לחדש
אדר ראשון שנת תקכ"ו לפ"ק

אברהם בהר"ר יצחק ז"ל נאמן דק"ק שארית ישראל

14. Certificate for a Shipment of Kosher Beef to Barbados, 1767
Courtesy, American Jewish Historical Society

15. Joseph Simson
Miniature by John Ramage
Location Unknown

Frankses worked closely with the Gentile interests which had entered into the ambit of the family through intermarriage. Jacob Franks's son-in-law Oliver De Lancey, who married his daughter Phila, came of a wealthy and influential family, and Oliver's firm of De Lancey & Watts, a partnership with his brother-in-law John Watts, represented the larger London army purveying firm whose chief member was Moses Franks, Phila's brother. Anne, one of the daughters of Phila and Oliver, married John Harris Cruger, scion of a very important mercantile family with excellent connections in New York and in Bristol, England. The De Lanceys themselves were related to the Van Cortlandts, the Schuylers, and the Coldens; and such connections were of great commercial value to the Frankses, since the social and political power possessed by their in-laws could be translated into land grants, contracts, and economic privileges.[43]

The Frankses of course were always elite in status, but what did one do if one was not born into a well-to-do family? In that case nothing would serve so well as marriage into the patriciate. Good connections were essential; they meant credit, and without credit even the most competent of merchants was debarred from success. In Europe apprenticeship to a merchant and entry via marriage into his firm were relatively common among non-Jews, but there was very little of that in the American Jewish community. Levy A. Levy, who clerked for Joseph Simon and married one of his many daughters, was Simon's nephew and thus already a member of the family before his marriage to Susannah Simon tied him even closer to his uncle.[44]

As was the case also with substantial Gentile merchants both in England and in the colonies, many of the Jewish businessmen in colonial America were connected by ties of marriage and blood. One might tend to find in business a rationale for these relationships, but there was a simpler reason. There were so few Jewish families in colonial America that Jewish businessmen had no choice if they intended to marry Jews. This would also explain why in America—very much in contrast to England—marital barriers between the proud Sephardim and their humbler Ashkenazic brethren were virtually nil. Early New York offers a noteworthy instance of family connections between Jewish businessmen. Of the seven Jewish businessmen who contributed in 1711 to the building of the steeple on Trinity Church, six represented families interrelated either by marriage or by betrothal.[45]

Marital interrelations can be documented in colonial America as early as the 1600's. Asser Levy, who came to New Amsterdam in 1654, had a relative Samuel Valentine Van der Wilden. Valentine's nephew was Michael Asher, whose brother Moses Mikal (Michaels) was a trader in the West Indies. Moses Asher's sisters Richea and Rachel married the merchant-shipper brothers Samuel and Moses Levy of New York. These two Levys had a London brother named Joseph who married a sister of Nathan Simson, thought to be the first of his clan in North America. Simson's chief New York agent after his departure to England in 1722 was Abraham Isaacks who was related to Mrs. Simson. Jacob Franks of New York, the greatest merchant of them all, was married to Abigail, a daughter of Moses Levy and thus a niece to the Joseph Levy who was Nathan Simson's brother-in-law.[46]

So much for now—though much more could be said—regarding London-New York marital ties. Marital as well as economic ties between the North American seacoast and Curaçao were also very much in evidence. During the years between 1685 and 1743, for example, five New York families married into as many Curaçaon families. Among these New Yorkers were the Riveras, from whose ranks came Sarah, Aaron Lopez' second wife, and the Gomezes, who were heavily concerned in the West Indian trade and had probably come to North America via the islands. In any event, all of Luis Gomez' surviving sons turned to the islands to find mates, as did also Jacob Rodriguez Rivera.[47]

Abigail, Aaron Lopez' first wife (and his niece), was a cousin of the Gomezes, and in the early years before Lopez became a successful merchant, he did considerable business with them. His daughters Esther and Abigail later married into the Gomez family. Uriah Hendricks, an Ashkenazi, married a Gomez in 1762. It was a good match, for Hendricks was very successful, while the Gomezes were an old and influential family. Uriah's second wife was Rebecca, another of Aaron Lopez' daughters, whom he married sometime after 1775. Family connections had always, of course, been important to

Uriah. It was family, certainly, that helped Uriah to get his start in this country, for he came here from London with a substantial cargo of goods, their payment very probably guaranteed by his relatives in London. Hendricks maintained close touch with his father, brother, and brother-in-law in London—they were his most frequent and probably his chief suppliers, though he also bought rather heavily from Moses Franks of London.[48]

Joseph Simon, the Gratzes, and the Bushes also comprised a maritally interconnected group that often worked closely together. Through his marriage to Rose Bunn, Joseph Simon was related to Mathias Bush, whose second wife Rebecca Myers-Cohen was a first cousin to Mrs. Simon. Michael Gratz, who became Simon's son-in-law in 1769, was one of five Jewish businessmen to marry daughters of Simon. The other four were Simon's nephew Levy Andrew Levy of Simon, Trent, Levy & Company; Solomon Etting, who later also married Barnard Gratz's only surviving child and thus became additionally a nephew-in-law to Michael Gratz; Levi Phillips; and Solomon Myers-Cohen, who was also a first cousin to Rose Simon and Rebecca Bush, and thus related to Joseph Simon even before marriage to one of his daughters. There can be no question that such intramarriages made for close economic relations, and while we cannot determine with certainty the extent to which economic advantages had inspired these matches in the first place, economic advantages surely posed no barrier to them.[49]

CHAPTER 32

THE MERCHANT: SUPPLIERS, STOCKS,

AND CUSTOMERS

WHERE HE GOT HIS GOODS

Nothing was more characteristic of the colonial businessman than the wide range of commodities he handled. But where did he secure the goods he offered for sale locally or shipped to other markets? Some of the produce, apparel, textiles, and the like in which he dealt were of native production and were obtained through purchase or barter from farmers, craftsmen or local shopkeepers. This was equally true of regional products shipped in from neighboring or more distant regions in North America. Commodities of European and West Indian origin were procured either directly from the countries of their production or from North American firms which traded in such wares.[1]

In 1760, for example, Aaron Lopez bought from Levy & Marache of New York manufactured goods they had imported from London merchants, which naturally added to the cost of the goods. At various times during the 1760's Lopez also contracted with local suppliers for fish in exchange for salt and barrels, purchased lamps from a specialist in that commodity, and secured a cargo of Pensacola red cedar lumber from another Newport merchant. Cattle, hay, and cheese came from a local supplier in exchange for cash and goods, anchors from an anchorsmith, and iron from the Browns of Providence. During the year 1766 Lopez typically received bricks from Taunton, Massachusetts, sails from a Newport sailmaker, mustard from another craftsman, cordwood from Westerly, Rhode Island, and small boats from a local boatbuilder. The grain Lopez sold had been imported from New York and Connecticut, the flour from Pennsylvania and Maryland, and the barreled beef from the Connecticut River valley and Long Island. Lopez obtained tobacco from Rhode Island and Connecticut as well as in all probability from Maryland and Virginia. These examples could literally be multiplied a thousandfold.[2]

New York Jewish merchants buying rum in 1748–1749 secured shipments from Boston, Newport, Elizabethtown, New Jersey, and Connecticut. The Louzadas of the Jerseys brought a shipment of rum from Boston via New York at the same time that the New Yorkers were buying some from Elizabethtown, New Jersey.[3]

Shopkeepers in villages and towns could turn to the largest nearby merchant for English wares. Meyer Josephson of Reading, for instance, looked upon the Gratzes of Philadelphia as his patron-suppliers and sent them country produce in exchange for manufactured goods. Indeed, as a rule small tradesmen looked to their regional metropolis for supplies, even if that entrepôt was rather distant. Thus Canadians very frequently purchased their goods in the New York market, their purchases being sent up the Hudson, over Lake Champlain, and down the Richelieu River to the St. Lawrence, though it is difficult to determine whether Canadian Jewry bought most of their goods from New York or London.[4]

Merchants in the same region and even in the same city traded with one another or lent one another goods in short supply. It was not at all uncommon for them to do business with one another to reduce surpluses, and in general they would barter with one another or with anyone anywhere if they could envisage an ultimate profit. James Lucena of Newport traded wines for Providence spermaceti candles although, since Newport was a great candle manufacturing center, this was nothing less than carrying coals to Newcastle! Obviously, however, Lucena was eager to get rid of his wines, even though accepting the candles in exchange probably meant he would take some loss. The Browns, to whom Lucena's wines were offered, might have gone along with the Newporter because the exchange was sweetened with specie and bills of exchange. In short, to secure payment for a debt a merchant might accept staples in payment, whether or not he had any need for those goods at that particular moment. One of the Providence Browns, for example, paid a debt to Aaron Lopez in rum and molasses.[5]

Certain food staples like molasses, sugar, cocoa, and rum were, as we have said, secured directly from the West Indies or by barter and purchase from North American merchants. Manufactured wares ultimately came from Europe, mostly from England. The typical larger merchant bought directly from London, although on occasion even a Lopez would turn to Boston for the English dry goods he needed. At times, however, smaller merchants and larger shopkeepers traded directly with England too, so that Isaac Solomons of Middletown on the Connecticut River, close as he was to the New York wholesale market, bought some wares directly from London. Inland merchants also dealt with England, and Samuel Jacobs of St. Denis, who traded with Montreal, Quebec, and New York, employed a substantial London firm as his supplier, while Simon & Henry of Lancaster and Mordecai Sheftall of Savannah occasionally bought directly from London wholesalers. Many American Jewish merchants, large and small alike, made trips to London to buy directly from the city's wholesalers and commissionmen.[6]

Before the mid-1700's, it is certain, the American Jewish merchants who bought and sold goods outside their own localities were tied to the New York region. This was true even for those doing business in Newport, Philadelphia, Charleston, and Savannah. After about 1750, however, those towns became in their own turn regional and metropolitan centers for local and outlying Jewish shopkeepers and merchants, though the probability is that New York still maintained her metropolitan character for all American Jewish buyers as late as the Revolution. Of course New York was completely dependent on London, although goods were also purchased in Holland throughout the eighteenth century.[7]

WHAT HE SOLD

Colonial tradesmen, whether they ranked as merchants or merely as shopkeepers, even very small shopkeepers, sold essentially the same wares. Merchants, to be sure, featured larger stocks but not necessarily a greater variety of goods. The entire stock of Hannah Moses in Philadelphia was, for instance, probably worth less than £100, but she carried a little bit of everything. Most shops, large or small, carried a variety of hard and soft goods and were in that sense very much like the present-day urban department store, or perhaps even more like the old-fashioned rural general store. One businessman very aptly called his establishment "The Universal Store or The Medley of Goods." [8]

The merchant sold dry goods (textiles and apparel), notions, jewelry, cutlery, china, mirrors, groceries (especially candles and molasses), fish, tobacco, snuff, and wet goods (liquors and wines). (The use of the term dry goods is an index to the relative importance of wet goods.) He handled drugs and medicines, Indian goods, cordage and sailcloth, naval stores, lumber, ships, and lottery tickets—and there were times when his merchandise included a "parcel" of Negroes to be sold or hired out, and white indentured servants. [9]

"A large and general assortment of merchandise" was not at all unusual, and the well-stocked Jewish merchant could have said with justice to his customers in the language of the twentieth century go-getter, "You ask it, we got it." He had it: coffin handles, Bibles, psalters, spelling books, millinery, bathing suits, perfume, and just about anything else that the eighteenth century American shopper might wish to buy. In addition to selling furniture, hardware, bricks, lime, paint pigments, and coal, the Jewish businessman was constantly trying to sell real estate or to rent rooms. He also outfitted ships, for which he would supply every item, and even served as an employment agency to place sailors. He sold passengers space, engaged in the freighting business, dealt in livestock—cattle, sheep, horses, shoats—and delivered oil for the flickering lights of the synagogue. Wines were always on hand, among them "brandy, geneva, mamsy, frontiniac and claret," and during the long war years the merchant carefully stocked soldiers' clothing and camp necessaries, gunpowder and swivel guns. [10]

Luxury goods, as we might call them, were also frequently in stock. Jewish shopkeepers specialized in cocoa and chocolate which they secured in large quantities from their coreligionists on Curaçao. As early as the second decade of the eighteenth century when well-established Americans were beginning to build beautiful homes, Nathan Simson sold pictures, and a generation later Aaron Lopez offered 116 violins at nine pounds each in Rhode Island old tenor currency, and a parcel of fiddle strings. Another popular musical instrument was the Jew's harp; Joseph Nunes' inventory included forty-two dozen in 1705.[11]

Lotteries were an additional commodity in which the Jewish merchant dealt frequently. Commissions for selling them must have been very attractive, for when Uriah Hendricks traded in lottery tickets during the 1750's, he expected to make a substantial profit on their resale. Even so, it is not easy to determine in all instances whether merchants bought lottery tickets for resale or held them as personal investments. In numerous instances there is no doubt that, hoping to win substantial prizes, merchants invested in lotteries for themselves. During the early 1770's, for instance, Moses Seixas of Newport bought chances in lotteries sponsored by the Presbyterian-affiliated College of New Jersey and some Presbyterian churches in Princeton, New Jersey, and the Delaware towns of New Castle and Christiana Bridge. In 1775 when Jacob R. Rivera purchased tickets in a lottery to finance the building of the First Baptist Church at Providence, he had a threefold purpose. He wanted to oblige "the very worthy Mr. [Nicholas] Brown" who was one of the lottery sponsors; he was glad "to promote and forward every publick building"; and not least to be sure, he was certainly hopeful of receiving one of the lucky numbers.[12]

Jews not infrequently served as managers of lotteries and handled the details of sale, the drawing of the lucky numbers, and the distribution of the prizes. Jacob R. Rivera, for instance, was employed in the administration of a lottery at Newport; Joseph Simon had been the treasurer or one of the managers of a lottery to raise money for the construction of a bridge over Conestoga Creek and to help pave the streets of Lancaster; Barnard Jacobs supervised a church drawing; and Levi Cohen was one of the managers of the lottery to buy a fire engine for Fredericktown, Maryland. In the 1760's the Gratz brothers bought some tickets in the Dublin Exchange lottery. Barnard referred to this Irish lottery as the *bezim* (eggs) lottery, though actually, its Hebrew designation notwithstanding, it had nothing to do with eggs as such. Barnard was simply punning. The Yiddish and German word for eggs is *Eier*; thus *Ire*land is "egg land." [13]

In short, a merchant would sell anything from a needle to an anchor, from a package of sarsaparilla to a cargo of mahogany, from a parcel of snuff to a farm. The degree to which variety is in fact "the soul of pleasure" or "the very spice of life" may be arguable, but there is no doubt at all that variety was the soul and spice of eighteenth century American merchandising. Unlike their London compatriots, however, American Jewish merchants were not in the bullion, diamond, jewel, or coral trade; they played no role in banking, textile manufacturing, or in the extensive sale of bills of exchange. The absence of Jews in such enterprises is due to the fact that almost no one in North America was concerned with these specialties. Important as the North American colonies were for the commerce of the empire, they were still on the outer rim; London was the hub.[14]

WHO BOUGHT LOCALLY FROM HIM

For whose benefit did the merchant maintain his "large and general assortment of merchandise"? Mostly for a local and regional clientele which bought at retail, for local and regional shopkeepers, and for an occasional fellow-merchant who turned to him for the purchase or loan of a special commodity. Retail tradesmen often used him as a wholesaler; they would buy finished goods and West Indian food staples from him at wholesale in exchange for the country produce and wares they in turn had received as commodity money in their shops. Thus the retailers who did business with the merchant were both his suppliers and customers.

As nearly every page of his account books indicates, Aaron Lopez enjoyed a built-in clientele, for practically all his house and shop employees as well as the dozens of suppliers, contractors, shippers, and sailors who worked for him, or did business with him, had to accept some goods of him in lieu of cash. His records show also that he had many Negro customers, both free and slave, but a study of the account books of other merchants is needed to determine whether Lopez was exceptional in this respect. In any case, as an intelligent, acute businessman, Lopez clearly was well aware of the buying potential of this substantial minority in Newport. Even slaves, he knew, had some money.[15]

Gentiles, of course, formed the great majority of every Jewish merchant's customers. The extent to which Jewish businessmen were dependent on sales to their fellow-Jews was small at best, and no Jewish businessman made a living from a Jewish clientele. There were simply far too few Jews in the country for that. As a clerk engaging in small ventures, young Barnard Gratz certainly did business with Jewish friends, but it is difficult to ascertain if the bulk of his business was done with them. Shopkeepers and merchants in the Canadian backcountry rarely if ever had Jewish customers, and this was true of most country shopkeepers and merchants. Aaron Lopez numbered Jews among his clients, but the percentage of his total business with coreligionists was negligible. Of the approximately sixty-five creditors of the bankrupt firm of Hays & Polock, no more than four were Jews, and an examination of Judah Hays's receipt book leaves no doubt that most or perhaps ninety percent of Hays's business dealings were with non-Jews. Still, the amount of business Jews did with Jews *was* far higher than the Jewish ratio in the general American population. Though Jews never constituted more than one-tenth of one percent in the general population of colonial America, they always exceeded that percentage in their business relations with one another.[16]

How He Did Business and How Much He Did

An important fact to recognize about the colonial period is that most merchants carried on business without the benefit of hard cash. We should not be surprised when we find Isaac Adolphus, a New York merchant, writing on one occasion that he did not have twenty pounds in the house. Of course units of money were used in bookkeeping, but little actual cash was employed. Most goods were paid for by other goods at prices agreed upon, with the result that much business consisted of a series of bookkeeping transactions and a periodic balancing of accounts between buyers and sellers. Frequently, of course, bills of exchange and some specie were used, particularly to pay London creditors who could not always absorb the commodities sent abroad to be credited against outstanding colonial debts.[17]

Most merchants, even the most successful, bought and sold on credit or country pay, and it is doubtful if there was a shop in any colony that traded only for cash. Credit was king. Goods were frequently sold on nine to twelve months credit, and many businessmen carried accounts for years. Businessmen gave notes to their creditors and accepted notes and mortgages from their debtors. The most adroit and distinguished merchants sometimes possessed little more by way of resources than ingenuity and courage; for them success lay in an ability to manipulate credit to their own advantage. The one essential was a reputation for integrity, a good name. Of course there had to be a final settlement of debts, and the successful merchant would then meet his obligations to overseas suppliers by paying them in cargoes and bills of exchange as well as hard cash.[18]

Aaron Lopez appears to have been remarkably fortunate in securing the aid of sound businessmen who not only supplied him with goods, but helped finance him as well—Henry Lloyd in Boston, Gabriel Ludlow and Henry Cruger Sr. in New York, Henry Cruger Jr. in Bristol, and William Stead, George Hayley, and Edmund Hopkins in London. Lopez must have been one of the most skillful credit manipulators in North America, for as one writer has said, he "built an empire on credit." Lopez' balances with his Bristol and London suppliers ran into many thousands of pounds sterling, but that fact did not deter him in 1775, at a moment when his obligations to one firm alone amounted to almost £23,000 sterling, from embarking with some partners upon a speculative venture involving an investment of some £40,000. For years this clever businessman managed to maintain his empire by temporarily placating the most importunate of his creditors. There may have been times when his creditors pressed him most insistently and impatiently, but Lopez was never forced into bankruptcy. What, one muses, would have been the fate of Lopez' career had he not accidentally drowned in 1782 on a trip to Providence with his wife and father-in-law? His estate was insolvent—hopelessly involved. Would it have been otherwise had he lived? Lopez' contemporaries Robert Morris and William Duer, both daring speculators, would die broken men in the postrevolutionary period.[19]

Credit aside, how was day-to-day business carried on in the North American colonies? In ways, we may be sure, often strikingly divergent from twentieth century patterns. David Ferera of seventeenth century New Amsterdam and Maryland conducted his business with tobacco—or the price of tobacco—as the unit of payment, while his contemporary Asser Levy of New York and Albany traded sheep against lumber and employed beaver skins as commodity money. After the turn of the century Samuel Levy's barber took his fee in yard goods, and Abraham Isaacks, in debt for almost £700 to Nathan Simson, paid off in feathers, flour, cider, a Negro slave, and some cash. During the French and Indian War, Jonas Phillips did business at Albany, then a military post, by selling dry goods and groceries in exchange for deerskins. The Charleston firm of Da Costa & Farr traded rice for rum; Isaac Elizer of Newport bartered molasses for rum; and Samuel Jacobs of St. Denis, Canada, exchanged rum for wheat, and as previously noted, offered to buy a farmer's tobacco if the man would sell him his wheat crop as well. The Gratzes of Philadelphia were offered Canadian furs for Pennsylvania corn whiskey and wine for flour, while Joseph Simon of Lancaster sent country produce to Philadelphia in exchange for textiles and sugar.[20]

When Samuel Brenton needed a hogshead of rum for Mr. Marsh, he sought out Aaron Lopez who issued an order on Overing the distiller. Overing gave the rum to Marsh and debited Lopez who in his turn collected from Brenton in kind or services or even some cash. On other occasions Lopez offered the Browns of Providence textiles in exchange for their pig iron, traded Levy & Marache of New York sugar and candles for their dry goods, and was quite willing to send Aaron Hart of Canada rum for his wheat. Indeed, when paying a debt or negotiating a deal was concerned, to judge from his records Lopez had recourse to as many variations as human ingenuity could devise.[21]

Customers frequently came into a tradesman's establishment, purchased items, and then presented an order for them from another merchant, or a responsible citizen, or one of the tradesman's creditors. Such orders or assignments of credit were in general gladly accepted. As a rule customers were loyal or indebted to a merchant, and if the supplier with whom a purchaser was accustomed to do business did not have what he wanted, the purchaser was given an order on another supplier.[22]

The services customers would render to liquidate their indebtedness to a merchant provide graphic testimony to the conduct of business in eighteenth century America. A Lopez account book for 1765 reveals that the printer Samuel Hall paid off his obligations to the Newport merchant by printing bills of exchange, commercial forms, and money tables; a cooper made barrels; a slave owner surrendered a slave to work for a year as a sailor before the mast; a tailor made suits; a painter painted; a bookbinder bound; a nurse took care of Lopez' ailing daughter; a seamstress made trousers; a common laborer dug ditches; and Sarah, an Indian woman, balanced her accounts with domestic labor.[23]

In 1738 a New York businessman epitomized much of the trading of the eighteenth century in a brief advertisement:

At Isaac Rodrigue's store in the Square, near the Slip Market, all shop keepers in town and country may be furnished with several sort of European goods lately imported from England, at prime cost or ready money, or in truck [trade] for porvisions [sic], likewise for credit on good security.

This was petty business, but in essence the more imposing dealings of American importers with their English suppliers were no different.[24]

Though no studies are as yet available on the volume of business carried on by the Jewish merchants of colonial America, there are relatively adequate materials for Nathan Simson and Aaron Lopez, and to some extent for Samuel Jacobs of Canada too. Many of the shipments Nathan Simson received early in the eighteenth century amounted to well over a thousand pounds. The revenue records for 1701–1703 disclose that in terms of value, Jewish merchants in New York imported about five percent of the dry goods unloaded there. A generation later, according to figures compiled by a competent scholar, the Jewish businessmen of that city "accounted for approximately eight to fifteen percent of the colonial trade for the years 1727 to 1739." [25]

In one of Lopez' account books for 1771 there are sixty-five entries—for one day alone of sales to and transactions with local and regional clients. Some of the amounts involved were fairly substantial. The lack of complete records and the complex problem of equating various currencies make it very difficult to compute the size of Lopez' local, coastal, and overseas business, but the substantial insurance carried on his cargoes, the huge debts he owed Cruger of Bristol and Hayley & Hopkins of London, and the sizeable taxes he paid in Newport all indicate amply that during the five years between 1770 and 1775 he presided over a trade which amounted annually to many thousands of pounds sterling.[26]

CHAPTER 33

JEWS AS MERCHANT-SHIPPERS

SHIPOWNERS AND MERCHANT-SHIPPERS

Merchant-shipping among the Jews began on a modest scale with the first Jewish settlements, for among the pioneers were merchants who carried on regional and transatlantic trading. They used shipping, of course, since that was the basic means of transportation. Still, even though they owned or employed ships, some at least of these merchants were only petty businessmen rather than merchant-shippers. The merchant-shipper, as we have already said, was a substantial distributor primarily concerned with large-scale wholesaling, importing and exporting. As a wholesaler he traded throughout the Atlantic basin, which made him a shipper, hiring shipboard space, chartering ships, or owning them. To satisfy the needs of his business, such a merchant arranged for or financed the manufacture of consumer goods, and thus became an industrialist. In his efforts to finance such undertakings, he prefigured many of the techniques of modern banking, and his eagerness to help himself and his associates, and to increase his economic leverage, led him nearly always into other areas of enterprise such as retailing, agency, and brokerage. Of very few of the seventeenth century Jewish pioneers could all this have been said.

Of course, as we had occasion to note earlier in these pages, no two Jewish merchants or merchant-shippers were exactly alike in the nature or extent of their business. Some were petty capitalists, part-time ocean-going peddlers, prone to sea-huckstering although already established as sedentary merchants; very few were mercantile capitalists. In general not many Jewish businessmen in the North American colonies ever rose into the ranks of the merchant-capitalists. Neither New York during the first half of the eighteenth century, nor Newport during the third quarter of the century, ever had more than a dozen at one time. Canada, Philadelphia, Charleston, and Savannah may each have had two or three at most during the quarter-century from 1750 to 1776, but with the exception of David Franks of Philadelphia, none was a merchant on a grand scale. They were all relatively modest entrepreneurs, for the typical Jewish tidewater merchants of the late seventeenth and eighteenth centuries were small-scale businessmen who employed shipping to buy and sell their wares. Most of them never attained affluence; most of them rose and fell in economic power, but with rare exceptions, even those who fell managed always to make a good living.

Some of the first businessmen who arrived from Amsterdam in the 1650's may well have come in their own ships. One of those early Sephardim, David Ferera, of whom we have spoken before, was trading in Maryland as early as 1656. He sold and transported goods by sloop and ketch at New Amsterdam and along the river plantations of Maryland. The last four decades of the seventeenth century never lacked Jewish merchants who employed shipping facilities in their businesses as they shuttled goods up and down the coast and across the Atlantic as far south as the West Indies and Surinam and as far east as England and Holland. Among the finished wares that they brought to seventeenth century New York were twine, pottery, glassware, dry goods, white and red lead, linseed oil, shoes, slippers, kitchenware, fowling pieces, and tombstones. Their exports to the West Indies featured provisions and barrel staves.[1]

It was after the turn of the century, with the growth of American commerce, that the Jewish businessman achieved more importance as a merchant-shipper. At least more is known about him than about his coreligionists of the late seventeenth century, for the first few decades of the new century witnessed the rise of a group of brilliant far-ranging merchant-shippers like Nathan Simson, Luis Gomez and his family, Abraham Haim De Lucena, Samuel and Moses Levy, Jacob Franks, and Rodrigo Pacheco. Though most of these magnates were related, however distantly, through intramarriage, they were often rivals, and the Gomezes, a numerous and powerful family, undoubtedly experienced sharp competition from the able and aggressive Levy-Franks clan. All of these merchants owned ships, almost invariably in partnership with non-Jews. One of these shipowners, Abraham Haim De Lucena, named the *Hester* after his daughter Esther. Another, Moses Levy, had his portrait painted, depicting him with a ship in the distant background in testimony to his maritime interests. One of Levy's vessels was the *Abigail*, probably named after the daughter who married Jacob Franks, an outstanding New York merchant-shipper, as we have noted, whose life and activity spanned six decades of the eighteenth century. Franks himself owned a ship called the *Charming Phila* after his daughter. In later years Phila's name was borne by another vessel that belonged to her uncle Nathan Levy and her brother David Franks. Shipowning gave merchants an added advantage with the coming of the French and Indian War; for privateering, in which Jews of the northern colonies were able to participate actively as shipowners, underwent a boom during the war years. Three Philadelphia Jews purchased and reconditioned ships privateers had seized from the French.

By the 1740's the Jewish communities of Newport, Philadelphia, and Charleston had taken root, and some of the Jewish merchants who had recently settled in those towns turned to the sea. Practically all the Newport Jewish traders, for example, owned shipping; there are about half a dozen familiar names. The most successful of the lot of course was Aaron Lopez, estimated to have controlled twenty to thirty vessels around the year 1770.[2]

Prerevolutionary Philadelphia sheltered only one noteworthy Jewish mercantile clan—the Levy-Franks combine which had come there from New York. To be sure, Jews of London residence had registered ships at Philadelphia as early as the 1730's, but it was not until the 1740's that the Levys and Frankses became shippers in Philadelphia. During the years between 1744 and 1751 they owned at least five vessels of modest tonnage. During the 1770's their vessels were larger and were probably employed to serve their owners' extensive operations as American agents for the London consortium of army suppliers. Among the vessels owned by this Philadelphia mercantile clan was the *Myrtilla* which brought over from Europe the bell later to be known as the "Liberty Bell." [3]

The Gratzes, whose maritime interests were never more than modest, for the most part freighted their goods. For a brief period they did own a ship which they had acquired, probably in payment of a debt, but it is doubtful that they ever used it. Beginning with the 1760's they made unsuccessful attempts to become merchant-shippers, and in order to establish themselves in the trade between Philadelphia and Curaçao, brought into existence the Philadelphia firm of Miranda & Gratz. The Curaçaon end of the business was handled by E. & I. Rodriguez Miranda. Apparently it was the new firm's purpose to enter into competition with the New England and New York provision shippers by exchanging Pennsylvania food staples for Curaçaon products, but nothing came of this ambitious attempt of the Gratz brothers. As far as the Atlantic trade was concerned, they remained venturers, and any success they achieved in business during the 1760's and the following decades was to be in the west across the mountains. [4]

The few and small Jewish merchants settled at Charleston were also among those who had some stake in shipping, and between 1744 and 1763 at least five of Charleston's Jewish businessmen owned vessels. The *Lindo Packett* belonged to Moses Lindo, the ebullient promoter of "indico" production in South Carolina. Lindo used his vessel primarily to trade with Curaçao and the British West Indies. During the late 1750's he imported a cargo of forty-nine Negroes from Barbados and shipped rice, indigo seed, and shingles to Jamaica in exchange for the island staples of sugar, rum, and molasses. In the early 1760's, together with a number of Christian associates, Isaac Da Costa sent out cargoes of rice, naval stores, and lumber to Barbados, and brought back salt from St. Martin and sugar and hides from Havana which at that time was still in English hands. [5]

Why so few Jewish merchant-shippers flourished in the South very likely stemmed from the fact that the southern staples of tobacco, rice, and indigo found such a ready market in England that a regular carrying trade between the two countries could be established. Freights were cheap, and ships bringing English wares were always certain of returning to England with a load of Carolina staples. Few if any of the Charleston Jews seem, however, to have entered into this carrying trade between England and South Carolina, perhaps because a good living could be made without ship-owning. The Carolinas, unlike the northern colonies, had no need for circular trading, the peddling of cargoes between three or more countries or continents in order to secure funds or products to pay off English creditors, and it was for such circular or triangular trading, characteristic of the North, that merchants required their own shipping.[6]

How to Start Out as a Shipper and Owner

It was not too difficult for a young beginner to engage in the coastal or overseas trade on a modest scale, since a shopkeeper, or a budding entrepreneur, or even a clerk could consign a parcel of goods to an agent in a distant port, or turn it over to the captain to handle for him. This was typical of the beginnings of almost every American Jewish merchant.[7]

When a man had some savings he could buy a small vessel, so that a seventeenth century trader like David Ferera found it possible to acquire a ketch and a sloop for trading on the Potomac in much the same way Jews two hundred years later would peddle their way up and down the lower Mississippi bayous from plantation to plantation. Enoch Lyon was one clerk who aspired—unsuccessfully, as it happens—to be a merchant-shipper. Another aspirant, Abraham Minis, transported supplies from Savannah to Frederica in a very small boat, which was no index, however, to his mercantile scope, since even the wealthiest merchants used small vessels. The *Four Sisters*, which belonged to Moses Levy of New York and traveled for him between Barbados and New York, was only a twelve-ton sloop. Lopez' *Abigail*—named either for her owner's first wife or for one of his daughters and engaged in transporting bales of goods from London—was only a fifty-ton sloop.[8]

Money, as we have had frequent occasion to note, was a scarce commodity in colonial America, and even a small ship purchased on credit may often have involved too much of an expenditure for one

[619]

man. In that case, however, a group could usually be found to band together for its purchase. A partnership was always an advantage, for the investment was small in the event of a loss, and if a man had more capital, he could spread it among several enterprises. Consequently, it was very common throughout the seventeenth and eighteenth centuries for Jewish businessmen to join with others, most frequently non-Jews, in the buying of ships. David Ferera, for example, in 1659 acquired one-third of a vessel in Maryland, and in 1694 Joseph Bueno of New York owned part of a brigantine.

Throughout the eighteenth century joint ownership of vessels was common in nearly every town of Jewish settlement. It was the rule rather than the exception, and the New York port records for the years between 1715 and the 1760's demonstrate quite conclusively that while individual Jews did possess ships of their own, the general tendency was to co-opt partners. Often four or five or even six businessmen would join together to buy one vessel. When Uriah Hendricks suggested to a London merchant that they pool resources to buy a sixty-ton sloop for the West Indian trade, he took pains to point out that the entire ship and cargo could be purchased for £1,400. Hendricks himself was willing to invest one-quarter of the necessary amount.[9]

THE COASTAL TRADE

Colonial Jewish merchants looked at most to five or possibly six metropolitan trading centers: Newport, New York, Philadelphia, Charleston (which to some degree included Savannah within her commercial ambit), and Montreal. The latter serviced the city of Quebec, the few Jews to be found in towns like St. Denis and Three Rivers, and of course the upper country fur traders. Newport rather than Boston, it will be noticed, was New England Jewry's commercial mart. Each of these centers had its backcountry, its natural hinterland with which it traded, in addition to its commerce with every other port of significance on the North American coast, in the West Indies, and across the seas.

Newport's regional ambit, while it extended into Massachusetts and eastern Connecticut, seems to have been limited primarily to Rhode Island herself. Business relations between Newport's Jewish merchants and the Providence Browns were constant, though it is also true that throughout the province Lopez of Newport maintained contact with a number of smaller clients to whom he sold goods at wholesale or retail.

New York Jewry, by contrast, had a far wider area of regional activity. Connecticut always belonged to New York commercially, and Jewish New Yorkers had been trading there ever since the seventeenth century. The Gomez ledger for the mid-1700's shows that as coastal traders the Gomezes did considerable business in the towns around New York, on Long Island, and in New Jersey, though they also had accounts as far north as Boston and as far south as Charleston.[10]

Philadelphia Jewry served western New Jersey as well as Maryland and Virginia, but most of their regional trading was with the little towns to the north and west of Philadelphia, as far west in fact as Pittsburgh and ultimately the Illinois country. On occasion, to be sure, the merchants of the interior towns did some trading among themselves, as when Meyer Josephson of Reading made some purchases in Heidelberg and Easton. Maryland was not an independent center, certainly not as far as her Jewish merchants were concerned, but fell well within Philadelphia's mercantile orbit. In the seventeenth century, however, the Jewish traders of Maryland had drawn their supplies from New Amsterdam, or New York as she was later called, and from the European continent.

Charleston was southern Jewry's metropolis, and the area to which her Jewish merchantry sent supplies included parts of North Carolina, the South Carolina backcountry, East Florida, and much of Georgia where Da Costa, the best known of Charleston's Jewish merchants, had considerable business dealings. Savannah served southern Jewry as something of a subcenter. The town had been a supply base for Oglethorpe on a modest scale as he launched his attacks against the Spanish in Florida, and it was from Savannah that supplies had been sent south to Frederica for the use of his troops. Some of the Savannah wares supplied by the Jewish merchants of those days had not come, however, as might be expected, from Charleston, but from New York, and there is evidence also that the Savannah merchants around the year 1740 received some of their goods directly from London. As Georgia took shape behind the coast, Savannah's merchants began to do business with the hinterland.[11]

The geographic boundaries of the regional areas in which, as we have seen in preceding pages, colonial Jews bought and sold do not tell the whole story of American Jewish commerce, for every regional center engaged in coastal trade beyond its own legitimate district and also entered to a greater or lesser degree into the West Indian and transatlantic trade. The great bulk of colonial American business, it will be recalled, was maritime because the important cities were on the ocean, while some of the smaller towns and settlements were most accessible by river routes. It was the function of coastal merchants to gather the raw materials of their regions and to send them for purposes of exchange to other colonies on the North American mainland, to the West Indies, and to Europe. The restrictive character of the trade and navigation acts, which severely limited non-English foreign trading, and the governmental encouragement given traffic with England and the colonies of the British Empire proved a stimulus for merchants to occupy themselves extensively with coastal commerce. This trade did not, to be sure, match the sum total of the overseas shipping to Great Britain and the West Indies, but in 1764, for instance, nearly half the ships sailing out of American ports cleared for other American ports. In 1768 Lopez sent five vessels to the West Indies, four to Europe, one to Africa—and thirty-seven up and down the American coast.[12]

Not every Jewish regional merchant, however, was engaged in coastal trading. The Canadian Jewish merchants were not merchant-shippers; with rare exceptions they neither owned nor chartered vessels, and many of their imports came up from New York by the shorter land and water route, since a continuous water passage north from New York was impossible, unless one sailed up the Atlantic coast and around Nova Scotia into the St. Lawrence. The only outgoing cargoes the Canadians cleared for foreign ports consisted of furs, which they freighted. Even the most substantial Canadian merchants like Aaron Hart and Samuel Jacobs were essentially large backcountry shopkeepers, businessmen without benefit of ocean-going vessels. It is true, as mentioned before, Samuel Jacobs had come to Canada with a schooner, but he sold it, and all he ever again owned or chartered were riverboats to do local interior hauling. Eleazar Levy had a brig that traded with London, and there may have been other Quebec and Montreal Jewish merchants with ships of their own. The extant records, however, would indicate quite clearly that they were not merchant-shippers, certainly not in the classical sense.[13]

Though colonial Boston had no Jewish community, there was nearly always a Jewish merchant or two in the city to carry on trade between Boston and New York. It has not been possible to determine, however, whether any of them used shipping of their own. At the other end of the coast, in Charleston and Savannah there were agencies of the New York Frankses during the 1730's and 1740's. Earlier in the century the first colony of Charleston Jewish merchants had probably been merchant-shippers. Some had come there from Jamaica; others, from New York. Mordecai Nathan, who hailed from New York, sent sole leather and calfskins to Rhode Island and certainly also trafficked in New York with his good friend and correspondent Nathan Simson. Joseph Tobias, Isaac Da Costa, and their friends, who constituted the second stage of South Carolina Jewish settlement during the second and third quarters of the eighteenth century, owned vessels and carried on a coastal trade. In addition to his riverboat, with which no doubt he serviced his planter-clients, Tobias had a schooner called the *Judith* after his daughter, whose name has persisted in the Tobias family of Charleston down to the present day. Da Costa solicited trade from Henry Lloyd in Boston, kept in close touch with his coreligionists at Newport, and transacted considerable business in Georgia. Men like these helped Charleston become increasingly important as a port.[14]

Savannah Jewish merchants, too, had some share in the coastal trade. Minis & Salomons, Isaac De Lyon, the Sheftalls, and the later Minises all imported and exported goods and produce, but rarely in their own vessels. The small boat the first Minis used to carry supplies from Savannah to Frederica for Oglethorpe during the Spanish wars can hardly be termed a ship. For a brief time during the

Revolution, Levi Sheftall owned a small schooner, the *Beggar's Benison*, which he had purchased from the estate of Button Gwinnett after this Signer had been mortally wounded in the duel with Lachlan McIntosh. Isaac Mendes of Pensacola, Florida, is known to have done business with Newport and London, but whether or not he possessed shipping of his own cannot be said.[15]

The coastal trade carried on by colonial Jews was concentrated for the most part among those living in Newport, New York, and Philadelphia. As early as the 1670's the Rhode Island metropolis had sheltered Jewish businessmen, and David Campanell commanded a sloop in the late 1690's. Well before the seventeenth century came to a close, Jewish Newporters were carrying on trade, albeit of no great consequence so far as can be determined, with Boston and New York, but it was not until the 1740's when their community was reestablished, that Jewish Rhode Islanders became important in trade and shipping. Beginning with the decade of the 1740's they owned and chartered vessels and were active in commerce up and down the coast as far north as Newfoundland and as far south as Georgia.[16]

Naturally enough, since theirs was the oldest settlement, the first evidence of Jewish coastal shipping is found among the New Yorkers, who as early as 1655 had begun sailing up the Hudson to Esopus (present-day Kingston) and Fort Orange (Albany) and down the coast to the South (Delaware) River in the neighborhood of the original Swedish settlements. They brought furs and wheat down the Hudson and sent up consumer wares. Trading for furs on the Delaware, they no doubt offered finished goods and liquor in exchange. Even in those early years, however, they reached out north along the coast to New England, and south to Maryland and Virginia where they bought tobacco. With the first decades of the eighteenth century, when the population of British America underwent a substantial increase and the North American littoral was dominated by a string of English settlements from Nova Scotia south to Frederica, Georgia, and later to Florida and Mobile, the New Yorkers became even more active in coastal shipping.[17]

Nathan Simson, whose mercantile net reached out to England, Holland, the Caribbean islands, and the slavecoasts of Africa, interested himself also in the coastal trade, and his correspondents and consignees were to be found all the way from Boston to St. Augustine in the years between 1715 and 1722. A number of petty Jewish shopkeepers in the Connecticut towns of Stamford, Stratford, and Hartford were carried on his books. He could claim at least two customers in the Jerseys, both Jews, and he also did business across the Delaware in Philadelphia. Excluding Charleston, South Carolina, where Simson had good friends, all his customers and agents south of the Jerseys were non-Jews. Visiting Philadelphia from the Pennsylvania backcountry, Isaac Miranda solicited his patronage, but there is no evidence that Simson did any business with him. Except for Miranda in Pennsylvania and a handful of Jews in South Carolina, there were few if any Jewish settlers at that time in the provinces south of New Jersey, and so Simson had Gentile agents and correspondents not only in Philadelphia but in the Carolinas as well. From North Carolina he secured pork; from South Carolina, tobacco, snuff, rice, cocoa, and deerskins; for all of which he exchanged provisions: English goods, gunpowder, and since parts of South Carolina were to remain hostile Indian country for almost another century, beads for the Indians. On some of his South Carolina ventures, Simson had as his partner Samuel Levy of New York; on another occasion Jacob Van Cortlandt joined him in sending a shipment of bacon to the Carolina planters.

Goods shipped to Charleston by Simson were either on his own account, the account of a partner, or the account of correspondents or agents. One of his agents in South Carolina used Charleston as a base for Simson's attempt at trade in the neighboring Bahamas, which proved to be a disastrous venture because of a Spanish attack in 1721. Still, though Simson did encounter difficulties in the Bahamas, he seems to have experienced no trouble in carrying on trade with Spanish-Catholic St. Augustine despite the fact that he was Jewish. Judging from their names, his correspondents in the Florida settlement were Englishmen, but then, Simson too is an old English name. Coastal trading was in any case hardly Simson's prime concern; it was the least important of his economic interests, for most of his traffic was carried on with the West Indies and London.[18]

The second decade of the eighteenth century found the Jewish merchants of New York, who were contemporaries of Nathan Simson, importing large quantities of English manufactures from Boston and Rhode Island. Trading with Philadelphia, they secured furs, and at New Castle farther down the Delaware, they bought grain and flour. In South Carolina they bartered provisions and consumer goods for rice and naval stores. Through the war years until 1743 they received furs, hides, tallow, deerskins, staves, naval stores, tobacco, and rice from the Carolinas and Georgia, in return for Northern products, liquors, and European goods. Rhode Island exported rum, fish, oil, molasses, and sugar to New York in exchange for provisions, while the Newfoundlanders imported from New York staves for their barrels as well as naval stores, rum, sugar, molasses, and some cotton —this last primarily to keep the women busy at their spinning wheels when the men were out with the fishing fleets. The fish caught by the Newfoundlanders paid for their New York purchases. New York's shipment of provisions to Georgia during the Anglo-Spanish war years of 1738–1743 was particularly heavy, and her imports of rice from South Carolina at the end of the next war in 1763–1764 also assumed relatively large proportions. The New Yorkers always balanced their accounts with edibles and European goods.[19]

Among the important New York merchant families involved in coastal shipping were the Levys, Frankses, and Gomezes, all of whom have appeared before in these pages. The Frankses, who frequently did business with the government, embraced an area of trade from Boston south to the Florida border and at various times maintained agencies in the larger coastal towns. The Gomezes, as their ledger indicates, traded up the Hudson, visited the Long Island ports, and moved north to New England and south to Pennsylvania, Maryland, and South Carolina. Mid-eighteenth century port records show that the Jewish merchants of New York, importing rum, wines, and cocoa, were in commercial contact not only with Rhode Island, but also with Boston, with Fairfield and New London in Connecticut, with Elizabethtown and Perth Amboy in the Jerseys, and with Philadelphia. Judah Hays, as his receipt books bear witness, was trading with Quebec in the 1760's, while the Henry Lloyd letter book testifies that Hays's New York Jewish contemporaries were carrying on business in Boston.[20]

The biggest Jewish firm in Pennsylvania was that of the closely knit Levy-Franks clan, but since nearly all the Levy-Franks papers have disappeared, it is practically impossible to gauge the nature and extent of their interprovincial shipping. We do know that from the 1750's well into the period of the Revolution, David Franks and his associates were actively engaged in army supply, which involved extensive use of shipping from Quebec all the way to the southern ports.

The Gratz brothers, one of whom had begun his commercial career under Franks patronage, constituted a much smaller firm during the colonial period. The fact that so many of their papers have survived should not mislead the student into exaggerating their consequence for the coastal trade. They achieved no marked importance until the Revolutionary and post-revolutionary periods when their western trading and land speculations did become quite extensive. The family has gained considerable recognition because of the part its second generation played in the commercial, cultural, and social life of early nineteenth century Philadelphia. Rebecca Gratz, Michael's daughter, was reputed to be the original of Rebecca, the beautiful Jewess of Sir Walter Scott's *Ivanhoe*, but there is no evidence to substantiate this romantic story. The limited scope—if not geographic range—of the Gratzes' participation in the coastal trade is evident during the fifteen years before the Revolution when Barnard and Michael used ships owned by others to send modest parcels of goods as far north as Quebec and Halifax and as far south as Spanish New Orleans. To Quebec, for instance, they dispatched scythes and gin, leather breeches and shoes; to Newport, flour; to Mobile, gin and butter; and to New Orleans, dry goods and saddles. In New York they traded with Peter R. Livingston, and with the brothers Samson and Solomon Simson who were in the market for indigo. The Gratzes were also invited to ship corn whisky to Montreal, to become partners in a vessel shipping flour to Georgia where they could secure rice and furs, and to barter molasses, earthenware, and a still for Virginia tobacco.[21]

LOPEZ AS A COASTER

The nature and extent of the coastal trade among Jewish merchants are seen to best advantage in the traffic of Aaron Lopez of Newport whose books, as already noted, record thirty-seven coastal voyages for 1768 alone. Such heavy traffic was, to be sure, hardly typical of the average Jewish businessman, for Lopez ranks as the leading Jewish merchant-shipper in the prerevolutionary decade. The fact that many of his papers are still extant, deposited in the library of the Newport Historical Society, makes it possible to describe and gauge his activities, which were of great significance since Newport was a clearinghouse for goods from many parts of the world. Lopez was her most distinguished merchant during the late 1760's and early 1770's. In monetary volume his coastal trade may not have borne comparison with his activity in the realm of West Indian and English imports and exports, but nonetheless, it was a trade of very substantial proportions. His correspondents were to be found in virtually every important North American town from Montreal to Savannah, and his dealings with them merit a somewhat detailed examination.[22]

To the Canadian markets Lopez shipped goods of English manufacture as well as liquors, rice, candles, and West Indian food staples like sugar, molasses, and rum, in exchange for furs and grain. There were times also when, serving as an agent, he merely assembled a cargo and shipped it on to his correspondents in Quebec. Captain George Sears, as has been noted, served Lopez as his factor in Newfoundland where he offered for sale the Newporter's marine supplies, English goods, naval stores, building materials, livestock, and provisions, particularly rum. Captain Sears was also instructed to sell the cargo-bearing ship itself whenever possible.[23]

Much of Lopez' business in Massachusetts stemmed from his involvement in the West Indian trade which required prodigious supplies of fish. At one point we find Lopez' brother David exploring, perhaps on Aaron's behalf, the possibility of trade with a citizen of Cape Ann, Massachusetts, through proposals to barter

Jamaica-bound fish in exchange for cordage, wines, and indigo. The West Indies' constant need for fish frequently led Aaron Lopez' captains to barter sundries for fish at Marblehead, Gloucester, and other places on the Massachusetts coast.[24]

In Boston, Aaron Lopez turned to a number of merchants who served as his correspondents, handling bills of exchange for him, or buying whale oil and head matter as well as candles on their own account or on commission. The Bostonian to whom he most often looked for business and personal services was, however, Henry Lloyd. Lopez sent Lloyd frequent shipments of whale oil and head matter, but there appears to have been no ascertainable pattern in the exchange of commodities between the two. Lloyd was ready to buy or sell anything that would find a market in Boston, and in addition to several other American Jewish businessmen, served Lopez as an advisor and agent, especially in collecting debts due in the Boston area.[25]

Lopez' chief correspondents in Dartmouth-New Bedford and on Nantucket were Joseph and William Rotch of the widely-ramified seafaring family and their various partners. The Rotches purchased cordage and spermaceti head matter for him, and he in turn sent them food staples, whale oil, naval stores, sole leather, and English goods, including tin cannisters for packaging foods.[26]

Closer to home, in Providence the Newport merchant bought cocoa from his Sephardic compatriot Daniel Torres, traded tea for candles with another merchant, and purchased candles, pig iron, ironware, spirits, oil, sugar, and rum from the Browns, to whom he sent in exchange English manufactures and liquors. In South Kingston he bartered English goods for lumber and fish and was offered some tobacco in exchange. He agreed to trade another Rhode Islander English wares and West Indian food staples for a new ship.[27]

Lopez' correspondence with some of his New York friends indicates that during the French and Indian War he was selling or sending on consignment candles, soap, chocolate, axes, spermaceti head matter, and whale oil in exchange for English dry goods, apparel, and china. Sometimes he sought lumber in payment or his New York correspondents offered him beaver and deerskins. On occasion he was asked by the New Yorkers to supply dry goods, flaxseed, sugar, wines, and indigo. When Levy & Marache, his New York correspondents of the early 1760's, lacked something Lopez wanted, they bought it for him and charged a commission for their efforts. The Newport merchant carried on a substantial trade in the Province of New York, particularly on Long Island. Throughout the 1760's and 1770's we find him purchasing beef, fish, and country produce in exchange for sugar, rum, indigo, raisins, and English merchandise. There were times when one of his captains would sail into a Long Island harbor with a load of West Indian and London wares and then proceed to barter as best he could for local provisions, which in reality was a form of huckstering.[28]

In New York City proper, where his New York trading was concentrated, Lopez had numerous customers and correspondents, mostly non-Jews. He carried on a great deal of business with Samuel Broome, the Ludlows, and the Crugers. Broome & Co. bought Lopez' candles and wine and forwarded sundries (English goods) and wine to a Lopez customer in the Jerseys. The Ludlows and the Crugers, the latter tied to Lopez through his Bristol correspondent Henry Cruger Jr., turned to Lopez for whale oil, potash, molasses, rum, and spermaceti candles, among other items, and on one occasion when Gabriel Ludlow sold a ship and cargo for Lopez in South Carolina, he made payment in cash, drafts, and a diamond ring.[29]

As he did in most provinces, Lopez had several correspondents in Pennsylvania, among them Benjamin Levy of the aristocratic New York family, who supplied him with large quantities of bar iron, and the Gratzes, who occasionally shipped him butter. Neither of these two Philadelphia firms, however, secured the bulk of his patronage. For many years most of his trading in Pennsylvania was carried on for him by Captain Joseph Anthony who made regular if unscheduled trips between Newport and Philadelphia. Lopez bought meat, flour, bread, wrapping paper, salt, lumber, and beeswax, in return for which he supplied the Pennsylvanians with staples of rum, molasses, whale oil, and candles.[30]

Despite the fact that Virginia was the largest of all the North American seaboard provinces and that both Maryland and Virginia were very important because of their great staple, tobacco, Lopez appears to have carried on little trade there. In 1761, before he became a merchant of distinction, Lopez had been a partner in small cargoes of sundries—yardgoods, furniture, hardware, turpentine, teakettles, and coffee—shipped to Maryland, and had participated that same year in two small voyages to Virginia where whale oil, rum, staves, and furniture were exchanged for grain. Though in succeeding years he apparently found little opportunity to do much business with Virginia, he did continue to explore the possibility of trade with neighboring Maryland. Throughout the 1760's Lopez made use of ventures consigned to captains or supercargoes and of partnerships in voyages to dispatch candles, molasses, rum, furniture, hardware, yardgoods, and provisions to Maryland and the growing city of Baltimore. The amount of business he carried on in the province was in sum, however, unimpressive.[31]

Lopez' coastal trade with North Carolina was tied up in large part with his traffic to the West Indies. He supplied the planters in North Carolina with the manufactured goods they needed in exchange for naval stores, lumber, provisions, grain, cattle, meat, hides, and fish, which he sent on to the islands or carried back to Newport. Occasionally, on their way back from the islands his vessels would stop in North Carolina to dispose of a few slaves or other commodities, and from time to time Lopez supplied the North Carolina planters with vessels for the shipments of fish they sent to the islands on their own account. Lopez' North Carolina traffic was not unimportant in his economy. His correspondent in Edenton was Cullen Pollok, a wealthy and prominent planter, and Lopez employed an agent in Newbern as well, Richard Ellis, to whom he directed many of his shipments. The first seven months of 1770, for example, saw at least seven of his vessels carry cargoes to North Carolina. In the early days of his career he had sought partners for his ventures to North Carolina, but after a few years the cargoes he sent there were his own.[32]

By 1761 at the latest, Lopez was shipping rum to South Carolina on his own "account and risk," and by the spring of 1764 he and his partner Rivera were importing rice from Charleston. That same spring Lopez put into effect a plan to take advantage of the opportunities in Charleston. He sent his brother Moses there with hay, provisions, oil, candles, and rum, and it was his intention to keep on sending such supplies to Moses who would remain in Charleston as a factor, receive his brother's New England goods and sell them for specie or bills of exchange to repay Lopez' English creditors, or barter them for rice, naval stores, and indigo to be shipped across to England or back to Rhode Island and Massachusetts. At his halfway station in Charleston, Moses would also be able to sell surplus slaves brought in by Lopez' and Rivera's Guinea ships coming up from the islands. No doubt too, brother Moses could dispose of some of the molasses Lopez' ships had taken on in the islands.

Though this plan failed, possibly because Moses was incompetent and soon returned to Newport, Lopez did not abandon his Charleston hopes, for the following year (1765) he consigned rum and candles to Isaac Da Costa. Apparently dissatisfied once more, however, he turned to the Charleston firm of Durfee & Russell whom he appointed his agents. It was the job of his new correspondents to sell what Lopez sent them and to remit in good bills or hard cash to Lopez' London creditor George Hayley. Thus a routine was established. He sent rum to Durfee & Russell who supplied him in their turn with rice and indigo or bills and cash. In buying indigo through Durfee & Russell, Lopez bypassed Moses Lindo, a Sephardic compatriot who was acknowledged to be the outstanding indigo expert in the province. Apparently, however, the Newport merchant was content to work through his tested Charleston agents.[33]

In pursuing his coastal trade Lopez developed a series of agents and correspondents stretching from Newfoundland to South Carolina. Typical of this far-flung operation was Lopez' decision to send the *Mary*, which had just come from Quebec, on to Savannah in 1771. Thus Georgia, one of the largest provinces and next to Canada the last one to take form, became another link in the chain, for it offered Lopez many opportunities. As a young pioneer colony—the newest frontier in fact—Georgia required basic consumer goods to maintain even the humblest of civilized amenities, and Lopez realized the potentialities in the situation. He may, indeed, have been responsible for his cousin James Lucena's removal to Georgia. In any event, whether prompted by Lopez or Rivera, or by the deteriorating

16. Jacob Rodriguez Rivera
Portrait by Gilbert Stuart
Courtesy, the Redwood Library and Athenaeum, Newport, R. I.

17. Interior of the Newport Synagogue
Photo, Kerschner, Newport, R. I.

political situation in New England, the Lucenas left Newport and by 1767 had settled in Savannah where James became Lopez' correspondent, and Rivera's too, since in practically all the shipments Lopez sent to Georgia from Newport, his father-in-law was also concerned as his partner.

Adapting the pattern employed for Charleston and the other ports, Lopez sent his Savannah kinsmen merchandise, foods, candles, oil for lighting purposes, furniture, axes, soap, a few Negro slaves, cordials, and large quantities of rum, in addition to hay to feed the horses raised on Georgia ranches and shipped south to West Indian sugar plantations. In exchange for what Lopez and Rivera dispatched to Georgia, Lucena and the ship captains to whom some of the outbound cargoes were consigned assembled return cargoes of skins, furs, tanned sole leather, rice, and lumber. Unquestionably, the trade relations Lopez and Rivera established with Georgia were of no small importance for the colony's economic development.[34]

CHAPTER 34

OVERSEAS TRADE

LOCALES AND TRADERS

The Acts of Trade and Navigation Laws, as we have seen, made it inevitable that North American overseas commerce would be focussed in the main on Great Britain and the British West Indies. Much of the business of the American maritime shipper had, therefore, to be carried on with the Anglo-American provinces, with England's Caribbean dependencies, and with Great Britain herself.[1]

The two British West Indian islands most favored by American traders were the wealthy sugar colonies of Barbados and Jamaica. The trade with Jamaica was particularly important. Curaçao, a Dutch colony, was also paid frequent visits by vessels in the service of American Jewish businessmen, while shipments to Dutch-ruled St. Eustatius were common enough, and there is even a record of a voyage to Bonaire for a load of salt. American ships also sailed into the harbors of the Spanish, French, and Danish islands in the Caribbean.[2]

North American Jews rarely carried on any direct trade with the Spanish-American mainland colonies, though London Jewry and the Jews of the Dutch and English West Indies were heavily engaged in that illegal traffic. Such direct trade to South America as involved American Jewish merchants was primarily to the Dutch colony of Surinam, and the New York Jewish traders, who had trafficked with Surinam since the late seventeenth century, continued their shipping throughout the next century. The North Americans dispatched to Surinam provisions, horses, lumber, and naval stores in exchange for typical Caribbean staples like rum, molasses, and sugar. No later than the year 1728, coffee, too, appeared in the invoices. Though by the middle of the eighteenth century Surinam's prosperity seems to have diminished, traffic between that territory and the North American mainland remained constant, with the Browns of Providence achieving a degree of eminence as specialists in the Surinam trade. Lopez of Newport, too, was in close touch with Surinamese merchants and in 1768 sent them at least three cargoes. There was, in any case, something of a special relationship between Newport and Surinamese Jewry, trade following the synagogue because the synagogue had followed trade! Their correspondents at Paramaribo's Neve Shalom congregation had contributed to the Newporters in their synagogue's time of need, and so at Newport on every eve of the Day of Atonement, benisons were piously and gratefully intoned for the well-being of the Sephardic Jews of Surinam as well as those of London, Jamaica, and Curaçao.[3]

Although the American coastal trade increased in importance with the growth of the mainland colonies, commerce with the Caribbean islands continued to be of great value until the American Revolution. In 1763, for example, of the 184 Newport vessels involved in foreign trade, about 150 cleared for West Indian ports. New York Jewish merchants were already shipping cargoes south to the islands no later than the 1660's, and all through the next century, up to the Revolution at least, New England and New York Jewish shippers continued to send provisions, lumber, and cattle to the Caribbean.[4]

Fortunately we possess many of the customs records for the port of New York during Queen Anne's War, and they permit us to gauge rather accurately the activities of Jewish merchant-shippers for that period. A study of the imports into New York harbor for 1703–1709 discloses that there were about twenty Jewish businessmen engaged in merchant-shipping. Five of them were important; the amount of business done by the rest was inconsequential. Nathan Simson is listed with but one entry; Jacob Franks is not even mentioned though he was already in the colonies. In the next generation these two were to become very distinguished merchants.

The New York Jewish businessmen of this period were dependent for their livelihood on other merchants and shopkeepers; not one of them enjoyed the patronage of the provincial government during these years, and not one of them fed at the public trough. Since they were importers, some of their wares came from Boston and Rhode Island; occasionally they secured goods from distant Madeira and even from the Guinea coast. Thousands upon thousands of gallons of rum were shipped to them from Barbados. Though London was the prime source for dry goods, most of their consumer wares were secured from the islands. Some European goods were billed to them from Nevis and St. Thomas, but their chief source for such supplies was Jamaica. Jamaica, in fact, shipped more manufactures to the New York Jewish merchants than all other sources lumped together, even including London. Yet, by the next decade in all probability, these men had emancipated themselves from the Jamaican middlemen and were dealing directly with the London suppliers. American trade was shortly to become more than a satellite of the West Indies; the North American colonies were coming into their own commercially.

How much business did these New York Jews do during Queen Anne's War? There were periods, the customs records indicate, when they were responsible for less than three percent of the imports, but there was one stretch when they alone could account for about eighty percent of all consumer goods unloaded on the docks. For the years in question, 1703–1709, over fourteen percent of all finished wares were shipped to Jewish businessmen in New York. It is probably correct to suggest that, for the first ten years of the new century, the Jews were significant in the import economy of the province, indeed relatively more important than they were to be in later decades.

The Simson papers enable us to follow the West Indian trading of the New York Jewish merchants during the second and third decades of the eighteenth century, but there is no reason to believe that non-Jewish businessmen pursued different routes or employed different methods. Trading with the French islands, with Danish St. Thomas, with the Dutch at St. Eustatius and Curaçao, and with the English at Barbados, Nevis, and Jamaica, the New Yorkers exchanged provisions—flour, beef, and vegetables—for molasses, sugar, rum, cocoa, snuff, indigo, and specie. The cocoa they secured came from Curaçao, Jamaica, and Haiti; rum and molasses were obtained from Antigua, Jamaica, Barbados, Curaçao, and St. Croix. Not infrequently Simson and the Levys resorted to the circular mode of traffic, which involved sailing with West Indian staples and specie from Jamaica and Curaçao to London where a cargo of sundries was picked up and then carried back to New York. Triangular trading of this type was obviously well-established at that time.[5]

Complementing the papers of Nathan Simson are the New York port records from 1713 to about 1760 which reveal that New York's Jewish merchants did business with practically all the islands. Sending in provisions, horses, naval stores, hats, oil, soap, candles, lumber, staves, and furniture, they received in return not only the typical West Indian triad of staples, but also Negroes as well as dyewoods, salt, indigo, hides, leather, mahogany, pimento, limejuice, cocoanuts, cotton, and even an occasional parcel of English manufactures.[6]

Disinterested in the intermediate step of distilling molasses into rum, the New York Jews imported less molasses than the Newporters. Much of the molasses bought by Newport Jewish businessmen came, however, from the French and Spanish islands where they could deal more advantageously. The fact that importing products from the foreign islands involved most shippers in questionable procedures and in smuggling rarely inhibited the Newporters. Merchants were never lacking for whom the profits gained justified the risks taken. During the French and Indian War, for instance, a New York merchant expected to realize profits of 100 percent by trading English wares for sugar at the still neutral Spanish port of Montecristi on Hispaniola. The profits derived from the sale of North American products in the West Indian and Caribbean area were used to help pay colonial debts to the English merchants, while return cargoes of molasses to Newport were distilled into rum for the Indian or fur trade, for the African slave traffic in which it served as a medium for barter, for the fisheries, and for the very heavy home consumption.[7]

When, along with the substantial Jamaican and Curaçaon trade, commerce with the "Mosquito Coast" (Honduras) assumed importance, a number of Jews availed themselves of opportunities to load their holds and decks with return cargoes of Honduran mahogany and dyewoods, especially logwood. About 1720, for example, Moses Levy of New York sent his brigantine *Rachel*—named probably for the daughter his new wife had borne him—on a voyage which included stops at Jamaica, then the Gulf of Honduras, and finally London. Though the *Rachel* was to have returned to New York, she was sold in London. Isaac Elizer later sent the *Free Mason*, whose name signalized her owner's interest in Masonry, to the Gulf of Honduras where her load of wine, provisions, naval stores, and hardware was exchanged for a cargo of mahogany and dyewoods destined for the Amsterdam market. Still another of Elizer's ships was instructed to barter a load of china, earthenware, and English goods at Honduras and the Haitian port of Môle St. Nicolas against native products and then to clear for Amsterdam.[8]

On the whole, trade with continental Europe and her African dependencies played no large part in the American Jewish mercantile economy, though voyages by ships of colonial Jewish ownership to the "Wine Islands" off the coast of Africa were not uncommon. Wine, of course, was a popular beverage in colonial America and rarely failed of a good market. The people of New York were so partial to Madeira that a special variety was named after them and a Philadelphian could write in 1754, "I make not the least doubt in a few years to read the Province of New York consumes the whole vintage of Madeira." [9]

Some of the New York Sephardim, notably the Gomezes who in all probability had special connections with crypto-Jews (Marranos) in the Wine Islands, applied themselves to the wine trade no later than 1710. They sent New York wheat to Lisbon and used the proceeds to buy wine in the Madeiras. When in 1710 the New York provincial authorities imposed an embargo on the export of wheat—needed for the newly arrived Palatine immigrants—Luis Gomez and one of his sons petitioned the government to encourage the barter of flour for wines with Portugal and her possessions. Gomez warned the New York governor and council that their failure to encourage such an exchange would only stimulate competition from New York's rival wheat-producing neighbor, Pennsylvania. The Gomezes themselves faced increasing competition in the Madeira wine trade from nearly every prominent New York Jewish merchant-shipper, but by the 1740's, judging from the New York books of entry and manifest books, they had outstripped their competitors to become the Jewish specialists in that trade. They were to maintain their lead and to encounter little if any Jewish competition in wine importing for the next two decades. During the 1760's, however, other New Yorkers entered the traffic again.[10]

What probably constituted a typical cargo for the Madeiras and the Canaries was loaded in 1764 by a Newport merchant: fish, leather, indigo, rum, snuff, meat, bread, and barrel staves for wine casks, since wine was undoubtedly to be the return cargo. Before the ship sailed, however, another Newport Jewish merchant bought the cargo on speculation, paying for it partly in cash and giving notes for the balance.[11]

As the Gomez ledger testifies, that family continued in the Wine Islands traffic throughout the middle decades of the century and occasionally even sponsored a voyage to Leghorn in Italy. Their Sephardic contemporary Rodrigo Pacheco may also have dispatched cargoes to Italy, for he owned a vessel called the *Leghorn*. Cargoes to Italy were rare; more common, though still infrequent, were Jewish consignments to Lisbon and other towns in Portugal, a land from which unbaptized Jews had long since been excluded. But American Jewry's insignificant part in the Portuguese trade stemmed less from the fact that professing Jews were not tolerated in that kingdom than from colonial America's inability to offer Portugal much except fish and barrel staves. By contrast, English Sephardic Jewry—equally detested in Portugal as heretics and infidels—enjoyed a brisk and lucrative trade with the Portuguese because the London merchants were able to supply the wide variety of manufactures and wares they needed. The London Jews were fortified, of course, by the domination of Portugal's economy the Treaty of Methuen had given England since 1703.

If American Jews dealt little with Portugal, they did traffick farther south along the African coast. Ever since the year 1719 Jews had been sending into the Gulf of Guinea ships laden with a diversity of trade goods to be exchanged for slaves.[12]

In addition to their ventures to the Azores, Madeiras, Canaries, and the Guinea Coast, American Jewish traders dispatched a vessel to Amsterdam from time to time, and in 1720 Nathan Simson was exporting sugar, beaver, furs, and tobacco to the Dutch metropolis. A generation later the Gomezes were carrying on with their Sephardic coreligionists in Amsterdam a very considerable trade, most of it in defiance of the navigation laws which prohibited direct trade with Holland. A sizeable portion of the Amsterdam trade involved smuggling, of course—with West Indian sugar dispatched to Holland and tea, an English monopoly, carried back for illegal importation. Such exchanges were consequently hazardous and the profits correspondingly substantial.[13]

As might be expected, dealings with Great Britain accounted for a very large proportion of the overseas trade. Witness, for instance, the Simson papers which run to something in excess of a thousand pages and concern themselves mostly with the London trade during the first thirty years of the eighteenth century. Still, commerce with the motherland was far from easy. The ofttimes stringent requirements of the acts of trade, added to America's need for articles of English manufacture and the constraint with which English buyers regarded American products, in the final analysis compelled every merchant-shipper to get his goods from England and to send back raw materials to pay for the wares he received. Practically all the apparel, dry goods, East Indian textiles, notions, and hardware used in the colonies came, therefore, either from or through the British Isles. Most American imports were secured from London; some were purchased in Bristol, and occasional cargoes addressed to Jewish merchants arrived from Dover, Cowes, Plymouth, Belfast, and Dublin. To balance their accounts, the Americans sent back timber, naval stores, large quantities of copper ore, flaxseed, furs, potash, pearl ash, indigo, rice, whale oil and fins, pig iron, snuff, tobacco, sugar, molasses, cocoanuts, spices, mahogany, dyewoods, and staves, in addition to specie and bills of exchange. As is obvious from this potpourri of goods, the American port towns were entrepôts assembling commodities from virtually every corner of the New World and transhipping them to England. One of the largest London firms catering to American merchants was headed by a native New Yorker, Moses Franks, with whom many non-Jews as well as Jews did business. Among the Jews were, of course, members of his own family—

his father Jacob and his brother David—Uriah Hendricks of New York and some of the Seixases. Among the non-Jews were his brother-in-law's firm of De Lancey & Watts, and James Beekman of New York.[14]

While American Jews were far from inactive in the transatlantic trade with England, there were salient aspects of this trade in which they were conspicuously absent. Very little on the eighteenth century commercial scene compared in importance with the export of grain from the Middle Atlantic provinces and of tobacco from Maryland and Virginia, and yet, though some of the New York Jews did export wheat and breadstuffs, neither the New Yorkers nor the Pennsylvanians were outstanding in that branch of trade. Even more striking, however, is the fact that Jews played practically no part at all in the tobacco export of the eighteenth century. The significance of their absence from this trade is seen in relief when we consider that up to 1740 the two tobacco colonies exported more of value to the mother country than all the other colonies combined, and that even as late as 1770, Maryland and Virginia accounted for about 80 percent of all North American shipments to England.[15]

Viewed, then, from the largest possible aspect, the Jews of colonial North America were hardly in the mainstream of Atlantic commerce or industry. North American trade in 1763 was concentrated in the tobacco colonies on Chesapeake Bay and the Carolinas, but the Jews were almost entirely absent from Maryland and Virginia and played little or no part in exporting tobacco from the Carolinas. Their largest communities were to be found in Pennsylvania, New York, and Rhode Island, colonies whose total trade with Great Britain that decade of the 1760's amounted probably to only about half of that of the Chesapeake colonies where not a single Jewish community was to be found. The historian, bound to maintain perspective, must conclude that though American Jews were not without consequence in the commerce of the provinces in which they lived, in an overall sense they constituted a group somewhat remote from the prime source of American wealth.[16]

Aaron Lopez

The general outlines of American Jewish coastal and overseas trading very often have to be reconstructed in the absence of documentary evidence, for much of the correspondence and many of the journals and ledgers which reflect these enterprises have long since been lost or fed to the flames. Fortunately, however, there are some exceptions to this melancholy rule. Many of the papers of Aaron Lopez of Newport are still extant and lend themselves to a study in depth of a distinguished colonial merchant. Here, too, as in the case of coastal shipping, an understanding of the colonial Jewish participation in overseas trading is best afforded by a somewhat detailed examination of the particulars—in this instance the dealings of one individual, Lopez.[17]

It is true, of course, that Lopez was not typical. Most Jewish businessmen were never entrepreneurs operating on a scale comparable to his, for after he hit his stride in the early 1770's, Lopez was on a par with the Browns of Providence and Thomas Hancock of Boston. He was, that is to say, a very great businessman, a merchant-capitalist of the first rank, and we find reflected in his career almost every aspect of merchant-shipping: the local, regional, and coastal trade, overseas commerce, and industrialism. Lopez' genius lay in a marvelous capacity for organization—an ability to carry on dozens of operations simultaneously, to send ships out to every part of the Atlantic world, to coordinate the intricate activities of his various shipping enterprises, and at the same time to supervise a host of mercantile and manufacturing interests—and all this with a minimum of clerical help.

BIOGRAPHY OF LOPEZ

Born in Portugal of crypto-Jewish stock about the year 1731, Lopez came to Newport in 1752 as a refugee with his wife Abigail, his daughter Sarah, and his brother David. He was about twenty-one years of age at this time. After his first wife's death in 1762, he married Sarah, the daughter of Jacob R. Rivera, and from then on the two men were constantly associated in business deals. The young émigré may have landed in Newport with some capital. Certainly there is no record of his ever having clerked for anyone on this continent. In all likelihood he lost no time in opening a shop and a store in Newport and began sending out ventures along the coast. He had come at an auspicious moment, just on the eve of the French and Indian War which was to bring prosperity to many. Before very long Lopez had established good relations with Henry Lloyd of Boston and Hayman Levy of New York. The New York Gomezes were related to Lopez' wife and undoubtedly offered him liberal credit. He began corresponding with them as soon as he landed in Newport. Less than a year after his arrival in Rhode Island, one of the Gomezes proposed lending him enough money to defray the cost of circumcising a child. Lopez, it is obvious, was struggling to keep his head above water. That same year of 1753 found him buying lottery tickets from the Gomezes, hoping to win the grand prize. Wherever he could, he borrowed cash and sought credit. Among his benefactors at the time were Jacob R. Rivera, his future father-in-law, and Jacob Franks. Indeed, one wonders whether it was not Rivera who had brought Lopez to Newport.[18]

By 1755, when the extant Lopez records are relatively detailed, he was already an established retailer and wholesaler, working closely with Lloyd and Levy. Carrying on his business as a merchant throughout the small province of Rhode Island, he bought and sold, dispatching goods to Boston and New York on his own account and on commission. From the very first it is apparent that candles played an important part in his economy.

Though ultimately to become one of the greatest North American Jewish merchant-shippers of the eighteenth century and probably the most daring one, Lopez seems not to have plunged early into the ownership of vessels. In fact it would be several years before he owned a ship. Owing, however, to the loss of the record books of the first four years of his career, it is not easy to reconstruct his development into an Atlantic trader. His first coastal ventures, it is evident, were modest, for he did not disdain the joint chartership of a six-ton sloop dispatched with a small cargo, in which he was only a quarter partner. More than once, it would seem, he shared in the cargoes of small coastal ventures which he had financed largely through supplying the bulk of their goods on credit. This, at least, is how he was conducting his affairs by the year 1761, less than ten years after his flight from Portugal.[19]

By the early 1760's Lopez had begun to interest himself in the overseas as well as coastal commerce, and by 1764 had already entered the slave trade and undertaken to buy cargoes of slaves on the West African coast. The following year found him active in fisheries, whaling, and the manufacture of spermaceti candles. By 1766–1767 he was heavily engaged in the West Indian trade.[20]

Lopez' mercantile importance is to be gauged by the fact that about half of the letters published in the two-volume, 1,000-page *Commerce of Rhode Island* deal with his activities. Typical of his operations during the period in which he extended the scope of his shipping is his record for 1770. During that year Lopez' vessels touched at Jamaica, Surinam, Haiti, Honduras, Newfoundland, England, Holland, Africa, Spain, Portugal, the Azores, and the Canaries. Lopez' boundless energy is reflected in a letter of July 20, 1774, which documents the fact that he was then clearing three boats for Newfoundland, buying coal from England and mules from the Mediterranean, selling ships to the British, shipping indigo from Jamaica and disposing there of cargoes of slaves, sending grain to Lisbon and England, and dispatching a brig on a whaling voyage. All told, twelve vessels in his service are mentioned in this one letter.[21]

Whether Lopez was an unusually daring speculator, or merely enterprising in the sense that all successful merchant-capitalists were, is hard to say, but he was certainly not content to make his living as a commission merchant or hesitant to risk his capital and credit. At the height of his career in the early 1770's, he had not yet reached his mid-forties.[22]

LOCALES OF HIS OVERSEAS TRADING

A study of Lopez' coastal trading reveals that his interests extended all the way from Quebec to Sunbury, Georgia, and his overseas operations were equally widespread, embracing dozens of lands and scores of cities. In July 1772, for instance, he was in touch with captains or agents at points as distant from Newport as London, Bristol, Newfoundland, Cuba, and Jamaica. Although his business with continental Europe and the North African littoral was relatively minimal, he bought and sold in Spain, Portugal, Gibraltar, the Barbary Coast, Madeira, the Azores, the Canaries, Sicily, Naples, Leghorn, and Amsterdam, not to mention Gothenburg, Sweden, and Emden, Germany. His slave ships sailed annually to the Guinea Coast; his cargoes were unloaded or his holds filled at Caribbean markets like Jamaica, Barbados, Montserrat, Haiti, Curaçao, Dominica, St. Kitts, St. Croix, the Gulf of Honduras, and Surinam; and through his agents he had business dealings in other areas too. On the eve of the Revolution, Lopez' whalers were making their way towards the Falkland Islands in the vicinity of Cape Horn.[23]

THE NUMBER OF SHIPS USED

Lopez had begun with modest shares in jointly owned ships, but in the course of time he purchased vessels and shipped goods in his own holds, which was typical of an expanding mercantile career. Beginners engaged in mercantile adventures generally freighted their goods on other men's ships, but as soon as he could, many a Jewish merchant dispatched his cargoes on boats he owned outright or shared with partners, Jews and Gentiles. A businessman who owned no ships could and did charter them, and if the vessels he owned or chartered were not full, he solicited freight from others in order to have a paying load. Some of the ships carried passengers as well, although there were times when shipowners found them more of a nuisance than a profit. Henry Davenant, one of Lopez' captains, once wrote to his employer, "I wish you had shipt four horses with us instead of four passengers, for they have been nothing but a plage to us."[24]

Like other merchants, Lopez chartered as well as owned vessels. He would charter a ship when his own could not be back in time and he wished to profit by dispatching a cargo in a hurry. He also carried freight for others and wherever possible sought to sell the vessels themselves in England or the West Indies if he could realize a profit.[25]

How many ships did Lopez own? This is difficult to determine. Ships were for him as much a commodity in themselves as they were an instrumentality for transportation, and ordering ships to be built for the market was a form of selling goods at a profit, since he paid for them out of his store. The records show that he was constantly buying, selling, and speculating in vessels, and it was not unusual for him to sell a ship he had used for only a voyage or two. How many vessels Lopez owned at any one time is thus rather perplexing; though in terms of the magnitude of a merchant's operations, whether he owned or chartered ships, or merely sent his goods by freight, is quite immaterial. A substantial overseas trader like Nathan Simson probably owned only one vessel, which he shared with others.[26]

Lopez' contemporary Ezra Stiles wrote that the Jewish merchant had "above twenty sail of vessels"; later historians have estimated that he owned outright or in partnership with others about thirty ships. During the years between 1765 and 1771 Lopez actually owned in whole or part twenty-seven vessels; at least fifteen were his alone. If we include chartered ships, however, the number of vessels under his control would sustain a substantial increase.[27]

HIS TRADE IN EUROPE

When we consider Lopez' trade in the Gulf of Guinea, with England or the West Indies, or along the North American coast, we can see that his commercial relations with continental Europe were of comparatively small importance, though he extended them when and where he could, maintaining correspondence with the Mediterranean, the Iberian Peninsula, Holland, Germany, and Scandinavia.

The cargoes he sent to Spanish markets consisted in the main of whale oil, furs, candles, staves, fish, and grain, which were traded for salt, wines, and fruits. Shipments of fish from Newfoundland were frequently dispatched by American merchants to Spain and Italy, and Lopez did not ignore that trade, nor would he fail to welcome a return cargo from the Canaries, which was certain to include wines and might in addition sometimes contain vineslips for American planting. In general, his Mediterranean-bound vessels carried provisions and lumber, in return for which they brought back salt, wines, fruits, and at times mules. Lopez' ships, after discharging their American cargoes and taking on southern European products, might go on then to London for a load of English manufactures before heading westward across the Atlantic to an American port. Sometimes a Lopez vessel would stop at Amsterdam where he had two correspondents, the firms of John Turner & Son and Daniel Crommelin & Sons. It was apparently his policy to make use of a firm until its proprietors began to press him heavily for payment. Then he would turn to other merchants in the same city. Of course he would continue to pay his old creditors, but with very modest sums. This policy was particularly obvious in London which was the chief source of his supplies.[28]

Did Lopez balk at skirting the law in his commercial transactions? There is no doubt at all that a voyage to Sweden for a cargo of tea offered by Scottish merchants could be construed only as a smuggling venture to circumvent the English tea monopoly. England's, however, was not the only law Lopez would seek to evade when he thought it advisable to do so, and though the Lisbon firm of Mayne & Company served as his agents in the Portuguese capital, he seems to have sent at least one substantial shipment of candles and hogsheads to Lisbon under a pseudonym. As a relapsed Portuguese Christian—a heretic—he may have feared the possibility that his cargo would be confiscated by order of the Inquisition. As a rule, however, Lopez corresponded quite freely with Catholic merchants in Portugal and Spain, and they in turn, constantly soliciting his business and acting as intermediaries in Lopez' contacts with his Marrano relatives on the peninsula, were apparently not in the least concerned with the fact that their Newport correspondent was guilty of heresy.[29]

As might be expected, a very large proportion of Lopez' trade was with the British Isles, the chief source of his consumer goods, and during the decade of the 1760's, he did business with suppliers in the English centers of Sheffield, Bristol, and London, as well as the Irish port of Cork where he secured, among other commodities, Irish indentured servants. No matter who or where Lopez' English correspondents were, however, the nature of his business remained much the same. He sent his suppliers rum, sugar, rice, naval stores, whale oil, dyewoods, lumber, hogshead staves and headings, pig iron, indigo, potash, saleable ships, and now and then, cash and bills of exchange. In return he received English textiles and hardware, coal, and—not least—insurance on his ships and cargoes.[30]

During the late 1760's and early 1770's his correspondents at Sheffield were Broadbent & Bland, a firm which apparently also maintained a branch in London where John Bland was located, but most of Lopez' English traffic in the decade or two before the Revolution was with the Bristol firm of Henry Cruger Jr. and the London firms of William Stead and Hayley & Hopkins. His Bristol business was particularly heavy. During the early 1760's his correspondents there had been Goodall & Barnes, but Lopez soon switched his patronage to the merchant Henry Cruger Jr., a member of the American mercantile family with which he was in frequent correspondence at New York. Lopez is likely to have turned to Bristol not only because she was a center for the West Indian trade, but also because there he could secure the almost unlimited credit needed to support his ever-expanding operations. And Lopez made the utmost use possible of the credit available to him, so that his trade with his English suppliers amounted in time to thousands of pounds sterling. At one point, for example, Lopez owed Henry Cruger Jr. alone over £11,000, which wrung from Cruger the anguished cry that "the ballance of your account must be reduced before I can be happy." Ultimately, though not rapidly, Lopez contrived somehow to pay Cruger most if not all the debts he had incurred.[31]

It is clear Lopez never confined all of his business in England to any one correspondent, possibly because the credit he required was simply too much for one house to extend. During the same years that he dealt with Cruger in Bristol, he was also carrying on a voluminous trade of the same type with William Stead of London, with whom relations had been established no later than 1763 and would continue on into the 1770's. Also, by the late 1760's Lopez and his partner Rivera had initiated a relationship with George

Hayley of the London firm of Hayley & Hopkins, to whom Lopez would become heavily indebted in the course of the next decade. Thus in the ten years or so before the Revolution, Lopez' three main English suppliers, Cruger, Stead, and Hayley & Hopkins, enabled the Newporter to maneuver, to manipulate his credit, and to conduct business on a truly grand scale.[32]

HIS WEST INDIAN, CARIBBEAN, AND SOUTH AMERICAN TRADE

By the mid-1760's Lopez became sharply aware that he was not making the progress he had envisaged. Up to this time his economic strategy appears to have stressed the importation of slaves and the offering of ships for sale in the English market. When by 1767 he discovered that despite all his efforts, he was heavily in debt to his English suppliers, he determined on a change and began then to emphasize the West Indian market, the natural market for North America.[33]

Though concentrating on Jamaica where his affairs were carried on by his captains, factors, and agents, he took care not to overlook other parts of the Caribbean area and for a time employed a New England sea captain as a special agent or factor in Honduras to trade his wares for the native woods. Lopez also maintained close relations with correspondents, including the American Jew Abraham Sarzedas, on Haiti, French Hispaniola. His agents there in turn carried on trade for him with the Spanish segment of Hispaniola. The ships he sent to the islands carried livestock, poultry, and provisions of every description, including pickled oysters; their holds and decks were loaded down with candles, fodder, naval stores, bar iron, bricks, lumber, all types of building materials, and on occasion, even fine silverware made by the well-known New England craftsman Jonathan Otis. His vessels in the Caribbean took on return cargoes of molasses, rum, cocoa, coffee, sugar, indigo, and Honduran mahogany and logwood. Some of these products—logwood for example—might be sold on Jamaica; other native staples were brought back to the North American colonies or sent on to England. In 1767 he assigned at least nine vessels to the West Indian trade and reached out a year later to Surinam. Through all of this, wherever possible Lopez

[649]

sought specie and good bills of exchange which, added to the cargoes he directed to England, would help him balance his accounts with his English suppliers. In 1776, following the break with England, he and his partners began dispatching cargoes not only to Spanish Hispaniola, but also to the Dutch Guianas, to Essequibo, Surinam, and to French Cayenne.[34]

When it seemed to the Newport shipper advantageous to do so, he did not hesitate to combine his North American coastal with his Caribbean traffic. No chance for profit was to be overlooked, and so Lopez ships carrying English goods to the Albemarle planters in the Carolinas would not always return to the North after trading their cargoes for Carolina naval products, barrel staves, and provisions. A captain might steer his vessel south to the islands, sell this Carolina cargo to the West Indian merchants and planters and even, if possible, dispose of the ship itself. Or a vessel that had cleared the islands, headed for Newport, might stop at North Carolina and trade its cargo of island food staples for one of raw materials. That the volume of his North Carolina trading was not inconsiderable is evident in the fact that Lopez might have three ships in the New Bern area at one time.[35]

There were many variations of this combined coastal-island traffic. A vessel, for instance, might sail from Quebec to Barbados, or from the Gaspé Peninsula in Canada to the Môle St. Nicolas on Haiti, or it might clear Newport with a cargo of hay for Savannah where a boatload of horses would be picked up and fed the hay en route to the West Indian market. Or a cargo of cheese and whale oil might be sent to Sunbury, Georgia, and the captain instructed to move on to Barbados if he could not dispose of his load in Georgia.[36]

HIS CIRCUITOUS TRADING

For an American merchant-shipper like Lopez, it was a basic and constant objective that his ships sell their North American products and secure in exchange either cash, bills, or a cargo that would find a market in England or, failing that, could be traded somewhere for some product needed by English purchasers. American merchants invariably confronted an adverse trade balance with the mother country, but that was no excuse when their English suppliers demanded a settling of accounts. No merchant-shipper could escape the exigency of ordering his vessels to move from port to port until their North American cargoes had been successfully converted into hard money or into something saleable in England. Circuitous trading and even sea-huckstering, though on a smaller scale, were therefore common features of American commerce in the prerevolutionary period, and Lopez resorted to such methods as often as any other merchant.

Sometimes Lopez might have a Carolina-bound ship load itself in a Carolina port, set sail directly for Spain and Portugal, take on a new cargo there, and then return to the home port in Rhode Island. On another occasion he might have a ship sail from Newfoundland to the West Indies and back again to North America if it had met with success in selling and buying advantageously. If it had not, the same vessel might continue on to Europe—say, to Sweden—before returning to the North American mainland. It might and did happen that a ship sailed from Newport for the Spanish Canaries off the coast of Africa and then moved westward across the Atlantic to Barbados or Dominica. Failing to sell anything at any of these ports, the captain might move on to Dutch St. Eustatius for a cargo of sugar and cordage. Or a vessel might make its way from Newport to Jamaica, to Dublin, to the Portuguese Madeiras, then back again to Jamaica and to the Gulf of Honduras, before returning once more to Newport. When Lopez' brig *Venus* cleared Newport in 1772, she would not see her home port again until she had called at Lisbon, Gibraltar, Surinam on the South American coast, and the Windward Islands in the West Indies—a voyage whose insurance amounted to £213 sterling.[37]

There were times when nothing would do but peddling, as in 1770 when a Lopez captain, after arriving in the islands from Newport, found it necessary to move on to Dominica, St. Kitts, St. Croix, and the Môle St. Nicolas in order to peddle his cargo of lumber, barrel staves and headings, candles, fish, and soap, for a return load of molasses and rum.

The orders Lopez issued to Captain John Heffernan reflected

the complexities involved in this type of circuitous trading. Heffernan was sent in the *Jacob* to Jamaica with an American cargo. On his first stop at Port Antonio, Jamaica, he was to unload his horses and then peddle the rest of the cargo in different West Indian ports. With the money acquired in this way, Heffernan was instructed to buy a load of sugar, molasses, and coffee destined for London. In the meantime he was to seek additional freight for the London voyage, and if a load of freight proved available without delay, the unsold part of his North American lading was to be turned over to a local agent and Heffernan was to hoist anchor at once for England. Another of Lopez' vessels, Heffernan was told, was due in Jamaica in three months and would close all unsettled accounts. On arrival in London the *Jacob* was to report to Hayley & Hopkins, surrender all goods and money to them, and pick up a load for North America. If, however, Heffernan found it impossible to procure London-bound freight at Jamaica, he was to remain on the island until his cargo had been sold, was then to reinvest the proceeds in molasses, rum, and sugar, and only then was he to return to Newport. There was nothing untypical about these orders, and we have no difficulty in understanding what Lopez meant when he wrote in 1767, "I am determined to reduce my troublesome navigation at all events, being really tired of so much laberynth as it occasions me." [38]

CHAPTER 35

PRIVATEERING, INSURANCE, AND FINANCE

PRIVATEERING

It happened invariably in wartime that an indeterminate number of ships were withdrawn from the normal channels of coastal and overseas shipping to be employed for military purposes under civilian auspices. Businessmen, in league sometimes with people who normally took no part in business pursuits, would form loose partnerships to charter or purchase vessels, arm them, secure letters of marque, and send them out to prey on enemy shipping. Though patriotism may have been a factor in all this, what moved most men to engage in privateering was profit, always a prime motive. It was, in short, characteristic of the eighteenth century for men to buy shares in privateers in much the same manner that men of later centuries would seek shares in munitions factories during times of war. Speculators hoped through the lucky capture of a prize to become rich overnight.

There is some evidence that North Americans turned to privateering during the first two Anglo-French wars to be fought in America: King William's War during the last decade of the seventeenth century, and Queen Anne's War during the first decade of the eighteenth. To what extent Jews were involved in such enterprises is uncertain. During King William's War—the American phase of the War of the League of Augsburg, lasting from 1689 to 1697—Lord Bellomont, the governor of New York, sent Captain William Kidd out in the *Adventure* to control piracy and harass French shipping. As noted before, the crew on that fateful voyage

[653]

included Benjamin Franks, but the *Adventure* was not really a privateer. We lack conclusive evidence, moreover, that any American Jews engaged in the traffic of hunting down enemy merchantmen during Queen Anne's War, the American phase of the War of the Spanish Succession, which lasted from 1702 to 1713. With the outbreak, however, of the War of Jenkins' Ear in 1739 and in King George's War, which continued to 1748 (both wars were American echoes of the continental War of the Austrian Succession), there can be no doubt of Jewish participation in privateering.

Becoming interested in privateering during the war years of 1739–1748, Jewish businessmen began then to buy shares in privateers bound for the Spanish Main to seize French, Spanish, and when the mood moved them, even Dutch shipping. The fact that captains and crews were rarely too scrupulous, so that privateering was frequently little better than piracy, inhibited no one. Eager for quick profits, Jamaican Jews fitted out a privateer at Newport in 1743 and set an example for their Rhode Island coreligionists, who themselves soon began to engage very actively in that traffic. One of the privateers, the *Defiance*, in which Abraham Hart was a partner, carried a complement of 110 men, fourteen carriage guns, and twenty-two swivel guns—a formidable armament. In 1748, the last year of the war, the *Myrtilla*, whose owners were Levy & Franks of Philadelphia, not only carried freight and passengers, but also ten guns and twenty men. She was prepared to defend herself, and if the opportunity offered, to pounce on enemy merchant ships.

It was during the French and Indian War, which reflected the continental Seven Years' War of 1756–1763, that privateering became a big business in America. More than 400 privateers were fitted out during those years, and a number of Newport and New York Jewish merchants took an active part in this speculative enterprise, though whether they were more interested in privateering than their fellow-merchants is difficult to determine. One does well to bear in mind, of course, that Jewish traders constituted only a very small percentage of the total number of merchants, particularly in New York.

It is worth noting that Aaron Lopez, the shining light of pre-revolutionary Newport's businessmen, was not numbered among the town's privateer-speculators during the French and Indian War.

Was it that, having been in America only two years when hostilities broke out, he felt himself simply too poor to hazard his meager capital? There may have been more to it than that, for later during the Revolution, as a rule Lopez continued to avoid privateering speculations, though he did make certain exceptions. In June 1776, for instance, he and Nicholas Brown joined forces to send a cargo of provisions, candles, hogsheads, and naval stores to Surinam on the *George*, a brig which sailed under letters of marque and carried twenty swivel guns and grapeshot. The armament served a double purpose: to protect their shipment and to enable the *George* to capture enemy vessels. What made Lopez' privateering ventures so rare, however, was no squeamishness on his part. Although willing to take chances on hazardous enterprises, Lopez probably regarded preying on English commerce as entirely too dangerous, and he may have seen in privateering little hope for an adequate return. During the Revolution he was himself the victim of American privateers who seized his ships and exposed him to losses and vexatious litigation.[1]

Some of Lopez' fellow-merchants were far less hesitant. At the time of the French and Indian War, the Harts of Newport, New York, and London entered very actively into privateering ventures and dispatched from their firm's Newport headquarters privateers as small as the twenty-ton *Diamond* and as large as the 350-ton *Perfect Union*. From 1758 to 1762 they and their associates were concerned in the financing of at least nine privateers. Various Jewish merchants in New York also purchased shares in privateers during this last Anglo-French colonial conflict. Uriah Hendricks, as a young beginner recently come from England, bought shares in at least two ships, probably for his family in London as well as for himself. Although Hendricks enjoyed some success—one of his vessels captured a French coffee and sugar ship—he apparently gave up that type of speculation. Privateers, he had found no doubt, were so expensive to outfit that the disbursements threatened to outweigh the gains.

The New York Jewish merchants most active in privateering were Judah Hays, Hayman Levy, and Sampson Simson. All three, who were known as able and successful merchants, sent out privateers on their own account or in partnership with others in 1757–1761, but the most daring speculator of the lot seems to have been Sampson Simson. During the years 1757–1759, either alone or with associates, he secured gubernatorial commissions for at least four privateers to attack and seize enemy shipping. One of his schooners, the sixty-ton *Samson*, carried a complement of sixty men and must have swarmed with fighters.

Were the Jews who engaged in such speculations successful? The answer seems to confirm Lopez' doubts about these enterprises, for there is no indication at all in extant correspondence and records that even one colonial Jewish merchant ever realized profits of any magnitude in privateering.[2]

INSURANCE

Colonial commerce was at best a precarious affair, but the very multiplicity of dangers merchants chanced gave rise to a business of no mean proportions—maritime insurance. Most cargoes shipped out were insured against storms, war, privateers, thieves, and arbitrary seizure by the authorities. Usually a group participated in underwriting the insurance to cut possible losses. Rates were low in time of peace, but high in time of war, and they varied radically. Underwriting insurance was highly speculative of course, at least as much so as privateering. Yet curiously enough, though the speculative hunger for a large profit induced Newport and New York Jewish merchants to outfit privateers or buy shares in them, the same fever seems to have deserted them when it came to maritime insurance. Few Jews had much by way of surplus capital, and some may have felt the profits to be derived from maritime insurance did not justify the risks, though lack of surplus capital rarely kept them from finding sufficient funds to help outfit a privateer.

Not that Jews were entirely absent from the underwriting of insurance. There were a few Jewish merchants who dabbled in insurance brokerage and parcelled out risks to the merchant-insurers. On occasion, for example, the firms of Levy & Marache, Hays & Polock, and David Franks arranged insurance for their clients and friends. Typical of the economic life of the time is the procedure to which Franks once resorted in insuring a client. Owing money to a correspondent in New York, Franks drew a bill of exchange on the insured party and directed him to pay Franks's creditor. When, however, circumstances later required the policy to be paid, the insured shipper had already assigned it to still another businessman.

Barnard Gratz at times served as a maritime insurance broker and once thought seriously of going into that business. In 1769, while on a visit to London, he was advised there to seek the insurance patronage of his New York and Philadelphia friends. Moses Franks, who was his mentor in London, thought that Gratz could secure patronage by not charging insured clients the usual broker's commission of one-half percent and by collecting fees instead only from the merchant-insurers. Nothing came of the project, however, because the American boycott of English imports effected a drastic reduction of business.[3]

In general, America's Jewish merchants did not concern themselves with the insurance business either as brokers or as insurers. They chose rather to insure their cargoes with Gentile businessmen. Aaron Lopez, for instance, preferred to have his Boston, New York, and English agents—all non-Jews—arrange for his insurance. The obvious advantage this procedure offered him was that it allowed all of his insurance to be handled on credit and thus afforded him additional monetary leeway in his numerous mercantile and industrial undertakings.[4]

FINANCE

One of the contrasts between eighteenth century Europe and colonial America lay in the fact that Europe had notable Jewish moneylenders and bankers. As early, indeed, as the late seventeenth century, Anglo-Dutch Jewish financiers had supported William III, and throughout the 1700's there were Anglo-Jewish men of affairs like Sampson Gideon who could, on relatively short notice, provide the government with £1,700,000 sterling to tide it over the crisis of the Young Pretender's invasion. Financiers of this magnitude were never to be found in the colonies.[5]

Why there were none is obvious. No banker of means would have chosen to settle in a North America which possessed nothing in the way of a financial center, enjoyed little or no direct trade with gem-producing lands like India and Brazil, and could not claim a single merchant, Jew or non-Jew, devoting himself exclusively to the buying and selling of bills of exchange. America had no central market for silver and gold bullion, and when specie and bullion made their appearance on this side of the Atlantic, they were dispatched at once to the London market to redress the colonies' endless deficiency in balance of payments. There was, in consequence, no place in the North American mainland colonies for the Jewish diamond merchants, bullion brokers, and bankers of England. Europe alone—and England in particular—could provide Jews with the physical security and the social and spiritual advantages that went with a well-established Jewish community; and Europe could provide something else: plentiful opportunities for enterprising Jewish financiers in a society constantly undergoing political, cultural, and economic improvement.

America had no comparable attraction to offer. Not even petty moneylenders, men who made a living exclusively in that fashion, were to be found on these shores. Was it that hard money was scarce? Or was it that Jews had learned too well, through bitter experience, that no one loves a moneylender? Whatever the reasons, colonial American records do not reveal even one Jewish pawnbroker or one individual devoted exclusively to the business of lending money. Even in eighteenth century England, as a matter of fact, the stereotype of the Jewish moneylender had become more a treasured prejudice and literary cliché than a historical reality.[6]

Still, though there were no pawnbrokers or merchant-bankers, it is a fact that all colonial businessmen borrowed or lent money at one time or another. As early as the 1670's Asser Levy, the butcher, from time to time lent money on interest. Indeed, he once charged a resentful debtor ten percent interest, but in the ensuing lawsuit, the court awarded him only six percent. It was reportedly through a loan made by Levy that the Lutherans were enabled to build their first church in this country. Levy was by no means the last Jewish businessman to offer money on loan. In 1700, for example, when the governor of New York had insufficient funds to pay his soldiers, Jewish merchants advanced him the needed money on bills which he drew on London. "Were it not for one Dutch merchant and two or three Jews," wrote Lord Bellomont, "I should have been undone." During the 1760's the General Assembly of Rhode Island, authorized to borrow money, secured funds from at least three Jews, including the "rabbi," though the amounts involved were very small. In 1770 Jonas Phillips, auctioneer and broker, advertised he would provide money on interest, and there is evidence that the Jewish merchants and shopkeepers of Canada also made loans now and then.[7]

Canadian Jews, even as modest moneylenders, performed a service, for in a primitive agrarian economy like Quebec's, an essentially non-mercantile culture whose middle class was all but entirely negligible, the moneylender constituted a necessity. This fact was no doubt clear to the Jewish merchant Gershon Levy, who advanced money to sailors at the request of General Amherst, and to his coreligionist Samuel Jacobs, who advanced the peasants money for their rent to the seigneurs. There is no evidence, however, that Jacobs charged the habitants any interest. A country merchant was, after all, expected to help his clients.[8]

In Lancaster, Pennsylvania, the town's outstanding merchant Joseph Simon lent money, took mortgages in payment of debts, and underwrote bail bonds on good security. In 1757 the inventory and will of the South Carolinian businessman Solomon Isaacs disclosed that he had left assets in the form of about thirty "bonds" as well as notes amounting to almost £8,000 in local currency, though the debts due him may have been incurred for goods sold rather than money lent.[9]

Every colonial merchant of any stature was involved, to some degree at least, in what we would call banking procedures—money changing, moneylending, advancing credit, and drawing and discounting bills of exchange. Banking was thus as much a feature of Jewish as of non-Jewish mercantile activity in the colonies, and while there seems to be no record of Jewish businessmen explicitly taking money on deposit subject to check or draft, such a procedure is evident in the fact that indebted merchants were constantly requested to make credit or cash available to a third person by written order. The scarcity of hard cash in North America and the fact that most business was done on credit necessarily involved purchases and sales in an intricate system of bookkeeping with long delayed balancing of accounts. When unpaid balances were finally established, of course debtor-merchants and clients were charged interest. Bills of exchange constantly had to be bought to pay obligations; they fluctuated in price, and fees were charged for buying and selling them.

As early as the first third of the 1700's Isaac Lopez, a Jewish merchant in Boston, dealt in bills of exchange drawn on London, but the precise nature of Lopez' banking activities is unclear. Unfortunately very little is known of Lopez, although he appears to have been a substantial merchant and landowner, in touch with a London house which used him to ship fish to Spain and Portugal.[10]

It is to the abundant Nathan Simson and Aaron Lopez papers that the historian must turn for a fuller description of the nature and scope of the banking activities of large-scale merchants and merchant-shippers. Simson would often pay one merchant at the request of another, lend money outright, and dispatch funds to European relatives of his clients and friends. On one occasion, at the request of the General Assembly of the Province of New York, he advanced the salary of a New York civil servant, and when a missionary for the Society for the Propagation of the Gospel in Foreign Parts wished to secure his salary, he drew a bill on London and sold it to Simson. Robert Hunter, the provincial governor, borrowed funds from Simson to pay the armed forces during Queen Anne's War; some of the bills, drawn by Hunter on the London army pay office to compensate the New York businessman for advances made, ultimately found their way to the countinghouse of one of the London Frankses. Thus the governor got his cash, Simson earned a commission, and Franks was paid for wares sold or services rendered to Simson.[11]

During the 1740's to the 1760's the Gomezes and Judah Hays also reflected banking techniques in the administration of their affairs, although the scarcity of their papers makes it difficult to gauge the nature of their commercial activities. It is quite clear, however, that the Gomezes, who seem to have come to the fore in

New York with the decline or disappearance of the Levy clan, lent money, forwarded bullion to Amsterdam, and dealt rather extensively in bills of exchange. Typical of the banking of that day are Judah Hays's dealings with Alexander Solomons & Company of Pensacola. When the Florida Jewish supply house bought, or received for services rendered, a bill of exchange from Major Robert Farmer, Solomons sent the bill for £700 sterling, drawn on the Lords of the Treasury, to his New York friend Judah Hays who credited the £700 to the account of his Pensacola client. Solomons then proceeded to assign various sums to his creditors and to draw on his credit or deposit with Hays as the need arose. Hays thus served as the New York banker for the Florida firm and as he saw fit, sold the bill, transferred it to his creditors, or turned it in for collection.[12]

In Newport the brothers Jacob and Moses Isaacks, merchants, advertised they dealt in New York bills, while their neighbors Naphtali Hart & Company, too, carried on an extensive business in bills. Inasmuch, however, as only one ledger of the Hart firm is extant, no more can be said of their banking transactions than that they advanced money and credit to other Newport merchants. Unlike the Harts, Aaron Lopez of Newport left behind over 100 account books which throw much light on his affairs, but strangely enough, the Lopez records show rather little evidence of the practice of mercantile-banking, possibly because Lopez was so engrossed in his own ambitious and adventurous projects, and so encumbered with endless minutiae, that he declined to concern himself with the details of banking operations. Obviously lacking capital in the early days, Lopez was in the market for loans, and later occasionally bought gold, frequently accepted promissory notes for debts due him, lent money—though not for large sums—and bought, sold, endorsed, and discounted bills of exchange. Craftsmen, who worked for Lopez and to whom he was in debt, discharged their obligations to others by issuing orders on him which he honored by cash or goods. When Hazzan Touro desired to liquidate a debt, he issued an order on Lopez, who paid the bill and then debited the hazzan's salary.[13]

New York-born Moses Franks of London transferred funds from England to this country and dealt widely in bills, but his base of operations was London and there is no record that he ever returned to New York after he sailed for Europe. His brother David of Philadelphia, however, either on his own behalf or as an agent for Moses, handled banking transactions with Europe and the West Indies. Thus David, together with Simson, the Gomezes, Judah Hays, Naphtali Hart & Company, and Aaron Lopez, was among the few American Jewish merchants who engaged now and then in banking and financial transactions quite similar to those of the European merchant-bankers.[14]

CHAPTER 36

INDUSTRY

E ssentially an agricultural country, colonial America had little industry. Protectionist mercantilist England, lacking either desire or intention to encourage industrial development in her North American mainland colonies, imposed a series of laws which placed legal obstacles in the way of large-scale manufacturing, although she was willing to encourage the rudimentary manufacture of some semifinished raw materials. Yet within the narrow confines of English prohibitions, the want of skilled workers and machinery, the high cost of labor, the absence of capital, and the rival pull of cheap lands, a modest degree of industry did develop in America, and colonial coastal towns were often manufacturing centers as well as commercial and maritime marts. Johann Doehla, a contemporary visitor, could say that Newport was a "sea and manufacturing city." [1]

The fact that eighteenth century colonial merchants had to process commodities for export made them of necessity manufacturers. Either directly or indirectly, the merchant secured his potash and pearl ash by having lands cleared and the woods burnt. These ashes he used at home or sent to England for processing into bleaches, soaps, glass, and fertilizer. He also saw to the preparation of turpentine, resin, tar, and pitch, the naval stores in contemporary demand. Shipbuilding was another of his industrial concerns, for not only did he supply the materials that went into the making of ships, he also ordered their building, though he himself did not supervise their actual construction. These vessels he used himself, offered for immediate sale, or sold at the end of a voyage. He had lumber cut to measure, saw to it that masts were prepared for sale and for export, and scoured the markets in all the colonies in search of staves, barrelheads, and hoops for the countless number of barrels needed for the North American and West Indian foods and provisions which he packed.

The American merchant was a lead, copper, and iron miner, a manufacturer of pig iron, and a miller of flour. His clients cured and packed meats to order for him. He himself processed tobacco into snuff, and was a tanner and a leather worker. His whaling and candle manufacturing were substantial if not large-scale industries, and he was also the driving force behind the catching, packing, and exporting of fish. Merchants were distillers of spirits, especially of rum, though more and more beer was brewed. There were businessmen who devoted themselves to glass manufacturing and sugar refining, and merchants by whom indigo was prepared and exported to Europe in hundreds of thousands of pounds and tobacco in millions of pounds. Despite the Wool Act of 1699, textiles were manufactured in the colonies, primarily for home use by farm women, and there was always spinning, weaving, and some manufacture of clothing, shoes, silks, and of hats from furs.

The factory system had not yet developed, and very few industries and workers were housed in central workshops. Most artisans worked in their homes or shops, and only on rare occasions did the merchant himself supervise the goods he produced; production and management were left to others. Much was manufactured on a petty scale in the home of the farmer-artisan. In the prevalent "put out" and truck system, the merchant-manufacturer gave orders to his manual workers whom he often supplied with raw materials like cotton, flax, wool, iron, leather, and lumber. When the finished product was delivered to him, he paid for it, partly at least, in an order for goods on his shop or warehouse.

If not many Jewish businessmen were industrialists, it is because industry was not vitally important in the colonies. Agriculture and commerce were far more significant in the colonial economy, and at least two generations were to elapse before the Industrial Revolution would make headway in North America. Yet by virtue of his being a "big businessman," the colonial Jewish merchant of stature had to be an industrialist, and as more and more new historical materials are studied, it will become increasingly evident that the Jewish merchant was concerned with the manufacture of the products he sold and exported. As a craftsman, as a manufacturer, as a merchant-capitalist supplying raw materials and ordering the manufacture of wares and commodities, the colonial Jew was present and active in every form of production except that of sugar refining and the making of iron. On the whole, most Jewish merchants were specialists in their manufacturing interests and limited themselves to one or two branches. It is only an Aaron Lopez whom we find engaged in a variety of industrial undertakings.[2]

WINE, SILK, COCHINEAL, AND INDIGO

In the South, where the raising and processing of tobacco, rice, and indigo were basic agricultural and semi-industrial activities, Jews had little to do with the production of tobacco and rice, but Moses Lindo played a significant part in the indigo industry.

The English government, in establishing colonies in the southern reaches of the North American continent, had originally intended to further the development of Mediterranean-type products and to emancipate itself thereby from dependence for wines and silks on the Mediterranean lands, the Wine Islands, and the Far East. England had cherished sanguine expectations that those two commodities could be produced in her own American colonies, and she had centered her hopes for a Georgia wine industry on Abraham De Lyon. Those hopes perished with the decline of the original settlement and the emigration of De Lyon, but more determined attempts were made to create a silk industry in Georgia. Silk reeling was, to be sure, nothing new in North America, for as early as Charles II's coronation in 1660, his robe had been made of silk manufactured in Virginia:

> Where wormes and food doe naturally abound
> A gallant silk trade must then be found.

Though the industry made no progress in Virginia or the Carolinas, it was thought the effort in Georgia would be more successful. It was said in classical mercantilist terms when the Georgia colony was being projected:

The value and usefulness of the undertaking [the manufacture of silk] will appear, as soon as we consider that all the silk consumed in this kingdom is now of foreign growth and manufacture, which costs the nation very great sums of money yearly to purchase; and that the raising our supply thereof, in his Majesty's Dominions in America, would save us all that money, afford employment to many thousands of his Majesty's subjects, and greatly increase the trade and navigation of Great Britain.[3]

The very first ship that docked in Georgia carried silk workers, some of them Italian, and they began reeling silk shortly after the colony's establishment. Very little was manufactured, although in 1741 a sample of the new Georgia fabric was sent to London where the merchant Sampson (Simpson) Levi, a specialist in the Georgia trade and an agent for Minis & Salomons, was asked to give his opinion on the quality and value of the Georgia product.

No real progress was made in silk manufacture until the coming of Joseph Solomon Ottolenghe. In 1752, a year after his arrival in Georgia, he turned his attention to silk culture, and the following year found him in charge of the Savannah filature. It was not long before he became the superintendent of silk culture in the colony, and giving the industry the technical and administrative skill required, by 1766 he had brought it to the peak of its production. Ottolenghe would remain the dominant personality in the industry until his retirement on a pension in 1769, and in January 1771, after his election to membership in the American Philosophical Society, he published a brief study on the subject of breeding silk worms. That same year, however, the Savannah factory was closed.[4]

Whatever success the manufacture of silk had achieved in Georgia was due to Ottolenghe, but the colony's silk production had failed materially to lessen the dependence of the empire on foreign sources. Unlike her wine industry, which never got into actual production, Georgia's silk industry had made some progress, producing hundreds of pounds of raw silk for export to England, but never fulfilled the hopes held out for it by the trustees. Even before the Revolution the industry was dead—along with Ottolenghe, the only colonial of Jewish origin ever to engage in the manufacture of silk.[5]

In pursuance of the policy they formulated for producing in Georgia commodities normally imported into the empire, the trustees of the Georgia colony also attempted to establish a dyestuff industry. One of the dyes the English clothworkers found serviceable was cochineal. Used for reds and purples, cochineal was an extract from an insect found in Mexico and Central America, and therefore the trustees were interested when two Jews approached them in 1738 with proposals for establishing the industry in Georgia. These two Jews are known to us only as Nunez and Belanger. One had lived as a Marrano in Mexico, where he learned how to prepare cochineal. When his Jewish origin was discovered, he had fled the country for fear of the Inquisition. The trustees negotiated with the pair for about two years, but the project never advanced beyond the stage of discussion.[6]

Far more important for the English cloth industry than cochineal was indigo, the chief dye for blue and reddish tints. Unfortunately for the English, however, they were dependent on French indigo, for which they had to pay in pounds sterling, a disadvantage whose burdensomeness increased when imports of that essential dye became scarce during the frequent Anglo-French wars.

Indigo had been grown and processed in the Carolinas ever since the seventeenth century, but it became profitable only in 1748 at the end of the War of the Austrian Succession, when a bounty of sixpence a pound was offered by the government. Though only some 134,000 pounds of indigo were exported to England at that time, in the course of a generation the plant became the most profitable crop in Carolina, next to rice. By the year before the Revolution, more than 1,000,000 pounds—worth £250,000 sterling—were being exported annually. With the possible exception of Eliza Lucas and Andrew Deveaux, who pioneered in proving the practicability of indigo cultivation, Moses Lindo of London and Charleston did more for the industry than any other person.

Back in London, Lindo had been a produce broker on the Royal Exchange and was a recognized expert in the field of cochineal and indigo. He had given testimony before the House of Commons on matters touching on indigo and claimed to be the best judge of dyes and drugs in Europe and America. Not a scientist, though he did possess some practical knowledge of the chemistry of dyes, he was primarily a sorter, an expert in judging and grading the material. Lindo's knowledge would enable him to establish standards for the crop and thus make its production and sale profitable.

On Lindo's arrival at Charleston in 1756, he had contracted with his clients in London to buy large quantities of the dye, and by certifying the materials which had his approval, he succeeded in imposing his standards on the planters and processors and therefore ultimately in creating a good market for American indigo. He seems to have been the chief channel through which the dye was sent to London, and when his contract expired, he remained on as a sorter and commission man, grading, buying, and selling. Lindo probably did some shipping on his own account as well, for he had a schooner to which he gave his name, and at one point he may even have been tempted to become an indigo planter, for he advertised for a farm of 500 acres and sixty to seventy slaves. That advertisement, however, may have been only a publicity stunt, for Lindo was well aware of the importance of publicity and was always eager to keep his name before the public. The South Carolina administration, the planters, and the merchants, realizing his value, secured for him an honorary appointment as surveyor and inspector general of indigo for the colony in 1762. The appointment undoubtedly gave him a great deal of moral authority and aided his efforts to further the industry.

Before Lindo died he had inspected millions of pounds and had seen the industry reach dimensions requiring the employment of 10,000 slaves. It was his hope that the English government would abolish the bounty on French indigo and impose a duty in order to keep it out and thus spur the growth and manufacture of the American dye. In the mid-1760's he expressed the opinion that a million and a half pounds of indigo might one day be grown in the colonies, a goal the planters were well on their way to achieving by the time of his death in 1774.

With the Revolution in 1775, however, indigo planting began to decline. England of course refused to grant the new American state a bounty for indigo, chemical dyes began to appear in Europe, and the invention of the cotton gin made cotton a more profitable crop in the South.[7]

METALS AND MINES

Jewish businessmen were interested in colonial America's metal industries, but for the most part only indirectly. Lopez of Newport, for example, kept in close touch with the Browns, from whom he purchased considerable quantities of pig and bar iron for export to the continent and the West Indies, where one of Lopez' Jamaican clients alone gave the Newporter orders for 300 to 400 tons per year. No doubt the iron was made up for Lopez in response to his instructions, although he employed his own blacksmith. From time to time the Newport shipper also ordered special metal parts made up for him, since he himself was not a producer of metal.[8]

Joseph Simon of Lancaster and one of his companies, Simon & Henry, shipped Pennsylvania pig iron to Pittsburgh, Baltimore, and London. The Baltimore shipment alone amounted to 100 tons. The firm's supplier was probably the Lancaster ironmaster Thomas Smith with whom Simon had close business relations, but Simon was himself an industrialist: a distiller on a modest scale, an arms manufacturer, and a fabricator of silver trinkets for the Indian trade. He and his partner William Henry of Lancaster were associated in the sale of hardware and the manufacture of rifles during the pre-revolutionary period, with Henry supplying the technical skill and Simon providing the capital and arranging for sales. In 1750, after the twenty-one-year-old Henry finished his apprenticeship, he and Simon organized a rifle manufacturing business. Their guns were sold during the French and Indian War and shipped to the frontier as far north as the environs of Detroit. In 1773 the still active firm was attempting to sell its rifles in New York and Schenectady, where Simon & Henry hoped to secure the patronage of Sir William Johnson, the northern superintendent for Indian affairs. The clerical work for the gun-manufacturing concern was carried on in Simon's countinghouse by his son-in-law Levy Andrew Levy. The rifles themselves were manufactured by workmen in their own homes, for Simon, like most contemporary manufacturers, conducted his industrial enterprises through outwork; he sent the materials out to be finished by craftsmen in their own shops and homes. It was not until the Revolution, when Henry entered government service, that the partnership was dissolved.[9]

As a large-scale dealer in Indian goods, supplying traders all along the frontier, Simon employed workmen to manufacture silver trinkets which, through the kind offices of the cultured Christian clergyman Thomas Barton, tutor to Sir William Johnson's son, he tried to induce the Indian commissioner to purchase from him. On two occasions in 1657 Barton recommended Simon to Sir William. The "eminent trader," said Barton, was "a worthy honest Jew" and "a man fair in his dealings and honest from principle." Sir William, who was colonel of the Six Nations, had constant dealings with the Indians and therefore was in the market for large quantities of trinkets—in demand as gifts, particularly when treaties were made. Simon must have been a large-scale manufacturer. One statement of March 1768 alone shows him billing Johnson's Indian agent George Croghan for 200 dozen of three different items. In addition to silver brooches and ear ornaments for the Indian traders, Simon also manufactured table silver; for example, he sent sauceboats to Canada.[10]

The manufacture of metal commodities was not the only metallurgic industry to which colonial Jews applied themselves. Nearly two decades before Simon settled at Lancaster, Isaac Miranda, Pennsylvania's Jewish pioneer, had investigated a mining property on the far side of the Susquehanna, and a generation later Michael Gratz was interested in mining at Whitemarsh near Philadelphia. By 1766, in fact, the Gratz brothers had already lost money exploiting a mine, probably in western Connecticut's Housatonic valley. The driving force in that project was the silversmith Myer Myers, a manufacturer of jewelry and a speculator in lead mines. In the 1760's Michael

Gratz, Sampson Simson, and Myer Myers were partners in mining and attempted to sell a mine they owned to Peter Hasenclever, one of colonial America's outstanding iron manufacturers. During the 1770's William Murray, sent to the Illinois country by the Frankses, the Gratzes, and their Christian associates, was charged with buying copper and lead properties from the Indians. Apparently the Gratzes were preparing to do some mining, for they attempted to interest Simon in a copper mine on the western frontier, where ever since the days of the Sieur de Bienville, mines were known to exist in the Mississippi valley.[11]

In staking a claim to a Connecticut "gold mine," one of the Gratzes' Jewish associates chiseled a Hebrew inscription on the mountainside. The carver must have been Myers, whose knowledge of lead mining apparently embraced the metallurgic aspects, since on the eve of the Revolution, the Connecticut authorities considered employing him to exploit lead deposits found in the neighborhood of Middletown.

Solomon Marache of Philadelphia was in the earthen and glassware business and filled orders for special types of bottles at a nearby factory, which may well have been that of "Baron" Stiegel. There is no evidence that Marache was ever more than a merchant placing orders for special products, but the Gratzes, always probing for new opportunities, did toy with the idea of establishing a chinaware and earthenware factory. They finally abandoned the plan when they encountered difficulty securing the proper clay for their purposes.[12]

TANNING, GRISTMILLS, VINEGAR, AND TOBACCO

There were a number of industrial enterprises in which individuals were concerned on a modest scale. Levi Sheftall of Savannah was for many years engaged in the hide-dressing business and owned a tanyard which he operated, apparently on a large scale, with slave workmen. Lopez of Newport was not a tanner, but following his usual procedure of securing goods through the outwork system, sent skins to be dressed and large quantities of raw hides to a tanner to be turned into finished leather.[13]

The Louzada brothers of New Jersey ran a gristmill, and far to the north in Canada, the grain buyer Samuel Jacobs seems at one time to have also had a mill. During the Revolutionary War he prepared his own flour for the troops he fed. Although grain and flour were important Pennsylvania exports, the Jewish merchants of the province were not outstanding for their participation in that trade, and there seems to be little record of their activity as flour manufacturers. Michael Gratz, however, once owned the Globe Mill where he may have processed grain.[14]

David Hays of New York ran a vinegar factory, and Moses M. Hays of the firm of Hays & Polock once embarked upon a partnership with others in a similar enterprise at Newport. In 1769–1770 the Gratz brothers, interested in setting up a vinegar, mustard, and snuff factory, attempted in vain to secure a competent worker from London.[15]

Although tobacco was one of America's great industries, Jewish merchants, as we have noted, played very little part in it. Colonial Virginia had no Jewish community; there were few if any Jewish tobacco planters in the southern colonies; and there is no evidence to show that Jews took any part in the work of growing and curing the leaf. If, however, Jews had little to do with the cultivation and export of tobacco, they were active as tobacconists, and this business was not uncommon among the Jews of the North. Many of those tradesmen also owned and operated snuff mills, and some, like the Gomezes of New York, seem to have been large-scale manufacturers. Another manufacturing firm of some proportion was the Scotch Snuff Manufactory whose members were Moses Lopez, Rivera, and one of the Cardozos, and whose Jewish clients often peddled its products all the way from Albany and Kingston on the Hudson to Virginia and probably even the Carolinas. These hawkers were permitted to return what they could not sell.[16]

FOOD PROCESSING

Among the industries in which colonial Jewish businessmen interested themselves was food processing. Aaron Lopez of Newport saw food-processing as ancillary to his involvement in the coastal and West Indian traffic. Since provisions were the prime staples sent by the New Englanders to the West Indies, it was with the islands in mind that Lopez contracted with various processors for thousands of pounds of cheese, while the chocolate he secured through outwork was destined for local and North American consumption.[17]

In 1721, long before Lopez' time, Aaron Louzada had been manufacturing chocolate from cocoa for Nathan Simson. Chocolate, in fact, may have been a Sephardic Jewish specialty, for the next generation found Isaac Navarro, Daniel Torres, Joseph Pinto, and Moses Mordecai Gomez engaged in that industry. In Newport relatively large quantities of chocolate were prepared for Lopez by Negroes whose Jewish masters may have taught them the art of making the confection. Prince Updike, one of Lopez' Negro workers, ground thousands of pounds for the Newport merchant. He received five shillings for every pound he prepared, and one batch of cocoa which he turned into chocolate weighed over 5,000 pounds. Another of the Negro craftsmen, a member of the cocoa-grinding Casey family, was so useful that when the man was thrown into jail for drunkenness, Lopez paid his fine and put him back to work.[18]

The West Indian planters, reserving their lands for the profitable sugar production, had no pastures to spare and few cattle. The islands were populous, however, and the dietary needs of their large population were met by America which exported substantial quantities of meat to them. Jews shared in this trade, and during the course of the eighteenth century in particular, meat-packing assumed rather sizeable proportions in the American Jewish economy. By the 1670's at the latest, New York Jewish merchants were shipping provisions to the islands, and by the second decade of the next century, Nathan Simson was regularly sending beef and pork to Jamaica. Even at that early date a good deal of beef was supplied by the small Jewish shopkeepers on Long Island who used it as a medium to balance their accounts with city merchants like Simson. Simson would provide the salt and barrels, arrange for the cartage, and even procure the rum to be given the men who did the packing under his supervision.[19]

From the 1730's to the 1760's the Gomezes of New York packed, through the instrumentality of others for the most part, large quantities of pickled beef and pork for export to the West Indies and at various times formed temporary partnerships for those packing ventures. In 1753 New York's Jewish congregation collected a purchase and sales tax of some £25 on 1,941 barrels of kosher beef shipped out by its members—an *imposta* which, like all taxes, represented at best a minimum estimate of what the members of the congregation had shipped. In much the same fashion as the Gomezes, Lopez, too, prepared or bought and sold substantial quantities of beef, much of it destined in all likelihood for the islands. One hundred barrels of beef—22,000 pounds—were offered Lopez in 1764 by Aaron Isaacs and Joseph Jacobs, two Jewish businessmen from the cattle lands of East Hampton and Southampton on eastern Long Island. In exchange for cash or beef, Isaacs was willing to buy salt from Lopez for pickling.[20]

When a rural Jamaican Jew named Henry Israell found it difficult in 1770 to "gitt such sort of provisions as is suitable to our religion," he turned for help to the North American mainland—to Lopez in Rhode Island. Other West Indian Jews, however, had long been looking to North America for "provisions . . . suitable to our religion," and in New York kosher meats were readied for the Caribbean market no later than 1704. In fact, by that early date Gentiles had already begun buying certified kosher beef for export. Since Jews alone could prepare kosher supplies and present certificates acceptable to their West Indian coreligionists, the New Yorkers of Congregation Shearith Israel could confidently anticipate a monopoly of the lucrative trade in kosher food, always more costly than nonkosher food. Throughout the century, indeed, the kosher meat export industry afforded a substantial revenue to those engaged in it.[21]

As early as 1714 Mordecai Nathan and Simon Valentine, at the time business partners in Charleston, packed large quantities of kosher beef, undoubtedly for the West Indian market. Charleston was, after all, ten days closer by ship than New York or Pennsylvania to the Caribbean market! One of the Charlestonians' shipments alone exceeded 10,000 pounds. Five years later the firm of Moses Mikal, Nathan Simson, and Joseph Isaacs was packing and shipping very sizeable amounts of kosher beef to Barbados, Jamaica, and Curaçao.

Isaacs, a butcher, was obviously in charge of production; Simson handled the New York end of the business; and Mikal, a Curaçaon trader, probably watched over the West Indian terminus. Some of the kosher provisions sent to the islands were purchased by Gentiles there either for resale or for their own use, since they appreciated the fact that kosher products prepared under supervision were usually superior in freshness and cleanliness to nonkosher foods.[22]

Very likely New York Jewish entrepreneurs applied themselves to this type of export business in every decade before the Revolution. In the 1730's Abraham R. Rivera was shipping fats and pickled meats to Curaçao; in the 1740's the firm of Levy Samuel & Lyon Lepmon (Lipman), armed with a killing knife and a branding iron, formed a partnership with the New York Gomezes to prepare kosher meats in the countryside. During the 1760's Philadelphia Jewish merchants, among them Michael Gratz and his cousin Henry Marks, exported kosher beef, turkeys, and fats to Barbados and Curaçao. Though these provisions were prepared in Philadelphia, the kosher certification or hechsher for the shipments came from New York as well as Philadelphia religious authorities.[23]

Newport Jewry, too, carried on a substantial trade in the kosher foods export business, primarily to the islands of Jamaica and Barbados, and to Surinam in South America. The foods shipped out from Newport were beef, fats, tongues, sausages, pickled geese, cheese, and the Passover salad called haroset. Surinam, for her part, exported or reexported kosher cheese to North America. It is by no means unlikely that the kosher cheese Pennsylvanians bought from Surinam had originally come from Newport! Thousands of pounds of kosher provisions were occasionally shipped from Newport in a single cargo, prepared under the supervision of the local religious functionary Hazzan Isaac Touro whose hechsher usually accompanied the shipment to assure the scrupulous that the food met ritual standards. Aaron Lopez—whose kosher cheese supplier, a Narragansett farmer, also supplied him with hogs for export—undertook to stimulate the Caribbean market for kosher victuals by forwarding samples to his West Indian and Surinamese coreligionists and offering to supply them with large quantities. Substantial orders for such provisions were, in fact, received at Newport, and the Rhode Islanders reaped considerable profits, even though in the Dutch colonies they had to compete with kosher imports from Holland, and on Jamaica, with ritually prepared foods from Cork and London. Even after the Revolution the Newport Jews maintained their interest in the export of kosher food, and forty kegs of beef—no small order— were shipped to Surinam in 1787.[24]

The majority of the Caribbean Jews were unwilling to abandon Jewish scruples in regard to the ritual fitness of the foods they consumed. New York's Shearith Israel sought, through congregational legislation during the years 1747 to 1758, to make absolutely sure that all meat exported to the Jews of the islands had been certified kosher by the hazzan or a responsible member of the Jewish community and that the food so certified would be shipped with the congregation's distinctive Hebrew brand *K. Sh. I., kasher* (Congregation Shearith Israel, kosher). By 1752, however, the kosher export trade had reached proportions which led the congregational authorities to adopt further legislation that local demands were to be met before kosher meat could be dispatched southward. The size of the West Indian kosher trade is suggested by the fact that Hazzan Machado was annually required to certify over 1,300 barrels of kosher beef for export.[25]

Undue depletion of kosher supplies for local needs was not the only problem the Jewish communal authorities of New York had to confront. It was also their responsibility to arrest any abuses that crept in. This was a serious matter, for some of the Gentile butchers appear to have shipped abroad nonkosher meat, represented as kosher meat, under cover of communal certificates, and it is possible that Jews too were guilty of the same legerdemain. Vigorous protests from the large communities of Curaçao and Jamaica about the nonkosher foods exported to them elicited assurances from the New York synagogue that the evils would be corrected, but providing kosher meat for local and distant communities never ceased to be fraught with many hazards. Kashrut was always to be a major problem for American Jewry.[26]

THE GARMENT AND SHOE INDUSTRY

Apparel manufacturing on a modest scale was probably characteristic of a number of Jewish merchants as well as, of course, many
Gentile businessmen. In 1764, for instance, Samuel Jacobs, assessing
the needs of the Indian trade, contracted with one of his branch
managers for the production of shirts, coats, stockings, blankets, and
other articles of clothing, and on a trip to London some years later,
Barnard Gratz proposed sending a shipment of secondhand clothes
to Philadelphia—a design to which Michael objected strenuously on
the ground that Philadelphia already had too many "slop shops,"
none doing sufficient business. "The poorest men here if he has got
20 shillings to buey cloths, he will have it new," wrote Michael,
adding, "However, shall make more inquiry; lett you know." The
result of Michael's inquiry was no doubt that Barnard forsook his
plan.[27]

Aaron Lopez, however, was at that time in the business of
making new clothes, as numerous entries in his account books indicate, though his interest in making clothing in larger quantities seems
to have manifested itself only in 1765 after the boycott on English
goods. Lopez then began to manufacture work clothes for sale in
his shop as well as for his numerous employees, and as long as he
remained in Newport, he continued to provide cheap clothing for
the use of low-income customers like the Negroes with whom he did
business in the town. Such clothing was also of use to Lopez for
African export and for his sailors who were clothed through the
truck system, receiving garments and other sundries in exchange for
their services on Lopez' vessels.

As a textile and garment manufacturer, Lopez was supplied with
cotton yarn and cotton wicks by the spinners who worked for him.
He also had at least one weaver producing cloth for him, and another
male craftsman who provided him with cloth bags. The Newport
merchant was apparently known as an outwork cloth entrepreneur,
for in 1766 Nicholas Brown & Company asked him to quote prices
on cloth to be woven for their needs. Another of his workmen made

children's stockings. Though Lopez' tailors made an occasional quilted petticoat, he concentrated production on shirts, smock frocks (men's work aprons), trousers, jackets, greatcoats, and men's baize gowns. The shirts, smocks, and trousers might be made of a variety of cloths: linen, "chex," or flannel. Jackets were classed as thin, thick, lined with linen, unlined flannel, thick flannel, plain, and ratteen.[28]

With the exception of his weavers, his cloth bag maker, and an Aaron Lopez Jr.—probably a member of his family who seems to have tailored for him—all of Lopez' garment workers were female. Some were Negro women; two were Jewish. A number specialized in spinning cotton, while others did tailoring only, and some probably did a little of both. All told, some twenty to thirty women worked for him at these different tasks from the 1760's if not earlier, until the outbreak of the American Revolution when Lopez fled Newport. Whether or not his employees were poor and compelled by circumstance to work for a living is impossible to determine. The two Jewish seamstresses were Mrs. Martha Lazarus and a Mrs. Isaacs. Mrs. Lazarus may have been a widow who had come upon hard times and needed a supplementary income. While Lopez was still in exile at Leicester, Mrs. Lazarus, by that time completely impoverished, became a pensioner of the congregation and was carried on the rolls till her death in 1787. Mrs. Isaacs may have been the wife of Jacob Isaacks, who is known to have suffered business difficulties during the early 1770's, and she may have wished in this way to help lighten her husband's burden. Another possibility, of course, is simply that both women, and most of the others too, were housewives eager to earn some pin money. There is, in any case, no reason to believe the women who spun and tailored for Lopez were farmers' wives. Most if not all of them might have come from Newport, but if some were farmers' wives, they did not limit their work to the winter months when the farm work slackened, for garments were brought to Lopez' establishment every month of the year.[29]

The system of household or domestic manufacture under which the Newport merchant-manufacturer produced his wares lacked even the semblance of mass production as the term is understood today. No power machinery was available for use in textile or garment production, in spinning or weaving, and the total cotton spun by all of Lopez' workers probably never exceeded several hundred pounds a year. Some spinners would take only five pounds of cotton, while others might process as much as 100 pounds. Plying his or her craft only intermittently and without the benefit of a sewing machine, a worker might produce a hundred garments a year. Some, like Mrs. Isaacs, produced more; others turned in only a few garments.

The laborer sold his labor only; the merchant-capitalist supplied the cotton for spinning, all materials for trimming, and even a pattern for the seamstress-tailor. All the work was done at home. Cotton spinners received a fixed wage of 28 shillings for every pound of cotton spun. A few of the clothing workers were paid by the day; the great majority did piecework and were compensated for every garment they finished. There was a set tariff for the manufacture of each item. In 1766 a pair of trousers brought the seamstress 10 shillings, a smock 15, a shirt 25, a jacket 50, and a greatcoat 60. By 1771 prices had risen materially; smocks and trousers brought 25 shillings each, and a greatcoat brought 70 shillings. For some reason jackets remained constant at 50 shillings, although in the following years their cost to Lopez rose to 70 and 80 shillings apiece, while baize gowns cost him 60 shillings each. By 1776, when the war for independence suspended imports from London, the need for clothing in volume became crucial. Jewish businessmen supplying the armed forces began then to manufacture garments in large quantities by the "putting-out" and even a primitive factory system.[30]

Lopez' interest in the apparel industry extended beyond garments to shoes. Shoes, in fact, played a far more important part than garment production in the economy of his enterprises—so much so, actually, that Lopez and his fellow-entrepreneurs may be said to have anticipated the role of the shoe industry in nineteenth and early twentieth century New England.

In a number of instances Lopez not only supplied his producers with leather and findings but also indirectly advanced them capital in the form of English wares. Such advances of capital, to be repaid in shoes, were fortified by interest-bearing notes, and if the finished goods were not forthcoming, the shoe supplier was compelled to pay interest on his notes. Some of Lopez' suppliers were themselves shoe-makers, but in addition Lopez employed agents to solicit shoes from farmers and others who manufactured them at home during their spare time. Most of the shoes that poured into his warehouses were assembled by special suppliers who collected them for him from the prime producers. Now and then, too, he would buy shoes in Newport from fellow-merchants who had scraped together a quantity in their shops. It was quite common for some of Lopez' suppliers to bring him small quantities, twenty to thirty pair at a time, but Mr. Tappan, of Newburyport, Massachusetts, sent him at least a thousand pair a year. Lopez also received shoes from Dartmouth, Massachusetts, and from nearby Bristol, Rhode Island, which was apparently a shoe manufacturing center in those years. The fact that he had at least seven suppliers in Bristol alone might lead one to believe that most of his shoes probably came from there, but Tappan, who seems to have been Lopez' sole supplier in Newburyport, may have shipped him more shoes than all the suppliers in Bristol put together.[31]

The shoes which found their way into his warehouses were for men, women, and girls. The women's shoes were cloth and leather; the men's were single-soled or double-soled, the latter no doubt for heavy duty purposes, as were the men's boots which he also manufactured. Customers could always find an assortment in Lopez' shop and warehouses, but the bulk of his stock in shoes ultimately found its way to Hayman Levy in New York. Levy in turn shipped large quantities of shoes to Phyn, Ellice & Company of Schenectady for transshipment to the Canadian northwest. Lopez had begun shipping shoes to Levy no later than 1757 and continued to do so as long as he remained in Newport. Levy would buy anywhere from 150 to 700 pairs or more at a time, and he paid for them in sundries, provisions, indigo, beaver, and even pig iron. Lopez had a better source for pig iron at the Brown furnaces, but it was not at all uncommon for a merchant to accept and trade any commodity that helped balance an account. The men's and women's leather shoes that Levy advertised in the *New-York Journal or the General Advertiser* during the early days of the Revolution probably came from his Newport correspondent.[32]

POTASH, PEARL ASH, AND SOAP

The manufacture of potash and pearl ash had considerable importance, during the colonial period, among the industries connected with forests. Often in colonial America the land was cleared by burning the timber, whereupon the wood ashes were leached to produce potash, a further refinement of which was pearl ash. These ashes found an excellent market in England. The British encouraged the potash and pearl ash industry, not only because of their need for these chemicals, but also because they served to pay for the English wares sent to America.

During the 1750's in particular, colonial America saw considerable activity in the production of potash, and Jews, too, interested themselves in the industry. The founding of Halifax in 1749 stimulated British efforts to clear the land in Nova Scotia and led in turn to the furtherance of potash manufacturing. Israel Abrahams, a former Newport merchant who was engaged in the manufacture of potash in England's Canadian enclave, urged the Board of Trade and Plantations in England to employ him to instruct others "in the buissness of making pot ash." If he were so employed, he wrote, the new industry would effectively "clear very large tracts of land," would "employ a great number of men in cutting and clearing the same," and would finally "be the means of making large remittances home"—that is, supplying a medium acceptable in England for the payment of English imports. Appeals of this sort for employment, grants, and monopolies were neither new nor original with Abrahams, but so common in fact, that they became conventional phrases in nearly all such applications.[33]

Nova Scotia was not the only part of England's Canadian domain to hold promise for the potash industry or to attest Jewish interest in potash production. No later than 1766 Samuel Jacobs, together with three other Canadian merchants, managed a potash and pearl ash manufacturing plant in Quebec. The enterprise seems to have been a large one, for its proprietors hoped to produce 1,200 pounds of the commodity daily and to make shipments to London

[681]

of no less than seventy tons. Jacobs' company bragged that it was the only potash manufactory in Canada.[34]

Further south, too, the industry had begun to grow. In Newport, Moses Lopez sought a monopoly in the manufacture of potash for export, and it was granted him in 1753. Years later he was still engaged in the same business and was trading formulas with a potash manufacturer in Boston. In 1765, when Samuel De Lucena sought a similar monopoly for an area within twenty miles of his factory at Norwalk, Connecticut, he was careful to point out that his was the first potash factory to be established in Fairfield County. At Albany, New York, Barrack Hays was looking for one or two sober young men to help him carry on the potash business, and at Lancaster, Pennsylvania, the firm of Joseph Simon and Dr. Samuel Boude owned the buildings and equipment in which they manufactured potash and pearl ash. Dr. Boude, as a physician, no doubt had the knowledge of chemistry needed to carry on the industry. The fact that businessmen like Abrahams, Moses Lopez, and Samuel De Lucena sought monopolies in the manufacture of potash lends credence to the belief that there was a real need for this chemical, that the industry was still in its early stages, and that potash producers expected special rewards—in the form of a monopoly—for their pioneering efforts.[35]

Related to the production of potash and pearl ash was the making and sale of soap, an industry in which Jews participated to some degree. During the 1720's Moses Levy of New York imported from Barbados and Antigua "Spanish" soap which he transshipped to Surinam, and decades later, Samuel Jacobs of Canada is known to have tried his hand at the manufacture of soap. To the south at Philadelphia, Michael Moses, a tallow chandler, manufactured and sold soap as well as candles in 1757. Moses was the technician of his firm; his partner, the merchant-shipper David Franks, supplied the capital for the concern. It employed a slave, and like most colonial manufactories, was a modest enterprise. After the death of Moses, Franks took other partners to keep the small factory open.[36]

The Jews of Newport may have been more interested in making soap than were their Pennsylvania coreligionists, although in the economy of the Rhode Island city the manufacture of that commodity never played an important part. In the early 1760's the Portuguese émigré James Lucena was granted a ten-year monopoly in Rhode Island to manufacture Castile soap in accordance with a formula used in the Portuguese royal factory, and Moses Lopez, another member of the Lopez-Lucena clan, also participated in the soap business. Lopez made hard and soft soaps, and his efforts to improve his product led him to exchange technical information with a Massachusetts entrepreneur. The Newport firm of Naphtali Hart & Company may also have manufactured soap.[37]

LUMBER AND COOPERAGE, BUGGIES, HOUSES, AND SHIPS

Lumber played no small part in the colonial economy, and most Jewish as well as Gentile merchants dealt in lumber, shingles, and oars, both for local sale and for export. The lumber they sold was cut to their specifications by craftsmen, and on occasion Aaron Lopez would advance money to skilled workers who then prepared the lumber he required. The Newport merchant also employed log-wood chippers to chip this dyewood for him and engaged sawyers to cut mahogany which he had stored in his warehouses. Army purveyor David Franks tried to induce the military authorities to sell him an old sawmill they owned in the neighborhood of Pittsburgh. Mordecai Sheftall purchased 1,000 acres of pine land in St. George's Parish, Georgia, and proposed to set up a sawmill there. Among other Jews in the lumber business were the Gratzes, who in 1769 were negotiating with Myer Hart of Easton, Pennsylvania, for the export of masts to England, although it is not known whether Hart owned and cut his own timber or, as is more probable, purchased masts from neighboring farmers when orders came in from tidewater merchants like the Gratzes.[38]

The most common lumber items handled by merchants were headings, staves, and hoops for barrels. Cooperage was, of course, a very important industry, since barrels were necessary for the packing of meats, fish, rum, salt, molasses, and flour, basic food staples in the North American colonies and in the islands. Casks and barrels were exported "shaken" or "shook"—unassembled in their respective parts—thus taking up less space in the hold. The sizeable amounts of material that Lopez shipped in barrels, casks, kegs, puncheons, and hogsheads made it advisable for him to buy staves, headings, and hoops in large quantities and set up a cooperage with his own craftsmen. Since one cooper could not hope to fashion all the casks needed in Lopez' business, the Newporter would customarily hire additional workers whom he supplied with raw material. In one case, Lopez even dispatched coopers on the long trip to Jamaica to assemble casks for the goods he expected to ship back to the North American mainland. Practically all of Lopez' manufacturing was of the domestic sort, and assembling or making barrels in his own workshop was one of his few enterprises of the factory type.[39]

Of more modest dimensions than the cooperage Lopez engaged in, was the buggymaking reflected in his contracts with the artisans who built sulkies for him. In a number of instances the materials were supplied by him and no doubt included iron axles, leather boots, broadcloth linings, moldings, and Turkish carpets.[40]

Lopez appears to have done far more business as a house builder, or more precisely, a building contractor. His was, in fact, one of the two Jewish mercantile firms in Newport to operate as building contractors. The other firm was Naphtali Hart & Company, the contractor for the Newport synagogue which was finally finished in 1764 after an earlier dedication. In all probability the Harts had subcontracted the job, and in similar fashion, Lopez did not directly supervise any house he erected. He would contract for a house with a master artisan and then sell it, for he was primarily a builder "for the market." In 1772, for instance, Lopez ordered a house built and on its completion sold it to a client—apparently for what it cost him! He had, of course, paid off the builders in European staples as well as cash and had thus made a profit through the disposal of his store goods. His customers were no doubt often happy to accept payment in manufactured commodities because paper money had a tendency to fluctuate in value.[41]

An even more enterprising phase of Lopez' activity as a builder was his preparation of building frames, prefabricated houses or "shell" homes, like those made to his order in Dartmouth and delivered to Newport. Structures of this type were then shipped by him to Jamaica or the Gulf of Honduras, where they were assembled by carpenters sent along on the voyage for that purpose and paid double wages for the time spent erecting these homes.[42]

One of the few sizeable manufacturing efforts the British government encouraged in America was shipbuilding, which fed England's eagerness to secure the bottoms she needed to capture the carrying trade of Europe. Through the navigation laws, therefore, the construction of ships was furthered in North America as well as in Great Britain. This very much abetted the American effort to find commodities and wares acceptable to the mother country in payment for the manufactures imported by the colonials. New Englanders in particular engaged so energetically in the building and selling of ships that by 1760 about one-third of all British ships were of American construction, while perhaps three-fourths of all American commerce was carried on in vessels built by American shipwrights. Able to compete successfully with English shipbuilders because of ready lumber at hand, the Americans found it an easy step to move from shipbuilding to freighting and transportation, and it was not long before they had won a good-sized share of the imperial carrying trade for themselves.[43]

Jewish merchants were concerned in almost every phase of the shipping industry. They were brokers, buying and selling bottoms on commission; they ordered vessels for delivery to others, rebuilt old ships, and after a fashion even supervised the building of new vessels. It was usual for Jewish merchants to construct new ships to carry their own cargoes to the English and West Indian markets where the ships, too, might be offered for sale, and a New England businessman like Lopez might discharge his debts to a creditor by building a ship for him. Though Lopez does not appear to have built hulls, he did quite commonly overhaul and repair vessels at his own wharf, would do all types of repairs and rebuilding, and even brought in technicians from other towns for a special job like the installation of a windlass.

In 1762 when he was just emerging as a ship entrepreneur, the thirty-one-year-old Lopez ordered the building of at least a half dozen vessels. The manufacture and sale of ships was for him a highly developed business. Others worked on a much more modest scale; for example, his father-in-law Rivera, who built and sold whale-boats, and the Monsantos of New Orleans, who provided the British army with flat-bottomed bateaux in the Gulf area.[44]

The financing of vessels, whether old or new, witnessed nearly as many variations as did transactions in far less bulky commodities. In one instance we find Lopez advancing money to Isaac Elizer, who then proceeded to order a ship built. Buying a ship on the open market from the carpenters who had finished it and were offering it for sale was common enough, but the classical form of shipbuilding, as exemplified in the Lopez papers, was to contract for a hull from a shipwright and then to make separate arrangements for the rigging, canvas, blocks, staterooms, and even the hencoop for the poultry. As a prime contractor Lopez often not only supplied the ironwork, but might arrange to have his own smith do the work. He also provided the tar, pitch, and oakum, but on one occasion at least, acting as a broker in ordering a slaver built for a client, specified the purchaser himself was to be responsible for "the awning, a second boat, caboose, colours, small arms, chains, and hand cuffs, with every other small utensil." Almost always Lopez, and other contractors too, would stipulate that the shipwright accept payment in English wares and in West Indian staples like rum and molasses, though once in a while the merchant also paid some cash. The Newport shipper in his own turn, when reimbursed for a vessel sold to an English correspondent, had to accept payment in London or Bristol manufactures, tea, and the like, though occasionally he might also receive some money.[45]

The final stage in the construction of a ship was the formal act of launching and its attendant celebration, which might take a week during which gallons of rum were used up—not by being poured over the hull of the new ship, but by being emptied down the gullets of the spectators and interested parties. Substantial quantities of food were also devoured, and there was a corps of Negro servants to wait upon the guests.[46]

Related to Lopez' shipbuilding and overhauling enterprises was another industrial facet—the supplying of rigging. On more than one occasion Lopez delivered hemp to an artisan who then processed it into rigging or cables to be used by Lopez either for his own ships or for assignment to a third party. Or the Newport merchant might give a man hemp and direct him to spin it into yarn, cod lines, or seine twine, which could then be turned over to another artisan to be made into pressing cloths for Lopez' spermaceti works. Other craftsmen, whom he provided with flax, made it into sewing twine and received thirty shillings per pound for the finished product.[47]

RUM AND DISTILLERIES

There's nought, no doubt, so much the spirit calms
As rum and true religion.

Americans may have quarrelled from time to time about "true religion," but practically no one in the colonies would have questioned the value of rum. Important both for home consumption and for export, rum was produced in prodigious quantities, and by 1768 New York alone had seventeen distilleries between Yonkers and Oyster Bay. The industry of rectifying spirits had attracted Jewish interest almost from the very beginning of Jewish settlement in America, and Jews were to be found in it within three or four years after the first Brazilian refugees landed in New Amsterdam. By the turn of the century, at least four members of New York's Jewish community were engaged in distilling rum from molasses, and they seem to have been among the pioneers in the production of this "kill devil" drink. Jews were in any event to continue as distillers in New York all through the eighteenth century.[48]

The Canadian businessman Samuel Jacobs had been a partner in a Nova Scotia brewery ever since 1759; three years later he was operating a distillery in Quebec. Rum was preferred in Canada to the more expensive British liquors, and Jacobs hoped to extract "corn spirits" from local grain during the French and Indian War. There can be no doubt that this enterprising sutler and commissary officer enjoyed a lively patronage on the part of the soldiers. The business had its difficulties, of course, and on one occasion when the firm of Jacobs, Price & Hay set out to hire a new brewer and distiller,

Jacobs observed sarcastically that he ought to be able to distill without yeast, molasses, corn, wood, or money! [49]

About the same time in Pennsylvania, Joseph Simon was interested in establishing a "stilling bussiness"—apparently on a very modest scale—and asked Barnard Gratz to procure the necessary utensils for him. Simon's in-laws the Gratzes, who hailed from Upper Silesia, were certainly not unfamiliar with the "bussiness," since Jewish tenants in their native Silesia frequently leased the distilling privilege from their landlords. There is no evidence that the Gratzes themselves engaged in distilling, but in 1775 on the frontier near Pittsburgh, one of their friends, Mordecai M. Mordecai, maintained a still on a plantation and sold his whiskey in his "ordinary." Simon bought Mordecai out, however, and it is not known whether Mordecai continued to distill for Simon. [50]

It was in New England that the production of rum reached classical proportions. By 1750 some 2,000,000 gallons of New England rum were being exported annually. Massachusetts alone could boast sixty-three distilleries, and Newport is reported as early as 1730, when there were few if any Jews in the town, to have sheltered twenty-two plants manufacturing rum. In 1764 there were more than thirty "distil houses" in Rhode Island, and Governor Hopkins spoke of the industry as "the main hinge upon which the trade of the colony turns." [51]

When the Jews began reestablishing their community in Newport during the 1740's some, like Israel Abrahams, Naphtali Hart & Company, and Myer Polock, turned to distilling after a few years, but it seems never to have become a favored full-time industry for Newport Jewry. Still, if there is little evidence that any of the town's Jewish merchants engaged directly and extensively in the manufacture of rum, they certainly did apply themselves to the "put out" phase of the industry. Huge amounts of molasses were supplied by Jewish businessmen to the local distillers who in turn rendered the molasses into rum for them. The distillers commonly returned a certain ratio of rum for every gallon of molasses delivered, or they received payment in consumer goods at so many shillings per gallon for distillation. Naphtali Hart & Company was involved in the industry in this way, and Lopez appears to have participated in it on a much larger scale, for there were times when he kept at least a dozen distillers busy rectifying thousands of gallons of molasses for him. There is no reason to believe that Lopez himself ever owned and operated a distillery, but where molasses importation and contracts for rum distillation were concerned, he was nothing less than a merchant-prince.[52]

FISHING AND WHALING

Together with whaling, manufacturing candles, distilling rum, and building ships, fishing was one of New England's great industries. Allied, if only remotely, with all the above pursuits, fishing was by 1765 one of the "commanding branches" of Aaron Lopez, whose active engagement in the fisheries in fact seems to have made him unique among American Jews. Buying considerable stocks of fish for export, Lopez had the sellers pack his purchases for him, and one of his coasters traded between Gloucester and Newport by exchanging sugar, rum, salt, and other products, primarily for fish.

In at least one instance a Lopez cargo was sold at Gloucester for one half its value in cash and the other half in fish for transshipment to Jamaica. When Lopez organized and financed fishing expeditions for cod to the waters off the Gaspé Peninsula, he provided the small auxiliary fishing boats as well as the salt, tackle, and utensils. Brought back to Newport, the catch was divided between Lopez and the crew, or taken directly to Jamaica where planters bought it to feed their slaves. Yet, though Lopez had a substantial interest in fishing and whaling and was not the least of the merchants devoted to those fields of enterprise in 1774, his voyages do not seem very numerous when one considers that a total of 138 ships cleared Rhode Island ports that year on fishing and whaling ventures.[53]

The eighteenth century had seen whaling achieve a notable and important place in the New England economy. Whales were sought for their bone and particularly for their oil, which was used for lubrication, lighting, and candles. So strong was the demand for whale oil in England that Parliament granted a bounty for the building and outfitting of whalers. At least 360 whalers are estimated to have been sailing the seas by 1774; they brought in thousands of barrels of oil and head matter which, when processed, produced the waxy spermaceti required for manufacturing the famous spermaceti candles, the finest candles of the time. Whaling and chandlery were, therefore, very closely associated.[54]

Not many Jews were active in whaling; it was candlemaking which interested them most. There were, however, some to whom whaling did appeal, among them Isaac Jacobs of Branford, Connecticut, and his New York partner Mordecai Gomez, who sought unsuccessfully in 1726 to secure a ten-year monopoly of "the fishery of porpoises" (whales actually) in Connecticut. Primarily entrepreneurs, Jacobs and Gomez claimed to "have, at great charge, travell, and expence, for a long time maintained and supported a skillful and knowing person in those parts of the world where the fishery of porpoises is best known and practised." A generation later Joseph Jacobs of Southampton, Long Island, was another Jew engaged in whaling. The outstanding Jew in the industry was, of course, Aaron Lopez.[55]

Shortly after Lopez' arrival on American soil in the 1750's, he entered the candle business and bought head matter from the suppliers. It was only a matter of time, however, before he found it necessary to ensure himself an adequate supply of spermaceti for his manufacturing requirements. When, like other American industrialists, Lopez encountered competition from English purchasers for the available head matter, he surmised that a direct interest in whaling was the best way to secure the raw materials needed for his candles and refined oils. In the early 1760's, therefore, he began to make agreements to finance, outfit, and provision whaling expeditions, and some of the ships he sent out were owned partly by him. The terms of his contracts afforded him a share of the catch and often, too, the right as sole agent to dispose of the entire cargo. Lopez' extensive use of head matter is suggested by the fact that in 1767 one of his purchases amounted to forty tons.[56]

Lopez' most ambitious whaling expedition—to the Falklands in 1775–1776—has already been alluded to. The vast and whale-rich expanses of the South Atlantic were not unknown to him. He had been among the first to send whalers there in the 1760's when his ships, on their way back to Newport, would call at the Dutch island of St. Eustatius and pick up bales of tea to be smuggled past the English authorities into Rhode Island harbors.[57]

By the spring of 1775, it was quite clear, the relations between New and Old England were deteriorating rapidly. The Restraining Act of 1775, excluding New Englanders from the North Atlantic fishing and whaling grounds, determined Lopez and his associates to dispatch a gigantic whaling fleet to the South Atlantic before effective boycotts and embargoes could be carried out by either the British or the Americans. Heavily in debt, Lopez probably calculated that a massive expedition to the Antarctic regions would, if successful, provide him with the means to meet his obligations. Accordingly, together with Rivera and others from Massachusetts, he set up a company to send about twenty whalers on the venture. It was no easy matter to arrange, for ways had to be found to circumvent the prohibitions of the Massachusetts assembly which forbade dealings with the English and also required the partners to post bond that they would return their cargo to that colony. The partners were aware, too, that the waters to the south were patrolled by English warships and that, in addition to traversing American and British waters, the whalers would have to skirt the unfriendly Spanish and Portuguese territories in South America. Sailors who fell into Iberian hands (one of Lopez' captains did) stood a good chance of being tried by the Inquisition for heresy. All this notwithstanding, however, one of the partners, Richard Smith, had London connections, while another, Francis Rotch of Nantucket, a Quaker, was a clever and devious businessman who knew how to deal with both the English and the Americans.[58]

There are indications that Lopez and his associates intended to bring their cargo back to America, but they were prepared for all eventualities. In a crisis their vessels were set to sail into an English or some continental European port, for which purpose they undoubtedly carried two sets of papers, probably with the connivance of the Rhode Island authorities. The partners were between the devil and the deep blue sea of English warships, irascible Massachusetts legislators, American privateers, and suspicious Spanish and Portuguese colonial administrators; they were playing a dangerous game, and they knew it.

The fleet sailed south with its bold design for a winter rendez-vous at the Falkland Islands where the oil could be barreled, the ships repaired, and plans modified as contingencies dictated. Infinite care and detail must have been lavished on the expedition—all to no avail, for the venture ended in failure. Some of the ships went down at sea; others were badly, even irreparably damaged. The vigilant British seized at least five, whose release Smith and Rotch had to seek in the English courts. It was a hazardous gamble, and the Americans had come away with nothing but defeat. The losses he sustained were beyond doubt a crushing blow to Aaron Lopez.[59]

CANDLE MANUFACTURING

Candlemaking was a lucrative industry in colonial America, and we are not surprised to find that during the mid-1700's candles made of wax, tallow, and spermaceti were manufactured and sold by Jewish businessmen. As early indeed as 1753, New York Jewish merchants found a ready market for the spermaceti candles sent them by their Newport friends and correspondents. Moses Lopez, Aaron's brother, and Abraham Lopez Jr. manufactured wax and dipped tallow candles on a small scale. Aaron himself, less than a year after his arrival, had already begun to manufacture the tallow type which, along with wax candles, he would continue stocking and selling, though his candlemaking appears ultimately to have been limited to the spermaceti variety. Eventually Aaron Lopez had at least two factories, one to process whale oil and head matter and the other to manufacture spermaceti candles.[60]

Lopez' stress on spermaceti candles was not unusual, for Jewish merchants appear to have manifested a particular interest in this aspect of chandlery, and there are some writers who maintain the spermaceti industry was introduced into America by Sephardic Jews like Jacob Rodriguez Rivera. Later local traditions notwithstanding, however, there is no evidence to support the contention that Rivera was responsible for the beginnings of the spermaceti industry in Newport. What is true is that in February 1751, just about the time Rivera moved from New York to Newport, a non-Jew secured a monopoly in the manufacture of spermaceti candles in Massachusetts, while that same year in June, other non-Jews established the first whale oil "refinery" on Goat Island near Newport. Jews and Gentiles were engaged in the manufacture of these candles no later than the 1750's, and the industry had grown so by 1760 that Newport alone reportedly had about seventeen factories manufacturing spermaceti candles and was annually exporting hundreds of thousands of pounds, especially to the West Indies.[61]

The decade before the Revolution found Newport Jews like Rivera, Jacob Polock & Company (the Polocks and Moses Michael Hays), Moses Lopez, Aaron Lopez, and Naphtali Hart & Company all actively occupied with the manufacture of spermaceti candles. Taken as a group the Jews were, in fact, the largest spermaceti manufacturers in Newport and in all probability had been induced to progress from sales to manufacturing by their eagerness to assure themselves a steady supply of the staple. Despite his involvement in the manufacture of candles, Aaron Lopez seems always to have been interested primarily in sales and distribution. Candles figured in many of the invoices of his cargoes to neighboring coastal towns as well as Canada, Savannah, and the West Indies. In less than nine months during the year 1759–1760, he sold 25,000 pounds of spermaceti candles, but even so, apparently never took an active part in the administration of the candle trust formed during the early 1760's.[62]

Money was to be made in the candle business only if the raw spermaceti could be bought at a reasonable price. The "catchers," the whalers with their headquarters at Nantucket, however, played the English market against the American and pitted American purchasers against each other. They were difficult to deal with and one was ill-advised, as Lloyd warned Lopez, to be "too nice and critical" with them, since they would simply not be tied "down to any measures they don't like." To the manufacturers this was an intolerable situation, and to protect themselves and their profits, they created in 1761 the United Company of Spermaceti Candlers, the so-called "Candle Trust."

Actually, the trust was a very loose voluntary confederation without any real authority to exert on its members the discipline the English Merchant Adventurers had exerted on theirs. First proposed by Richard Cranch & Company of Boston, the trust may have found in Rivera the driving force to unite the producers and later hold them together. This is not improbable, for it was Rivera who pleaded in 1768 with the formidable Browns of Providence to remain in the company: "As the advantages of such social concern have hitherto answered very salutary purposes, I doubt not you'll think a continuance to be worth your notice." Certainly he was the leader of the Newport Jewish candlemakers who, to judge from their allotment of thirty-three out of every one hundred barrels of head matter in 1763, formed the largest bloc in the trust. Rivera was also the troubleshooter for the United Company and it is worth noting than an effort was made to avoid meeting on Fridays, Saturdays, and Jewish Holy Days out of respect for the religious scruples of Rivera and his coreligionists.[63]

Seeking to reduce competition in purchasing the indispensable raw material, these New England candle manufacturers fixed the price they wished to pay for head matter and agreed, if the price rose too high, to engage in whaling themselves. They regulated the commissions to be paid the agents who handled the head matter, promised not to manufacture candles for anyone who was not a party to the United Company, and even fixed the price of the finished product, though a later agreement abolished price-fixing. The members also arrived at an understanding that they would use their joint offices to prevent the rise of rival factories. Though no quotas for head matter were specified in the first articles, later contracts provided for proportional allotments.[64]

In 1761 when the first agreement was signed, the United Company included at least eight participating firms from Newport, Providence, and Boston; three were Jewish or had a Jewish partner. Two years later some Philadelphians were added. Of the ten firms which constituted the United Company in 1763, four were Jewish. Though the Newport Jews as a group were the largest producers, three Gentile firms were each larger than any Jewish manufacturer, but despite the fact that the Providence Browns had the largest factory in the United Company, the center of production was in Newport. Three of the four Newport Jewish candlemakers were members of the Rivera-Lopez clan, though they ran their establishments independently of one another. By 1770 four out of ten firms were still Jewish but were now to be numbered among the smaller manufacturers.[65]

When they could, the members of the United Company suppressed competition ruthlessly. In 1763, for example, when some Quakers and a Jew, Samuel De Lucena, tried to set up a factory in Philadelphia, a member of the United Company, through a business associate in that city, set out successfully to besmirch the character of De Lucena, and the project for a Philadelphia factory died. A decade later, however, two New York firms were added to the association— James Jarvis & Company and a Jewish consortium, Sampson and Solomon Simson & Company. The United Company had been corresponding for several years with the New York Jewish group, which included at least four New Yorkers and one Newporter, and the two New York firms had been brought into the trust by Rivera to help control production and prices. Grateful for his efforts, they wrote to him, "We are greatly obliged to you, good sir, for the trouble you have taken for us and agree with you in sentiment that we had better work a small quantity to advantage then [than] a large one to no profit." Rivera's role in this affair established beyond question the fact that he was a brilliant business strategist and organizer.[66]

Actually, we cannot say how significant the New York Jews were in spermaceti candlemaking, since the lack of source material on New York Jewry's participation in industry generally makes it impossible to determine their relative importance as manufacturers. By contrast, the plethora of material on Aaron Lopez tends to emphasize his industrial role and that of the Newport Jews. Though there is little supporting evidence, it is not at all improbable that there were Jewish industrialists in New York during the second half of the eighteenth century. In any case, no later than 1752 Daniel Gomez of New York employed a number of slaves to make wax and tallow candles for the West Indian market.[67]

One historian has made the statement that the United Company "for some time absolutely controlled the entire industry from the price of raw materials to that of finished product, including all phases of marketing both." Certainly this is what the trust sought, but reality fell short of aspiration, and the abundant correspondence on the United Company in the John Carter Brown Library utterly fails to substantiate any claims to power and success on the part of the trust. If anything, the reverse is true, for it was always difficult to control purchasing and keep out interlopers, while relations among the associates were marked by constant trouble. There was trickery and cheating on fixed prices for the head matter, and rebates on agents' fees and commissions were common. The Achilles' heel of the inadequately organized trust was internal administration. Still, the United Company did hold on until the Revolution, and we may assume that, though the price-fixing of raw material could not be completely controlled, it was not without its effect in moderating the demands of the catchers.[68]

18. Abraham Halevi of Lissa, Poland, writes Aaron Lopez
a Hebrew-Yiddish Bread-and-Butter Note, 1770
Courtesy, American Jewish Historical Society

19. Rabbi Haim Isaac Carigal, 1773
Location Unknown

CHAPTER 37

THE SLAVE TRADE

THE SLAVE AS A COMMODITY

A most iniquitous trade in the souls of men" was the way the Reverend Ezra Stiles of Newport regarded the importation of Negro slaves into the colonies. Stiles could not think of the traffic "without horror," and there were other Rhode Islanders, such as Moses Brown of Providence and the Reverend Samuel Hopkins of Newport, who shared his sentiments. Most Americans, however, were completely indifferent to the moral implications of slavery and the slave trade; they rarely looked beyond the economic advantages of the system, and by the time of the Revolution, nearly every fifth person in England's North American colonies was a Negro slave. Most of these bondsmen were in the South, but there were large numbers in the North as well. Colonial America needed nothing so much as cheap labor, and Negro slaves helped fill that need. In the South they were necessary as farm hands for clearing and tilling the fields and planting and processing the tobacco, rice, and indigo on which the southern economy depended; and in the homes and cities of the South, too, there was great need for them as servants and artisans. The northern colonies, including Canada, always suffered a dearth of domestic help, and slaves were valued there as much as in the South. Many of the Negroes succeeded in developing skills, and an entrepreneur like Aaron Lopez frequently employed both free and slave Negroes in his business operations, particularly as chocolate makers and sailors. Some slaves were rented out to Lopez on a yearly basis by their masters.[1]

The moral issue in the purchase and sale of human beings would impress the colonial businessman far less than the fact that supplying slaves to the plantations of the West Indies and the North American South promised substantial profits. Ever since the seventeenth century, consequently, American shippers had entered that trade in the hope of making money through the use of their shipping and through the commodities and cash they acquired in exchange for the "servants" they sold. Jewish merchants saw the trade no differently than did non-Jewish merchants. A slave was merchandise, a commodity, and Jewish businessmen dealt in all types of goods. An advertisement in the *New-York Gazette* for May 4, 1752, was quite typical: "To be sold by Abraham Pereira Mendes, a parcel of likely young Negroes, piemento, old copper, coffee, etc." Ever since 1683 Jewish merchants had handled this line of goods and continued to do so throughout the colonial period.[2]

How many slaves passed through the hands of Jewish dealers? Merchant-shippers in need of a servant or two are known to have introduced slaves primarily from the West Indies, but the numbers imported in this manner over a period of decades barely amounted to one sizeable load for a large-scale entrepreneur in the traffic. Thus, less than eighty slaves were brought in by New York Jewish merchants and their Christian partners during the years 1715 to 1742, and it is very probable that those businessmen employed some of the Negroes in their own homes. Purchases and sales of slaves by Jewish merchants in other provinces were comparably small. Nathan Nathans, a pioneer Newport Jewish merchant, sent three slaves to Virginia; Moses Lindo of Charleston bought two Negro boys, and another Charlestonian, Israel Levy, served as a broker for a free Negro who voluntarily indentured himself as a slave for a period of seven years. Isaac Lyon and his two Gentile partners seized a French prize and brought eight captured Negroes into Georgia. The Jewish merchants of Montreal repeatedly asked their New York correspondents to send them domestic servants. Canadian Jews probably preferred Negro slaves to free white peasants for purposes of domestic service, not because of any possible monetary saving, but because in ritual observances, food, and the like, Negro slaves posed fewer problems than devout Catholic habitants.[3]

ABRAHAM GRADIS AND HIS SLAVERY PROJECT

The Canadian Jewish slave-trading connection went rather far back into Canadian history. Many years before the first Anglo-Jewish traders established themselves in the Laurentian region, Abraham Gradis proposed the establishment of a company based on the slave trade. Through *La Société du Canada* (Canadian Company) established in 1748, he and two other associates exercised control over Franco-Canadian trade for the next eight years. Gradis' company seems to have envisaged, ultimately, a three-cornered trade between Bordeaux, Quebec, and the French West Indies. French wines, brandies, and dry goods were to be sent to Quebec, Canadian produce was to be forwarded to the islands, and the island staples in turn were to be dispatched to the home country, France herself. The partners hoped in addition to carry on a direct shuttle trade between New France and the French West Indies.

That same year (1748) Gradis proposed the organization of a Louisiana Company, similar in some respects to his Canadian Company. In his overall strategy of tying together all of New France from the St. Lawrence valley in the North to the Mississippi delta in the South, the Franco-Jewish merchant-prince seems to have taken as his model earlier plans of the Company of the Indies and a memoir of the Sieur de Bienville, the founder of New Orleans. Influenced in all likelihood by these French commercial and imperialist hopes for the domination of the Mississippi valley, the Spanish-American Southwest, and Mexico with her mines, Gradis planned to develop trade with the Spaniards to exchange French goods for gold and silver. Efforts to people the wilderness with white immigrants had failed dismally, and Gradis suggested to the French authorities at Paris that large numbers of slaves be brought into the Lower Mississippi valley to work in new agricultural colonies to be created there. No doubt Gradis had tobacco plantations in mind, and he intended to import about 10,000 slaves directly from Africa, with the financial aid of the French government, which would be invited to fix the price of the slaves. The company hoped to develop the agricultural and timber resources of the Gulf region, to rehabilitate those areas neglected in the 1740's during King George's War, and to deal England a blow by cutting into her slave trade. These two companies, the Canadian and the Louisiana, would have enabled him to fashion strong political and commercial links between the French West Indies, the adjacent Spanish colonies, Mexico, the entire Mississippi valley, and Canada. Conceived though it was with characteristic brilliance by Abraham Gradis, the Louisiana Company came to nothing, for it was envisaged in 1748, just about the time the Ohio Company of Virginia proposed moving into the upper Ohio and thereby threatening an important French route south to the Mississippi. Only the Canadian Company flourished.[4]

LARGE-SCALE IMPORTERS

Nearly a generation before Gradis unveiled to the French king his grand plan for a slave-trading company, two New York Jewish merchants had been engaged in the importation of slaves, albeit on a much more modest, yet still substantial scale. In 1720 "Simon the Jew" was shipping Negroes from the West African Guinea Coast, obviously in large lots, while Nathan Simson, together with his Jewish and Gentile associates in London and New York, imported one load of about 115 slaves directly from Madagascar. After 1742, however, practically no slaves were imported by the Jews of New York, possibly because they had been frightened, like other New Yorkers, by the "Negroe conspiracy" of 1741 when it was reported Negroes were about to burn down the city and kill the whites.[5]

In Pennsylvania there were few Jewish slave dealers, though on one occasion David Franks imported slaves and served as an agent for a slave cargo from Africa. During the French and Indian War, when German servants were scarce and white laborers had been drawn into the armies, there was a call for Negroes to meet the high cost of labor and thus reduce the price of food. When the government took this opportunity to impose a tax on slaves, David Franks and his uncle Benjamin Levy were among the merchants who protested, asking for a deferment that they might cancel their orders for slaves.[6]

Far more important than New York or Philadelphia as a slave market was Charleston, South Carolina. There in 1755 the New Yorker Solomon Isaacs engaged in the trade on a wholesale scale, and a few years later the firm of Da Costa & Farr was also importing slaves. In 1760 the firm was responsible for 200 out of the total of 3,573 landed at Charleston that year; in 1763 Da Costa & Farr imported or served as factors to dispose of 160 more. Some of the firm's business was done with Henry Laurens, the largest slave dealer in the colony and a future president of the Continental Congress. In neighboring Georgia, Aaron Lopez' cousin James Lucena was engaged in the trade and on at least one occasion sent a slaver to the Guinea Coast. Lucena himself owned twenty slaves and no doubt hoped for a good market in the province, which had been opened to slavery less than two decades earlier. Though other Jews, like the Minises and Sheftalls of Georgia and Francis Salvador of South Carolina, owned slaves, they were not dealers in that commodity.[7]

THE RHODE ISLAND JEWISH SLAVE IMPORTERS

Nowhere in America was the slave trade as highly developed as in New England. As early as the 1730's Rhode Island merchants, none of them Jews, annually sent about eighteen vessels to the Guinea Coast. By 1770 there were 150 Rhode Island ships in the business. Still, although individual Jewish merchants bought and sold small parcels of Negroes, it was not until about 1754 that a Newport Jew engaged in importing them from the African coast. That year found Jacob R. Rivera in the trade, and he was soon followed in the early 1760's by others in the Jewish community, especially Aaron Lopez.[8]

The acquisition of slaves, it should be made clear at this point, was not always and perhaps even rarely the goal of slave-trading voyages. Their prime purpose was not to acquire a cargo of slaves, but rather to sell the goods exported—munitions, rum, molasses, sugar, rice, tobacco, candles, provisions, cattle, poultry, hardware (knives, brass rings, and bar iron), naval products, and cheap ready-to-wear garments—and an ideal voyage envisaged the sale on the African coast of the American ship and cargo for bills of exchange. It was not to import slaves, but to secure good bills to pay off English creditors, that African voyages were undertaken. Since, however, slaves were a medium of exchange for payment by the white or Negro vendors on the African coast, slaves were often brought back in lieu of hard cash.[9]

The slave business was carried on circuitously as triangular, or occasionally hexagonal trading. Typical were the sailing orders for the *Prince George* owned by Isaac Elizer and Samuel Moses in 1762. Though the cargo on this trip was not specified, in all probability the *Prince George* carried a large quantity of rum, the basic medium for trading on the African coast at that time. Elizer and Moses ordered their captain to buy a cargo of "merchantable young slaves" there and to proceed then to the West Indies, the prime American market, where the slaves were to be sold for cash or for local products, sugar and molasses. If slaves were not in demand on the islands, the human cargo was then to be carried on to Charleston and consigned to Da Costa & Farr, or in the last eventuality, brought back to Newport where some of the Jewish merchants may have had slave pens to keep their Negroes until they were sold. From Newport the surplus slaves could be peddled off in various parts of the country, particularly in the South, or sent back again to the West Indies when the market there improved.[10]

The Jews of Newport seem not to have pursued the business consistently, but this hesitancy proceeded far less from moral scruples than from the slave trade's speculative nature. Only too often the price demanded in the African market was too high, while the middle passage from the African coast to the West Indies frequently occasioned disastrous losses. The slaves, cramped and abused, died of disease or committed suicide; many rebelled and were killed. In 1765 on one voyage alone, the Providence Browns lost 109 Negroes and only twenty-four were sold.

Even if a ship finally arrived with a sound lot, the owners were often cheated by their agents, received bad bills of exchange, or found that the planter-purchasers were "poor pay." Nonetheless, though Aaron Lopez complained the trade was not profitable, it is a fact that he and his partner Rivera remained in the traffic as long as they could. From about 1762 to 1776 the two merchants averaged about one ship a year to the African coast, and in some years they sent two or three. Even the act of June 1774, limiting the importation of Negroes into the colony of Rhode Island, does not seem to have deterred Lopez and Rivera from sending slavers to Africa, for they dispatched at least two more ships there in the years 1774–1776. They consigned their cargoes not only to the West Indies, but occasionally also to their correspondents Da Costa & Farr in Charleston. Slaves brought a good price in the South Carolina port because of the colony's increasing rice and indigo production. In its price list the firm of Da Costa & Farr quoted four categories of Negro slaves—men, boys, women, and girls—along with rum, rice, and corn.[11]

The degree to which Jews participated in the slave trade cannot be determined with any exactitude. When, however, we compare the number of vessels employed in the traffic by all merchants with the number of ships sent to the African coast by Jewish traders, when we consider the statistics in Donnan's *Documents*, and when we bear in mind that Lopez and Rivera were the only Jews known to have engaged in the traffic on a substantial basis during the 1770's, we can see that the Jewish participation was minimal. It may be safely assumed that over a period of years American Jewish businessmen were accountable for considerably less than two percent of the slave imports into the West Indies and North America.[12]

How Jews Treated Their Slaves

According to Maimonides, one of the greatest legal and philosophical minds to emerge from the ranks of medieval Spanish Jewry, though Jewish law found no fault with the imposition of rigorous labor on slaves, "piety and wisdom command us to be kind and just." Nevertheless, there is no evidence to suggest that American Jews were any more considerate than Gentiles in their behavior toward slaves and indentured servants. Slaves were simply a commodity and were treated as such, while manumissions were exceedingly rare. The widower Benjamin Gomez appears to be one of the very few who manumitted a slave. In his will he left instructions that Katty, an octoroon or mulatto, be freed "as a reward for her fidelity." We have no reason to believe that any of the Jews of colonial North America concerned themselves about the morality of slavery. In an age when even outstanding clergymen like Ezra Stiles and Jonathan Edwards owned slaves, the Jews, too, were troubled by no moral scruples in keeping bondsmen.[13]

That Jews treated enslaved Negroes no differently than their Christian friends did is evident in the fact that the alleged New York Negro conspiracy of 1741 involved the slaves of Jewish as well as Gentile owners. It is evident also in contemporary newspaper advertisements, which indicate that Negro slaves and white indentured bondsmen frequently fled from their Jewish masters. What prompted these unfortunates to flee was most probably ill treatment, or their belief they were being mistreated, and their desire for freedom. Indentured servants were scarcely better off than Negro slaves, and it is worth noting that the indenture of Thomas Eskett of Charleston refers to bond servitude for a period of seven years as slavery.[14]

Even servant girls who were not under indenture often found themselves subjected to harsh treatment, although not all the wrong was on the side of the employers. Some of the girls were coarse, unreliable, and immoral, while others were only children, and it was not uncommon for mistress and maid to come to blows. In 1665 Asser Levy went to court to compel the return of Aucke Jansen's daughter, who had walked out on him before having served out her time. During a period of twenty months in the 1760's the Judah Hays household hired and lost ten female servants; the girl who served the longest lasted three months before being discharged for breaking china, the cost of which was deducted from her wages.[15]

Slavery, to be sure, posed many problems for the masters. Meyer Josephson, for example, complained in a letter to Michael Gratz that his "nigger wench" was "drunk all day, when she can get it," and also "mean," so that his wife was "afraid of her." When Michael's brother Barnard attempted to sell a domestic slave, he was informed by his agent that the slave could not be sold, since "he protested publickly that . . . if any one should purchase him, he would be the death of him." The slave had to be "chained and handcuffed on account of his threats." Colonel George Croghan knew that slaves were not always amenable to the wishes of their owners, for when he asked Joseph Simon to send a teen-aged Negro girl to him at Fort Pitt, where he planned to turn her over to an Indian, he cautioned Simon, "Lett the wench be likely, but don't lett her know she is for an Indian." A slave belonging to Simon's son-in-law Levy Andrew Levy felt differently about the Indians; he ran away with them, obviously preferring freedom with savages to servitude with whites. Simon himself owned a slave named John who had to be shackled and thrown into the dungeon at Lancaster after he had almost killed a man. Simon then sold the slave at a cheap price in order to be rid of him.[16]

CHAPTER 38

ARMY SUPPLY

JEWS AS ARMY COMMISSARIES

England began building an empire in the New World early in the seventeenth century. In North America, the western frontier of her new empire, she warred with the Indians and also with the Dutch, Spanish, and French. That struggle continued until 1763 when the defeated French surrendered New France—Canada and the cismississippi West—to the English and Anglo-American victors.

The English crown's century-long war for hegemony in the Western World was waged on a front which extended from Surinam on the South American coast, through the West Indies, north to Canada. So prodigious a struggle could not have been carried on for any length of time without an adequate supply system. Though they had organized a quartermaster corps, the British were dependent on civilian contractors and civilian sources for much of their matériel. The commissariat, the subsistence department, was still a civilian branch of the service and looked to civilian contractors and their agents not only to supply the army with food, but frequently to feed prisoners of war as well. These contractors were also called upon in time of crisis to provide temporary hospital facilities, transportation for baggage, and similar services. Naturally enough, the British officers entrusted with purchases attempted for reasons of economy to buy what they could in American markets, while the American provincial militias bought almost all their equipment, even their small ordnance, from local purveyors. In the field, both the regulars and the militia were accompanied by a host of sutlers peddling anything from shoe buckles to barrels of rum. Army supply was, in consequence, a big business, and it was a business which the Jews knew well.

Ever since the seventeenth century enterprising and daring Jewish merchants attached to the staffs of European princes and princelings had performed notable services in army supply during the continental wars. Some of them were massive suppliers, involved in operations requiring sums of money in the millions; others were petty sutlers or army peddlers. Jewish army entrepreneurs, primarily subsistence men, had been enticed into England ever since the late seventeenth century by her involvements in the wars of Europe, and the 1690's found Sephardic Jews like Machado and Pereira dunning the Lords Commissioners of the Treasury for the thousands of pounds due them for the services they had rendered English armies in Ireland and the Netherlands. Outstanding among these financiers and army provisioners was Solomon de Medina, who maintained close relations with the Duke of Marlborough and the government from 1689 to 1712. In accordance with the customs of the day, the duke received substantial sums for his personal needs from de Medina, and a popular couplet shows that the arrangement was no secret:

A Jew and a general both joined a trade.
The Jew was a baker, the general sold bread.[1]

The English armed forces which came to America during the early decades of the eighteenth century to begin their drive for the conquest of the French crown's transallegheny domains may very well—though as yet documentation is lacking—have brought Jewish commissaries and sutlers along with them. The Jewish immigrant shopkeepers and merchants who were already here are known to have begun serving the army and the militia as provisioners no later than 1693, at the time of King William's War, when Joseph Bueno furnished powder and goods to the fusileers at Albany. In 1711 during Queen Anne's War, New York Jews helped provide food for the English conquerors of Newfoundland, Acadia, and Hudson Bay.

[707]

Among the supplymen who had come with the troops may have been Jews, and some of them may have remained in New York and helped build her growing Jewish community. During the next contest, King George's War which was fought between 1740 and 1748, one of the Levys was the Jewish member of a politically influential company of five partners who shipped provisions to American troops stationed in Virginia; Pacheco, then in London, was exporting large quantities of guns to the colonies, and one of the Gomezes was selling muskets, swords, and bayonets to George Clinton, the governor of New York. The records of the French and Indian War, which lasted from 1754 to 1763, reveal that there were Jewish sutlers and supplymen active in the vast territory between the Altamaha River in southeastern Georgia and the St. Lawrence River in Canada.[2]

The conquest of Canada was, of course, a major military operation, and it involved numbers of Jewish tradesmen. There is a tradition that some Spanish-Portuguese purveyors and commissaries accompanied the army of conquest, but even if the tradition reflects historic fact, none of them seem to have remained. If, however, we know nothing of the Sephardim—if any—attached to the invaders, we can document the fact that a sizeable number of Anglo-German Jews accompanied the troops and remained in Canada after the conquest to become fur traders, among them Ezekiel Solomons, Levy Solomons, Chapman Abram (Abraham), Benjamin Lyon, and Gershon Levy. In 1767 Levy was still selling provisions valued in the thousands of pounds to the garrison of Michilimackinac, then under command of the notorious Major Robert Rogers. With the army of Lord Amherst came Aaron Hart, a Bavarian Jew who was destined to become a notable Canadian businessman in the postrevolutionary period.[3]

Typical of the army traders who appeared on the scene at that time was a man whom we have already had occasion to meet in these pages, Samuel Jacobs, a Jew of German or perhaps Alsatian origin— at least he had a marked French accent. This may have been Jacobs' second trip to these shores, for he reminded a colonel that he had served his regiment back in 1747 during King George's War. In 1758 at the latest, he was doing business with British troops stationed in Nova Scotia. In 1759 Jacobs sailed up the St. Lawrence in his own schooner, loaded it would seem with supplies for the troops. Immediately after the conquest his ship was commandeered by the army to haul cattle and other provisions to Quebec, although he had hoped that year to send a cargo of fish to Oporto and to return with a lading of Portuguese wines. The next four or five years, as the conquest was consolidated, found Jacobs, with his headquarters at Quebec, busy as a sutler, grain trader, and general merchant importing wares direct from England. His primary job was to serve as a commissary and supply man at various army posts in northern New York and Canada where he established branches. Many years later Jacobs was still trying to collect debts from some of the officers who had long since sailed away, and one of his debtors, an army captain, had gone to that haven whence no soldier ever returns.

Jacobs prided himself on seeing to it that the troops were well fed, in which respect he was far more conscientious than Thomas Hancock's suppliers during King George's War. Jacobs never received the sort of letter that had been addressed to Hancock in 1748:

I had like to omitt acquainting you of the sad dog of a butcher that salted the barrell of beef. I dare engage that the bullock or cow must have been forty years old. It's so hard it can't well be cut with a knife after four hours boiling. And my servants have actually refused to eat it, and say they could with pleasure eat [the] butcher.

When the Revolution broke out in 1775, Jacobs resumed his interest in army supply and undertook to provision British regulars and German mercenaries in Canada. Although the Continental troops who had occupied the Richelieu valley appealed to Jacobs for credit and supplies as they marched to besiege Quebec during the spring of 1776, Jacobs was and remained a staunch Anglophile. He had no sympathy for the Americans moving north under General Richard Montgomery to seize Montreal.[4]

In many of the North American provinces to the south of Jacobs' Richelieu valley, Jewish merchants and shopkeepers had offered and sold goods to the authorities for the use of the military during the French and Indian War. Rhode Island Jewish businessmen, for example, shipped dry goods to the troops at Crown Point and sold the provincial committee of war clothing, powder, lead for bullets, and duck for tents. The few Jews in Connecticut had little to sell the militia, but the New Yorkers did a thriving business as sutlers and shopkeepers, satisfying the wants of soldiers and militiamen. Still, though retailers of army goods to individual soldiers and officers, they were not army purveyors, and some were in reality only army peddlers. One recent immigrant, Jonas Phillips, had a shop in Albany where he catered to soldiers fighting the French around Lake Champlain. Jewish sutlers were also stationed with the troops at Fort William Henry on Lake George and Fort Edward on the upper Hudson, and one of them, a trader named Lyon, was at Fort William Henry when the Marquis de Montcalm moved against that stronghold with his Indians in 1757. When Montcalm took the fort in August, Lyon was fortunate enough to escape the ensuing massacre by the Indians. Manuel Josephson, another sutler working at nearby Fort Edward, reported the massacre to Hayman Levy who was probably his employer and who specialized during the war in military goods, including camp equipages and scarlet broadcloth for uniforms.[5]

The Anglo-Dutch merchant Uriah Hendricks was another who dealt in military supplies at that time, and among the goods he imported from England were muskets. Hendricks reported that "Little Loew" (Lyon?) and his associates "do trade considerably in the army and get money, but on the other hand their expences to follow the army is great." There were a few businessmen who operated on a somewhat larger scale, although the swivel guns advertised by Samuel Judah were intended most likely for privateers, not for men-of-war. A year before the war with France started, Naphtali Hart Myers, then temporarily in London, had shipped lead and gunpowder in relatively large quantities to his agent Jacob Franks. The year following the war found Sampson Simson and an associate sending soldiers' clothing to South Carolina.[6]

It was also during the French and Indian War that Jewish merchants from Philadelphia and Lancaster helped supply the army and the militia in their efforts to crush the Indians on the transallegheny western frontier. However, with the exception of the Franks family, the transactions of these businessmen were actually of no more than secondary importance. Joseph Simon served during the war as a sub-agent, furnishing provisions and transportation for the troops moving westward to occupy the country around the forks of the Ohio. One of Simon's firms, Simon & Henry, made rifles for the militia, and subsequently at the time of the Revolution, sold guns to the Continental Congress. In 1774 during Cresap's War, which saw the Indians rise to save their hunting grounds from the oncoming settlers, another of Simon's firms, Simon & Campbell, sold supplies to the Virginia troops in Pittsburgh and also helped outfit and finance the soldiers and workmen repairing and building Fort Pitt and Fort Fincastle (present-day Wheeling). Mathias Bush, another member of the Lancaster-Philadelphia Jewish merchantry, supplied Pennsylvania with relatively large amounts of arms and munitions. (The same accounts credit Benjamin Franklin with 100 tomahawks, which he no doubt supplied for the use of loyal Indian allies.) In the adjoining province of Maryland, Sampson Lazarus sold blankets for the use of the militia on the frontier, and farther down the coast in South Carolina, Moses Parmiento was listed as a sutler.[7]

At the outbreak of the American Revolution, Aaron Hart of Three Rivers became, whether voluntarily or involuntarily, a purveyor for the invading American troops under General Montgomery's command; a generation later he was still trying to collect payment from an indifferent Congress. In Montreal herself, Levy Solomons, David Salisbury Franks's brother-in-law and a Canadian of marked Whig sympathies, served the American occupiers with loyal devotion and was appointed by General Montgomery purveyor to the American hospitals, for which he provided housing, food, and transportation. Solomons continued to supply the American troops when they attempted to take Quebec, but after Montgomery's death and Benedict Arnold's withdrawal, he was rewarded for his services to the American cause by Arnold's confiscation of much of the stocks he had stored up for trading with the Indians in the Upper Country. When the British consolidated their position in Canada, they too rewarded Solomons for his services: General John Burgoyne had Solomons thrown out into the street—on July 4, 1776.[8]

Aaron Lopez also interested himself in military supplies, and the years of transition from protest to outright revolution found him selling a whale boat and small quantities of ammunition to the Rhode Island colony. In no sense, however, did Lopez or any of the New England Jewish merchants achieve in the slightest degree the status of army purveyors. Even less important in 1776 were the commercial activities of an obscure sutler to whom in June of that year General Philip J. Schuyler issued a license, Haym Salomon. This petty trader, a Polish immigrant, became a fervent American patriot. During the Revolution he fled to Pennsylvania. There he would distinguish himself by his self-sacrificing devotion to the Whig cause and his outstanding capacity as a bill broker, and would become a valued aide to the French army in America and to Robert Morris, the superintendent of finance. Salomon's Philadelphia co-religionists, the Gratzes, had begun selling flints to the American commander at Fort Pitt by the turn of the year 1776. They also sold goods to the Maryland and Virginia conventions and even aspired to outfit a Virginia battalion with leather breeches, stockings, shoes, and garments.[9]

THE FRANKS FAMILY AS LARGE-SCALE PURVEYORS

All the individuals mentioned thus far in connection with army supply were sutlers, commissaries, and unofficial purveyors, shop-keepers and merchants who catered to the regular army and the provincial militias, but aside perhaps from the Canadian consortium of Ezekiel and Levy Solomons, Chapman Abram, Benjamin Lyon, and Gershon Levy, none of them were of any real significance. There was only one Jewish family which played an important part in British army supply—the Franks family. An interest in army purveying may indeed have been what brought Jacob Franks, who represented the second generation of his family on American soil, to New York during the first decade of the eighteenth century. He may have come to New York when he did to take advantage of the business opportunity offered by Queen Anne's War. It is certain, at any rate, that from the War of Jenkins' Ear in 1739 into the period of the American Revolution, the Frankses of England and America were active in providing supplies for the British authorities in North America and in the Caribbean islands.

On their own account the New York Frankses were importing cannon for privateers by the late 1730's at the same time that they were serving in an official capacity as carriers and agents for the London contractors charged with victualling the military forces on Jamaica. About 1740 Naphtali Franks, then living in London, entered into a partnership with the English merchant Simpson Levy. The partners, who enjoyed an official relationship with the British government, dispatched cargoes of English goods to New York where their agents Jacob and Moses Franks, Naphtali's father and brother, traded them for provisions and building materials. These in turn were then sent to the London partnership's Jamaican correspondent John Colebrooke for the naval command on the island. On the final leg of this triangular voyage the *Charming Nightingale* which the Londoners had chartered was expected to carry a load of sugar back to England. Some time later Moses, who had already settled in London by 1739, became the key member of the army supply syndicate which assumed such importance on these shores during the French and Indian War. Among Moses' close associates as food contractors in the decade of the 1760's were members of the Colebrooke family, related in all probability to the John Colebrooke with whom Naphtali had worked during the 1740's.[10]

Directly as well as through their agents in Charleston, Savannah, and Frederica, Georgia, the Frankses helped Colonel James E. Oglethorpe secure supplies for his attack on the Spanish in Florida, and their sloop *Oglethorpe* made frequent runs between New York and Georgia. Their Charleston agents were Samuel Levy and Jacob Franks's nephew Moses Solomons, while their Savannah interests were handled through the firm of Minis & Salomons. The Salomons in this firm may have been another of Jacob's nephews; Abraham Minis, however, had been serving Jacob as a correspondent ever since 1736. Minis' financial agent in London was also close to the English branches of the Franks and Salomons families. When Oglethorpe attacked the Spanish bases in Florida during the years 1740–1743, Minis shuttled supplies, sent by the New York Frankses, from Savannah to the forward base at Frederica. The Frankses watched

[713]

carefully over their affairs in Georgia. When Moses Solomons was detained or jailed for debt at Charleston in 1743 and when a Georgia-bound ship was sunk, David Franks, Jacob's twenty-three-year-old son, was sent down to South Carolina and Georgia as a trouble-shooter.[11]

Supply as big business came into its own during the vast military operations required by the French and Indian War. The large French and English armies had to be provisioned, and both armies looked to Jewish suppliers for food. The chief purveyor for the French forces under Montcalm was the Bordeaux Jewish firm of David Gradis & Sons whose military contracts amounted to millions of livres. It is doubtful whether any of the Frankses, either in England or in America, were comparable to Abraham Gradis, the head of the Bordeaux firm, in his dogged devotion to the cause for which he labored. An ardent French patriot, Gradis devoted himself whole-heartedly to the promotion of French imperialism in the Americas, and from the time of the War of the Austrian Succession during the 1740's, his firm was significantly linked to the development of New France. Dispatching provisions on behalf of his government to French colonists and troops in the New World, Gradis' company became in itself an entire quartermaster corps during the French and Indian War.

Gradis constantly urged the French crown to greater efforts for its North American colonial empire and supplied Montcalm with provisions, munitions, and transport for the French general's push into northern New York. When the French tide began to ebb during the crucial year of 1758, Gradis assembled a fleet of ships, some of which he owned, others of which he chartered, and sent them to Montcalm's aid. One of Gradis' ships was captured, but others evaded the English blockade in 1758 and thereby enabled the French to hold out in Canada for at least another year. In his heroic effort to help save France's North American domain, Gradis dispatched many ships to Canada, but even those which did succeed in piercing the blockade fell into enemy hands on their way back to Europe. Gradis' zealous efforts were simply unequal to French dilatoriness, ineptitude, and discord during the fateful year of 1759, the year of Montcalm's death and Quebec's fall.[12]

The Frankses never played quite the part in England's war effort that the Gradis family played in the French war effort, but they were the closest Anglo-Jewish parallel to the Bordeaux firm. The Frankses were to become England's chief, though not sole agents for army supply during the French and Indian War. Sometime in the 1750's their relations with the government at London became more intimate, more official. By then, as we have noted, two of Jacob's sons, Naphtali and Moses, had settled in London and entered the ranks of the city's outstanding and highly respected merchants. In 1775 on the eve of the Revolution, the French ambassador in London could report to his government that Moses was "particularly esteemed by their Britannic Majesties." Moses established close relations with a number of important London entrepreneurs—some of them members of Parliament and able consequently to exercise considerable political power—and may have been responsible for his father's appointment as agent of the king in New York and the northern colonies. The appointment was probably made during the war and gave Jacob Franks some status as an official purveyor to his majesty's armed forces.[18]

The precise financial and commercial relationship between Jacob and his son Moses is not clear, but in all likelihood the son was the permanent member of a rather protean syndicate which became the chief supplier of provisions to the British troops on American soil from March 25, 1760, into the period of the Revolution. England's war effort had bogged down during the mid-1750's, due in no small part to the breakdown of army supply, but conditions improved materially when Moses Franks and his syndicate took over. The syndicate's principals included notable and politically powerful merchants like Sir James Colebrooke, George Colebrooke, Arnold Nesbitt, Sir Samuel Fludyer, and Adam Drummond. As their political fortunes waned, various partners dropped out of the syndicate, but Moses remained a constant member—possibly the only constant member—into the 1780's. The very disqualification he bore politically as a Jew made him largely invulnerable to political change. It was his syndicate, the largest among the army purveyors, that secured the contracts for victualling his majesty's forces in North America, including the thirteen colonies along the coast below the Bay of Fundy, the Canadian provinces, the transallegheny frontier, the Illinois country, and the Old Southwest along the lower Mississippi. The syndicate reached out into the West Indies as well and shipped provisions to the armed forces in the Bahamas and on Bermuda, Martinique, Guadeloupe, and Jamaica. In addition, moreover, to provisioning the army, Moses Franks and his associates undertook some mercantile activity in America and did a considerable amount of banking. There can be little doubt that the amount of government business, which the syndicate did from the time Moses Franks became active in it, reached into the hundreds of thousands, if not millions of pounds.[14]

The syndicate's two most important subagencies were located in Philadelphia and New York. The New York agency, managed for the syndicate during and after the French and Indian War by the firm of De Lancey & Watts, serviced the military in the provinces of New York, New Jersey, New England, and Canada, and on occasion provisioned troops in other colonies, including the West Indies. The Philadelphia agency served army needs in Pennsylvania, Virginia, and other southern provinces as well as the transallegheny frontier, and was managed by David Franks, Moses' younger brother. The De Lancey & Watts partnership consisted of two brothers-in-law. Oliver De Lancey, probably the firm's chief partner, was the brother of Lieutenant-Governor and Chief Justice James De Lancey and as such exercised substantial political influence. As Phila Franks's husband, Oliver was also brother-in-law to Naphtali, Moses, and David Franks, and it is likely the firm's services had been co-opted by Moses Franks. Intermarriage among the De Lancey, Watts, and Franks families made for a close working relationship between the New York and Philadelphia agencies.[15]

Just as Moses Franks was the constant partner in the changing London syndicate, his brother David was the constant element in the Pennsylvania branch where he worked with a number of politically powerful notables, among them William Plumsted, mayor of Philadelphia. The peak of the Philadelphia agency's activities was reached most probably during and right after the French and Indian War. In the course of the campaign against the French, David Franks, acting in his separate capacity as a merchant, helped outfit some troops under Colonel Washington and provided for the Virginian's personal needs in the field. During the late 1760's and early 1770's David Franks's partner in army supply was his uncle Isaac Levy. Their firm was known as Levy & Franks, and Isaac, who was a brother of the late Nathan Levy, was very probably a partner in an earlier firm of the same name. During the 1740's, 1750's, and 1760's at any rate, Isaac spent many years in London where he served as the Philadelphia firm's purchasing agent and resident partner.[16]

David Franks seems to have been the leading Jewish supplyman in North America for more than twenty years from about 1755 until about 1778. His territory covered the area south of the province of New York, primarily western Pennsylvania, the Illinois country, and in all probability the Old Southwest. Though he and his associates were engaged chiefly in provisioning the troops as agents for the London contractors, they never overlooked the fact that they were merchants, and they took advantage of opportunities to sell merchandise on their own account to the soldiers. When, for instance, the army at Fort Pitt, following the suggestion of Sir Jeffrey Amherst, Captain Simon Ecuyer the commander, or William Trent, gave blankets and handkerchiefs infected with smallpox to some dangerous Indians, it was one of David Franks's partnerships, Simon, Trent, Levy & Company, that replaced the goods expended in this bacteriological phase of the French and Indian War.[17]

David Franks's supply agency, like that of his French opposite Abraham Gradis, was a many-faceted organization. In addition to providing food, its basic job, it offered a courier service, forwarded news and political gossip, supplied carriage for baggage, impressed vessels, transported detachments, established depots wherever troops were stationed, and later during the Revolution, also fed and clothed prisoners of war in the hands of the American army. Not surprisingly, of course, the problems of such an agency, as reflected in the Colonel Henry Bouquet and other papers, were at times nearly insurmountable. Writing to Moses Franks in 1764, John Watts remarked morosely, "Dealing with generals and armys . . . and God knows who . . . would often discompose the philosophy of Socrates." On another occasion he said of the London army headquarters,

"The management is so unintelligible at home [England] it would puzzle a Newton." General Thomas Gage quarrelled frequently with David Franks and charges of bad faith were hurled about.[18]

David himself had to travel constantly to the depots stretching west from Philadelphia to Lancaster, Carlisle, Fort Loudon, Bedford, Fort Ligonier, and on to Fort Pitt, but never went down the Ohio to the Illinois country, though his contract covered that area as well as stations farther down the Mississippi. He and his associates presided over a farflung and often exasperating empire of wagons and packtrains. A string of 200 provision-laden horses was not unusual, nor was a shipment of 50,000 pounds of flour dispatched on horseback along roads which winter made almost impassable. Even in summer the trails across the mountains were difficult, but drovers kept moving on the roads with the live cattle kept in reserve for meat, and butchers were sent along to slaughter, salt, and pack the cattle and hogs. It was not uncommon for food to go bad in storage. Though he numbered among his most trusted agents Jewish merchants in Easton and Lancaster, Franks had to deal with a host of subagents, not all of whom were models of honesty. There were also Indian attacks to be feared; provisions already contracted for had to be purchased in an inflationary market, and rival trading companies out to make trouble—Baynton, Wharton & Morgan, for one—had to be guarded against. Proper administration of the empire never failed to involve an infinite amount of detail and a mountain of correspondence with agents and with Colonel Bouquet, General Gage, Sir William Johnson, Sir Jeffrey Amherst, and a host of others. Yet somehow, the supplies were sent, the armies were fed, and Canada and the West were won for the crown of England. Certainly, in helping secure the transallegheny country to King George, the Philadelphia suppliers performed a prodigious feat.[19]

CHAPTER 39

THE WESTERN TRADE

The fur trade was one of the earliest forms of commerce in America. For the Indian, furs were useful not merely as apparel, but of equal importance to him, as money, commodity money. The savage had certain basic needs. He required hardware, guns, ammunition, textiles, ornaments, tobacco, and liquor—essentially, that is, the very same commodities sought by the settlers, particularly those in the hinterland. The Indians were thus in the market for much the same type of goods as the white settlers, but could pay for them only in furs. The trader who bartered his consumer wares for the Indians' furs had no interest in the furs as such; he too valued them as money, money through which he could pay for the supplies secured from the merchant. Furs were a medium of payment. In the early days, during the seventeenth century furs loomed large in the settler's economy. But as soon as he succeeded in his efforts to produce the staples of field and forest, furs tended to diminish in importance, so that by the year 1770 the furs shipped from the thirteen colonies amounted in value to less than two percent of the exports from British North America.[1]

The first trading in furs began on the narrow coastal strip, in the tidewater country. As the game fled west, however, the Indians and the fur traders followed, and the mid-1700's found Americans interested in four basic fur-trading areas. Far to the north lay the Hudson Bay country. Below it stretched the so-called Upper Country, the basin of the St. Lawrence River and the Great Lakes, an important fur-producing region which tapped the lands west to the Rockies and was dominated by Quebec and Montreal until the nineteenth century. Farther south lay the territory of the Ohio River, the Mississippi, and their tributaries, and still farther south was the backcountry of the Old South and the Old Southwest. Jewish traders were concerned with all those areas except that of the Hudson's Bay Company, although even there, as we have seen, one of the company's chief factors was a Jew.[2]

The Indian, not the trader, did the trapping at this period, and he either bartered his furs with white visitors to his village, or more typically, went to the nearest white outpost to do business. Such outposts were to be found on the Great Lakes, the Ohio, and the middle Mississippi, at Niagara, Detroit, Mackinac, Presque Isle, Fort Pitt, Vincennes, Fort de Chartres, Cahokia, and Kaskaskia. The presence of colonial Jewish traders or their agents is documented at every one of these places except perhaps Vincennes.

Fur trading was a costly and often hazardous venture. As a rule the trader who dealt with the Indians, or who sent a hired man to the Indian villages to haggle for the furs, secured his goods from a merchant in Quebec, Montreal, Albany, Schenectady, New York, Philadelphia, Lancaster, Charleston, or Savannah. The merchant usually bought his wares on credit from a wholesaler or commissionman in London. Thus the bales and barrels of goods the trader exchanged for furs had to travel the formidably long distance from London to the North American seaboard by ship and then on to the frontier settlement by riverboat, wagon, or packtrain. Every mile added to the cost. Even when the merchandise arrived on the frontier, the trader was not at the end of his difficulties, for he still had to reckon with Indian or outlaw attacks, and sometimes even the capture and death of his men. No less distressing to the trader in his little counting-house was the fact that the Indians were notoriously poor credit risks. Often enough they had to be carried on one's books, but there were times when they could not or would not bring in furs to discharge their debts. A final hazard lay in the fact that, once the furs had finally been obtained and were baled, they had to be freighted on the rivers or across the mountains to the coast for transshipment to distant England. There they would be auctioned off and might, as was not infrequent, chance on a bad market. Clearly, therefore, the supply of furs could not be guaranteed nor could the market price be controlled—which made the fur trade very much a speculative industry.[3]

Its Importance for the Jew

Though the fur trade is associated with the seventeenth century beginnings of colonial commerce and in the next century was no longer a foundation stone of the American economy, probably no chapter of history strikes the modern reader as more interesting, or because it involves the Indians, more romantic. As far as Jewish businessmen were concerned, it was primarily the Jews of Canada, and to some extent of New York and Pennsylvania, who occupied themselves with the trade. To the Canadian Jews it was particularly important, since for them as for all Canadians, furs constituted the chief article of export. In New York, however, the furs exported by the entire mercantile community during the first half of the eighteenth century amounted in value to no more than 25 percent of all the goods shipped out, and this had fallen to about two percent by 1775. In Pennsylvania fur never constituted more than some seven percent of all exports to the mother country during the three-quarters of a century preceding the Revolution. Jewish merchants and fur traders in Canada, New York, and Pennsylvania, a miniscule handful of the population in absolute numbers, shared at most in only a small percentage of this trade. In general, then, for eighteenth century American businessmen—a term embracing most Jews—fur trading was simply part of the job of being a merchant, and they regarded it highly only so far as it enabled them to sell goods in exchange for furs.[4]

Though the Canadian Jews were fur traders, at least initially, Jews engaged in the traffic in the other thirteen provinces were primarily suppliers; they were among the merchants from whom the fur traders secured their supplies. Not very many Jews took up the fur business, for it required overly extensive resources of money and credit. Many of the Jewish newcomers to America lacked capital; they had to husband their credit in England and were generally too cautious to engage in a speculative enterprise like the fur trade. Even out on the frontier at the trading posts, the Jewish adventurer was as much a shopkeeper as he was a fur trader, and his clientele included farmers, frontiersmen, and habitants, as well as Indians. Thus for him pelts were not always the prime medium of exchange.

The Jewish businessmen east of the mountains and along the seaboard never looked to the trade in furs as their primary interest, and for most of them, that traffic provided a negligible source of income. A great merchant like Lopez, for instance, rarely bothered with furs, though on occasion he did handle a parcel, as any businessman would. The situation was different, however, for the businessman in the interior, and the closer a shopkeeper was to the forest, the more intensive was his interest in furs, hides, and pelts. The isolated Jewish shopkeeper in the backcountry, in the region between "the forest primeval" and the tidewater, commonly enough handled the hides and skins which were brought to him down the river or were traded with him by the neighboring farmers and settlers.

As the Indians moved westward, receding with the frontier, the lands they vacated were opened for trade, settlement, and speculation. Of course the sedentary Indian trader, the petty frontier shopkeeper, and the seaboard merchant who stood behind them both had all been contributory factors in driving the Indian farther west and in helping prepare the country for immigration and settlement. It was the fur trader, hovering over the eastern fringes of the Indian country, who made possible, through his basic stock of goods, the westernmost penetration of the whites, for often he became shopkeeper to both Indians and white frontiersmen. Some of the traders probably did as much business with the whites as with the redskins, and the entire gamut of their activity—selling goods, bartering for furs, and speculating in land—constitutes the story of the western trade.

New York Jews in the Fur Trade before the French and Indian War

The Indian fur trade beckoned to the Jews almost immediately on their arrival in North America. As early as 1655 trading opportunities with the Indians were drawing the Jews of New Amsterdam up the Hudson to Fort Orange (present-day Albany), and Stuyvesant's conquest of New Sweden was soon followed by the appearance of Jewish businessmen on the Delaware River, where again they undertook to carry on trade, primarily with the Indians. In 1665 Jacob Lumbrozo petitioned the Maryland authorities for a license to do business with the Indians, and the latter years of the seventeenth century found one Moses Levi supplying the New York provincial authorities with tobacco to be offered as a gift to the Indians who, as an early eighteenth century verse makes clear, were an ever-present danger:

> For none that visited the Indian's den,
> Return again to the haunts of men;
> The knife is their doom, oh sad is their lot;
> Beware! Beware of the blood-stained spot.

By 1700 New York Jewish merchants were stocking beads for the Indian traders, and less than two decades later, the hazards of the Indian trade notwithstanding, the Gomezes established a stone trading post on a tract of land some six or seven miles north of present-day Newburgh, New York. Strategically located close to the Hudson River on an important Indian trail in the Devil's Dance Chamber area, the house still stands and is one of the oldest monuments to Jewish settlement in this country.[5]

As the furs supplied by the Indians diminished during the 1700's in their relative importance in the economy of the New York merchant, the Jews paid less attention to the trade. Still, the port records indicate that merchants like Nathan Simson, Moses Levy, Jacob Franks, and the Gomez brothers constantly included substantial quantities of furs and skins in their London-bound cargoes. Once in a while they sent a shipment to Holland as well. As long as he remained in America, Rodrigo Pacheco forwarded numerous fur consignments to Bristol, and on his return to England, received furs in London. All the while these merchants were shipping furs and skins of North American origin to London and Bristol—roughly between 1715 and 1735—they were also importing hides from Curaçao and even from Jamaica. That is, they were not fur merchants in any sense of the term, but merely used the pelts they had obtained from their debtors as a means of balancing their own accounts in England. Most of the furs that they dispatched overseas came from the territory to the north and west of New York, though an occasional load might also be secured from Philadelphia during the first quarter of the century. By the 1730's relatively large shipments were received by Pacheco and Jacob Franks from the Carolinas and Georgia. The back areas of both these provinces were just opening up; they formed a new frontier.[6]

When the French and Indian War began in 1754, New York was still an important fur-exporting depot. Some of the peltries that appeared in the city had even been diverted from French-controlled Montreal and Quebec, for the New York merchants lost no opportunity to do business with the French fur traders whom they supplied with superior English goods at reasonable prices. Through those traders, who came down over Lake Champlain, and also through England's Iroquois allies, the New York merchants were enabled to tap the furs of the Great Lakes region by way of Lake Ontario and the Mohawk River. The Jewish merchantry as a whole had long since abandoned any substantial interest in furs, but individual New York Jews like Hayman Levy were active participants in the trade.[7]

Second only to New York in the exportation of furs was Pennsylvania. By the second decade of the eighteenth century Isaac Miranda of Conoy Creek was already trading with Indians in Lancaster County on the Pennsylvania frontier. Miranda was probably Pennsylvania's first Indian trader of Jewish origin. A few decades later his son George would cross the mountains and barter for furs with the Shawnees in western Pennsylvania. The year 1739 found another Jewish businessman, Judah Israel, whose commercial undertakings at various times touched Philadelphia, New York, and Newport, shipping furs from Virginia to England.[8]

The first permanent Jewish merchant in Philadelphia was Nathan Levy who by the 1740's had already established the pattern that would remain typical of the Pennsylvania Jewish businessmen throughout most of the century. As a supplier, Levy outfitted fur traders whom he debited with goods to be paid off ultimately in furs. During that same decade he took his sister's son David Franks into his business, and about the same time the Lancaster merchant Joseph Simon also became a partner in the firm of Levy & Franks. Regrettably few of Simon's papers have survived, but this Lancastrian was one of the leading Jewish Indian-trade suppliers in all America. Though the Levy-Franks mercantile group was richer than Simon, the trade in furs was only incidental to them—as it was not to Simon who, it is probable, initially secured most of his goods through the Philadelphians. In later years Simon's in-laws, Barnard and Michael Gratz, would become his chief correspondents, agents, and suppliers in Philadelphia.

Active in his efforts to equip many of the Scotch-Irish Indian traders, Simon served as a middleman between them and the merchants on the Atlantic coast, and before long the need to protect his interests compelled him to enter into partnership with his debtors. While much of Simon's Indian business was thus carried on by and in the name of his partners, some of it was in his name alone, and in order to oversee his proliferating operations down the great valley of Virginia or across the mountains at Fort Pitt, Simon found it advisable to ride the trails hundreds and ultimately thousands of miles. In the 1740's Simon and his clients, and soon enough the Philadelphia merchants as well, were competing for furs with the French on the upper Mississippi, the Ohio, and the Great Lakes, and with the New Yorkers on the Mohawk River. By 1754 the Ohio Company of Virginia had moved to the forks of the Ohio in an effort to control the fur trade from that strategic vantage point as well as to bring in settlers and to threaten French communications between Canada and Louisiana. The French of course did not remain passive before this British thrust at their stake in the fur trade, and their Indian allies began to wage war on the traders, to capture and torture them, and to loot their packtrains. Simon and the Levy and Franks firm, too, suffered losses from these Indian raids, but reverses of even greater severity were in store for them.[9]

THE FRENCH AND INDIAN WAR
AND THE INDIAN UPRISING

The French were right to be very much disturbed by the English entry into the upper Ohio valley, for furs were New France's chief item of export to the mother country. The English, they saw, were crowding them on all sides. The far north was a scene of pressure from the Hudson's Bay Company, while to the south of Hudson Bay furs that should have been French-bound were being siphoned off by New Yorkers, Pennsylvanians, and Virginians. Worse, once on the Ohio the English would have gained access to the Great Lakes and the Mississippi valley and could move both north and south into French territory. For the French, then, protecting their lines of communication and saving their fur trade meant keeping the English east of the mountains, which they were determined to do. The first skirmish took place in 1749 when the Lancaster-outfitted packtrains were attacked. The French and Indian War itself began in 1754 when French forces seized the all-important forks of the Ohio in accordance with their policy of building posts on Lake Champlain and the Great Lakes, and in the Ohio and Mississippi River valleys, not only to keep open the lines of communication between Canada and Louisiana, but also to encircle and contain the advancing English. Once more the traders were despoiled of their goods, and once more Levy & Franks and Simon lost heavily.[10]

In the ensuing hostilities the English were on the defensive till 1758, but the following year they seized Quebec. The end was in sight then, and within a few years the formal peace of 1763 added Canada and the cismississippi West to England's empire. Again, however, for a brief period in 1763 the frontier flamed with war, led this time by the Ottawa Chief Pontiac. Incited by the French and fearful of the threat that English mass settlement posed to their lands and game, the western Indians rose almost spontaneously in a last desperate attempt to save their heritage. By wiping out English garrisons all the way from Mackinac to Fort Pitt, they hoped to drive the English back over the mountains. The Pontiac uprising of 1763 led to Indian seizure of the traders' packtrains for the third time in less than fifteen years. Some Jews were captured; two, reported killed, later turned up. With nearly a dozen posts attacked and all but three destroyed, traders everywhere, among them Jews in Canada, New York, and Pennsylvania, suffered heavy losses. When the "Suffering Traders" of 1763 in the Pennsylvania sector alone appealed to the British government for reparations, they produced a bill for some £50,000 sterling. Over a third of the losses suffered by all the western traders fell to the account of the Levy, Franks, and Simon group.[11]

Much more is known about the Pennsylvania Jewish fur-trade suppliers than about their Canadian counterparts—and rivals—since sources touching on the Canadian Jewish fur traders between 1761 and 1776 are so scanty. It is beyond question, nevertheless, that the Canadians carried on a larger traffic than the Pennsylvanians. They also hazarded more. The Pennsylvania Jews were shorn of their property in the Pontiac uprising, but the Quebec and Montreal Jewish traders, caught out in the field when the Indians began their attacks, hazarded their lives as well as their goods in the spring of 1763. The little syndicate of Ezekiel and Levy Solomons, Gershon Levy, Chapman Abram, and Benjamin Lyon had made a vocational shift from army supply to the western trade. Forming during the war and in the postwar period a series of companies of which little is known save their names, the various members of the syndicate worked out of Montreal, Quebec, and Albany, and traded as far west as Lake Superior, where they tapped the furs at the back door of the Hudson's Bay Company. As post or sedentary traders, they sent subordinates to do the actual bartering in the Indian villages. Undoubtedly, like other English fur entrepreneurs, the Jewish businessmen had adopted the traditional French Canadian system and had become interior traders (bourgeois), employing voyageurs or *engagés* or coureurs de bois.

Some of the syndicate's wares may have been shipped in from London, and the five traders were also linked to Hayman Levy of

New York who was one of their chief suppliers. When they went down, they dragged the New Yorker down with them. Though the exact nature of their partnership is not known, it is likely to have been a purchasing syndicate with a common responsibility for all debts incurred. As a pool of fur-trading businessmen who merged some of their interests, the five antedated by almost a generation Canada's North West Company of the 1780's. What makes it so difficult to sort out their business relationships is the fact that the western trade included at least three Jewish firms with a partner named Levy—there were at least four Levys then in the business! The syndicate's losses in the Indian uprising of 1763—losses further exacerbated by the postwar restrictions England imposed on the trade with the Indians—forced it into bankruptcy. The five owed their creditors £18,000, and after this failure, apparently they dissolved the company, each trader thereafter going his own way.[12]

After the fall of Quebec and Montreal the five partners had divided the territory among themselves. Although they did not always do business at the same home station, each of them did tend to limit himself to a favorite village, whether it was Mackinac, Detroit, Sandusky, or Niagara. Seeking credit or bringing furs, the Indians flocked to those posts where a trader, accompanied by a large number of French employees, offered them dry goods, provisions, liquor, guns, shot and ball, and hardware.[13]

Ezekiel Solomons had come to Mackinac in 1761 as one of the earliest licensed English traders in the Upper Country. There, at the time of the uprising in 1763 the Indians, pretending engrossment in a ball game, gained access to the stockade and massacred the garrison. Solomons fled for his life to a French friend while his stocks and furs were looted, but betrayed to the Indians, he was held captive for some time before being taken to Montreal to be ransomed. Shortly after, however, he was back again in Mackinac to carry on his usual traffic. Levy Solomons, who was probably Ezekiel's cousin, escaped from the Indians and reached the safety of besieged Detroit, but some Jewish traders coming in from Sandusky were captured. Two traders named Levy were seized; one of them was certainly Gershon Levy, who may have been the head of the syndicate. The other, who was initially reported dead and seems to have been cap-

A

SERMON

Thomas H Webb

PREACHED AT THE

SYNAGOGUE,

In NEWPORT *Rhode-Iſland,*

CALLED·

" The SALVATION of ISRAEL :"

On the Day of PENTECOST,

Or FEAST of WEEKS,

The 6th day of the Month *Sivan,*
The year of the Creation, 5533 :
Or, *May* 28, 1773.

Being the ANNIVERSARY
Of giving the LAW at *Mount Sinai :*

BY THE VENERABLE HOCHAM,
THE LEARNED RABBI,

HAIJM ISAAC KARIGAL,

Of the· City of HEBRON, near JERUSALEM,
In the HOLY LAND

NEWPORT, Rhode-Iſland : Printed-and·Sold by
S. SOUTHWICK, in Queen-Street, 1773·

20. Title Page of a Sermon by Rabbi Haim Isaac Carigal
This is the First Sermon in English, by a Jew,
Published in North America, 1773
From Facsimile in PAJHS, XXX, 70

כתבם יא נשתנה ּ יראו עיניך מסקנת הגמרא בסברת
התנאים דלא נשתנה כלל ּ ויפה כתב ר' ברטנורא
דעל השקלים היה כתוב שמרית אבל התורה לא
נשתנה כלל ּ ואמת הדברים ּ כה דברי כותב יחותם
בנופרט בראד לאנד ה' ימים לחודש סיון יצנת התקל"ג
ליצירה אני הצעיר מעיר הקודש חברון

להיקר החכם עזרא שטליס

21. Last Page of a Hebrew Letter
of Haim Isaac Carigal to Ezra Stiles, 1773
Courtesy, Yale University Library

מבטן קדוש ליהוה · יברך האל וזרעיך למיןו היוה נר לך
תמיד בישראל · וכיון וישלח את אגרת כתוב אל אישתך בחני
הקרב לירושלם בארץ צבי שאלתי לה ולביתי בשמי לשלום כי
האהבתיך למענד אהב אני כולם ·וישמחו אבך ואימך כען
תזהר עם אצלי קדש ובקרב השרפים ·אז יבקע כשחר אורך
וארכתך מהרה תצמח והלך לפניך צדקך כבוד יהוה יאספך
ישע נ"ה ·ואלה הדברי כותבים בנופורט ראד־אי־לאנד
לאמריכא כח ימים לחודש תמוז שנה התק"לג ·אני הצעיר
התלמידי ישוע הנצרי

22. Hebrew Letter of Ezra Stiles to Haim Isaac Carigal
The Signature is in Arabic, 1773
Courtesy, Yale University Library

tured by the Wyandottes, was Levy Andrew Levy, the partner and son-in-law of Simon of Lancaster. This Levy was not one of the Canadian Levys, but the storm which broke in 1763 found him and his ten employees competing for pelts with the Canadian traders in the Lake Erie region.[14]

Benjamin Lyon or Lyons, another member of the syndicate, may have been the sutler Lyon reported to have barely escaped with his scalp intact from the Indian massacre at Fort William Henry in 1757. If he was that same Lyon, then his was the dubious pleasure of experiencing two Indian wars within six years. But these men, intent on earning a livelihood, were somehow not deterred by the dangers they faced. Many years later, Lyon was still in Mackinac where he subscribed himself as a witness when the Indians transferred the island to the crown. By then, of course, the syndicate had long been broken up, and Lyon was probably a rival of Ezekiel Solomons in that town.

Chapman Abram had preempted for himself Detroit, a very important spot commanding the east-west and north-south fur traffic. Approaching the fort at Detroit during the Pontiac uprising, Abram was captured by the attacking Indians. One contemporary account has it that he had hidden himself, but was betrayed and tied to a stake. About to be burnt alive, he asked for a drink and was given some hot water which he promptly threw into his tormentor's face. Convinced he was mad, the Indians set him free. The poet Stephen Vincent Benét used this version of Abram's captivity in his story of a Jewish fur trader, "Jacob and the Indians," but another and much more prosaic account of Abram's experience reports only that he was finally exchanged for a Potawatomi chieftain. In any case, like Ezekiel Solomons, Abram returned to his post as soon as the Indian rebellion was crushed.[15]

By 1764 the uprising was under control, Pontiac had lifted the siege of Detroit, and the fur traders were again moving west with their loaded canoes and packtrains. Levy Solomons transferred his headquarters from Albany to Michilimackinac and at length to Montreal where, in 1770 Benjamin Lyon insisted to Aaron Lopez, Solomons had become the largest fur buyer in Canada. Anxious to win a contract for Solomons and himself from Lopez, Lyon may have exaggerated his friend's importance, but no doubt Solomons was doing well. Samuel Judah, too, was probably prospering, though the claim that he exported furs to the value of £30,000 is patently wrong. In Three Rivers, Judah's cousin Aaron Hart acquired a competent French-Canadian partner and ventured into the fur trade. Hart, it may be assumed, provided the goods and the credit, and then sold the furs his French partner and employees had secured from the Indians. His London connections enabled him to trade his furs there for English wares, and there is every reason to believe that Hart made money in the trade, for he was a businessman destined for success.[16]

Fur Trading after the French and Indian War

Troubled by the Indian uprisings which had followed on the heels of the French and Indian War, the Hillsborough ministry determined to secure the western frontier against further disturbances. In October the Proclamation of 1763 was issued, declaring it the king's "will . . . to reserve . . . for the use of the . . . Indians, all the land and territories not included within the limits of our . . . three new governments" of Quebec, East Florida, and West Florida, "as also all the land and territories lying to the westward of the sources of the rivers which fall into the sea from the west and northwest." In short, the vast western hinterland was cut off from Canada and the coastal provinces to be turned into one huge Indian reservation. England hoped by this means to pacify the Indians and to reduce the cost of her army of occupation. Unfortunately, however, though appeasing the Indians, she struck at the interests of the English traders who, in succeeding the French along the St. Lawrence, had inherited the French tradition that the Upper Country and the transallegheny West all the way to the Mississippi properly belonged to Canada. A territory of 100,000 or less in population, Canada was almost entirely a wilderness, a wilderness whose prime business was the acquisition of furs. For what had the war been fought, asked the aggrieved Anglo-Canadians, if not to drive the French out of the fur trade so that English merchants and traders in Canada might benefit? In this they were united with their New York, Pennsylvania, and Virginia rivals, for all were at one in opposition to royal constraints on the fur industry.[17]

The old competition between the French and the English for the furs of the West did not come to an end after the peace of 1763; the old roles simply had new players. Now it was the English, rather than the French, in Canada, who carried on the older rivalries with the New York, Pennsylvania, and Virginia traders. All of them were, of course, hampered by the Proclamation of 1763 which had made of the West an Indian reservation. Under later regulations the traders were licensed, the prices they charged for their goods were fixed, they were compelled to pay attention to governmental restrictions by the posting of bonds, and were required to trade only at the posts where they would be under the surveillance of the government's commissary. Fortunately for the traders, who resented all governmental restraints and frequently did not scruple to cheat their drunken clients, most of the restrictions had been removed or disregarded by 1768.[18]

In the free-for-all race that now ensued, Canada forged far ahead of her rivals to the south. The English traders in Montreal enjoyed the benefit of competent assistance from the voyageurs, and since the conquest, of course had faced no French competition in Canada. The coureurs de bois helped them maintain good relations with the Indians, and English manufactures as well as an adequate supply of rum were available to them at moderate prices. Consumer goods of English origin could be obtained at Albany, and the furs could be shipped to England with relative ease over Lake Champlain, down the Hudson River, and thence across the Atlantic. Thus the English who came into Canada to replace the French had many advantages denied the prewar French traders—all the advantages of English goods and English markets—and the absence of French rivalry. By the late 1760's Canadian profits in the trade had begun to rise markedly as the political difficulties of the thirteen colonies to the south, and particularly their boycotts of English goods, made it difficult for Canada's competitors to secure trading supplies. The act of 1774, restoring the West to the province of Quebec, constituted an additional stimulus to Canadian success, for it guaranteed that the furs of the upper Mississippi, the Upper Country, and the region across the Great Lakes would be floated down the St. Lawrence.[19]

Furs played little part in the economy of the New England Jewish merchants. To be sure, from time to time Lopez would buy or accept beaver from a Canadian correspondent; in order to trade with the Canadians, he had to take their prime staple in payment. In general, however, though he certainly would not disdain furs for their value as commodity money, he seemed to prefer trading his rum for Canadian wheat. Georgia, like Canada, was fur country, and here too, in order to balance his accounts with his customers from the Deep South, he would not refuse furs; but on the whole, Lopez emulated the Boston Hancocks and the Providence Browns in fighting shy of the fur business. New England in the prerevolutionary decades was no market for furs, and the western furs commonly bypassed her by going down the Hudson to Albany and New York.

Unlike the case in New England, furs were important in the South—although, little as is known about the Jewish fur shippers and traders in Canada, even less is known about those in the Old South. The fur and hide trade was relatively significant in the sparsely settled South and Old Southwest during the colonial period. Much of the South was at that time a wilderness; ranching was important, but next to rice and indigo came hides and skins. The centers of the southern fur trade were Augusta, Savannah, and particularly Charleston.[20]

As we have seen, Pacheco had imported deerskins from South Carolina in 1731, and at the end of the decade, Jacob Franks received them in exchange for the English consumer goods he dispatched to Georgia. Da Costa of Charleston advertised Indian goods in 1757; Isaac De Lyon and James Lucena of Savannah shipped out deerskins in the 1760's to pay for their English imports; and back in the woods the Nunez brothers traded with the Indians among whom they lived and fathered a brood of half-breeds. As early indeed as 1750, Moses Nunez had become an important trader among the Upper Creeks in present-day Alabama. There he risked his life and goods among the Indians whom the French at Mobile, eager to drive the English out of the western trade, incited to hostility.[21]

Scarce though they are for New England and the South, sources touching on Jews in the Indian trade after the French and Indian War are more adequate for the two middle provinces of New York and Pennsylvania. New York still played a substantial part in the trade, and at least one New York Jew, Hayman Levy, continued to interest himself in this line of business. An old and possibly accurate tradition has it that John Jacob Astor, newly arrived from his native Waldorf in South Germany, was first employed in America by Levy, for whom he beat out furs at a dollar a day. Albany, too, remained an important fur-trading center, though there is little evidence that Jewish traders or merchants were active there in the years following the French and Indian War. Most of them had probably moved north to Canada, particularly as political and economic conditions in the thirteen colonies began to deteriorate in the late 1760's. The papers of Sir William Johnson, who was superintendent of Indian affairs for the Northern District, indicate that a number of New York and Pennsylvania Jewish merchants did business with him. Johnson's considerable influence with the Indians made him an important person to know.[22]

Among the merchants who did not shift their base of operations to Montreal was Hayman Levy; he remained in New York City and continued as one of the outstanding fur traders of the prerevolutionary period. Levy was one of the chief suppliers of the frontier firm Phyn, Ellice & Company, whose letter books for 1767–1776 enable the historian to study in detail Levy's fur-trading transactions. The fact that the Phyn-Ellice records contain over 115 letters addressed to Levy make these letter books a superb source—better even than the Gratz letters—for evaluating the business operations of a Jewish fur-merchant. (This is not to imply in any sense whatsoever that the commercial activities of Levy were appreciably different from those of non-Jews.)

In 1767 Phyn, Ellice & Company had their headquarters in

Schenectady, hard by Albany. From there they had easy access by river, road, and lake to Montreal, but their attention was directed primarily toward the Great Lakes and Upper Canada. Doing business on a large scale at Niagara, Detroit, and Michilimackinac, they trafficked with the fur traders, the English military, the Indian Department, and the French settlers. During this antebellum decade Hayman Levy served Phyn, Ellice & Company as a chief supplier, shipping them commodities amounting in value to thousands of pounds. The peak years of their relationship were 1768 and 1769, although the two firms continued to trade with one another at a progressively diminishing rate into 1776. While Phyn and Ellice maintained an office in Schenectady, they had shifted their headquarters to London by 1774, and no later than 1775 were securely ensconced in Montreal. The approaching Revolution may account in part for the firm's move to England and Canada and the loosing of their ties to Levy, who was a fervent Whig.

During the late 1760's Indians would bring their furs to Michilimackinac, Detroit, and Niagara to barter them there for their needs with the trader-merchants. More often the Indians would receive the traders in their villages. In turn these traders, some of them businessmen of real substance, then shipped their bales of furs, skins, and leather to their suppliers, firms like Phyn, Ellice & Company. Sometimes the Schenectady firm bought the bales and packs of furs outright; at other times they received them only on consignment, to be sold on commission, but in either case, Phyn and Ellice balanced their accounts with commodities. The Schenectady concern was still essentially an intermediate supplier; most of its goods were secured from New York merchants. For a few years its primary New York contact was Hayman Levy, a specialist in furs who operated on a sizeable scale.

Levy negotiated directly with individual traders in the Upper Country, but seems in general to have carried on his business with secondary supply houses like the Scotsmen Phyn and Ellice. In dealing with them, the New Yorker either bought their furs outright or accepted them on commission. Like the intermediate supplier, he too balanced his accounts with staples and luxuries. Occasionally Phyn, Ellice & Company did not barter furs for the goods received from Levy, but satisfied him with good bills of exchange. There were times when the Schenectady firm went into the market as Levy's agent, bought beaver for him at a commission of 1.25 percent, and drew bills on him to cover themselves. The beaver, raccoon, and other furs purchased on Levy's account, or received by him, would be shipped to Albany where a sloop picked them up and carried them downriver to New York. There in Levy's warehouse, all the furs were carefully checked, culled, and transshipped to London. As was typical of the age, innumerable variations in trading are discernible. Now and then Phyn and Ellice received consignments of consumer goods from Levy and disposed of them on a commission basis; every so often Levy would store goods purchased by Phyn and Ellice till the canny Scotsmen had a need for them. They would encourage him to hold onto the furs when that commodity was scarce and higher prices were in prospect. Sometimes the New Yorker might ship goods directly to one of their clients—a compass, for instance, to a mariner who had a sloop on Lake Erie.

What were the staples which Levy sold Phyn and Ellice and which they transshipped from the Mohawk to the upper and lower lakes? With a few notable exceptions, they were essentially the very same commodities in demand at Newport or New York or Philadelphia: brandy, beer, ale, porter, rum, wine, cheeses, tobacco, pork, flour, molasses, spices—and pills from Mr. Rivington. Tea was always available despite the anti-British boycotts. Iron, steel, copper, rope, paints, dry goods, needles and other notions appear in many an invoice. As a big shoe jobber and wholesaler, Levy would frequently be called upon to ship men's, women's, and children's shoes in large quantities. Moccasins, it is clear, were not the only footgear of the Upper Canadians; as far west as Mackinac, farmers, soldiers, clerks, and a host of others wore Levy's shoes in sizes "as large as possible." The letters of Phyn and Ellice also called for indentured servants and for "blacks," Negro "boys" or "Affrican gentlemen"; once in a while, a slave would even be shipped south to Levy for sale in the New York market. Typical Indian goods sent north by Levy were blankets, black and white wampum, guns, powder, ball, lead, vermillion—and scalping knives.

As we have already had ample opportunity to observe, merchants in their relationships with one another were commonly more than mere purveyors of goods, and this fact is well documented in the letters Phyn and Ellice addressed to Levy. The New Yorker, always courteous, would not hesitate to make the rounds of other merchants to secure special commodities for his Schenectady clients; he forwarded letters for them and even shipped their furs on to London if he himself were disinclined to accept them. He bought bills of exchange for them, paid off their obligations in the city, and accepted the drafts the creditors of the Schenectady firm drew on him.

All this spelled time and trouble of course, but Levy and his Mohawk valley associates were confronted with many more problems. The correspondence between the two firms reflects a relationship brimfull of bickering and mutual suspicion. Perhaps the numerous complaints to be found in the letters represented only another phase of haggling, a jockeying for better prices and more concessions. Phyn and Ellice were constantly charging Levy with errors in quantity, quality, and prices. Goods were improperly packed, edibles were spoiled, and even the iron stoves Levy supplied lacked feet on which to stand or pipes to carry away the smoke. Not infrequently Levy could not assemble the goods his correspondents ordered and was unable to get them to Schenectady in time for the departing sloops on the lake and the bateaumen on the rivers. Pontiac's War of 1763 had left its mark on the fur merchants, and when an Indian threat seemed likely, trading came to a standstill. Levy, moreover, was constantly grumbling about the quality of the furs he received, and when he culled the packs, Phyn and Ellice groaned because they had to keep separate the accounts of the packs consigned to them by individual traders. Accounts current submitted by Levy and by the Schenectady partners were subject to careful scrutiny. Differences would be ironed out when one of the Scotsmen came down to the big city, or when Levy or one of his Jewish associates, an Etting or an Isaac Moses, paid a visit to Schenectady. Both firms were on their toes; they kept such a wary eye on the ultimate balance sheet that when the day of reckoning came, it did not find them too far apart.

Remembering the massacres, attacks, and sieges by the Indians in 1763, and noting the scalping knives listed in the invoices, the gentle reader of today might shudder to think of the primitive life which characterized the upper country frontier. Before he wastes his pity on those wilderness settlers, however, let him scan this list of items sent to the upper lakes by Levy through the agency of Phyn and Ellice: children's toys, hair powder, pickled oysters, pineapples and oranges, colored silk umbrellas, violins, gold lockets, horn books, spelling books, almanacs, looking glasses and playing cards, gold and silver thread, copies of the *Gentleman's Magazine* for 1768 and 1769, and pear and cherry trees ready for transplanting. Through the efforts of enterprisers like Levy and his Scottish confrères at Schenectady, even so remote and forbidding a wilderness as the North American interior was not to remain beyond the ambit of Atlantic civilization.

PENNSYLVANIA

It was, in particular, the Pennsylvanians who were alert to the opportunities in the West after 1763. The main entrance to the West, the Ohio, was in their backyard, and they were quick to see in the recently conquered transmontane lands a vast area for exploitation, an area offering new opportunities for selling and trading goods. For the first time in nearly a decade, profits beckoned in the West.

War had, of course, seriously hampered fur traders ever since 1754, and the two relatively peaceful years of 1761 and 1762 had been succeeded by the Indian troubles of 1763 and 1764. Just at the time the western trade appeared to be emerging from its difficulties, profits in the coastal traffic were diminishing for every colonial merchant in Pennsylvania and elsewhere, due to England's postwar abandonment of "salutary neglect" and her new policy of regulating commerce and collecting duties. Business was further disturbed by the boycotts which the Stamp Act provoked. No wonder, then, that merchants, though still looking hopefully at the old, sought for new markets and new ways to make money. In the West many found an answer, for with the pacification of the Indians, the fur trade could secure a new lease on life. Using Pittsburgh as a headquarters, merchants could now ship goods down the Ohio as far as the

Mississippi and barter them for furs. The whole western market, including the transmississippi West, was no longer impenetrable, for now the river routes and the portages north to the Great Lakes could be controlled, fur shipments diverted from the Great Lakes and the St. Lawrence could be channeled up the Ohio toward the Pennsylvania seaboard, and the Anglo-Canadian traders and suppliers could be outmaneuvered.[23]

This was the vista that opened for Pennsylvania merchants and traders after 1763. It was a vista which appeared all the rosier when the merchants understood that the troops in the Illinois country at Fort de Chartres would have to be fed and that the army could be provisioned only through Pittsburgh. New Orleans after all was in Spanish hands, and therefore the Mississippi was not always open to English transport. As the Pennsylvania traders assessed their prospects in 1765, they saw new markets available to them in the distant western traffic with the Indians and the fur traders, in army provisioning, in sales of merchandise and liquor to the soldiers and the French settlers in the Illinois country, in commercial contacts with the petty shopkeepers on the frontier. The interest of the Pennsylvanians and of other eastern entrepreneurs was further aroused by their belief that, despite restrictions on the purchase of western land, there would be a rush of settlers across the mountains and down the Ohio. Here, of course, was another attractive opportunity, for the far-sighted merchant would be able to sell land, build colonies, and ride the crest of a new wave of agricultural and commercial expansion.

Of particular value to the historian is the fact that licensing was required of Indian traders. These recorded licenses make it possible for him to know what he otherwise could not; for instance, that immigrants like Michael Hart of Easton and Jacob I. Cohen of Philadelphia and Richmond, who in later years became successful storekeepers and merchants, began their careers as Indian traders licensed by the provincial authorities. Since they apparently confined their activities to eastern Pennsylvania in the years after the French and Indian War, when the frontier was on the Ohio and the Indian trade was centered at Pittsburgh, these men were in reality peddlers. On the other hand, it is significant that Joseph Simon and the Gratz brothers were never licensed as Indian traders; they were primarily suppliers, although on rare occasion they might bargain with the Indians themselves. Clearly, the Pennsylvania merchant who was involved in the western commerce did not commonly engage in direct trading with the Indians, but depended usually on partners and agents in Fort Pitt and in the Illinois country, where barter was carried on with the Indians and the whites who brought in the peltries. Levy Andrew Levy, who dealt with the Indians in his company's store at Pittsburgh, was a notable exception. To be sure, backcountry Jewish shopkeepers like Levi and Jacobs still continued to trade textiles, notions, and provisions for furs brought in by the farmers and hunters, but the bales of furs assembled by the licensed trader or the village shopkeeper were inconsequential when the volume of the industry was viewed as a whole.[24]

The western trade in any case held little profit for the small man. The West tendered large opportunities, but these opportunities entailed tremendous expenses and required a huge outlay of capital. The fur trade was a hazardous business, not only because of the fickle nature of the Indian traffic, but also because of the continuing competition offered by the French and Spanish, north from New Orleans to St. Louis, and by the Anglo-Canadian traders and merchants who operated out of Montreal and Quebec.

Even before the war was over—no later, that is, than 1760—the Philadelphia and Lancaster Jewish merchants and merchant capitalists were already associating themselves with William Trent and other Indian traders to exploit the West. They knew the war had been won and that it was only a matter of time before businessmen could move into the area. The new company formed by Trent, Simon, Levy, and Franks looked for its capital to Philadelphia and Lancaster, primarily to David Franks and Joseph Simon. From the vantage point of Pittsburgh, goods were sent as far north and west as Sandusky and Detroit, though some furs were probably also brought up from the South through the Shenandoah valley and on to Philadelphia. The store the new firm operated in Pittsburgh pursued such an aggressive mercantile policy that a competitor bitterly complained about its readiness to extend credit to the Indians, to supply them with rum, and to cut prices. Simon, Trent, Levy &

Company were not the first firm to penetrate the new Far West, the Illinois country. They had been preceded by their more powerful rivals, the Philadelphia firm of Baynton, Wharton & Morgan, with whom the Indian trader George Croghan had close business relations.[25]

In 1765 Croghan, deputy superintendent for Indian affairs in the western Pennsylvania area, had set out for the Far West to bring the Indians there within the English ambit. The supplies Croghan carried on his memorable trip to open the West in 1765 were, however, confiscated by the vigilante "Black Boys" who objected to giving savages gifts of guns, ammunition, and scalping knives. Croghan appealed to Simon, Trent, Levy & Company, and they reequipped him for his trip west with everything from fine ruffled shirts to seventeen tomahawks and nineteen dozen Jews' harps. Working closely as a silent partner with Baynton, Wharton & Morgan, who hoped to control the trade in the colonization of the Illinois country, Croghan led a second expedition to the Far West a year later. Baynton, Wharton & Morgan also attempted at that time to establish on the Scioto a trading post which would enable them to intercept the Indians bringing their furs to Pittsburgh. Their attempt at a monopoly of the western trade did not go without challenge, and among those who protested to Sir William Johnson was Joseph Simon's Pittsburgh firm of Simon & Milligan.[26]

Simon and his associates must have impressed Croghan, for the following year 1767 found him beginning to turn away from Baynton, Wharton & Morgan, who were already on the decline—and to whom he was heavily in debt—and switching his loyalties to the Philadelphia-Lancaster group, which included Simon and a number of other Jewish businessmen. By 1768 these businessmen had already made substantial inroads into the western trade. Levy & Franks of Philadelphia were given the army provisioning contract for Fort de Chartres by the London contractors and were also able to engage in a general mercantile business with the Indians, the French settlers, the English, and other traders moving up and down the Mississippi.[27]

By means of various companies and temporary partnerships, David Franks, his uncle Isaac Levy of Philadelphia and London, Simon of Lancaster, the Gratzes of Philadelphia, and a number of

Pennsylvania non-Jews extended their trading interests westward to the Illinois country in 1768. Working independently but in harmony, or as partners in special ventures, they sought to capture the trade of the middle Mississippi, if not the entire valley, and to frustrate the monopoly Baynton, Wharton & Morgan had been attempting in that area since 1765. The Franks-Levy agency on the Mississippi reached south to New Orleans, west to the Rockies, and north to the Great Lakes and Canada.[28]

Few entrepreneurs in the Indian trade were more persistent and enterprising than Joseph Simon. From his headquarters at Lancaster, one of the most important fur centers in the middle Atlantic provinces, he continued in the postwar period to serve as a prime supplier for the western traders. As we have already had occasion to note, Simon built his little empire by means of partnerships. Beginning in 1760 when the fall of Montreal finally opened up the West to the English, he held partnerships in a number of fur-trading companies, all having their main offices or headquarters in Pittsburgh; but in all probability, Simon kept changing his partners, and the Pittsburgh firms in which he was concerned did not all exist coevally.[29]

Always closely associated with Simon were his kinfolk, the Gratz brothers. Barnard, serving Simon as an agent since 1762 if not earlier, disposed of the Lancastrian's furs or shipped them to the London market. Michael was Simon's son-in-law. That same year of 1762, the brothers had already entered the western traffic in a very modest way, for one of them entrusted a parcel of Indian goods, including scalping knives, to the trader Hugh Crawford. Isolated to some extent in inland Lancaster, Simon needed someone in tidewater Philadelphia to sell the furs he had acquired in Fort Pitt from his own firms there or from traders in debt to him, and the Gratzes met that need. Working intimately with Simon throughout this period, they were his chief Philadelphia agents and also supplied him with English wares, rum, and a variety of native and foreign products in exchange for his furs. Then too, there were times when the Lancastrian, serving merely as an agent to sell the furs of his customers, sent them on to the Gratzes for sale—which illustrates, from the fur trapper's point of view, the inherent weakness in the trade. If the Gratzes in turn sent the furs on to the London auctions, as they probably did, the English brokers, constituting a third selling agency, also collected a commission. What, then, was left for the trader at Fort Pitt? What profit could the Indian hunter or the trapper hope to realize? [30]

Up to about 1765 the Gratzes were engaged primarily in the coastal and West Indian trade. Freighting their goods in the ships of other men, they were not and were never to become truly great merchants. Even in the western trade they were very probably overshadowed by Simon, and David Franks was richer than all of them, though it is true his degree of participation in the traffic is somewhat obscure. This is not to say that the western commerce of the Gratzes was negligible.

The report that Joseph Simon and Barnard Gratz had a secret sales agent in the French villages of the Illinois country during the early part of 1768 may be untrue, but it is certain that later in the year Barnard and his brother were openly concerned in business there. In entering the Illinois trade they were probably allied with David Franks and some of his associates, but there can be no question that they soon began to do a substantial western business on their own account, and they even sent adventures, parcels of goods, in the names of their children. It is not unlikely that the two brothers, who had worked together for nearly a decade, joined then in a formal partnership as B. & M. Gratz, a relationship that was to endure almost to the end of the century. Two men were to be closely associated with them in their Illinois venture: George Croghan and William Murray. Leaving Baynton, Wharton & Morgan, Croghan turned to the eager and ambitious Gratz brothers, who set about making their firm one of his chief east coast suppliers. Murray, a former army officer turned businessman, served the Philadelphia-Lancaster "Jewish" business group as their chief factor and business agent in the Mississippi valley where he advanced their interests in army provisioning, fur trading, and land speculation from 1768 on well into the Revolutionary period.[31]

The Gratzes, like all merchants, had diverse interests, but their prime concern as of the second half of the 1760's lay with the western trade. Much of their business on the frontier was done with traders at Fort Pitt where Barnard, acting as a field man for the

Philadelphia-based firm of B. & M. Gratz, undertook to seek furs for disposal by the company. The Gratzes thus solicited consignments which they sold on a 2.5 percent commission and remitted in the form of English wares, Indian goods, and provisions. Despite the fact that George Croghan was constantly in debt to them and had to balance his accounts with additional shipments of furs or transfers of land, the Gratzes certainly derived no great profit from their relations with him prior to the Revolution.[32]

The accounts of William Murray with Levy & Franks in the Illinois trade during the early 1770's amounted to many thousands of pounds; like Baynton, Wharton & Morgan, the Frankses, the Gratzes, and their associates were also hazarding large sums in this new traffic. Possibly, of course, the Gratz brothers hoped in 1768 that Murray would be able to sell their goods to great advantage because the nonimportation agitation had so radically cut the supply of English wares. The lack of imports from England tended to make staples scarce and costly, but the Gratzes apparently had stocks, and moreover planned to bring in more supplies as needed through the ports of Baltimore and Newport where nonimportation surveillance was lax.[33]

Around 1770 the Pennsylvania Jewish merchants lost their chief rival when Baynton, Wharton & Morgan prepared to withdraw from the Illinois country. A combination of problems—bad merchandising, failure to secure the army provision contract, the expensive haul from Pennsylvania, and competition from French fur buyers on the other side of the Mississippi, from the traders at Detroit, and from the aggressive David Franks and the Gratzes—put an end to their grandiose schemes of western commerce and colonization. As they pulled out, they sold their wares to a company their competitors had formed to dispose of the Baynton, Wharton & Morgan goods. The new concern, David Franks & Company, was a loose federation of economic interests, including Franks and the Gratzes in addition to a number of Gentiles who held a majority of the shares. Carrying on trade in the French-founded towns of the region, the new company continued no doubt to use the trading posts George Morgan had opened in Vincennes, Kaskaskia, Cahokia, and Fort de Chartres.[34]

The interest of the Philadelphia and Lancaster Jews and their Gentile business associates in the Far Western trade, throughout the territory near the mouth of the Ohio and northward, was in consonance with their hope of exercising more control of the traffic along the entire course of the Ohio. Their business rivals believed no doubt that they were trying to monopolize the trade, and they probably were, even as Baynton, Wharton & Morgan had attempted the same before suffering bankruptcy. In any case, with Pittsburgh assuming more and more importance as the gateway to the West, Joseph Simon continued to make that town the base for expansion of his involvement in the western trade. Simon's chief associate in Pittsburgh during the early 1770's, while he was seeking to extend his mercantile sphere of influence, was his partner John Campbell of the firm of Simon & Campbell.

The Pennsylvania attempt to capture the Ohio valley trade met with serious opposition, for Pennsylvania and Virginia, with conflicting claims to the upper Ohio, found themselves at cross purposes. Early in 1774 Lord Dunmore, the governor of Virginia, advanced into western Pennsylvania to protect Virginia's interests against Pennsylvania's claims to the upper Ohio and to save the western reaches of the Virginia hinterland from being swallowed up by the new colony of Vandalia. As Virginia occupied Pittsburgh and marched against the Indians, who had risen once more to keep the Americans out of their hunting grounds, Simon and his partner Campbell decided to throw in their lot with that colony. If Virginia succeeded in dominating the Ohio, Simon & Campbell could extend their mercantile influence on that river from the source to the mouth and implement some of the commercial and colonization plans of the defunct Baynton, Wharton & Morgan Company. Therefore, in the course of Lord Dunmore's westward push against Pennsylvania and the Indians in 1774, Simon & Campbell made financial advances to Dr. John Connolly, Virginia's vicegerent in the Pittsburgh area, and protected their loan by taking a mortgage on lands in present-day Louisville. It may be they planned to open a store in that area, although Simon himself played no part in laying out the town that arose during the Revolution at the falls of the Ohio.

The year 1775 spelled an end to all these schemes. War broke out that year between the Americans and the mother country, and the western fur trade again declined. The Mississippi garrison maintained its loyalty to the crown, which meant the West would remain under English control and the fur country would be closed to American traders. For all their efforts and investments, the entrepreneurs in the western trade were to make no fortunes in the decade after 1766.[35]

CHAPTER 40

THE WESTERN MOVEMENT

Writing to Sir William Johnson in 1766, George Croghan remarked, "One half of England is now land mad and every
body there has thire eys fixt on this cuntry." It was, of course, not
only English "eys" that were drawn to "this cuntry" (the territory
beyond the Appalachians), but also Anglo-American feet, the feet of
white settlers moving westward in an unending, though still trickling
stream. What was it that beckoned to these eyes and these feet? [1]

As already suggested, the development of the transallegheny
area involved substantial economic undertakings—fur trading, army
supply, and commerce in English goods—but associated with these
activities was also a large-scale attempt to carve colonies out of the
wilderness. The businessmen who had sent goods across the mountains for the armies stationed there, and for the Indian traders and
the white pioneers in English forts and French villages, knew that
it was only a matter of time before thousands of immigrants from
America and Europe would move westward to settle upon the waiting farmlands. These eager and ambitious eighteenth century merchants conjured up visions of farms, cities, and commerce extending
to the Mississippi. They anticipated for themselves great opportunities, great wealth, and that is why so many eyes were "fixt on
this cuntry."

The growth of the West would ultimately become the saga of
American expansion to the Pacific coast. That saga began in 1754

when a serious attempt was made by the Ohio Company of Virginia to settle the site of present-day Pittsburgh. A few months later, at the Albany Congress summoned to confront the threat of war with the French and the Indians, Franklin unveiled his plan to unite the colonies against their common enemies. Among his proposals was the suggestion that new settlements be created in the transmontane territory. Nothing came of Franklin's proposal, but the treaty of peace signed in 1763 gave the English and the Americans mastery of the cismississippi West from Canada to the Gulf of Mexico. Even before that, however, as early indeed as 1758, when the settlers— driven back to the Allegheny ridges in 1754—saw that the French had abandoned Fort Duquesne, they began moving westward again into the upper Ohio valley. Ultimately they occupied the old French outposts as far west as Mackinac. The Indian uprising of 1763 was only a temporary setback to the eager frontiersmen. Now the French no longer threatened, the Indians were soon beaten down, the roads were open, and large numbers of settlers moved into what is today western Pennsylvania, West Virginia, Kentucky, and the states to the south. By the time of the Revolution thousands of Anglo-Americans had moved across the mountains; all of Canada could not have boasted many more white settlers. If vast reaches of land could be cheaply secured by grant or purchase and sold to the oncoming set- tlers, fortunes could be made, and it was precisely this hope that animated many distinguished American planters, merchants, and politicians in the decades before the Revolution.

The colonial land company was nothing new on the European or American scene, for trading and land companies had been formed ever since the sixteenth century to exploit both the East and the West Indies, South America, and the coastal regions of much of North America. The proprietary provinces of Maryland, Maine, New York, the Jerseys, Pennsylvania, Delaware, and the Carolinas were all to a considerable degree land promotion companies, estab- lished with certain exceptions to sell land and to make a profit for their owners. The disaster of the "Mississippi Bubble" during the first quarter of the eighteenth century, when John Law's Company of the Indies was permitted by the French government to attempt the development of a huge business establishment for the exploitation of French Louisiana, testifies to the great interest which such speculative enterprises aroused in Europe.

Here in the colonies the Ohio Company of Virginia had been organized by 1747 to settle people on the Virginia and western Pennsylvania tributaries of the upper Ohio, and the next two or three decades saw dozens of companies created to settle the West and to sell land. A typical instance was the Mississippi Company of Virginia whose sponsors, among them George Washington and some of the Virginia Lees, hoped to secure a large grant at the junction of the Ohio and Mississippi Rivers, and from the vantage point of that strategic triangle, to control commerce and trade in several directions. Neither the Ohio Company nor the Mississippi Company ever accomplished anything, which apparently discouraged no one, for by the time of the Revolution the territory from Pittsburgh west and south on the Ohio all the way to the Mississippi was largely staked out on paper by rival and overlapping land companies. The riparian regions stretching north along the east bank of the Mississippi and along both banks of the Illinois River to the Great Lakes were also preempted by ambitious speculators. Every businessman involved in such schemes hoped for impressive profits from the Indian trade, from the buying and selling of furs and land, and from supplying merchandise to new settlers, but practically none of those large-scale colonizational projects ever went beyond the planning stage. Most of them, indeed, were never more than bright gleams in the eyes of avid promoters, and the new dispensation formulated in Whitehall after the French and Indian War went far toward darkening even these gleams.

The debt-ridden British government wanted nothing so much as peace in the transallegheny Indian country, and the desirability of this goal was only underscored by the turbulence of the Pontiac uprising. As we have already noted, England's eagerness to pacify the Indians led to the Proclamation of 1763 which forbade settlers to establish themselves west of the Appalachian watershed. Determined on rigorous enforcement of her policy of excluding settlers and keeping the West as an Indian reservation and Indian trading area, England manned outposts in the area and made strong efforts to regulate the fur trade and to protect the Indians from encroachment and exploitation.

There were, of course, many who sympathized with the imperial regulations of 1763 and wished those regulations to be upheld. The Indians and the Canadian traders hailed the new policy, and those who saw in it a means of reducing the expense of supporting an extensive series of military outposts also favored it. Those who wished to maintain the area as an Indian reservation also opposed the establishment of transallegheny colonies on the grounds that once across the mountains, the new colonists would be beyond reach of British arms and might even be tempted to manufacture their own consumer goods. Speculators and other vested interests, however, were less pleased and exerted tremendous influence on the government to modify its attitude. Their efforts were undermined by the growing antagonism between England and the thirteen colonies, for the more obstreperous these colonies became, the more inclined some groups were to reward the loyal and submissive fur-trading Canadians who wanted to leave the West untouched.

Other Americans and Englishmen stoutly insisted the colonies had the right to develop the hinterland as they saw fit. Some of the Americans were, to be sure, far more interested in eastern than in western lands. Enough, however, wanted to establish new colonies and were ready to argue that the new settlements would serve the East as a protective buffer against the Indians, that the militiamen who had fought in the Indian wars were entitled to land bounties, and that the settlers would create a western market for English goods. The proponents of this viewpoint hoped, of course, to make fortunes in commerce and the sale of lands.

An intermediate position recommended itself to a number of American as well as English politicians, bankers, and merchants whose desire was both to establish colonies and to encourage the Indian trade. This group opposed the principles of the Proclamation of 1763 and was eager to open the West for settlement—but slowly, gradually. Such, in all likelihood, was the attitude of the Lancaster-Philadelphia Jewish-Christian group. They sought four strings to their bow: a tripartite trade—with the Indians, the habitants in the Illinois country, and the oncoming Anglo-American settlers—plus the marketing of lands.

The existence and competing claims of these different groups and interests prevented the British agencies from establishing and pursuing a consistent policy in relation to the proposed colonization of the area, and all the while as the government debated the pros and cons of colonization, Indian pacification, and the fur trade, the settlers kept moving over the mountain trails, through the gaps, and down the rivers to the ever-beckoning new lands. By 1768 the hammering of vested interests in England and North America had thoroughly pulverized the policy of excluding settlers. Even those who advanced conflicting financial claims were united in their determination to remove governmental controls, whether in the establishment of colonies or in the exploitation of the Indians and the fur trade. The ministries could not withstand the pressures and intrigues of "big business"; they had to back down. In March 1768 Lord Hillsborough persuaded the cabinet to move the proclamation line of 1763 west, roughly speaking to the Ohio River. A number of supervisory posts were abandoned by the economy-minded British government, and the colonies were now permitted to regulate trade with the neighboring Indians. Of even greater importance was the fact that vast tracts within the area bounded by the new 1768 line and its predecessor of 1763 were to be made available for settlement, despite the prohibitions and the continuing hesitation of the government in London. Traders and landjobbers could now once again cherish great expectations.

There were still a number of problems the land companies would have to cope with. The basic one, which was never resolved, involved securing unequivocal imperial permission to settle between the 1763 and 1768 demarcation lines. Another difficulty, equally annoying for planters, capitalists, and promoters, lay in the conflicting provincial claims to the new lands. Virginia, for instance, claimed the territory west and north to the Mississippi River, including the upper Ohio valley, a region claimed in part by Pennsylvania too. Pennsylvania of course had long been in conflict with Virginia— ever since the early 1750's when the advance of Virginia's Ohio

Company promised to cut Pennsylvania off from her western hinterland and her stake in the fur trade. Moreover, Virginia's interpretation of her charter moved her to see threats not only in Pennsylvanian resistance to her claims, but also in the proposed colonies of Indiana, Vandalia, and those to be established in Kentucky and along the Illinois and Wabash Rivers. All of them were in her backyard. In 1774, as we have already noted, Virginia moved into action against the threats she feared. Governor Dunmore seized western Pennsylvania and then took to the field against the Indians who rose in resistance. When his forces defeated them in a few short months, Kentucky and the great highway to the West, the Ohio River, lay open despite provincial rivalries and imperial obstructionism.[2]

In one respect the year 1774 induced a large measure of unanimity among the contending provincial parties which were all extensions of what South Carolina's 1776 constitution would call "the free Protestant English settlements." Pennsylvania, Virginia, and the other "free Protestant English" colonies deeply resented the Quebec Act, promulgated in May of that year, which reattached the "vast tract of country" north and west of the Ohio to the "Catholic" province of Quebec. The rebellious Americans were now to be prevented from encroaching on the new lands of the Northwest where they could not and would not keep peace with the Indians. Lord Dunmore's War seemed to offer some relief to the frustrated Americans, but less than twelve months after the Indians had been driven back, skirmishes were fought at Lexington and Concord, and the Revolution divorced America and England. Settlements under British auspices were no longer possible, and the way west was blocked.[3]

Ultimately, of course, the westward movement was to be a great success and the American West was to be settled in its entirety—all this despite the fact that the prerevolutionary western land colonies had failed so abysmally. The colonists and the organizers, hampered by the French and the Indians, had enjoyed no extended period of peace before the Revolution, and the irresolute British government had never been able to make up its mind to confirm Indian grants or purchases for new colonies. The rivalries of the empire with the colonies and the colonies with one another, added to the overlapping claims of the different land companies, had hindered mass settlement, so that not a single prerevolutionary colonization scheme achieved realization. After the Revolution the western lands were in large part ceded to the federal government, and the Indian grants and purchases were not recognized. Nothing would remain of this episode in the history of early America but a memory of the bold, imaginative, and—premature—vision eighteenth century English and American businessmen had entertained.[4]

JEWS AND THE WESTERN MOVEMENT

Without distorting the historical focus, it may be said of Jewish businessmen that their participation in the western colonization movement is deserving of some notice. Even before the French and Indian War, from time to time European Jews had shown some interest in America's colonizationist potential. It has already been pointed out that as far back, indeed, as the beginning of the eighteenth century, Benjamin Levy, a London Jewish capitalist, had become one of the proprietors of West New Jersey, and that during the 1740's the Spanish-Portuguese Jews of London had flirted with the idea of underwriting mass Jewish settlements in the Carolinas, Georgia, and Nova Scotia.

In America herself a number of Jewish merchants who had control of some capital interested themselves in the possibilities of transmontane colonization. Participation in the establishment of colonies beyond the Alleghenies was of necessity limited to a very few, for only those with sufficient funds could hope to engage in such large-scale enterprises. It is worth noting, too, that these promotional ventures appealed to some as a means of salvaging earlier investments. When all is said and done, the history of Jewish participation in those colonization schemes is a history of failure, but a study of Jewish investment in such schemes is able, nonetheless, to illuminate what was, after all, a widespread economic activity of the prerevolutionary generation.[5]

Though there were many settlement and colonizing schemes,

the historian of American Jewry is interested in only five: George Croghan's first Illinois venture, and the Indiana, Grand Ohio-Vandalia, Illinois, and Wabash companies. Jews, both English and American, had some connection with these enterprises, and it may be a tribute to their realism and acumen that some at least of these projects came close to realization.

CROGHAN AND THE FIRST ILLINOIS VENTURE

One of the most important men in the attempt to create western colonies was the Indian trader George Croghan. Active in the Ohio valley since the late 1740's, Croghan became in the next decade a deputy superintendent for Indian affairs under Sir William Johnson. In 1765 Johnson sent Croghan out to the Illinois country to induce the Francophile Indians of the region to submit to the English crown, now that France had ceded the territory to England. After his supplies and presents for the Indians were seized by vigilantes in western Pennsylvania, Croghan turned to the Pittsburgh firm of Simon, Trent, Levy & Company to be outfitted anew. Even these wares and offerings, however, were not fated to reach their final destination, for they too were seized, this time by hostile Indians who attacked Croghan's party. Croghan suffered tomahawking, though happily no mortal wound, in that encounter—the tomahawk used against him may very well have been one he had intended as a gift to the Indians.

Despite everything, the mission was a success, and on his return Croghan made plans to create a huge new colony that would include much of present-day Illinois as well as parts of Indiana and Wisconsin. Closely associated with him in this enterprise was the large Philadelphia firm of Baynton, Wharton & Morgan, the rivals of Trent, Simon, Levy, and Franks. Baynton, Wharton & Morgan saw the undertaking as an opportunity to establish a combination trading company and proprietary colony, but their hopes had faded by 1768 when the British decided definitely not to make the grant on which the scheme's success depended. Though the firm of Simon, Trent, Levy & Company had been helpful to Croghan in the course of his initial expedition into the Illinois country, there is no evidence that the firm was to be concerned in the development of the proposed colony.[6]

THE INDIANA COMPANY

In 1766, at the same time that Baynton, Wharton & Morgan, together with Croghan and their patrons, were seeking a royal grant on the Mississippi for their first Illinois Company, they—or some of them—were also negotiating for a similar grant on the upper Ohio. Though the Philadelphia-Lancaster Jewish merchants had no formal relationship with the first Illinois Company and were in fact in rivalry with its sponsors, they were associated with the simultaneous effort to secure a grant on the upper Ohio.

Three years before, a group of traders and merchants had met at Philadelphia and set up an organization to press the government to secure compensation for them from the Indians for goods seized during the Pontiac uprising and for "wantonly and inhumanely putting our people to death, torturing some of them whole days and nights." Croghan as well as Baynton, Wharton & Morgan, and Simon, Trent, Levy, and Franks were all behind the new company. These "Suffering Traders of 1763," as they were called, prepared a statement of the pillage and submitted claims for about £80,000 in Pennsylvania or New York currency, or £50,000 in sterling. Some of their accounts were undoubtedly padded, but there can be no question that their losses had been sizeable. The heaviest losses, more than one third of the total, were those suffered by the firm of Simon, Trent, Levy, and Franks, although at the company's subsequent and more formal organization the Baynton, Wharton & Morgan group held the largest number of shares.[7]

A plan of campaign to influence the home government was laid out, and Croghan was sent over to London in 1764 to explore the possibilities of securing compensation, possibly in land grants on the Mississippi or the Ohio. Croghan of course was an expert on Indian affairs for those areas, and behind him with his great influence stood Sir William Johnson, who expected to reap substantial benefits from the organization of a successful company. David Franks, the agent for the army provision contractors, was probably responsible for suggesting that Croghan work through politically powerful notables like Arnold Nesbitt, Moses Franks, and William Colebrooke. Moses Franks was to be the company's chief lobbyist in London, although he would have the support of the able Benjamin Franklin. Croghan and Moses Franks were each to receive five percent of all net sums granted as compensation by the government. Though Croghan accomplished nothing on that trip, by 1765 the group had organized itself formally as the Indiana Company and decided to ask the crown for Indian lands to indemnify them for their losses.[8]

Three years later the company's position improved materially when the Fort Stanwix Conference, at which Sir William presided, moved the Indian boundary westward and arranged for all of the new territory between the Appalachian divide and the Ohio to be sold by the Iroquois to the crown. A sizeable segment of that "sale," about 2,500,000 acres in present-day West Virginia, was given by the Indians to the king as trustee for the "Suffering Traders of 1763" in compensation for their losses. With this first of its major goals attained, the Indiana Company saw as its next step an effort to secure royal confirmation of its particular Indian grant, and Samuel Wharton and William Trent, representing the two largest trading groups, were sent to England the following year to accomplish this purpose. Again, however, the effort came to nothing, for though the king did approve the larger Fort Stanwix purchase, he withheld approval from the specific grant to the Indiana Company. His majesty recalled no doubt the report on the western problem he had received from the mercantilist-minded Lords of Trade in March 1768, and their warning that "consumption of British manufactures . . . would not be promoted by . . . new colonies, which being proposed to be established . . . in places which upon the fullest evidences are found to be utterly inaccessible to shipping, will . . . be probably led to manufacture for themselves." The Lords had also advanced the argument that "the extension of the furr trade depends entirely upon the Indians being undisturbed in the possession of their hunting grounds" and "all colonizing does in its nature, and must in its consequences, operate to the prejudice of that branch of commerce."[9]

By 1769, therefore, the Indiana Company had come to an impasse despite its Indian grant. Wharton, lobbying at London that year for the company, realized the intended grant would not be confirmed. Only too conscious of the difficulties raised by the over-lapping claims of rival land companies and the conflicting boundary pretensions of the seaboard provinces, he knew he would have to recruit a great deal more political influence if the opposition at White-hall was to be checkmated. To accomplish this, Wharton and his advisers proposed the establishment of an even larger colony, one which would include the Indiana Company shareholders, other rival land companies, and a whole series of important English financial, commercial, and political personalities. The proposed new colony of Vandalia was never to come into being, but following the formation of the United States Government, the Indiana Company would be reorganized, would proceed to conduct its affairs independently of the Vandalia Company, and would run afoul of the state of Virginia, which refused to approve the company's Indian grant and declared she had never recognized England's right to dispose of Virginia lands. The United States Congress, to which the Indiana Company turned next, and the United States Supreme Court were also un-responsive. During the Revolution the Gratz brothers were to find themselves involved in the problems of the Indiana Company—in their capacity no doubt as creditors of George Croghan whom they had served for some years as factors and bankers and had carried financially. The traders, merchants, and speculators who created the Indiana Company, or became associated with it as shareholders, were never in fact to receive any compensation for their claims, nor were they to make any money unless they succeeded in unloading their shares onto others.[10]

Still, the "Suffering Traders of 1763" were better off than others; for instance, the consortium of five Canadian Jewish traders, apparently organized under the name Gershon Levy & Company, who had joined with other Canadian fur entrepreneurs to urge Sir William Johnson to compensate them for their losses at the hands of the Indians. Unable to muster the political influence available to the Pennsylvania merchants, the Canadians made no progress at all in furthering their claims, but they were not alone in seeing them rejected. Among the Pennsylvanians who had incurred losses in the uprising of 1763 were several who had also suffered French and Indian depredations at the onset of the war in 1754. These "Sufferers of 1754" included Joseph Simon, David Franks, and the latter's kinsman Benjamin Levy, the socially-prominent Philadelphia merchant. Even before the declaration of war in May 1756, they had claimed compensation for their losses and after the war some of them continued their appeals to Johnson and the British government for monetary restitution or land grants. Working at various times through Croghan, Wharton, Trent, and in particular, Moses Franks of London, they too sought in vain to secure official acknowledgment that theirs was a just claim against the Indians or the British government. The London authorities simply replied that the French and their Indian allies had been responsible. No reparations were accorded them, therefore, and their claims were not included in the Indian grant made for the benefit of the "Sufferers of 1763." [11]

VANDALIA

In suggesting the creation of a colony to be known as Vandalia, the American lobbyists seeking royal confirmation of the Indiana Company's grant had hoped, as we have said, that their proposal would harmonize—or overshadow—the conflicting interests of the province of Virginia, the old Ohio Company of Virginia, the Indiana Company, and a variety of other colonizing or land-jobbing groups, to say nothing of the oppositional forces within the English ministries. Though the proposed colony itself was to be called Vandalia, the new company called into existence in 1769 for the purpose of establishing Vandalia was the Grand Ohio or Walpole Company, named after Thomas Walpole, an English banker. The group proposed to buy from the crown some twenty to thirty million acres in the western part of Virginia, territory which today is part of West Virginia and Kentucky. The greatest of prerevolutionary schemes, Vandalia was essentially an English, not an American enterprise. The Indiana Company and other American groups had little say in the proposed new proprietary colony and government, nor were the

"Suffering Traders of 1763" directly integrated into the project, though of course they expected to secure compensatory grants in the new colony.[12]

In the developing rivalry between English and American capitalists for new investment opportunities, the more powerful English succeeded in excluding many of the Americans from participating or playing a dominant role in the proposed new colony. Most of the shareholders were British. There was not a single American Jew among the founders, but three of the London Frankses, including Moses, were involved along with two of Moses' Christian army provisioning associates. These three London Frankses were to be sure of American birth; two were brothers to David Franks, while the third was one of David's sons. In January 1770 the three London members of the family turned their share of the Vandalia Company over to David. Either they had served as a front for him, or more likely, they noted the colonies were drifting away from the mother country and believed their Vandalia interests would be best served by transfer to a man on the scene.

The years 1770–1772 saw the plans for the colony approved by the king and the Privy Council, and in 1773 a charter was drafted. That same year the new government seemed ready for organization, and the Indians began assembling for their expected gifts. Croghan, who was managing that end of the business, turned once more to Simon and his associates and was advanced the goods he needed. That year of 1773 proved, however, to be not only climactic but also catastrophic for Vandalia. Virginia objected to the new colony's formation in territory she believed her own, and made it clear that she had no intention of allowing any rival province or company to cut her off from the West. As if this were not enough, the quarrels, boycotts, and the like preliminary to the Revolution soured the English on the thought of a colony across the mountains, and the Quebec Bill of 1774 restored that western wilderness to imperial control and bound the Indian country once more to Canada. Vandalia's title was, therefore, never to be confirmed by George III, and no final action was ever taken to put the charter into effect. An American-sponsored Vandalia company was later organized, but it too failed to accomplish anything.[13]

Apart from the case of the Indiana Company, the relationship of American Jewish businessmen to the land companies was, it is clear, tangential. Jewish merchant-suppliers were concerned in the Indiana Company rather heavily through Joseph Simon, Levy Andrew Levy, and David Franks, while William Trent, another member of the company, was in debt to these Lancaster and Philadelphia entrepreneurs. If, however, the Gratz brothers were interested in any of the land companies described above, it was only through their financial services to George Croghan who was very much involved in the Indiana and Vandalia Companies. Had those projects ever eventuated and had Croghan made money and wielded influence, the Gratzes of course would have benefited accordingly, and they had certainly counted on that.[14]

In 1773, however, the Gratzes took upon themselves a direct interest in one attempt to establish an American colony, this time in the "Far West," the Illinois country where they had been doing business since 1768. Together with the Frankses, they prepared to buy land for the establishment of a colony in the same general area chosen a decade earlier by the Mississippi Company of Virginia and by the first Illinois Company of Baynton, Wharton & Morgan.

There were a number of factors which brought the second Illinois venture to birth. The Anglo-American traders in the Illinois country were on the lookout for something to improve their economic position, while David Franks & Company, then the dominant mercantile group, no doubt discovered that the trade had not proved the bonanza they had anticipated and that land deals were necessary to supplement their profits. The year 1773 was decisive for them, for by that time it seemed certain to almost everyone that Vandalia would be organized as a new government. William Murray wrote to the Gratzes in May "that the New Colony was fixed" and that its governor was "to be over in June." It seemed beyond question that the British government had finally committed itself to the establishment of western settlements. The entire Ohio River country was beginning to receive white inhabitants. The vanguard had already penetrated Kentucky, and it was only a matter of time before the river would be dotted with villages along its whole length from Pittsburgh to the Mississippi. The West, everyone could be sure, was bound to grow; its white population was increasing daily.[15]

On July 5, 1773, Murray, acting for his principals in eastern Pennsylvania, purchased from the Indians two strategically located pieces of land for over $37,000 worth of barter goods; that at least was the amount the scheme's promoters claimed to have spent. Neither Murray nor his associates worried overmuch about the fact that they were encroaching on "reservation" territory, lands beyond the 1763 and 1768 demarcation lines, both of which were south and east of the Ohio. There was simply no doubt in their minds—a confidence they shared with George Washington and others—that settlements would be created beyond the established Indian boundaries. Nor were the would-be colonizers much concerned about royal confirmation of the title to the lands they had purchased, for they had come upon, albeit in a garbled version, an opinion of Charles Pratt (later the Earl of Camden) and Charles Yorke, two eminent English jurists, to the effect that certain East Indian grants and titles required no royal letters patent. Murray in fact reported to the Gratzes that during Croghan's London sojourn, "Lords Camden and York personally confirmed . . . the opinion respecting Indian titles," but whether the Americans who involved themselves in this new colonization venture took the opinion seriously or whether they deliberately acted on a gamble is hard to say. In any event, their conviction that the future lay with them made them willing to back up that gamble with a substantial sum.[16]

Of the two areas they purchased, one was the triangle of land formed by the confluence of the Ohio and the Mississippi Rivers; the other extended north along the Illinois River from its mouth toward Lake Michigan. The parcels were obviously chosen with great care, for the lower Ohio-Mississippi triangle might well enable its proprietors to dominate the trade of that whole area and even tap the transmississippi commerce as far as the Rockies, while the Illinois River parcel would allow its owners to intercept furs going north to the Great Lakes and perhaps even divert southward the ever-increasing west-east fur traffic moving toward the St. Lawrence. The colonizers could also employ the Illinois River as a highway into Canada. There is, however, evidence that another of Murray's prime motivations in penetrating the Illinois country was his desire to purchase and exploit lead and copper mines on behalf of his clients. The Gratzes in particular, as we know, were very much interested in lead mining in the East. Thus the businessmen concerned in the Illinois venture hoped, in one well-coordinated operation, to combine fur buying, the sale of merchandise to Indians and settlers, army provisioning, land settlement, mining, and colonization. Now that the rival firm of Baynton, Wharton & Morgan had been eliminated, there was, they believed, nothing to prevent them from moving in to fill the Illinois vacuum.[17]

The grantees in the new land company—"the Land Affair," as Murray called it—originally numbered twenty-two; eight were Jews, four of them Frankses, and the remaining four related to one another. Two of the non-Jews were in-laws to David Franks, but in fact, nearly all the grantees were very closely integrated into the Lancaster-Philadelphia "Jewish" mercantile group in which David Franks undoubtedly held a leading, if not indeed the dominant position. Certainly he was far more influential than the Gratzes, for with him came the London branch of his family and his politically powerful kinsmen, the Hamiltons of Pennsylvania. Franks looms larger on the scene than historians have heretofore conceived him. By 1770 he had taken over the Vandalia interests of his London relatives; he controlled the largest army provisioning effort in the West, had competed successfully with Baynton, Wharton & Morgan, and had come into possession of their stores and trading posts throughout the Illinois country. In addition, he had land interests around Pittsburgh and by 1773 had combined his relatives and business associates into a new Illinois Company. A year later he had also acquired the shares of the English members of his family. As a speculator, Franks lacked the stature of Robert Morris and William Duer, but he was nonetheless an enterpriser of singular daring and vision.[18]

None of this helped in the end. The historic factors that aborted the Vandalia design operated even more decisively against the Illinois Company. The purchases made by Murray were hundreds of miles west of the Indian boundary line of 1768, a line which had been set up to exclude settlers, not to encourage their coming. The Illinois Company's interpretation of the Camden-Yorke opinion was at best self-deception, and by 1774 the aroused and resentful British government had made the West "part and parcel of the province of Quebec." Virginia too was troublesome, for she had not limited to the Vandalia scheme alone her protests against settlements in territories she claimed; she protested with equal vehemence the new Illinois Company's activity in her backcountry which she intended to reserve for exploitation under her own auspices. Virginia documented her determination in 1774 by moving against Vandalia, the Indians, and Pennsylvania. At this stage of the game the Illinois Company thought to retrieve its fortunes by moving into the Virginia camp. The company had no choice actually and appealed to Lord Dunmore to take it under his wing. In its petition for the governor's protection and patronage, the company pointed out that its members sought colonization by industrious British subjects who would create a barrier protecting the eastern settlements against Indian attacks and would pacify and civilize the aborigines, keep out unauthorized squatters, and further British trade.[19]

Dunmore's good will was won when provision was made for him the following year (1775) in the development of a related venture, the Wabash Company. The new Wabash Company, whose only Jewish members were David Franks and his family, included two substantial areas along the Wabash River, one of them contiguous to the Ohio-Mississippi triangle of the Illinois Company. Substantial sums of money were invested in these new purchases, which through the Wabash River offered additional access via portage and the Maumee River to Lake Erie and Canada. Governor Dunmore's recommendation that the Illinois and Wabash purchases be approved now followed, but Indian hostilities, British objections, and the outbreak of the Revolutionary War rendered actual colonization impossible.

In 1778–1779 during the Revolution, both companies merged as the United Illinois and Wabash Land Companies and claimed about 60,000,000 acres. The Gratzes, it is of interest to note, had not been included in the original Wabash Company of 1775, since they may well have felt at the time that they were getting out of their depth, but with the establishment of the united companies, Barnard Gratz reappeared as the secretary of the new venture. Clearly, David Franks and his group were still in control.

After Virginia took possession of the western country under the leadership of George Rogers Clark, the united companies appealed in vain to the Virginia state legislature for confirmation of title to their purchases. The Virginians invalidated Richard Henderson's Indian purchases in Kentucky as well as those of the Indiana and the Illinois-Wabash Companies, and in later years, after the federal government claimed the western lands as the heir to the crown, fruitless appeals were made to Congress for confirmation. By 1823 all hope was gone, for the United States Supreme Court had by then definitely decided that Indian titles to land under grant to individuals in the territory northwest of the Ohio River could not be recognized in American courts.[20]

Traffic in Undeveloped Lands

The Jewish merchant, balancing the accounts of his speculations in the Indiana, Vandalia, Illinois, and Wabash colonization schemes, could not have been but dismally aware that his losses had been heavy. There would have been, he might come to understand, more profit for him in buying, selling, and speculating in undeveloped lands which lay well within the defined borders of a province, for such ventures as a rule involved no problem of title. In fact, many of the colonial Jewish businessmen did buy and sell acreage and tracts within provincial boundaries, and speculations of this type would be characteristic of American merchants and promoters generally until the closing of the last frontier at the end of the nineteenth century. Colonial Jews, however, were marginal citizens, politically at least, and were in consequence rarely accorded substantial grants of lands by the authorities. They had to make their fortunes the "hard way" —and often they did.[21]

David Franks, together with his partners and associates, bought land, particularly in western Pennsylvania, from Croghan who, as deputy superintendent of Indian affairs, possessed the authority to "buy" from the Indians and never hesitated to take advantage of his opportunities and prerogatives. During the 1760's and 1770's, therefore, Jewish businessmen like Franks, Joseph Simon, Levy Andrew Levy, and the Gratzes purchased from Croghan, or received from him through mortgages, tracts of 10,000 to 50,000 acres in Pennsylvania and New York. Since their earliest days as merchants, the Gratzes had handled land sales on a commission basis. Such undertakings were an all but negligible part of their business until Croghan became financially involved with them and they set out to sell large parcels of thousands of acres for him. As his indebtedness to them increased, Croghan assigned large tracts to them, just as William Trent, similarly in debt to his Jewish partners Simon and Franks, mortgaged to them a tract of 7,500 acres. In 1774, the reader will recall, Simon & Campbell lent money to Dr. John Connolly who gave them a mortgage on part of the townsite that was soon to become the city of Louisville.

Mathias Bush of Philadelphia speculated in Virginia tracts, and the decade before the Revolution found Aaron Levy beginning his career as a trafficker in Pennsylvania lands. During the postrevolutionary period Levy would become a land agent buying hundreds of thousands of acres for his principals, Robert Morris, James Wilson, and others. In the course of the 1760's a number of New York Jewish merchants acquired lands, very probably for speculation, in Connecticut and in the New Hampshire backcountry—present-day Vermont. That same decade Samuel Jacobs of St. Denis on the Richelieu owned land in Nova Scotia, and his fellow merchant Aaron Hart became the largest Jewish landowner in Canada after the Revolution. Hart was no speculator, however, and his acquisitions were farm lands. Some of them he may have bought as investments, but it is more likely that the seigneuries he gradually secured came to him through debts for merchandise or fell to him when mortgagers defaulted on their payments.[22]

There were, of course, hazards in land dealings even in the more settled provinces. Isaac Levy of Levy & Franks found this out in 1754 when he bought a half interest in the three Georgia Sea Islands from the notorious Anglican clergyman Thomas Bosomworth. Completely disregarding Levy's equity, Bosomworth blandly sold two of the islands to the crown, and with the approval of the Georgia government, retained the third one, St. Catherines, for himself. When Levy's appeal for justice to the Privy Council brought him no relief, he offered to compromise his claim for the right to exploit a coal mine on Cape Breton Island. Not improbably, his attention had been drawn to the mine by his London relatives, the Frankses, whose business associates had some interest in the Cape Breton coal mines. Levy hoped to compensate himself by importing coal into the American colonies and promoting it as a fuel rather than wood. The Lords of Trade, however, frowned on the use of coal which, they feared, would increase the manufacture of iron and thereby ultimately threaten British industry. They preferred to placate Levy by offering the unfortunate investor a small monetary compensation in 1769— fifteen years after the original Georgia investment. That same year of 1769 one Isaac Levy, along with twelve others, successfully petitioned the New York authorities for a grant of 13,000 acres on the west side of the Hudson in a tract purchased from the Catskill Indians. If this was the same Isaac Levy victimized by Bosomworth, it is evident he was more than casually involved in the land business. In any case, as a brother-in-law to Jacob Franks and thus an uncle not only of the powerful Frankses of England but also by marriage of Oliver De Lancey, he was one of the few Jews in America who could muster influence with the provincial authorities, if not with the Lords of Trade.

The Reverend Thomas Bosomworth, Levy's nemesis, did not retain St. Catherines, his share of the three Georgia Sea Islands, for very long. By 1765 the clergyman had sold it to Button Gwinnett, who in 1770 gave a second mortgage on the island to the Savannah merchants Mordecai and Levi Sheftall. When Gwinnett affixed his signature to the mortgage, the Sheftalls and no doubt Gwinnett himself would have thought it a huge joke had anyone suggested to them that a century and a half later in 1927, a letter bearing Gwinnett's signature along with the autographs of five other signers of the Declaration of Independence would fetch $51,000.[23]

REAL ESTATE

All told, no more than six or seven American Jewish merchants ever participated in the attempt to develop western colonies. Many more of course speculated in the buying and selling of parcels and tracts of land. In fact, however, there was hardly a Jewish craftsman, shopkeeper, or merchant who did not at some time own a piece of property, so that the buying and selling of urban property—lots, houses, gardens, and wharves—can be duplicated in almost every town and village of Jewish residence during the eighteenth century. In this sense colonial American Jewry was unique among the Jewries of the world, for many European cities and provinces either denied Jews residence altogether or, if not prohibiting them outright from buying land, at least restricted and delimited them in their land purchases. This was not so in America, and after an initial prohibition against Jewish houseowning in New Amsterdam, Jews, as we have had occasion to point out, were allowed to buy and own property anywhere.[24]

Land was inexpensive here and so, like others, Jews bought and sold as their desires prompted and as their means permitted. Even before New Amsterdam became New York, Asser Levy owned a house and a lot in the village of Beverwyck (present-day Albany), and his kinsman Simon Valentine van der Wilden was probably the first Jew to own a town lot or part of one in Charleston, South Carolina. The New York tax records for 1695–1734 list numerous Jews as possessors of property, and Isaac Lopez of Boston was a heavy investor in real estate in that city during the same period. Between 1722 and 1726 alone, he bought six parcels of land. During the same decade Aaron Louzada was already acquiring property in New Jersey. When Georgia was settled in 1733, the Jews who followed a few months after Oglethorpe's landing received town lots and gardens; others increased their holdings by purchase or grants.[25]

As urbanites conscious of the possibilities that lay in the rapid growth of well-favored towns, Jews bought and speculated in town property. The name of Joseph Simon, for instance, occurs over twenty-five times in the deed books of prerevolutionary Lancaster County, Pennsylvania. Some of the lands, houses, and lots that Simon and his in-law Mathias Bush owned were acquired by them through mortgages received from Indian traders and farmers to satisfy judgments for unpaid goods and loans. An eye to speedy profits led Mordecai Moses Mordecai to buy lots from James Allen in the future city of Allentown as early as 1760, and the next decade found Aaron Levy purchasing a lot in the far western Pennsylvania town of Sunbury just a few months after Northumberland County's establishment. The Canadian Jews were no less active in such enterprises. Even before the British conquest of the Laurentian valley, Naphtali Hart Jr. owned a substantial amount of urban property in Halifax; he had purchased it within five or six years after the town's founding. Shortly after the conquest Samuel Jacobs, army commissary and merchant, acquired land and houses in Montreal, Quebec, Sorel, St. Charles, St. Denis, St. Ours, and probably in other towns and villages as well. Off in distant Detroit, Chapman Abram bought and sold houses and lots in the decade before the Revolution when the little French settlement sheltered less than 700 whites.[26]

Actually, there was nothing very remarkable about this possessory urge, for owning a lot or a house was almost a necessity for the businessman who sought recognition from his peers. Property helped a man's credit rating and enhanced his economic status. That, however, was only one motivation for such purchases. Jews also bought lands and homes because they were useful and made for better living. Some of the more successful merchants had their own homes not only in the city but in the countryside too; for example, Moses Levy, the well-to-do merchant-shipper who had a house and acreage in Rye, and Levy's son-in-law Jacob Franks who summered in Flat Bush and Harlem. In the latter village he owned or rented a house with a lovely view of the river. But, unlike their English coreligionists, American Jews were not primarily interested in buying country estates to improve themselves socially. In England estate owners were gentry; the American Jew, however, with very few exceptions, had no such pretensions. His immediate goal was to become a merchant rather than a gentleman.[27]

CHAPTER 41

HAZARDS TO SUCCESS

ANTI-JEWISH PREJUDICE

M any were the hazards that a merchant had to face before he attained what was often an only too brief and fleeting success. The economic historian is fully aware of all those hazards, for they are most generously recorded in the sources. Fortunately or unfortunately, much more is known of the pathology of business than of its soundness. The waste books, ledgers, and letter books of successful merchants rarely survived their authors' retirement, for the accounts of such merchants were balanced and their papers destroyed. Very often the records that have survived reflect the careers of men whose estates were in litigation. In all probability, however, the enterprising merchant did not fret too much about the numerous perils which threatened him—although he protected himself as well as he could. Had he lingered overlong on the barriers to success and brooded about them, he might never have attempted any venture. The fact that individuals and groups left a town or province is sufficiently eloquent testimony to the insurmountable economic, social, or even political barriers they had met. What other explanation is there for the disappearance of Newport's Jewish community of the 1680's?

To what extent, we may ask, was a Jew handicapped in business by virtue of his religious faith? Apparently the road was open to him in commerce and in landholding, for he could speculate where and as he wished, with no restrictions except those imposed by the limitations of his capital or his credit. Actually, however, the

Jewish businessman was disadvantaged economically by virtue of his religion, for as a Jew he experienced a variety of social disabilities, and social disabilities inevitably curtail economic opportunities. Of even greater significance is the fact that in colonial times office-holding helped materially in securing land grants, contracts, and the like—while Jews as Jews could hold no office.[1]

The extent to which the Jewish merchant had to cope with anti-Jewish prejudice—the extent to which Judeophobia was an effective economic deterrent—can only be conjectured, for no one can peer into the hearts of men. People who cherished anti-Jewish sentiments and refused to do business with Jews rarely documented their attitude openly, but Jewish businessmen certainly knew that Bishop Warburton spoke for many in England and America when he stigmatized the Jews as "a people long since abandoned of God." The Jew never doubted that a certain degree of prejudice against him was present in some quarters, and he took this into account. On the whole, however, anti-Jewish prejudice was not a discernible barrier to the success of a Jewish businessman.[2]

THE HAZARDS OF SHIPPING

Judeophobia was probably the least of the risks a merchant ran. Especially as a shipper, he faced many worse hazards. The voyage across the Atlantic was often long and expensive; crossings of fifteen to twenty weeks in duration were not uncommon. Freight rates were not always low, and the charges on lumber and provisions to the West Indies might well equal the cost of the lading itself. Owners of vessels had, moreover, to cope with the prospect of deserting sailors and imprisonment of personnel by government agencies, nor was it unusual for the crew and even the captain to embezzle or steal from the cargo.[3]

Insurance was never cheap; it was particularly high in areas of danger, in time of war, and in localities where storms were common or pirates flourished. There was no insurance to cover insurrection by Negroes on a slaver from the Guinea coast. In wartime a vessel might be commandeered by the government, and though the owner was frequently paid for its use, it is questionable if the compensation was adequate.[4]

Wars were frequent, and with them came not only enemy warships but the plague of privateers. Missing a convoy could be a serious matter, and all too often in any case, the privateers of one's own country were as much to be dreaded as those of the enemy. Individuals attacked by pirates lost their ships, cargoes, and personal belongings, and were fortunate to escape with their lives.[5]

Customs officers presented another problem, as a seventeenth century New York merchant found when a vessel he had dispatched to the Virgin Islands was driven back into port by French privateers and the local customhouse refused to release it. Customs officers were frequently a headache for the businessman; whether they were incorruptible or not, one faced the difficulty of evading them, and their interpretations of the trade and navigation acts were constant sources of trouble for shippers.[6]

There was no end to the trials of a merchant. When Isaac Cohen de Lara transported goods from Rhode Island to New York, he had no intimation that the master of his sloop was in collusion with privateers or pirates and would turn the cargo over to them. Nor could Michael Gratz foresee that a voyage to the West Indies in which he was interested would end in disaster with the boat captured by Spanish privateers and the captain hauled off to be held for ransom in Europe. Jacob Rodriguez Rivera did evince foresight in 1767 when, even though it was not a war year, he instructed a factor in Jamaica to send a cash remittance by two different ships in order to minimize the possibility of loss by seizure. No one, however, could arm himself against the epidemics which might break out on ship or be encountered in foreign ports. No one could be sure that the supply of water would not give out on long voyages. On the eve of the Revolution, Lopez suffered the loss of a captain and his mate, seized by the Portuguese off the Brazilian coast and dead of the smallpox in a Rio jail. A few months later another of his captains, "in consequence of those infernal storms riseing which threttens our destruction"—he meant the Revolution—sold Lopez' *Venus* in London at a considerable loss in order to avoid the even greater loss of confiscation by the British.[7]

The fortunes of an early eighteenth century Boston merchant provide vivid testimony of the dangers to which traders were exposed, especially if they accompanied their cargoes. In September 1705 the Boston newspapers reported Samuel Frazon lost at sea. Actually, as we know from later reports, Frazon had been driven out to sea by a storm that lasted for six days. Cast adrift during this time, he had no food at all, and making his way at length to an island, was stripped naked by the Indians. Two of Frazon's men died of exposure, his Negro slave was taken from him, and for three months he was kept prisoner by the savages until they took him to Martinique where he was ransomed. By way of Nevis and Barbados, he returned to Boston, ready to do business again. Evidently Frazon was no man to be trifled with, for he was once haled into a Boston court for beating someone else's Negro servant.[8]

Frazon's experience was not altogether untypical, for among the constant dangers shippers had to face were storms. Most eighteenth century ships were small—frequently under 100 tons—and very vulnerable to strong winds which commonly took a heavy toll, nowhere more so than in the Caribbean. Isaac Elizer, for example, lost three ships in two years, two of them in successive months. Another merchant lost three men on one voyage through sickness and bad weather. One of Lopez' captains reported to him that of fourteen vessels driven ashore by a gale, five had been destroyed, and one had gone down without survivors. It is no wonder merchants made out their wills before accompanying their cargoes or embarking upon a long ocean trip. At Curaçao it was customary for a Jew on his arrival or return from a lengthy voyage to repair to the synagogue and there give thanks to God for his manifest blessings.[9]

No document points up the hazard of an ocean voyage better than the sailing orders Lopez and Rotch issued to John Lock, the captain of the *Minerva*, one of their whalers making for the Falkland Islands. In that one letter the captain was enjoined to beware of scurvy, storms, the wrong course, leaky ships, and the Spanish and Portuguese Inquisition. Nothing was said about the ever-present possibility that the *Minerva* might not catch an adequate number of whales.[10]

If in addition to severity of weather, a merchant was confronted with an imprudent unbusinesslike captain in charge of his cargo, if his ships were too small to make a profitable run or old and in need of constant repair, if the selection and destination of the cargo were unwisely chosen, or if thousands of gallons of Madeira wine turned sour on the homeward voyage—if these or a thousand other threats came to pass—then the merchant-shipper would invariably sustain heavy losses.[11]

HAZARDS ON LAND

The difficulties with which shippers contended at sea were matched by those which merchants met on land. Fire and water threatened the wheat stored in the hangars, and the riverboat that sank probably carried no insurance. Partners fought frequently, and the dissolution of partnerships raised vexatious issues. Problems of theft in overland transportation were rarely to be avoided. Only too often drivers tapped the rum barrels, and wantage after a trip was a common complaint. Stupidity could be disastrous. In the war year of 1776 the Gratz clerk made a slight mistake in a shipment over the mountains to Pittsburgh. He sent a barrel of mustard seed instead of gunpowder! And what was a merchant to do when a clerk—he may have been a relative—was short in his accounts? [12]

In 1762 Levi Michaels of Brookhaven South, Long Island, was wiped out by a fire which gutted his shop and "reduced" him "to the lowest circumstances." He then began all over again by immigrating to Montreal, but three years later he was back in New York, and it was not long before he appealed to the congregation for a loan to enable him to return to his new home in Canada. Fire and robbery posed great threats in a day when such losses were not insurable, so that the theft of a diamond ring or a pair of earrings was serious even for a well-to-do person. And pilfering of goods, especially silver plate, was frequently reported by Jewish merchants. A peddler bound from New York to Albany might disappear for months or never be heard from again. Either he had absconded with a load of goods, or he had been robbed, murdered, and his body buried in the woods.

Wartime losses at sea through pirates and privateers had their counterparts at home in Indian attacks and enemy inroads. The "Suffering Traders" lost heavily in 1754 at the outbreak of the French and Indian War and again in 1763 during the time of Pontiac's uprising. Indian trade goods were on occasion lost in transit due to the lack of good roads and of adequate means of transportation. Added to such hazards were attacks by "white" Indians like the "Black Boys" of Pennsylvania—frontiersmen who confiscated the guns, powder, scalping knives, and other English wares eager merchants dispatched to Fort Pitt and the Illinois country. Then there were misfortunes like those of "Little Levy" who had been captured by the French in 1758 and taken to Canada. He finally succeeded in returning to London, but it is not known whether, chastened by his experience, he remained in England, or came back once more to the colonies to meet their challenge and profit by their opportunities.

The uncertainties of nature were of necessity taken for granted by the speculating merchant. Far harder to bear were the arbitrary injustices inflicted by men in authority. Consider, for example, the case of Eleazar Levy, a Montreal merchant appointed agent in 1763 to handle the estate of the bankrupt Thomas Wilson. One of the officers of the English army of occupation wanted to be treated as a preferred creditor, and at the officer's request the Montreal military council, then in control, seized Levy's *personal* estate and sold enough of his goods to pay the officer's claims. The remainder of Levy's goods—*not* those of the bankrupt Wilson—were stored in the provost marshal's office where they were later destroyed in a fire. After the civil courts were established in Canada, Levy appealed to them for justice, carried on litigation for eleven years to recover the value of his personal estate, and made two trips to London to bring his grievances before the Privy Council. He won the case, but never collected a cent. The suit itself had cost him some £1,500.[13]

COMMUNICATIONS, AGENTS, MARKETS,
AND CURRENCY PROBLEMS

The twentieth century business mind must surely boggle at the difficulties besetting colonial merchants who, without adequate knowledge of local market conditions, had to ship their wares great distances. Carrying on trade without benefit of rapid communication or speedy transportation was an enormous handicap, for it rendered virtually impossible any effective guidance or control of far-off partners, captains, supercargoes, and agents.[14]

Collecting debts and apprehending thieves were particularly difficult and time-consuming. Da Costa of Charleston once spent seven months in Georgia chasing employees who had cheated him, while Samuel Jacobs of Quebec, who had sold goods to British officers during the French and Indian War, was faced with the problem of collection when a number of them sailed away, one as far as Barbados. Through an agent, Jacobs once had to track down a debtor all through England and into Ireland before catching up with him and collecting. Lopez sent his Jamaican-born son-in-law Abraham Pereira Mendes to represent him on that island. The shipments he was entrusted with were of vital importance to Lopez, but Mendes proved to be an impossible choice. Unreliable and incompetent, the young man spurned orders to return home to his deserted wife and seems also to have sabotaged the efforts of Benjamin Wright, the shrewd Yankee sea captain Lopez had appointed his successor. Even the incomparable Wright once forgot to insure a cargo.[15]

The business of a merchant was further complicated by the fact that it took so much time to ship goods from the supplier to the purchaser. The swiftest shipment of manufactured wares from London required four to six weeks. Facilities for dispatching wares were inferior, while scanty knowledge of market conditions often made it difficult for a merchant to determine what goods should be shipped to a specific market. Sending a cargo for which there would be no demand could be a very expensive error, as Nathan Simson discovered in 1722 when his onions would not sell at Port Royal, Jamaica, because a shipment of 1,000 barrels from other sources had preceded them there. In later years Henry Lloyd wanted to return a consignment of spermaceti candles to Rivera of Newport because they were a drug on the market in Boston. Such disappointments were common, and a sated market—an oversupply of slaves for example—was a decided economic hazard. Stagnation in trade, a vessel returning without freight, underselling, the rotting of perishable goods, the return of unsold goods from distant markets—all these involved the seller in losses.[16]

Distances inevitably made deceptions easier to perpetrate and costlier to bear. London merchant-agents often failed to inspect goods put up by the suppliers, so that unwanted substitutes were foisted on the luckless Americans who would have to make shift with what they were sent. Merchants, it is true, frequently did return goods to England because they could not use them, but such returns were expensive. Once Levy & Franks of Philadelphia, when presented with a bill drawn on them by a responsible Maryland client, discovered only through accident that it had been forged by the man who presented it. Or it was common enough for a merchant to receive a mortgage and later discover to his dismay that there were other creditors with prior judgments and liens.

When favors were sought, committees of the provincial assembly had to be wined and dined, and many a busy merchant had to chase around doing unremunerative favors for clients. In order to carry on his operations successfully, a merchant-shipper required accurate and speedy commercial information about markets and detailed credit data about clients. His chief sources were reports of returning ship captains and travelers, and intelligence derived from letters and newspapers, which might come late, contain misinformation, or be lost altogether. Often a merchant was in doubt as to what ports to select, what cargoes to send, and what prices to charge. It was not easy to get good bills of exchange without paying a heavy premium, and even after a merchant had honored a bill of exchange from a good client, he lacked any guarantee that he would be paid promptly or at all. The government was often dilatory about payments, and there was little the unhappy creditor could do about it.

Good customers had to be carried; one charged them interest of course, but the money outstanding was worth a great deal more to the merchant himself, who was always short of working capital. And in any event, how could one cope with prices that fluctuated twenty percent in one month? By May 1776, to cite a particularly staggering example, goods were up 400 to 500 percent.[17]

Few features of the colonial scene could have been more exasperating than the currency problems which were nearly always present. The eighteenth century had evolved no commercial banking system as the term is understood today; there was no good continental medium of exchange in the colonies, and currencies were seldom stable. In 1749 £1,100 in Massachusetts "old tenor" might be equal to £100 sterling, but one could not rely on that, since inflation forever disturbed and confused buyers and sellers alike. In 1764 Rhode Island paper "lawful money" was worth 23⅓ times as much as the colony's "old tenor," though lawful money was itself worth less than sterling. Even a hasty glance at almost any of Lopez' waste books or ledgers will demonstrate the complexities of exchange, for Lopez found it necessary to keep his accounts in a bewildering variety of currencies: New York money, Rhode Island old tenor and lawful money, Boston money, sterling, and Spanish specie.[18]

Paper money was common until 1764 when Parliament limited its use as legal tender, which infuriated the colonists for whom the end of the French and Indian War had spelled a depression. They wanted soft money, since a shortage of metallic coin was endemic then and later in every province. Samuel Jacobs, for instance, questioned in 1772 whether there were twenty dollars circulating cash in Cumberlandshire, Nova Scotia. Economic life was only further jumbled by the fact that foreign coins were in common use by merchants, while both hard and paper counterfeit money was so prevalent that during the Revolution, South Carolina issued paper bills with Hebrew letters scattered about them indiscriminately in order to confuse would-be counterfeiters.

One attempt to cope with some of the difficulties inherent in the contemporary economic scene was the Chamber of Commerce established by a group of New York merchants. Among its other functions, the new institution was to encourage arbitration among businessmen when differences arose to threaten their economic relations. The eleven merchants who were given the task in 1770 of obtaining a charter for the chamber included one Jew.[19]

CREDIT DIFFICULTIES

Securing adequate credit information about customers was on the whole a rather formidable problem for manufacturers, wholesalers, jobbers, and suppliers in general. This could prove hazardous, since in an undeveloped land like America, there were bound to be some customers who were very poor credit risks. New countries, frontier areas of cultural and economic life, have of course always sheltered a percentage of unprincipled men quick to flee from the more advanced and better policed areas of culture and business.

Actually, such people were rarer in the colonies than might have been expected and as a rule, if the client of a major supplier did not pay promptly, it was because he in turn had been unable to collect from the individuals to whom he sold at retail. For example, the correspondence of Meyer Josephson of Reading reflects his own problems of collection as well as his efforts to keep a London supplier from bringing drastic proceedings against him. Writing to the Gratzes in 1767 about his creditor, a Mr. Cooper, Josephson said: "I have to keep him out of money as long as I can, that is, at least for two years. I cannot help myself in any other way at present, because times are so bad, and I must make my payments to other merchants, as you gentlemen well know." The letterbook of Uriah Hendricks for 1758–1759 is full of complaints from his London family, who were among his suppliers there, because his remittances were so seldom prompt. Hendricks was slow in remitting because he himself found it difficult to collect from his customers. In all probability one of the reasons he placed heavy orders in London with Moses Franks was that this Anglo-American merchant, possessing large capital reserves, did not push Hendricks too strenuously.[20]

Conditions, in any case, were generally such in colonial America that most clients almost everywhere were slow to pay. Merchants in

North America were fortunate if their capital turned over once a year; more often they had to wait several years. One of Lopez' clients in Jamaica, where the Newporter held large outstanding debts, took seven years to discharge his obligations. When he had no choice, Lopez was willing to take payment in local produce for debts due him on the island. He and his partner Rivera had one customer at Barbados in debt to them separately and jointly for over £3,000 sterling. To collect this debt they commissioned as their agents two North Americans, Samuel Hart and Samuel Hart Jr., who were leaving for Barbados. Samuel Hart's tombstone on Barbados is mute evidence that he died there of the "putrid fever" in pursuit of his duty.[21]

During the last two years of the French and Indian War, the Canadian Jewish consortium of Gershon Levy & Company found itself in debt to Alexander MacKenzie and Samuel Jacobs. Though hard pressed by his own creditors, Jacobs agreed to wait. Imagine his dismay when the Levy furs finally arrived from the Upper Country and the firm proceeded to assign them to Jacobs' rival Isaac Levy. Jacobs lost no time in asking Governor James Murray to attach the beaver and other furs in payment for the debt due him and MacKenzie.

An interesting tradition tells us that Jacobs had arranged for the parish priest in St. Denis to help him collect debts by naming the delinquent customers after the Mass. That this was not necessarily a special courtesy accorded the Canadian merchant is clear from Jacobs' papers, which reveal that it was quite customary to make public announcements at or after church services. On one occasion the New York merchant Manuel Josephson offered all sorts of inducements to a Canadian debtor to get him to pay. The insolvent client was told that if he settled his accounts, Josephson would say nothing to other creditors, and what is more, would send the debtor more goods.[22]

Merchants in debt sometimes had difficulty in staying out of a debtors' jail, but large-scale suppliers as a rule were exceedingly patient, if only because merchants pressed too hard went into bankruptcy. It paid to be considerate and to hope for the best when one dealt with a competent and honorable man like Aaron Lopez.

Around the year 1767 this Newport shipper owed William Stead over £5,600, in 1768 he owed Cruger of Bristol over £11,000 sterling, and by 1775 he was indebted for twice that amount to Hayley & Hopkins, his London suppliers. Lopez may have used his credit with those three suppliers as capital to carry on a series of mercantile and industrial undertakings. The Newport merchant was something of a financial juggler, and when Cruger pressed him too hard for payment, Lopez threatened to transfer his patronage to others. One thing is certain—Lopez always managed to remit enough to maintain his credit in England. Cruger was paid off ultimately, although Lopez had found no means to settle his debts with Hayley & Hopkins by the time the Revolution broke out. Still, financial juggler though he was, Lopez appears to have been a model of honesty—by the standards of his own day.[23]

LITIGATION

Law Is a Bottomless Pit was the title John Arbuthnot gave a pamphlet in 1712, but a host of circumstances inherent in the very nature of business enterprise during the seventeenth and eighteenth centuries saw to it that the bottomless pit never lacked for visitors. Buying, selling, and storing, shipping and freighting, employing agents, extending credit—all these features of economic life made litigation inevitable and relatively frequent in colonial America. This was as true of Jews as it was of Gentiles, and the fact that the Jewish community was small and bound together by ties of kinship rarely precluded recourse to the courts when disputes arose between Jews in commercial matters. Indeed, the very smallness of the Jewish community bred rivalries in business and gave rise to social affronts, real or imagined, that made for bad blood, mutual recrimination, and inevitably expensive litigation. Brother sued brother, families contended over inheritances, and a widow even refused to pay for her husband's coffin.[24]

Only two or three weeks after the twenty-three landed in 1654, two of the refugees were suing one another, and some years later a New Amsterdam Jewish businessman sued a coreligionist in Maryland. Not long thereafter, when the little Dutch Jewish community on the Hudson had almost evaporated, two of its remaining members, Asser Levy and Rabba Couty, were embroiled in a lawsuit. Migrating from New York City, probably in the late 1680's, Simon Valentine van der Wilden carried on mercantile activities at Port Royal, Jamaica, until he was ruined by the famous earthquake of 1692. His business and his records both destroyed, he then sailed north to Charleston where he was successful and where he was sued for a substantial sum by Jacob Mears of Jamaica. Neither could produce any records, however, and Valentine claimed that Mears owed *him* money as the two took their differences to court! [25]

Beginning with the year 1700 when Joseph Bueno dragged his opponent Jacob Do Porto into court in New York and lost the suit, there is ample evidence throughout the eighteenth century that business differences led Jews to sue one another. The New York merchant Moses Levy may have been related by marriage to Nathan Simson, but that did not prevent bad blood from boiling up between the two, and their feud was to continue for at least a decade during the early years of the century. A generation later Solomon Hays publicly offered 100 pistoles—a large reward—for information about the "several scandalous Jews" who were hurting his "character and credit." That he himself was hardly lily-white is eloquently documented in the minutes of Shearith Israel Congregation, whose leaders resolved in 1755 that "for . . . the scandalous things he has reported of us about the city . . . he be no more look'd upon or deemed a member of our holy congregation." He was not readmitted to membership until some four years later, after paying a fine of £20 and promising to "deliver up a certain book in his possession wrote against our society." [26]

The decades of the 1760's and 1770's saw some of the Jews of New York and Canada resort to the press to charge one another with financial misconduct, and at Newport a bitter business quarrel raged for years between Isaac Elizer, Jacob Isaacks, and Issachar Polock, who all accused one another of bad faith, if not worse. Jacob Isaacks apparently had the last word in the press when he quoted from the forty-ninth chapter of Genesis, "Issachar is a strong ass." [27]

Notwithstanding the numerous actions Jews brought against their coreligionists, most of the surviving records deal with suits between Jews and Gentiles. Though this fact lacks any social significance beyond the recognition that Jews did most of their business with Gentiles, the litigation is historically valuable in that it enabled the courts to document the existence of early American Jews who might otherwise have remained unknown to us. In most of those cases the Jew appeared as a plaintiff, suing for the payment of debts, and one sometimes suspects that an action in court was almost a normal method of collecting money due. *Caveat venditor* (catch me if you can) seems to have been the taunt of many a customer, and one writer has pointed out that "the courts were a virtual collection agency." Jewish businessmen even brought suit to secure the payment of gambling debts. They were determined to "cash in" on what they had won at piquet, for the stakes were often high. As early indeed as the 1650's, Lumbrozo and Ferera of Maryland brought suit against customers for non-payment of debts, as did the Massachusetts firm of Gideon & Baruh (Barrow, Baruch) during the 1670's. In the course of the next century New York merchants were constantly to be found filing claims in their home province and in Connecticut. The case was much the same in neighboring New Jersey, where not only New Yorkers but Pennsylvania and Jersey Jews as well repeatedly turned to the courts to secure payment for goods they had sold. Between 1719 and 1752 Aaron Louzada of Bound Brook was a litigant in at least ninety cases, in most of them as plaintiff. The amounts in question concerned sums of anywhere from £5 to £117 in local currency. The inventory of the estate of Henry Benjamin Franks of Bridgetown and Mt. Holly, New Jersey, reveals that his shop goods amounted to £413, while the bonds, notes, and book debts due him came to £140. Many of those obligations undoubtedly had to be collected in the courts by his executors.[28]

In litigation, as in so much else, Aaron Lopez appears to have been quite exceptional, for this great merchant avoided the courts as he would the pestilence. What has been said of Lopez—that he was "singularly averse to controversy"—finds confirmation in a letter he addressed in 1770 to Nicholas Brown & Company. The Browns were seeking a reconciliation after having offended him, and Lopez declared to them in his typically formal and pompous style, "I value myself both by principle and inclination in averting, in the course of my little business, any altercations, even at the expence of ceding my own right." Lopez' pacific attitude was in sharp contrast to the view Meyer Josephson of Reading expressed four years earlier. Though himself struggling to stay out of the courts—and out of jail—for non-payment of his debts, Josephson inveighed bitterly against a client who owed him money: "Hope he may be kept in prison till lice eat him up!" [29]

Despite the frequency with which it was employed, recourse to the courts was not a simple matter. At best it was expensive; at worse, calamitous—and suits might be protracted for years. One of the Gomezes was still trying in 1753 to collect an obligation incurred twenty years earlier, while during the 1750's Jacob Isaacks of Newport was party to a suit touching on a debt contracted by his father in New York no later than 1743. Dragging on for years, the case was tried in several courts and was finally won in 1758, only after an appeal to the Privy Council in London. A substantial sum was at stake, but the expenses Isaacks had to bear must certainly have been very heavy. Isaacks seems, in any event, to have had a propensity for litigation—or misfortune—for he was involved in two other appeals to the Privy Council, and the high costs of these proceedings probably contributed to his insolvency in 1771–1772. One particularly hapless Jewish merchant, who had gone to Europe on business, discovered to his dismay that he had been sued in his absence and his creditors had secured a judgment for double interest and double costs. He had no choice but to go into the courts and show that his European sojourn had prevented him from answering the suit and that in any event he had already paid the largest part of the debt. [30]

There is one much protracted case which, better perhaps than any other, vividly reflects the problems and hazards confronting eighteenth century businessmen. During the year 1718 the London firm of Solomon de Medina Mossesson & Company was shipping a cargo of tobacco from Spanish Cuba in the *Victory*, a French vessel, when hostilities broke out between Spain and England. Seizing the *Victory* as a prize, the British man-of-war *Diamond* brought her and the cargo into New York harbor, where the courts speedily restored her to her owners. The captain of the *Diamond* appealed the verdict, however, and thus initiated a suit which was carried on for seventeen years. Part of the cargo, awaiting the court's disposition, had been deposited for safekeeping with two apparently reputable New York merchants who subsequently and fraudulently withheld part of it, and thus themselves became defendants. The pair made every effort to avoid surrendering the tobacco in their possession and induced a British naval officer to claim part of the cargo for the crown on the ground that it had originated with the Spanish foe. That maneuver also failed, and at the final moment the defendants fled. In the meantime the New York Jewish merchants representing the London Jewish plaintiffs had paid £290 in fees to their lawyer James Alexander, who was some years later to be John Peter Zenger's preliminary counsel. These £290 certainly did not exhaust the expenses attached to a case that was argued for so many years—a case in which, as the complete record shows, the attorneys and the plaintiff they represented encountered embezzlement, chicanery, and prejudice on the part of the courts.[31]

In view of the fate that might await a merchant in court, it is no wonder that other remedies recommended themselves to many a plaintiff. Awareness that litigation was costly, and that courts were occasionally corrupt, often persuaded Jewish merchants—and non-Jews too of course—to resort to arbitration. Statutes imposing arbitration on Jews in business matters, while found in the regulations of Sephardic synagogues in Amsterdam, London, Brazil, and Curaçao, appear to have been alien to congregations in colonial North America. Nonetheless, arbitration was not uncommon on these shores, and when both litigants were Jewish, they frequently selected Jewish arbitrators, although there seems to have been no fixed rule to this effect.[32]

DEPRESSIONS, FAILURES, AND BANKRUPTCIES

"The dismal science," as Carlyle dubbed economics, never seemed more dismal than in the wake of the constant wars fought in the Americas. Invariably, though wartime brought prosperity, the concomitant was postwar recession, for after a war was over commerce would decline, prices would fall, and local manufacturers would curtail production. There would be a surplus of farm products, unemployment, and general economic distress. Merchants would be ruined.

Business depressions disturbed every decade from 1750 to the Revolution, and to these periodic economic upheavals was added the political unrest that began after 1763 as the empire attempted to implement its new colonial system. The new revenue and taxing acts, the duties on imports, the serious effort to curtail smuggling, the political disturbances—all these factors made for further economic distress with which the merchant had somehow to cope if he could, and many could not. By 1774 many Americans had embarked on a policy of nonimportation, nonexportation, and nonconsumption. The English soon retaliated with countermeasures, and the merchants were in trouble.[33]

It is quite obvious from a study of the hazards that faced the business community that its problems were numerous and serious. No businessman found it easy to survive, and Pastor Henry M. Muhlenberg summed up with terse eloquence the difficulties against which storekeepers had to strive unceasingly:

Anyone who wishes to support himself and his family in these times by keeping a store or a shop, either in the country or in a town, must have the eyes of a falcon, the alertness of a rooster, the fluency of a Jew, the patience of a mule, capital to invest, etc. The profits are not remarkable, they undersell one another, it costs a great deal to keep a clerk, some of the goods will become old and lose their value, and the storekeeper may be robbed or defrauded if debtors run away or declare bankruptcy, etc. The common proverb declares that it requires no great art to become a merchant, but it does to remain one.

It is not surprising that many a businessman went down in the struggle, and the Jew was no exception, for a large number of the better-known Jewish businessmen at one time or another in their careers suffered bankruptcy or were forced to make settlements with their creditors. Just what the causes of failure were is not always or even often easy to determine, but there can be little doubt that the constant and recurring economic depressions were contributing causes, and misfortunes at sea probably took their toll, though most shippers were careful not to sail without maritime insurance. Were those who failed invariably men of incapacity? In view of the fact that some of them fell only to rise again, one is inclined to the opinion that not all bankrupts were incompetent.[34]

It may well be symptomatic of the colonial Jewish economic experience that Solomon Franco, the first known Jew in the North American colonies, came to the attention of historians because he appealed for aid. There is, in fact, hardly a decade in which we find no record of Jewish shopkeepers and merchants in the courts for bankruptcy and in jail for debt. By 1685 Ansell Samuel Levy, a relative of Asser Levy, was in prison for some economic reason, while early in the next century Isaac Naphtaly, a butcher, fled because he could not meet his obligations. The 1720's found the merchant-shipper Abraham Haim De Lucena insolvent and at the mercy of his creditors. Michael Asher had been imprisoned in Boston for debts by 1716, and Isaac Emanuel and Daniel Nunez, both of New Jersey, fled in the 1720's to escape imprisonment for the same reason. Emanuel took refuge in South Carolina, where Moses Solomon, a nephew of Jacob Franks, was jailed for liabilities incurred by the Carolinian firm of Levy & Solomons. The same year (1743) that Solomons of Charleston suffered arrest, Solomon Hart of New York ran away, leaving his wife and child with relatives. Hart's rich brother Moses had refused to come to his rescue and Abigail Franks, indignant at the wealthy Moses' unfraternal conduct, wrote to her son in England: "It's commonly said the rich man is God's steward. Moses Hart is a very saveing one whoe will lett a brother perish when such a triffle as £200 might make him happy." [35]

Two years later Solomon Hays was running away from the sheriff—and a £50 reward—but shortly thereafter contrived somehow to resolve his difficulties with his creditors. The year 1745, toward the end of King George's War, brought insolvency to the Newport firm of Nathan(s) & Abrahams. Isaac Navarro of New York (unlike most of his Jewish associates, he was always to remain a poor man) was locked up for debts in New York at the beginning of the French and Indian War. Moses Lopez of Newport was bankrupt and in jail by 1756, and it may well be that Rivera too was in distress at the time, since a family tradition holds that Rivera failed, but years later paid off all of his creditors.[36]

After the conquest of Quebec in 1759 the war boom collapsed, and a number of Jewish merchants either absconded, failed, or found it necessary to make settlements. Among the merchants who fled in 1760 was one named Israel Joseph; a man with the same name turned up during the Revolution in South Carolina, where he became a distinguished patriot. The ending of the French and Indian War and the Pontiac uprising which followed took another heavy toll of Jewish businessmen, and Jewish bankruptcies were to continue in the 1770's, reflecting the warning Hays & Polock addressed to the Providence Browns: "You must be very sencible that the late disunion and obstructions of trade are felt by every person in business." Jewish fur traders and merchants in New York City, Albany, and Montreal were hard hit, and Gershon Levy's Canadian consortium of sutlers, army suppliers, and fur men was forced into bankruptcy. Hayman Levy, the New York fur trader, appears to have been involved with the ill-fated consortium, although tradition has it that like Rivera, he too later paid off all his debts along with the accrued interest. The injuries the postwar economic decline imposed on Jewish businessmen were, however, not exceptional, for practically all businessmen suffered when war buying came to an end. An anonymous letter for the year 1762 in the Gratz-Joseph collection declared that bankruptcies were frequent among all kinds of dealers, except the principal traders. The scarcity of cash, continued the writer, required great circumspection in business and covered the countenance of most people in trade with looks full of care.[37]

In South Carolina, Isaac De Lyon and Joseph Tobias were in the custody of the provost marshal as insolvent debtors in 1767, and De Lyon was again—or still—bankrupt in New York during the 1770's. De Lyon was not alone, for during that same decade Isaac De Costa and Philip Jacobs of Charleston and Mordecai Sheftall of Savannah were all in trouble. In 1761 Sheftall had set up a trust in the form of a release to his wife, in order to protect her and the children, but found it necessary in 1770, as he veered toward insolvency, to sell some of the property that had been reserved for his wife and family.[38]

The exacerbation of the quarrels with England brought nothing but distress to many Jewish merchants. The wealthy Benjamin Levy of Philadelphia, for example, went down in 1768, and the following year found a Mr. Moses in the debtors' jail at Jamaica, Long Island. Moses was still there in 1770, although his imprisonment could not have been too onerous, for it did not prevent him from becoming the father of two boys.[39]

Establishing oneself in a small town was no guarantee of less competition or of easier economic survival, and Jews in the villages of New York Province fell victim to the times as speedily as those in the metropolis. Daniel Mendez da Castro, a shopkeeper in Lancaster, Pennsylvania, gave his Philadelphia creditors Levy & Franks a first mortgage on a Lancaster lot, but finally lost the lot, as well as a house on it, in order to satisfy a judgment of the Phila-delphia firm. Meyer Josephson of Reading, constantly struggling to satisfy his creditors, in a wry letter to one of the Gratzes requested the speedy return of his one coat in the hands of a tailor: "I have no other coat to wear and do not want to show poverty inside and out." In the small town of Easton one of the local Jews was in the debtors' jail by 1773; ten years later the town magnate, a Jew, was also insolvent.[40]

The Newport Jews had no better luck than their coreligionists in other American ports. Judah Israel, for example, had been a merchant at Newport in the 1730's, but was reduced by 1759 to the position of a beadle in the New York congregation, while Nathan Nathans and Israel Abrahams, very probably New Yorkers who had settled in Newport to operate a business partnership there, were insolvent about 1746. It was in 1763 after the Treaty of Paris, how-ever, that Newport's Jewish merchants began to experience a post-war depression in all of its severity. Myer Benjamin, one of the congregational employees, was bankrupt by 1764, and 1768 saw de-cline set in for substantial merchants like the Polocks and the Harts. During a nine-month period in 1771 and 1772, four of the best-known firms in Newport were forced to the wall: Isaac Elizer, Naphtali Hart & Company, Jacob Isaacks, and Hays & Polock.[41]

[787]

As late as 1768 Moses M. Hays, cocky and jocose, could write to his good friend Michael Gratz, with whom he was trading, "If you behave well, and do things well, I will make your fortune for you." But Hays was bankrupt by 1770, and the Gratzes survived. Hays's self-confidence notwithstanding, the Gratzes and other Jewish merchants were apparently wary of doing much business with his firm, Hays & Polock, for only three Jews, including the "rabbi" of Newport, were to be found among the sixty-five creditors who presented claims against the bankrupt company. Following the Revolution, however, Hays moved to Boston where he became a wealthy and prominent merchant and a leading Masonic figure. Elizer and Isaacks, who had both been merchants and shippers of substance and had failed in Newport around the same time as Hays, never recovered financially. In his later years, Elizer had to rely on charity while Isaacks dabbled in chemistry and tried to get a grant from Congress for his work in the distillation of seawater.[42]

Only Aaron Lopez never suffered bankruptcy. His commercial skill and the confidence he inspired in his creditors kept him from ever being too hard-pressed despite the huge debts he piled up. Yet after his death, it soon became obvious that his estate was insolvent. Had he survived, of course, he might have managed to extricate himself from his difficulties and even to have remained a very wealthy man. Over twenty years after Lopez' death, however, his estate was still in liquidation, and it is to be doubted that his creditors, including the Hayleys whom he still owed £11,000 sterling at the time of his death, ever received as much as a tenth of what was due them.[43]

Further study and research would reveal no doubt that many other Jewish merchants were crushed—though some only for a time —by the difficulties inherent in the colonial economy.

CHAPTER 42

SMUGGLING AND CRIMINALITY

SMUGGLING

Somehow, despite all the hazards which bedevilled colonial merchants and shippers, most of them managed to survive—and not only that, but many of them made a comfortable living, while some, if very few, even acquired substantial wealth. To what extent extralegal stratagems were responsible for this capacity to survive is an interesting question, and one wonders how dependent upon smuggling the successful conduct of business was.

It is well known that smuggling in exports and imports was quite characteristic of colonial trade during the eighteenth century and even earlier. The New Englanders certainly persisted in an extensive illegal import of sugar, molasses, and rum from the foreign—the non-British—West Indies where such staples were obtainable at far less expense than from the islands under English rule. Every effort was made to evade payment of the requisite duties, and the core of the navigation laws, the requirement that most imports and exports from and to Europe clear through English ports, was often flouted. Smuggling in tea, dry goods, and gunpowder, not only from the Dutch West Indies, but also from Holland herself, was something less than uncommon.[1]

There seem for the most part to have been no strong moral scruples about smuggling. Substantial merchants like the Browns, the Hancocks, and Lopez all smuggled, whenever the opportunity to do so safely presented itself. That such opportunities did not lack their share of governmental connivance is clear, for until about 1764, when a strict new imperial economic policy terminated the years of "salutary neglect," English officials had frequently ignored the illegal activities of the merchants. Bribery had been common enough for one historian to record that "a guinea being placed over one eye had considerable effect, while another guinea rendered them blind to what was going on"—even though economic historians today believe that most foreign trade was carried on in legitimate channels.[2]

In any case, whether smuggling was truly a large-scale "industry" or not, there is ample evidence that in matters of contraband and the like, Jewish merchants were at one with their Gentile counterparts; they smuggled when they could. As early as 1655 one of the pioneer Jewish merchants of New Amsterdam was accused of smuggling tobacco, and in 1686 two other New York Jews were fined for boarding a vessel before the master had reported its arrival to the authorities. After the turn of the century charges of bribery were brought against Joseph Bueno, a well-known New York merchant who, it appears, had enjoyed the connivance of the collector and receiver general of the province. In 1718 we find Abraham Haim De Lucena, merchant and amateur "rabbi," seeking the return of some of his wares seized in Pennsylvania for nonentry. De Lucena pleaded for relief because of "his poverty and numerous family." Even the papers of Nathan Simson, which are in general singularly free from any indication of smuggling on Simson's part, reveal that in 1719 he sent one of his London partners three pieces of embroidered silk in a barrel of cocoa! The silk cloth was valued at £21.[3]

Moral scruples were so slender where smuggling was concerned that it was but a step from illegal trading with England's traditional enemies, the French and the Spanish, to doing business with them during periods of open warfare. Not that trafficking with the enemy was a new problem for the British, since there is reason to believe that as early as King William's War in the late seventeenth century, the Schuylers, the Rensselaers, the Livingstons, the De Lanceys, and two Jewish freighters, Saul Brown and David Robles, had engaged in collusive trading with French Haiti. The classic period of this type of trading was, however, during the French and Indian War when, with French vessels powerless to run the English blockade, the French sugar islands were desperate for food. Under the guise of flags of truce carrying returning French prisoners, the Americans, with the active connivance of their colonial officers, carried on an extensive barter of provisions and English wares for French sugars, either directly with the enemy islands or through their "neutral" Dutch and Spanish neighbors. The Beekmans of New York and the Browns of Providence were heavily engaged in this traffic, and Uriah Hendricks of New York was also eager to cash in on the trade by doing business at Montecristi, Hispaniola, with the Spanish, who were in reality a bridgehead for the French in adjacent Haiti. Rhode Islanders were notorious for their participation in this traffic, and Jewish businessmen like Naphtali Hart & Company, along with the other merchants, sought their share of it, too.[4]

The numerous business papers of Aaron Lopez afford considerable evidence of his involvement in smuggling, and Lopez' son-in-law knew whereof he spoke when he wrote to the Newporter that "you was always a great shipper with the coasters." Although on rare occasions one of his captains—possibly without his permission—smuggled rum into England, Lopez' contrabandist activities were limited for the most part to bringing in molasses from the West Indies and wines from Europe. Dutch tea and bolts of duck picked up at Surinam would be tucked away cosily between barrels of molasses and introduced undeclared into Newport. The products of the islands were not always of foreign origin, and once, when Lopez imported a cargo of molasses from the British West Indies, he instructed his correspondent there to clear only two-thirds of the return load in order to save on duties at the cargo's Rhode Island destination—"provided you can do it with safety." When cousin John C. Lucena ordered a cargo of provisions and groceries from Lopez for father Lucena in Savannah, the son wrote, "Please to let as small a quantity of gallons of rum be mentioned in the clearance as possible." Captain Wright, Lopez' factor in Jamaica, never hesitated to scatter a few shillings judiciously about in order to save several pounds, and Lopez himself was always glad to warn other merchants "to be upon your gard" when the customhouse officers were in their neighborhood.[5]

Wines, which Lopez' ships had unloaded in Rhode Island at

"the back part" of Aquidneck Island or at some other lonely un-guarded spot on the coast, were smuggled by his men into New York and the Jerseys. The querulous, gossipy, and occasionally inaccurate Ezra Stiles confided to his diary in August 1772 that Lopez had an understanding with the customhouse officials, who showed him "all lenity and favor" and permitted him to smuggle almost with im-punity—and it is certainly true that Charles Dudley, the collector of customs, was one of Lopez' friends! In the same indignant entry, Stiles reported that Lopez, caught smuggling wine, would suffer the condemnation of his vessel and cargo, but that "favor and partiality" would enable him to buy them both back for "far less" than the duties involved. A more generous contemporary, discovering on the beach one of Lopez' casks of wine which had apparently been thrown overboard to escape the coastal patrol, wrote Lopez of his find and offered to return it to him: "I imagine that the sea, more merciful than the customhouse officers, hath spared one of them." The friend who winked thus at the return of contraband was none other than Samuel Ward, a former governor and chief justice of Rhode Island! [6]

Ward, however, was not nearly as wicked as Stiles might have thought when we consider that the British government itself was willing to wink at one aspect of the contraband trade. The govern-ment clearly had no qualms at all about encouraging, especially on the part of its Jewish subjects, the illicit—and lucrative—traffic with Spain's dependencies in the New World. No less a personage than Lord Chancellor Hardwicke openly alluded in Parliament to this form of smuggling as "the trade which gives life to the whole, a trade which I do not for very good reasons chuse to name, is chiefly carried on by the Jews, by means of the correspondence they have with their brethren in other parts of America, and without which no such trade could be carried on." [7]

CRIMINALITY

Meyer Josephson could brag in 1764 that no Jew had ever been jailed in Reading, and some eighty years later in an address delivered before the Redwood Library of Newport in 1847, United States

23. Barnard Gratz
Portrait by Charles Peale Polk
Owned by Mrs. S. F. Goodrich, Princeton, N. J.

24. Mrs. Aaron Lopez and her Son Joshua
Portrait by Gilbert Stuart
Courtesy, the Detroit Institute of Arts

Senator William Hunter could claim, "From a close examination of the records of our courts of justice, I find against no one of the Hebrew faith an indictment." Still, if we can accept Josephson's boast easily enough—after all there were never more than three or four Jewish families in Reading at any one time—we might ask how true Hunter's statement really was of Rhode Island and of the other colonies as well.[8]

The English jurist Sir William Blackstone defined crime as "an act committed or omitted in violation of a public law either forbidding or commanding it." Certainly smuggling was such an act, and ample evidence is available to show that Aaron Lopez, like other merchant-shippers, engaged in smuggling rather extensively. Of course Mr. Hunter, knowing the moral climate of prerevolutionary Rhode Island, might not have considered smuggling a crime but have seen it rather, with the eyes of an American patriot, as in reality a virtue during the decade before the Revolution. Lopez himself had once written that the duties imposed by the British were "unnatural" —hence wrong and properly evaded.[9]

If, however, Lopez cannot be regarded as a criminal, a like claim cannot be made for Abraham Peters, a Maryland Jew. Legally at least, Peters was a criminal, and he may have been one in fact as well as law, for many if not most Maryland indentured servants were originally criminals who had been sent over to work out their time. Peters was one of the indentured servants who had run away from their masters in Harford County, Maryland. The abuse to which they had been subjected was probably more than they could bear, and it is not without significance that the fugitives fled two days after the Battle of Lexington. The spirit of liberty, of revolt, was in the air, and certainly they too sensed it.[10]

Two years after his boast Meyer Josephson may have wished to revise his views of Jewish rectitude in Reading—but was Esther Josephson a criminal because she had been "ketcht with one Clarke of Reading Town" and turned out of her house by her irate husband? Or was a Mr. Levy of New Jersey to be deemed a criminal because he welcomed into his arms Deborah, the runaway wife of John Farnsworth? Deborah's husband had advertised that he was no longer responsible for her debts because "she likes the said Levy better than me and . . . intends to live with him as he will maintain her as a gentlewoman. I have waited on Mr. Levy respecting the affair, from whom I have received no other satisfaction than insolent language." [11]

Mr. Levy, Mrs. Farnsworth, and Mrs. Josephson were in all probability guilty of fornication or adultery, not uncommon "crimes" in colonial America. As early as 1656 one of the Sephardic settlers of New Amsterdam was accused of having illicit relations with his Negro slave, and Jacob Lucena, a New York peddler in Connecticut found guilty in 1670 of "lascivious dalience and wanton carriage and profers to severall women," was fined and ordered out of the colony. The General Treasurer's Accounts for Rhode Island in the 1680's report a number of men and women, black and white, fined for fornication, among them Abraham Campanall. We have seen elsewhere that the tradition of the Jewish peddler seducing the farmer's wife tended to become part of American folklore and appeared and reappeared as a "comical affair" in the eighteenth century American press.[12]

In general the record is quite clear: for the most part the crimes of Jews involved petty cheating in commerce. In 1659, for example, David the Jew was fined twenty shillings in Connecticut for going into homes, when the family heads were absent, and trading provisions with children. During the 1670's Asser Levy, too, was charged with business infractions, and before the end of the century, Mrs. Aaron Isaacs was arrested for selling liquor without a license, while Isaac Rodriguez Marques was charged with altering entries in the weighhouse books. Complaints of a more serious nature, however, appeared in early Georgia where one Jew was named among those accused of conspiring against the colony's trustees, two Jews were punished for "scandal" and "defamation," another was arrested for assault and battery, and still another was charged with mistreatment and nonsupport of an illegitimate child. Still, tough as some of these Georgia Jewish pioneers were, they seem on the whole to have been a decent lot, if one can believe the distinguished clergyman John Wesley, then in Savannah: "I began learning Spanish in order to converse with my Jewish parishioners, some of whom seem nearer the mind that was in Christ than many of those who call him Lord." [13]

Though American Jews in general were disinclined to violence, harsh words and exchanges of blows were not unknown. Less than two years after the first émigrés landed at New Amsterdam, two of the pioneer fathers were trading blows in Abraham De Lucena's store, and almost a century later Moses Gomez of New York was arrested for assaulting Solomon Hays.[14]

Bitter accusations made by one Jew against another need not always be taken too seriously. When, for instance, Levy Andrew Levy attacked Benjamin Nathan as a "worthless rascal," he probably meant that Nathan, who had just lost a member of his family, was not observing the prescribed days of mourning but was instead going to taverns, drinking to forget his troubles, and then staggering back to business. His failure to observe the amenities of mourning like a self-respecting Jew made him "a worthless rascal" in Levy's eyes. Nathan, who ran a branch store in Heidelberg for Levy's uncle Joseph Simon, also had a falling out with Simon, who threw him out of the business, attacked him physically and verbally—"Get out you dem sona vebitch"—and seized some of his possessions as security for unpaid debts. Nathan's Heidelberg compatriot Barnard Jacobs was no luckier, since he spent some time in the local or county jail for apparent mismanagement or misappropriation of lottery funds. Jacobs indignantly denied the charges against him, but the merits of the complaints involving these Pennsylvania Jewish businessmen are hard to judge from the meager sources now available—though none of them were "criminals" as the term is understood today.[15]

There is no question that individuals did cut corners. A New York merchant reproached his father for sending him watches enclosed in a letter in order to escape freight charges, and New York Jewish merchants were in several instances charged with and found guilty of selling demented and unsound slaves they had warranted as sound. The cases of Jews who appeared before the New York Mayor's Court deal for the most part with business matters, loans, debts, sharp business practices, and the like.[16]

More serious are the cases involving bankrupts. But here, too, there were variations in "criminality." Some "absconding" businessmen were without doubt honest unfortunates who fled penniless in order to escape imprisonment for debt, but Hays & Polock when bankrupt, so it was intimated by one informant, sold or turned over assets to a relative. The charge cannot be sustained, but it is a fact that facing inevitable bankruptcy, individuals sometimes attempted to protect their families by increasing and hiding assets, while others deliberately absconded with goods in order to make money. As a rule creditors were cognizant of those who had criminal intent—and certainly there were some who had such intent.

Levy Marks, a young man from the West Indies, called on the New York merchant Manuel Josephson and gave him a hard-luck story. Touched by the recital, Josephson offered him some £30 to £40 of goods on credit and—what was even more generous—at prime cost. Young Marks, however, disappeared with the goods, and a furious Josephson wrote to Michael Gratz, asking him to have the young villain arrested if he appeared in Philadelphia. Isaac Jacobs and Emanuel Lyon, who shipped goods to Lancaster and New York in 1772, seem to have been no more honorable; there is little doubt that they were trying to defraud their creditors. Large quantities of the stocks this pair had purchased from the suppliers were shipped to New York and sold there at auction by Jonas Phillips, but perhaps the latter failed to realize that the partners were bent on cheating the wholesalers. Myers Levy of Spottswood, New Jersey, fled in 1760 with £2,300 of unpaid supplies and left his creditors, who offered heavy rewards for his capture, convinced that he had set out to swindle them. Three other Jewish businessmen ran away to Holland to engage there in "new scenes of villainy," though the fact that one of them left some assets behind would imply that he was an honest bankrupt. Debtors who would not or could not pay were of course "villains." [17]

When a court finds someone guilty of wrongdoing, it brands him, justly or unjustly, as a malefactor or a criminal which, for the historian, is usually an adequate classification. It is not always so easy, however, to categorize people attacked and defamed in contemporary accounts. Simon Valentine, for example, was accused of working closely with a Carolina governor in a shabby financial deal that may have involved trading with the enemy during King William's War, and in 1766 Joseph De Palacios (Pallachio) of Mobile was accused of selling British army flour on behalf of the local commandant to the Spanish at New Orleans. In neither of these cases, however, was the accusation proven.[18]

There were, to be sure, thoroughly unsavory characters among the Jews—Dr. Lumbrozo of Maryland for instance. A man of some prominence, he was nonetheless always in trouble, and even if he is undeserving of the epithet criminal, he was certainly no delectable individual. Facing many accusations in his day—abortionism, attempted seduction, fornication, receiving stolen goods—he was very probably guilty of some if not all of them. Lumbrozo, it will be remembered, found his life in danger when charges of blasphemy were brought against him, and it is to his credit—and he needs some credit—that he stood up manfully, admitting that as a Jew he had denied the Trinity and the Resurrection.[19]

Years later, during the 1720's two Jews found themselves in serious trouble at New York. One of them, Isaac Jacobs, was indicted for robbery, then a capital offence, and was defended by James Alexander who was instrumental in getting him a pardon. Jacobs was fortunate enough to have powerful friends in Mordecai Gomez and Moses Levy, but Moses Susman was not so lucky. Susman was, in fact, the only Jew known to have suffered capital punishment in eighteenth century America, and his nemesis was the same Levy who had befriended Isaac Jacobs. A German immigrant who knew no English, Susman was accused in 1727 of stealing gold, silver, and some jewelry from Levy. Found guilty, he was sentenced to be "hanged by the neck till he be dead" in July 1727. The fact that New York's small and apprehensive Jewish community failed to intercede for him suggests that Susman must have been regarded as an incorrigible criminal. Possibly he had originally been a transport, one of the 50,000 convicts the British authorities shipped to the American colonies.[20]

Other immigrants of dubious antecedents were Henry Hart and "Isaac Jones" (né Solomon Isaac), both of whom were very probably transports. Hart, a tailor, was a servant in Maryland in the 1740's and had likely been sent over to serve out his time. Constantly in trouble, he was suspected of being a receiver of stolen goods and was found guilty in a bastardy case. Jones, a native of London, spoke

"High Dutch" (Yiddish?) and was known as a Jew. He served for seven years in Virginia or Maryland and then moved on to New York and Philadelphia. Caught stealing in both cities, he was flogged and imprisoned, and in 1775 was sought as a runaway servant by his New Jersey master who had "bought" him in December 1774.[21]

Criminality within their ranks was a source of anguish for the Jews; they were definitely and understandably sensitive when their status was concerned. As early as 1663 the first Jews in Restoration England had enacted a communal statute proscribing intercession for a known felon. Such a criminal was to be "punished by the law according to his crimes, as an example to others, and that thereby the stumbling-block in our midst be removed, and God's people be free." Nearly a century later two former Americans, Naphtali Franks and Naphtali Hart Myers, as leaders of London's Ashkenazic community, collaborated with the police in ridding England of Jewish evildoers through deportation, which was how England frequently solved her problems of criminality.[22]

Some of London's Jewish undesirables were shipped to America, and at least one of them is documented in the colonies in 1771. That year two travelers came to Lancaster from Philadelphia, where as suppliants they had received extraordinarily generous treatment from the Jews. One of these newcomers had been given a coat and a camisole by a clerk and had been presented with a hat, wig, shirt, and stockings by the butcher's son. Another Philadelphian had gone surety for a horse, the beadle's son had furnished some cash, and the local Jewish engraver had written a letter of introduction. Thus mounted and accoutered like gentlemen, the pair arrived in Lancaster where one of them claimed to be a cousin of the merchant and fur trader Levy Andrew Levy. The other professed himself a lawyer and may also have been a Jew, though he apparently passed himself off as a Gentile. The humble Philadelphians who showered them with kindness had of course been unaware that Levy's "cousin" was a transported criminal, and never suspected that together with his "lawyer" companion, he would proceed in Lancaster to rook Jew and Gentile alike with fine impartiality! The twosome took advantage of the Lancastrians to pass counterfeit money at one of the inns and then disappeared. They were never heard from again. A year later Meyer Josephson of Reading received a letter from a relative in England asking for help. The writer's son, a fifteen-year-old lad, had been found guilty of theft and was being transported to the colonies to be sold into servitude. The heartsick father asked Josephson to ransom his son so he would not have to live among Gentiles.[23]

Jewish apprehensions soared at Charleston in 1773 when a Sephardic Jew was convicted of receiving stolen money from a slave. The Negro was executed, and the Jew was flogged, fined heavily, and pelted with rotten eggs as he was locked in the pillory. Such criminals were especially feared and hated by the Jews because they gave their coreligionists a bad name. Nearly every Jew in eighteenth century America was, after all, very insecure. Struggling hard to acquire and maintain economic and political rights, the Jews believed, not without cause, that all they hoped for was jeopardized by fellow Jews who were criminals; the community was always apprehensive that it would be held responsible for the derelictions of individuals. This communal sensitivity undoubtedly helped to curb criminality, but it was not the only factor which kept the ranks of Jewish felons small.[24]

Presumably, a large percentage of the criminals in colonial America came from the class of indentured servants, a class whose members are estimated to have constituted one-third to one-half of the entire colonial population. There were, however, very few Jews among these bondsmen.

Most of America's Jews were urban dwellers, engaged in some form of business or commerce; few were in actual want. Colonial Jews suffered no egregious civil or economic disabilities; they were not packed into overcrowded ghettos, nor humiliated by narrow-minded civil servants and bureaucrats. Consequently, they bore no resentment against the society in which they lived and when faced with misfortune, had no need to commit acts of criminality in order to secure the means to sustain themselves. The local Jewish community was an ever-present source of help. Paupers, itinerants, and unsuccessful businessmen were supported out of synagogal funds;

help was forthcoming for food, fuel, and medical care; cash loans and credit were at hand. Survival required no resort to violence, and so Jews convicted of evildoing never formed more than a miniscule company.

CHAPTER 43

RELIGION AND FRIENDSHIP IN BUSINESS

RELIGION AND BUSINESS

There is every reason to believe that a well-organized counting-house, ample stocks of seasonal goods, constant help at home, and loyal and intelligent agents abroad made for mercantile success, but it would be worth determining also whether a North American Jewish merchant received more help, more consideration—in short, more business—from a fellow-Jew by virtue of the religious ties between them. Samuel Hayne, an imprisoned and embittered seventeenth century English civil servant, was convinced that the Jews of Holland, England, and the American colonies worked closely together, carrying on their trade "in a lump" and collaborating to undersell, cheat, smuggle, bribe, and defraud the English government of its just customs and duties. Hayne's animus against the Jews, whom he held responsible for his misfortunes, was absent from the feelings of Joseph Addison, one of the editors of the *Spectator*. Addison too supposed that Jews cooperated with each other, but he nursed no hatred for them and wrote in 1712 that the Jews

are, indeed, so disseminated through all of the trading parts of the world, that they are become the instruments by which the most distant nations converse with one another, and by which mankind are knit together in a general correspondence. They are like the pegs and nails in a great building, which, though they are but little valued in themselves, are absolutely necessary to keep the whole frame together.[1]

The American Jewish historian Max J. Kohler quoted Addison's remarks with approval and contended that the Jews were well-qualified to carry on business and, he implied, to succeed because of their dispersion, fellowship of blood and vernacular, knowledge of languages, similarity of customs, mutual confidence, and common interests. Kohler appealed also to Oscar S. Straus, the American diplomat, who had declared in a presidential address before the American Jewish Historical Society that the Spanish-Jewish refugees had turned to one another for help in the New World and "in the several countries wherein they settled soon established mercantile correspondence with one another."

How true, we must ask, was all this? To what—if any—extent were Jews "the instruments by which the most distant nations converse with one another"? One fact strikes us immediately, that despite the inclusion of the Mediterranean basin in the Diaspora of the Spanish and Portuguese Jews, North American Jews carried on very little business in that region. More business was conducted with Spain and Portugal, but even there, as we have already had occasion to note, the volume was in no sense appreciable. The population of Spain and Portugal included a number of crypto-Jews, but we are unable in most instances to determine whether the Iberian correspondents of North American Jewish merchants were crypto-Jews or "Old Christians" whose Jewish ancestry was nil. At least some of Lopez' Spanish and Portuguese agents were, judging from their names, of Anglo-Saxon Christian origin. Jews did business in the Spanish West Indies, too, particularly during the early eighteenth century, but again there is no way to determine whether their correspondents in the Spanish islands and on the Spanish Main were Marranos or not. On the other hand, though Holland sheltered a sizeable Jewish community, North American Jewry maintained no extensive trade with that country, since the proscriptions of the navigation and trade acts made it necessary, and also advantageous, for North American Jewish merchants to confine most of their trading within the limits of the British Empire.[2]

Still, within the areas in which American Jews did carry on business (England, the British North American colonies, and the West Indies), whether they were British, Dutch, French, or Spanish, did their correspondence favor, where possible, Jewish businessmen? Naturally, where there were no Jews, as in Newfoundland and Boston, they had no choice but to do business with Gentiles, but what did a merchant like Aaron Lopez do when he had a choice? Benjamin Lyon of Canada—and this is interesting—asked Lopez to employ Levy Solomons of Montreal as his correspondent there instead of Isaac Werden; he argued that Solomons was more competent. Although nothing was said, Lopez understood that Solomons was a Jew and Werden was a non-Jew. As far as we know, however, Lopez disregarded Lyon's appeal. Bristol, England, where Lopez worked through Henry Cruger Jr., had only a few Jews and no merchant big enough to do business with the ambitious Newporter, but in London, where Lopez could have turned to eminent Jewish suppliers, for reasons of his own he preferred to deal exclusively with Gentiles.[3]

Only a formal relationship emerges from an analysis of the correspondence between Jews who had enjoyed no prior personal friendship. The correspondence between Lopez and Aaron Isaacs of East Hampton is a case in point. Of course Lopez, a Portuguese Marrano who had risked his life to come to America, may have had little use for the German-born Isaacs who, in a land of religious freedom, had voluntarily divorced himself from his ancestral faith by intermarriage. Where, however, there was a mutual respect between Jewish correspondents, even if they had never met in person, a perceptible cordiality obtained. Jewish correspondents who knew and esteemed each other usually exchanged holiday greetings and manifested their common religious interests, though nowhere in any of the letters between Jews is there a bald statement: Do business with me because I am a Jew. Such an utterance was never explicit, but there is no question that some Jews did expect consideration from coreligionists by virtue of their common religious ties.[4]

The New York and Rhode Island Jews never hesitated to appeal to the Jews of England, the British and Dutch West Indies, and Dutch Surinam for aid in erecting American synagogues. Was this so because they did business with one another, or were such pleas grounded primarily in religion and kinship? Probably all these factors were involved, but there can be no doubt that the primary appeal was not mutual business advantage, but the inexorable tradition that Jews must help one another in matters religious.[5]

[803]

Were Christians disadvantaged as such in their commercial relations with Jews? This is difficult to believe when we consider that the mercantile world of the British Empire was so preponderantly Christian and Protestant. An unwillingness to accord Christian correspondents full courtesy could only have hobbled Jewish commercial enterprise in a mercantile structure which featured nothing less than a Protestant Christian Diaspora, where Christians could turn to their fellow-Christians if they so desired and it was to their mutual advantage.[6]

Even had the Jews of North America and the West Indies preferred to do business with one another, they would rarely have been able to act on such a preference. In North America particularly, Jews formed so small a group that they had no choice but to do business where and with whom they could—and most of their business was done with non-Jewish merchants and consumer-customers for the simple reason that Gentiles outnumbered Jews by 1,000 to 1. The profit motive was, of course, always all-compelling, and a check of the correspondence in the two volumes of the *Commerce of Rhode Island*—a selective list, to be sure—shows that the letters Aaron Lopez exchanged with non-Jews were roughly about five times as numerous as those with Jews. An examination of all the Lopez letters would demonstrate, undoubtedly, that the proportion of letters received from non-Jews was far larger than five to one. The entries in the Gomez ledger for the mid-eighteenth century suggest that about 67 percent of the firms and individuals with whom the Gomezes dealt were Gentile, which indicates actually a very high percentage of Jewish customers—about 33 percent. The Gomezes were specialists in the Curaçao trade, and most of their correspondents there were fellow-Sephardim.

In the final analysis it is probable that common religious ties did constitute a factor on which Jews reckoned, as did the Quakers when they engaged in business with one another. Wherever there was a Jew, there was a possibility of mutually advantageous trade. Jews were always closely bound to each other, particularly if they shared the same national and cultural origins, and the business letters of Jews who knew each other are replete with religious references. All things being equal where economic advantages were concerned, a Jew *was* prepared to give another Jew special consideration. Not that Jews were always willing to believe this! For example, the Harts, whose financial reverses in North America had led them to resettle in the Caribbean, wrote Lopez that they found the Christian merchants of Barbados and St. Eustatius readier than the Jews to help them: "There is no sincerity among those of our society, being jealous of each other." But the Harts had been soured by their misfortunes. More characteristic, in any case, was the reception Manuel Josephson and Samuel Judah tendered a total stranger, a Jew from the West Indies, whom they staked to substantial credits.[7]

FRIENDSHIP AND BUSINESS

Though religious ties between Jews did not necessarily contribute to successful dealings with one another, their significance should not be discounted. Acts of friendship among Jews, as well as the knowledge of the binding power of a shared religious heritage, certainly played their part in furthering and cementing relations between merchants. Jewish businessmen showed one another courtesies which required time, effort, and occasional expense. Minor business courtesies could be demanding and onerous, and it is not always easy to analyze the motives that prompted such courtesies. Expediency, the prospect of gain, was involved, though sometimes there were disinterested acts of friendship. One cannot always be sure whether acts of friendship preceded or followed business relations, but a certain fellowship, a guild spirit so to say, required even rivals to help one another at times. Such courtesies were expected; they were characteristic of that day.

Michael Asher of early eighteenth century Boston served as an agent for some of his New York Jewish suppliers and collected debts for them. Asher may, of course, have received a commission on the debts he collected, so that his kindness was not necessarily altruistic. Self-interest, however, was probably far from Lopez' mind, when the young daughter of a Jamaican merchant sent him limes on a venture. The parcel seems to have been small, most of the limes arrived rotten, and one of Lopez' hired hands had to go to the trouble of sorting the good from the bad. This was a nuisance consignment, but Lopez accepted it affably, even though he could hope at the most for a few shillings profit. Lopez himself received such courtesies. When one of his captains touched at Charleston, Da Costa & Farr met the vessel and gave the captain special sailing orders sent there from Newport. This was a courtesy—and a bother. Da Costa, writing business letters to Lopez on his own account, always lapsed into the Portuguese vernacular. The relationship between the two Sephardim was close. Yet when a young Ashkenazi, Esther Hart of Charleston, went to Newport for her health, she was introduced to Lopez not by Da Costa, but by Nathaniel Russell, Lopez' Charleston Gentile correspondent. Da Costa may not have been friendly with Joshua Hart, Esther's father, a local shopkeeper.[8]

Merchants could be and were very neighborly to one another without the prospect of immediate gain. Abraham I. Abrahams of New York was a petty businessman and a mohel or circumciser who had inducted a number of the Lopezes, children and Marrano adults, into Judaism. His affection for the Newport businessman led Abrahams to go out of his way to arrange a trade of Lopez' spermaceti candles for logwood in the hands of a New York Gentile. Mordecai M. Mordecai, a Russian Jewish businessman in Pennsylvania, helped Joseph Simon buy a slave and accorded courtesies also to Simon's in-laws, the Gratzes. In turn, because of his close relations with the Simon-Gratz clan, Mordecai did not hesitate to ask Michael Gratz to intercede for him with the rich Myer Hart of Easton when he was about to open a shop in Baltimore and wanted Hart to advance him credit or goods. Hart was Mordecai's brother-in-law, but in all likelihood there was bad blood between the two. Meyer Josephson, a customer and good friend of the Gratzes, sent them a haunch of venison as a gift from Reading, and from Falckner's Swamp came a kosher turkey from Aryeh Loew, the son of Moses London. Barnard Gratz enlisted the aid of the influential David Franks, his former employer, when he proposed to open a maritime insurance agency in London and wished to secure the patronage of the New York De Lanceys, with whom the Frankses were intermarried.[9]

Merchants forwarded letters for one another and helped trace fugitive debtors. Hyam Myers of New York and Canada was a friend of Samuel Jacobs of Canada. Out of friendship for Myers, Jacobs stored some goods destined for Aaron Hart and sent Hart a courier to inform him that there was a shipment awaiting his orders in Jacobs' warehouse. Jacobs did all this despite the fact that he had little love for Hart.[10]

Merchants acted as executors of estates for their friends and acquaintances and forwarded useful bits of information to their colleagues. When, for instance, Philip Minis was in the West Indies, he chanced to meet Lopez' problem son-in-law and immediately sat down to write the Newport shipper that he had found the young man "in a very bad state of health." This was not extraordinary, for Jews would rarely hold themselves aloof from their fellow-Jews—or from their difficulties. Early in Jonas Phillips' career he asked Moses M. Hays to put in a good word for him with a Gentile supplier. The request to Hays ended with the pious hope: "We pray that the Almighty may reward your children for your intended goodness to a poor but honest family." When Phillips got into some sort of trouble, his former employer Moses Lindo rallied to his support with a deposition: "This deponent further declares that he beli[e]ves the said Jonas trustworthy even of gold untold." [11]

Friendship between Jewish businessmen was cultivated through visits, home hospitality, friendly notes, the exchange of holiday greetings, and the sending of gifts. Letters which tradesmen sent one another frequently contained a delightful admixture of personal and business concerns, as when Lopez' friend Daniel Torres sent him from Providence an intimate letter in Portuguese: "And how is Moses Lopez, your brother; I am sorry he is not well. I have had an earache since the second day of Rosh ha-Shanah; and how shall I send the three barrels of cocoa?" Writing to Da Costa, Aaron Lopez expressed the hope that his (Lopez') recently deceased brother Moses might enjoy eternal felicity, and then proceeded to offer Da Costa some choice candles. Or Lopez might send a salmon to Joshua Hart of Charleston, and in season receive some oranges or new potatoes. In short, the American Jewish businessman felt, with Ecclesiasticus, that he who finds a faithful friend finds a treasure.[12]

How did Jewish merchants treat the non-Jews with whom they

did business? Did they show non-Jews the same courtesies they extended to Jews? In fact, there is ample evidence that Jews were punctilious in the acts of friendship they offered their Gentile business associates. Lopez, for example, served as a rating agency for his Bristol supplier Henry Cruger Jr., and took pains to warn the Browns of Providence that the customs officers were prying about in search of law violations. Sarah Lopez, Aaron Lopez' wife, and Ann Pollok, the wife of a distinguished North Carolina planter who corresponded with Lopez, were good friends, and Sarah wrote to Ann frequently, sent her gifts, and in all probability, welcomed Ann as a house guest on her visits to Newport.

When the French and Indian War approached its end, Moses Franks of London wrote to discuss the situation with his client James Beekman, for peace invariably brought a sharp decline in the price of goods. On another occasion Franks went out of his way to have some silver pieces manufactured for Beekman, and hearing that some absconding Jewish debtors had fled to Europe, did not hesitate to ferret them out for his New York Gentile clients.[13]

A Lopez ship bound for Bristol might well carry a box of apples and cranberries for Cruger—and this at a time when the Newport merchant had already discharged much of his indebtedness to his Bristol correspondent. When Cruger signed himself "Your affectionate humble servant" in a letter to Lopez, we have no reason to doubt the sincerity of his sentiments.[14]

CHAPTER 44

SUCCESS AND WEALTH

SUCCESS

Multiple as the hazards of doing business were in the colonial period, they by no means precluded the possibility of success, for no merchant-shipper found himself confronted at one time or on one voyage by all the perils described above, although one may be sure that some shippers thought so. Poor, harassed Henry Cruger, for example, once confided to Lopez: "Good luck seems the lot of some people. I never was of the party. Every year and almost every other connection I make produces something unpropitious." Still, even Cruger might have admitted that while a bad voyage or two could almost break a man, a few good voyages or a few good years could insure success. And if it be asked, what is success, the answer is, a comfortable living. The difficulties of colonial commerce notwithstanding, it must be borne in mind that generally even those merchants who were insolvent and bankrupt made a living, often a comfortable living, as they began their ascent once more in the world of trade. They fell only to rise again; very few were permanently impoverished, and most of them always remained part of the solid middle class. With certain notable exceptions, the names of the bankrupts are not to be found on the charity rolls of the synagogue. Isaac Elizer of Newport and Eleazar Levy of Canada and New York do seem to have been permanent casualties; yet theirs was not a typical fate. The Revolution, it is true, crushed many of the Jewish businessmen who were Loyalists, but often that was because they had left the country. Equally true is the fact that Jewish merchants who were Whigs suffered heavily, for with few exceptions the war made them refugees compelled to abandon their property and businesses as they fled from the British-occupied tidewater towns.[1]

What made for Jewish business "success"? Some Gentiles ascribed it to a magical faculty they believed Jews possessed—an inscrutable quality of Jewish "fitness" for the commercial life. What impressed Gentiles was the high degree of visibility which belonged to the successful Jewish businessmen on Front Street. Of course, there were always some Jews who were patently successful, but what an observer might not have seen so clearly was that they were not always the same Jews. The wheel of fortune was constantly turning.

Chaplain John Sharpe said in the early eighteenth century that the Jews had learning and intelligence; they were "ingenious men." And it was true—they were nearly all literate to some degree. Customers believed that they could do better at the Jew's store. As Gerard G. Beekman wrote to a Rhode Island Channing: "There is no such thing as perswaiding the shop keeper that yours is better, and cost more, but think Mr. Levey's as good as yours." For that same Beekman, "Jew" was a term descriptive of indefatigable, persistent, dogged activity which inevitably and ineluctably brought success in its wake.[2]

Gentile concepts of the Jew were compounded in part of myth and reality, but how much truth was there in them? What was myth, what was reality? Jews *were* for the most part reared in commerce; the ways of business, hammered into them from a very early age, became almost second nature to them. They understood in detail the techniques and intricacies of business, and they were mobile and competitive. Frequently, too, they had relatives willing to give them a helping hand, and they could always turn to the local Jewish community for advice and help. The eighteenth century Jew had a compulsion to improve himself, and the compulsion became even more driving in North America where he realized his hopes were not idle dreams. The law of this land actually made it possible for him to succeed, if success was in him. The Jew's need to better himself economically, and through his wealth to rise socially and to reach out for political privileges, made him willing to work, to labor, to slave at his task, in order to achieve success. His industry was only another facet of the restless, tireless energy his checkered history had developed in him. On the whole he was sober, thrifty, and trustworthy, not disdaining, for instance, to augment the family income by renting rooms out, as did the Israels and the Hayses of New York when they made living quarters available in their homes to a fencing and dancing master. The Jewish businessman was not reckless; he was speculative when the chances he took looked like an excellent gamble, but he rarely entered into a commercial adventure of small or vast proportions unless he felt reasonably certain it would "answer." [3]

Thinking of a younger brother who was a prospective immigrant to America, Barnard Gratz laid down a formula for success in 1758: "honesty, industry, and good nature, and no pride." It may seem curious that nothing was said about intelligence and ability, but Barnard took that for granted. James Lucena of Savannah, watching the accomplishments of his cousin Aaron Lopez, developed his own formula; he attributed Lopez' success to the Newporter's financial "credit," his "reputation," and his "plentifulness"—Lopez' ample supplies of goods—all of which he hoped would bring Lopez "some rest and satisfaction." Lucena was not certain that success was to be found in Rhode Island, "but I know that you are the proper man, to find it even in the most inappropriate place." Lopez himself, commiserating with the bankrupt Hayman Levy, consoled the unfortunate man with the thought that his industry and experience in trade would again carry him to the top. Barnard Gratz, Lucena, and Lopez were at one with the Gentile Beekman in agreeing that assiduity—"indefatigable industry," as Lopez put it—was indeed characteristic of the successful Jewish merchant.[4]

"Indefatigable industry" was certainly exemplified in the career of Levi Sheftall of Savannah. Even as a child of twelve Levi was determined to succeed in the world of business. Borrowing some money from his father, he began to dress deerskins and finally cleared five shillings. It was hard, disagreeable work, but he kept at it and after two years had made £20 sterling. Taking the advice of Captain John Milledge of the Georgia Rangers, Sheftall—then about eighteen years of age—finally entered into the butcher business with a German Christian partner. In order to acquire capital, he saved every cent he made, never spending a shilling on himself except for the barest necessities, literally working day and night, and reducing his sleep to an absolute minimum. In the first year of his partnership he saved £150, working with a slave—and like a slave. By the early 1760's Levi owned a house, a lot, and six or eight Negroes, and could boast that in a period of six years he had never spent a penny on himself and had not tasted his first drink till he was twenty. Then he turned to another business, and the £1,500 he had saved disappeared. In 1768, after a couple of unhappy love affairs, he married and soon lost his second fortune—through no fault of his own, for he had forfeited it very likely by signing notes for the family or close friends. Once more he addressed himself to making money. He continued in the butcher business, opened a tanyard, acquired a wharf, a plantation, and forty-four slaves—all this in four years. Then came the Revolution and once more Levi lost everything, a fortune he valued at more than £10,000. He was then about thirty-five years of age.[5]

Another element that made for the success of the Jewish merchant—and obviously this was not typically Jewish—was luck. Lopez' luck ran out in 1775 when the troubles between England and America became acute, and his huge whaling expedition to the Falklands failed, leaving him without the means to recoup his losses. One had to be favored by the accident of circumstances: good weather, good agents, good markets, good clients. A good client was one who not only could but would pay—promptly.

Did integrity play an important part in a merchant's success? Probably it did, though this is of course a presumption difficult to prove. One can assert on the other hand, however, that the absence of integrity did not help a merchant. For example, one of the New York Harts was not necessarily a dishonorable merchant, but he was "poor pay," and Gerard G. Beekman would not accept his paper—whereas Jacob Henry, quite without means, was given thousands of pounds credit by London Gentile suppliers because of his reputation for honesty. There is an early tradition dating from the 1820's that the insolvent Jacob R. Rivera, a man "very much respected for his integrity," was unable to "remain easy until he paid all his former creditors the utmost farthing." Another, somewhat later tradition—it dates from 1838—adds to this story the folkloristic embellishment that Rivera gave a party, invited his creditors, and placed under the plate of each the exact sum due, with the exact amount of interest calculated down to the last day.[6]

Integrity would seem to have been Aaron Lopez' hallmark. Ezra Stiles appears to have taken delight in reporting defamatory gossip about Lopez, but when he recorded in his diary the Newport merchant's death, he paid him this tribute: Lopez, he wrote, had been "for honor and extent of commerce probably surpassed by no merchant in America." But mayhap one should turn to his creditors for the measure of a man. After carrying Lopez for many years—and for huge amounts—his two largest creditors were still able to address him in terms of the highest praise. Cruger of Bristol wrote to Lopez in 1773, "I long for an amicable and an affectionate shake by the hand of a gentleman for whom I have conceived the warmest regard." Two years later Hayley & Hopkins of London congratulated Lopez for "that integrity of which we have seen many instances in the course of our correspondence and [which] does you great honor." A generation after the death of Jacob R. Rivera and Aaron Lopez, a man who signed himself "A Christian" would write in a Newport newspaper: "Reflecting on the excellent character and benevolent conduct of these worthy gentlemen of the Hebrew nation, may we not be allowed to use the words of that Divine Jew, who said to his followers, 'Go and do so likewise.' " [7]

The belief on the part of his customers and correspondents that a merchant was honest and responsible certainly ranked as an important element in his success. Jews distinguished for their integrity were not unconscious of the esteem in which they were held, and that awareness could not but help mould their conduct in the future.

As important as honesty—or a reputation for honesty—in a successful career was a capacity for enterprise. It was a sine qua non which involved versatility, daring, courage, imagination, innovation, energy, and a talent for speculation. This quality had become evident among Jewish businessmen almost immediately on their settlement in mid-seventeenth century America. There had always been a number of enterprising Jews since the very earliest days, so that New

Sweden on the Delaware had hardly been conquered by the Dutch when the Jews, not yet fully tolerated by Stuyvesant in New Amsterdam, asked and ultimately secured permission to trade in that area and to exploit its commercial possibilities. In 1700 two or three Jews in New York City evinced a sense of enterprise by lending the governor money to pay his troops at a time which found most of the merchants sabotaging his administration. In 1771 a Rhode Island Jew named Levi patented a specially designed ship to export lumber to England—a raft-type vessel which might be expected to carry 1,200 tons of lumber in one shipment. Three years later another Rhode Islander, Aaron Lopez, encouraged the breeding of mules for the West Indian market and offered what was in effect a bounty for them. Lopez had realized that it was cheaper to raise mules in Rhode Island than, as hitherto, to import them from the Barbary Coast via Gibraltar.[8]

The spirit of enterprise was again expressed, if in a modest way, when Hyam Myers organized a "Wild West" show. Like many of his fellow merchants in the Canadian fur trade, Myers had suffered reverses during the French and Indian War and presumably in the Indian uprising that followed it. To recoup his fortunes, he had his friend Sampson Simson intercede with Sir William Johnson for formal permission to exhibit some Mohawks in Europe. Myers sailed with the Indians before the proper certificate was forthcoming from the Indian Commissioner, and had already begun to parade them in Holland and in the taverns of London when the Lords of Trade urged Lieutenant-Governor Cadwallader Colden in New York to have Johnson put an end to the undertaking. From all indications Myers made no money on his grand European tour, for he ended up owing the Indians money—or refusing to pay them. Then, as now, there was "no business like show business"! [9]

Enterprise showed itself in other forms as well. In 1773 when the first transallegheny colony, the Vandalia grant, was in the process of preparation, some 400 Indians from seven different tribes gathered in the Pittsburgh area for the great occasion. When, however, the expected inauguration failed to materialize and the assembled Indians were denied provisions and presents, difficulties with them were feared. In that crisis, George Groghan was able to turn to

Simon & Campbell and to secure from them on credit the necessary supplies with which to pacify the Indians.[10]

A less spectacular example of enterprise is afforded by the Canadian Aaron Hart who, ensconced in the town of Three Rivers, is said to have been the first merchant there to buy goods directly from Europe. Then there was Sampson Simson's father Joseph who in 1755 pointed out to the New York City Council how dangerous it was for the city to tolerate the scattering about of highly inflammable naval stores like pitch, tar, and turpentine. Appealing to them for the right to build a storehouse in a remote place, he petitioned the city fathers for a monopoly on such storage, which they rejected. The venturesome spirit of American Jewish businessmen was again in evidence when they interested themselves in the manufacture of potash and of spermaceti candles. Jews were, as we have noted, among those pioneers who addressed themselves seriously to those phases of colonial industry. Myer Hart, the first merchant in Easton and one of its founders, demonstrated a similar spirit when he undertook to ship wheat from the backcountry down the Delaware to Philadelphia, while Hayman Levy was almost modern in anticipating some of the advertising lures of the twentieth century merchant. In those pre-parcel-post days, he offered to send goods free of all charges as far as Albany to prospective customers fighting with the army on the New York frontier. Levy made the bait even more appetizing by declaring his willingness to forego any commission in filling their orders for goods which he himself did not handle. What could have been more enterprising in the year 1757? [11]

Naphtali Hart Jr. announced that he would sell as *low* as anyone in Newport or Providence. That was in the *Newport Mercury* of June 1, 1767. The following week the same newspaper carried a notice of Issachar Polock that he would sell at a *lower* price than anyone else. Such advertisements show how eager and industrious Jewish merchants were, although this is not to imply that Gentile businessmen were their inferiors in the aggressive pursuit of business.[12]

The correspondence of Lopez with the Browns reflects his very polite, but nonetheless vigorous and constant appeal for patronage. When he sent some wine bowls to Moses Brown of Providence, he suggested that Brown return them without ceremony if he found them unsuitable. And turning to Nicholas Brown & Company, Lopez claimed his goods were as cheap as any on the continent. In another note, he informed his Providence friends that a ship of his had come in with goods from England and they should come down and see what he had to offer. The Lopez account books testify further to the Newport merchant's venturesomeness. The accounts are full of memoranda indicating that Lopez encouraged men to take home shoes, stockings, and mitts on approval to their wives—and as frequently the memoranda report that the goods were returned. In any case, every courtesy was shown the customer, even though the sale was relatively inconsequential. Enterprise of a higher order was evident, of course, in Lopez' daring decision to embark with his associates on their huge and ill-fated whaling expedition to the Falklands. The Newport shipper was, however, not to be crushed by the weight of his bold mercantile undertakings. Always venturing, always moving and trying to better his position, he embodied a genuine versatility which, for all its daring, never tempted him to wanton recklessness.[13]

The Gratzes were fully conscious of the persuasive powers of a proper potation. One Gratz account book contains entries for rum, limes, and the like, expended on a party of gentlemen from New York. The enterprising Joseph Simon was not to be outdone, and through the good offices of George Croghan, sent samples of his silver work for the Indian trade to Sir William Johnson, superintendent of Indian affairs.

The Philadelphia-Lancaster group of Jewish merchants and their Christian associates cherished the ambitious dream of dominating trade not only at the forks of the Ohio, but farther down the river to the Mississippi as well. Those Jews—Franks, Simon, Levy A. Levy, and the Gratz brothers—dreamed of controlling both the Ohio River and Mississippi River trade, of competing for the transmississippi business, and of tapping the Canada-bound traffic as it moved north and east up the Wabash and Illinois Rivers. Sending their packhorse trains across the mountains, they fully hoped to dominate the western trade from the vantage point of the Ohio-Mississippi River triangle, to control mercantile sales, to build new towns and colonies, and to populate the vast territory between the Alleghenies and the

Mississippi. The Philadelphia firm of Baynton, Wharton & Morgan had had such a vision and had set out to implement it before the Philadelphia-Lancaster Jewish entrepreneurs, but the Philadelphia Gentile firm's failure did not discourage the Jewish group from attempting to carry on the design.[14]

Doing business in the colonial transallegheny West required more than a modicum of both physical and moral courage. The Canadian Jewish fur traders who reached out to the foothills of the Rockies for furs had to be prepared to experience all the rigors of a brutal Indian captivity. Houtelaas, a Gentile partner in the Jewish firm of Solomon & Chapman, was "killed last autum [1771] by a Chippewa Indian." Houtelaas "was much given to liquor," but most Jewish fur traders stayed (reasonably) sober—and stayed alive. There were plenty of Indians about, and also rude, truculent frontiersmen ready to take the law into their own hands. The Jewish sutlers, fur traders, and petty merchants, going about their business from Michilimackinac in the Upper Country to Frederica, Georgia, on the border of Spanish Florida, could not be unconscious of the physical dangers that lay in wait, but they seem to have been undeterred by such threats. The letters of those Jewish businessmen, it is interesting to note, never mentioned weapons, except in the invoices.[15]

Certainly there were special circumstances which helped some individuals to achieve and maintain their success. Luis Gomez, for example, was materially aided in all probability by his several sons associated with him in business. This was equally true of Jacob Franks and his sons. Aaron Lopez certainly benefited from his close relationship to Jacob R. Rivera, whose daughter he married after the death of his first wife. But, special circumstances notwithstanding, in the final analysis the factor that was probably most important in making for success was ability. Isaac Seixas could claim excellent family connections, which he further improved by marrying into the Levy-Franks clan, but he never made anything of himself financially or commercially. In matters of business he was simply not able. There were Jewish shopkeepers whose lack of ability accounted for their failure to rise to the status of merchants; they suffered constant financial distress, and on occasion their ineptitude led to imprisonment in the debtors' jail.

[817]

The truly able man took advantage of circumstances, of the help he had, of the opportunities that presented themselves, and he made the most of them. Men of capacity knew the sources of production and the consumers' markets; they understood bookkeeping; they were skillful in the use of currencies, and adept in the intricacies of securing and using bills of exchange. Above all, they knew how to manipulate credit, to extend it if necessary almost to the breaking point, and yet always to have ample credit in reserve for a crisis or for a new opportunity. They were clever and versatile, and alert enough to survive in the highly competitive business world of New England and the Middle-Atlantic provinces.[16]

An ability to develop "decent human relations" was often as important as an ability in credit and finance. Politeness, charm, affability, and considerateness are in large part cultivated—they are not necessarily innate—and they form a vital part of that larger ability without which success is rarely achieved. Aaron Lopez displayed these qualities to a high degree, but seems by instinct and nature to have been a kind and considerate person, even in his dealings with an insolvent debtor. A Jamaican Jewish merchant once wrote to the Newport shipper: "Your politeness, good nature, and benevolence cannot [but] help to gain you the esteem of every person. They have captivated my heart, together with that of every gentleman of your acquaintance." And after Lopez' death, Ezra Stiles said of him, "He did business with the greatest ease and clearness; always carried about him a sweetness of behavior, a calm urbanity, an agreeable and unaffected politeness of manners." The human sympathies of which he was capable were responsible to no small extent for the fact that Lopez was esteemed by his contemporaries as a very successful businessman. Two centuries later, of course, the advantage of hindsight may move historians to question the success, and even the ability and judgment, of the great merchant-shipper whose sudden death left his feeble successors in charge of a hopelessly involved and insolvent commercial empire.[17]

Lopez' older contemporary, the Gentile Thomas Hancock of Boston, displayed other qualities. Hancock probably achieved his considerable success by attention to small ventures. He engaged in many different types of business, chose his agents and partners care-

fully, was vigorous and able, and proved himself a skillful adminis-
trator. In the main Lopez had specialized in a limited number of
ventures, had avoided partnerships, and though engaging in substantial undertakings, had shown himself generally more cautious
than Hancock. Altogether unlike Hancock, he liked people and was
ready to help them. His interests went beyond his own home and
his own countinghouse. Hancock once wrote to a client, "As to the
proffet you git on your goods, its your look out, not mine. I expect
my money of you when its due, according to agreement." Lopez
would never have written such a letter to a customer; it was not
within him to do so. In an age when selfish interest and frequently
unbridled ruthlessness were characteristic of businessmen, Lopez
stood out for his gentility and humanity. In 1662, a hundred and
twenty years before Lopez was drowned, the following epitaph graced
the last remains of a Hartford, Connecticut, merchant. It could with
equal propriety have been inscribed on Lopez' tombstone:

> Who can deny to poore he was reliefe.
> To marchantes as a patterne he might stand,
> Advent'ring dangers new by sea and land.[18]

WEALTH

Success for the colonial Jewish businessman can be defined only
in terms of his wealth. The typical well-to-do Jew was a merchant
engaged in trade, commerce, and shipping. Medieval disabilities in
Europe had limited the Jew's opportunity to commercial fields.
Even on his arrival in British North America, the continuing political disabilities to which he was subjected, coupled with his past
training and with a positive desire for business activity on his part,
made it all but inevitable that the Jew would remain a merchandiser.
He owned property, but with few exceptions had no interest in
land speculation on a grand scale, and the few Jews who did undertake large purchases of land apparently derived no substantial revenue
from that type of business, certainly not in the prerevolutionary
period. Merchants who were prosperous owned their own homes,

occasionally some farm or uncultivated lands, perhaps some urban real estate, and a slave or a bond servant. They might have one or more shops, some cash in the till, a few notes due, and a considerable amount of money outstanding in book debts. Taxes were small, and though Jews seem to have been thrifty and to have saved where they could, they lived and dressed well and gave their children the advantages that came with education.

In estimating the wealth of colonial Jewish merchants, it must be constantly borne in mind that a substantial number of them had come to America during the French and Indian War. Typically, therefore, merchants enjoyed a few good years, 1755 to 1758, but between 1759 and the Revolution the situation was far different. These prerevolutionary years were plagued with economic upheavals and political distress; most of them were lean years, and merchants who made money found it hard to hold onto. In any case, even the wealthiest Jews in the land seem never to have achieved the success of a Thomas Hancock of Boston, an Oliver De Lancey of New York, or a Governor James Wright of Georgia. A man like Lopez was no one's inferior in ambition or vision, but he never rose to the heights of Hancock, who reputedly left an estate of close to £70,000, or De Lancey, whose estate was worth £100,000, or Governor Wright, who owned over 500 slaves, twelve plantations, and some 19,000 acres of land.[19]

THE POOR

Jews, however, were rarely to be found in the ranks of the impoverished. With the exception of a few indentured servants and a very modest number of the "poor and struggling," colonial Jews were securely ensconced in the middle class. On the whole they were to be divided into three economic groups in an ascending scale, the "fairly comfortable," the moderately wealthy, and the wealthy.

The earliest American Jews were in straitened circumstances. It took time for the New York community to get on its feet financially. Though the congregation was established at New York (or New Amsterdam, as the colony was called at the time) about 1654 and reestablished in the 1670's or 1680's, the Jews were unable to build a modest synagogal structure of their own before 1730. Prior to that time they rented rooms for synagogal purposes. That some members of the group were always struggling to make a living is documented by the fact that a number of children constantly had to be given free religious instruction because their parents could not pay the teacher. Many Jews were imprisoned for debt in the course of their careers, and the minute books eloquently testify that once affluent members who had come down in the world were pensioned by the congregation.[20]

THE FAIRLY COMFORTABLE

Most Jewish shopkeepers and merchants were "comfortable." That is to say, they made a good living and lived comfortably. Many of them owned their own homes, while practically all had at least one domestic slave and could afford to lose twenty shillings at cards— once a week—at the club. In New York City during the French and Indian War, young Uriah Hendricks was prosperous enough to be able to buy large cargoes of English wares from Moses Franks of London, on credit of course.[21]

In the town of Reading, Pennsylvania, on the outskirts of civilization, Meyer Josephson owned a house and lot, a horse, a cow, and a stock of goods; although frequently but one step ahead of the sheriff, he was never in real want. In Philadelphia during the 1760's Josephson's good friends and patrons, the Gratz brothers, were just getting on their feet. Successful enough to secure credit for goods worth about 14,000 livres (pounds?) which they dispatched to the Illinois country, they were nonetheless in no sense wealthy or notable merchants. In Easton on the Delaware the richest man in town was one of the founding fathers, Myer Hart, who in 1768 owned two houses, a bond servant, six lots, a horse, a cow, and his stock in trade. Deemed a wealthy man in Easton, Hart would not have been considered wealthy by the standards that prevailed in the metropolis of Philadelphia. In New Jersey, Henry Benjamin Franks of Mount Holly or Bridgetown left in 1758 an estate appraised at less than

£1,000, New Jersey currency. The estate consisted of cash, shop goods, and book debts, and it is safe to assume that Franks was among the wealthiest householders in the village. In the South, Benjamin Sheftall, who had come to Savannah a few months after Oglethorpe, left a house, a lot, three slaves—two of whom were children—some land, book debts, and some cash, but he was certainly not rich, even by Georgia's standards of that day.[22]

THE MODERATELY WEALTHY

It is not always easy to place the moderately wealthy in their proper setting. Some of them may have belonged to the "fairly comfortable," while others might be more accurately assigned to the truly wealthy. One does well, in any event, to remember that the standard of wealth, to say nothing of the purchasing power of money, varied tremendously from the 1670's to the 1770's. In 1664 Asser Levy was to be found in the lower half of the assessed taxpayers. Ten years later he was assessed at 2,500 florins, but there was at that time one man who paid taxes on 80,000 florins. Yet, of the sixty-odd taxpayers in that listing, twenty-eight owned 2,500 florins worth of property or less. By 1676, however, Levy had risen into the top third of the taxpayers, and his estate was inventoried in 1683 at about £550. He was by no means a poor man, for Governor Andros had once said that a man commanding £500 to £1,000 was a substantial merchant. The inventory of Levy's estate included fine linen, pictures for the walls, silver plate, and no less than fourteen rings.[23]

In 1701 the home of Abraham Haim De Lucena, the merchant-shipper and "rabbi" of New York, was assessed at £20; in 1703 the assessment was £55 for his house and lot; in 1720 £75. Obviously he was going up in the world. A generation later Samuel Myers Cohen, after remembering relatives, friends, and the synagogue in his will, bequeathed to his wife and four daughters the rest of his substantial estate, consisting of city property, silver plate, furniture, and slaves. Aaron Isaacs, of East Hampton, Long Island, was a successful small-town merchant and at his death owned a ship, houses, lots, farms, and part of a wharf.[24]

Two Jews of Lancaster County, Pennsylvania, were well-to-do by the first half of the century. Isaac Miranda, Indian trader, farmer, politician, and convert to Christianity, owned two houses in Philadelphia, silver plate, and a farm, in addition to several thousand acres of land. He was sufficiently well-off in 1735 to allow himself the hope that his daughter would marry into one of Pennsylvania's most aristocratic families. The other Lancastrian, Joseph Simon, was already a man of substance in the 1750's; he owned real estate and stores and was an important figure in the Indian trade.

In Charleston, South Carolina, Simon Valentine was a respected and successful merchant in the year 1701. Solomon Isaacs, whose will was probated in 1757, left a substantial inventory of goods, a house, books, mahogany furniture, colored prints, silver plate, several Negro slaves—three of whom were children—two horses and a chaise, and a quarter ownership of a sloop. In addition to all this, there were about £8,000 in notes, South Carolina currency, due his estate. His contemporary in Charleston, Joseph Tobias, owned a schooner, slaves, a tract of 950 acres, and in 1761 left an estate of about £11,000.[25]

Among the colonials belonging to this group of the moderately wealthy were Moses Mordecai of Philadelphia and the well-known Georgians, Mordecai Sheftall, Abigail Minis, and her son Philip. Since none of her sons survived Abigail, her entire estate was bequeathed to her five daughters, "who with great affection have always treated me as their fond mother, and by their industry have helped not only gain what I possess but by their frugality to keep together my estate."

A study of the inventories of the estates of Moses Mordecai, Mordecai Sheftall, and the Minises throws light on the furnishings of the home of a Jew in good circumstances. The furniture was of mahogany and walnut, with an occasional piece of maple and cherry. There were desks, chairs, stools, and benches, tables, a clothes press, a sofa, a chest of drawers, commodes and bidets, a rum case, a card table, and a bookcase. There were bed and table linens, blankets, quilts, and counterpanes, bolsters, pillows, and mattresses. The well-appointed home had its silver and pewter plate, china, glassware, crockery, mirrors, a clock, pictures, curtains, and carpets. There were fire dogs and firescreens, brass and iron shovels, tongs, candlesticks, and pokers. The kitchen included ovens, gridirons, spits, pothooks, knives, forks, spoons, pots, pans, skillets, coffee mills and tea kettles, bottles, candle moulds, and cotbedsteads for the servants. And in the stable, particularly in the South, were a chaise, harness, a saddle and a bridle, a horse and a cow. Mordecai Sheftall still cherished an old musket.[26]

GREAT WEALTH

As Daniel Defoe noted in 1727, the wealthy Jews of London were by then moving out to estates in the London suburbs, particularly Highgate and Hampstead, where during the summer they entertained their Jewish and Christian friends. A similar move soon began taking place across the Atlantic.[27]

Arriving at New York in 1748, the traveler Peter Kalm reported that the Jews there had "houses, and great country-seats of their own property," and "likewise several ships." Long before that, however, in a list for 1674 Rowland Gideon, a Jew, had been the highest "town" taxpayer registered on the rolls of the city of Boston. (Some who had "country" estates as well paid more.) Gideon was either rich or, and this is improbable, he was being mulcted. In 1708 when the will of Joseph Bueno de Mesquita was admitted to probate, it was obvious that he had been a wealthy man by the standards of his time. He had occupied two houses rented from Colonel De Peyster and his estate, amounting to about £1,000, included plate, rings, slaves, and—no small item—a manuscript Scroll of the Law with its silver orna·ments.[28]

When Nathan Simson of New York returned home to London in the 1720's to spend the last few years of his life, he brought with him an estate of nearly £60,000 sterling; in later decades his grand-nephew Sampson Simson would become one of New York City's outstanding businessmen. During the 1730's Nathan Simson's friend Rodrigo Pacheco also returned to London a very wealthy man. The wealthy New York Jews whom Kalm had in mind were very probably the Levy-Franks clan and the Gomezes. The details available about the estate of Luis Gomez are insufficient even to estimate his

25. Michael Gratz
Portrait by Thomas Sully
Location Unknown

26. Gershom Mendes Seixas
Photo, Peter A. Juley & Son, New York, from a miniature
Courtesy, Columbia University, New York

wealth, but there can be no question that he and his son Mordecai were men of great means. At the latter's death in 1750 his will contained a bequest to charity, arranged an annuity for his mother-in-law, and left slaves, silver plate, snuff mills, and at least nine houses and lots, including a countryseat in the suburbs of New York—present-day Greenwich Village.[29]

When Samuel Levy died in 1719, a relatively young man of about forty-three, his estate included, among other items, seventy-six pounds of silver plate, shares in two vessels, an annuity for his wife's mother, and some bequests to relatives. More precious than Levy's wealth, however, was the good name he left behind him. His lawyer James Alexander, who certainly knew him well, praised him as "the honestest Jew that has been in this place and a man of most easy temper." Like most other wills of the day, that of Samuel's brother Moses, who died in 1728, leaves the researcher with few details, but there can be no question that he, too, was among the wealthiest Jewish merchants—he may have been the wealthiest—in New York City.[30]

Moses Levy's son Nathan, the founder of Philadelphia's Jewish community, was undoubtedly the city's richest Jew at the time of his death in 1753. Nathan had lived exceedingly well, for his detailed inventory includes mahogany furniture, glass, china, silverware, pictures, card tables, music books, a library, linens, rugs, ruffled shirts, and a wine cellar. Nathan Levy's brother-in-law Jacob Franks was the outstanding Jewish merchant of New York City during the years between 1730 and 1765. His rise to economic power in the second half of the century testified to the financial ascendancy of the Ashkenazic element both in England and in North America. Nothing is known of the details of Franks's estate, but it can be stated with assurance that he had no peer among the Jewish merchants of his time. Jacob's American-born sons, who had then been living in England for a generation, were among the wealthiest Jews in the empire. Still, no Jewish families in North America were comparable in wealth to the English Gideons, Levys, Salvadors, and De Medinas, or to the Anglo-Jewish diamond merchants during the heyday of their financial and commercial eminence.[31]

Two of America's wealthiest Jews during the second half of the century were Aaron Hart of Canada and Aaron Lopez of Newport. Though Hart died in 1800 the wealthiest Jew in Canada, his prominence as a merchant, landowner, industrialist, and small-town banker had probably not been achieved until after the Revolution, while Aaron Lopez' wealth, despite the fact that thousands of pages of his papers are extant, is almost impossible to determine because of his credit manipulations. What can be said about this most attractive figure is that he lived on a baronial scale, maintained an entourage of over thirty persons, including the necessary slaves and hired servants, and had his own stable and two chaises. When his daughter Sally married one of the Jamaican Pereira Mendeses in 1767, the New York press reported the event and described the bride as a lady of merit and fortune. This much is certain: 1775, the first year of the Revolution, found Lopez paying the highest tax in Newport; he was obviously the town's most prosperous businessman. In what might be considered a typical year, 1768, Lopez dispatched nearly fifty ships with cargoes. Ezra Stiles's necrology of this distinguished trader characterized him as probably the greatest merchant in America, which was an exaggeration, but Lopez certainly enjoyed remarkable success in the judgment of his contemporaries.[32]

Some Economic Statistics

A study of the taxes paid by Jews to the government—and also of their contributions for religious purposes—is helpful in estimating the relative wealth, success, and class structure of colonial American Jewry.

New York City assessment and tax lists for 1676 included four Jews, two of whom paid taxes on property valued at £400; one on property worth £200; and one on property assessed at £100. In relation to the generality of the New York taxpayers of that year, the four Jews were all in the "middle" bracket, since there were very roughly about as many who paid higher taxes as there were those who paid less. The lowest assessment for the generality was £50; the highest, £3,000—indicating thus that the wealthiest Gentile taxpayers were some seven and a half times as rich as the wealthiest Jewish taxpayers. In another New York City tax list, this one for December 1695, nine Jews are identifiable, two of whom were assessed for property valued at between £100 and £150; five for property worth from £20 to £40; and two others for property worth from £5 to £10. Another list, for July 1699, includes thirteen Jews, two of whom paid taxes on estates valued at from £110 to £150; eight on property assessed at between £20 and £50; and three on property worth from £5 to £10.[33]

Seventeenth century New York Jewry appears thus to have included a few who were well-to-do, a few who were in the lower brackets, and a more sizeable number who were in a middle bracket. Relating the Jews to the entirety of taxpayers, we see that most of the Jews seem to have belonged in the middle-middle or lower-middle income groups. This structuring is further confirmed by an analysis of the income and expenditure entries for the New York congregation some years later in 1720–1721, which reveals that six men (16 percent) supplied 60 percent of the budget, while the remaining thirty-one members in good standing (84 percent) were to be found in the middle or lower-middle classes.[34]

A study of the New York City tax lists for 1699–1734 throws further light on the data derived from the congregational records. Some of the years of Queen Anne's War (1703–1713) would seem to have been prosperous ones for the small Jewish community. An unusually large number of Jewish businessmen—at times about half of all the Jews assessed—were to be found in the higher brackets. In 1707 well over ten percent of all citizens in the high brackets were Jews, even though they probably constituted no more than one percent of those taxed. For some individuals, the fluctuations in taxation, and presumably in wealth, were very marked during this war. Jacob Do Porto, for instance, was assessed £10 in March 1703, £100 in February 1706, and £30 in December 1706. Such variations in the war years were not untypical. During this period New York Jewry was to be counted in the upper middle class, or at the least, in the middle class.

The picture changed between 1722 and 1734, years of peace. With some exceptional years, less than ten percent of the Jews appeared then in the high brackets, though there were very wide variations in the percentages of those in the middle brackets. One year 70 percent of all Jews taxed were in the middle category; another year saw as few as 14 percent in that category. In general the percentages of Jews in the middle bracket ranged from 20 to 44 percent. Except for one year, at least 50 percent of all Jews taxed were in the lower categories. It must, however, be borne in mind that during the years 1699–1734 many of those in the lower bracket owned their own homes; they were not poor or impoverished. If during the years 1722–1734 those in the upper-middle and lower-middle groups are added to the middle category, then it is safe to say that the Jews formed part of a broadly conceived middle class, or at the worst, of the lower middle class.

The picture did not change radically in the second and third quarters of the century. A 1728 list of subscribers to a cemetery fund in New York City shows that 76 percent of the money was given by 33 percent of the subscribers, or by further dissection, that 45 percent came from 15 percent of the subscribers. Some 70 percent of the congregants, that is to say, were in the lower and lowest brackets. A 1747 assessment list from the synagogue in New York suggests that 77 percent were in the lower and lowest brackets. In 1750, when members were taxed for congregational seats, about 66 percent of them were to be found in the two lower brackets, while 37 percent of the money collected was supplied by some 15 percent of the contributors. A study of twenty-four Shearith Israel ketubot or marriage contracts for the years 1759–1776 indicates that three men settled £2,000 New York currency on their brides; one man promised his bride £800 sterling, fourteen assigned from £300 to £500 to their wives; and six were able to offer only from £100 to £250 New York currency.[35]

Newport Jewry appears to have achieved a somewhat more ample degree of prosperity. The seventeen Newport Jewish taxpayers whose names appear in what seems to be a complete tax assessment list for 1760 paid over four percent of the taxes, though they formed less than two percent of those taxed. Of the seventeen, approximately a third or about 35 percent were in the low bracket, while some 17 percent were in a middle bracket, and about 47 percent were in higher brackets. Only 9 percent of Newport's Gentile taxpayers were in those same high brackets, but—and this is significant—not one

Jew was to be found in the very highest bracket, which included twenty-one Gentiles. Still, Jews as a group, it is clear, were in a relatively high bracket and were better off than most non-Jews in Newport. This is confirmed fifteen years later when a Newport taxroll for 1775 lists eighteen Jews (roughly 1.5 percent of the taxpayers) contributing a little more than 8 percent of the taxes. Whereas about 80 percent of the non-Jewish taxpayers were in the lowest brackets, approximately 18 percent in the middle category, and perhaps one percent in the highest bracket, about 50 percent of the Jewish taxpayers were in the lowest group, some 39 percent in the middle group, and perhaps 11 percent in the highest group. The Jews, as businessmen, were obviously better off than the general run of taxpayers.

The tax paid by Aaron Lopez according to the 1775 tax list is of interest. Lopez' share was equal to about *half* the total paid by *all* the other Jewish taxpayers in the city, which does not reflect their low status, but his outstanding wealth and success. All the other Jewish taxpayers in Newport paid about £66; Lopez was assessed over £32. The next highest Jewish taxpayer, his father-in-law Rivera, paid a little over £9.[36]

When these rather crude statistics are evaluated, it is clear that the magnates included a very small number of men. The number in the lowest brackets was large, but not unduly so, and when the middle and lower—but not lowest—income and taxpaying groups are lumped together, they constitute a not inconsiderable proportion of the whole, which suggests that economically American Jewry was a very healthy body.[37]

Turning now to a consideration of gifts to the synagogue, we may ask whether any distinction can be made between the Spanish-Portuguese and the Germans or Ashkenazim in their contributions. Judging from an analysis of the names and amounts given as reflected in the New York records, an Ashkenazi, Jacob Franks, was the biggest giver from 1728 on, when the New York synagogue was being built. Up to about 1750, however, the numerically smaller Spanish-Portuguese group gave more money. Whether the Sephardim were wealthier, or merely more generous, is difficult to determine, but it may be that they came to America with larger capital reserves— in contrast to the Central Europeans who, as far as we know, brought with them to these shores relatively little capital. Still, in any case, generalizations as to the wealth of the respective Spanish-Portuguese and Central European groups are hazardous, for even a casual glance at the financial records of Shearith Israel in the colonial period will show that its members included many Spanish-Portuguese Jews of modest means and many Central Europeans of substance. On the whole, however, the men in the lowest brackets were of Central European origin. They might well have been recent immigrants; there were very few Spanish-Portuguese newcomers to New York after the middle of the eighteenth century.[38]

CHAPTER 45

CLASS STRUCTURE, ECONOMIC MOBILITY,

INFLUENCE, AND STATUS

CLASSES AMONG THE JEWS

Colonial America may have been, as Crèvecoeur described her, a land in which "the rich and the poor are not so far removed from each other as they are in Europe," a land whose "dictionary . . . is but short in words of dignity and names of honour." It is a fact, nevertheless, that colonial American society developed three more or less distinct classes—an upper, a lower, and a middle class. The upper class included large-scale planters and landowners, great merchants, industrialists, titled aristocrats, and some professional men such as officeholders, lawyers, clergymen of the established churches, and probably some physicians as well. The men in whom power was resident during the mid-eighteenth century were the merchant capitalists, the large landowners, the lawyers and legislators.

We know of only one Jew, Francis Salvador of South Carolina, who might have been termed a landed magnate. Compared to those of the notable Virginia and New York plantation owners, his holdings were modest, but there is no question that he moved within the magic circle of South Carolina's Whig aristocracy. Salvador's career, as it happens, was too brief for him to make any impact on the society of his time, since he landed in the late winter of 1773 and was killed in a skirmish with the pro-British Cherokees in August 1776.[1]

It was as merchants, not as landowners, that Jews entered the upper ranks of colonial society. The Levy-Franks clan of New York, Philadelphia, and Baltimore was accepted socially by the ruling groups, but the third quarter of the eighteenth century already found them on their way out of the Jewish fold. Some intermarried, others were converted to Christianity, and still others—the charming, clever, and gossipy Rebecca Franks, for instance—were Christians by birth and sentiment. Prominent Jewish merchants like the Levys and the Frankses hovered in the twilight zone between the patricians or aristocracy and the peak of the upper middle class. As a merchant with substantial capital, Jacob Franks of New York was on the fringe of the élite and his family, as it married into the landowning and politically powerful New York De Lanceys and the Pennsylvania Hamiltons, was in later generations to achieve more political power, although by that time the Frankses had practically ceased to be Jews. The Gomezes, the Lopezes, and the first generation of the New York Frankses had, however, never removed themselves socially and religiously from their fellow Jews.[2]

The typical American Jew of that period was a middle-class urbanite—a fact tempting the historian to speculate about the extent to which the Jew's middle-class status stemmed from Gentile policies designed to exclude Jews politically and socially from the top social level. Certainly, if Gentile rejection retarded the richer Jews in the process of their defection from Jewish identity, that delay would enable newer immigrants, through the generally rapid anglicization characteristic on these shores, to find complete social acceptance within the larger Jewish group.[3]

The lower classes or ranks in colonial America included in their midst small farmers, frontiersmen, some artisans, laborers, and servants, both free and bond, in addition of course to the large number of Negro slaves. Not very many Jews were to be found in the lower strata, for even the humblest Jewish artisan probably had a shop of some sort. There was, to be sure, an occasional Jewish criminal who had been transported to this country, and we know of a gunner on a privateer during King George's War. Then again, John Davidson, one of the soldiers who served under Oglethorpe in Georgia—and deserted—was said to have been a Jew. There were also cobblers and house painters, debtors who had been in jail for years, servants, and a number of the "genteel poor" who were supported by the community, but many of the Jews belonging permanently or temporarily to a lower-income bracket had status and were not looked down upon.

The functionaries of a Jewish community, for example, were usually in a low-income group, but on the whole they were respected. The hazzan, the shohet, and the shammash augmented their modest incomes by teaching, and often by doing a little business on the side. Frequently enough, these synagogue employees were businessmen only temporarily distressed and destined ultimately to become successful, as in the case of Hyam Myers, Samuel Myers Cohen, and Jonas Phillips, all of whom had functioned as ritual slaughterers, and Joseph Simson, who had once served as a beadle for the synagogue. Abraham I. Abrahams, another synagogue employee, was never to become a successful merchant, but he did well enough nevertheless to send a son through King's College and to see him trained for the practice of medicine. He may have lacked money, but he never lacked status among the Jews, and his correspondence with a merchant-prince like Aaron Lopez evinces a high order of mutual affection and respect. Meagerness of income clearly did not always go hand in hand with social debasement, and there was thus among colonial Jews very little in the nature of an immutably poor or pauperized group.[4]

INDENTURED SERVANTS

The total absence of a Jewish helotry cannot be claimed, despite all said above. Very close to the bottom of the colonial American social ladder—next indeed to the slaves—were the indentured servants and redemptioners. Those who came here voluntarily had signed an indenture obligating them to serve a number of years for their passage; they were in effect sold on this side of the Atlantic to the highest bidder. Redemptioners were redeemed on arrival by friends, family, or coreligionists, or if unable to defray the expenses of their passage, they too would be sold to the highest bidder. No less, in fact, than one-half of the immigrants to these shores in those early days were in these two categories; some were religious refugees, others were political or military prisoners, a few were outright rogues and convicts. The explosive Samuel Johnson may have had this in mind when he declared on the eve of the Revolution that the Americans were "a race of convicts and ought to be thankful for any thing we allow them short of hanging." Most of the immigrant bondsmen, however, had accepted the yoke in the hope ultimately of improving their lot in life.[5]

Back in Europe, Jewish paupers and vagrants, if they were not evildoers, were not customarily turned over to the authorities for deportation, but were fed, clothed, housed temporarily in a hospice, and shunted from town to town. Still, there were cases of impoverished Jews determined on emigration. Usually they found a friend or relative to pay their way, or came over at the charge of a European congregation eager to lighten its charity load. Sometimes, however, they were unable to achieve their goal except at the price of indenture. Thus, though there were not many Jewish indentured servants in colonial America, there were some. Now and then American Jews would redeem coreligionists who had signed servitude bonds for their passage. In most instances, of course, bondsmen who arrived desired to live among Jews so they could enjoy the social and religious life typical of the urban Jewish community.[6]

Jews feared mistreatment by Gentiles, and for a bondsman to be compelled to live isolated among Christians on an outlying farm was almost equivalent to apostasy. Such a bondsman would be cut off from religious services, be denied kosher food, and possibly even constrained to eat swine's flesh. It was not unusual, therefore, for Jews to redeem their fellow Jews on arrival. Women, too, were found among these bond servants. Tradition has it, for example, that Rachel Phillips, the wife of the merchant and land agent Aaron Levy, had once been an indentured servant. Employed by the Chews, she was working on a Sabbath morning when Levy discovered her weeping because she was compelled to desecrate the Sabbath. He then redeemed and married her.[7]

The first Georgia Jews brought over with them indentured servants, both Jews and Gentiles. A Jew living as a servant with Jews would of course have no need for immediate redemption, though this did not mean he would not crave his freedom. The silversmith Myer Myers had an engraver, very probably a Jew, indentured to him, but this skilled craftsman, even though living in the "large" Jewish community of New York, fled from his Jewish master.

An Italian proverb has it that "no one is born a master." In America, the proverb could have been expanded to "no one need die a servant." In 1772 three Jewish indentured servants landed on American soil. One of them, named Michael Levy, might well be the same Michael Levy who in 1786 married Rachel, the daughter of the merchant Jonas Phillips. Dr. Benjamin Rush attended that wedding and described it in a detailed letter to his wife Julia. Jonas Phillips, who had originally clerked for Moses Lindo of South Carolina, may himself have come over to America under the terms of an indenture. Jonas' grandson by Michael and Rachel Levy was Uriah Phillips Levy, who was destined to become a wealthy and distinguished officer in the United States Navy.[8]

Economic Mobility

"The most opulent families, in our memory," Lieutenant Governor Cadwallader Colden once wrote, "have arisen from the lowest rank of the people." Eighteenth century America, that is to say, was a land of marked socioeconomic fluidity, and perhaps no Jew typified that fact more graphically than Jonas Phillips, who arrived in the colonies as a clerk or as we have said, possibly even an indentured servant, and became a successful merchant.[9]

Like Jonas Phillips, most Jews who came to the colonies succeeded ultimately in bettering themselves financially and socially. In many cases the type of business they followed here enjoyed more status than the occupational interests which had characterized them in Europe, for America did offer opportunities to mount the social and economic ladder. It is worth noting in this connection that Isaac Rodriguez Marques of New York paid a tax on property worth £20 in 1695; a mere nine months later he paid a tax on property valued at £100. This was economic mobility with a vengeance, but it was a fact that the clerk and petty venturer of one decade might well be the broad-visioned merchant of the next. Michael Gratz, for example, came to America in 1759 and had relatively little capital, between £200 and £300 at most. In less than ten years, however, he would become a merchant, doing business in partnership with his older brother Barnard and enjoying a credit in the thousands of pounds. The year 1773 found Barnet Levy imprisoned for debt in an Easton jail; six years later he was a smalltown shopkeeper, apparently successful.[10]

There was, to be sure, another side to the coin of mobility—the scale of fortune rises, but it may also sink. In 1782 one of the aristocratic New York Gomezes, a refugee in wartime Philadelphia, contributed to the Mikveh Israel building fund about one percent of what Haym Salomon gave. The Gomezes had been Americans for eighty years; Haym Salomon, an East European immigrant, had been an American for only about seven years.[11]

Status within America's overwhelmingly middle-class Jewish community was never very rigid. On the whole, even new immigrants were accepted by and assimilated into the still fluid little Jewish community of colonial times. Joseph Simon, the wealthy Lancaster merchant, for example, never thought it beneath him to maintain close touch with a number of Philadelphia Jews, even though some of them were in humble circumstances. There were simply too few Jews, and changes took place too rapidly, for status to become very easily crystallized. The once princely David Franks was only too happy during the postrevolutionary years to borrow money from his prewar clerk, while David's father Jacob, the wealthiest Jew in mid-eighteenth century America, never sought to flee his Yiddish-speaking, Hebrew-educated, German immigrant roots. The Jewish tradition of reverence for learning was so much a part of Jacob Franks that it would certainly never have occurred to him to snub the beadle Joseph Simson, who knew more Hebrew than he did! And just as certainly Jacob would have had respect for a young sutler, Manuel Josephson, who was better versed in rabbinic law than he was and probably wrote and spoke better English.[12]

THE MIDDLE CLASS

Colonial American Jewry was, as we have said, overwhelmingly "middle class" and constituted a community in which class distinctions were at a minimum. This does not mean, however, that the community was completely homogeneous. On the contrary, there *were* distinctions because of wealth, nor did the fact of Jewish kinship preclude intra-Jewish prejudice.

Social distance among Jews was by no means unknown in the colonies, and not merely between the Spanish-Portuguese and the Central Europeans. Among the Central Europeans themselves, distinctions were not rare. Bohemian-born Mathias Bush, for example, writing in 1769 to his "in-law" Barnard Gratz, then in London, spoke unkindly of recent Jewish immigrants, impoverished fellow-Ashkenazim, and urged Gratz to "prevent . . . any more of that sort to come." As this letter indicates, early immigrants could be prejudiced against later immigrants. American Jewry, tiny as it was, had its full share of envies and hatreds arising from wealth, knowledge of English, status in the larger general society, familiarity with the social amenities, and fear of newcomers who offered older settlers economic competition and threatened their power within the Jewish community.[13]

The newer immigrants gave occasional expression to their resentment against the older group by seeking to organize their own conventicles, as they did for a brief time at Philadelphia in 1769 and at Charleston during the 1780's. In the end, however, the leveling influence of America made itself felt, and the newcomers were assimilated to the common pattern. Social and economic reasons led them to join the older group, which abandoned its antagonism and accepted them.[14]

Ultimately, then, the process of integration was accelerated and all the Jews became one group. Distinctions in synagogue membership existed, it is true, but these were purely financial in nature, so that a man able to pay more was admitted to the fuller and more privileged rank of the *yehidim* on the synagogue roster. In America's small Jewish community, where every man was needed for ritual purposes, the older groups simply could not afford the luxury of excluding newcomers, while recent immigrants, however resentful, dared not divorce themselves from the community. Jewish life did experience its frequent and bitter internal struggles, but a hardworking struggling businessman was entitled to certain pleasures in a frontier country—and quarreling was one of them.

The fact that American Jews formed for the most part only one socioeconomic group, neatly and comfortably ensconced between the colonial aristocrats and the lower classes, made all but impossible the development of permanent, frozen class distinctions rooted in family, birth, or wealth. Jewish life in colonial America gave rise to no acknowledged aristocracy, engendered no class consciousness, and unlike contemporary Anglo-Jewry or tidewater American Gentile society, knew no sharp cleavage between rich and poor. Plutocracy and proletariat were equally alien to the Jewish community, essentially a guild of shopkeepers in whose tight little world society remained fluid and flexible. There is no human society free of the social distinctions that come in the wake of wealth, but any Jew who made money could hope to share the status of his wealthier coreligionists. Social stratification was present, to be sure, but social immobility was not the rule. Some of the older families are very likely to have looked upon themselves as aristocrats, even after they were bypassed by others in wealth, but it was not too difficult for the young Anglo-Dutch immigrant Uriah Hendricks to marry into a proud but declining Sephardic family after he had attained a degree of affluence. Then, as today, an upthrusting socioeconomic mobility was characteristic of American Jewish life.[15]

Who was included in the rather extensive middle class that comprised the great bulk of colonial American Jewry? Impoverished but respected businessmen, even those living on the congregational dole, communal employees, clerks, and craftsmen were all as much a part of that class as artisan-shopkeepers, large shopkeepers, merchants, and merchant-shippers. Few if any farmers were included, since it is highly doubtful that any middle-class Jews made a living exclusively from their farms.

A study of the Jews admitted as freemen in New York City between 1696 and 1775 reveals that twenty-five of the forty-six men identified as Jews were shopkeepers, retailers, and merchants. Of the remaining twenty-one, four were candlemakers, three were snuffmakers and tobacconists, two each were barbers and perukemakers, goldsmiths, tailors, and watchmakers, and one each was a distiller, a butcher, a baker, a cordwainer, a brazier, and a saddler. It is probable that most if not all of those twenty-one artisans also had shops where they sold their own and other products. All of them may have been self-employed.[16]

The fact that practically all the Jews in New York were businessmen is confirmed by the description of those naturalized under the act of 1740. Of the thirty-four listed, thirty-one were merchants and traders, one was a minister, one a tallow chandler, and one a butcher. The butcher Hyam Myers soon became a merchant, and the chandler Isaac Hays probably had his own shop. Of the six Jewish rebels proscribed in Georgia by the British through the Disqualifying Act of 1780, all were businessmen, though one was classified as a butcher and another as an army officer.[17]

In some respects the American Jewish middle class differed strikingly from its counterpart in England. American, unlike English, Jewry had few nabobs and few paupers. On the whole English Jewry was much wealthier at the top levels, including a number of stock and produce jobbers, jewelers, and diamond merchants. Such brokers or jewelers were not to be found among American Jews, though some handled jewelry. There were, however, quite a number of silversmiths and watchmakers here, and in this respect the American Jewish vocational distribution did not differ from the English. Hatters, diamond polishers, and necklace makers, found in England, were not represented here, and while there were some embroiderers among American Jews, there were more in England. London had far more Jews than America engaged in the production and distribution of luxury goods because of the mother country's larger wealth and more extensive clientele. England also had many peddlers, old clothes traders, and impoverished "businessmen" struggling to eke out a bare livelihood, but there were very few peddlers among American Jews, and there was no one who traded exclusively in old clothes, probably because the American gentry customarily turned their old garments over to their domestic slaves. The American people preferred cheap new clothing to renovated castoffs, even of good quality. There was, in any case, very little need to peddle secondhand merchandise when it was so easy to open a shop and begin one's rise up the social and economic scale.[18]

STATUS AS A RESULT OF ECONOMIC INFLUENCE

"Here are no aristocratical families," wrote Crèvecoeur, but there was an American aristocracy. It was not based on hereditary title or on military rank, of course; it was based rather on political and economic influence. This meant that though most Jewish merchants, by virtue of their being Jews, could never hope for entry into the upper-level power cliques and were in fact excluded from membership in the ruling aristocracy, they were far from powerless. The urban elements in American society were the dominant elements, and so some Jews, as urbanites and as merchants, were inevitably part of that elite power constellation. Because wealth was king, Jews of means, skills, and powerful Jewish and Christian connections both here and abroad, lacked neither respect nor influence. Jacob Franks and his family were always welcome guests at the gubernatorial mansion; their economic power and their influence in London saw to that, just as they saw to it that Jacob's brother Aaron in England could secure an audience with George II and intercede for the oppressed Jews of Bohemia. Jacob and his brother, and other Jews like them, would be careful of course to avoid political involvements, for they had no desire to incur the enmity of influential factions and were, moreover, as natives of Central Europe, only too well aware of the risks to life and fortune braved by the court Jews of the German lands. Still, they would not hesitate to exert pressure in the economic, as distinct from the political realm.[19]

Respect for the successful businessman, even if he was a Jew, had been characteristic of England ever since Cromwellian days, and on the American continent Jewish merchants were encouraged to concern themselves with those economic issues which touched on the public welfare. Thus, as early as 1705 five New York Jewish merchants were invited to sign a petition asking the governor's help in establishing a fair standard of value for foreign coins, and a generation or two later New York and Philadelphia Jewish merchants were invited to work with other local merchants on such diverse monetary projects as regulating the rate of exchange, furthering the acceptance of Connecticut bills of credit in New York, and protesting against the importation of British copper coins which threatened to depreciate the currency. In the third decade of the century an office seeker, eager for an appointment to the royal customs service in America, begged Nathan Simson to influence the London Jewish merchants to intercede on his behalf with the all-powerful Sir Robert Walpole. Simson and his associates were highly respected; they had important friends. When Simson, Moses Levy, Moses Mikal, Moses Hart, and Mordecai Nathan—all substantial New York businessmen—sought to become denizens of Great Britain, they apparently had no difficulty in enlisting the aid of a high-ranking personage like Henry St. John, Viscount Bolingbroke.[20]

There are numerous other examples of Jewish involvement in public issues. In 1733 when the projected molasses act, designed to give the English sugar planters monopolistic advantages in the North American colonies, was being discussed in Parliament, Rodrigo Pacheco was one of the London merchants in the American trade who were asked to protest the bill before Parliament. His help was needed in the struggle against this proposed law, which would limit the importation of sugar and molasses from the foreign West Indies, and by diminishing the profits of American traders, impair their capacity to pay for English finished products. The New York Assembly requested Pacheco, then living in London, to appear among the protesting businessmen. Pacheco, who had been a New York merchant for many years, obviously enjoyed the assembly's esteem. It was to the same Pacheco that the lawyer James Alexander turned in seeking restoration to his former position on the New York Provincial Council. For many years Alexander, a notable New York and New Jersey politician, had business and professional relations with Pacheco, and Mrs. Alexander, a successful businesswoman, was among the Jewish merchant's customers. Now Alexander solicited his friend's influence in London.[21]

In 1749 when the shopkeepers and traders of Fairfield County, Connecticut, asked for remission of taxes after King George's War, three Jews signed the appeal to the provincial assembly. Though not a founder of the New York City Chamber of Commerce, Sampson Simson was one of its important members and served on a number of committees. He was among those deputized to prepare a draft charter for the chamber and to petition the governor for its granting. Among the committees on which Simson worked were those to regulate commissions charged on exports and imports, to conserve the value and stop the clipping of gold coins, and to encourage whaling in New York. In 1764 five Newport Jewish businessmen joined with their fellow merchants in the Rhode Island city to protest against the fees charged by the customhouse officers. The Jewish signers constituted about ten percent of all the signatories.[22]

No Jew in Newport was more influential than Aaron Lopez, and so in 1772, when Henry Cruger Jr. of Bristol wished to secure advancement for a young man named Wyatt in the Rhode Island customs service, he was confident that Lopez could arrange for the promotion. A weightier testimony to Lopez' influence was taking shape just about the same time. During the early 1770's ambiguity with respect to beach and forest privileges in and near the Gulf of St. Lawrence and a monopolistic bill before Parliament threatened Rhode Island's rights and opportunities to carry on codfishing in Canadian waters. The provincial merchants, Aaron Lopez among them, appealed to the colony's general assembly to protest to the British ministers against the proposed monopoly. In response to the merchants' plea, the assembly appointed a committee to draft its letter to the secretary of state in London, and Lopez was one of the members of that committee. Thus the assembly, which in 1761 had denied him naturalization and suggested that he depart Rhode Island for Canada, now honored him by appointment to an important committee. The cause of the Rhode Island entrepreneurs was supported by a Gaspé magistrate, Felix O'Hara, one of Lopez' customers, and it is obvious that the astute Newport merchant was the guiding force in this effort to protect the rights of Rhode Islanders on Canadian fishing grounds. It was O'Hara who had confidentially alerted Lopez to the monopolistic grab in the Gaspé and was now secretly directing the Rhode Island protest.[23]

CHAPTER 46

SUMMARY AND EVALUATION OF THE JEW'S ROLE

IN THE COLONIAL AMERICAN ECONOMY

The Jewish Businessman
in an Agricultural Economy

The North American colonies were essentially agricultural. Even in New England, where commerce and industry were most intensively pursued, only a small fraction of the population was involved in nonagricultural enterprises. Clearly then, in a young country like British America on the periphery of the empire, businessmen were very useful and Jews, as shopkeepers and merchants, had a very important function to perform, both for the North American provinces and for the manufacturing heart of the empire in London. People here craved manufactured commodities, consumer goods, and luxury merchandise. The businessman imported those wares and sold them or distributed them to others for sale. The staples he sent eastward across the Atlantic helped pay for the imports and thus contributed to the promotion of English industry. The American merchants, Jews among them, exported the raw materials and the semifinished goods of their provinces to European and West Indian markets. By virtue of this export-import economy in which they participated, Jewish merchants helped make possible in America a European standard of living. And along with English textiles came English culture.

Not only commerce but civilization, too, was advanced by the merchant and the shopkeeper. American Jewish traders, because of their skill, experience, and contacts with Jews in other commercial centers, particularly in the West Indies, were able to participate vigorously, along with other American businessmen, in the furtherance of North America's local, coastal, and international traffic.

[843]

It is not without significance that Aaron Lopez had friends and relatives, fellow Sephardim, on Barbados and Curaçao; with some of them he was in touch only months after his arrival in Newport. The British colonies, it is clear, benefited economically by the presence of such newcomers, and that is the essential reason why they were tolerated and encouraged. The celerity with which the Rabba Couty case was handled by the Privy Council can mean only that the emerging British Empire was determined to encourage and protect the commercial activity of naturalized Jews. The Jews of course knew their value and were not hesitant to press it upon the government. As early as 1696, in a petition to the House of Commons, a group of London Jewish businessmen pointed out the obvious fact that "those of the Hebrew nation . . . in the plantations" bought English wares, made returns in local products, and generally acted "to the great advantage" of the colonial economy. Though only a very small percentage of the merchants, the Jews *were* merchants, and a progressive and enterprising group of merchants at that; as such they were most helpful in furthering North American civilization.[1]

This word—civilization—has not been used lightly. Even Hannah Moses in her little shop at Philadelphia made her contribution to the task of raising and maintaining the standard of living in an agricultural land. She sold not only shirts and stockings, but also reading glasses, mother-of-pearl buttons, needles, razor straps, enameled fountain pens, and four-blade instrument knives. Jacob Abrahams may have made the minimum contribution to Shearith Israel, but who will deny the civilizing contribution of a humble shopkeeper who sold pineapples? Perhaps only those who have lived in small towns and in out-of-the-way places before the days of good roads and automobiles can really appreciate the shopkeeper's importance in the towns and villages of the seventeenth and eighteenth centuries. It was these shopkeepers—the Jews among them too—who brought to the town and the hamlet the hardware, dry goods, sugar, molasses, coffee, tea, and rum so necessary to the backcountry villages and the frontier settlements. The village shopkeeper was nothing less than the transmitter of the civilization of the time. Myer Hart was for years the only storekeeper in the town of Easton, and by virtue of that fact he was, in a way, the town's most useful citizen. Who can gauge the importance of an Abraham Cohen at Georgetown, South Carolina, in 1762, or attempt to assess the "value" of the goods Abraham Minis brought to remote Frederica, Georgia? [2]

The towns were the hearths of culture, and the Jews were an urban people. They maintained a community in every important tidewater city but Boston. Yet their trading and its consequent beneficent influence were not limited solely to cities of Jewish settlement, for they did business in every province and with nearly every town of size. The agents and customers of an Aaron Lopez extended all the way from the St. Lawrence in Canada to Savannah in Georgia.

Wherever Jews lived they helped build the towns that gave them shelter. They provided markets for farmers and fishermen, jobs for industrial laborers, work for shipbuilders. They may not have accumulated much capital, but they did have access to extensive credit, and they built, owned, rented, and chartered ships and wharves, shops and warehouses. They bought, sold, and manufactured. Thus on this side of the Atlantic, Jewish merchants helped create a little world of commerce and industry which tied the colonies together, and it is difficult to overemphasize the merchant's importance in creating a common culture, a common country, a common spirit. In a world of particularism, where each colony was an isolated duodecimo enclave nursing its own prejudices, the Jews of the tidewater strip were undeniably a factor making for cohesiveness and national unity. Through his regional and overseas commercial activity, the Jewish merchant was an important element in the decomposition of parochialism. Through his sales and purchases he helped unite scattered American colonial settlements and helped bring disparate and diverse groups closer together. In short, he helped further the growth of a national consciousness.

CANADA

The Jewish contribution to the Canadian economy was particularly significant. Since Canada was more of a "wilderness" territory even than the thirteen other British colonies, she had a relatively greater need of trade, and commerce was more important for Canada's development than it was for her sister colonies to the south. A decade before the English came into the St. Lawrence Valley, the Gradis family of Bordeaux, through its commercial activity and through the Canada Company, had already been keeping a constant stream of supplies flowing into New France. What the Gradis interests had attempted was continued and expanded by the Jewish traders who came to Canada with her British conquerors. Those Jews who, together with other businessmen, distributed English wares throughout the colony served the function of exposing a feudal Catholic society to the more advanced culture of England and in addition helped the Canadian population, peasants and seigneurs alike, not only to maintain but also to raise its standard of living.

Coming into Canada as pioneers and establishing themselves there from the beginning of the English regime, Jewish merchants played their part in promoting the country's growth. This is more readily apparent when we bear in mind that in the decade between 1760 and 1770 there were probably less than 100 merchants in all Canada. About ten of them were Jews, including Aaron Hart, the leading merchant and the first British businessman in Three Rivers, Canada's third most important town.[3]

CRAFTS AND INDUSTRY

The colonial Jewish contribution to American craftsmanship and industry merits consideration. Though there were never many Jews in the crafts, there had always been some Jewish artisans ever since 1654 when Asser Levy landed at the Battery in Dutch New Amsterdam. In later years Jewish entrepreneurs performed an important industrial function in marketing indigo and in expanding the field of chandlery, and possibly also in developing the production of clothing. As an indigo expert, Moses Lindo of Charleston probably did as much as any other individual to further this product, the third crop in the South. Lindo's proficiency in sorting, grading, selling, and maintaining the quality of South Carolina indigo enabled him to benefit the American economy in a very substantial sense. Taken as a group, the Newport Jewish chandlers did much to promote the manufacture of spermaceti candles and also to spur the development of the whaling industry on which spermaceti chandlery was totally dependent. Who can measure the cultural significance of the improved reading habits made possible by the use of the spermaceti candle? Where garment manufacturing is concerned, only a study of the relevant data in the ledger and account books of other colonial merchants can determine whether Aaron Lopez was a pioneer in that field.

Jews were important industrially, not so much for what they themselves produced, as for the stimulus they gave others—shoemakers, candle-box makers, distillers, and shipwrights. Jewish businessmen were instrumental in finding markets for New England pig iron, lumber, oil, and rum, for New York and Pennsylvania grain, flour, beef, and furs, and—though singularly devoid of any influence in the tobacco industry—for Southern rice, indigo, and naval stores.

THE WEST

The American West and the advancing frontier were important for the development of an American national self-consciousness and a desire for autonomy. In that connection, as Frederick Jackson Turner discerned, the trader was a key figure, for by providing settlers and frontiersmen with supplies, he brought civilization close on the heels of the advancing riflemen. The Jewish merchant who channelled goods into the ever-growing West and its retreating frontier may have been less daring than his contemporaries who moved along the often perilous trails in search of greener meadows and taller timber, but the services he rendered were certainly as important as those of the frontiersman. By freighting indispensable goods and wares, merchant-suppliers kept pushing the frontier farther and farther back. They provided the manufactures the frontiersmen needed for survival, and it was those goods that made it possible for still more settlers to move into the West.

The merchants' packtrains and bateaux went everywhere. Following the rivers, lakes, and trails, traders penetrated ever farther and deeper into the wilderness with their heavily laden canoes and packtrains, and in the end their efforts led to the building of towns where the tidewater culture could take root again. The packsaddles of the horse-trains bulged with the wares which bound the frontier villages around Fort Pitt in western Pennsylvania or Fort de Chartres in the Illinois territory to the businessmen of Philadelphia, and even London. It was primarily as tidewater merchants that Jews shared in the taming of the frontier, for the merchants of the American tidewater towns made their great contribution to the opening of the West by supplying and financing the traders who traveled the vast transallegheny region in quest of furs.

Canadian Jewish merchants and traders like Ezekiel Solomons of Michilimackinac tapped the fur resources of the North American wilderness as far west as the Continental Divide. Other Canadian Jewish businessmen moved over the Great Lakes and the river portages to the Mississippi, and down that stream to the neighborhood of present-day St. Louis. There is even some evidence, the presence of a French Jew at Kaskaskia in 1768, that Jewish businessmen had come north up the Mississippi to bring in goods, for which in all likelihood they took back with them furs and agricultural products. Commercial exploits of that sort helped to establish the French settlements more firmly in the mid-Mississippi valley.

One Jewish merchant, Joseph Simon, participated in the struggle for control of the strategic Ohio valley as early as the 1740's, when it was still a bone of contention between the crowns of England and France. Jews were also, of course, to be found in the Philadelphia-Lancaster group of merchants who had begun financing many of the western traders no later than the 1750's. Even before Daniel Boone made his first exploratory trip to Kentucky in 1767, Simon and his associates had outfitted George Croghan as he moved on to the Illinois country, and Jewish merchants specializing in the western trade were among the first to help open up regions which later became the states of West Virginia, Ohio, Indiana, Kentucky, and Illinois. The Philadelphia-Lancaster group of Jewish merchants offered formidable mercantile competition in the Illinois country to the Philadelphia firm of Baynton, Wharton & Morgan and maintained the lifeline of supplies when its Philadelphia rivals failed to accomplish their multiple purposes.

Like other Anglo-American merchants, entrepreneurs, and land speculators, the eastern Pennsylvania Jewish merchants envisioned a trading empire of their own along the strategically located Ohio and Mississippi Rivers and sought to divert the Mississippi River fur trade from Canada and to channel it eastward to Philadelphia. Eager to link the Mississippi valley to the Atlantic coast and active in their efforts to serve as a source for English goods, they helped weaken French and Spanish influence in the Illinois country. Though the transallegheny towns, colonies, and settlements of which these Jewish merchants dreamed were not to eventuate until after the Revolution, the goods Jewish merchants sent into the region not only made it possible for already established settlers to remain there, but also made life easier for those who continued to come. Believing in the future of those vast reaches beyond the mountains, Jewish merchants were thus instrumental, if only to a modest extent, in opening the transallegheny West.[4]

THE EAST

That the economy of the eastern seaboard benefited from Jewish commercial activity cannot be doubted, for in the East, where most of North America's Jews lived, they helped build the commerce of the towns in whose midst they had settled. Very often the local Jewish shopkeeper was an important or leading man in his town or village. Jews were always the harbingers of urbanization. One of their contributions, apparently a most effective one, was to train others in the field of commerce. The Newport merchant Samuel Rodman, for example, secured his early training in the Rivera countinghouse, and reportedly, in later years Rodman asked Jacob R. Rivera to sit for a portrait by Gilbert Stuart. James O'Hara, who has been referred to as the first important industrialist in Pittsburgh, clerked as a boy for Simon & Campbell.

America's largest community of Jewish merchants was to be

[849]

found in New York City where the Franks family, in particular, was outstanding for its vast operations in the area of army supply during the French and Indian War. It is highly probable, however, that New York Jewish businessmen as a group exerted their greatest influence during the first quarter of the eighteenth century. By the decade before the Revolution the city's once notable Jewish merchantry was to some extent in eclipse, which appears to constitute something of a classic pattern. Further studies in American Jewish life may very well show—this applies to the nineteenth century as well—that while Jews were often among the very first businessmen in a town, they soon disappeared or were overshadowed after a while by the non-Jewish merchants who came in and built on the foundations the Jews had helped to lay. Then, in later decades a new generation of Jewish businessmen would establish itself in the same town, but in areas of economic endeavor which on the whole were secondary. This seems to have been true in colonial New York, in Savannah, and also to some degree in Newport.[5]

There is no lack of evidence that Jews achieved considerable economic—and sometimes even civic—importance in various communities, particularly in the South. In the seventeenth century, for instance, Jewish tradesmen in the recently established Carolinas were especially useful in meeting the pressing economic needs of those colonies. When on March 10, 1697, sixty-four aliens were naturalized in South Carolina, eleven of them were merchants and of those, four were Jews, including Simon Valentine, who was sufficiently important in Charleston to be appointed one of the town's police commissioners. The situation was not otherwise in Georgia, where during the first decade of the colony's existence, Jews played a disproportionately notable role in the provincial economy. A generation later the Jewish merchant Mordecai Sheftall was one of Savannah's outstanding Whig leaders.[6]

The Jewish role in colonial Newport is legendary and somewhat exaggerated. Still, if Jews did not create the greatness of mid-eighteenth century Newport, as some writers have enthusiastically maintained, they certainly did contribute heavily to the town's growth and prosperity. They did not make the town, nor did the town make them, but it would more closely approximate the truth to say that

Newport and her Jews helped make each other. It has been said that Newport did not survive the departure of her Jewish merchantry during the Revolutionary and postrevolutionary years, and it is a fact that important families like the Riveras, Lopezes, Harts, and Pollocks had either died out, been driven out, or lost their enterprising spirit by the end of the Revolution. Newport declined in commerce and no more Jews came to settle. One might speculate about Newport's fate had the brilliant and versatile Aaron Lopez survived the Revolutionary years to resume his career as one of the town's most important merchant-shippers, if not indeed her most important businessman. It would be, however, an idle speculation. The work of a man like Aaron Lopez does, of course, testify to the large-scale, diversified businesses which Newport's outstanding Jewish merchants and merchant-shippers developed. Rejecting the lingering traces of a feudal economy, they were in the vanguard of economic individualism and nascent capitalism. As manufacturers, and as the clients of manufacturers, they may be numbered among the better-known harbingers of nineteenth century industrial capitalism.[7]

Considering the economy of the British Empire as a whole, the Jews of North America were not very significant. They participated very minimally or not at all in either the East Indian or Mediterranean trade; they were not outstanding in the importation of sugar and played practically no part during the eighteenth century in the all-important export of tobacco. Only one Jewish merchant, Lopez, busied himself with the fisheries, and only two, Lopez and his partner Rivera, persevered in the African slave trade. The role of American Jewish merchants—and it was the classical role assigned the colonial businessman in a mercantilist world—was to buy and pay for English wares. This meant that the Jew, like his Gentile fellow merchant, was involved primarily in shipping provisions to the Caribbean Islands, bringing back West Indian staples, and sending the English cash or needed commodities. Within this framework the handful of Jewish commercial specialists on the western flank of the empire served a useful purpose. As a group, to be sure, the colonial Jews showed ability; they furthered commerce and worked as a force for good in the towns in which they lived. Their significance on the American, if not on the general imperial economic scene, is of some

note when it is remembered that commerce was certainly a supporting hinge of colonial prosperity. In a tract on Maryland written in
1666, a writer said:

> Trafique is earth's great Atlas, that supports
> The pay of armies, and the height of courts,
> And makes mechanics live, that else would die
> Meer starving martyrs to their penury.
> None but the merchant of this thing can boast,
> He, like the bee, comes loaden from each coast,
> And to all kingdoms, as within a hive,
> Stows up those riches, that doth make them thrive . . .

The Jewish merchants of colonial America were without question
eager, intelligent, and diligent contributors to this "trafique." [8]

PART VII

RELIGION, SOCIAL WELFARE,

AND JEWISH EDUCATION IN THE LIFE

OF THE NORTH AMERICAN JEW

CHAPTER 47

THE RELIGIOUS LIFE

Colonial America's Jewish community was an offshoot of European Jewry. Nearly every American Jew came from Europe and it was only natural, therefore, that the Jewish immigrant, carrying his religious institutions with him, would attempt as far as possible to re-create on American soil the pattern of his old community in Europe. He found here no Jewish model to which he could conform. Here in America he was a pioneer, a Jewish "Pilgrim Father," as it were. Jewishly, this was for him the end of the world, a spiritual wilderness with nothing religious to offer him. Of course, in seeking to make a life as European as possible, he did not differ notably from his Gentile neighbor, for everyone who came to America looked to Europe as *the* source of culture, and religion.

The legal basis for Jewish corporate existence in continental Europe had been determined by royal grants extending back to the first pre-Christian millennium in the ancient Near East. Jews had enjoyed a communal life of their own even in the Babylonian exile which followed the destruction of Jerusalem and the Judean kingdom. With some exceptions—notably England—the European Jewish communities were legally constituted and recognized by charters. An organic document, a *privilegium*, authorized Jews to settle in a specific area, to do business there, and to collect taxes from their coreligionists for the use of the state and for the needs of the established, recognized Jewish community. The state saw to it that those taxes were collected and paid. The Jews also had their own rabbinical courts exercising control in civil cases, and Jewish leaders could turn when necessary to the Gentile authorities for aid in implementing the decisions of the Jewish courts.

The Jewish leaders, as a result of the power vested in them by chartered *privilegia*, were able to hold sway, a far-reaching sway, over the members of their community. In effect the European Jew was born into the Jewish community. He was part of the Jewish people. If he lived with Jews, he had to remain a Jew; if he wished to leave the ranks of Jewry and to establish a home of his own beyond the reach of the Jewish community, he had almost inevitably to become a Christian. The two worlds of Judaism and Christianity offered few if any interstitial spaces into which he could creep.

Unlike the situation on the European continent, no Jewish community in colonial North America lived under a charter, and Jewish settlers here lacked authority to create a formal Jewish community in the continental European tradition. Jews could not and did not achieve corporate status under English rule in the colonies, but that did not prevent them from establishing Jewish communities, and a de facto parish or *Gemeinde* or kehillah system came to prevail in every colonial American Jewish settlement. It was simply assumed that every Jew in a town and its environs belonged to the "community." Jews were thus able to achieve a functional solidarity for, though lacking the *privilegia* of Europe, they clung to the European spirit. Exercising authority now through their own desire rather than through Gentile fiat, American Jews employed Jewish public opinion, moral pressure, and the threatened denial of basic religious privileges to impose a communal will on recalcitrants. It is probable the urge toward the organization of a "synagogue community" was furthered by the communal spirit which prevailed in Congregationalist New England and the Anglican South. In essence what both of these churches strove toward was the integration of their communicants into one rounded-out religious, social, and eleemosynary whole.

The individual Jew never faced exclusion from an American town or village by virtue of the fact that he was a Jew, but if he craved a social and religious life, he had either to become one with the Christian world or to fashion a Jewish society of his own. Characteristically, he chose the latter, and eager for an organization which would exercise social control in order to perpetuate his ancestral traditions, readily gave the past an unyielding and passionate loyalty. There was actually very little question as to what the Jew would do if there were other Jews in town. With the rarest of exceptions, he certainly wished no church membership; conscience and habit made it inconceivable for him to live except as a Jew, and he wanted his own socioreligious community, his own way of life. Unless prepared to abandon the Jewish heritage, the colonial Jew neither dared nor cared to separate himself from his fellow Jews. After all, he needed ritually prepared foods, and if he broke with his coreligionists, they might refuse him a Jewish burial! The reluctance of an individual to challenge the communal will was only fortified by the fact that no colonial American Jewish community ever sheltered more than one permanent synagogue, and the local synagogue virtually exercised a monopolistic control over every Jew within its ambit.[1]

In the final analysis, then, membership in the American Jewish community was no more than theoretically or apparently voluntary. Like the Dissenters, Jews found themselves compelled by a need for their own sancta and their own way of life to establish communities of their own. Dissenters and Jews dispensed with state support in America. They throve in the intensity of their convictions and in their desire to be together. And in addition, the Jew always had a certain knowledge that served to buoy him up: behind him, supporting him with sympathy, and often enough with hard cash, was the body of World Jewry.

The motivations prompting American Jews to unite into a group were in substance identical with those which had moved their fathers in the Old World. As Erasmus had said, "If it be the mark of a good Christian to hate Jews, what excellent Christians we all are!" And so there could be no thought of accepting Christianity, which was synonymous with hostility and persecution. There was, after all, no Jew on whom the Christian world of the seventeenth and eighteenth centuries did not impose disabilities, whether great or minimal. The socioreligious world of the Christian was utterly foreign to the Jew; it was unacceptable to him and strange to his way of thinking.

[857]

There could be no choice. The Jew had to create a community of his own, no less in America than in the Europe from which he had come.[2]

If the Jew was to be a religionist, then of course it was Judaism he wished to follow. There was no question at all in his mind. His faith was the only true one. His being a Jew made him part of an age-old history, heir to a magnificent tradition which centuries ago even a Christian scholar, the Venerable Bede, had called "the pure source of Hebrew truth." If, then, the Jew was insular, it was a voluntary insularity; if he exulted in his own ethos, if his universalism was embedded in a welter of particularistic ceremonials, it was because of his determination to maintain intact a religio-ethical-spiritual heritage he believed superior to all others. The typical Jew was thus a very proud man, and this was important, for no one lives by bread alone.

Still, he was frightened too, because he was so alone. Spiritually a European, he was only too conscious that in America he dwelt exposed on Europe's westernmost Atlantic frontier. If he was to find happiness, he would have to transport Europe across the ocean; he would have to surround himself with the familiar sights and familiar institutions of his European heritage; he would have to see his own folk around him. As a Jew he had always belonged to a tight kinship group, had always been part of a people with the same cultural pattern, the same rites and practices, and in large part even the same economic role of purveying merchandise. Community life afforded him a chance to enjoy a feeling of oneness with his coreligionists; it strengthened the already existent Jewish group solidarity and offered Jews a much better opportunity to survive as a minority. The Jew had a total Jewish consciousness. He felt better, knew himself more secure, when he lived as a Jew, nursing his own special prejudices and cherishing his own special ideals. In a very specific sense, a community life of their own made it possible for Jews to marry their own and to enjoy religious services, Jewish educational opportunities, and a wide variety of religious and social-welfare services. From birth through and even beyond death, from circumcision to the cemetery, the Jew could be sure that he would be cared for by his own people, that provision would be made for him at every juncture of his life, and this was the prime motivation that induced him to create and maintain communal forms of living. The Jewish community did even more than that, however, for it gave the Jew a base from which he could function economically. Individual fellow Jews might on occasion cheat him and take advantage of him, but the community as a whole was always, and justifiably, to be trusted. A decent Jew was rarely if ever disappointed by the community, and among his coreligionists he could attain the prestige and status denied him by the Christian world.

Try as he might to bring his European homeland along with him to these shores, the Jewish immigrant could not succeed completely. The Jewish community that soon began to rise here diverged inevitably from its European source. Oligarchy characterized the European ghetto, whose ruling body, essentially a council of the rich and the learned, enjoyed state support in its control of the communal agencies for religion, culture, and social welfare. In European Jewry's complex of well-integrated institutions, the synagogue may have been central, but not necessarily or even typically dominant. In America, however, the synagogue was destined to become the chief, indeed almost the sole Jewish communal agency. The community's basic institution, absorbing and including all other communal agencies, the synagogue was the spinal cord, if not the body of American Jewish life; it was the instrumentality whereby Jews could strengthen and further their sense of community. Its leaders became the community leaders; the community itself became a synagogue-community. Virtually all the activities of the organized Jewish group, whether religious, cultural, or philanthropic, were subject to the direction of the synagogal heads. The one known exception, the Newport Jewish social club, was no rival to synagogue authority, nor is there convincing evidence that even one Jewish confraternity came into being in all colonial North America. It was the local synagogue which governed all communal concerns. It was the local synagogue which held a full and undisputed hegemony.

One might, of course, have expected such a development in a land of Protestant orientation, and to be sure, in its hegemonic aspect the colonial American synagogue did parallel contemporary Protestantism. The fact remains, however, that even pre-American and pre-Protestant Jewry had exhibited characteristics which to a large extent would typify Protestantism in North America, for most of the

Jewish communities of medieval and early modern Europe were independent, enjoying autonomy. Within the framework of religious customs the individual American Jew was thus master of his own soul. Any man who could make synagogal offerings and pay for his seat was by and large as influential as the next. The powerful religious dissent which shaped itself in Protestant America merely strengthened Judaism's already established antihierarchical tradition. Jews made no attempt here to organize themselves on a regional basis or along diocesan lines, for the two closest synagogues were nearly a hundred miles apart.

The Jewish church in America betrayed similarities to all the Protestant churches, yet it was like none of them. It was formal and liturgical, yet not aristocratic. It gave rise to no unrestrained emotionalism, yet its members sang out lustily and prayed loudly. Surely it had an air of exoticism about it, with its worshipers swaying, muffled in their prayer shawls, intoning Hebrew orisons in Oriental modes. Its exoticism was, however, far less pronounced than the variety manifested in those Christian conventicles whose frequenters ranted and moaned and rolled on the ground indoors and out in the emotional extravagances of the Great Awakening. The synagogue was no stranger to respect for learning, even though few American Jews could claim to be truly learned; illiterates, no matter how pious, played no part in the leadership of the community. The synagoguegoer found himself constantly subject to discipline and control and censure, yet congregations on the whole were democratic, both administratively and religiously, for all men were accounted equal in the sight of God. Spiritual, mystical "conversion" went without recognition as a religious concern and would in any case have offered no advantage in the synagogue; the Jew was too firmly convinced that all men, made in the image of God, lived on one spiritual plane. Compared to any or all of the Protestant denominations, American Jews and Judaism represented a phenomenon apart. On the other hand, the Jewish church could hardly have exercised any influence on Protestant America. It has been estimated that there were in the thirteen colonies at least 3,000 congregations, of which only seven all told were Jewish, even if Lancaster and Montreal are included.[3]

Divergent as it was in so many respects from other American

churches, the colonial synagogue was, nonetheless, uniquely American. The problem of the Jew in the European Jewish community was never one of Jewish loyalties and identification. If European Jews faced internal problems, from the seventeenth century on they involved questions of easing Jewish communal control and securing a toehold in the outer world of Christian western culture. There was no danger in Europe of a Jew's ceasing to be a Jew. The American Jew, however, confronted an altogether different problem from that which beset his European brethren. Here in America on the religious and cultural frontier of Europe, there were inadequate communal controls, few Jewish institutions, no overpowering Jewish environmental and cultural influences. Christians here did not oppress Jews, did not push them into spiritual ghettos and thus make of them, if only through arousing their resentment, better and more observant Jews. The comparatively bright and warm sun of American tolerance invited assimilation. Thus the real question here for the individual was: How can I remain a Jew? How can I have a Jewish life? The answer was the synagogue-community and all that it implied. The synagogue-community was a natural development on the American scene. Jewish immigrants began with the one basic and primary Jewish institution, the synagogue, and everything that developed out of it during the colonial period, all Jewish non-economic activity, remained within its ambit.

If there was any European pattern Jewish immigrants were able to adapt to their experience on American soil, it was the rural type of European community, small and democratic. No elaborate apparatus was needed in the American synagogue, because all Jewish congregations here were small and unpretentious. In these miniscule American Jewish communities all Jews, irrespective of their ethnic backgrounds or their personal religious beliefs or disbeliefs, were gladly and eagerly accepted. Affiliation was easy in this folk community, and the synagogue-community evolved in America emerged as a simple, coordinated, organic structure admirably suited to the requirements of a small pioneer group of Jews. In one unifying institution all Jews, whatever their origins, were held together by their need and desire for a Jewish way of life. Within the embrace of this one unifying instrument they were able to organize worship, secular and religious education, philanthropic concerns, and opportunities for meeting and mingling socially. The synagogue-community was home and a homeland in a physical, spiritual, cultural, and emotional sense.[4]

CHAPTER 48

THE SYNAGOGUES OF NEW YORK,

NEWPORT, AND MONTREAL

NEW YORK

The oldest Jewish community in North America is that of New York—New Amsterdam as she was known by her Dutch founders. Actually, that Jewish community was the only one to emerge on the mainland during the 1600's, with the possible exception of Newport. Even in New York there would be no other synagogue for over 170 years.

How did the Jews of New Amsterdam conduct their religious life? Not a great deal can be said, but to the best of our knowledge, no "professional" readers were employed at Jewish services during the period of Dutch rule. Worship was led by voluntary hazzanim, while one of the butchers probably acted as shohet or slaughterer and circumciser. The slaughterer was paid for any service he rendered his fellow Jews, and one may assume that there were laymen who taught the children Hebrew, and that marriages and funerals were conducted by the members themselves.

The Jews of New Amsterdam were among the very first groups to assemble for worship in what is today New York. Preceded by the Dutch and French Calvinists, the Jews were already conducting religious services during the 1650's—about the same time, that is to say, as the Quakers and the Lutherans. It was only later that Anglicans, other Protestants, and Catholics held services in the town. Sometime, however, before the Dutch under Stuyvesant struck their colors in 1664, the Jews ceased to meet together as a congregation. The requisite religious quorum was no longer available in the colony and New Amsterdam Jewry as a *community* had faded away. Even the original cemetery of New Amsterdam Jewry vanished with the decline of this tiny community. The experience of the town's earliest Jewish settlers would not be unique, however, and the appearance and disappearance of local Jewish groups would prove in fact to be typical of the American Jewish community. Not only in New Amsterdam-New York, but in Philadelphia, Newport, and Savannah as well, more than one attempt would have to be made before a viable religious group survived.[1]

The English who occupied New Amsterdam in 1664 maintained the status quo so far as the religious privileges of the few remaining Jews were concerned. The Jews were certainly allowed to worship in private, but public worship may well have been another matter. As late as 1673, back in England Jews experienced difficulty in securing permission to worship publicly, and there is no reason to believe that the Jews of New York would have found it any easier, had they been able to assemble a quorum of ten congregants. True, as the reader will recall, Governor Andros was instructed in 1674 to accord "the free exercise of their religion" to "all persons of what religion so ever," but such "free exercise" may not have meant freedom to worship in public. At any rate, from 1683 to about 1691 the English authorities of New York held "that noe publique worship is tolerated . . . but to those that professe faith in Christ, and therefore the Jews' worship [is] not to be allowed." The Jews in town were, however, not much inhibited by the English refusal to grant them "liberty to exercise their religion," for there are certainly evidences of a reactivated congregation in the decade of the 1680's. Ground for a burial place was purchased in 1682, and services were also conducted that year, though probably in a private home behind closed doors.

By 1685 the growing Jewish community had set out to attain recognition and more privileges. The spearhead of the community's attempt seems to have been Saul Brown, a Dutch-born wanderer named after his distinguished ancestor Rabbi Saul Levi Morteira, who had been a scholarly leader of Amsterdam Jewry and had sat among the judges presiding over Spinoza's excommunication. Brown's name, which his sojourn among the English had led him to change from Pardo to its English equivalent, was among the most distinguished names in the religious history of European and American Jewry. Thus he had a brilliant and illustrious family tradition of religious leadership. Coming to North America by way of the West Indies, possibly Barbados, he settled briefly at Newport as a businessman no later than 1684, but moved shortly thereafter to New York. Emerging in that city by 1685 as a merchant and a lay religious leader, he was the first New York cantor known by name.

That same year New York Jewry unsuccessfully petitioned for the right to hold public religious services. Charles II had just died, and it was hoped his Catholic brother and successor James II would accord religious liberty to all, if only to secure it for his fellow Catholics. The following year, in fact, the new king did instruct his Catholic governor, Colonel Thomas Dongan, to allow religious freedom to all, and it may well be that Saul Brown then became the lay hazzan of the community. In 1692 the French visitor Antoine de la Mothe Cadillac noted that Jews were holding services, while three years later John Miller, an English chaplain, reported the existence of a "Jews' Synagogue" on Beaver Street. The chaplain identified Saul Brown as the "minister" of the Jewish community of twenty families. From that year on at the latest, Jews were undisturbed in the conduct of public religious services, and by 1704 if not earlier, the location of the synagogue was well-known in the city. In all likelihood Brown officiated till 1702 when he died while on a visit to Curaçao.[2]

Another businessman, Abraham Haim De Lucena, was probably Brown's immediate successor as congregational "minister." In 1710 De Lucena petitioned the governor for those privileges and exemptions accorded the Christian clergy which "ministers of the Jewish nation" had customarily received in the past. De Lucena, apparently a well-to-do merchant, shipped supplies needed for the attack on New France, and together with other Jewish merchants, contributed toward the erection of the steeple on Trinity Church. It said something for the improvement of Jewish-Christian relations, particularly in the North American settlements, that a Jewish minister should have made a voluntary contribution to the building of a Christian church.[3]

Abraham Haim De Lucena probably ceased acting as hazzan about the year 1714, when Moses Lopez de Fonseca may well have taken over as the "sweet singer of Israel" for Congregation Shearith Israel. Like Brown, Lopez de Fonseca came from a West Indian rabbinical family and had been given an excellent Hebrew education. A tradesman in New York, possibly as early as 1709, he may have succeeded De Lucena long before the latter's death in 1725. When the synagogue was being erected on Mill Street, Lopez de Fonseca was already serving as hazzan with a fixed salary, though it can hardly be doubted, since the duties of a hazzan were not onerous, that he continued to carry on his business. In 1736, after the death of his wife, he finally returned to Curaçao, whence he had come, and officiated on the island as a rabbinical judge and hazzan. Even there, however, he continued as a businessman.[4]

David Machado, who followed Lopez de Fonseca as hazzan, was reputedly a native of the Iberian Peninsula. A Marrano who found refuge and ultimately a home on the banks of the Hudson, he entered the New York business world, acquired some knowledge of Hebrew and Hebraic lore, married the daughter of Dr. Samuel Nunez of Savannah, and capped his career with the office of hazzan at Shearith Israel. Machado served his fellow Jews in the New York area from 1736 to 1747 as precentor, Hebrew schoolmaster, and overseer certifying the kashrut of meat exported to the West Indies. After his death his epitaph was stamped on a lead plate, but many years later during the Revolution, the lead was torn from the marker and melted down for bullets, which was in a way a fitting prelude to the career of his descendants, Revolutionary War veterans and eminent American patriots.[5]

Machado's successor, Benjamin Pereira, another New Yorker, was doing business in Virginia when he was called back to conduct services and to teach the children. Pleading illness, he gave up the position in 1757 and sailed for Jamaica where, however, he kept in touch with his former congregants and tried to help them when they urged him to find them a teacher.

It was obvious to the leaders of Shearith Israel that they would have difficulty in securing a replacement from abroad where the professionally skilled men were to be found, and so they turned once more to a fellow congregant, Isaac Cohen Da Silva, to whom they gave the job on a temporary basis. He served for less than two years (1757–1758), and was succeeded by a man of greater competence, but in 1766 he again assumed the post, only to lose it in 1768 when he went into hiding as a bankrupt and the congregation was compelled to dismiss him.[6]

Joseph Jessurun Pinto, who had been elected hazzan after Cohen Da Silva's first tour of duty, like Brown and Lopez de Fonseca before him, belonged to a well-known rabbinical family. There is every reason to believe that this man, who had come to New York via London from his native Amsterdam, was a competent Hebraist, well-qualified to do his work. He knew Dutch, Spanish, and Portuguese, and as his reports to the *mahamad* eloquently testify, he wrote English as well and in a fair hand. When he returned to London in 1766 to claim an estate, in an act of uncommon generosity for that day and age, the congregation paid his way back. Pinto's last post was with the Sephardic synagogue in Hamburg, where he probably added German, and Danish as well, to his linguistic repertory.[7]

The Cohen Da Silva debacle of 1768 must have induced caution in the selection of the precentor who was to take his place. The choice fell upon a native America, Gershom Mendes Seixas, whose family had been playing a not unimportant part in the congregation's life ever since the first decade of the century. Prior to Seixas' time all the ministers of Shearith Israel were foreign-born as well as foreign-trained, and it bespeaks a considerable measure of religiocultural progress that in 1768 the congregation was able to appoint a native as its reader. The twenty-three year-old Seixas had been able to acquire a very useful working knowledge of the sacred tongue, was a man of good character, thoroughly American, and intelligent. He served his fellow-Jews in New York faithfully till 1776 when, like most of them, he fled before the British and took refuge in nearby Connecticut. During the war he was called to Philadelphia to minister to the newly reorganized Whig congregation. The minority of members left behind in New York, Loyalists and neutralists, conducted services under the English during the Revolution, but with the British evacuation of the city in the fall of 1783, the Jewish Whig refugees returned, summoned Seixas back to the New York pulpit, and began a new chapter in the religious history of American Jewry.[8]

Long before Seixas' appointment as hazzan, however, the congregation had begun making good progress. It had already achieved some form of organization by 1706, when a constitution was adopted to provide "wholesome rules and restrictions." As a recognized and tolerated group, the Jews had advantages denied Christian Dissenters. Indeed, the very year this constitution was written, two Presbyterian ministers were arrested for preaching without a license. The third decade of the eighteenth century brought with it an upsurge in the congregation. Business had been good, New York enjoyed economic expansion and considerable inflation, and Jewish newcomers in small but steadily increasing numbers swelled the size of the little community. There were by then about 175 Jews in town, forty of them "householders," although not all married. Nathan Simson, a rich German-born merchant-shipper, held the presidency in 1720–1721 and was succeeded in September 1721 by an equally distinguished businessman, Jacob Franks. The professional paid staff of the synagogue consisted of a hazzan, a beadle, and a shohet who also served as a teacher. The congregation's total budget amounted to about £128, New York currency, which indicates how small the community still was.[9]

Beginning with the 1720's much more is known about the congregation, for its minute books from 1728 on have been preserved. That year the constitution of 1706 was revised, and the leaders set about raising money to buy land, erect a synagogue, and increase the size of the cemetery. The time had come, they believed, to build a house of worship. Ever since the 1650's they had been meeting in private rooms or rented quarters. By the 1690's they had a rented building to themselves, and the years 1700–1704 found them renting a modest frame house on Mill Street—Jews' Synagogue Street. New York Jewry was to worship on Mill Street until well into the nineteenth century.

By 1728 the congregation had become known as Shearith Israel (Remnant of Israel). How that name came to be chosen is a matter of some conjecture. It is possible, of course, that the Jews of New York looked upon themselves as the "remnant" that had survived the fall of the seventeenth century Brazilian Jewish community, and as early indeed as 1646 Hakam Aboab had referred thus to those who had withstood the attacks of the Portuguese enemy. It is far more likely, however, that the name Remnant of Israel was taken as an allusion to the messianic hopes of a scattered Jewry which had never ceased yearning for the day of its restoration to the ancient homeland in Palestine. Prior to 1728, and occasionally even in later years, the congregation also called itself Shearith Jacob, which may have referred to the prophet Micah's proud boast that in time to come, "the Remnant of Jacob" would stand "in the midst of many peoples, as a lion among the beasts of the forest." [10]

The new synagogue lot purchased on Mill Street in 1728 cost the congregation £100 plus a loaf of sugar and a pound of tea. Even so, the building which was erected could not be owned by the Jewish community as a group, for the Jews were forbidden communal incorporation and could hold neither land nor property in the name of their community. Title to the synagogal and cemetery lots and buildings had instead to be vested in members who gave bond to their fellow-Jews that they would faithfully perform their duties as trustees of the congregation. The new cemetery ground, purchased specifically for the "Jewish Nation," was deeded to the Gomezes, New York's most influential, powerful, and numerous Jewish family in that decade of the 1720's. Themselves quick to make liberal contributions, the Gomezes in turn gave bond to the other members of the congregation that they would not sell the land, but would use it only as a burial ground for Jews. This contrivance worked, but not always smoothly.

Denial of the right to hold property in the name of the Jewish community as a corporate group would occasion the Jews a great deal of trouble in later years. The descendants of the Gomezes tenaciously held on to their legal rights as trustees, and one member of the family had to be paid off in the nineteenth century before he would finally sign a release clearing the deed to the cemetery. In Philadelphia, too, the title to the cemetery lands was originally held by individuals as trustees for the Jewish community, and the Philadelphia community later had similar problems and disputes with respect to its burial ground. Refusal of the right to incorporate was a disability imposed not only on Jews but also on Protestant Dissenters as late as the decade before the Revolution. It was, in fact, not until after the Revolution that the Jews and some other religious groups throughout the country received the privilege of incorporation and proceeded to take title to their lands and buildings.[11]

By 1729 the building committee had begun to erect the synagogue, for which a Jewish artisan was employed as a painter. The construction itself was carried on by local non-Jewish laborers and craftsmen, although some of the materials were purchased from members. The congregation itself was either not rich enough to pay the entire cost of the building or, in accordance with the eleemosynary standards of the day, was simply not prepared to raise and expend the necessary funds. That was not a generation trained to give generously. The total expense of some £600 had to be shared by about forty families, several of them in very modest circumstances. Funds were raised by selling the four cornerstones, which in some cases were auctioned off on the Sabbath. Even widows were expected to contribute their mite. Ultimately, however, the local subscribers sought help from others in this country and abroad. Though they asked support from the three or four Jews in Boston, their primary appeal was directed to the rich Jewish communities of London, Jamaica, Barbados, Surinam, and Curaçao. Over one-third of the total cost came from abroad before the synagogue's final dedication during the Passover season of 1730. The new synagogue was the first to be built on the North American mainland.[12]

The congregation continued its slow but steady growth. Its membership increased as children grew up and immigrants came from Europe. Behind the synagogue a permanent or semipermanent booth, a cabana or sukkah, was erected for the observance of Sukkot, the Feast of Tabernacles. A year after its synagogue was dedicated, the community consecrated a school building on the grounds. Called Yeshibat Minhat Areb (Offering of the Evening or West), taken in all probability from Daniel 9:20–27, where it was associated with "skill and understanding" and a messianic restoration, the building was at times referred to as the school (yeshibah), house of study (beth ha-midrash), or meeting hall (hebrah). Congregational and board meetings were frequently held in it, and the teacher sometimes lived there. This Yeshibat Minhat Areb was an additional evidence of the community's dependence on overseas philanthropy, for it was given to the congregation, no doubt in memory of his parents, by a distinguished philanthropist of Marrano origin, Jacob Mendes da Costa Sr., a native of Bayonne, France, who moved to Amsterdam and finally settled in London. Jacob and his brother Benjamin had also contributed to the building fund of the synagogue, and a few years later the family would give the Georgia Trustees money to help them settle the new colony on the Savannah River.[13]

Shearith Israel was ultimately to have a religious compound on Mill Street. In addition to the synagogue, the cabana, and the school, the congregation had a house and lot, used for the most part by the beadle. By 1759 the members could boast of a small stone building, used as a ritual bath primarily by the women for their monthly purificatory ablutions. Tradition has it that prior to the time it was built, the women of the congregation had bathed in a creek flowing into the East River. Shearith Israel, it is clear, had made great strides since its beginnings in the 1650's. On the eve of the Revolution the congregation owned on Mill Street a plot of ground containing at least five buildings and on Chatham Square maintained an extensive cemetery.[14]

"All go unto one place," Ecclesiastes had said. "All are of the dust, and all return to dust." The Jew was well aware of that, of course, but he wanted the dust to which he would return to testify to his Jewish identity as much at least as his living frame had. Proper burial and proper burial grounds were thus never less than matters of profound concern.[15]

The Jews established at New Amsterdam were granted a cemetery in 1656 by the Dutch, as we have noted, but that cemetery had disappeared a generation later when the Jewish settlers reviving the community under British rule procured a second one in 1682. That year Joseph Bueno de Mesquita purchased a plot of ground on St. James Place below Chatham Square, to be used as a cemetery for his own family and it is probable for other members of the local Jewish community as well. Developing a cemetery under private auspices was not unusual, and many a Jewish cemetery began in colonial times as a private burying ground owned by a family, but opened eventually to other Jews. The Philadelphia and Charleston cemeteries began in this way; the Savannah cemetery was a gift from one of the Sheftalls to the community; and the Boston cemetery, which lasted only a generation, was also originally the property of two partners.

The New York cemetery initiated in 1682 is now known as the Oliver Street, New Bowery, or Chatham Square burial ground. The second oldest Jewish cemetery in the country, it is also the second oldest extant graveyard of any denomination in the city. The "House of Life" in Newport, acquired during the late seventeenth century, ranks probably as the oldest still existing Jewish cemetery in North America, although its oldest dated tombstone harks back only to 1761. The first burial in the New York Jewish burial ground took place in 1683 when Benjamin Bueno de Mesquita, a relative of the owner, was laid to rest there. In those early days the New York cemetery lacked reserved family plots. Following the Sephardic practice of London and Hamburg, graves were not clustered together by family, but individuals were buried next to each other successively in the order of their death. By 1728 the original Bueno de Mesquita field had been filled, and the congregation was compelled to buy additional ground adjacent to the older holdings. The new purchase of 1729 gave the New York Jews enough ground for more than a century. It was used till the early 1830's when it was finally closed to further burials.[16]

New York was the only town in the Hudson River basin to develop a Jewish religious community. Individual families in surrounding settlements and provinces maintained kashrut and owned their own burial plots, but could establish no community. The Louzadas of Bound Brook, New Jersey, for example, were fully observant Jews, but they were simply too few to set up a synagogue. The same was true in New Haven, where a family of Venetian Jews held services in the early 1770's. Nothing, however, is known about those immigrants except that they came from St. Eustatius and were numerous enough to assemble for religious exercises. Even their name remains unknown, and it is probable that they did not linger very long in America. Four years later Jewish Whig émigrés from British-occupied New York certainly conducted services during their sojourn in Connecticut, but Connecticut was to support no permanent Jewish community until the coming of the German Jews about 1840.[17]

Individual Jews were to be found in Boston no later than 1649 but, as in Connecticut, no Jewish community was established there until the 1840's. Although Jewish businessmen were always to be found in the city during the late seventeenth and eighteenth centuries, there were apparently never enough for a religious quorum. Still, even an isolated family in the countryside requires a cemetery plot, and this was true of Boston too. In 1734 two Boston Jewish businessmen set aside a lot for the "Jewish nation" but, though the cemetery is known to have existed for a decade or two, it went unmentioned when the plot was sold in 1762.[18]

NEWPORT

New York's early Jewish community, its minutes still largely extant, unfortunately is the only congregation with extensive records for the colonial period. By contrast, only a few letters, fragments, and financial notations survive to cast a feeble light on the beginnings of the Newport, Philadelphia, and Charleston synagogues. The first appearance of Jews at Newport, for example, cannot be stated with any certainty. Jews may have come to the Rhode Island port from New Amsterdam, Brazil, or Holland as early as the 1650's, but there is no evidence to that effect. The first authentic datum seems to be a deed of purchase for a cemetery at Newport in 1678, and this document is clear in its implication that a number of Jews had once lived in the town but had left. Some two centuries later, however, a soured if not altogether anti-Semitic investigator of considerable capacity, Sidney Rider of Providence, would maintain that the "pretended deed of land for a Jew cemetery in 1677 [old style] is neither more nor less than a deliberate fraud." The extant copy of the Newport deed, it must be confessed, is characterized by a number of irregularities. The original deed itself has been lost or destroyed, and what does exist is a certified copy of the reputed original made in 1767 by the Newport town clerk. There is, on the other hand, no question at all that the existence of a "Jews burial ground" in the city can be documented from the original land records no later than 1693.[19]

Though there are in the cemetery no dated tombstones antecedent to 1761, it should be kept in mind that from about 1690 to about 1750, very few Jews lived at Newport; there were times, no doubt, when not a single one was in town. Stones must have been carried off, eroded by the elements, or destroyed by the youthful vandals who haunt all deserted graveyards. As late as the nineteenth century old and broken stones were known to have been buried or thrown away when repairs were made, and archaeological research on the grounds might well bring some of these old stones to light.

Evidence, albeit indirect, is not entirely lacking to substantiate the existence of the cemetery prior to the 1690's, for the presumptive grantees of the cemetery in 1678 were Barbadian Jews, and it is known that those Barbadians did build the first Newport community. One of them, Mordecai Campanall, is documented at Newport in the 1680's, while the other, Moses Pacheco, was in Boston no later than 1675. In the early 1700's the body of Joseph Frazon, a Boston Jew and apparently a Barbadian immigrant, was carried by coach and boat to Newport for burial. Though there were few if any Jews at Newport in 1713, the area of the old cemetery was designated on a map of that year as Jews Street. During the late 1760's the cemetery appears to have been enlarged by the purchase of additional ground and to have been fenced off and securely padlocked against vandals. In all likelihood this Newport cemetery, still to be seen at the head of Touro Street, is the oldest extant Jewish burial ground in the country.[20]

By 1684 Newport certainly sheltered a quorum of Jews and even a congregation of sorts, with Saul Brown serving as its lay reader. Newport's Jewish community is thus the second oldest in the country, but here too, the settlement was not continuous, for it did not last out the decade. The year 1685 found Brown in New York, struggling to secure privileges for the Jewish religious group there, and it is doubtful whether any organized synagogal life emerged in Newport again until the middle of the next century.[21]

The economic activity attendant on King George's War and on the French and Indian War brought about the rebirth of Jewish congregational life in Newport. A number of Jews began drifting in from New York during the 1740's and Jewishly, Newport became a spiritual colony of New York; as late indeed as 1750 Newport Jews still owed money to Shearith Israel. Whether these debts were membership dues or whether they were offerings made by Newporters whose business affairs made them commuters to the New York market cannot be easily determined, but no later than 1754 and perhaps even earlier, there was a congregation in Newport, and services were conducted in a private room or a house. Zachariah Polock and Jacob Isaacks were the officiants and slaughtered meat according to ritual requirements, although it seems no one in town was capable of performing a circumcision.[22]

The guiding spirits of the new synagogue in all likelihood were the Riveras, whose paterfamilias Abraham had several times been a president of New York's Shearith Israel; Jacob Rodriguez Rivera, Abraham's son, had once sat on the New York congregational board. The different merchants in Newport took turns serving as parnas, and Aaron Lopez, Jacob Rivera's future son-in-law, held the presidency, probably for the first time in 1756–1757. Many years later a nephew of Aaron Lopez would claim that Aaron had been "founder of the Newport Synagogue," but there is not much evidence to support this pious contention of the 1820's. As early as 1757, it is true, Lopez had requested a London merchant to send him lamps, prayer books, and mezuzot, but these purchases may have been made for his own home and rapidly expanding family, rather than for the new congregation over which he was presiding. By the late 1750's, in any event, the congregation had grown enough to attract the outstretched hands of Palestinian messengers, ever on the alert to collect money for themselves or for the perennially destitute communities of the Holy Land. They knew where to turn and had already begun appearing in Newport.[23]

As was typical of all colonial communities, the Newport Jews first held services in private homes, then in rented quarters, and finally in a new building of their own. In 1759 a substantial lot on the edge of town was purchased, and the dozen or so Jewish merchants in Newport, after first making gifts and advancing loans which were to be repaid them, sent out appeals for help. Some of these businessmen

may have had money, but few of them—perhaps none of them—
were rich in the 1750's, and they believed at any rate that other
communities were in duty bound to help them. They turned to
New York, of course, and also to London, Jamaica, Curaçao, Surinam, and probably Barbados as well—in short, to the same communities that Shearith Israel had petitioned thirty years earlier.[24]

Then they set themselves the job of building. Three members,
the richest of the group no doubt, were constituted a building committee and trustees for the property. One of the town's Jewish
firms, Naphtali Hart & Co., served in a supervisory capacity, engaging contractors and workmen, purchasing supplies, and making
necessary disbursements. That same year (1759) six cornerstones
were laid, four for the synagogue and two for the annex to house
both school and sexton. A year later Shearith Israel lent the Newporters the defunct Georgia community's Scroll of the Law, and if
this was their first scroll—which one may well doubt—then prior
to that date the Newporters had obviously been holding services
without benefit of a manuscript Pentateuch. This contrasts sharply
with the situation nine years later when the Newporters could boast
of six treasured Torahs in their ark. The synagogue at its completion cost about £2,000 sterling, a large sum, too large apparently
for the resources of a congregation which included at the most ten
merchants of any real substance.[25]

In 1761 and 1762 the Rhode Islanders appealed to their coreligionists in New York for money, ornaments, furniture, lamps,
and wax for candles. They did not appeal in vain, but it was the
congregation's misfortune that its members had not begun to build
until the war boom was over. The Newporters found themselves in
real trouble. They were saddled with a large debt in the midst of the
financial depression which had set in with collapse of the war economy. In consequence, some of the congregations which the Newporters asked for aid had little choice but to turn a deaf ear to
them. Nevertheless, the dedication of the new synagogue was finally
celebrated on December 2, 1763, during Hanukkah, the Feast of
Dedication or Lights. The dedication was a colorful ceremony, high-
lighted by the procession of Jewish leaders carrying the pentateuchal
scrolls, and the affair featured in addition the traditional chants and

the curious and respectful glances of the provincial officials invited to grace the occasion with their distinguished presence. Pastor Ezra Stiles, that untiring notetaker and diarist, was in attendance and returned home to record that "Dr. Isaac de Abraham Touro performed the service." Hazzan Touro thus became the second of his breed to receive the accolade of what we might call a doctoral degree, *honoris causa*; the first was a Charlestonian, "The Right Reverend Moses Cohen, D.D.," who had departed this world almost two years earlier.[26]

The Newport congregation seems to have been known originally in 1754 as the "Scattered Ones of Israel" (Nephuse Israel). That name was inspired by Isaiah 11:12—a messianic verse which supplied names for two hopeful congregations in the Western Hemisphere: Barbados as well as Newport—"[God] will assemble the dispersed of Israel [Nidhe Yisrael, which the Jews of Bridgetown called their synagogue] and gather together the scattered of Judah [Nefuzot Yehudah, which the Newporters adapted to their purposes]." By 1764, however, the community at Newport had assumed a more positive attitude to the messianic redemption, and now sanguinely called itself Yeshuat Israel (Salvation of Israel), a phrase from Psalm 14:7.[27]

Not that the Newporters had much cause for optimism in 1764, since the postwar depression had scarcely ceased plaguing the congregation. Indeed, by 1764 the community was unable not only to amortize its three-year-old mortgage, but even to pay the interest on it, and the Jews were in some danger of losing their building. In their distress they turned to a Christian Curaçaon Dutch businessman then in Newport, and asked him to intercede for them with their Curaçaon coreligionists.[28]

The Newporters managed to survive that crisis; times got better, and by the early 1770's the congregation was flourishing. It now had a synagogue, a school, an oven to bake unleavened bread for Passover, and even a little mortuary chapel where last honors were paid the bodies of the deceased. The congregation's religious needs were met not only by the hazzan but also by a slaughterer, Myer Benjamin, and a beadle, Benjamin Myers, the father of Major Mordecai Myers, a veteran of the War of 1812. There had also settled at Newport a Hebrew teacher, Moses V. Calo, but whether he worked exclusively for the Lopez family or served the entire community is uncertain.[29]

Unfortunately, this eager and vigorous Jewish community was not destined to enjoy many years of happiness. The Revolutionary War saw to that. When the British occupied Newport in 1776 the Whigs among the Jews fled, and even some of the Jewish Loyalists slipped away for fear of the local patriots. The Jewish community never recovered from the blow of military occupation. By the time the war ended Newport was on the decline, and her Jewish community was moribund by the end of the century.

MONTREAL

The first Jewish settlement in Canada was at Halifax where, within a year after the town's founding in 1749, a Jewish cemetery had been established and worship services were being conducted, though in all likelihood only sporadically. Even unobservant Jews have always and everywhere been ready to assemble for recitation of the kaddish, the memorial prayer for the dead, but there is no indication that a community was actually organized at Halifax.[30]

It was not until the British conquest of 1759–1760 that Jews began settling in the province of Quebec. By 1760, however, the province had more than enough Jewish supplymen for a religious quorum, and there is every reason to believe they held religious services. The Jewish sutlers who accompanied the British armed forces may not have been particularly observant—how observant could they be in time of war?—but nonetheless some of them are to be numbered among the founders of the Canadian Jewish community. After the end of the war in 1763 those supplymen and other Canadian businessmen were able to fashion a new Jewish community. Montreal began to grow and along with her the local Jewry as the fur trade received a new lease of life. Montreal's Shearith Israel Congregation is thought to have had its beginnings in 1768, and if one may judge from the congregation's name and the very close commercial relations its members enjoyed with New York Jewry, it is obvious that the Jews of Montreal were spiritual scions of the community on the Hudson.

The year 1770 saw the Harts of Three Rivers set aside a family burial plot in their town, while five years later the Montreal community established a cemetery near present-day Dominion Square which at that time was outside the city limits. Inasmuch as no Jewish congregation could be incorporated in Canada till 1831, the cemetery land was held in the name of Lazarus David. The congregation's first parnas known by name is said to have been Philadelphia-born David Salisbury Franks in 1775. Franks did not remain in Canada during the Revolution, but left to become one of the newly independent nation's most distinguished Jewish patriots. He would attain the rank of lieutenant colonel before his separation from the American army.

Two years after Franks's reported presidency, the congregation built a stone synagogue on Notre Dame and St. James Streets and a year later, in 1778 adopted an elaborate constitution. Phoebe, the widow of Lazarus David, gave or lent her coreligionists ground for the sanctuary, and Abraham Judah soon presented them with a Scroll of the Law for the synagogue's ark. Clearly, the community was thriving, for in the short space of three years it purchased a cemetery, built a substantial though modest house of worship, and brought Jacob Raphael Cohen over from London to serve as a reader. Cohen, the community's first minister, was also to function as teacher and slaughterer. A North African living in London when invited to Canada in 1778, he sailed for New York after a somewhat hectic career in Montreal and was at length summoned to Philadelphia, where he officiated into the early nineteenth century. By 1780 Shearith Israel of Montreal had acquired at least four Scrolls of the Law; two additional scrolls had been presented by the Sephardic mother synagogue in London, and one had been purchased by subscription. All during the 1770's, it is worthy of note, this young, vigorous, and contentious congregation could probably never claim more than a dozen members.[31]

CHAPTER 49

THE SYNAGOGUES OF PENNSYLVANIA

AND THE SOUTH

Philadelphia

To Nathan Levy of the well-known New York Levy-Franks clan belongs the credit for founding the Philadelphia Jewish community; though to be sure, the term "community" should not be taken too literally, since some three decades were to pass before a permanent congregation came into existence. By 1738 Levy had purchased an emergency burial plot, and two years later he secured another piece of ground on Spruce Street as a family cemetery. The graveyard on Spruce Street, later increased through purchases by Levy and others, was in use by the 1760's as a communal cemetery. Still on the edge of town during the 1750's, the cemetery was not closed until the second half of the nineteenth century and is today one of Philadelphia's best-known Jewish historic sites. The burial ground's gradual but steady growth in size affords an index to the development of the Jewish community.[1]

Thus it can be said there must have been at least a dozen or more families in town during the 1740's, which would seem to substantiate the tradition that Jewish services were held that decade in rented quarters on Sterling Alley. The lack of a formal community during the 1750's is suggested by the fact that Nathan Levy, the most important Jew in town, was still paying dues to the New York synagogue, while Samson Levy as late as 1754 had to import a mohel from New York to circumcise a son. From the 1760's on, however, religious functionaries were always available to the Jews of Philadelphia and the backcountry for ritual slaughtering, circumcision, marriages, divorces, and scribal needs. Kosher meat, prepared locally, was exported to the West Indies.[2]

As in every town of Jewish settlement, the early years of the French and Indian War brought Philadelphia a noticeable degree of prosperity and an influx of newcomers. By 1760 there was even talk of building a synagogue and the following year, a few weeks before the High Holy Days, a group of Jews from Philadelphia and the outlying towns borrowed a pentateuchal scroll from New York. The scroll, it is very probable, was used for services held in Philadelphia, but there was still no organized congregation. Wills made out by Philadelphia Jews left money for the local cemetery, but contained no legacy to a local synagogue, and a deed of trust executed in 1764, listing all American Jewish congregations, omitted Philadelphia altogether. New York Jewry, sending an itinerant on to Philadelphia in 1768, apparently knew of no Jewish organization in the city at that time, and a directory for the years 1767–1768 made no mention of a Jewish house of worship. In 1769 Rachel Moses wrote to a Christian minister that there was no "rabbin to apply to here." (There may indeed have been no Jewish clergyman in Philadelphia at the time, but the fall Holy Days would see *two* rival services!)[3]

The year 1771 was the magic year for the Jews of Philadelphia. They rented quarters and settled down to establish a permanent congregation. The press took notice of the congregation's existence, the Reverend Gershom M. Seixas came down from New York to officiate at its consecration, and Hazzan Touro of Newport called the new synagogue to the attention of Ezra Stiles. It may well have been then that the simple draft constitution found among the Yiddish papers in the Gratz-Joseph collection was written. A scroll and prayer books were purchased in London; Myer Myers, the goldsmith, made the Philadelphians some beautiful ornaments for their Torah; Shearith Israel gave them a silver pointer; and even they themselves were affluent enough to support a permanent beadle. Philadelphia Jewry had arrived![4]

A minute of 1773, one of the few references to the prerevolutionary congregation, indicates that the new congregation was already known as Mikveh Israel. If this record has been accurately quoted, it would seem that the Philadelphians had taken as their namesake the

Curaçaon community established during the preceding century. Since, however, the Yiddish draft constitution of about 1770 and the Ezekiel Levy employment contract of 1776 do not use the name Mikveh Israel in speaking of the synagogue, it is by no means improbable that the name was first adopted in 1782 and may well have been proposed at that time by one of the new congregation's founders, Mordecai Sheftall of Savannah's Mikveh Israel synagogue. The Philadelphia congregation's president in the early 1770's was Barnard Gratz and its treasurer was Solomon Marache, a New York businessman who had moved to fast-growing Philadelphia. Still, though the new congregation was conducting services and distributing charity to needy Jews, other Jewish communities seem to have remained unaware of its existence, for when Mordecai Sheftall made a deed of trust for the Savannah cemetery in 1773, he included Charleston, Newport, and New York, but not Philadelphia. Nevertheless, the Philadelphia synagogue was firmly established, and the year 1776 found it employing young Ezekiel Levy in the triune position of reader, shohet, and Hebrew teacher.[5]

EASTON AND LANCASTER

North of Philadelphia on the Delaware lay the little town of Easton, whose founding fathers included a Jew. There were nearly always four or five Jewish families in town. Michael Hart kept a kosher home there, for which he performed his own ritual slaughtering. When General Washington passed through Easton he was entertained by the well-to-do Hart and enjoyed the rare privilege of eating a kosher meal.

It is hardly to be doubted that there was an occasional quorum of Jews in Easton, and services were certainly held there. Still, though a group settled permanently in a town might be expected to have an imperative need for a cemetery, there is no record of one at Easton in colonial days. The town, however, did have at least one man, a "Rabby Israel," competent to serve as a religious factotum—documented by the fact that New York found in Easton a candidate for the job of shohet and teacher. "Rabby Israel" was probably employed professionally in Easton, where he may well have taught their children and performed all other religious functions for the town's handful of Jews. The religious services he rendered may have been an avocation on his part, and it is not improbable that the "Rabby" derived his real living from clerking or peddling. There is no indication that Easton ever developed an organized community, although there, as in Lancaster, the line between formal organization and informal gathering was fine indeed.[6]

The frontier town of Lancaster, larger and more substantial than Easton, saw the establishment of what might be called a Jewish community—a rather unique Jewish community at that. In Philadelphia, in Savannah, and probably in other towns too where Jews maintained synagogues, one man appears to have "carried" the community, at least for a period of time. Cases in point were the leadership of Nathan Levy in Philadelphia and of Mordecai Sheftall in Savannah. Lancaster, however, was even more of a patriarchal or family community. Not only were her Jews very probably organized and held together by one man, but his death some fifty years later meant the death of the community. The paterfamilias of Lancaster Jewry was Joseph Simon, the richest Jew in the area, who had Jewish partners, several sons-in-law, and marital ties to a number of people. It was around him that Lancaster's one-man synagogue revolved.

As early as 1747 a cemetery had been purchased in trust for the Society of Jews settled in and about Lancaster. Within a decade Jews had taken up residence in a number of the surrounding towns —as far west as Northumberland, and by the time of the French and Indian War, even in Pittsburgh. With at least ten adult males as a nucleus, a synagogue was established at Lancaster about the middle of the century, most likely in Simon's home; it is doubtful whether the local Jews ever worshiped in a separate building. Ultimately, the community was able to boast of having its own ark, two Torah scrolls along with silver ornaments for them, and a synagogal treasury. Since some of the local businessmen traveled about frequently, it was probably impossible to assemble the necessary quorum for services every Sabbath, but there is ample evidence that the major holidays were observed. Jews in the surrounding settlements found it easier to travel to the relatively large town of Lancaster for the holy days than to undertake the long trip on poor roads to distant Philadelphia.[7]

Lancaster Jewry seems to have had everything essential for communal life. Kosher meat, for example, was always available, since a number of the men in town were trained in shehitah. By the 1750's Simon was employing a ritual slaughterer and teacher in his home for his numerous progeny, and there can be no doubt that all the Jews in town took advantage of the presence of such a functionary. Even when the shohet and teacher left him for greener pastures, Simon could turn, temporarily at least, to the ubiquitous Barnard Jacobs. Still, if Simon quarreled with the local slaughterers, or if his own factotum deserted him, he found himself in a great deal of trouble religiously. When his daughter Miriam married the young merchant Michael Gratz, the bridegroom took pains to bring Hazzan Seixas to Lancaster all the way from New York. Was that because Simon was currently feuding with the local "clergy"? Or was it simply that for so important an occasion, Simon preferred the services of a professional from a big city? Another of Simon's sons-in-law owed money to the Philadelphia synagogue, but this need not have reflected trouble in Lancaster; it might have meant no more than that while on a buying or selling trip to Philadelphia, the visiting Lancastrian had made an offering for the Philadelphia shul. It is, in any case, a fact that when the Revolution broke out, Lancaster Jewry was a flourishing community, a "city of refuge" during the war.[8]

CHARLESTON

Jews had been settled at Charleston since the late seventeenth century, and it is by no means unlikely that the four Jewish merchants who lived there were able, through the aid of visiting Jewish businessmen, to conduct occasional services. Nonetheless, real evidence of Jewish religious life and an organized Jewish community does not antedate the late 1740's or early 1750's. By the 1740's Charleston Jewry had received a substantial number of recruits from the moribund colony of Georgia; enough at least had established themselves there to help lay the foundations of a Charleston community.

Nathaniel Levin, a nineteenth-century writer who had access to records now lost, reported that services were first held during the High Holy Days of 1749, and Levin's account would have it that the congregation began with a full-fledged rabbi, a hazzan, and a president. This is all highly improbable, however, for Jacob Olivera's will, dated 1751, left money to a London synagogue, but made no mention of a local sanctuary. A generation later Isaac Da Costa was to claim that he himself had "in 1754 instituted a synagogue at Charleston," and it is also known that regulations for the growing community had been adopted no later than 1756. Thus, though 1749 seems to be a fanciful date for the congregation's founding, there is no reason to doubt the existence of an organized community in the mid-1750's, and by the 1760's the Charlestonians were receiving gifts of ceremonial utensils from a Curaçaon family.

Two men in particular deserve the credit for helping organize Charleston's Jewish community: Isaac Da Costa and Moses Cohen, both businessmen and in all probability volunteer readers. These two sires of the Charleston synagogue happen to have had more than rudimentary Jewish learning. Cohen died in 1762 and his proud family then, or perhaps at a later time, denominated him on his tombstone as "The Right Reverend Moses Cohen, Doctor of Divinity." Da Costa served the congregation as its reader till 1764 when he quit after a quarrel. Another of the founders was Mordecai Sheftall of Savannah, to whom belongs the distinction of having helped create three colonial Jewish communities: Savannah, Charleston, and in 1782, Philadelphia's reorganized war-time synagogue.

No later than 1751, the year Olivera died, there was a cemetery in town, and a group of men performed the traditional ablutions for the corpse. Some ten years later Da Costa established a family graveyard in which his fellow-reader Moses Cohen was interred. It was this burial ground which Da Costa sold in 1764 to several people, to be held by them in trust as a cemetery for Charleston Jewry. The trustees he chose, in addition of course to the local designees, were residents of London, Jamaica, Barbados, Newport, Savannah, and

New York. Da Costa and his associates believed, it would seem, that there was safety in numbers, and it is obvious, too, that in designating those he did, Da Costa was drawing the boundaries of his commercial world.

In the cemetery's deed of trust the Charleston congregation was called Beth Elohim (House of God), which may have represented an abbreviation of Beth Elohim Unveh Shalom (The House of the Lord and Mansion of Peace), the congregation's full name as we know from later records. Another possibility—in view of the far from placid nature of these early American Jewish pioneers—is that the double name, documented for the first time during the 1780's, reflects a merger of two rival conventicles.

No later than 1766 Abraham Alexander was serving as hazzan, and there is every indication that he was brought over from London to act as Beth Elohim's first professional reader and factotum. He had probably been summoned to replace Da Costa. Alexander would serve the congregation as a salaried functionary until postrevolutionary days, when he became a civil servant. There seems to be no question that by the time of the Revolution, the congregation had acquired a full complement of officials, both honorary and paid; it had emerged as a fully developed community in every sense of the word.

Since its founding the congregation had changed its rented quarters at least three times, but by 1775 it was ready to build. Da Costa at that time purchased a lot in his own name, payment to be guaranteed by five members of the synagogue. Following the traditional pattern of seeking help elsewhere, the Charlestonians turned to New York for aid, but were refused, understandably enough, for the Revolution was imminent, times were bad, and the New Yorkers were very apprehensive. Their hopes for a building of their own thwarted, the Charlestonians that same year of 1775 accepted from Joseph Tobias a seven-year lease for two rooms on Hasell Street to be used as a synagogue. Tobias, indeed, may have offered the lease as a gift, for the congregation voted him a public blessing for his generosity. During the Revolution, however, the community did secure quarters of its own; a factory was rented, rebuilt, and remodelled into a house of worship, later known as the Old Synagogue.[9]

SAVANNAH

Savannah Jewry came to America as an organized group of colonists. Forty-two—including a baby who died during the crossing—had set out on the voyage. Landing in the six-month-old colony on July 11, 1733, these pioneers brought with them from England a Scroll of the Law, a set of circumcision instruments (gifts from a London well-wisher, a Mr. Lindo), and reportedly a wooden box to serve as an ark for housing the scroll. Dr. Samuel Nunez, the physician who accompanied the group, may have served as the circumciser.

There is every reason to believe that the Jewish newcomers held services on disembarking and regularly after that. Not long after their arrival Oglethorpe gave them a plot on the commons for use as a cemetery, and in 1735 a more formal communal organization was attempted, with the congregation taking as its name The Hope of Israel (Mikveh Israel). Obviously, the name had been inspired by the Curaçao synagogue, one of the oldest, largest, and richest in the Western Hemisphere.

Factious though they were and split by Sephardic-Ashkenazic antagonisms, the Jewish colonists who united into a formal congregation were probably impelled to do so by missionary advances on the part of the neighboring Anglicans and the Lutheran Salzburgers. Despite hard times in pioneer surroundings, the congregation grew. A year after its founding Mikveh Israel had a teacher. In 1737 the community received another Torah, as well as a Hanukkah lamp and some prayer books, from Benjamin Mendes da Costa, a well-known London philanthropist who was the first president of the Board of Deputies of British Jews and gave substantial sums every year to Christian and Jewish charities. The following year there was talk of building a synagogue. The Jews could not unite to accomplish that end, however, for the traditional gulf between the town's Sephardim and Ashkenazim simply proved too wide. In this respect Savannah was unique among North American Jewish communities. Though the Ashkenazim were decidedly in the minority, it would seem that no building program could be carried on without them. Nevertheless, services still went on under the direction of a salaried young hazzan who seems to have been learned and competent.

Within less than a decade, however, it became apparent that in Savannah at least, "the Hope of Israel" was not long for this world. By 1740 the entire Georgia colony, not alone its Jewish enclave, had begun to disintegrate as a result of restrictions both on slaveholding and on the buying and selling of land. Georgia could not hope to rival the more attractive conditions other provinces offered, and so the colony collapsed, its first Jewish community dying with it. Except for two or three families, Georgia Jewry abandoned the colony, and it was not until the French and Indian War that the Jewish group began to reconstitute itself. The war-time prosperity attracted new Jewish settlers, and some of the children of the original pioneers returned. Even before the colony fell to the crown in 1752, the trustees had undertaken to relax their prohibitions against slavery and to ease their restrictions on land sales.

The renewed vigor of the Savannah congregation is reflected during the 1760's in its struggle to acquire burial grounds, a struggle which elicited an intriguing response from some of Savannah's Christian residents. Fearing a Jewish cemetery in Savannah would adversely affect property values in the burgeoning community, a number of the townspeople claimed that Christians would not "choose to buy or rent a house whose windows looked into a burial ground of any kind, particularly one belonging to a people who might be presumed, from prejudice of education, to have imbibed principles entirely repugnant to those of our most holy religion." Lest the reader conclude that nothing more than Judeophobia stood behind this statement, it should be noted that the petition of the Jews was not the only one to be rejected about that time—a similar petition of the Presbyterians was also refused.

Persuaded by 1773 that no concessions would be forthcoming from the Savannah authorities, Mordecai Sheftall gave the Jewish community a five-acre tract of land for a new cemetery and a synagogue building. Sheftall's grant specifically declared in its deed of trust that the plot was open to all Jews. This field appears to have been originally a private burial ground for the family, and that same year Levi Sheftall set aside exclusively for the Sheftall family another burial plot on ground immediately adjacent to his brother Mordecai's grant. Thus both of Savannah Jewry's two extant colonial cemeteries were established by the Sheftall brothers.[10]

Mordecai Sheftall did not limit his activity to the founding of a cemetery. Apparently there had been as yet no formal reorganization of the community, but in 1774 Sheftall invited the Jews to worship in his home and to reestablish a synagogue. The South seems to have been prospering during the early 1770's; the Charlestonians, for example, it will be recalled, even thought of building their own synagogue on the eve of the Revolution. In Savannah too, however, the war brought ambitious plans to an end. Occupied by the British, the city was administered by the Loyalists; its Jews, most of them Whigs, thought themselves well-advised to flee, and resumption of a congregational life would wait perforce until 1786.[11]

CHAPTER 50

SYNAGOGUE ART AND ARCHITECTURE

SHEARITH ISRAEL OF NEW YORK

Two synagogues were built as such in colonial America—or three if we include the Montreal building erected in 1777. A stone edifice with a tall red roof, the Montreal building and its yard were surrounded by a high whitewashed wall. The other two structures built for synagogal use were Shearith Israel's Mill Street Synagogue in New York and the Newport synagogue. There was nothing specifically "Jewish" or even Oriental about the architecture of those three houses of worship.

The no longer extant New York sanctuary, finished in 1730, was a small simple structure of blue-faced brick, thirty-five feet square and twenty-one feet high. Surmounted by a hipped or peaked roof sloping on all four sides, the synagogue had for its entrance a tall central door on the west side and also two windows, long enough to give light, on the west, north, and south sides. The floor was laid with square Bristol stones, and a stove provided heat in wintertime. Small as this synagogue was, it was larger than the Baptist and Quaker meetinghouses and was very attractive. Running around three sides of the building were galleries reserved for the women who, following traditional Jewish practice, were segregated from the men at worship. During prerevolutionary days a special bench on the north side was set aside for the aristocratic Gomez women, but that choice spot was given up by them after the war when a more democratic procedure prevailed and the Gomezes no longer owned the wealth or exercised the influence that had once distinguished them.

The entire building and its pulpit were—again in accordance with Jewish tradition—oriented toward the east in deference to the Holy Land. On the synagogue's extreme eastern side was the ark (*hekal*) containing the Scrolls of the Law. Encompassed on its three sides by a railing of banisters, the ark had three or four steps leading up to the doors by which it was opened. Above the ark rested a wooden representation of the Tablets of the Ten Commandments, and in front of the Decalogue hung a glass lamp containing the eternal light. In the center of the floor, facing east, sat the pulpit or reading desk, an elevated platform called the *tebah* or *shulhan*, surrounded by a low banister.

Around the north and south walls were benches. On the north side there was a special seat or *banca* for the president, and on the south side a similar seat for his alternate. Special seating provisions seem also to have been made for honored Christian guests. Later, some seats were placed around the center *tebah* where the children could sit under the watchful eye of the hazzan. Much of the floor space was left free for the standing worshipers and for the procession carrying the Torah from the ark to the reading desk. In all probability the floor of the Mill Street Synagogue—and of other colonial Jewish sanctuaries too—was covered with sand. Tradition would have it that the sand symbolized the desert through which the Israelites had wandered for forty long years in their flight from slavery to freedom, and it was also said to recall the original Tent of Meeting erected in the wilderness. Less romantically, but a good deal more realistically, one may venture the guess that far from reflecting the ancient Sinaitic milieu, the sand in the New York as in the Curaçaon synagogue was no more than a cultural lag from the Middle Ages when the floors of unheated public buildings were sand-strewn as a hygienic measure.

Illumination for the Mill Street building came from four chandeliers, each of sixteen candles, hung from each corner of the ceiling, and in the center a fifth chandelier of thirty-two candles. There were also candlesticks on the banister corners facing the ark and on the central reading desk. Some of the candles were as thick as a man's arm.

All synagogues owned ritual silver and costly textile covers. Shearith Israel beautified its Torah scrolls with silver scroll bells or ornamental finials fitting over the two staves of each scroll. These stylized stave-crowns, called *rimmonim* (pomegranates), had hanging bells. One pair was dated 1737, and around 1765 Myer Myers made another pair for the New York synagogue. Later this distinguished goldsmith also fashioned two sets of *rimmonim* for the newly organized Philadelphia synagogue. The New York congregation possessed pointers of precious metal for reading the Torah as well as silver cups and goblets for wine. There were lavers for the ritual washing of the hands, and rams' horns (shofarot) were sounded on the High Holy Days to call the worshipers to contrition and repentance. The inner walls of the ark were covered with damask, while there were also hangings within the ark in front of the scrolls, richly decorated mantles for the scrolls themselves, and cloths for the central reading desk. One of the cloths used for the desk was of red tapestry fringed with silver lace; some were made of silk, and still others were lined with taffeta. At the entrance to the synagogue stood a mahogany receptacle with the inscription "charity box." There is no doubt at all that the Mill Street Synagogue enabled its congregants to "worship the Lord in the beauty of holiness." [1]

NEWPORT

The Newport synagogue—known today as the Touro Synagogue in commemoration of the Touro brothers, its nineteenth-century benefactors—is the oldest *extant* Jewish sanctuary on the North American continent. It is younger by some decades than the present-day Mikveh Israel synagogue on Curaçao and the Sephardic synagogue in Paramaribo, Surinam, both of which date from the 1730's. The structure, for which ground was purchased in 1759 and on which work probably began two years later, was nearing completion in December 1763 when its consecration took place. Originally surrounded by a wooden fence, the synagogue was the only brick church in Newport. Its designer, the English-born Newport farmer and merchant Peter Harrison, was one of the best known architects in colonial America and succeeded in producing an edifice of exceptional beauty.

Harrison, an amateur who is believed to have worked without fee, was gifted with great artistry. Most of his plans, which he skillfully blended or varied, were drawn from English books reproducing architectural drawings. Harrison had already helped design Newport's Redwood Library, which had a few Jewish members and which all the Jews in town had ample opportunity to view, while some of the Newport Jews had no doubt also seen his King's Chapel in Boston. They were soon to see another of Harrison's productions, the Brick Market which arose in Newport about the same time as the synagogue.

The design for the synagogue's exterior, unaffected and unlimited in concept by any Jewish tradition, was left entirely to the architect. Harrison conceived it as a two-story Georgian structure of imported brick with a four-sloped roof. Built on a lot 92 by 106 feet, the synagogue was 35 feet wide, 40 feet long, and 48 feet high. Though its exterior lacked anything distinctively Jewish, the synagogue's interior, as in New York and indeed in all synagogues, was conditioned and governed by the traditional layout of the floor and the needs of Jewish worship. Hazzan Touro had no doubt told Harrison about the ark, the reading desk, the galleries, and the orientation to the east, and the architect may also have once visited the Bevis Marks synagogue in London. It is more likely, of course, that Harrison had visited Shearith Israel in New York, and he may even have seen pictures of eighteenth century Sephardic synagogues. Interestingly enough, the ark designed by Harrison is similar to his design for the altar of King's Chapel—a circumstance rather memorably foreshadowing the mutual tolerance American exigencies were to impose on all religious groups in the next decade.[2]

Harrison's design featured two colonnaded aisles of twelve columns on the lower floor and twelve in the gallery. The number twelve was probably not fortuitous and may have been reminiscent of the twelve tribes of Israel. The Amsterdam and London Sephardic

[893]

synagogues also had twelve columns. Above the ark was a painted representation of the Ten Commandments, surmounted by the traditional three *ketarim*—the crowns of study, priesthood, and Davidic royalty. As in all synagogues of that time, the usual perpetual lamp or eternal light hung above the ark, and in the center of the floor rested the raised platform with its reading desk facing east. Under that reading desk is found a very short passageway which has aroused considerable speculation. Some, conscious of the harried existence the crypto-Jews endured under the Inquisition, have suggested that the passageway is part of an escape tunnel, but in all probability it is nothing more than a secret storage room, typical of many buildings in eighteenth century America.[3]

As was also the case in Shearith Israel, the Newport synagogue had benches built around the walls with an enclosure on the north side for the honorary officers and their guests. The seats on this *banca* were decorated with inlaid Chinese mosaic work, reflecting the Chinese influences which were very strong in the world of eighteenth century art and are even visible in some of the stylized scroll bells of the New York silversmith Myer Myers. Lighting was provided by five large and small chandeliers hanging from the ceiling. The gifts of members, some of them were not installed until 1770; one portrays human heads and is rumored to have been donated by a Marrano priest from Catholic Spain. It is far more likely, however, that this chandelier is the work of a Christian craftsman who knew nothing of the prejudice some Jews harbored against graven images, especially in synagogal art.

By 1769 six scrolls reposed in the ark, some as loans from members of the congregation, others as gifts. One of the scrolls had been sent over by the London Sephardim, and another had been received from the Amsterdam Sephardic synagogue. Six years earlier, at the building's dedication Pastor Stiles had reported only "three vellum copies, rolls of the Law," including the one presented by the Jews of Amsterdam. That gift from Amsterdam is, incidentally, an interesting example of Jewish religious solidarity, for it evinces Amsterdam Jewry's capacity to surmount the feeling of envy England's imperial success had aroused in her Dutch rivals.

Newport Jewry not only had an ample supply of Torah scrolls, but also colorful mantles for the Torahs and at least two pairs of scroll bells made by Myer Myers. The synagogue was graced as well with two wooden "charity boxes" and with costly candlesticks sent by a pious London mother in honor of her son, a young Rhode Island businessman. By contrast with the partition or banister in Shearith Israel, which reached about to the chin, the women's gallery on the second floor of the Newport synagogue featured a relatively low balustrade, but it is not likely the women could be seen very well or could themselves see very much, since the bench they occupied was set back against the wall. Again by contrast with the New York synagogue, whose women's gallery was probably approached by an outside staircase, the gallery in Newport was reached through inside steps to the second floor of a building attached to the northern side of the synagogue. This wing, designed by Harrison for use as a school, was constructed at the same time as the house of worship. The Reverend Andrew Burnaby, who visited Newport in 1760 and saw the synagogue annex under construction, complained that despite the synagogue's elegant interior, the exterior would be "totally spoilt" by the school annex. Burnaby's criticism may have been esthetically justified, but for Newport Jewry esthetics took second place to education. A school building, they felt, was of paramount importance, and so they did not hesitate to spoil their synagogue by annexing to it a two-story addition intended to serve as a school, sexton's quarters, and meeting place for the officers and congregants.[4]

That Newport's new synagogue was an "edifice the most perfect of the temple kind perhaps in America," as Ezra Stiles noted, is not to be gainsaid, but the structure's exterior was nonetheless rather modest—probably not by happenstance. The modest exteriors of both of America's mid-eighteenth century synagogues mirrored, it is possible, not only the severity and frugality of the times, but also a desire on the part of the congregants to avoid undue attention to themselves and their doings. This was, after all, an age in which anti-Jewish disabilities still persisted, and the Jews had no wish to invite envy and enmity by pretentious buildings. That they had no lack of pride in their synagogues is bespoken by the elegance lavished on their interiors, as in Newport. The exterior of the Newport synagogue is not impressive; the beauty lies within. The synagogue owes its rank as one of colonial America's finest structures to the exquisite design Harrison adopted for its interior, and to the fine craftsmanship of the skilled workmen who carried out the architect's plans. Although the interior walls and ceiling are now painted in attractive delicate tints, the original color scheme remains undetermined; the small porch at the entrance may have been painted white or cream originally, while the brick of the building may have been painted yellow.

The religiocultural significance to be derived from the very appearance of Newport's eighteenth century Jewish sanctuary has not gone unnoted by later generations. No one has expressed it better than a biographer of Peter Harrison, the synagogue's architect:

There could be no more fitting symbol of the sweet reasonableness pervading the religious atmosphere of eighteenth-century Newport than the spectacle of a congregation professing an oriental faith asking a Christian of the Anglican persuasion to plan its synagogue, and of the Episcopalian, entirely without remuneration, responding with the finest interior design of his career—and that based on pagan Greek and Roman forms.[5]

The synagogue exteriors in Newport and in New York were not alone in their lack of ostentation. Even less artistry was lavished on the tombstones to be found in the Jewish cemeteries of the colonial period. There was no absence of floral scrolls, rosettes, portrayals of sacerdotal hands outstretched in blessing, or Levitical ewers and basins, but unlike the contemporary cemeteries of Curaçao and Amsterdam with their beautifully sculptured stones depicting deathbed scenes and symbolic representations of life's transitoriness, the stones in American cemeteries were invariably simple, invariably devoid of elaborate delineations. This, however, is to be ascribed to no traditional prejudice against graven images, but to the cost involved in fashioning splendid tombstones and to the absence of craftsmen adept in such work.[6]

CHAPTER 51

THE SYNAGOGUE AND ITS ADMINISTRATION—I

A PLACE FOR PRAYER, EDUCATION, CHARITY, MEETINGS, AND GOSSIP

The synagogue—which Renan justly characterized as "the most original and fruitful creation of the Jewish people"—has always been something more than a house of prayer. In seventeenth and eighteenth century Europe the synagogue was commonly a complex including a number of buildings where people met for common worship, where adults and children studied Hebraic lore, and where the community or its leaders gathered to discuss serious problems. In colonial America too, while the synagogue's main building was almost solely a place for worship and an occasional sermon, the annex (adjacent and auxiliary structures) housed classes in Hebrew for the children. There is no indication that any form of Hebraic study for adults was offered in the synagogal environs or anywhere else for that matter, but the *mahamad*, which met frequently, assembled by choice in the annex to decide matters touching on administration, education, discipline, or philanthropy. In a congregation with but one structure at its disposal, the board carried on its deliberations in the synagogue itself. What was true of the *mahamad* was true also of the congregation as a whole when its members were summoned to meetings by their leaders or, spurning the *mahamad*, assembled on their own initiative.[1]

The Jews, it is clear, did not gather together only or merely to intone prayers out of their well-thumbed liturgies. They constituted a people with a common background of tradition, of history, and not least, of problems, and they took delight in their gatherings. As a rule they met in the sanctuary only on formal religious occasions, but the synagogue also served to some degree as a communal club, though never as a dining or card club. It was the community's religious, cultural, and associative center. Though no "social center" in the modern sense of the term and apparently much less a community center than the New England meetinghouse, the colonial synagogue was not without its convivial aspects. Board meetings held on the synagogue premises often included collations at congregational expense, and the autumnal Festival of Booths provided worshipers with an occasion to meet in the cabana for a snack. In New York, it is reported, the worshipers adjourned one Simhat Torah (Rejoicing of the Law) during the 1760's to the cabana or one of the adjacent congregational houses, and there enhanced the festivities by frequent draughts that both cheered and inebriated.

For most immigrant Jews during the colonial period—this would prove no less true of nineteenth-century immigrants—the synagogue was both a religious and secular meetinghouse. The Jew rarely made much distinction between sacred and profane. Life for him was of one piece, and its communal hub was the house of God. The synagogue typified the Jew; nothing else so truly symbolized him, and even his Gentile neighbors understood this. Thus it is not surprising that a prominent New York Christian, John Watts, writing about the Jewish merchant Jacob Franks, referred to him as the "Synagogue." [2]

It is no exaggeration to say that every Jew who went to services looked forward to them. To be sure, the average Jew did not go to services primarily for a good time, but the house of worship was also a house of gossip. Between prayers, and if truth be told during prayers as well, neighbors at worship talked of business or of whatever else interested them. Their synagogue was the one place in which they all met together regularly. Within its walls was noise, was vitality, was interest—and an exuberant healthy devotion. This was the meeting which gladdened, comforted, and enriched the participant. This was the one place in which the colonial Jew could be sure of welcome and social warmth.

LEADERSHIP IN THE JEWISH COMMUNITY

What was the nature of Jewish congregational or communal organization in colonial America? How did colonial Jews cope with the problem—a serious problem, removed as they were from centers of Jewish life and learning—of regulating their religious affairs? The first members of the New Amsterdam-New York congregation came from highly organized metropolitan communities and were certainly conversant with administrative needs and procedures. The simplest forms of organization were obviously sufficient for these pioneers, but it is probable that as early as the 1690's some of the officiating personnel were compensated for their services.

It is not, however, until 1720, when the New York congregation's extant records begin, that the names of most of the leaders are known to us. The affairs of the community and its synagogue were administered at that time by a board and a presiding officer. The salaried officials included a hazzan, a shohet, a shammash, and a subsidized teacher, while the institutions of the community included, in addition to the synagogue, a school, a ritual bath, and a cemetery together with a modest mortuary chapel or hut. Congregants were offered worship services, elementary religious education for their children, kosher food, and not least, an array of social-welfare benefits, including medical care of the sick, fuel, mazzot and the haroset salad for Passover observance, and loans of money without interest. The community never failed to make provision for boarding and transporting itinerants. Relief and pensions were also available to elderly synagogue employees, transients, and impoverished members, while efforts were undertaken to meet the needs of orphans and widows. Money was collected to help support Palestinian Jewry, and cemetery lots and burial were supplied every Jew in the city.

Colonial America's Jewish community never experienced domination by a religious or lay hierarchy and produced no religious leaders whose authority rested on sacramental or charismatic powers. All control was vested in lay leaders, elected for a limited period of time by their peers. The New York congregation's oldest surviving constitution, a document dating from 1728, put it simply thus: "With the fear of God" the synagogal leaders were to "act as their conscience shall dictate them for the well governing" of the congregation. These leaders, however, did *not* include the reader or minister of the congregation, who actually had very little influence and in this respect was not to be compared with Protestant clergymen in the colonies or with rabbis in Europe. The various synagogal constitutions—this was particularly true of New York—saw to it that, theoretically at least, power was resident in the president or parnas and his board. The parnas served as the recognized head and leader of the community; a sermon published at Newport on the eve of the Revolution characterized him "the ruler of the synagogue." The extent of his leadership, the degree to which it proved effective, was determined by his personality, his capacities, and his wealth. It was the parnas and the elders who chided the people for religious laxity. In the final analysis, however, even the parnas might find himself subordinate to the rich merchants in the congregation. They were the real communal bosses, in all likelihood exercising considerable control even over the annually elected presidents and board members. By contrast with Europe there were, of course, in continental North America no men of great learning to work closely with the lay leaders and to share authority with them.[3]

No better example of what might be called elitism in colonial Jewish life is available to us than the Gomez clan. Wealthy Sephardim with aristocratic pretensions, they exercised a great deal of influence in New York during the first half of the eighteenth century. When they had means they gave liberally according to the standards of the time, and by 1750 members of the family had served eight presidential terms; seven members of the clan held the presidency for nineteen of the forty-seven years from 1729 to 1776. The family's prestige is reflected in the special consideration shown the Gomez women in the synagogal gallery. Though, unlike many Christian churches, the synagogue maintained no preferential pew system and individuals were not seated downstairs on the first floor according to rank or class, it is nevertheless certain that the choice seats were purchased by the wealthy.

Initially, New York's synagogal leadership was Sephardic, but by

1720 leadership in the growing community had to be shared with the Ashkenazim or Central and East Europeans. The wealthy Ashkenazic businessman Jacob Franks, for example, was elected president for seven annual terms from 1730 to 1764. Still, no one lay leader monopolized or controlled elective or appointive offices for an extended period, even though the wealthy and influential had much to say, whether they held office or not. The five decades between 1729 and 1776 saw only three out of thirty-three presidents serve more than three annual terms.

Did lay leaders of genuine distinction emerge from the ranks of colonial American Jewry? There is no ready answer to such a question, but Luis Gomez, about whom, unfortunately, too little is known, was probably an outstanding leader in New York, as was also Jacob Franks, undoubtedly a power at Shearith Israel for many years before his death in 1769. Toward the end of Franks's life, Hayman Levy and Manuel Myers, New York shopkeepers and merchants, had begun to manifest qualities of leadership which were in time to make them frequent officeholders. In the deep South, Mordecai Sheftall was virtually synonymous with Georgia Jewry, and Isaac Da Costa's leadership of Charleston Jewry was certainly not undistinguished. The Jews of Philadelphia, too, seem to have enjoyed able leadership from the Gratz brothers during the ten or fifteen years before the Revolution.

Officeholding in the community was never limited to the topmost social echelons. The various members of the congregation, shopkeepers as well as merchants, did assume office and did exercise some measure of authority. The attitude of officeholders toward the Jewish group and the faith itself was a positive one. What motivated them to take active part in American Jewish religious life was, above all, the European upbringing which tended to commit them to the teachings of their youth. The preponderant majority of all the parnasim up to 1776 were, after all, immigrants. They were very conscious in a traditional European Jewish sense, that it was not only a great privilege, but also a religious obligation to further Judaism and the religious community in which the Jewish faith had its embodiment. Nonetheless, its European inspiration notwithstanding, the nature and motivation of the communal leadership exercised here differed radically from the situation in Europe. Parnasim in many of the continental European Jewish communities had to be confirmed by the state, collaborated very closely with the governmental authorities, and in a caesaropapist sense, were little more than the creatures of the state. Very often, of course, they were rich, and their standing as court Jews or its equivalent enabled them to enrich themselves still further and to throttle aspiring economic rivals among their coreligionists. In Europe, therefore, control of the community spelled real and substantial politico-economic power, but of this there was literally nothing in the voluntaristic Jewish conventicles of the American colonies.[4]

BOARD AND MEMBERS

While, as we have noted, individuals did wield a great deal of influence on the American Jewish religious scene, the authoritarian nature of the synagogal constitution vested exercise of power in a lay board, variously called, following Sephardic usage, the junta, junto, *adjunta*, or *mahamad*. This body—its Hebrew designation *mahamad* goes back for about two millennia and may be translated literally as the "standing committee"—met frequently and actually governed the community. Appointments or elections to the board were for one year, but there were no limitations on reelection, since congregants were only too happy when they could get competent people to serve again.

Even the largest of America's Jewish communities was relatively small—Shearith Israel, for instance, probably never had more than about fifty active members—and so the board, despite the authority vested in it, often hesitated to take upon itself sole responsibility for important decisions. It was not unusual for the *mahamad* to co-opt substantial members of the community in order to secure their advice on pressing matters. Then too, past presidents probably constituted either an official or semi-official group of elders (*ancianos* or *velhos*) exercising an undefined but still considerable authority. Thus though under normal circumstances the congregation as a whole was expected to convene but once a year for the elections, "normality" was actually never much in evidence. Faced with constant financial crises and problems in hiring and firing salaried officials, the board commonly hesitated to take action without convening the entire membership.[5]

Judaism developed no creedal church, and admission to synagogue membership had very little if indeed anything to do with a formal declaration of religious conviction. Any Jew had a moral and religious right to membership if he could meet the—primarily financial—requirements of the constitution. The Philadelphia congregation, to judge from its draft constitution, was so eager for members that it omitted any article touching on membership qualifications. Nearly anyone could join. Montreal Jewry was most exceptional in exhibiting a very particularistic attitude: charter members were to have "a double vote hereafter for ever, them, and all their oldest sons," while no "stranger" (newcomer) was "to be admitted without the consent of the junto." Strangers were also to pay an entrance fee, "to enjoy no office for three years, to have no vote for two years, and then to have only a single vote afterwards." And all this in a congregation of about twenty members! One wonders whether the Montreal Jews were as severe in actual practice as they were in constitutional theory.

Most congregations were only too happy to welcome newcomers who had been for some time in town, had met with the approval of the board, and were willing to support the synagogue financially. Such persons generally became first-class or select members (*yehidim*). The *yahid* was entitled to claim a good seat, had the privilege of voting and of holding office, and could also expect ritual courtesies in the worship service. He would be called up to read or at least pronounce the traditional blessings over the Torah and to open and close the ark. If he was about to take a wife, special recognition was accorded him during the service on the Sabbath preceding his marriage, and the reader later took note of his presence at worship when he and his wife appeared in the synagogue on the first Sabbath after the birth of a child. The *yahid* had a right to the ministrations of the congregational functionaries on all occasions of joy and sorrow, the reader, beadle, and circumciser standing ready to help him at a circumcision, a wedding, or—God forbid!—a funeral.

The age for admission to synagogue membership varied from

[903]

eighteen to twenty-one. If a candidate for membership was cognizant of his privileges and obligations, and if the board accepted him, then the potential *yahid* became a "subscriber"—he signed his name below the signatures of the other *yehidim* "on the foot of" the constitution. In effect this act of his constituted a moral obligation to comply with synagogal rules under the threat of stated penalties.

In general restrictive regulations about admission to membership were made only to be broken. The financial burden of synagogal maintenance and the eagerness of the *yehidim* to ease that burden through sharing it with others saw to it that membership would not be too difficult to acquire. Montreal *yehidim*, for example, unless "married and had a child," were to be at least twenty-one years old, but the two Davids who signed as members of the Montreal shul in 1778 were twelve and fourteen years of age! [6]

Vast numbers of Christians in early America were unaffiliated with any church, and no doubt there were Jews too who did not identify themselves with their fellow Jews. On the whole, however, the Jew in the colonies appears to have been eager to join with his coreligionists, and most Jews in a town were affiliated with the local synagogue. Some, to be sure, did not affiliate; they lacked the means, or they were in transit, or indifferent, or even in the process of "passing," of drifting away religiously. How many defectors there were will never be known, but not all who refused to join the local or nearest congregation were defectors. Some were certainly observant Jews, but had removed themselves out of anger at some real or assumed slight. How else are we to explain the absence of the wealthy and orthodox Aaron Hart of Three Rivers from the Montreal roster? And this may also account for the fact that Levy Solomons, Chapman Abram, Jacob Moses, Samuel Isaacs, and the New York shopkeeper Joseph Simons do not appear in the records of the New York congregation. Naturalized in New York, most of these men are known to have been committed Jews, *not* escapists. [7]

Some congregations had what might be called contributing members—out-of-towners from whom support was received. In 1737 and again in 1747 the straitened Shearith Israel congregation in New York ordered, under threat of a mild form of the ban, "every family or private person, that carries on trade in the country[side], and that is in circumstances," to pay a stipulated annual sum into the synagogal coffers. Anyone refusing would "not be call'd to Sepher [Torah], have any misvoth [religious privileges] nor be loock't upon as a member of this congregation." Shearith Israel was at the time the only synagogue in North America, with the exception of one in the newly established colony of Georgia. Shearith Israel received support, then, not only from Jews in the surrounding towns and villages, but also from individuals like David Franks of Philadelphia, from men in distant Boston, and even from London, to which Pacheco, a former member, had permanently moved. The Newport and Philadelphia synagogues, too, received help in later years from families and friends who lived at some distance or even in remote parts of the continent. Philip Moses of Savannah was a loyal contributor to the Newport synagogue, and in general the Savannah Jews were benefactors of the Charleston synagogue. On one occasion when the New York merchant Uriah Hendricks visited Newport, he was called up to the Torah and responded to this courtesy with an offering of eighteen shillings. Eighteen was a magic number in Hebrew, for it spelled *hai* (living).[8]

Distaff members were unheard of in eighteenth century synagogues, and if women were to exercise any influence in the congregation, it had to be exclusively through their husbands. Still, though women could never hope to become *yehidim*, they were encouraged to attend worship services, particularly on the Sabbath and on holy days. They made their contributions if the spirit moved them through monetary gifts, legacies, and gifts of expensive cloth hangings, mantles, and covers for the scrolls, arks, and pulpits. Long after they were dead, blessings were gratefully and piously recited in memory of the generous New York and Newport women who had made gifts to their congregations.[9]

Not everyone was or could be a *yahid*. Those who gave no adequate financial support or who had just come to town were deemed strangers. Second-class members, they were accorded ritual honors only after the *yehidim* had been recognized, and they were not given the choice seats. Nevertheless, a congregation desperate to find officers might well elevate a second-class member to the rank of a *yahid* and immediately elect him to office. It should be emphasized in any case that people were never denied religious privileges, even if they were too poor to pay for them. Admission to the synagogue, to the prayer service, was open to all, whether financially able to contribute or not.[10]

HONORARY OFFICERS

In general, it would seem, Shearith Israel in New York followed the pattern of organization established at the Spanish-Portuguese Bevis Marks Synagogue in London. There were, however, decided differences between Bevis Marks and its colonial counterparts. In 1663 the London Sephardim had adopted a constitution whose prototypes went back via Amsterdam, Venice, and Salonika to late medieval Spain and Portugal. Many of the ordinances which recommended themselves to the Londoners were meaningless to their American brethren. The London-Amsterdam prohibition against carrying "weapons of offence" into the synagogue—perfectly understandable and natural in fifteenth century Spain—would surely have appeared ludicrous to an eighteenth century North American synaguegoer. By the same token, the effete London Sephardi would doubtless have laughed at—if he were not shocked by—the admonition in late eighteenth century Savannah that no worshiper should mount the lectern with boots. (What could the Londoner know of Georgia dirt-farmers?)

The first Jews here in the seventeenth century were familiar with the structure of the Amsterdam, Recife, and London synagogal organizations. They knew that those congregations—Bevis Marks especially—reflected an establishment of self-perpetuating lay rulers and boards and that no individual but only the *mahamad* had the right to speak for the community. That state of affairs had not arisen ex nihilo. Despite Dutch willingness to "accord freedom of religion to all," the Jews of sixteenth and even early seventeenth century Amsterdam had certainly thought it best not to publicize the fact that they belonged "to a religion different from that of the rest of the city's inhabitants," and English Jewry had known even less security during the mid-1600's. The first Jews to settle in England and to organize a synagogue there during the 1650's had been crypto-Jews, frightened newcomers whose all too recent escape from the Inquisition was very much in mind. Lacking legal recognition in England, they had wished above all to keep undercover, and in order to protect themselves, had insisted on a rigorous social control. Following the Iberian Catholic pattern they and their fellow Sephardim in Amsterdam knew best, they were autocratic and dictatorial.[11]

Not only was the religious life of the individual English Jew carefully supervised, but his ethical and business practices were no less subject to synagogal regulation. The English Jews and the early American Calvinists had much in common in this respect. Looking to earlier traditions, the London congregation not only scrutinized the economic conduct of its members, but also taxed the business transactions of individuals to provide support for the Jewish community. The caution and fears of English Restoration Jewry were reflected in the stern prohibition of proselytism, in the Jewish community's refusal to help Jewish criminals, and in the censorship imposed on all publications—because "it thus conduces to our preservation." [12]

The governing apparatus of London's Bevis Marks Synagogue was extensive, featuring a bicameral board: an upper house of past officers or elder statesmen called the Elders, and a lower house (*mahamad*). There was in addition a well-organized committee system to control all communal activities. The congregation employed a full-time ordained rabbi, called the hakam. Unlike the twentieth century American rabbi, he did not function primarily as a preacher or pastor. Although the hakam of Bevis Marks preached regularly, he was preeminently a judge versed in rabbinical law and a scholar; he decided ritual and legal cases and also taught Talmud to advanced students. The secular language employed in the synagogue for announcements and preaching was Spanish or Portuguese.[13]

The North American synagogue-community differed strikingly in its pattern of organization from the system which characterized Jewish life in London or Amsterdam. To be sure, authoritarianism was attempted in the small congregations of America, but it rarely succeeded in maintaining itself for any length of time. A large measure of democracy proved inevitable and necessary in a group whose constituency was small and whose members were practically all to be found in the same social class.

The extant congregational records which begin in detail in the 1720's indicate that New York's Shearith Israel was at the time governed by a board of three, a president elected by the membership as a whole and two associates appointed by the president himself. Traditionally called *hatanim* (bridegrooms), the two associates served a liturgical as well as an administrative purpose, for they were privileged to officiate at the autumnal Festival of Booths in the course of which the annual cycle of pentateuchal readings simultaneously comes to a close and is recommenced with the reading of Genesis. Between 1728 and 1751, however, the electoral process was inoperative, with the board of three, if only by default, naming its own successors. In this, Shearith Israel was at one with the age in which it lived, an age which preferred appointments over elections. The mayor and governor of New York were also appointive officials, and in the South some of the Anglican vestries, too, were self-perpetuating. The congregational board or executive committee of three—all its members to be married men—served for a year and could always be renominated; elections or appointments took place either in the spring before the Passover or in the fall before the High Holy Days.[14]

This simple, almost patriarchal system of government had begun to break down by 1746; King George's War had been in progress then for six years, and everyone was so busy that there were occasions which found not a single officer present when needed. No one wanted to hold a time-consuming presidential office, and there was talk of remedying the trouble by the adoption of a new constitution. Now even a man of thirty and unmarried would be acceptable as parnas— if one such could be found. About 1750 past presidents and past officers, the substantial members, began to assume authority, if only an extralegal authority. Following the European pattern of Elders, these worthies took increasing power with the decline of the presidential office and the executive committee. Not that the institution of Elders had been previously unknown, for there are intimations as early as 1706 that Elders were in existence. Unfortunately, however, the constitutional documents now extant throw no more light on their jurisdiction in the 1750's than on their function in 1706, and the term Elders may have referred simply to past officers.[15]

In September 1751 the congregation employed a new device to solve the problem of reluctant presidents. Resorting to a well-known Sephardic precedent, the New Yorkers decided to elect *two* presidents, a *parnas presidente* and a *parnas residente,* each one to serve only six months. Thus the term of responsibility was halved for each president. This made the New York synagogue unique in North America, for so far as we know, the term of office for a president in all other North American colonial synagogues was and remained a period of one year. In 1751, then, New York's miniscule community introduced a bicameral structure: a body of Elders whose authority, though advisory, was nevertheless recognized, plus a *mahamad* of two presidents and two assistants. The actual administrative and executive duties devolved on the respective semiannual president.

A year later the two presidents and their two assistants were being elected by the Elders and the two outgoing presidents, but the problem of finding proper leadership continued to resist solution because so few were willing to serve. It was cheaper for a busy merchant to pay a heavy fine for his refusal to accept office, and the French and Indian War only exacerbated the problem, for it opened new economic opportunities which no officer wished to spurn. Then too, new immigrants were constantly arriving, and all this meant that the president who carried the administrative load found himself burdened with a full-time job. American Jews were not, of course, singular in their reluctance or refusal to accept office; this was a malaise characteristic of Jewish communities in many lands, since it was exceedingly difficult nearly everywhere for Jewish merchants to find time for congregational duties in addition to their commercial interests. Refusal to assume office and willingness to pay fines are documented in every important congregation, not only in North America, but elsewhere as well.[16]

Once more the congregation tried to solve its problems—this time by appointing a constituent committee of past presidents—and in 1761 the new committee was instructed to draft a constitution which would automatically be accepted on presentation. This constitution of 1761 and its predecessor of 1728 are the only colonial New York synagogue constitutions extant, although there may have been others in the intervening years. It was in force, with modifications, from its adoption in 1761 to the Revolution, and under its terms the status of the Elders was regularized as a body of assistants, usually numbering five, although at times less, and occasionally seven. Some of these Elders were elected for life; others were elected annually by the congregation as a whole. The Elders functioned also as an electoral college and chose the two new semiannual presidents and the two "bridegrooms" or board members.

New York's innovation of a five-member board of Elders may have influenced the nascent congregational group in Philadelphia, for the executive in Philadelphia at that time was also a board of five. At Montreal too, in 1778 the junto consisted of five members—a president, a treasurer, and three juntomen. Unlike New York, however, the executive of five in both Philadelphia and Montreal came to office through direct election, and the Canadians also elected two *hatanim*, although they were probably not members of the junto. Whether the adoption of an elective system in Philadelphia and Canada indicated a growing democracy in those emergent communities over against a more conservative tendency in the already venerable New York synagogue is difficult to determine.

The New York constitution of 1761 had been operating only eight years when Shearith Israel appointed a new constituent committee, though no formal constitution appears to have been adopted—at least none is to be found in the records. The trouble was, of course, the same; no one would accept office. Between 1771 and 1775 the situation worsened, with the organizational structure breaking down completely as a result, primarily, of the political unrest overtaking the entire country. The Revolution was in the making, and the congregation's members, mostly merchants, found their livelihoods threatened. As Whigs, most of them would ultimately pack up, quit the city, and be virtually compelled to start life over again. They had little time and possibly less inclination to occupy themselves with the details of synagogal administration.

By 1771 the congregation had reverted to the old system of 1729–1750, a self-perpetuating board of one parnas and two "bridegrooms." Each year one new member was appointed to the board, and the officers succeeded automatically to the presidency. There was this difference, however—the office could now be imposed on an unwilling candidate who could refuse only after paying a substantial fine. One is reminded of the onerous duties inflicted on unfortunate municipal officials like the *decuriones* during the troubled days of Roman imperial decline.

Two years later, in 1773 the congregation turned back to the semiannual presidential system. Throughout this entire period, of course, from 1761 to the outbreak of the Revolution, the Elders in the background had been monitoring the changing executive committee. Nothing availed and in 1775, with the coming of the Revolution, the congregation dissolved for the time being. Even the Elders refused to serve, although the executive of four—two presidents and two assistants—continued in force, and at length control over the synagogal administration was relinquished to one man, Hayman Levy, unanimously elected by the members in the last documented act of New York's colonial congregation. In December 1783, when the minutes were again recorded, the Revolution was over and Shearith Israel had become part of a new and independent republic.[17]

CHAPTER 52

THE SYNAGOGUE AND ITS ADMINISTRATION—II

FINANCES: INCOME

J udging from the situation reflected in the New York congregational records, colonial synagogues never found it easy to meet
their budgetary needs or their current expenses. This is not difficult
to understand when we consider that a substantial percentage of the
members could never afford to make more than small contributions
to the synagogue and that very few of the congregants were rich.
People of wealth did not commonly leave Europe to settle a frontier
land, and while there were pioneers who acquired some wealth in
America and others of substance, eleemosynary standards were low.
In Amsterdam, Recife, and London, communal taxation of commercial sales was an established institution, but the practice was not
adopted by any North American synagogue-community—not at any
rate after 1728. The only sales tax that an American synagogue ever
levied was on kosher meat prepared primarily for export; the revenue
from this tax fell to the hazzan.

Congregations obtained their income in a variety of ways, and
not all of the methods employed were characteristic of every synagogue. Some money was raised through initiation or entrance fees,
but much more was derived from the sale of ritual honors, publicly
auctioned off from the reading desk to members who were, for instance, eager for the privilege of "reading" a portion of the Holy
Scriptures. In New York offerings (*nedarim*) constituted the chief
source of income, but some congregations after a time fixed on a
minimum of dues. When such a minimum was set, a man was en-

titled to a specific number of public honors or courtesies for which no additional charges were assessed. If, however, the total of his honors exceeded the amount of his dues, he had to pay the difference. In most congregations the annual dues were equivalent to a charge for a seat; that is, members paid minimum dues for the right to a seat in the synagogue. It is not known what the seat dues were in Newport, and the Rhode Island congregation may have depended entirely on offerings. Aaron Lopez is reported to have been generous in his prosperous days; one Passover he offered the Newport synagogue about $20 in specie and Pastor Ezra Stiles, who was present on that occasion, was very much impressed. Holidays, however, generally offered wealthy members opportunities for friendly rivalry to bid up the monetary value of special honors and thereby benefit the congregation.

Members and visiting strangers, called up to the reading of the Law, frequently made memorial offerings (hashkabot) especially on behalf of their dead relatives. Also, as we have already noted, the New York synagogue at times compelled "our brothers dwelling in the country" (members in outlying rural areas) to contribute an annual minimum to the congregational treasury. In addition, various types of free-will monetary donations and collections (*nedabot*) were common at all holidays, but they were not an important source of income for Shearith Israel in the mid-eighteenth century. From time to time cash subscriptions and contributions were received, as when a wealthy Philadelphia merchant promised Shearith Israel a substantial grant in honor of his father who had just died in New York. If a new Scroll of the Law was needed, members were asked to raise the necessary amount by subscription.

Like Christian congregations, Jewish ones imposed fines for nonattendance at services and meetings, for refusal to accept office, and for many other causes. One might suppose that these fines, so constantly threatened for all sorts of disciplinary breaches, minor and major, would have provided a substantial income. No doubt some fines were collected, but it is to be doubted they went very far toward helping to balance the annual budget.[1]

Some income accrued to the New York community from the rental of its property. A portion of the cemetery ground might, for example, be leased out on a long term as a lot for building a house. In the twentieth century, of course, most congregations have made money from the sale of their cemetery lots, but it was otherwise in colonial days when burial and graves were free to members. Nonmembers were required to pay, but the sums annually received even from that source were inconsequential. The sale of cemetery lots was certainly not a business during the colonial period.

A study of the New York synagogue's chief sources of income indicates that prior to 1728 the congregation was supported primarily by offerings, and after 1728 by the annual sale or allotment of seats. For a brief period of about eighteen months during the late 1740's the congregation met its financial needs by a special tax on the wealth of its members. By 1750 the tax on seats had become compulsory, so that in effect the members were assessed annual dues. Philadelphia, too, depended on the sale of seats as a prime source of income, but the seats in the Montreal synagogue had been sold in perpetuity, so the prime additional source of income in that community was undoubtedly through offerings made in public.[2]

In addition to the income to be derived from monetary offerings, the rental and sale of seats, and monetary gifts from members, from generous friends in other towns, and from individuals or communities abroad, congregations also received contributions in the form of furnishings for the sanctuary. A New York merchant might give his synagogue several candelabra, and an ambitious young clerk in Newport might donate some beautiful brass lamps to his congregation. When the Newport synagogue was under construction, a number of New Yorkers made gifts in the form of public offerings, but one man sent the Newporters 100 pounds of wax for candles, another supplied the perpetual lamp, and a third gave some candlesticks for the ark and the reading desk. The leaders of a Portuguese Jewish educational confraternity in London provided Newport with a Scroll of the Law, and Aaron Lopez donated another—a truly substantial gift, for a manuscript Torah written with meticulous care was very costly. Both of these scrolls had artistic silver ornaments washed with gold.[3]

People who gave valuable gifts to the synagogue were repaid three-fold. They gathered merit for the world to come and were honored during their lifetime by public announcement, while blessings (hashkabot) were recited posthumously on the anniversary of their passing as well as at the New Moon services and during the High Holy Days. In New York on the seventh day of Passover, the anniversary of the Mill Street Synagogue's consecration, special blessings were recited to honor the four men who had given most liberally. Such hashkabot were also recited to memorialize faithful communal servants whom the congregation remembered gratefully. Unfortunately, the records are silent as to the precise deeds and devotion of such worthies; it is only on infractions that the records lavish detailed accounts. The minutes are replete with information about the exuberant souls who were constantly making trouble and struggling under the yoke of communal discipline.[4]

Past benefactions were passed in review by Shearith Israel on the Eve of Atonement when the congregation's benisons testified to the generosity of Jewish communities in Amsterdam, London, Curaçao, and Surinam. Pious women were also not forgotten, and a special blessing was recited for those who in the early days had made the white Torah mantles and ark curtains used on the High Holy Days. The Newporters, too, remembered their benefactors: Daniel Gomez of New York, who had been particularly generous, fellow Newporters who had made special gifts, and all the foreign communities that had befriended the Rhode Island synagogue.[5]

Piety also achieved tangible expression in the form of memorial gifts and legacies for the congregation. One could leave money without restriction, or specific provision could be made for its uses. The widow Burgos of Barbados memorialized her husband and provided for hashkabot in her own memory by giving the New York congregation £40 for a wall around its cemetery; another woman asked that a Scroll of the Pentateuch be purchased with her bequest; and Joseph Isaacs, a merchant, left £50 to support a Hebrew school. All those donors were assured that on certain days of the year prayers would be recited in their memory.[6]

It is an adequate commentary on the frontier character of Shearith Israel to note that its total income in 1732 was less than £180 New York currency, while the income of London's Bevis Marks Synagogue less than a decade earlier in 1726 had been £6,742, *ster-*

ling! Bevis Marks did, it is true, employ a sales tax, but in general both congregations drew their incomes from similar sources: the sale of mazzot and haroset, emergency imposts, pew rentals or sales, freewill gifts, legacies, fines, rentals from properties, and above all, offerings.[7]

Newport, and it is likely some of the other synagogues as well, submitted statements on printed forms. The actual collection was probably left to the beadle, but practices varied, and at times any member of the congregation, or any honorary or paid official, might serve as an agent to transmit funds to the disbursing officer. In the 1720's some of the New Yorkers paid their dues in kind or services rather than in cash—they would send a Negro slave to clean the synagogue or would supply wax for the huge Yom Kippur candles. During the 1760's and 1770's Hazzan Touro and the other Newport communal servants took part of their salary in goods at the Lopez shop, and Lopez simply charged their purchases to the sedakah, the synagogal treasury.[8]

FINANCES: EXPENDITURES

The congregational treasury in colonial days was referred to frequently as the sedakah, a Hebrew word whose basic meaning is righteousness and which came in talmudic times to mean charity. North American synagogues made no distinction between funds for charity (*obras pias*) and funds for direct congregational needs; they were one and the same. It must be understood, of course, that no congregation was ever free of financial stress. There were always members delinquent in their dues, and Shearith Israel in New York even went so far as to mark certain congregants as "bad."

Whether or not synagogal coffers were adequate, the parnas and board had to meet constant recurring charges. Before 1730 when New York's Mill Street Synagogue was built, there were rents for the old sanctuary and for a neighboring house, while after 1730 repairs always had to be made, the synagogue had to be scoured thoroughly, and the street in front of it swept clean. Salaries had to be paid to the reader, the slaughterer, and the beadle, and a subsidy had to be provided for the teacher. There were expenses for fuel, a basic ingredient in all salaries and charitable grants, as well as for unleavened bread and haroset on Passover, for building and decorating the cabana during the Feast of Tabernacles, and for procuring a load of sand for the synagogue floor.

To light the synagogue and other congregational buildings, it was necessary to purchase oil for the lamps and also wax, wicks, and molds for the candles which were often made by the beadle. Not every congregation was as fortunate as Newport, where the beadle had no need to make candles, since good ones, indeed the best, were secured from Aaron Lopez, the generous-hearted manufacturer who supplied them cheaply or often as a gift. Lead had to be bought for the tags used by the slaughterers to identify kosher meat; eatables of various types had to be purchased for holiday collations; and new decorative cloths and ritual silver were always required in the synagogue. There were in addition expenditures for *obras pias* which, in New York at least, formed one of the most important items in the budget. Finally, of course, there were the costs of cemetery maintenance: keeping fences in repair, buying burial utensils, paying gravediggers, and making coffins. A study of the New York congregational budget for the years between 1729 and 1750 shows that the budget jumped prodigiously during King George's War in the late 1740's as a result, quite possibly, of inflation or the arrival of new families which imposed new responsibilities and required heavier expenditures. After the war, however, when money became scarcer, the budget was cut by more than half.[9]

PARNAS, BOARD, AND COMMITTEES

The parnas never had an easy time of it. Although the semiannual parnas of the New York congregation served but six months, he may well have felt, in view of all that a parnas was expected to accomplish, that his term of service was six months too long. Certainly the demands of his office were troublesome enough. He was in charge of the minutes and probably acted as secretary to the congregation. It was his responsibility also to keep the financial records, to control all expenditures, and to dispense charity from the congregational funds. If the amounts involved were large, he generally co-opted his board, and in any event he submitted to the board members periodic financial reports which they audited. He had in addition to keep a watchful eye on the progress of the services, to maintain decorum, to distribute—or impose—the ritual courtesies and honors that were passed out at each prayer meeting, and to assign seats to members and transients. It was the job of the parnas to supervise congregational elections, to authorize weddings, and to see to it that the congregation had an ample supply of kosher meat and that kosher meat for export had been properly prepared and certified.

These, however, were only some of his duties. The parnas was also expected to settle quarrels among members, to regulate burials, to watch, supervise, and discipline the congregational functionaries, and to prescribe minor routines. He was responsible, moreover, for the congregational buildings, the cemetery, the school, the ritual bath, and the houses owned by the congregation and occupied by the salaried officials. On occasion he might find it necessary to set the dues—and even go out to collect them himself. He called congregational and special board meetings and imposed fines. When there were no funds in the synagogal treasury, he frequently had to advance his own monies, and if he exceeded his budget, he was held accountable for unauthorized expenditures. At times he and the board had no choice but to raise money among themselves to help pay the salary of the hazzan.[10]

It is not surprising that an officer burdened with such responsibilities, and occupied in addition with the equally or more pressing concern of making a livelihood for himself, would tend toward autocracy. The autocratic tradition was particularly strong at New York's Shearith Israel, which was closest in age, and in other respects as well, to London's well-disciplined Bevis Marks congregation. Even in New York, however, dictatorial tendencies were radically ameliorated by the refusal of members to serve in office and by an absence of pride in the synagogue. It is significant that Shearith Israel's earliest extant constitution provides for arbitration of the difficulties between the president and his two associates on the board. In both Philadelphia and Montreal the power of the parnas was carefully circumscribed. The Philadelphians made it quite clear that they did not want a parnas who was "quarrelsome and tyrannical."

Even in New York the president worked closely with his board, although board meetings were held very irregularly. Sometimes the *mahamad* would come together two or three times in the same month, but there were occasions when it would not be convened for many months, if one may judge from the surviving records. The provision in the 1761 constitution that the board meet monthly was apparently never enforced.

The boards of the various American congregations varied in size. No board ever had fewer than three members, and the number might even reach eleven. At the actual meetings, however, absences were common, and there were often only a handful to make the decisions.

No colonial community seems to have had a secretary in any formal sense, although it is obvious that records were kept—by the president or a board member in all likelihood. Possession of the records often proved a fruitful source of dissension, for an angry officer might thumb his nose at his colleagues and refuse to surrender the congregational papers he had at home. There was trouble on this score both in New York and in Philadelphia during the days before and after the Revolution. New York finally resolved the custody of the congregational archives by deciding that the president was to remain in possession of the records, but was to sign a large bond that he would transfer them to his successor. Congregations might have seen no need for establishing a secretarial office, but they were more easily convinced of the necessity for a treasurer. The existence of such an officer—the gabbai—is documented in Philadelphia and Montreal, but strangely enough, American Jewry's largest congregation, Shearith Israel of New York, failed to develop the office of gabbai. Very likely Shearith Israel simply followed Bevis Marks in requiring a member of the board, usually the parnas, to act as treasurer.[11]

Busy organizations and societies today commonly apportion their work to standing committees, but so simple a truth does not seem to have characterized Jewish administrative procedure in colonial North America. The Spanish-Jewish communities had already learned this lesson in the late medieval period; the Central European Jews had learned it by the sixteenth century, and much of their communal business was handled by *hebrot* (pious associations or confraternities). During the 1600's and 1700's dozens of such societies developed in Amsterdam, at least nine or ten in London, and a series also in the metropolitan communities of Brazil, Surinam, and the West Indies. These *hebrot* were in charge of education, orphans, free loans, trade apprenticeships, dowries for poor girls, redemption of captives, Palestine relief, care of the sick and the dying, and burial of the dead.

Still, the historian who confidently expects to find such associations documented in New York will be disappointed, for there is no positive proof of the existence even of a *hebrah* for the sick and for burial. This lack of evidence in regard to the presence of a sick-care and burial society in New York, or for that matter anywhere in North America, is all the more curious when one considers that such a society was to be found in nearly every European town which had even a handful of Jews. It may be, of course, that there was a *hebrah* of this sort in New York and that all record of its existence has disappeared. More probably, however, the American communities were so small that the functions of such a confraternity were performed here by the congregation itself, that is, by the community as a whole. In the absence of such *hebrot*, such permanent semi-autonomous committees, much of the responsibility they would have undertaken fell inevitably upon the shoulders of the parnas, which just as inevitably led many individuals, seeking status themselves, to resent the autocratic authority and attitude of this arbiter of their many-faceted communal life.[12]

American Jewish communities had learned, of course, to assign some tasks to individuals or groups, so that ad hoc committees were formed to write synagogal constitutions, while individuals were at times specially designated to collect money for Palestine. The construction of the New York and Newport synagogues was overseen by a special committee, two men were appointed to supervise repairs on the New York cemetery walls, and the year 1750 saw a committee appointed in New York to assess members and assign seats.

Much of the communal disorganization and the consequent burdening of the parnas stemmed from the fact that congregants were economically so insecure. Harried by the necessity of making a living, too many were unwilling to make some sacrifice for the sake of the community, and it is a tribute to some of the communal leaders that they were able to hold their people together and to keep their synagogues going. After the Revolution congregations began appointing secretaries and treasurers, and a formal committee system of apportioning the synagogal work was finally adopted.[13]

CONGREGATIONAL AUTHORITY

The Jews of colonial America had to decide for themselves where power lay, and at first glance it might appear that they decided in favor of the parnas and the board. The Philadelphia congregation, for instance, obligated its members "to pay heed to what the president orders in the synagogue and, God forbid, not offer him any affront." In fact, however, the congregation—the congregants themselves—always had the final say. In Montreal quarterly financial accounts were submitted to the congregation, and an officer expelled by his associates could always turn to the members for redress. Even in Philadelphia board members were to be "people who will dispense justice," and an aggrieved individual could appeal to the householders over the head of the board. With rare exceptions, it was everywhere the body of the members as a whole which elected and discharged salaried officials. When important decisions were to be made, the congregation was called together; boards were only too happy to shift the burden of a decision to the members of the larger body.

New York, whose synagogue had a self-perpetuating board during the second quarter of the eighteenth century, was exceptional, for congregations elsewhere usually elected their honorary officers, if not always directly, then at least secondarily through an electoral committee. Constitutions reflected popular sentiment by virtue of the fact that the *yehidim* chose the constituent committee or required that the organic statute be submitted to them for ratification. There were very definite limits to arbitrary procedure in a small congregation where the defection of one paying member would throw a financial burden on others. A robust democracy was a practical necessity, not a virtue. The small American Jewish conventicles had little money, while financial, social, and ethnic rivalries could be disastrous. Compromise was, therefore, called for on all occasions.[14]

DISCIPLINE AND DECORUM

A stiff-necked people with a thirty-five-hundred-year-old tradition of exuberance, Jews never found it hard to multiply breaches of synagogal discipline. Problems of decorum were thus in no sense unique to North American Jewry. No Jewish congregation anywhere escaped being plagued with infractions of rules designed to preserve order. The congregant who had a complaint or wished to draw attention to himself would unfailingly discover some way to disrupt congregational devotions and to insult and pester his fellow members. Some worshippers might talk incessantly; others might walk in and out of the service; still others might quarrel in the synagogue itself, or in the synagogue yard, or whether coming or going, on the streets leading to the house of worship. In the synagogue an ebullient member might raise his voice unduly and try to outsing or outshout the cantor. Taking the wrong seat either deliberately or accidentally, and disputes over seats assigned the womenfolk in their gallery, offered occasions on which violations of decorum could not but thrive. Then, of course, there was the unhappy member who declined, for reasons best known to himself, a ritual honor accorded him by the president. Such rebellion brought a penalty in its wake—and an additional fine if the congregant refused to pay. Indignant refusals to pay fines were frequent pretexts for disturbance, and the harassed parnas who omitted or failed to collect a fine was in turn responsible and could himself be fined for his forbearance.[15]

Some members refused to attend meetings or to support the synagogue. Whatever the reason may have been, it was not poverty, for the poor were always given consideration, and no man without means was urged to contribute. There were always factious people determined not to pay offerings, dues, and seat assessments. Some of the *yehidim* talked too much of what they had heard at board meetings in executive session; they betrayed confidences and set member against member. There were also men quick to hurl verbal insults, defame fellow members, and engage in mutual vilification. Especially troublesome were those who wrote lampoons attacking individuals, officers, and the congregation as a whole. Not that the Jews were the only ones to issue such diatribes. Christians, too, tried their hand at attacking men and institutions. *The Hidden Life of a Christian*, ridiculing religion, so it was said, appeared at Boston in 1743 and was proscribed by the provincial authorities. The Jews dreaded "literary" fusillades by their coreligionists—and not only because of their scandalous content or because they challenged the power of synagogal officialdom in an age which viewed rebellion as a cardinal crime. Such productions were dreaded most because they drew the attention of the civil government to actual or imaginary abuses of power by the Jewish leaders. Throughout the centuries European Jews had been at the mercy of apostates and delators, renegades who betrayed their own people and invited unsympathetic and brutal rulers to scrutinize the timid, insecure denizens of the ghetto. Such troublemakers were deemed *moserim*—criminals of the darkest hue. That lampooners ever wrought such dire consequences for colonial Jewry is much to be doubted, but the social historian must regret the failure of any colonial Jewish pasquils to survive. They would have made most interesting reading for him.[16]

Difficulties arose also from the salaried officials. Exasperated probably by officious bosses and even more officious members, they would from time to time squat on their haunches and balk at constituted authority, which brought about mutual recriminations, fines, grudging apologies, and an abundance of ill will. The man who had given his congregation the gift or loan of a scroll constituted another source of aggravation. Jealous to see that his scroll was taken out and used, he would deem it a personal insult if his Sefer Torah lay neglected in the ark.

Young children in the synagogue offered problems all their own, for they tended to become restless and unruly at a service which could and did continue for hours. They had to be watched and were seated in a special corner or section under the wary eye of their Hebrew teacher, or in the shadow of the reading desk where the hazzan could frown down upon them. Jews resident in the countryside were often, as we have already noted, an affront to the more zealous officers and congregants, for some of them were notorious for trading on the Sabbath and violating the dietary laws. Fierce threats were unleashed against those sinners, but never implemented for fear of driving them from the congregation or, God forbid, encouraging them to throw themselves into the arms of the waiting Gentiles.

Congregational life was thus not very decorous, but then decorum is a relative term. Though a great deal of leeway—audible reading and singing, walking about, and even gossiping with neighbors—was tolerated in all synagogues, no congregation wished to promote anarchy or disorder, and North American Jewish communities did what they could to limit noisemaking and interruptions during religious services. From the vantage point of later centuries, however, no one need be shocked at the lack of decorum which most frequently characterized worship during colonial days. After all, the Orthodox synagogue even today is not, and never has been a house of awe. The notion that a sepulchral silence must reign in the House of God is not rooted in Jewish experience. Believing Jews, guided by a sense of intimacy, have always been at home with their Deity. And because Jews were not awestruck by the nature of the synagogue, they felt quite free to quarrel within its precincts, to insult the parnas, and if so impelled, even to fight. Their weapons were fists and words. The synagogue was not only God's house, it was *their* home, and they did what they pleased—until the long-suffering officers called a halt.[17]

Christian churches and Jewish synagogues alike kept a careful watch on their members and communicants, but there were radical differences between the church and the synagogue in their respective approaches to questions of infraction and discipline. As an institution, the synagogue concerned itself only secondarily with the personal morals or orthodox thinking of its members. The morality demanded of Jewish congregants was a communal morality. It insisted on ritual conformity and was designed to ensure group discipline vis-à-vis the world "outside." Though the Jewish community made no overt ethical demands on its members, moral imperatives were implicit in the biblical and rabbinic teachings and traditions. Right living was always the solid substratum of Jewish belief and practice.

Still, churches cared far more than synagogues about the ethical behavior of the individual communicant and about the orthodoxy of his belief. To achieve their ends, the churches set up disciplinary committees to ensure conformity in ethical, moral, and religious conduct.

In some measure, to be sure, there was such social control in the tightly disciplined Jewish communities of Europe and in the larger congregations of the Caribbean and of seventeenth century Brazil. London's Bevis Marks congregation, for instance, did exercise a close surveillance over its members and even censored all Jewish books and publications; the Amsterdam Sephardim forbade dealing in prohibited coins, and the Jewish communities of Brazil and Curaçao imposed restrictions on gambling. There was, however, nothing of this in the North American colonies with their smaller, weaker congregations. The individual Jew was much freer on this continent because the Jewish community was much more dependent on him than was the case in Europe or the West Indies.[18]

Usually, after an infraction of Jewish communal rules the man who had committed the disturbance was asked to mend his ways. If, however, he persisted in his insubordination, he would be admonished by word of mouth or through an official communication. Frequently this was enough to frighten the offender and to obtain from him a plea for pardon. Fines, as we have seen, were also commonly imposed. There were many methods a synagogue-community could use to discipline a man and compel him to behave. He might, for instance, be denied a seat, in which case he would receive few or no ritual honors—a shameful blow to a man's pride. One congregation employed capital letters to enter in its records the name of an offender and the "crime" he had committed. The obstinate could also be punished by denying their children ritual naming, by depriving rebels of office and even of membership, and finally by withholding from them the privileges of marriage and burial. For those who toyed with the thought of intermarriage, there was one ever-present threat: loss of Jewish burial. An illegitimate child, too, could be and in at least one instance was denied burial in the cemetery proper.[19]

Extreme cases called for denunciation from the reading desk and expulsion from the congregation. Though formal excommunication or the threat of it was not infrequent in Europe and in the large Jewish communities of the Caribbean and South America, the records reveal no formal ceremony of excommunication in North America. Still, the effect of congregational action in severe disciplinary cases was tantamount to the ban. When, however, an offender saw the error of his ways and made his peace with the congregation, he was always readmitted, and no grudge appears to have been held. The offender of yesteryear might even turn out to be the parnas of tomorrow.[20]

Was the discipline severe? Yes. It was an age which had no tolerance for nonconformity, an age of hierarchical paternalistic authority. Discipline was severe everywhere, in family life, in the courts, and in the churches. But the Jewish leaders, with only a handful of members struggling to stay alive in a tiny community, never looked for trouble. They took drastic measures only when they had no recourse, and in general they found that the threat of extreme action was effective. The typical Jew dreaded social ostracism with its attendant impairment of his status. The alternative which faced the defiant—to live with Christians or as a Christian—was no less unacceptable. At the most, recalcitrants held out for a few years, but ultimately they returned to the fold.[21]

CHAPTER 53

THE SALARIED OFFICIALS

THE RABBI

Every North American congregation numbered among its salaried officials a hazzan who served as cantor or reader, but the hazzan was *not* a rabbi. No rabbi, in fact, would serve on the American mainland until the 1840's, when Rabbi Abraham Rice occupied the pulpit of the Ashkenazic congregation in Baltimore. In short, it was to be nearly 200 years from the first landing of a Jew in New England before a fully ordained rabbi was elected to lead a North American synagogue. By contrast, most European congregations of any size maintained a rabbi, and certainly the larger Sephardic communities of Western and Central Europe employed hakamim, as they frequently called their rabbinical leaders. There were also men of rabbinical ordination and learning in the Caribbean communities of Jamaica, Barbados, Curaçao, and Surinam.

To what extent—if any—North American Jewry was disinclined to engage rabbis is an interesting question. Certainly, American Jews believed themselves unable to afford rabbinical leadership, and in any case felt no pressing need for a learned ministry. For the most part unreflective, however devoted, as religionists, they had little interest in higher Jewish education and were content simply to practice their faith—with equal indifference to the fine points of halakah, rabbinic law, and to the anti-religious influences of rationalism. To be sure, problems of Jewish religious law did arise in the colonies, but they could usually be settled by learned laymen able to consult the standard rabbinic codes. New York in particular always sheltered a number

[927]

of congregants who had enjoyed a good Hebrew education, like Joseph Simon and Manuel Josephson. Involved problems and moot questions of law could always be referred to rabbinical authorities in London, Amsterdam, or The Hague.[1]

It is by no means improbable that the Jewish laymen of New York, even had they been able to secure a rabbi, would not have elected one to their pulpit for fear of limiting their own authority. Excepting seventeenth century New England, it was the laymen of America, Christians and Jews, who generally assumed leadership in religious matters, and they were always wary of clerical prerogatives and pretensions. The occasional need for a sermon or a sermonic announcement, as required by the state, could be met well enough by the reader, and any layman could say what words were necessary at a funeral. Competent, learned, rabbinical leadership might, nevertheless, have made a perceptible impact on colonial Jewish life, both culturally and religiously, for no Jewish community in the Diaspora has ever achieved a significant development without rabbinical guidance. Trained rabbis, however, had no desire to exile themselves to a frontier America whose Jewish communities were too small and too poor to offer good salaries. Moreover, there was little learning here in this land, and a rabbi would have had little status here; what he had to give would have found no market.

Still, though North American congregations never employed rabbis in colonial days, both Sephardic and Ashkenazic rabbis did come to these shores—and not infrequently. They came, however, on religious missions for Palestine or to collect funds for themselves. Some were probably only itinerants, schnorrers, adventurers of a sort, and it is something of a tribute to their enterprise that they undertook the long and hazardous voyage across the Atlantic. They passed through Newport, New York, Philadelphia, and no doubt— though their coming there in prerevolutionary days has remained undocumented—through Charleston as well, because Charleston was on the way south to the lusher pastures of the West Indies and Surinam. During their sojourns in North America these visitors might deliver a guest sermon, decide tangled questions of law, and examine the qualifications of the local slaughterers.

The Hebraist Ezra Stiles noted in his diary six "rabbies" who visited Newport between 1759 and 1775. Actually, there were at least seven, but not all of them may have been ordained scholars like Haim Isaac Carigal of Hebron in the Holy Land. One of the most distinguished of the Sephardic worthies to come to these shores, Hakam Carigal was the scion of a notable Palestinian family. Landing at Philadelphia in 1772, he moved on to New York for half a year and then sailed north to Rhode Island. There, in Newport, he spent considerable time with Stiles, who devoted to "the Chocam Rabbi" several entries in his diary. It is a pity that New York had had no diarist to record Carigal's doings at Shearith Israel. The New York records contain but two brief mentions of him, reporting that he was sent on to Newport after he had approved the qualifications of the local shohet.[2]

THE HAZZAN

In the absence of rabbinical leadership, the actual officiants in North American communities were hazzanim or readers. Any man of competence the congregation was willing to hire could become a hazzan. An aspirant needed some training, but that was not very difficult to come by, and neither ordination nor certification by a higher authority was required. Such as it was, the authority of the hazzan was from man, not from God. The hazzan was no priest. Warranted by no hierarchy and graced by no sacrament, he was simply a layman hired to do a job. In that sense he had something in common with the Puritan minister.

New York seems to have been the only community with a succession of professional hazzanim, and all the officially appointed hazzanim there throughout the colonial period were of Spanish-Portuguese stock. No doubt the congregation's Sephardic minority insisted on this requirement, and it may have been the price of peace in a community dominantly Central European in numbers, but Sephardic in ritual. Ashkenazim, however, did acquaint themselves with the Sephardic ritual and chants, for there were times when Abraham I. Abrahams, an English-born Ashkenazi of Lithuanian descent, officiated very satisfactorily. On one occasion in 1758 Abrahams was given a piece of plate worth some £20 "for his zealous services to the synagogue." In all likelihood the New Yorkers had used readers ever since their congregation's establishment in the mid-1600's, but it was not until about 1720, as the budget for that year discloses, that the readers received a full salary. Before that time they may have been paid on a part-time basis.[3]

Hazzanim did not always get along well with the congregations which employed them. Hyam Myers, a Canadian trader who went to London, undoubtedly on a business trip, during the late 1770's, had been instructed by his Montreal coreligionists to find a hazzan for the newly built synagogue. The Canadians had confidence in Myers, who had himself been shohet of Shearith Israel in New York for about nine years before becoming a businessman. It is obvious, however, that Jacob Raphael Cohen, whom Myers hired at London in 1778 to serve the Montreal community as hazzan, shohet, mohel, and teacher, did not give satisfaction to all the members, for Cohen was suing the congregation in court before his departure from Montreal during the Revolution.[4]

The Newport hazzan Isaac Touro seems to have given more satisfaction. The Touro family, a very distinguished one, had branches in Holland and the islands, particularly on Curaçao where the first Touro had come, it is possible, as early as the 1650's. Hazzan Touro, a native-born Hollander, was employed by the Newporters in 1759 or 1760 at the recommendation of the Amsterdam parnasim. Some years later he married Reyna, the daughter of Judah Hays, a prominent New York merchant. Touro's employment as a fulltime officiant gave the Newport congregation a large measure of stability and strength. He remained in Newport for about two decades until the congregation's disruption by the English and French military occupations. During the Revolution he finally left for British-occupied New York. Though he was a loyal Dutch citizen and presumably a neutral, his sympathies lay with the British.[5]

The Philadelphia congregation apparently managed for a generation with volunteer hazzanim. At any rate there is no indication that the Philadelphians paid anyone to act as their reader until 1776, when they employed young Ezekiel Levy, who was given a contract under bond to serve for one year as hazzan, shohet, and teacher.

It is interesting to note that the Philadelphia congregation's Yiddish draft constitution, which dates from around 1770, makes no mention at all of a hazzan—which would imply that at that time the congregation expected to conduct its affairs with the aid of volunteers from among its own members. In Charleston, too, the reader was probably a volunteer until Abraham Alexander's employment in 1766. The young cantor in Savannah during the days of the colony's organization received compensation for his services, but as the Jewish community declined, it is most likely that services, if held at all, were performed by one of the few remaining laymen.[6]

When a precentorship fell vacant the news got about, and occasionally aspirants might write in to solicit the position. As a rule, however, "notice" would be given in "foreign parts"; congregations would write to friends and business associates in London or the West Indies to ask for candidates. If necessary, expense money for the ocean voyage would be advanced to the candidate who had been chosen, and the congregation would of course pay for the passage. All the hazzanim who served in New York were foreign-born until the time of Seixas, the last precentor to be employed before the Revolution. Several of them hailed from Holland, and Abraham I. Abrahams, who served as the perennial substitute when anything went wrong, was a native Englishman. Isaac Da Costa, the first volunteer hazzan of Charleston's Beth Elohim congregation, was also of English birth. Unlike their New York coreligionists, the Jews of Montreal, Newport, and Charleston looked abroad to Europe for hazzanim, once they had organized themselves and felt that their communities were solidly established. No doubt the New Yorkers would have done likewise, especially after the completion of the Mill Street Synagogue, had they not believed—for the most part rightly—that suitable chaunters were to be found among their own members

In 1757, however, the New Yorkers did ask their London brethren to recommend a new hazzan, and in the course of this correspondence the qualifications held necessary for the position were specified. First of all, however, it seems to have been taken for granted that the man had to be a Sephardi, since it was difficult though not impossible to secure an Ashkenazi versed in the Sephardic chants. The Ashkenazic majority in the New York congregation, and probably in all the others as well, offered no objection to the adoption or continuance of the Sephardic rite, and it would be interesting to know whether the young Ashkenazi Ezekiel Levy, in leading services in 1776 for a congregation whose ethnic composition was overwhelmingly Germanic, used the Sephardic ritual and knew the Iberian chants. What the New Yorkers asked of Bevis Marks was "a young man, of good morals and strictly religious." Their hazzan had to be an observant Jew in every sense of the term, but he was also to possess the "advantage of an agreeable voice" and to know enough Hebrew to read or chant the Pentateuch and the worship services after the Sephardic fashion. A "capacity for teaching of Hebrew, and translating it into English as well as Spanish" was an additional requisite, though before long a knowledge of Spanish would not be required. The New Yorkers did not insist on a man who was skilled as a sermonizer, for the hazzan infrequently addressed the congregants. In no sense was he a preacher like many of the Protestant clergymen who edified their auditors on political and social issues. An American hazzan would never hold forth unless authorized to do so by his board, and in any event he would adhere rigidly to the limited topic which prompted the rare sermonic occasion.

Congregations preferred someone unmarried—"a young man"—because of the smaller expense involved in his maintenance, but they would accept a married one, particularly if his family was small. Hazzanim in some towns served also as communal slaughterers, and New Yorkers like Machado knew shehitah and licensed other precentors, Pereira for example, to slaughter, though there is no evidence that the cantors of New York ever practiced there as shohetim. In most congregations the hazzan was expected to function as the Hebrew and religious teacher for the children and to prepare the boys for the ceremony of bar mizvah in their thirteenth year. In 1762 the New Yorkers finally saw the need of hiring or subsidizing a special communal teacher to conduct Hebraic and secular studies in their local all-day school; the duties of the hazzan were then separated from those of the "ribby" or teacher, although future cantors were not prevented thereby from teaching privately or even for the community as a whole.[7]

The hazzan commonly did more than function as a chaunter. It was incumbent upon him also to supervise the kashrut of the community and to issue certificates for the export of kosher meat. Before the Passover season he was expected to keep an eye on the baking of unleavened bread and to ensure the mazzah's ritual fitness. Reflecting his professional training, Hazzan Pinto submitted formal annual reports of births, marriages, and deaths in the New York community, and after Pinto's departure those records were continued in a less formal fashion by Abraham I. Abrahams, the omnibus factotum of Shearith Israel. Not only did hazzanim officiate at weddings and funerals, but from time to time they functioned also as mohels and performed circumcisions. There were even occasions when a hazzan might exchange pulpits with a colleague in another community.

An eighteenth century writer like William Cowper might look upon the clergyman as "God's ambassador," but that was certainly not the way colonial American Jews tended to see their precentors. In fact, the status of the colonial hazzan left much to be desired. Authority, even in religious matters, lay primarily in the hands of laymen, and it was not the hazzanim but the parnasim who "like faitful sheeperds call into the fold the wandring sheep." At most, the hazzan would occasionally talk to his flock about peace and unity and urge them to attend worship services. He enjoyed no surfeit of respect. Even a kindly grande dame like Abigail Franks was so unimpressed with Hazzan Lopez de Fonseca that she told her son, "He, poor man, is mad for Esther Lucena, but she has the sence to refuse him." Many decades were to pass before the typical reader of a Sephardic synagogue would attain a measure of prestige, and even then in the mid-nineteenth century, he would find himself only too frequently the object of shabby treatment by the parnasim who were his employers. In no sense was the cantor's position comparable to that of a European rabbi. Rarely a scholar, the hazzan was in essence a hired hand who could be penalized—actually fined—for dereliction of duties. He was expected to "behave himself in every respect," and "good behavior" was a condition for election.

There was one factor which worked in the hazzan's favor—the tendency on the part of Christians to see the hazzan as they saw their own clergymen. Slighted he might be by the Jews, but not by the non-Jews! Ezra Stiles, for instance, once referred to Touro as "Doctor," and when one of Pinto's prayers was published in 1760, the New York hazzan was designated "Dr. Pinto" on the title page. Even Jews, speaking or writing of a hazzan, occasionally called him the "dominie." Actually, as early as the 1760's the hazzan's status was being ameliorated by virtue of the attitude which Christians manifested toward their own and other spiritual leaders. *Wie es sich christelt, so juedelt es sich.*[8]

In the hierarchy of salaried functionaries, the hazzan occupied the top rank. Outside of New York this meant little, since one and the same man often acted as hazzan, shohet, mohel, and teacher. Until about the 1760's the New York precentor received a base annual salary of £50, probably in local currency, not sterling. That sum was roughly twice what the shohet was paid, and the shohet invariably received more than the beadle. During the 1760's the hazzan's wages rose to £80, and in 1775 Seixas was promised £120. These increases do not, however, necessarily mean the pay was getting better; they may merely have reflected inflation and the rising cost of living. Still, the cantor had more than his salary on which to depend; he was given fuel, mazzot for Passover, a parsonage for his living quarters, gifts and offerings made at services, perquisites from marriages and in all probability from funerals, fees for schooling and training the children religiously, and benefits for certifying kosher foods for export. These additional emoluments were certainly not negligible in his economy.

All their additional sources of income notwithstanding, hazzanim found it hard to make both ends meet; they hovered on the fringes of impoverishment. This did not keep the New Yorkers from threatening in 1761 to cut their hazzan's salary by £20 in order to procure additional funds to pay for a teacher. Later, the year the Revolution broke out it was Hazzan Seixas himself who did some threatening. He would resign if his salary were not increased. "The perquisites of his office," he pointed out, were "verry inconsiderable," and he was kept so busy with his congregational chores that he had no time to supplement his income by engaging in commerce. The £30 plus "board and lodging" which was the annual salary of the Philadelphia factotum would ensure Ezekiel Levy's living modestly, but Levy was luckier than Cohen of Montreal. Hired in 1778 at the yearly salary of £50 lawful money, Cohen had at length to sue his employers in order to collect![9]

The earliest of the New York hazzanim—and probably of most congregations during their formative years—were businessmen who served as volunteers. If they did receive some remuneration, they were not dependent for their livelihood on what the members of the congregation gave them. It was through commerce that they provided for their basic needs. Even in the early 1700's when the New York congregation began employing full-time professional ministers, the picture did not change radically, and most of the New York hazzanim maintained an interest in business. Lopez de Fonseca, Machado, Pereira, and Cohen da Silva had all been tradesmen before mounting the pulpit as professional readers, and they continued to woo commercial fortune after accepting ministerial office.

Even "Dr." Pinto, the most professional of the mid-eighteenth century hazzanim, had a "business" of his own. He advertised in the local press that he was prepared to give lessons in Hebrew, Spanish, and Portuguese. So far as we know, however, Seixas, one of Pinto's successors, did not engage in business, although after the Revolution he may have carried on a modest traffic in books from the privacy of his home. Hazzan Touro of Newport certainly engaged in commerce with local Gentiles as well as Jews and on occasion sent parcels of goods to Jamaica where he had family. It may well be that in requiring Hazzan Ezekiel Levy to "bind himself for and in consideration of £30," the Philadelphians sought to make sure not merely that he would perform his manifold duties, but that he would not succumb to the temptation of earning an extra shilling or two at the expense of his congregational responsibilities.[10]

The hazzan was not the only religious functionary to interest himself in business. The shohatim and beadles of all congregations were always involved in ventures—making sausages or buying fodder, selling bricks or retailing notions, and even engaging in petty overseas transactions. Congregants seem not to have objected, and there can be no question that great merchants like Nathan Simson and Aaron Lopez even went out of their way to help the synagogal staff members make a little money on the side.

The Church of England was, of course, second to none in size and influence on the colonial American scene, but her pastorate, particularly in southern colonies like Maryland and Virginia, was not always a model of probity. Only too often Anglican clerics were men of dubious repute, men of "notorious badness" and "immoral conduct." Colonial hazzanim appear in this respect to have been far superior to many of their Christian colleagues; though they quarreled occasionally with their congregants and even contended with them in the courts, they were generally men of unblemished moral character. Marylanders might despise their Anglican Church because she "permitted clerical profligacy to murder the souls of men," but it is much to be doubted that any Jewish congregation would have tolerated a hazzan whose personal life gave evidence of "profligacy." Inasmuch as—unlike his Anglican counterpart—the Jewish minister was not a sacramental personality, he was always subject to dismissal, and laymen could step up to carry on the service.

Shortly after the young hazzan Joseph Jesurun Pinto arrived in New York, he seems to have had trouble with his board, but so far as can be determined from the correspondence, Pinto's transgressions were not of a moral nature; he could tell the board, "after earnest reflection," that there was "nothing sinful clinging" to his hands. Even in the case of Pinto's successor, the Reverend Isaac Cohen Da Silva, whose conduct was undeniably "indiscreet and scandalous," it was a commercial misfortune but no immorality which ultimately brought about his summary discharge.[11]

THE SHOHET

Since nearly all Jews in colonial America were religiously observant, they had to have kosher meat and qualified shohatim or slaughterers to prepare it. There was never a dearth of such functionaries, although at times a congregation might encounter difficulty in securing a shohet because the pay offered him was so meager. Butchers had been found among the Jews ever since their first coming in 1654, and in all probability some of those early pioneers had been trained shohatim. Asser Levy had been a butcher, or soon became one after his arrival in 1654. In 1660 the New Amsterdam authorities excused him and another butcher, Moses De Lucena, for religious reasons from killing hogs, which lends support to the assumption that they were shohatim. Some men, about to emigrate and anxious to ensure themselves a supply of kosher meat, no doubt studied the art of ritual slaughter in Europe, while others learned shehitah only after their arrival on these shores. Hazzan Machado of New York is known to have licensed eighteen shohatim, one of them a recent bar mizvah, thirteen-year-old Myer Myers, who was later to become a highly competent gold- and silversmith.

Shehitah appealed to some individuals as a means not only of providing themselves with meat, but also of serving their Jewish neighbors in the small towns where they might settle. Those who mastered it as a trade would be enabled thereby to support themselves until they could learn the ways of the new land and make the transition to a life of commerce. Shehitah was commonly a profession for beginners and failures: the first resort of the poor and the last resort of the incompetent. For example, the Canadian trader Hyam Myers who founded a family of merchants was originally a shohet for the New York Jewish community. In Rhode Island a retired silversmith became the Newport shohet. A shohet might be poorly paid, but he would not be poorly treated. The New York congregational records for 1728 indicate that Benjamin Elias, who had served the community for a generation as shohet, was retired with a pension of "twinty pounds . . . per annum" plus "two cords of wood and passover cakes." [12]

Even in those early days a considerable amount of kosher meat was sold, for a shohet slaughtered for the several Christian butchers from whom the Jewish community bought its meat. The New Yorkers, it seems, always made an effort to maintain one individual as the community's official shohet; he was the professional. The list of communal shohatim known by name includes twelve between 1728 and 1776, but there were many others who could be called in for emergencies when the incumbent stepped down.

In towns outside New York—Montreal for instance, or Lancaster and Philadelphia—shehitah was performed by the local religious man of all work. There was scarcely a town or village sheltering even one Jewish family which lacked someone who could act as shohet. Even in the remotest communities Jews could and did provide kosher meat and food for themselves and their families. Although in 1695 Newport is unlikely to have had more than three or four Jewish families, Isaac Naphtali was recorded there that year as being a "Jew butcher"; Michael Judah of Norwalk, the Louzadas of Bound Brook, and Michael Hart of Easton provided kosher meat for their own tables.[13]

Neither poverty nor isolation spelled a disinterest in kashruth. Meyer Josephson of Reading was nearly always in financial straits, but nonetheless he managed to keep his own personal shohet who doubled in brass by clerking in the store. Josephson's correspondence testifies to his determination to maintain a kosher home. He imported three "killing knives" from London, shipped ritually-slaughtered deer meat as a gift to the Gratzes, and importuned them to order him some kosher cheese from London. In Lancaster one of the town's early Jewish settlers, Isaac Nunes Henriques, had studied the art of ritual slaughtering in New York with his fellow Sephardi, Hazzan Machado; Henriques fortified himself with a Spanish book on shehitah published at London in 1733. Like Josephson, Joseph Simon of Lancaster and Aaron Levy of Northumberland had personal shohatim, probably young men who mainly tended store for them and in their leisure hours performed shehitah. The Lancaster shohet and mohel Barnard Jacobs once issued a shohet's license to the young Lancastrian Solomon Etting, but limited him to the privilege of slaughtering for his own use only. Jacobs probably did not think the young man proficient enough to slaughter for communal needs. Mordecai Sheftall's attachment to kashruth was such that when calling on a Gentile friend in the Georgia backcountry, he brought his "sharp knife" along with him to slaughter a sheep ritually.[14]

In a community like New York the shohet was expected to give three months' notice before he quit. The congregation, on receiving such notice, would proceed to advertise in the synagogue for a successor, and if no one in town was willing to take the job, the board would write letters to other American communities. Ultimately of course, a candidate was found. After being examined on his knowledge of the slaughtering ritual, the aspirant would at length be elected, usually by vote of the congregation as a whole, though there were times when the board assumed authority and appointed a shohet.[15]

The shohet's primary job was to slaughter cattle and fowl, to supervise the processing of kosher meat by the Gentile butchers, and finally to "keep the markets sufficiently furnish'd with meats for supplying of this congregation" and also for foreign export. The congregation was particularly eager to have an adequate supply of meat in the stalls before the Sabbath and the holidays. The slaughtering was done in different abattoirs, all of them controlled by Christians, who had to be watched lest for the kosher meat they substitute terefah—something ritually unfit. Careful supervision was particularly important in the export trade, where meats had to be properly sealed with lead tags marked "kasher," or where casks had to be branded and certificates issued. Despite all precautions, deception and cheating were commonplace in the export trade; not only were foods falsely represented as kosher shipped abroad, but often taxes on kosher products were not paid to the exporting community. The shohet had to guard against these duplicities. He was never a free agent. Subject in ritual matters to the hazzan, the shohet was answerable even more directly to the board and the honorary officers.[16]

The shohet's pay was always modest. In 1720 the shohet of the New York congregation received £15 annually in local currency, in 1728 his salary was £20 a year, and by 1775 it had risen to £50. Frequently, to be sure, there were additional emoluments and grants. The shohet might, for instance, be given free housing in one of the congregational buildings. The tongues of the animals he slaughtered usually belonged to him, and he could eat them or sell them. He would also receive fuel or a fuel allowance, mazzot, ferriage to the slaughterhouse if he had to cross a river, and lead for the seals. Often, too, the congregation supplied the slaughtering knife. At times, however, there were no allowances for the shohet; he was given a salary and nothing additional. To protect his meager income, he was granted a monopoly of all congregational shehitah in New York, in all probability including the slaughtering of fowls for individuals as well as all slaughtering done for export. For such work he undoubtedly received extra compensation from all those who used his services.[17]

The shohet's lot was hardly a desirable one, and there was an unending series of complaints from the communal shohatim in New York that they could not make a living. As one of them put it in 1768, "his labor is very heavy, and the sallary small and no perquisites." The job seems indeed to have been a difficult one and men often resigned or were discharged. The average tenure of office was about four years. The rigid supervision and periodic reexamination to which shohatim were subjected must have been extremely galling. Congregational presidents, loyal to tradition, were certainly exacting if not captious with regard to the qualifications of the slaughterers under their control, while congregants were indignant if for some reason or other there was insufficient meat in the stalls.

Some of the shohatim, to judge from complaints lodged against them, were apparently not overly meticulous in the performance of their duties and had to be closely watched. Threats of dismissal for carelessness were constant. The synagogal officers were always at pains to guard against the slaughterers leaving their sealing-tools around lest an unscrupulous butcher make use of them to certify unfit meat as kosher. On one occasion a shohet was accused of carelessly mixing together kosher and unkosher tongues and of "sealing" (declaring ritually fit) a lamb killed by a non-Jewish butcher. Then, it might happen that shohatim would obstreperously refuse to submit their knives to the inspection of a competent person. Slaughterers found to be negligent were reprimanded and sometimes even suspended.[18]

THE SHAMMASH

The Hebrew word *shammash* (shammas, samas) literally means servitor. A shammash was the sexton or beadle elected by the congregation as a whole. Always a Jew, the holder of this office is not to be confused with the laborers employed to clean the synagogue, though it is not improbable that in some communities the sexton was his own janitor. His duties may have been onerous and his position humble, but the shammash was not necessarily a nobody, and occasionally a learned man knowledgeable in Hebraic lore occupied the position. Joseph Simson was such a person. Shammash at New York in 1738–1739, a decade later he had risen to the presidency of Shearith Israel. Simson's ascent, however, was not only a tribute to the social mobility that characterized New York's Jewish community; in all likelihood it was also a compliment to the business acumen of Simson's sons who became prominent New York merchants. As their power and influence increased, they undoubtedly carried their father along with them.

Most congregations hired a sexton as soon as they had established a formal organization—certainly as soon as they began to rent quarters for worship services. The Montreal and Philadelphia congregations, small as they were, are known to have had beadles, and the Newporters too, with their substantial building and its annex which included living quarters, commanded the services of a shammash. The New Yorkers had employed shammashim since 1720 at least and probably even a generation earlier.

In a sense the shammash served as the executive arm of the board. His work was significant, as is clear from the enumeration of his duties. The shammash's presence was required at all prayer meetings, and he had to call the congregants to services on Friday afternoons. When early-morning penitential prayers were recited in the fall, it was his duty to make the rounds about midnight to awaken the people and summon them to the house of worship. He saw also to the cleaning of the synagogue, and merely looking after the ninety-six candles in the chandeliers of Shearith Israel was in itself no small task. There were other candles aglow in the candelabra before the ark and on the reading desk. Sometimes in New York the shammash was expected to make the candles himself. All the ritual silver had to be cared for and polished, the eternal light had to be kept burning, and the can where people washed their hands had to be supplied with water.

The shammash's responsibilities included care of the cemetery, and he was present as a majordomo at circumcisions, weddings, and funerals. It was his job to make certain that the ritual bath was in order, and that the water was properly tempered. In addition he made the rounds collecting dues, debts, offerings, and—one may be sure—gratuitous insults. Since the shammash's house, like that of the shohet, was used as the local hospice, he would be called upon now and then to lodge and board the poor, the sick, and the itinerant, albeit at the expense of the congregation. Above all, it was his duty to "stricktly obey the orders of the parnas," and a shammash who wished to hold onto his job "chearfully agreed and returned thanks."

For all this, in New York the shammash was given a base annual salary of £2.20 in 1720 and £15 in 1728—though the salary rose in later years. As did the hazzan and shohet, the shammash too might usually expect additional emoluments and perquisites from those whom he served on occasions of joy and sorrow. He also received an allowance of fuel and unleavened bread as well as free rental or a house at a modest rental—so long as he was willing to permit the use of its facilities for baking the Passover mazzot. Individual worshipers may have made offerings for the shammash during the services as they certainly did for the reader. No doubt, however, there were shammashim who neglected their duties in an effort to augment their income by work or business on the side, and such shammashim found themselves discharged or threatened with substantial fines.[19]

CHAPTER 54

BELIEF AND PIETY

The Affirmation of Judaism

B ecause most colonial American Jews were positive in their religious identity, they lost no opportunity to fashion synagogal
institutions in which they could give voice to the philosophy and the
sancta of Jewish life. Jewish history, checkered though it was, had one
continuous thread—a belief in the fellowship of all Jews everywhere,
a desire to implement the religious and moral ideals of the Jewish
faith, and a determination to observe the customs, rituals, and ceremonies inherited from one's immediate forebears.

The Jews of North America were enabled to remain firm in
their religious loyalties by the constant contact they maintained
with Europe, and in addition by their ties with the larger Caribbean
Jewish communities, where ancestral religious traditions were inflex-
ibly preserved. The unyielding adherence of American Jews to the
teachings of their fathers was further fortified by continual arrivals
of religiously-minded immigrants from the continent and England.
In actuality the Montreal congregation and the tidewater synagogue-
communities to the south were extensions of London Jewry, such
that when Richa Franks lost her father, this cultured heiress left the
land of her nativity and returned "home" to England. There, she
knew, her brothers Naphtali and Moses and her widely-ramified
family lived as Jews—by contrast with the situation in the colonies,
where her sister Phila and her brother David had both intermarried
and were rearing families of Christians.[1]

American Jewish religion and religious practices centered, as we have already indicated, not in the hazzan-minister, but in the layman. The Jewish communities here were built by the initiative of merchants, shopkeepers, and artisans who needed and wanted religious institutions in which they could express themselves as Jews. To most American Jews no other but a Jewish way of life was conceivable; their folkways were bred, as it were, in the bone. Some of the Jews were truly pious, while others were observant in a mechanical fashion, but all who identified themselves as Jews were determined to live Jewishly. Within a comforting communal ambit of their own creation and their own choice, they lived and practiced their own distinctive religious way from cradle to grave. They organized congregations, held services, and speedily rented rooms or buildings for their religious purposes. Rarely possessed of sufficient funds to erect structures of their own, they hesitated even more rarely to turn to their fellow Jews both here and abroad. Neither they nor their coreligionists overseas ever failed literally to bear in mind the ancient rabbinic adage that Jews are responsible for one another. In 1759, for example, Newport Jewry, involved in the process of "establish[ing] a regular congregation," did not hesitate to urge the New Yorkers to raise funds for them on Passover in the Mill Street Synagogue. The response of the New Yorkers was typical —"Your pious design was a sufficient inducement to promote the success of your request"—and a substantial amount was raised for "the holy building."

A great deal needed to be raised, of course, for when Jews set out to fashion a religious community, every effort was made to secure the cult utensils required for proper synagogue and home observance: pentateuchal scrolls, ritual silver, prayer books, prayer shawls, phylacteries, special lamps, and mezuzot to post on doors. Some of the ritual silver was made by American Jewish silversmiths, but most of the other utensils and supplies were secured probably through gifts from distant congregations and individuals or, as was often customary, by purchase from London.[2]

THE RELIGIOUS OUTLOOK OF THE AMERICAN JEW

The degree to which, or indeed whether, theology ever made any intellectual impress on the consciousness of the typical Jew in colonial America is highly debatable. Nevertheless, the colonial Jew did possess a theology, which was reflected in a variety of ways. It was the characteristic, traditional theology of his European home-land—a complex, we might say, of Diaspora religious notions which had originated in talmudic if not in pre-Christian times. This theology did not constitute a system of beliefs of which the Jew was particularly conscious; it was, on the contrary, an unemphasized aspect of his religion. The Judaism to which he clung was a God-centered, God-motivated ethical way of life which featured an elaborate series of folkways and practices very precious to him. Judaism was not for him something one debated intellectually; it was something one practiced, lived—and enjoyed. It was the substratum of his life, automatically and spontaneously expressed, and in the last analysis very real. In actual practice, it may be said, Judaism was a socio-ritualistic faith, a culture-religion, if not indeed a religious culture.

Basic to the theology of the Jew was his devotion to a unitarian concept of a Deity who had revealed himself to the Children of Is-rael. This belief in God and in his divinely revealed, immutable laws was founded on the Five Books of Moses, but those laws had in turn been interpreted for all generations by the sages of the Talmud and were codified for speedy reference in the *Shulhan Aruk* (The Prepared Table) of two eminent sixteenth century legal authorities. That code had accompanied the immigrants across the Atlantic, and its prescriptions, held binding on all Jews, were accepted without hesitation, certainly without any perceptible protest, by American Jewry.

Ever since the twelfth century, to be sure, the Jews had had a formal statement of faith prepared by one man, Maimonides. All Jews knew the creed, read it frequently in their prayer books, took it for granted—and blandly ignored it. Subscription to its thirteen articles was no doubt assumed, but no one was ever asked by any rabbinical authority to affirm them. Their acceptance was the criterion of an orthodoxy that was never tested—certainly not in colonial America. The Maimonidean articles of faith may have been something to embrace, but they were not something to discuss. The Jewish "church" was simply not a community of doctrinally convinced and tested believers.

The religious outlook of colonial Jews found what was in many respects its most distinctive expression in wills. Despite their formulary character and the fact that they were frequently prepared by non-Jews, the wills of colonial days emphasized the traditional and basic ideals which preoccupied the minds and hearts of Jews at the most critical moment of their lives. It is evident from their wills that colonial Jews were not threatened by an overpowering sense of sin. Certain Old Testament teachings notwithstanding, their God was not a God of vengeance or of inexorable justice, for rabbinism had long since transmuted the God of anger into a God of mercy and love. Notions of eternal damnation were alien to the colonial Jew, and the battle against sin and the devil, so characteristic of Christian revivalism during the Great Awakening of the eighteenth century, left him cold and disdainful. Unlike his pious Christian neighbor, the Jew of that generation was never *overwhelmed* by sin, but this is not to say that sin had no reality for him or that he felt no personal responsibility for his own evil deeds on the final day of reckoning.

The Jew certainly had a sense of sin, and particularly for the Jew of Sephardic ancestry, this sense of sin may have been exacerbated by the teachings of his forebears who had been reared as Christians on the Iberian Peninsula. It is a Spanish-Portuguese Catholic influence which may be reflected in Jacob Olivera's will written in 1751:

I commend my soul to the Almighty God of Israel, Creator of Heaven and Earth, imploring His most gracious pardon for all my past sins and transgressions of which I most sincerely repent and, hoping His infinite mercies will extend to me also, I most vehemently and sincerely invoke His holy name, saying, Hear, O Israel, the Lord our God, the Lord is One.

The final phrase may well have been the passionate affirmation of a former Marrano who had been constantly compelled in his Christian guise to affirm a belief in the Trinity. A feeling of guilt, of being weighed down by sin, is voiced in a personal religious supplication by one of the Gomezes. It is one of the few original nonliturgical prayers to survive the colonial Jewish experience:

Be merciful to me, O Lord. Forgive my iniquities. I am mourning for my transgressions. They compass me with terror of your wrath. Being sensible of my sin I beg for forgiveness and, as your goodness is great, I rely on your mercy and beseech your blessing that I may be preserved under the shade of your wings. Not for any worthiness in me but for your goodness sake. May my soul cleave to Thee and Thy commandments, and may I walk in uprightness that I may be one of your beloved chosen Israelites. Amen.[3]

In their wills American Jews craved pardon for their sins and expressed the hope that God's infinite mercies would reach out to them, sinners though they were. Not infrequently wills contained an invocation to "the one God" who was "the God of truth" (Psalm 31:6), and it is quite probable that this last phrase was polemical, directed against a Christianity whose man-God was, in Jewish eyes, neither One nor a God of truth. The Jews of the seventeenth and eighteenth centuries may be said to have believed, as the New Testament put it, that "salvation is of the Jews," and that it could come only through the God of the Jews.[4]

Many of the pious phrases adverting to death reflected a hope for physical resurrection, a hope interlaced with the messianic coming and the final judgment. Death was but a step to a better life. One who died had been "gathered" to his God, had "passed away" and was "with God," or had been "liberated for Paradise." A common phrase coupled with the report of death and expressing the hope for a future life was: "May his blessed soul be gathered to the peace of the saints [pious ones]." The dead person was "fortunately blessed," and when it "pleased the Almighty to take Mr. Moses Heyman out of this trublsom world," Isaac Adolphus hopefully expressed the wish that his friend was "in the Garden of Eden." The tombstone of Abraham R. Rivera bears a poetic effusion and pun:

He shines now with effulgent light a
   denizen above,
In realms reserved for all who here
   revere a god of love.

A touch of skepticism was, however, not to be gainsaid. That death
was not always the joy and blessing that some of the pious phrases
implied asserted itself in more sober, more practical statements like:
"May the Almighty . . . grant us all long life in His holy service."

As is common enough even today, reference to the dead was
most frequently followed by the parenthetical phrase "of blessed
memory," and occasionally the bereaved wife was remembered by
"May God comfort her." Though for the most part such pious ut-
terances were automatic and lacking much thought, they did express
the Jew's universal hope for the resurrection of the dead. In a will
signed in 1716 Abraham De Lucena most succinctly summarized the
theology of the Jew as he faced possible death: "In the name of
God, Amen. I, Abraham De Lucena, of New York, merchant, by
God's grace proceeding on a voyage to Jamaica, considering the
dangers of the seas . . . I bequeath my immortal soul into the hands
of the Almighty God of Israel, my creator, trusting in his mercy for
pardon of all my sins and hoping for a joyful resurrection to life
eternal."

Ezra Stiles once discussed resurrection with Rabbi Carigal in the
presence of Jacob R. Rivera and his wife, who had been the Widow
Sasportas when Rivera married her. Certainly not with tongue in
cheek, for he was a most orthodox Christian, Stiles put to the rabbi
the same question that the Sadducees had posed to Jesus many
centuries before: Would there be "any relations of husbands and
wives in the resurrection"? Unlike Jesus, Rabbi Carigal answered in
the affirmative, and Stiles, "joyned" by the Riveras, asked then
which of Hannah Rivera's two husbands would be her mate in the
world to come. Carigal, "at a loss," had no answer except that "God
Almighty only could determine." He was certain only that "the
resurrection state would be happy and glorious, though he did not
pretend to be able to answer and solve all questions and mysteries
concerning the circumstances of the resurrection state." [5]

Most Jews no doubt were as puzzled as Rabbi Carigal by the

"mysteries" of "the resurrection state," but they did all they could to make sure that the translation to the next world would be effected properly and speedily, and that the memory of the dead would be cherished. Money for this purpose—for prayers after death—was left in wills or provided by the family. These hashkabot (prayers of "repose") articulated the hope that the deceased would find and enjoy tranquility of soul in Paradise, under the wings of the Almighty. The colonial Jew, after all, never doubted there was a very substantial life after death, and the tombstone of "Rabbi" Moses Cohen of Charleston blazoned forth the conviction of his survivors that his soul had gone "to shine and glorify in Heaven," where "among the seraphims" the departed would surely fix his "dwelling amidst the glorious transparent pavements." [6]

Synagoguegoers did not question that the hashkabah prayer promoted the repose of the dead or that the dead needed such help from those who had remained behind and were moved by filial piety to intervene for them. Prayer was needed by all, for no man was so righteous that on his death he would immediately partake of the joys of Heaven. This notion—that the dead would attain repose in the hereafter through the prayers and the charities of their survivors—certainly harked back to the medieval Catholic theology and practice to which all European Jews had been exposed for over a millennium. Much more indigenously Jewish, however, was the belief in the importance of accumulating mitzvot (meritorious deeds) by following the commands of God, fulfilling his religious injunctions, and observing his laws. Such moral and ethical acts assured one of long life in this world and of bliss in the world to come. When the Rhode Island Jews encountered difficulty in amortizing their new synagogue, they wrote their fellow Jews on Curaçao: "We flatter ourselves that since the practice of mitzvot is so deeply ingrained in your spirit, you will unanimously agree to come to the aid of this effort:" The Curaçaons would surely be recompensed with "long life, increased favor [with God], and prosperity for many years." Virtue, that generation believed, was the best passport to heaven. As the dying Jacob Olivera of South Carolina put it, "I . . . recommend to my . . . son to walk in the fear of God and in the path of virtue, which is the last and best legacy I can leave him."

Who were the men who would inherit future bliss? The epitaphs of colonial Jewry pointed up the answer in no uncertain terms. Samuel Levy, who died in 1719, was remembered because he had lent money to the poor and orphans, because he had spoken the truth, and because he had been honorable in business. This Levite had stored up mitzvot. Toward the end of the century the inscription on Jacob R. Rivera's tombstone praised him as one who had "profess[ed] and patronize[d] the principles of Judaism," "observe[d] the strictest integrity in extensive commerce," and "exhibit[ed] unbounded benevolence for all mankind." It was for their good deeds that men like Levy and Rivera were distinguished, and in the minds of their contemporaries they were assured the "superlative happiness" of future life. Writing to her son Naphtali on the death of his father-in-law in 1737, Abigail Franks summarized the theology of postmortem survival through good deeds: "All the difference after death is a man's works here on earth, for that never dyes, and one that has left soe great and good a name may be said to have lived full of days and dyed in a good ould age."

And a woman? How could she attain Paradise? The answer to this is found in the Latin inscription on the tombstone of the thirty-six-year-old Abigail Lopez of Newport: *Virtute insignis charitate ardens.* She had been distinguished for virtue and charity; she had been faithful to her husband, a good companion, and the tenderest of parents.[7]

From a long rambling Hebrew letter describing his own religious philosophy, which Hazzan Joseph J. Pinto addressed to the New York congregation, one can adduce a summary of the theological goals of the individual. A man had to seek for righteousness through the performance of good deeds. The knowledge of what God requires was to be found in Torah, that is, in the study of God's law as it appeared in the Bible and as it had been interpreted in later rabbinic literature. Marriage was important, for the family that came of it was also to be reared to study God's commands. If these laws and ordinances were followed, then prosperity and long life would ensue in this world, and there would come in God's own time redemption for the Holy Land of Promise.[8]

Sin, Fate, and Torah

Though he gave himself very little to brooding about sin, the colonial Jew, as we have seen, was certainly not deficient in a sense of sin. Just as personal sin played a considerable role in the life of the individual, even so did a sense of collective sin pervade the "economy" of American Jewry vis-à-vis its God. The Jewish fate was no puzzlement to those eighteenth century religionists: the Jews were in exile because of their sins; the Temple of Jerusalem had been obliterated by the Romans in the first century of the Christian era because the Judeans had transgressed religiously. When the synagogue at St. Eustatius was laid waste by a hurricane in August 1772, it was "our sins," wrote the leaders of St. Eustatius Jewry to their coreligionists in New York, which "caused us to see our holy synagogue destroyed."

Earlier that same year in Newport, Enoch Lyon, a local Jewish businessman, visited Pastor Stiles for "some religious conversation," and the two fell to discussing the problem of sin. Sin was certainly fundamental to Christian theology, which emphasized the redemptive and vicarious sacrifice of the sinless Jesus and his coming to save a wicked world. Lyons, too, believed in "the infinite evil of sin," but saw no "necessity of . . . a Messiah's atonement." God, Lyons told Pastor Stiles, was "infinitely merciful," and there was, therefore, no need for Jesus to have died on the cross to expiate the transgressions of mankind.[9]

Rabbi Carigal too, as he addressed the Newport congregation on Pentecost in 1773, saw God as "the merciful creator," and he too spoke of sin. "The calamities . . . endured" by the Jews, he said, had "not been casualties or accidents"; they had proceeded from sin, and the sin which the community as a whole had committed in the past—and of which its members were still guilty—was disregard of God's ancient injunctions. "The loss of Jerusalem," he declared, quoting a talmudic sage, "was owing to the contempt and ignominy with which they treated every one who applied himself to the *divine study*." But, said Carigal, though the Jews were in exile for their "crimes and abominations," they had not been rejected by God. The

Babylonians and the Romans, God's instruments to punish the Jews, had already been destroyed, but when the Jews as a community expressed "true contrition" and "promise[d] amendment," they would surely experience God's redemptive mercy, entailing an ultimate restoration of the Holy Land and of the Temple with its divinely prescribed and atoning sacrifices.

Repentance, insisted the rabbi, had to include study in the home, in the academy, and in the synagogue. (Perhaps Carigal emphasized "divine study" so strongly because he wanted the Newport community to accord him special courtesies as a rabbinic scholar.) The generation of Newport Jews to which he addressed himself in these terms knew what study meant. It meant the Law and its practice as ordained by Moses and Ezra and the rabbis. And it was the obligation of every congregation—may God preserve and multiply them!—to study the word of God and to immerse itself in, as Carigal put it, "the holy law, which subsists man in this world and in the world to come," and in "the divine tradition which instructs in the true way of living." "Nothing," said the rabbi, "is more advantageous and beneficial towards our being established and fixed in the true belief than the frequentation of the sacred colleges and synagogues, where we daily hear the word of the Lord. But the true intent of this frequentation must be directed to the sole purpose of penetrating and observing the divine precepts, and acquiring the fear of the Lord." Study was the best antidote to sin. Through study, one learned God's moral requirements, the "epitome" of which was the Decalogue.

In speaking of study, Carigal digressed momentarily to asperse the Gentile rationalists who criticized the Bible, made improper interpretations, and questioned the rationality of Scripture. Such attempts to "deface the purity, lustre, and truth of the divine tradition" he branded as nothing but "ignorance, arrogance, and presumption." It was, in any case, incumbent upon the Jew to obey the law not because the law made sense, but because the law had been commanded by God, "the great sovereign monarch." The law was not to be changed; it was "permanent at all times and places, except when the divine legislator commands the contrary." The only changes that Carigal recognized were "in the precepts relating to the sacred worship of the temple, and others that depend on our residence in the Holy Land."

This matter of the Holy Land was important. Ultimately the purpose of observing the Law was to bring about the restoration of the Jewish people to its own homeland. "Let us have a firm belief," argued Carigal, "in the innumerable prophecies that predict our restoration." God could be expected to expedite the restoration if his people obeyed his moral law by "faithfulness and integrity" in their commercial dealings, by establishing "fixed times for the meditation of the law," and by loving their neighbors as they loved themselves. At the final restoration the whole world would accept the ethical monotheism of the Jew and would say "as with one voice," "In that day there shall be one Lord, and his name one." [10]

Carigal was, to be sure, not a permanent settler in North America, and he may have used his sermon wherever he went, but there can be little question that his address reflected the thinking and beliefs of his Jewish auditors in Rhode Island. The Jews of Newport and their coreligionists on this continent rarely devoted time to theological cogitations; nevertheless, Carigal spoke for them, and they accepted the substance of his theological outlook without demur. His was, of course, the religious philosophy of all the observant Jews of that generation in all lands. Their fathers had sinned; they were in exile; there would be a final restoration in a messianic age. The belief in the ultimate advent of the Messiah was a real one which recurred in the daily and holiday prayers and in nearly every official congregational communication with other Jewish groups. Though no specific literature on the subject emerged in colonial America, the Jew here was concerned about redemption; he believed it would surely come. An apostle, sent out from Constantinople in 1760 on behalf of the sufferers of earthquake-ravaged Safed in Palestine, did not fail to remind the leaders of Shearith Israel in a letter to them, that their charity to the unfortunate Palestinians could hasten the coming of the Messiah—". . . by your acts, Omnipotent God may redeem us from our bitter and prolonged captivity."

Why—the reader might ask—should the American Jew of the seventeenth and eighteenth centuries have concerned himself with the possibility of a restoration to Palestine? To begin with, he believed God had promised the Jews would come back to the Holy Land. Above and beyond that, however, many genuinely hoped for the creation of a Jewish politico-religious empire in Palestine with Jerusalem as its capital. The first Jews to settle in America included many whose parents or friends had been hounded by the Spanish and Portuguese Inquisitions. Relatives had perished in Iberian dungeons or died at the stake because of their Jewish sympathies. The German and Polish Jews of the 1600's and 1700's had no less reason to crave the messianic advent. They had suffered bitterly from legal disabilities, and particularly in Eastern Europe, from outright massacre. The conditions they found in North America were much, much better, but here too, Jews were still second-class citizens and were never unmindful of their inferior status. Restoration had much to recommend it and that is why, as we have pointed out, most of the early American synagogues carried names of messianic significance with their intimations of an ultimate restoration.

The Holy Land was never very far from the consciousness of American Jewry, if only because the Jews of the colonies were frequently called upon to support the rabbinical academies and the poor of Palestine. That was the land to which God had promised they would return in the messianic age, and certainly they prayed daily for that return. Many a Jewish letter closed with the familiar entreaty that God might soon send a Redeemer to Zion. Pastor Stiles's conversations with the Jews about messianic matters document his own concern rather than Jewish preoccupation with the subject, but Jews had been for centuries very much interested in the restoration. They were constantly juggling with the chronology of certain obscure verses in the Book of Daniel, and there was in fact no time in which world Jewry did not engage in messianic computations. The eighteenth century was no exception, so that some New Yorkers, on the basis of certain calculations by European rabbis, expected the Messiah to appear in 1768. The following year Stiles reported that the Jews thought the Messiah might make his appearance in 1783. In 1770, still curious, Stiles discussed with a visiting Jew from Poland the possibility of the Messiah's speedy advent. The Pole told his host that the Jews "looked for him every day." [11]

The subject must have fascinated Stiles. (Did he harbor an unconscious fear that the appearance of a Jewish Messiah would be tantamount to a denial of the messianic character of Jesus?) In 1773 he spoke with the visiting Carigal about the coming of a Jewish redeemer. Carigal expressed the traditional view that the Messiah would appear in an age of "universal tumult and confusion," but the times, he said, were now no more unsettled than in any previous age. A week before, however, the rabbi had speculated that the Messiah might appear "daily, probably within forty years." In all likelihood the typical American Jew who prayed daily for the return did not dwell overmuch on the content of a prayer he could neither understand nor translate. Had he been asked about his belief in the messianic coming and in the restoration, he would have declared no doubt that such was God's promise. In his own mind, however, the restoration was always in the future—tomorrow. He did not seriously envisage the prospect of return; after all, he was relatively happy where he was.[12]

Observance

The pattern for what later generations would call orthodoxy was set by the very first arrivals in the colonies. The inventory of the personal possessions of Asser Levy, the founding father as it were of American Jewry, reveals that he owned a ritual spice box, a Sabbath lamp, kiddush cups, and a parcel of old books—undoubtedly well-thumbed dog-eared Hebrew liturgies. This Jew carried a treasured world in his seabag, but how typical was Levy? On the whole most of the Jews who lived in organized communities were nominally loyal and observant in matters of religion—a conclusion which may be prejudiced by the fact that most of the sources touching on religion are synagogal records. Some Jews were no doubt loyal only because of the moral pressures exerted on them by the Jewish community, but there were certainly a great many whose attachment to Jewish ways stemmed from tradition, training, and conviction. The vast majority of "Christians" in America may have been unchurched, but not the Jews. Whatever their motivations may have been, most of them affiliated themselves with a synagogue and attended services with some frequency. To be sure, there must have been some who hid their Jewish origin, as would happen early in the nineteenth century when Cincinnati Jewry, the first Jewish community to be established west of the Alleghenies, bought a cemetery in order to bury a man who had lived as a non-Jew. In his last moments he would make himself known to the Jews and would ask for Jewish burial.[13]

Hart Jacobs, the last shohet of prerevolutionary Shearith Israel, petitioned successfully for exemption from service in the city watch on Friday nights because military duty on the Sabbath was inconsistent with his religious scruples. The Jews of that day were Sabbath observers; they interrupted all commercial correspondence shortly before nightfall on Friday, and as the numerous Lopez account books testify, kept their shops closed on the Sabbath and on all holidays. A Gentile associate of the Gratz brothers was "chagreened" to discover in May 1774 that no business, however urgent, would persuade Michael Gratz to abandon his devotions on Pentecost—"as the Devil will have it . . . Moses was upon the top of a mount in the month of May—consequently his followers must for a certain number of days cease to provide for their families." Not every Jew was so scrupulous of course. That mordant wit, Samuel Jacobs, who was anything but observant, had no use for the piety of his fellow Jew, Hyam Myers, the former shohet of Shearith Israel:

I don't blame you for not breaking our Sabath, particular as it was to pay cash to a person in want. Tho', I dare say, the [Christian] bearer would have waited till next day and broke his [Sunday rest] in order to relieve me. But I blame you for having sleep'd so many hundred working days and broke the most part of the Ten Commandments by indeavoring to keep that one of not paying cash of our Sabath.[14]

There were individuals who were rigidly observant. For instance, during the French and Indian War Uriah Hendricks looked with distaste on those Jewish sutlers who in their travels with the army broke the Sabbath, ate forbidden food, and manifested no regard for their religion. Even in later years when he became a man of position and wealth, Hendricks remained adamant in opposing concessions to time and circumstance and even refused to attend services in Newport because the portion of the week was read out of a printed and vocalized Pentateuch rather than out of a manuscript scroll. Something of a minor cause célèbre occurred in Philadelphia during the Revolution when a zealot accused a fellow Jew of shaving "on a Sabbath at Baltimore." The congregational leaders considered the charge to be a serious one and summoned the alleged offender to appear before them to exculpate himself.[15]

According to the Talmud, "he who remains unmarried impairs the divine image." The typical Jew thus attached great importance to marriage and preferred his community leaders, both lay and religious, to be married men. In New York only married women were allowed to sit in the front row of the women's gallery where they could look out on the men. After the Revolution an exception was made for Rachel Pinto—who was nearly seventy years of age! Of course, when circumstances demanded it the community modified some of its convictions, and lacking at the time another candidate for the position of hazzan, employed the young bachelor Gershom M. Seixas.[16]

Difficult as it was, there were in the backcountry villages Jewish families who made herculean efforts to retain their religious identity and to bring up their children in the ancestral traditions. Aaron Hart of Three Rivers went all the way to London to marry his cousin Dorothea Judah, whom he brought back to Canada to keep a ritually proper Jewish home for him. Rearing his children as he had been reared, Hart made every effort to develop their loyalty to the dietary laws and to observance of the holidays. As they grew up, he sent them across the border to the new United States to be educated among Jews. Isaac Solomon of early eighteenth century Boston was another who did his best to live as a Jew. Though there were practically no other Jews in town, Solomon wrote to his New York supplier and asked for the loan of a High Holy Day prayer book. Lacking accoutrements like a prayer shawl, phylacteries, prayer books, and a slaughtering knife with its honing stone, no Jew could hope to express himself religiously, and so even in the most isolated hamlet which harbored a Jewish settler, such items were standard religious equipment. They were so necessary for the maintenance of Jewish spiritual life that when Joseph Simon seized the goods of Benjamin Nathan for debt, he forebore to deprive Nathan of his religious "tools." A letter of the period reports that a country Jew living near Baltimore was so anxious to provide his children with Jewish associations and religious opportunities that he was prepared to make a substantial financial sacrifice by leaving his place of business and bringing his family to New York.[17]

When the term observance is used in connection with Judaism, it refers among much else to a congeries of pietistic "minutiae" (as some would call them) which were and are part and parcel of Jewish religious expression. Judaism requires, for example, that a host of blessings be recited daily in accordance with a variety of activities and circumstances. A blessing is to be recited on arising in the morning, on washing one's hands before meals, on partaking of food, and so on. There is also the recitation of grace after meals. All these customs were observed by Jews in colonial America. The diarist Ezra Stiles mentioned the fact that Jews had a friendly phrase for the man who had "accidentally sneezed." He reports also that during a thunderstorm in July 1769, the Newport Jews threw open their doors and windows and began "singing and repeating prayers . . . for meeting Messias." There are, to be sure, stereotyped blessings for sneezing and thunderstorms. The pastor's informant on this matter was probably some member of the congregation who recalled the rabbinic statement that the messianic age will be ushered in by "birth pangs" such as famine, death, and thunder. Stiles noted and accurately described the custom whereby a Jewish father blessed his children on Friday evening at the home or in the synagogue by the laying on of hands. "I have seen old Mr. Moses Lopez do it to his boys in the synagogue after service," he wrote.[18]

It has been suggested that for many Jews religious observance was ritualistic and magical in its quality. It is true enough that the majority of those who worshiped in North American synagogues and piously rattled off the Hebrew prayers and psalms are likely to have had at best only an inkling of their meaning. Yet there was in such practices a constant affirmation. The Jews believed the under-lying purpose of their observances was the furtherance of holiness, godliness, and ethics; they believed honor, integrity, and morality were the real goals of prayer and ceremonial. Theirs was essentially an optimistic faith, and they were convinced their personal conduct could make this world a good place in which to live. It was their bounden duty, as they saw it, to work toward that end through the religious regimen they had taken upon themselves.

RELIGIOUS APATHY

The observance and piety to which the typical colonial Jew paid at least formal tribute does not preclude indifference on the part of a number. Indifference to Jewish life was far from uncommon. To be sure, most North American Jews maintained a formal affiliation with a synagogue, but their attendance and interest, nonetheless, very often left much to be desired. Some Jews had no wish at all for synagogue membership, although it is not easy to determine just how many refused to associate with their fellow Jews. Disinterest can rarely be documented without difficulty in colonial times. One has the impression, however, that the early Sephardic settlers in Georgia were not very observant, and as early as 1735 the Portuguese Jews of Savannah were reported to have dispensed with many of the Jewish rites. In the 1740's Pastor Henry Melchior Muhlenberg branded the handful of Jews in Philadelphia as "practicing atheists." The missionary-minded pastor may have exaggerated the situation, but conditions must have been rather less than satisfactory in Philadelphia, for Mikveh Israel's draft constitution of the early 1770's threatened Sabbath desecrators with severe punishments and recommended certain sanctions against "people in the community who do not want to make any contribution, and separate themselves from the group, and do not want to help to support the community."

Discipline was tighter in the well-organized New York community, but even there problems of laxity and indifference were much in evidence. The motivation for Shearith Israel's new constitution of 1728 was that the "wholesome rules and restrictions" of 1706 had "been neglected to be put in due force for some time past." As we have seen, Peter Kalm reported in 1748 that the younger Jews, pursuing their business out of the city, often ignored the dietary laws, and the *mahamad* of Shearith Israel, disturbed in 1757 by rumors that some of the country Jews "do dayly violate the principles of our holy religion," threatened with expulsion from the Jewish community those who persisted in eating forbidden food and in trading on the Sabbath.

In June 1776 Lieutenant Isaac Bangs, an army surgeon and a Christian, wandered into the New York synagogue on a Saturday afternoon and noted that though services were in progress, "no person sat" in the women's gallery. This, of course, hardly testified to disinterest, since by tradition women were not expected to attend all services, and certainly not those held on a Sabbath afternoon. Had the lieutenant come in the morning, he would have found a number of persons in the women's gallery. Still, the records of Shearith Israel do abundantly demonstrate that some of the members manifested disinterest. They refused to accept ritual courtesies, declined to hold office, and frequently absented themselves from services and meetings. There may have been personal reasons for such conduct or misconduct, but it all added up to a distressing degree of indifference and waywardness.[19]

PIETY AND PIOUS PHRASES

The piety of the colonial Jew found its verbal expression in reverential phrases. Some of them were no doubt purely formal and automatic, but whatever their motivation, they do indicate that the Jew saw all life as lived under the protecting wings of the Divine Presence. Virtually every event offered opportunity for some pious expression. A fire, for instance, would be followed by the fervent ejaculation, "May God deliver us from a similar disaster." A betrothal would occasion the practical supplication, "May the God of Israel be pleased to grant us many happy years, and in its time give us the fruit of [his] blessing." At the birth of a child a proud father might write, "It pleased the Almighty to bless us with a beautiful son," and after his son's circumcision a parent might voice the hope, "May God permit us to raise him for the welfare of his holy service." Variations of the theme were such phrases as "The Lord make him His faithful servant" and "May the Lord cause him to grow up to the study of the Law, to the wedding canopy, and to good deeds." That this last invocation was, in part at least, formalistic is eloquently underscored by the fact that no Jew in the American colonies is known to have ever been specially or solely dedicated by his parents to what Carigal called "the divine study."

Understandably enough, phrases touching on death were very numerous. Of a deceased father it was written, "May his blessed soul be received into eternal happiness and be seated among the just." For a departed son or daughter a distraught parent wrote, "May the Almighty be contented!"—and take no more of our children? The gravestone of a wife who had died in childbirth bore the inscription, "May her blessed soul enjoy eternal glory." And tombstones then, as many of them still do in the twentieth century, often carried the traditional formula, "May the memory of the righteous be for a blessing" or "May his [or her] soul be bound up in the bundle of life . . . with the souls of the righteous in the Garden of Eden." [20]

Many, even most American Jews were, as already noted, observant, but cultic practice is no real measure of religiosity. Piety of course is deeper than words. Yet, what the nature of Jewish piety was in colonial days is almost impossible to determine in any detail. Since the Jews of that day left no edificatory or devotional literature, one is forced to fall back on personal correspondence, but here too, unfortunately, the pietistic locutions that appear and reappear may have been no more than inherited formulas and thus in no sense reflective of an inner religiosity. Europe certainly had Jews who devoted their lives to religious studies and to pious confraternities, but so far at least as the sources indicate, such enthusiasts were not to be found in America. Here there were few, if indeed any Jews whose sole aim in life was the pursuit of the religio-ethical commandments enjoined in the teachings of the rabbis. The most, then, one can hope to do is gauge the inner religiosity of the colonial Jew in negative terms—by what it was *not*. That is possible.

Unquestionably, such religious frenzy or revivalism as revolutionized Christian religious thinking and feeling on this continent during the eighteenth century had no analogues in the Jewish community. It is no exaggeration to say that the evangelical spirit was totally foreign to the psyche of the Jew here, as it was also by and large to the Jew abroad. A colonial Jewish merchant would have looked with distaste, if not with horror upon the often unrestrained emotionalism of those who had been "awakened" in a revival. A Jew would surely have been shocked to see a "justified" or "regenerated" sinner "cry out, fal down, and fome at the mouth like a man in a convolshon fit." It is true that contemporary pietism, common to both America and Europe, had generated a somewhat similar movement—Hasidism—among the Jews of Eastern Europe, but there is no reason at all to believe that any of the Hasidim had found their way to this side of the Atlantic. Since there was no oppression in this land, there was no need here to seek escape through emotionalism, mysticism, or ecstatic flights of the imagination. The colonial Jews never "illuminated their hearts by beclouding their minds." All the available evidence suggests that religious emotionalism was simply not a feature of the colonial synagogue. Nor does the American Jew of that day seem to have laid store on any inner religious experience leading to a personal, almost mystical conversion. Such conversions—the Hasidim excepted—were not typical of normative Jewish life anywhere in the world.[21]

If for American Christianity revivalism occupied one end of the colonial religious spectrum, the other end of the spectrum was characterized by secularism, rationalism, and what might be designated scientism. As an immigrant group, the Jews were relatively immune to modernist influences—their prior indoctrination coupled with the lack of secular education among them saw to that. To be sure, some of their native-born children may well have absorbed such influences, if one may judge from the books they actually read, from their libraries, and from their sympathy for the radical political ideas of the postrevolutionary "democrats," but on the whole secularism made no impact upon prerevolutionary thinking and piety. If he existed at all, the religious liberal confronted in America no spiritual oppression moving him to protest, for the synagogue never made any overt theological or doctrinal demands upon him. Jewish religious liberalism as a movement of any consequence still lay far in the future.[22]

Typically, colonial Jewish shopkeepers, which most Jews were, followed a via media between the secularists and deists on the left and the emotionally riven, sin-beset, salvation-minded Christian fundamentalists on the right. It was a generally placid, "no-nonsense" approach to faith that recommended itself to American Jews. Contemporary records—an ethical will, an epitaph, an original prayer—reveal the pious Jew had faith in God, worshiped Him in reverential fear, and hoped for some form of life in a future world. Virtue, charity, and honesty in business were the prime manifestations of colonial Jewish piety. That piety, almost completely this-worldly, was preeminently a social phenomenon in a traditional setting of rites and customs; it was a piety which expressed itself through conformity and ethical living.

On occasion a colonial Jew would reveal—and unwittingly summarize his ideal of religiosity. One of the Gomezes did so in a prayer which, there is every reason to believe, typified the ideals of his fellow-congregants:

I pray to the great God of Israel to have mercy on my soul and enlighten me in His holy Law, forever to give me understanding, that I may not disobey His holy commandments and never forsake them. And that He may always direct me in the paths of life and refrain me from all evil, to advise and direct me to get my honest living . . . And that I may always be charitable to the poor and needy. . . .[23]

CONVERSION TO JUDAISM

Believing as they certainly did that theirs was the one true religion, pious Jews might have been expected to encourage conversion to Judaism, but this was not the case, and there were very few converts to Judaism in the North American colonies during the colonial period. (Unlike the Surinamese Jews and some of their coreligionists in the islands, North American Jews made no attempt to convert Negro slaves to Judaism.) Moses Mordecai had married a convert, Elizabeth Whitlock, a young Englishwoman who signalized her espousal of Judaism by taking the name Esther. She became the ancestress of the distinguished Mordecai family of Virginia and North Carolina, and after her husband's death married Jacob I.

Cohen of Richmond and Philadelphia, an outstanding merchant of the postrevolutionary period. Esther Mordecai Cohen, however, was an exception, for she seems to have been a formal convert. There can hardly be any question, of course, that some of the Jews had Christian consorts who may or not have been formal converts but kept Jewish homes for their husbands and reared their children as Jews.[24]

The fact that there were so few conversions to Judaism is not difficult to understand. It stemmed from Jewish fear of Protestant resentment. Jews were certainly aware of the English law of 1698 "for the more effectual suppressing of blasphemy and profaneness," a law which made it a crime for Christians to "deny the Christian religion to be true." That law—which was still on the statute books of England in the twentieth century—was taken seriously by English Jewry. In fact, a generation before its passage fearful Sephardic newcomers to London had incorporated into their constitution of 1663 an article forbidding, under penalty of excommunication, conversion to Judaism of anyone except, of course, Spanish-Portuguese "Catholic" refugees, crypto-Jews. The London Sephardim dreaded "to disturb the liberty which we enjoy and to make us disliked," though several of them were intransigent enough to marry female proselytes of Christian origin anyhow! About a hundred years later Shearith Israel of New York adopted severe penalties to prohibit the making of converts or marriages between birthright Jews and proselytes. It is obvious that attempts were made in this country to induce the Jewish authorities to approve such conversions and marriages, and it is equally obvious that the Jewish communal leaders here feared an outraged Christian public opinion.[25]

There was an additional reason why the Jews of that day opposed marriage with proselytes to Judaism. Not only did they dread what the Gentiles might say and do, but they realized also that marrying converts was only one step away from intermarrying with unconverted Christians. Intermarriages aroused alarm because there always lurked within them the possibility that the Jewish spouse would ultimately embrace Christianity. Outright conversion to the Christian faith was scarcely uncommon, and certainly the children of mixed marriages were frequently lost to Judaism. Nevertheless, individual Jews ignored Jewish law and congregational ordinances forbidding wedlock with Gentiles. Intermarriages with unconverted Christian women did occur in colonial times, even though the Jewish members of such unions often remained in the Jewish fold. The laconic fashion in which Barnard Jacobs once recorded the circumcision of a child—he mentioned only the mother's name—would suggest either the child had been born out of wedlock or the father was a Christian.[26]

CHAPTER 55

LITURGY, PREACHING, AND THE HOLIDAYS

Liturgy, Minhag, Prayer Books

Though Judaism is rich in liturgical rites, there have long been but two basic liturgies, the Sephardic or Iberian and the Ashkenazic or "German." The Ashkenazic rite (minhag Ashkenaz) is followed not only by the Jews of Germany, but by those of Poland as well. Both minhagim employ Hebrew along with some Aramaic, and both are what we should today call theologically orthodox. The two rites feature a number of minor liturgical variations, but what chiefly differentiates them is their pronunciation of Hebrew.

The Sephardic ritual (minhag Sefarad) was used universally in the New World during the colonial period, even by a so-called German (Ashkenazic) congregation in Surinam. It had been traditional here since its introduction into Dutch Brazil by the Sephardim during the first half of the seventeenth century. In the course of time it became the American rite, and even non-Sephardic newcomers accepted it rather automatically. On occasion Ashkenazim might protest, but not for long or with singular vehemence. At New York in the early 1700's there may have been some doubt as to the universal acceptance of the minhag Sefarad, for the Curaçaon Jews refused to help the Shearith Israel congregation build its Mill Street Synagogue until assurances were forthcoming that New York's Ashkenazic majority would accept the Sephardic liturgy. When the first Jewish settlers came to Savannah in 1733, they squabbled about the choice of a ritual, and as late as 1761 a sarcastic and skeptical letter writer implied it would be difficult to establish a synagogue in

Philadelphia since its members might be expected to quarrel about the type of *Ashkenazic* ritual to be adopted—would it be "Hambro, Pragg, or Poland fashion"? Local variations of the Ashkenazic rite were common, and there were always belligerent devotees willing to do battle for the liturgical usages to which they had been bred. Information about the minhag adopted by Lancaster Jewry, a community of Ashkenazim, is lacking, but the Lancaster rite was probably Sephardic, since some of the town's first settlers had been Sephardim and Joseph Simon maintained contact with New York's Sephardic Shearith Israel.[1]

Why German and Polish immigrants should ultimately have accepted the ritual of the Sephardim and the Sephardic form of synagogal organization is an interesting question. In all likelihood what prompted this abandonment of Ashkenazic norms is not only the fact that the minhag Sefarad was already established in the colonies, but the even more cogent fact that in both Europe and America, Sephardim represented a higher socioeconomic group. By adopting the Sephardic ritual and identifying themselves with the Sephardic heritage, the German and Polish newcomers were upgrading themselves. An equally important or even weightier consideration, in New York at any rate, was Sephardic control of the communal buildings and the religious apparatus. A rebellion to establish an Ashkenazic synagogue might have proven very costly, and most immigrants on landing in America could ill afford the luxury of founding a new congregation. Then again, Jewish communities were so small throughout the eighteenth century that it was imperative for all Jews to join together if even *one* form of worship was to be maintained.

Nonliturgical English prayers of original composition were written and used by some individuals, but to what extent this practice was general, it is difficult to say. At his death in 1743 Abraham Isaacks left a manuscript copy of a translation of some of the daily prayers. Who the translator was is not known; there is a bare possibility it may have been Isaacks himself, for if one can infer anything from the career of Abraham's son Jacob, an amateur chemist, the Isaacks family was one of some learning.[2]

Unique to the American Jewish experience was the publication

[967]

of portions of the Sephardic liturgy in English translation. In 1761 there appeared at New York a work entitled *Evening Service of Roshashanah and Kippur, or the Beginning of the Year and the Day of Atonement*. This first volume of Jewish prayers printed in America contained no Hebrew text, for numerous Hebrew editions of the liturgy were available, and the printing of an American edition would have been very expensive. The translation of 1761 was idiomatic and well done. It has been ascribed to Isaac Pinto, but there is no proof that the work was prepared by him. In 1740 Hakam Isaac Nieto of London's Bevis Marks community had published a Spanish translation of the entire Rosh ha-Shanah and Yom Kippur service, and Nieto's work may well have been used by the editor of the American translation. The only English version of the Jewish liturgy to appear in print prior to the American work was a malevolent "translation" of the minhag Ashkenaz. It had been issued in 1738 by an apostate English Jew, Abraham Mears, who wrote under the nom de plume, or better, nom de guerre of Gamaliel ben Pedahzur.[3]

It is curious that the American translation of 1761 was anonymous. Did the local congregational leaders object to the translation because English was a profane language? Did the New Yorkers fear the Sephardic authorities in London would take offense? As far back as 1663 the Bevis Marks congregation had declared, under threat of excommunication, that no religious book was to be published by a Jew without the approval of the synagogal board, and the New Yorkers might have been afraid that their toleration of an English rendering would open them to accusations of undermining the sanctity and study of the Hebrew language. The translation of the liturgy into Spanish was quite a different matter, for among the Sephardim, Spanish had assumed an almost sacred character. Indeed, it was not until 1773 that an English translation of the Sephardic liturgy first appeared at London.[4]

Five years after the publication of the New York work there appeared another volume, lugubriously entitled *Prayers for Shabbath, Rosh-Hashanah and Kippur, or The Sabbath, The Begining of the Year, and the Day of Atonements, with the Amidah and Musaph of the Moadim, or Solemn Seasons, According to the Order of the*

Spanish and Portuguese Jews. In this case, however, the translator's name was supplied; it was Isaac Pinto. Pinto undoubtedly published this work as a commercial enterprise with a view to its sale not only in North America but also in the English-speaking British West Indies. Taken together, the two books constitute a translation of the Sabbath, High Holiday, and festival liturgy. The daily prayers had been omitted, possibly because only men who were very observant—and presumably knew some Hebrew—met for daily devotions. Since the translation of 1761 had provoked no repercussions in New York or London, Pinto probably felt it safe to publish his translation of 1766 and to take public credit for his work.[5]

There had been no explanatory preface in the prayer book of 1761, but Pinto did supply the translation of 1766 with a brief foreword in an apologetic vein. Acknowledging "the very great advantage" he had received from Nieto's "elegant Spanish translation" of the High Holiday liturgy, he expressed the hope that any defects in this English version would "meet with indulgence from the candid reader." He emphasized the importance of Hebrew as not only the language "in which it pleased Almighty God to reveal himself to our ancestors," but also as the tongue destined one day to "be re-established in Israel." Inasmuch, however, as Hebrew was "imperfectly understood by many" and "by some, not at all," a version in the vernacular was necessary. The Spanish translation, said Pinto, served that purpose in Europe, for the Sephardim there knew that tongue, but that was not the case "in the British Dominions in America" where the Sephardim did not all understand Spanish. It was for this reason that Pinto had prepared an English translation, with the "hope that it will tend to the improvement of many of my brethren in their devotion." Pinto was right of course, for the New Yorkers, most of them Central European in origin, knew little or no Spanish or Portuguese. Nieto's Spanish version was of no help to them. The only language common to all the Jews of America was English, and the differences among American Jews made it imperative for them to accept as a common vernacular the language of the land in which they lived, the language they employed in business.

Neither of the two English translations was actually used for worship. They did not represent complete translations of all the standard prayers, and their editors never intended them to replace the Hebrew liturgy or to modify it theologically. The publication of the two books was in no sense an indication of Reform tendencies. The translations were made solely for the benefit of worshipers who knew no Hebrew, even if some of them could read it mechanically. Although Pinto did not state so specifically, he intended his work for men, women, and children—girls especially—who lacked familiarity with the ancient tongue. Those who could read but could not translate Hebrew found transliterated rubrics, initial phrases, in the English text to guide them as they followed the services. The translations were no doubt brought to synagogal services and were also employed in private devotions.

What was unique about these two American volumes is that they were the first Sephardic prayer books published in English anywhere in the English-speaking world. The conservative Spanish-Portuguese Jews of London all knew English too, of course, but they were enamored of Spanish. Favoring Spanish as their vernacular, they had encouraged the appearance of Spanish translations during the first half of the century. The power of censorship which they exercised enabled them to prevent the publication of English versions, though they appear to have existed in manuscript. It was thus in America that English renderings of the Sephardic liturgy first appeared in print. It was American Jewry, freer, less disciplined, less controlled, which tolerated an English translation.[6]

While the Sephardic rite became the American rite, there was by no means an absolute uniformity of liturgical detail in every congregation. Manuel Josephson, a learned Jew who had been observing the American congregational scene since the French and Indian War, said in 1790 that American synagogues had "no regular system." Lacking "fixed and permanent rules to go by," they were "continually . . . in a state of fluctuation." Their members, moving about as they did with such frequency, were apt to carry with them from congregation to congregation their own liturgical traditions, and newcomers were constantly introducing innovations. The different hazzanim added to the "state of fluctuation" by "patch[ing] up" ceremonial systems of their own, bringing with them to each new post the customs they had practiced or witnessed elsewhere. Apparently then, even within the general framework of the American Sephardic liturgy, there were a number of petty and minor differences which, Josephson averred, contrasted rather sharply with "the large and old established congregations abroad" where "even the most minute" liturgical forms had been "reduced to a regular system, from which they do not deviate on any account." [7]

Preaching and Special Patriotic Services

Preaching, we have pointed out before, was not characteristic of the American synagogue till about the middle of the nineteenth century, and even then its recognition was due primarily to the influence of Protestantism, which frequently gave it a central role in the service. During the colonial period, however much the sermon formed the core, the essence, of the worship service in the New England meetinghouse, it remained for the American synagogue extraneous and fortuitous—so much so in fact, that no place was reserved for it in the published Hebrew liturgies. Nonetheless, though irregular, there was preaching in colonial synagogues, primarily by the itinerant rabbis or money-collectors who came to these shores from Europe and Palestine and displayed their homiletic wares week after week. The Newporters heard Tobiah ben Judah Loew, an Ashkenazi, preach in Dutch. Though a Polish Jew, Tobiah had lived for twenty-six years in Amsterdam. One wonders how many of the congregants understood him. Jacob R. Rivera, who had lived for a time on Curaçao, was probably one of the few able to follow the rabbi. It is interesting to note that Tobiah did not speak in Yiddish, his mother tongue.

Carigal of Hebron preached in Newport at Pentecost in 1773 before a distinguished audience which included the governor and some of the outstanding members of the judiciary. His sermon, which lasted some forty-seven minutes according to the meticulous Stiles, was presented in Spanish, quite possibly not contemporary Spanish but the antiquated Ladino the Sephardim had taken with them from Spain at their expulsion in 1492. One of the local Jews made an English translation of the sermon which was then published independently and offered for sale in the *Newport Mercury*. It is a tribute to the English knowledge of Abraham Lopez, a Portuguese émigré, that he could have prepared so excellent a translation despite the fact that he had been in America but six years.

One suspects that Carigal's distinguished audience was not so much entranced by his address, which they could scarcely have understood, or his "fine and oriental" elocution and gestures, as by his garb which must have filled them with admiration if not with envy. Carigal, Stiles tells us, wore on that occasion a "fur cap, scarlet robe, green silk damask vest, and a chintz undervest—girt with a sash or Turkish girdle—beside the alb [prayer shawl] with tzitzith [ritual fringes]." An attractive man with a large black beard, he must have cut a most impressive figure. The piquancy of the Pentecost service was further enhanced by the fact that Abraham, the small, undersized son of Jacob R. Rivera, was invited to participate in the proceedings—he read the first chapter of Ezekiel—even though he had not yet reached the age of thirteen as required for inclusion in the minyan or quorum of ten.[8]

As part of the general colonial community, Jews, like all others, were expected to hold special services in their houses of worship on patriotic occasions. After the fall of Montreal, New York Jewry, undoubtedly at the suggestion of the authorities, prepared a morning and afternoon service in Hebrew to commemorate the victory of September 1760 when French Canada surrendered to the English. The morning Hebrew service included a prayer of thanksgiving for victory, some psalms, the usual prayer for the welfare of the government, a passage attacking all the enemies of the royal house, and finally a fervent plea for "a firm and lasting peace." The afternoon prayers also featured psalms as well as other biblical writings and a blessing for the royal family. These services were never published in their original Hebrew, but an English translation was issued under the rather baroque title, *The Form of Prayer, which was performed at the Jews Synagogue, in the City of New-York, on Thursday, October 23, 1760, Being the Day Appointed by Proclamation for a General Thanksgiving to Almighty God for the Reducing of Canada to His Majesty's Dominions.* The title page also informed the reader that the service had been "Composed by D. R. [Doctor!] Joseph

Yeshurun Pinto in the Hebrew Language and Translated into English by a Friend to Truth." This "Friend to Truth" may well have been Isaac Pinto, no relative of the hazzan, as far as is known. Of particular interest is the fact that in all probability this publication was the first English work of an unconverted Jew to be printed in the North American continental colonies.[9]

Two years later the authorities of the province of New York ordered a service of "solemn humiliation before the Almighty God" because a peace treaty had not yet been signed with the French. It was a day of prayer and fast, and the hazzan took the text for his sermon, which was certainly delivered in Spanish or Portuguese, from the fourteenth verse of Psalm 60: "Through God we shall do valiantly, for He it is that will tread down our enemies." This sermon was not printed and is not extant. In August 1763 the government asked that a general thanksgiving celebration be held to commemorate the signing of the treaty of peace and the ending of the long French and Indian War. Hazzan Pinto preached once more, this time on the verse, Zechariah 2:10:

Ho, ho, flee then from the land of the north, saith the Lord, For I have spread you abroad as the four winds of the heaven, saith the Lord.

The hazzan had chosen a most appropriate text, for the French crown had indeed been forced to "flee . . . from the land of the north"—Canada. Pinto's sermon, which is no longer in existence, was very probably preached in Spanish or Portuguese. Pinto knew both, as well as Dutch, and is unlikely to have spoken in English, though he had spent some time in London.[10]

In Newport on Thanksgiving Day, November 28, 1765, the Jews assembled in their synagogue to listen to an original Hebrew prayer by Hazzan Isaac Touro. A few days later a translation of Touro's prayer appeared in the *Newport Mercury*. Following a few introductory sentences of thanks for God's bountiful mercies, for the land that had yielded her increase, and for the trees that had brought forth their fruits, the hazzan turned to what troubled him and his congregants most. He pleaded for "internal peace" and expressed the hope that the royal counsellors and Parliament would be moved to concern themselves with the "whole British Empire." The immediate past months had witnessed the enactment of the obnoxious Quartering and Stamp Acts, the rise of the Sons of Liberty, a demand for economic sanctions by the rebellious Americans, and a precipitous decline in business. Newport, like other commercial centers, had been grievously affected.[11]

The eve of the Revolution brought new occasions for prayer and preaching. The Continental Congress recommended a fast day to be observed throughout the colonies on July 20, 1775. Newport's Anglican minister, loyal to England, refused to preach; all the Anglicans would do was read prayers—reluctantly. The Jewish community, however, did conduct special services in Newport on that day, and Rabbi Samuel Cohen, visiting emissary from the Holy Land, delivered the sermon. Precisely what the rabbi said, we do not know, but a perusal of the text he chose—Numbers 25: 11–12—gives a clue to the content of his message: "Behold, I give unto him my covenant of peace." The following year on May 17, 1776, the Congress again called for a day of religious devotion. Gershom Mendes Seixas of New York, the patriotic minister who was to go into exile together with many of his congregants that very year, preached and pleaded for peace. His address, like the sermon Rabbi Cohen had delivered in Newport, is no longer extant either, but one may be sure in any case, that those colonial rabbis and hazzanim were by no means comparable as preachers to the distinguished Christian clergymen who exercised so much influence through their election-day sermons.[12]

RELIGIOUS PRACTICES

DAILY SERVICES

As an individual, the devout Jew prayed the traditional liturgy daily, morning, afternoon, and evening, in the privacy of his home. Typically, he donned phylacteries (tefillin) for his weekday morning prayers and wrapped himself in his prayer shawl with its ritual fringes. Phylacteries and prayer shawls were favored gifts to Marrano émigrés, who of course had not dared to wear them in Portugal or

Spain. Still, his private devotions notwithstanding, it was in a synagogue that the Jew preferred to pray, in company with at least nine other adult males, so he would be counted in a minyan (quorum of ten), and thus be able to read out of the Torah. Whenever and wherever Jewish males over thirteen years of age assembled, they attempted to hold a common service. No "clergyman" was necessary for such orisons, for Jewish practice and law made no distinction, religiously, between professional readers and laymen, and a layman frequently officiated in the American synagogue even when a hazzan was present.[13]

Throughout the eighteenth century efforts were made to hold daily services in the morning and in the late afternoon and evening, but it is much to be doubted that these congregational efforts were crowned with more than occasional success. In 1759 for instance, during the French and Indian War, Uriah Hendricks was unable to assemble a minyan to recite prayers on the Jahrzeit (anniversary) of his mother's death. Even when quorums would have been possible, difficulties were encountered in gathering them for daily services due to indifference on the part of some individuals or the pressure of economic necessity. On Mondays and Thursdays, days which were liturgically special, it was easier to secure a quorum, and towns of any size invariably saw services on Saturdays and holidays. The pious were at pains to keep the fast days and all the holidays, and anyone in doubt as to when these observances fell could always turn to his liturgical calendar for information. The Sephardim included among the fast days to be observed the anniversary of a parent's death.[14]

It was not long before every colonial congregation of any size had several Scrolls of the Pentateuch reposing in its ark, but these scrolls posed problems in their very numbers. Members who had lent or made gifts of Torahs demanded that theirs be read at stated times. In New York peace was preserved by reading out of every scroll, on certain occasions, according to the seniority of their owners or donors.[15]

Not infrequently, Christians attended the services, and some of these visitors left us in their writings impressions of what they saw and heard. Different visitors came away with different impressions. The huge candles would be noticed, and of course the men garbed in hats and praying shawls. To Dr. Alexander Hamilton of Annapolis, the women of New York's Shearith Israel, some of them "very pritty," appeared penned in the gallery like so many hens in a coop (apparently there was lattice work above the banisters or railings of the women's gallery). Visitors would be struck by the active participation of the congregants in the public devotions, by the vigorous reading, chanting, and singing of the worshipers—though Ensign Caleb Clapp, witnessing a service at New York in 1776, "was not able to distinguish between reading and singing." When shortly thereafter Isaac Bangs attended Shearith Israel "to observe the method of the Jewish worship," the singing sounded to him at times like "jabering." One onlooker in New York found the hymns "dolefull," while another in Newport thought them "exceeding fine and melodious." [16]

SABBATH

The Sabbath in every Jewish community spelled the cessation of all business activity, and any Jew bold enough to transact business during that twenty-four-hour period would have been chastised by his coreligionists. All Jewish congregations imposed severe penalties for desecrating the sanctity of the Sabbath, and neither writing, riding, nor commercial dealings of any sort were tolerated after sundown on Friday. A common phrase in many letters was "You'l please excuse my curtailing, being Friday afternoon, therefore not able to enlarge." Non-Jewish servants would be called into the synagogue to trim the candles on Sabbaths and holy days, such work being forbidden Jews on those days. Even in remote and isolated Lancaster, Joseph Simon sedulously kept the seventh day, and the fish sent to him from Philadelphia were probably destined to grace his Sabbath table in accordance with an age-old Jewish culinary tradition. A Christian missionary who passed through Lancaster on a Sabbath in 1772 was pained to discover that Simon would do no business with him on that day of rest.[17]

Aaron Lopez reportedly made it a rule not to dispatch a ship on the Sabbath—which was certainly true. His account books document his practice of closing his shop from Friday night to Monday morning every weekend as well as on all the Jewish holidays and on election days. When this distinguished merchant fled Newport during the Revolution and opened a shop in Leicester, Massachusetts, he continued his practice, and his Christian neighbors were quick to note that out of deference to them he kept his place of business closed on Sundays as well as Saturdays. A similar procedure characterized the firm of Levi & Jacobs in the backcountry of Lancaster County, Pennsylvania. In postrevolutionary years when the Newport Seixases became the executives of the first bank in the state of Rhode Island, the father and son would not go to their office on the Sabbath. Instead, one of the young Channings would call on them and take their keys to the Christian who had been left in charge of the bank on that Jewish day of rest. For his services George G. Channing was rewarded with mazzot on Passover and a traditional confection called "Haman's ears" on Purim.[18]

The missionary may not have appreciated Joseph Simon's regard for the Sabbath, but the Gentile community at large showed consideration for Jews who kept that day. As far back as the time of Peter Stuyvesant, a Jewish businessman was excused from appearing in court on Saturday, and during the American Revolution, as we have seen, the New York authorities excused a Jew from performing militia duty on his day of rest. Writing to Isaac Da Costa's Christian partner, the Charleston merchant Henry Laurens said, "I must not obtrude business upon him [Da Costa] on this day [Saturday]." [19]

James Sheldon, a Providence farmer and distiller, called upon Aaron Lopez in Newport during the Passover holy days to settle his bills, only to discover Lopez would not receive him. Sheldon does not seem to have objected to Lopez' treatment, probably because he lost nothing by it, but there were occasions when the refusal of Jews to transact business on the holy days proved costly to a Christian associate. John Watts, for example, suffered a sizeable loss because Jacob Franks would settle no accounts during the High Holy Day season. By the time the holy days were over, the rate of exchange had mounted considerably, and Watts found himself the victim of a heavy penalty.[20]

PASSOVER (PESAH)

By the onset of the Revolution there were enough Jews in New York City to justify the inclusion of the Jewish calendar in the almanacs published by James Rivington, the New York journalist. Thus every Jew, no matter where he happened to travel, could always prepare himself to keep the holy days. The Sheftalls of Georgia, desiring more detailed information, preferred a *calendario* appended to a European Sephardic holiday prayer book. Such calendars covered decades, and Jews who made use of them were easily able to determine the dates on which the ceremonials associated with Passover, Pentecost, the Seventeenth of Tammuz, the Ninth of Ab, the New Year, the Atonement fast, Tabernacles, and the Feasts of Dedication and Lots were to be observed.[21]

Businessmen writing to one another never failed to offer greetings at the Passover season, "I wish you and every one of your family a merry Pascua de Pesah [Passover], and that you may see many of them with felicity and happiness." Country Jews came into Jewish centers from the surrounding areas, and transients and businessmen on the road made every effort to be in a town at that time of the year so they could have Passover food served in ritually clean utensils. During the Passover period Jacob R. Rivera would attend no meetings of the "candle trust," in whose affairs he played so large a role. To their dismay, some merchants were unable to celebrate the holiday in the company of their families. Barnard Gratz found it necessary to spend the Passover of 1776 in Pittsburgh. Since he could not write to his Philadelphia relatives during the opening and closing days of the holiday without violating Jewish law, he had a Christian business associate write for him.[22]

Even Jews who were not meticulous in their observance of the dietary laws were eager to observe Passover properly by eating mazzah, the prescribed unleavened bread, during the eight-day festival. Though there were no professional Jewish mazzah bakers in colonial times, unleavened bread was prepared in the larger American Jewish communities under the control and supervision of the religious authorities. From time to time at both New York and Newport, mazzah was baked in the homes of the beadles or in ovens maintained in the synagogue yards. Mazzah was provided, at a price, to the members of the New York congregation, but large supplies were distributed gratis to the poor and to the congregational functionaries. Both the New York and the Newport congregations maintained supervision over the production of mazzah, but for a number of reasons—among them in all probability, the inconvenience of recording sales—the actual baking and distribution were frequently left to Christians. Some householders brought their Passover flour to a Christian baker who made the mazzah for them, presumably under some sort of ritual supervision.

The mazzah produced in the larger centers was not always used exclusively for local consumption. There is no clear indication that mazzah baked at New York was exported to the West Indies, but the New Yorkers certainly dispatched supplies to Newport and the Newporters in turn sometimes sent shipments of mazzah to the New York market. Lopez once ordered 250 pounds from New York, but probably not as a commercial undertaking. Inasmuch as his family and relatives were a host in themselves, it is likely he intended this shipment for his own entourage. By the Passover of 1776 he had fled from Newport to Portsmouth, Rhode Island, to escape the British and their blockading fleet. From Portsmouth, however, he sent the Newport beadle 100 pounds of flour to be made into mazzot for the congregation. The mazzah that Lopez ate that year in his exile from Newport was truly what the Passover liturgy calls it—"bread of affliction."

Mazzah is not the only food characteristic of the Passover holiday. A special fruit and nut salad known as haroset is customarily eaten at the festive Passover eve meal to symbolize the mortar the ancient Israelites used for making bricks during their servitude in Egypt. The New York congregation would make haroset and distribute it to the members, but Lopez undertook a more ambitious task. Not only did he have a quantity prepared for his own use, but he exported some of the haroset to the islands for the delectation of the West Indian Jewish settlers.[23]

PENTECOST (SHABUOT)

The late spring harvest festival of Pentecost would find the synagogue decorated with flowers and foliage, and following a cabalistic practice, the worshipers would gather to read excerpts from the Bible and the Mishnah all through that holy night. This *tikkun lel shabuot*, as the vigil of the eve of Shabuot was called, was customary in Newport and probably in the larger community of New York as well. Those who participated in the long vigil were fed at congregational expense. Pentecost, in addition to its harvest character, also commemorates the giving of the Torah on Mount Sinai. Michael Gratz had not forgotten this fact, as William Murray was dismayed to learn when he sought in vain to discuss business with him on that holiday.[24]

THE FASTS OF TAMMUZ AND AB

The colonial Jew was remote from the centers of Judaism in Europe, but not from the observances that rendered the Jewish calendar so distinctive. Rites like the summer Fast of the Seventeenth of Tammuz, recalling the breaches made in the walls of Jerusalem first by Nebuchadnezzar and centuries later by Titus, had their place in his life. On the Sabbath following that fast, Ezra Stiles was intrigued by an interesting custom he observed in the Newport synagogue. Hakam Carigal, after chanting the prophetic portion—the first chapter of Jeremiah—in Hebrew, "chanted the same in Spanish" or Ladino, as it may have been. Somewhat similar practices still prevail in Sephardic synagogues even today.[25]

Equally colorful, but in a different way, were the services held in the synagogue on the midsummer Fast of the Ninth of Ab, a holy day which commemorates the destruction of the Jerusalem Temple in biblical and again in Roman times. The razing of the Temple marked the downfall of the first and second Jewish commonwealths, and this sad anniversary was observed, especially by the Sephardim, with deepest mourning. In the Newport synagogue the ark and the reading desk were covered with black cloth, the lamps were extinguished, and the hazzan, standing before the ark, wrapped himself in the black curtain that had been hung there for that special occasion. The prayers—various dirges and the biblical Book of Lamentations—"were exceedingly melancholy," wrote Stiles, impressed in particular by the manner in which Hazzan Touro "slowly mourned out a most solemn weeping, and doleful lamentation, for . . . the destruction of the holy of holies." Even the Scroll of the Law, Stiles noted, was encased in a covering of black cloth. Removed "without any ceremony" from the ark, it was not carried to the elevated reading desk, but was opened and read at the foot of the platform. The Ninth of Ab ceremonies at Shearith Israel in New York were no less impressive. *"Hermanos, Casa de Israel, oyid!"* the hazzan would intone at a dramatic moment in the ritual:

Brethren of the House of Israel, hearken. On this sad and doleful night there are . . . years since our second holy temple was destroyed by the cruel Romans, and since then we have been captives away from our land and scattered to the four corners of the world, without a king or settlement, being the scorn of the peoples and the contempt of the nations. The crown has fallen from our head. Woe unto us that we have sinned! [26]

NEW YEAR AND THE DAY OF ATONEMENT

Falling nine days apart in the autumn are the High Holy Days, Rosh ha-Shanah and the fast of Yom Kippur, which were rigorously observed by colonial Jewry. During the solemn season of 1768, for example, Lopez did not hesitate to keep his shop closed on four successive days. On Saturday and Sunday, and then Monday and Tuesday, the first two days of the Jewish New Year, the wheels of the burgeoning Lopez empire ground to a halt. Earlier that decade in Lancaster, Joseph Simon, eager to look his best for the New Year, had reminded his Philadelphia correspondent Barnard Gratz to send him a new beaver hat and a pair of breeches "before the holydays." At the same time Simon generously supplied Barnard with some beaver fur to make a new hat for himself. The approach of Rosh ha-Shanah in 1776 found Barnard detained at Pittsburgh and unable to return to his family; he wrote his brother to ask that his

Hebrew prayer books be sent him posthaste. Letters exchanged during the High Holy Day season were replete with pious wishes that the recipients would be inscribed *besefer hayyim tobim* (in the book of good life) for the coming year.[27]

THE FESTIVAL OF BOOTHS (SUKKOT)

The Feast of Booths, following the Atonement fast by a few days, is one of the most engaging of the Jewish holidays. It was during this autumnal harvest festival that some of the synagogal officers were elected for the ensuing year and that the cycle of pentateuchal readings was recommenced. At New York the newly elected officers were evidently expected to provide liquid refreshments in the cabana erected in the synagogue courtyard—with the result that the celebrants returned to their homes in a very exhilarated mood. The Sukkot celebration at Newport was an equally joyous occasion. The cabana was beautifully decorated with yellow, green, purple, and red ribbons, pinned to the walls or hanging as streamers, while the lulab (a bundle of palm branches, myrtle twigs, and willows used in the ritual) was carefully wrapped in yards of colored ribbon. A table in the cabana held ample servings of fruit, bread, and rum.[28]

THE DEDICATION FEAST (HANUKKAH)

One holiday appears to have been little mentioned in colonial days— Hanukkah, the Feast of Dedication or Lights, which begins in December on the twenty-fifth of the Hebrew month of Kislev and commemorates the Maccabean victory over Antiochus Epiphanes during the second century B.C.E. Unlike American Jews today, colonial Jews tended to deemphasize the festival, possibly because Christmas, which Hanukkah parallels somewhat both in season and in the saliency of lights, was of small consequence in colonial America. Nevertheless, congregations—and many individuals as well—owned the traditional eight-branched candelabra which were kindled during the eight-day celebration. The first Jews to settle in Georgia brought such a lamp with them on their arrival in 1733, and the menorah used by Shearith Israel in the Mill Street Synagogue is still among its beautiful treasures. In Newport too, as Lopez' account books testify, the Hanukkah lamp was provided with "sweet oil," and the holiday was observed in a formal fashion.[29]

THE FEAST OF LOTS (PURIM)

Purim, celebrating the deliverance of ancient Persian Jewry from the wicked Haman, was a popular holiday. Jewish merchants wished each other the compliments of the season, and roguish Meyer Josephson of Reading once invoked upon the head of Michael Gratz the blessing, "I wish you a Merry Purim and a Good Haman." If a postrevolutionary celebration in Richmond was typical of prewar Purim parties, the Purim joy came manifestly rather less from the food than from the potations—porter, spirits, brandy, and gin. Joseph Darmstadt, a Hessian Jewish sutler with poetic ambitions, undoubtedly caught the spirit of an eighteenth century Purim when he wrote:

> All this I say and no more:
> May He who knows us all bless you as before,
> And keep you many Purim merry,
> And I will drink your health in a glass of sherry.[30]

CHAPTER 56

THE LIFE CYCLE CEREMONIES

CIRCUMCISION AND THE CIRCUMCISER

The Jews of America, with relatively few exceptions, enjoyed the folkways of their fathers. It is very difficult, of course, to determine the motivations which prompted individuals to comply with Jewish ritual, but it is a fact that the colonial synagogue never lacked for members well informed in matters of custom and tradition. An eager participation in the ceremonies of the life cycle was certainly nothing uncommon.

In the folk-mind scarcely anything was more important than circumcision, the covenant of Abraham. Though Jewish theology asserts no sacraments, circumcision assumed for most Jews a sacramental character. Circumcision *made* the Jew. The Jews of colonial America betrayed few subtleties in their mode of thought: no circumcision, no Jew—and no burial in a Jewish cemetery. When a young son of Ezekiel Solomons died in Canada, the father had some trouble in providing him with a Jewish burial, for the lad was uncircumcised and the son of a Gentile mother. Solomons was one of the Montreal congregation's honorary officers at the time, and he finally did secure permission to bury his son "according to the rules and customs of Jews," but the congregation made it very clear that the courtesy afforded Solomons was singular indeed:

Several circumstances favourable to . . . Ezekiel Solomons appeared to us, for which reason we allow his [child] being buried. But at the same time, we do hereby unanimously agree and declare that no man or boy, whomsoever shall be, after sixty days from this date [November 30,

1778], be buried in the burying place of the congregation unless circumcised.

Michael Judah of Norwalk thought circumcision so important that he induced his New York friend Abraham I. Abrahams to circumcise young David, Michael's son by his Christian wife. Come what may, Michael was determined to make David a Jew—though his determination would be thwarted when the circumcised boy grew up to take a Christian wife of his own and to abandon his Jewish identity.[1]

Since circumcision was required of every Jewish male child, it was imperative that there be someone in each community to perform the rite, and in fact most communities did have a mohel or circumciser. Ritual slaughterers would have possessed the necessary skill, and some of them are likely to have served as mohalim. Though the mohel was never a communal official—even in contemporary Europe—he may well have been a "professional." While he served some of his clients without compensation, from others no doubt he received a fee. One of Ezra Stiles's Jewish informants told him that circumcisers "in America got a living by it," but that was surely not so. In America, a pioneer land with only a handful of Jews here and there, no one could hope to make a living from circumcisions, even if he traveled about like Barnard Jacobs of Pennsylvania.[2]

Country Jews waited until the mohel got around to see them or until they could spare the time to visit the nearest town where a competent practitioner was to be found. Frequently enough, parents would bring their infant sons to a metropolitan center from the villages and towns in which they lived. One need not conclude from this that no mohel was available in their vicinity; there may have been one, but perhaps they distrusted or disliked him—he may even have been a business rival. Then again, the parents may simply have wanted a holiday in the city. At any rate, they would make the trek to the big town and bring along their child to be circumcised—not, as was traditional, on the eighth day after his birth, but sometimes weeks, months, or even years later.[3]

On occasion berit milah (the covenant of circumcision) might take place in most unusual surroundings. Normally, of course, the operation was performed as a home ceremony, but what if the father had been imprisoned for debt? No father would wish to be absent from his son's circumcision, so if need be, the surgery would be held in the debtor's jail—and this happened more than once.[4]

Influenced in all probability by their Marrano Catholic background, Jews of Portuguese ancestry made much of the godfather and the godmother at the circumcision ceremony. Occasionally they even used the Old World terms *padrinho* and *madrinha*, and preferred to confer those honors on relatives.[5]

No record books of the circumcisions performed in Savannah and Charleston are known to have survived, but it cannot be doubted that men adept in the surgery were present in those communities. As a matter of fact, a circumcision kit accompanied the first group of Georgia Jewish settlers in 1733, and Mordecai Sheftall, who performed his own shehitah, also circumcised his sons. In Canada during the late 1770's and early 1780's circumcision was one of the duties of the minister Jacob R. Cohen who, strangely enough, in a period of at least three years reported operating on only four infants. Before Cohen's time some of the Canadian Jewish children were probably left uncircumcised, or there may have been other mohalim in Montreal. Some of the Montreal families undoubtedly brought their sons to New York or Newport for the ceremony, though they may have waited for months or years after the births of their sons before setting out on a wearisome and hazardous trip. Canadian Jews who took the sea route to Rhode Island by way of the St. Lawrence and the Atlantic imposed on themselves a journey of well over a thousand miles. This may explain why the parents of Jacob Hays, who was probably of Canadian birth, delayed bringing him to Newport for his circumcision by Moses Seixas until 1796 when he was almost five years old.[6]

From the 1750's to 1790 eastern Pennsylvania, including Philadelphia, was fortunate in having the services of Barnard Jacobs, a businessman who spent several years in and around Heidelberg in Lancaster County. His circumcision book, still extant, indicates that Jacobs traveled about in the towns and villages of eastern Pennsylvania wherever he was needed—as far west as York and as far east as Philadelphia. When Jacobs headed for the backcountry he would journey by boat or on horseback, and some of the Pennsylvanians apparently waited for years till their favorite officiant came along. Jacob Mordecai, later to become a well-known educator in North Carolina, was not circumcised by Jacobs until he was nearly eight years of age.[7]

As might be expected, New York never had a dearth of mohalim, both professional and amateur. Throughout the eighteenth century members of the wealthy and prominent Gomez family were adepts at the art. For a number of decades Benjamin Gomez not only circumcised children of the widespread Gomezes, but was also free and generous with advice to all his friends. The Gomezes were certainly volunteer mohalim and primarily interested as such in storing up religious merits for the world to come. A "Doctor" Marks of New York performed circumcisions when he was not in jail for debt, but the city's most active functionary in matters of milah was Abraham I. Abrahams, who supplemented his business affairs by serving as a Hebrew teacher, a congregational reader, and a mohel. Abrahams' circumcision book has also been preserved, and it shows that in addition to carrying on his religious work in the city proper, he traveled up the Hudson, crossed over into New Jersey, ventured into Connecticut, and sailed as far north as Rhode Island. The fact that Abrahams went to Rhode Island would suggest that there was no circumciser in the province, but one was very probably available there. (Rhode Island certainly had a shohet.) Some Newport parents, however, for reasons all their own may have dreaded using the local practitioner. Abrahams was a close friend of the Newport Lopezes and was called in when the Abrahamitic rite had to be undergone by newborn or very young children.

Sometimes Abrahams' services were not required for Lopez youngsters, but for New Christian relations who had escaped from Portugal. It was, of course, a moment of great satisfaction for American Jews, particularly those of Sephardic origin or ancestry, when a Marrano family fled the Iberian "fiery furnace" to the safety of these shores and openly embraced the Jewish religion, as most *refugiados* did. Such a moment occurred in 1767 with the arrival in Newport of Michael, Aaron Lopez' older brother, and Michael's wife, three sons, and a daughter, all of whom took new biblical names on espousing Judaism. Abraham I. Abrahams was invited to Newport to serve Aaron's brother and nephews as the "meritorious instrument of their obtaining the covenant which happily characterize us a peculiar flock." Abrahams was assured that he would find Michael and his sons receptive to *milah*, for they wished to glorify the "Protector of Israel." These newly escaped Marranos, Aaron wrote, "are inspired with a spark of our old [biblical] father's [Abraham] zeal and ready to obey the divine precept." The operations took place in the privacy of the Hart farm at Tiverton, Rhode Island, and Aaron was soon able to say, "My brother and his children received five days ago the divine covenant with success." Although the New Yorker was probably paid for his services to others, it is to be doubted that he was recompensed when he went to Newport. He would not have wished or sought a fee from the Lopezes with whom, on one occasion when called to Newport professionally, he remained as a family guest for several weeks.[8]

Precisely because circumcision betokened the covenant between the Jew and his God, Moses Seixas, a young Newport businessman, wished to become adept in its performance—even if he had to rely on a "correspondence course" from Abrahams of New York. Through the mails, therefore, he received instruction from the New Yorker who described in every detail what was to be done and what medicines were to be used. Judging from this correspondence, Abrahams knew his business well. "The first and principal thing," he wrote Seixas, "is to have a good heart, to perform the operation with courage intermixed with tenderness." And in time Seixas probably became an expert, for he did not hesitate to circumcise his own children as well as the sons of others. Yet more than half the infants he circumcised died within a few months or in the course of a year—not necessarily from postoperative sepsis. Infant mortality was everywhere terribly high in colonial days, and statistics show that as many as half of all infants succumbed.[9]

Bar Mizvah

Following his circumcision, the next public or social step in the life of a Jewish boy was taken at the age of thirteen. It was then that he became a bar mizvah (Son of the Commandment), in token of his having reached religious maturity and his having assumed responsibility for his own spiritual welfare. Beyond any doubt, practically all Jewish boys whose parents were synagogue-affiliated underwent preparation for the bar mizvah ceremony, in which they chanted the requisite portions from the Pentateuch and the Prophets. Unquestionable as this is, however, surprisingly few records of such ceremonies have come down to us from colonial times.

This much can be said: Jews in the smaller towns, lacking adequate instructors and finding it difficult to purchase praying shawls and the basic Hebrew prayer books, were faced with all but insurmountable difficulties in readying their sons for this important moment in their lives. The problem is reflected in a letter Benjamin Sheftall addressed to an acquaintance in London during King George's War. Greatly distressed, Sheftall complained that the bar mizvah books for his young son Mordecai had not yet arrived. "I hope Your Honour will soon find it out wether that ship [bringing my son's books] is taken by an enemy or lost at sea. . . . I live [leave] Your Honour to guess in what grife I am in to be so misfortenabel, my eldest son b[e]ing three months ago thirteen years of age, and I not to have any frauntlets [phylacteries] nor books fit for him." [10]

Marriage and Domesticity

In due course, once he had become bar mizvah, the Jew was expected to marry. Unlike most Gentile Americans, however, he rarely married early. A study of marriages among American Jews prior to 1776 reveals that of twenty-four bridegrooms, fourteen were over 30 and ten were under 30, but not even one was under 21. The typical male married at 30. Women married earlier. Of twenty-six brides, eight were teenagers, while the rest were over 20. The typical Jewess seems to have married at 23. The women, it may be assumed, waited till their parents could dower them, and the men in all likelihood postponed marital ties until they had established themselves in business and could support their wives fittingly. [11]

Marriage among colonial Jews, as among the better-class Gentiles, was closely associated with a dowry, and there seem to have been very few marriages in which the dot did not figure. It was always a Jewish father's concern to give his daughter a proper *nedunyah* or dowry so she would be able to secure a suitable husband. Such weight was attached to this that in Europe Jews founded special religious brotherhoods to help poor and orphaned girls by providing them with *nedunyot* and thus making it possible for them to marry. One of the most famous of these *hebrot* was and still is Amsterdam's Holy Society for Dowering Orphans and Virgins, which annually arranged a Purim drawing and distributed substantial sums of money for dowries, not only in Holland but abroad as well. In 1692 an American girl, the orphan Rachel Dovale of New York City, won 450 florins for her marriage portion.[12]

Not only fathers, but other relatives too might assume responsibility in dotal matters. Immigrants to America, concerned about sisters whom they had left behind in Europe, made every effort to dower them. Uriah Hendricks, still young and unmarried, offered a substantial amount from his own small capital in order to secure a young New Yorker as a husband for his sister Rosy in London. The man he had in mind was either Myer Myers, the goldsmith, or Sampson Simson, the merchant—either of whom would have been an excellent prospect for Rosy—but unfortunately, Uriah promised the prospective groom too meager a sum. Hendricks himself was considered a catch and was offered a generous dowry to marry a lady of good family and good parts, "but no money will tempt me against inclination." He was going to marry for love! [13]

Once a man chose his wife—or had been chosen for her—a Hebrew prenuptial agreement might be signed, penalizing either party if the marriage did not take place. In 1711 the twenty-three-year-old Jacob Franks put his name to such a contract stipulating that he had agreed to marry Abigail Levy, daughter of the merchant-shipper Moses Levy. The agreement, for some reason, was written in English, which is rather strange since, though there was no rabbi in New York City, it is difficult to believe that the local Jewish community included no one learned enough to write a formal contract of this nature in Hebrew. At any rate, Franks was fortunate, for Abigail proved to be an exemplary helpmate.

Even proxy marriages were not unknown, for one took place in 1762 when Hazzan Pinto deputized a Jewish judge in London to marry him there to Rebecca de la Torre. She was then sent over to him in this country where the final ceremony took place with both parties present.[14]

At practically all nuptial ceremonies the traditional Aramaic marriage contract (ketubah) was prepared, read publicly, and signed, usually by the groom and two witnesses, with the officiant (hazzan) also appending his signature on occasion. The use of a holograph ketubah was standard procedure at marriages, and the instrument would be prepared by a competent person, usually the hazzan, who generally engrossed it on parchment. Copies—in New York at least —would then be made of the contract for the synagogal records. Hazzan Pinto, evidently unsure of himself, employed for his guidance a blank form with detailed instructions for filling it out. The blank form seems to have been prepared for him before his coming from Europe in the 1750's.[15]

The ketubah, a lien upon the husband's estate, was designed primarily to protect the woman from arbitrary divorce and to provide support for her on his death. Most of the ketubah's stipulations, financial and otherwise, had been fixed for centuries by tradition and law. Added, however—and variable—were the dowry brought by the wife and the *tosefet ketubah*, the supplement to the standard ketubah, granted by the husband. The New York contracts usually stipulated, further, how much of the wife's estate was to revert to her family in the event of her death. Sometimes, as in the marriage of Mordecai Sheftall of Savannah to Frances Hart of Charleston, a release was made by the husband, who appointed a trustee and turned lands, houses, and slaves over to his wife. Under normal circumstances after such an indenture was prepared, the husband would continue to use the income of the property and chattels assigned to the wife, but should he become impoverished, the property and income reverted to her and the children. This served the wife as a protection against her husband's creditors.[16]

Quite common in Europe among both Ashkenazim and Sephardim was a custom whereby a groom secured free board and lodging with his wife's family for a stipulated period. Apparently this arrangement—the Ashkenazim called it *Kest*—was sometimes made even in colonial communities, for Uriah Hendricks, after marrying Esther Gomez, secured maintenance from his father-in-law's estate.[17]

Since very few eighteenth-century American Jews were paupers, after marriage most of them lived in relatively comfortable quarters, and even the homes of those in modest circumstances were adequately furnished. Where those who had some means were concerned, inventories garnered from various colonial archives document the fact that their homes were more than plentifully supplied with furniture, linens, and kitchen utensils, while the wealthy lived, as one might expect, in luxury. But even the average middle-class Jewish businessman had slaves and servants—and servant troubles. As early as 1664 in Dutch New Amsterdam, Asser Levy sued to compel the return of a maid who had been taken away by her father and had gone to work for someone else.[18]

Colonial homes may generally have been small, but colonial families were frequently large, for very few if any made efforts to practice birth control. Only too often, of course, children died in infancy, but despite all the hazards of children's diseases and the odds against survival, large families were to be found in every town. Aaron Hart of Three Rivers had at least twelve children; Aaron Lopez of Newport fathered at least seventeen from two wives; Jonas Phillips of Philadelphia was presented with twenty-one by his—one —wife; and Joseph Simon of Lancaster sired a brood of no less than ten sons and daughters. Grace Levy of New York, the second wife of the merchant-shipper Moses Levy, was widowed at thirty-four with seven little ones, the youngest only a few days old. By his first wife her husband had had five children, all of whom seem to have detested their stepmother. Seven years after Levy's death, Grace married another widower, David Hays, apparently something of a schlemiel. Five years later, in 1740 at the age of forty-six, she departed to her, one would think well deserved, "eternal bliss." [19]

Much as we know or can guess about Grace Levy Hays's relations with her stepchildren, there is little we can say about her relations with her husbands—a rather typical failing on the part of colonial sources. The letters of Abigail Franks to her children in Europe are in this respect unusually revelatory, for they reflect quite vividly a home in which wifely and motherly devotion were to be met with at every turn. Even more, Abigail's letters breathe a remarkable intimacy and camaraderie with her children. Her attitude to and treatment of them seem to have been devoid of authoritarianism, and the atmosphere in her home, which still harbored younger children, was apparently a permissive one. If Abigail's letters are at all representative of colonial Jewish domesticity, the typical Jewish family was closely knit, women and children were well-treated, and every effort was made to provide for their material welfare and happiness.

In one respect Abigail's letters would seem to depart far from the contemporary norm. They reflect an absence of the paternalism characteristic of most homes in those days when parents busied themselves arranging the marriages of their children and the disobedient were punished by disinheritance. Nothing in the Franks letters parallels, for instance, the will of Judah Hays, which threatened three of his children with loss of their patrimony, and one of his daughters was cut off with five shillings. Even a minister of Shearith Israel congregation was not exempt from the watchful paternal eye, and when twenty-four-year-old Gershom Mendes Seixas rode horseback to Philadelphia to officiate at the nuptials of Michael Gratz, Seixas *père* recommended his son to the "particular notice" of the bride's father Joseph Simon. Gershom, he wrote, "has never been so far from home, and if you find anything amiss in his behaviour . . . kindly admonish him for it." [20]

Discipline there was aplenty in the colonial family, but not that alone. Samuel Myers, a former New York shohet who was just getting on his feet as a businessman, undertook the further burden of supporting a brother and marrying off a sister. Constantly recurring in the journals of Aaron Lopez are entries for cash opposite the name of his brother Abraham—mute but eloquent testimony that Aaron was maintaining Abraham and even paying for his barber. The will of Isaac R. Marques documents a tender love and consideration for his mother:

It is my will and minde that my deare mother Rachell Marques be maintained out of my estate and live with my wife or my daughter dureing her naturall life. But if she cannot agree with them or like to live by her self, the sume of fifty pounds currant money of New Yorke, and a good serviceable Negro woman shall alsoe be purchased for her out of my said estate to attend her duering her naturall life. . . . And I doe give hereby a strict charge to my wife and children to be dutifull to my said deare mother.[21]

Not that Jewish home life was always peaches and cream! It may be true, as rabbinic tradition would have it, that marriages are made in heaven, but they do have to be lived in this earthy realm. The year 1767 supplies a case in point—the marriage of Abraham Pereira Mendes of Kingston, Jamaica, to Sarah (Sally) Lopez, the eldest daughter of the great Newport merchant. In January of that year Aaron sought information about Sally's suitor from a fellow Sephardi in New York; he inquired whether it was a "genteel family" to which the young Jamaican belonged and whether the prospective son-in-law's personal character and behavior were all they should have been. He did not, it is of interest to note, so much as touch on young Mendes' Jewishness; his loyalty to Judaism was simply taken for granted. Young Mendes, wrote the boy's elder brother from Jamaica, was well-educated and endowed with very "bright qualitys." The Mendes family—the widowed mother and Brother Isaac—gave the match their approval; they were pleased not only with Sally's "ameableness," but also with "the bright character and honour" of the Lopezes both in Portugal and in America.[22]

When one considers the dot provided by Lopez, it is not hard to understand why the Jamaicans should have been so well pleased. Lopez gave Sally a dowry of a thousand Spanish milled dollars, a munificent sum for those days. Nothing comparable to it appears in the New York marriage contracts. In the course of the year Lopez paid the entire dowry—part of it, to be sure, by deducting the debts Mendes had already accrued with his father-in-law. The young couple seems to have been very much in love, and their wedding must have been a most costly and luxurious affair. Henry Lloyd scoured Boston to secure beautiful silks and brocades for the bride, and intending no sarcasm, wished Sally and her husband "every felicity the marriage state affords." After the marriage Lopez set his daughter up in housekeeping and supplied her with everything she might possibly need. Young Mendes was then sent off to Jamaica as a factor for his father-in-law and soon proved to be a dismal failure. For years he refused to return home, patently a sick man physically and emotionally. As late as 1770 his mother pleaded with Lopez to take her son back—she promised to visit Sally and spend a year with her! Ultimately, no later than 1775 the errant husband returned, was given a job by Lopez, and soon became the father of a boy, Samuel, who was circumcised by Moses Seixas. The long-suffering Lopez no doubt breathed a sigh of relief.[23]

Actually, there are very few references to unhappy marriages, and the record of disreputable unions is scantier still. During the 1730's a connection of the Frankses reportedly had an affair with a maid employed by one of the New York congregants; she "swore her self with child by him," and his aggrieved wife apparently left him. A generation later Meyer Josephson's wife was unfaithful to him and their marriage, too, ended in divorce. When Josephson later re-married, he took to wife a Gentile who bore him children. That union, however, ended as disastrously as his first, and during the Revolution the second Mrs. Josephson abandoned him, took the children with her, and prepared to rear them as Christians.[24]

Isolation in small towns was undoubtedly one factor which promoted unhappiness for Jewish families accustomed to larger communities and Jewish associations. During the 1760's, for example, one Levi of the firm of Levi & Jacobs, doing business in a Lancaster County hamlet, divorced his wife, and she then proceeded to marry Levi's partner Barnard Jacobs. No moral turpitude seems to have been involved, but years later when Barnard's son Solomon wanted to marry a Philadelphia girl of good family, for some reason the parnas of Mikveh Israel tried to stop the marriage on the ground that Solomon's mother had been a divorcée.[25]

THE MIKVEH

Since traditional Jewish practice requires women to immerse themselves ritually after menstruation, a mikveh or ritual bathhouse is likely to have been provided in New York from the earliest days of Jewish settlement there. Initially a running stream was used but later, so tradition has it, the New Yorkers constructed a ritual bathhouse over a brook near the Mill Street Synagogue. At any rate, no later than 1759 a mikveh was built for the prescribed female ablutions. Savannah had a mikveh as early as 1738 and Newport, too, is said to have had one. The records make no mention of similar facilities elsewhere, but there can be no doubt that other colonial Jewish communities of any size also maintained such bathhouses.[26]

KASHRUT

When the Scandinavian botanist Peter Kalm visited New York in 1748, "several men of credit" told him that there were local Jews who paid less than strict heed to the demands of kashrut. "Many of them," he wrote, "especially among the young Jews, when traveling, did not make the least difficulty about eating this [pork], or any other meat that was put before them." As Kalm himself observed, however, the Jews of New York "commonly eat no pork," and the evidence at our disposal fortifies the view that colonial Jewry did in general comply with the requirements of the dietary laws. The colonial Jew wanted to maintain kashrut, and when he found himself in a Jewish community, he *dared* not do otherwise unless he wished to invite social and religious ostracism. Certainly, whatever he might do "on the road," no affiliated Jew would be bold enough to eat non-kosher food openly in town or to keep an unkosher home. One old Sephardi went so far as to use a kosher toothpick box, and most likely, kosher toothpicks as well. A Christian observer, Pastor Boltzius, reported from Savannah in 1738 that the "German Jews" (Ashkenazim) there "would rather starve" than eat forbidden meats; the Sephardim, he was told, were "not so strict." Sephardim in New England, however, were apparently more insistent on kashrut, for Aaron Lopez would seem to have kept in his shop a supply of kosher food for the use of his family and relatives.[27]

Levy Andrew Levy of Pennsylvania was probably typical in many respects of the Jewish businessmen whose interests in the backcountry or on the frontier required them to absent themselves from their homes for weeks at a time. Though at Winchester in Virginia's Shenandoah valley he refused to eat bacon, a drinking and eating party in Pittsburgh found him willing to taste barbecue turtle, so succulent a dish that—for him at least—it *had* to be kosher. Still, this Lancaster fur trader never took kashrut lightly and years later expressed a deep and most poignant regret at having been compelled to live in a small town where it was very difficult to rear his children as Jews and where, it would seem, he had not always been able to keep kosher. "For a family to be remote from our [Jewish] society is shocking." [28]

To such an extent did the colonial mind identify Jews with abstention from eating pork that Dr. Alexander Hamilton's refusal to take bacon with his eggs during his Connecticut journey in the 1740's led bystanders to think him a Jew. Indeed, a body of folklore about the Jewish aversion to swine's flesh was already current in the eighteenth century. A local Massachusetts historian reported, for instance, that when the mother of a child in the Lopez-Rivera ménage learned that it had innocently tasted some pork, she immediately administered "a powerful emetic." Easton, Pennsylvania, supplies a similar anecdote about the Jewish merchant Michael Hart, who was afflicted with stuttering. Hearing that his son had eaten a piece of pork, the outraged father choked the offender till he disgorged the unclean meat, and then Hart exclaimed, "N-n-n-ow the divil is out." [29]

Most of the immigrants who came to these shores were young unmarried men, and it was imperative for them to live in Jewish homes where the dietary laws were observed. Even though documentation is lacking, the existence of kosher homes which accommodated boarders in New York is beyond question as early as the 1600's. Such boardinghouses were apparently found in every Jewish community. No later than 1709 Moses Hart, then a humble businessman, ran a kosher boardinghouse in New York and numbered among his guests aspiring young and still unwed merchants like Nathan Simson and Jacob Franks. Establishments like Hart's did not go unscrutinized by the parnasim and board of Shearith Israel, whose ears were always open to complaints about violations of kashrut. Thus in 1774, when the widowed Hetty Hays brought into her boardinghouse some meat whose ritual fitness was suspect, she was made to cleanse her utensils to ensure their fitness for use in a Jewish home.[30]

The colonial Jewish boardinghouse did not confine itself to serving the needs of young immigrant bachelors. From time to time it was also employed as the local congregational hospice; in New York, as already noted, the home of the beadle or the slaughterer occasionally served as the Jewish inn. This was also the case at Newport where Myers, the shammash and "Jew butcher," in addition to boarding Hazzan Touro before his marriage and feeding the country shopkeepers who came to town for the holidays, gave food and lodging to needy itinerants who were constantly landing in the town.[31]

DEATH AND BURIAL

"He that goeth down to the grave," observed the author of Job, "shall come up no more." The colonial Jew may not have taken Job's theology literally, but *how* one went "down to the grave" was a matter of great concern to him. Lacking the pious confraternities which in Europe concerned themselves with the dead, the entire Jewish community in an American town had to assume responsibility for funerals. Jews were not unique in this respect, for Christian groups, too, worked cooperatively in the villages and countryside to provide funerals for their neighbors, friends, and fellow believers. Burial costs were minimal; in 1751–1752 the New York congregational budget was credited with an income of a little over three shillings for an interment. New York Jewry could boast of its own hearse since the mid-1760's, and the cemetery grounds in Newport as well as New York, and undoubtedly in other towns too, included a *matar* house or mortuary hut where ritual washings of the corpse were performed.[32]

Both Christians and Jews frequently practiced the custom of laying flat stone slabs down in the cemetery, directly on the ground or on a slightly elevated brick foundation, over the bodies of the deceased. To be sure, not all graves were covered with stones, for they were expensive, and the poor could not afford such luxuries.

After all, the stone for Mordecai Gomez' grave cost some £15, and the marble one which marked Judah Hays's last resting-place cost a little more even than that. Such a sum was equal to the salary paid his housemaid for twenty months.

Mourning customs were generally observed, even by an assimilated Jew like David Franks who, though he had married out and was rearing his children as Christians, did not shave for thirty days after his father's death. Prayers for the dead were prescribed, and immigrants here, far away from home, were eager to know the anniversary of a parental death, so that the prayers could be appropriately recited. Henry Marks of Philadelphia thought the matter important enough to warrant a letter to his brother Zanvil in Europe. He had had no contact with Zanvil for twenty-five years, but how else was he to secure information as to the date of their mother's death?[33]

CHAPTER 57

DISSENSION

O ne must bear in mind that most of the Jews in colonial America were immigrants from lands where they had endured a host of civil, political, and economic disabilities. Some had suffered persecution, and many of them, even here in an America, were never able to rid themselves of their fears and apprehensions. For the Jew, as for many a Gentile too, much of America was frontier territory, and the difficulties inevitable and inherent in life on the frontier tended often to exacerbate and distort human relationships. Not infrequently the richer Jews were inclined to ignore their poorer coreligionists. It was not unusual for new settlers to find themselves at odds with the old settlers, despite the fact they often hailed from the same European country. There were business rivalries, economic envy, and social snobbery. During the first third of the eighteenth century, for instance, some of the older Spanish-Portuguese families, fearful in all likelihood of compromising their hard-won status in the larger Christian community, looked down on German-Polish newcomers.

Many of the Jews felt themselves, as it were, boxed in—if only by virtue of their being Jews—and so they were unhappy. Upset by the new and strange life that confronted them in American surroundings, these immigrants were prone to quick irascibilities. Because they dared not vent their unhappiness on the Gentiles about them, their bitterness found convenient outlets within the confines of the Jewish group. Colonial congregational minutes and personal correspondence tell an ever recurrent story of pettiness, insults, quarrels, hatreds, and expressions of meanness—even in the synagogue itself. No community escaped such dissension; as late as 1789 Hazzan Seixas was obliged to implore his congregants "to relinquish" their "prejudices against each other." [1]

The religious quarrels which erupted from time to time were probably nothing more than rationalizations of personal animosities, for nowhere do the records indicate that Jews ever quarrelled about the creed, the prayer book, or the pattern of synagogue organization. Theology played no significant part in their lives; dogmas were taken for granted and ignored; the fighting was personal, not theological, and the synagogue was the scene, not the source, of bickering.

ASHKENAZIC AND SEPHARDIC DISSENSION

To what extent was congregational quarreling expressive of a group conflict between two disparate ethnic, cultural, and liturgical factions —between, that is, Sephardim and Ashkenazim? There is no easy, uncomplicated answer to such a question. Unquestionably, during the seventeenth and early eighteenth centuries New York Jewry was dominated by the Sephardim, and all too often they looked askance at the Ashkenazim—the *Tudescos*—to whom, after all, they were at the time certainly superior in secular education and in familiarity with the social amenities.

The Sephardim were, of course, always conscious of the Ashkenazim; even in 1654 when the first Sephardic émigrés landed at New Amsterdam, an Ashkenazi, Jacob Barsimson, was waiting to greet them! In 1737 Rodrigo Pacheco, who had by then taken up residence in London and held membership in the Bevis Marks congregation, voted for the imposition of penalties on a Sephardi who was frequenting an Ashkenazic synagogue. As late as the 1740's Pacheco was to be numbered among the Sephardim who regarded marriage with an Ashkenazi as a *mésalliance*. When Pacheco's New York nephew Isaac Mendes Seixas married into the Ashkenazic Levy-Franks clan, Abigail Franks reported that he was "displeased." She did not know, she went on to say, where Isaac "could have mended himself in anny thing but a fortune, but I fancy Mr. Pecheco's quarle is her being a Tudesco." Abigail was undoubtedly right in her fancy, and such social snobbery on the part of some Sephardim was to linger even after the other barriers between Sephardim and Ashkenazim had broken down. The Gomezes, New York Jewry's most influential family during the first decades of the eighteenth century, resisted intramarriage with Ashkenazim till the third generation; they preferred, if it came to that, finding properly Sephardic wives in the islands. The Ashkenazim were not content with the status assigned them by some of their Sephardic brethren. Abigail Franks, as we have seen, was not at all cowed by "Mr. Pecheco's" prejudices, and it was not much more than a generation after the Mill Street Synagogue's erection that Hayman Levy, an aggressive Ashkenazi leader, besought the aged Daniel Gomez to "appoint trustees of the Aschanazim, as well as of his own family," for the cemetery.

The Sephardim had been in New York for about seventy years before their hegemony was seriously threatened. Up to 1740 more Sephardim than Ashkenazim served as parnasim, which of course gave the Sephardim an opportunity to entrench their own liturgical rite. In Georgia, too, the first Jewish settlers, who came over with Oglethorpe, were predominantly Spanish and Portuguese. Fresh from Europe, they brought with them their social exclusiveness and hostility toward the *Tudesco* minority that accompanied them. To be sure, the two groups did hold a common service and had a young hazzan to lead them, but they quarreled and could not agree on the building of a synagogue. Superficially at least, their differences appear to have been liturgical. It is curious, however, that though the problem resolved itself with the dissolution of the community about 1740, the remaining two families, both of them Ashkenazic, finally adopted the Sephardic rite when they reorganized the congregation, and even they quarreled among themselves about the liturgy.[2]

THE CENTRAL EUROPEANS AND THE SPANISH-PORTUGUESE LEARN TO LIVE TOGETHER

The socioethnic picture had already changed in New York by 1720, for by then Ashkenazim outnumbered Sephardim. The Central Europeans did not, of course, come to power suddenly, though some of them served as presidents of Shearith Israel as early as the second decade of the century, if not earlier; that is to say, even before the new Mill Street Synagogue was erected. It is true that the Sephardim were dominant in the synagogue's reorganization of 1728, but more than half of the subscribers to the new cemetery fund were Ashkenazim. By the decade of the 1730's the Ashkenazim were ready to swamp the Spanish-Portuguese. When the cornerstones of the synagogue were laid in 1729, two of the four donors were Ashkenazim, and after 1732 most of the congregation's presidents came from Ashkenazic ranks. After 1728, in fact, parnasim of Ashkenazic background outnumbered by more than four to one the Sephardic parnasim, all of whom, with one exception, stemmed from the Gomez family.

One might have expected this socioethnic revolution to have engendered intrasynagogal dissension, but the records fail to justify such an expectation. In fact, few if any of the recurrent synagogal quarrels which disrupted eighteenth century American Jewish life were due to an alignment of Sephardim against Ashkenazim. The reverse seems to have been the case, for an analysis of the names of the disputants demonstrates that combines of Central Europeans and Iberians were pitted against opposing Ashkenazic-Sephardic groupings. North American Jewry was in this respect, as in others, sui generis.[3]

Unlike all other Sephardic-Ashkenazic settlements, the North American Jewish community became a melting pot. The solidarity general among the early settlers reflects itself in the fact that of the seven Jewish contributors to Trinity Church in 1711, four were of Germanic stock, while three were born Sephardim. This solidarity was achieved at the expense of Ashkenazic distinctiveness. What happened in North America was that German and Polish immigrants as well as the incoming English-born sons of Ashkenazim simply adapted themselves to the Sephardic ritual; they observed Sephardic customs, abandoned their own Ashkenazic pronunciation and cantillation of Hebrew, and even surrendered their own form of memorial prayers for the dead. That amalgamation with the Sephardim was cemented by the imperative need to employ a common vernacular, English.

The Ashkenazic settlers intermarried with the Sephardim and set about rearing Sephardic families. It was inevitable, of course, that the numerical dominance of the Ashkenazim and their rise in the economic scale would lead to intermarriage between the two groups, and the process was only accelerated by the fact that very few Sephardic immigrants arrived after 1760. Nearly all the Sephardim already here began, then, to marry into German or Polish families. Zipporah De Lyon, the American-born daughter of a Portuguese pioneer in Georgia, for instance, was apparently only too happy to marry Mordecai M. Mordecai, a Lithuanian immigrant. Zipporah would probably have felt otherwise had she lived outside North America, in the islands, say, where the Spanish-Portuguese formed the majority and discouraged intramarriage with Ashkenazim. The cleavage was even more pronounced in London, whose Spanish-Portuguese community was constantly being replenished from other parts of Europe and where the Sephardi who married an Ashkenazi risked virtual ostracism.[4]

In Europe, of course, the Sephardim could afford to be selective. There, wealthy Sephardic aristocrats married among themselves for financial reasons and in order to maintain the purity of their strain —their own *limpieza de sangre*. One historian, speculating that obsession with "purity of ancestry" may have originally been a Spanish Jewish concern, has argued that such considerations were taken over from the Marranos by the Spanish Christians and subsequently applied by the so-called Old Christians against the Jewish-descended New Christians. At any rate, the fact that Jewish Iberians of Marrano stock had suffered in Spain from the measuring rod of *limpieza de sangre* never inhibited application of that rod not only against the Ashkenazim but even against the humble within Sephardic ranks.

Limpieza de sangre never assumed importance in the American Jewish community due to the paucity of North American Sephardim. Here the Sephardim could not in the long run afford the luxury of such ethnic prejudices, for if their children were to marry within the Jewish fold, they had to content themselves with German mates— or remain single.

The unification of Sephardic and Ashkenazic Jews, or if one prefers, the Ashkenazic assimilation to Sephardic culture, was thus uniquely American and was already evident by the second quarter of the 1700's. Sephardic hazzanim gladly entertained Ashkenazic scholars who came to these shores, and no distinction—no doubt with an exception here and there—was made between the two groups socially. In most American towns they were all, Sephardim and Ashkenazim alike, tied together by the bonds of blood and marriage.[5]

One wonders whether union between the various ethnic components in American Jewry was not encouraged by the prevalence of tolerant attitudes in the culture at large. Certainly this is possible, but other influences may well have been more compelling. Above all, Jews wanted to live as Jews, and had they declined to unite and cooperate, they would have been faced with almost insuperable difficulties in maintaining their religio-communal life. Well aware that if driven to it, the Ashkenazim could and would establish their own conventicles or shuls, the Sephardim had no choice but to act with tact and discretion. Constantly subject to a proportionate decline, they had to accept non-Sephardic Jews or die out. Theirs was a choice between amalgamation with Ashkenazim or with Christians —and they preferred the former. In the ensuing symbiosis the Sephardim emerged—nominally at least—as the victors, for their ritual, their ethnic linguistic phrases, and their way of life in large part remained intact. It was the Ashkenazim who abandoned their distinctiveness, but the Ashkenazim were never denied office and status, and their acceptance by the Sephardim did keep them from organizing separately. Then, too, some of the Ashkenazim very probably believed that there were social advantages in adopting the Sephardic heritage.

At this point a caveat should be uttered with respect to the religious relations of the Ashkenazim and the Sephardim. They did not constitute two separate denominations. They were all "Orthodox"

Jews, always one "church." Apart from the variations in their liturgies, their differences were primarily social, cultural, and ethnic, but the ethnicity which stood out abroad was relegated to a minor role in North America, whose Jews all shared a common fate and included a large percentage of immigrants. Merger between the two elements of North American Jewry, the Central Europeans and the Iberians, was promoted by a common anglicization, by the economic rise of many of the Germans, and finally by the fusion that religious survival demanded. Actually, by 1776 the "Sephardic" Jew was an American of Iberian, Central European, and even East European stock, and in this he set an enduring pattern. The "German" Jews of nineteenth century America were to have no more valid claim to ancestral "purity," embracing as they would French, Hungarian, Polish, Russian, and other non-Teutonic antecedents. The American Jew who has emerged since the quota laws, which cut off European immigration during the 1920's, comes forth, then, from a crucible into which have been poured Iberians, Germans, East Europeans, Mediterraneans—and an ever growing number of Gentile converts to Judaism.[6]

The Anatomy of Dissension

The religiosocial life of colonial Jewry amounted all too often to a precarious balance between natural tendencies to dissension on the one hand, and the demands and expressions of kinship on the other. Living together constituted nothing less than a major problem for congregants, and one is almost tempted to assert that the smaller the group, the more the trouble. The Canadian constitution of 1778 was a case in point. Motivated in large—and distressing—part by the problem of internal strife, it made mention of disturbances and controversies in the House of God, touched on misconduct by individuals, and spoke of members who threatened to quit. As happened also in some of the Christian churches, special provisions had to be adopted to suppress quarreling among congregants, and it was necessary for the board to call an arbitrational procedure into being. Within no more than a year after the constitution's promulgation, tensions in the Montreal community had become so acute that disputatious members were bidden "to take the oath by the Laws of Moses"—before the open ark—that they would "never hereafter speak against the characters or prejudice the persons of each other on any pretence whatsoever." Finally, the president himself was accused of having "made use of expressions to the manifest injury of this congregation" and suffered suspension, though he was back in the fold before very long.

Jewish communal life was no more peaceful at the other end of the continent. In Charleston, South Carolina, the congregation, which probably boasted some twenty members, was split into two dissentient groups during the early 1770's, while the even tinier community of Lancaster, Pennsylvania, saw the fury directed against its richest member, Joseph Simon, undoubtedly the boss of the congregation. When Michael Gratz married Simon's daughter Miriam at Lancaster, Simon, it would seem, deliberately bypassed a local Jew competent to perform the ceremony—probably Moses Lazarus, whom Simon had employed as a shohet and teacher, but had discharged the preceding year. Lazarus was reportedly so incensed that he removed sheets from his erstwhile employer's Scroll of the Law to render it unfit for use. Without a "kosher" scroll, it would be impossible to conduct a service, which was such a shocking sacrilege for an observant Jew that a son-in-law of Simon said, in commenting on it, that the culprit deserved excommunication.

Such incidents render far more plausible the sarcasm which informed Jacob Henry's pen in 1761. Hearing the "great and mighty news" that the Philadelphians were about to establish a synagogue —"it convinces me Eternity is nigh at hand"—he asked which one of the *Ashkenazic* rites they would choose. "For my part," he wrote, "I think it will be best after the old mode of Pennsylvania." In other words, since the Philadelphia Jews could not be expected to agree on any mode, they ought to imitate the Quakers and have none at all! Henry seems to have known his Philadelphians. A century and a half later in his article on America for the *Jewish Encyclopedia,* Cyrus Adler could write that quarrels between German and Polish Jews in Philadelphia inhibited the establishment of a congregation in that city, and Adler would appear to have based himself on an authentic eighteenth century tradition. The year 1769 witnessed the eruption of severe dissension in the Philadelphia community, with new Jewish settlers pitted against their predecessors, although without exception both groups comprised men of German and Polish origin. A "parcell" of "new Jews" composed a pasquil against the older settlers, and the attack centered on the Lancastrian, Joseph Simon, who seems at that time to have been affiliated with Philadelphia Jewry. Secession progressed, and the seceders held their own holy day services in the fall. When a constitution was prepared about that time for the tiny community, mention was made of those who disturbed the synagogue, and provision was made for the arbitration of all difficulties. Intramural quarrels were not uncommon even in London's comparatively sedate Bevis Marks congregation, and aristocratic resentment toward "new people" appears to have characterized most colonial American Gentile groups as well.[7]

Actually, little can be said about the *Sturm und Drang* of Jewish life in colonial Philadelphia; much more is known about the problems and the bickerings of New York Jewry. Constant quarreling took place in Shearith Israel, especially after the commencement of the French and Indian War when new immigrants began arriving. There had, to be sure, been trouble enough long before that, as the preamble to the constitution of 1728 documents in asserting that these new rules were intended "to preserve peace, tranquility, and good government." In the body of the constitution itself there was mention of persons who offered "to give . . . affront or abuse." The next extant constitution, that of 1761, contained two paragraphs governing disorderly behavior and disturbances. Troubles reached a climax in the congregation in 1769 when six members rebelled and were threatened with expulsion unless they made "proper, reasonable, and satisfactory concessions" to the authorities.

Curiously enough, dissension in Philadelphia, too, had reached its height in 1769. Whether these two rebellions were in any way related to each other is unknown, though it is by no means improbable that Jews everywhere in the colonies were very much influenced and disturbed by widespread American protests against an increasingly harsh British imperial authority. No one could escape the effects of the nonimportation boycott resolutions and the consequent decline in trade; everyone breathed the air of frustration, fear, and revolt. The trouble in New York's Shearith Israel—a general opposition to constituted authority—seems to have expressed itself particularly in refusals to accept synagogal responsibility, to be associated in office with a personal enemy, and to pay offerings. Apparently King Hezekiah's admonition in II Chronicles 30:8—"Now be ye not stiffnecked as your fathers were"—was not much taken to heart by Judah's latter-day descendants.

The president in office was frequently an object of attack, and his antagonists would show open contempt for him by making scandalous offerings during the services. Public offerings were never an unmixed blessing. The bidding or auctioning of honors in public was often fatal to decorum, while humorous, sarcastic, and nasty bids were made on occasion by petty or embittered people. The bidding might even lead to a fight in the shrine itself. Some congregations tried to stop such indecencies by arbitrarily fixing the price of honors, and parnasim, worried that they had no authority to eject offenders forcibly, sought legal advice. The fact that synagogues were not incorporated societies seems to have left parnasim little redress, but the law did make it possible for them to protect themselves by bringing suit against troublemakers for disturbing the peace. Of course, not all offenders were recalcitrant or belligerent. Abraham I. Abrahams, the religious functionary of Shearith Israel, once punched Abraham Seixas during the service, but hastened to offer the board his apologies. Still, as late as the last year of the Revolution, Hazzan Seixas hesitated to return to Shearith Israel because, as he wrote:

I am informed that many parties are formed—and forming—to create divisions among the reputable members of the congregation, by which means a general disunion seems to prevail instead of being united to serve the Deity, consonant to our holy law.

Hayman Levy, the army supplier and fur trader, must have been an obstreperous character. In 1756 he was fined twenty shillings for "the indecent and abusive language" he had used against the parnas in the synagogue yard, and in 1765 he directed his anger against the hazzan. When he himself became president, however, he received a dose of his own medicine, for he in turn had to endure abuse. Baruch (Barrak) Hays, for one, offered him "repeated insults." The Hayses were the most factious family in the congregation, but not because they were newcomers fighting for recognition, since they had immigrated to this country as early as the 1730's. One quarrel—about seating in the women's gallery—involved Judah Hays in a three-year tug-of-war with the synagogue officers, while Judah's brother Solomon defamed the congregation through a pasquil and was physically beaten in the ensuing imbroglio. After an unsuccessful attempt to sue his attackers, Solomon was denied congregational membership for five years, but finally paid his fine and was readmitted. Nine years later, however, he was in trouble again. All told, Solomon's wars with his fellow Jews lasted for at least fifteen years. If Solomon's name, which means "peace," was ill suited to his temperament, his son Baruch, too, was scarcely better named, for Baruch was anything but "blessed," as his name declares. Baruch Hays was thrown out of the synagogue bodily and sued. Convicted of being a nuisance, he was put under a minor ban, but on his apologizing, the congregational leader Hayman Levy withdrew the suit he had initiated. Hays agreed to pay the costs, but exerted every effort to prevent publication of his apology; he offered £100 to keep it out of the press.[8]

Moses Lazarus had battled with Joseph Simon at Lancaster in 1768. In 1771 he appeared in New York City as a temporary shohet, and three years later when he was embroiled in difficulties, made accusations against the president and the congregation. Refused the privilege of speaking at the funeral of one of the Hays brothers, he told the parnas that he presided over a lunatic asylum, "the bog [bug] house." To prevent his preaching, he was ejected, and as he cursed the president, Lazarus' coconspirator Manuel Josephson uttered a solemn "amen." Both men were denied ritual courtesies until they paid a heavy fine. Josephson finally paid his, but there is no record of what Lazarus did. Josephson later became an outstanding leader at postrevolutionary Mikveh Israel in Philadelphia and on behalf of American Jewry congratulated Washington on his election to the presidency. Lazarus was a great-granduncle of Emma Lazarus, whose famous sonnet was inscribed on a plaque at the base of the Statue of Liberty. Obviously, Emma's words about "huddled masses yearning to breathe free" would have applied strikingly to her mid-eighteenth century immigrant forebear.[9]

CHAPTER 58

KINSHIP AND SOCIAL LIFE

ANALYSIS AND MANIFESTATION OF KINSHIP

It is true that dissension among the Jews of colonial America was constant, bitter, and mean. In the context of history, however, it was not overwhelming. The quarreling was very real and terribly annoying, but no community was destroyed because of it. Centripetal forces were stronger than those making for divisiveness. Once a community was firmly established it managed to endure. The bonds that united Jews were very strong; they were tied together by a religio-ethnic kinship—a common experience of suffering and a common confidence in survival. It was their sense of kinship, their feeling of intimate fellowship allied to their pervasively middle-class character, that made for social integration within colonial American Jewish ranks and served as a foundation on which to build a communal life. The North American Jewish community persisted because it was buttressed by a high degree of economic stability. The demands of religion and kinship and the desire to be together had a stronger impact on the community's members than the divisive forces assailing Jewish life. An apprehensive group, always and perhaps even pre-ternaturally aware of the outside world whose hostility they had endured throughout the ages, they huddled together for comfort, and on the American frontier the synagogue was their blockhouse and stockade. Despite the centrifugalities lurking on the American scene, the desire for Jewish communality prevailed, so that the community could survive and grow. The history of the colonial Jewish community reflects the attempt to preserve the balance in favor of unity as against disruption. And it is the history of a successful attempt.

Kinship, like charity, began at home, and close family ties were usually the rule. Isaac M. Seixas of New York sent his sister in London some pickles; she sent him some Spanish peas and sugar. Even though an immigrant was thousands of miles from his native heath, he bore in mind the needs of his often financially hard-pressed dear ones. Money would be sent them, and legacies left them. Only two years in this country, Michael Gratz sent his sisters in Silesia a substantial sum—out of the first profits he had made. A Jew imprisoned for debt was aided by the community. The New York hazzan whose debts had forced him into hiding may have been discharged from his office, but efforts were made to help him nonetheless. Typical of the generosity Jews showed their coreligionists is the fact that emissaries from the Holy Land rarely returned empty-handed. Even the itinerant rabbis and scholars who landed on these shores to collect funds for none but themselves were treated courteously and almost without exception, generously. The American-born Frankses in London were most gracious to Barnard Gratz when he visited them, and Michael Gratz in Philadelphia was hospitable and attentive to young Gershom Seixas when the hazzan of Shearith Israel came to town.

Jews were always willing to help one another, particularly if the suppliants were honorable people, but they were quick to flare up if their hospitality and generosity were abused. As we have noted, the New Yorkers did not hesitate to testify against a fellow Jew who had stolen from one of them, even though theft was a capital crime and their testimony brought about the criminal's execution.

In business matters, kinship sometimes went out the window. Whether for reasons of kinship or sound business, Jewish creditors frequently made settlements with their Jewish debtors, but it is also recorded that on occasion a Jew would refuse to settle with a fellow Jew and would be prepared, if necessary, to send the debtor to jail. Myer Myers, it will be recalled, had an English Jew for an indentured servant, but the servant finally ran away. Apparently the kinship that should have held these two together proved weaker than the forces impelling the servant to solve his problems through flight.

It was his sense of kinship, however, which bade a Jew visit a neighboring city to participate in a synagogue dedication; he wished to rejoice with his fellow Jews. Again, it was kinship which often led congregations to aid one another financially, though at times their help was inadequate, or at least the recipients thought so. But kinship might be relegated to second place when it came to establishing the rights or lack of rights due newcomers to a congregation. A constitution such as that adopted by the Canadians might solemnly declare in its opening paragraph that the newly established synagogue was "meant for the use and service of all Israelites who conform to our laws," and then in following articles proceed to set up rules and restrictions whereby all subsequent joiners would in effect be granted only second-class membership. It is clear the pioneer Jews of early America were fallible human beings.[1]

INTERCOLONIAL COOPERATION

Although Jews in seventeenth and eighteenth century Central and Eastern Europe manifested tendencies towards some sort of national organization, nothing comparable developed in the American colonies. America possessed not the slightest vestige of a national Jewish organization. Independency was everywhere the rule, and each American congregation was a law unto itself. There was, to be sure, nothing unprecedented in this situation, for the inherent right of every congregation to govern itself constituted a venerable Jewish tradition with roots at least a thousand years old in Europe. Self-government among Jews thus long antedated the similar polities of New England's Protestant churches. Like the churches of Massachusetts, American synagogues did have relations with one other, but their ties were voluntary, and the sense of political unity which grew among the rebellious colonies during the 1770's brought about no formal religious unity among the Jewish congregations. Yet, despite their lack of a formal national organization, the synagogues of America were bound together by a close bond of ethnic and spiritual kinship, enhanced by the prevalence among them of a common Sephardic rite. These religious bonds were fortified by advances in communication and transportation. The development of interurban and intercolonial commerce, better roads, and improved postal services made it increasingly easier for Jewish individuals and communities to keep in close touch with one another, so that there was in fact, if not in form, one overall American synagogal spirit. There is, for instance, no evidence of sectionalism in the relations and attitudes of Jews in the North and the South, and the sense of community was very probably much stronger among Jews throughout the land than among American Protestants.

New York's Shearith Israel—actually the only continuously functioning synagogue prior to 1750—was considered the mother synagogue of American Jewry because it had been the first established here and was the largest and richest. Congregations and individuals turned to it for help and advice, and relations between Shearith Israel and Jewish communities elsewhere in the country were strengthened by virtue of the fact that Jewish businessmen from all over America made frequent trips to the New York market. Once in town, they customarily attended services at the New York congregation, made offerings, and renewed friendships. Of course many of those who came to New York had once lived in the city; they had landed at that port originally and were, so to speak, returning home.[2]

Jewish communities, especially Newport, New York, and Philadelphia, had to keep in touch with one another, for to them fell the common task of dispatching itinerants and visiting rabbis to farther destinations. As Jews, their members accepted certain responsibilities of interurban and intercolonial religious cooperation. When, for example, the first Savannah community disappeared about 1740, the congregation sent its Sefer Torah to New York Jewry, which turned the scroll over to Newport's renascent congregation around 1760. At Savannah Jewry's reconstitution as a community in 1773, the Simson brothers of New York were made trustees of the Savannah burial ground, just as New York, Newport, and Savannah Jews had been included among the trustees when the Charleston congregation consecrated one of its cemeteries in 1764. Later, in 1775 when the Charlestonians thought to build a synagogue, they appealed to New York for money to further the project.[3]

Such cooperation was a well-established pattern. During the 1760's a group of Philadelphia Jews, setting out to create a formal synagogue community, turned to New York and borrowed a scroll. And when in 1771 the Philadelphians reorganized their community for the third, but not the last time during the eighteenth century, they brought Hazzan Seixas down from New York to officiate on that auspicious occasion. The Lancaster Jews had a little synagogue of their own, but they too maintained close relations with Philadelphia and New York, while Newport, like Philadelphia, was a direct offshoot of Shearith Israel. The business, social, and religious relationships between the Newport and New York congregations were very close, and when the New Yorkers found themselves temporarily without a shohet, they might advertise in the Rhode Island community for a candidate to fill the job. Newport in turn secured a great deal of financial help and encouragement from New York when she began to build her synagogue. Boston was another colony of New York, albeit a very small one. Since no Jewish community was established there in colonial times, the New Yorkers living in that New England city continued to contribute to Shearith Israel's Mill Street Synagogue.[4]

INTERNATIONAL COOPERATION

The universal brotherhood of all Jews is axiomatic of course, no less during the eighteenth century than today, and yet colonial American Jewry maintained no close relations of an institutional nature with foreign Jewries. Judaism—in contrast to Catholicism, the German Reformed church, or Anglicanism—had engendered no formal international organizational structure uniting under one aegis Jewish congregations in one land with those in another. Ties among Jews were essentially sentimental; the only centripetal force in Judaism was spiritual, and it was in these terms—sentimental and spiritual—that American Jews saw their relations with Jews abroad.

The Jews of the North American colonies kept in close touch with the West Indian islands whose Jewish communities they supplied in part with kosher meat. Europe, from which practically all of North America's Jews had come, was close to their hearts. They even revered the European Jewish heroes, and the walls of one

American Jewish home were graced with a picture of Manasseh ben Israel, the distinguished seventeenth century Amsterdam rabbi. Following standard eighteenth century Sephardic liturgical practice, the New York, Newport, and Philadelphia congregations recited blessings for the welfare of the Jewish community of Jerusalem, for Jews held captive, for those who were in the hands of the dreaded Inquisition, for the men and women who traveled by land and sea, and for all who were sick.[5]

What holds true today held true in the 1700's. The moment a Jewish community is formed, even at the end of the world as it were, other Jews will unfailingly appeal to it for help. In colonial times, for instance, representatives of Palestinian Jewry, suffering under tyrannical Turkish pashas, wrote to their North American coreligionists to ask for aid. On occasion they might turn directly to an American Jewish notable whose name they had somehow secured, or they might appeal indirectly through the mediation of a well-known European Jewish community or religious leader. At times they might even send messengers to solicit funds in person. When an earthquake wrought terrible havoc in one of the Palestinian communities, the New Yorkers received an urgent appeal for aid from a Constantinople rabbi who had been delegated to raise funds for the earthquake victims, and a similar call came on behalf of the Jews of Smyrna, Turkey. After Smyrna's Jewish quarter burned down, the London Jews responded generously and then pressed—unsuccessfully in this instance—New York Jewry to help relieve the suffering. When, however, a hurricane destroyed the synagogue at St. Eustatius in the Dutch West Indies, the New Yorkers did offer aid and received in turn a grateful promise of "fervent prayers for the prosperity" of Shearith Israel. From time to time distant communities in the West Indies and even in Europe shipped their poor to North America; they knew that American Jewry would do its duty, even if it meant no more than shunting the itinerants along to another town or another land.[6]

In general, however, the communities on this side of the Atlantic received more than they gave. North American Jewry after all was dependent on the Caribbean and Europe financially, culturally, and religiously. Shearith Israel of Montreal, for example, was generously helped in its first years by the Sephardic congregations of London, Surinam, Curaçao, and New York, while Shearith Israel of New York, when it proceeded to build its first synagogue, asked for and received aid from individuals and communities on Jamaica, Curaçao, and Barbados, as well as in London. With the exception of Dutch Curaçao, these were the important Sephardic communities of the British Empire. When the Newporters, too, began to build a generation later, they turned successfully to these same communities, and Dutch Surinam, whose business relations with Rhode Island were close, also responded to their request for help. Again, in the 1760's when financial troubles threatened Newport Jewry with the loss of its synagogue, appeals for aid to both Curaçao and Surinam resulted in liberal donations from the Sephardic community of Paramaribo, the Surinamese capital, and the Ashkenazim, who also had a community of their own in Paramaribo, promised to be equally generous. Indeed, the ties between Surinam and Rhode Island were such that when a Palestinian messenger in search of assistance for his clients in the Holy Land prepared to leave Surinam for Newport, a Paramaribo Jewish physician gave him a letter of introduction to Newport's richest and most openhanded Jew.[7]

The ties between Rhode Island and Surinam notwithstanding, North American Jews and New Yorkers in particular, as British subjects, were naturally in closer touch with the British West Indies and London than with the Dutch possessions. London's Bevis Marks Synagogue, as the Sephardic alma mater of the Jews in the British Empire, always maintained close relations with North American Jewry, which looked to London for advice and financial aid. The first Jewish schoolhouse on the North American continent was built by a London philanthropist, and it was to the Spanish-Portuguese synagogue of the imperial capital that New York Jewry turned when it needed a hazzan. It was from London Jewry that the Canadians, the Rhode Islanders, and the Georgians received necessary religious and ritual appurtenances, especially highly prized Scrolls of the Law.[8]

Despite the rigidly parochial nature of Bevis Marks, the London Sephardim never lost their sense of identity with World Jewry. They responded to appeals for help from Jews in all parts of Europe without regard to liturgical rite or ethnic origin. Still, there can be no doubt that the unusual composition of American Jewry, the community's admixture of Sephardim and Ashkenazim, did make it easier for the colonials to issue effective appeals for aid to the Sephardic congregation in London as well as to the city's separate Ashkenazic community. During the 1720's and 1730's, for example, individual Sephardic Jews were most generous in helping an already preponderantly Ashkenazic New York Jewry build and establish its religious and educational institutions. Nor were the Ashkenazic Jews of London less generous, even though it meant aiding a Sephardic synagogue at New York in a generation when those very London Ashkenazim were excluded from membership in Bevis Marks! The fact that the minhag Sefarad had prevailed in New York did not prevent London Ashkenazim like the Frankses, Levys, and Polocks from contributing to the new Mill Street Synagogue, and a generation later Shearith Israel looked to Naphtali and Moses Franks of London's Ashkenazic community for help in building a wall for the Chatham Square cemetery. The New Yorkers, their attachment to the Sephardic rite notwithstanding, had every expectation of meeting with a favorable reply, since Jacob Franks, the father of the two American-born Franks brothers, was buried in the Chatham Square cemetery.[9]

THE ACCEPTANCE OF MARRANOS AND NEW CHRISTIANS

In evaluating the sense of fellowship that Jews cherished for each other, it is of interest to explore the attitude of colonial Jewry toward the Marranos, Christians of Iberian Jewish origin, who had been drifting onto the shores of British North America ever since the seventeenth century. How Jewish were they? How were they received?

Some of the Marranos or New Christians had lived as Roman Catholics for generations in Spain and Portugal. A number of them, accustomed to travel outside the Iberian Peninsula merely to do business, had no thought of starting life all over again in a non-Catholic environment. Actually many, perhaps even most of them would have remained Christians, had the Inquisition let them be. Once, however, the Holy Office suspected, justifiably or not, the religious loyalty of a New Christian, the hapless victim was intimidated or tortured until he confessed to Jewish practices, even if he had not engaged in them. It was thus a desire to escape from the Inquisition that led some of the Marranos and New Christians, even those among them who were believing Christians or harbored no interest in Judaism, to flee Spain and Portugal when they could. Such émigrés might return to Spain or Portugal if they felt it safe to do so. Benjamin Mesquita de Bueno, for instance, had been expelled from Brazil as a Jew, but went back to the Iberian Peninsula to live as a Christian. Quitting Europe again, he spent his last days in New York where in 1683 it was his distinction to be the first Jew buried in the Chatham Square cemetery.

Though all the Marranos were of Iberian origin or ancestry, not all of them came to America directly from Spain or Portugal. The Robles family, which landed at New York in 1687, had fled France after Louis XIV's Revocation of the Edict of Nantes two years earlier. In all probability they were Protestant—Huguenot—Marranos. Since no Shearith Israel records have survived for that early period, the extent if any to which they cherished Jewish religious loyalties cannot be determined. Shortly after 1700 another French Marrano family, the Gomezes, landed at New York, but their Jewish loyalties are well documented; they were pious, observant, and completely devoted to Judaism. They soon became pillars of the New York congregation, and their loyalty to the Jewish faith was expressed in the family's motto:

> Boundless as the fishes of the sea,
> Was honour and integrity of the Gomez family.
> Supported by lion's strength they did their faith uphold,
> Nor would they change it for a crown of gold.[10]

Many of the Jewish settlers who landed at Savannah in 1733 had come from Portugal or Portuguese Brazil via England. They would not have been sent over by London's Sephardic community had they not professed Judaism, although some of them seem not to have been particularly observant. Among those émigrés was nineteen-year-old Zipporah Nunez who had been reared as a Catholic, but in America would marry the "rabbi" Hazzan Machado. Family tradition has it that one of the Machados had been burnt at the stake by the Portuguese Inquisition and that some of the women of the Nunez-Machado family habitually employed a rosary as they recited their Jewish prayers here on American soil. Whether Zipporah Nunez Machado held to this practice cannot be said, but in any case she was to be the ancestress of several notable American Jews.[11]

The Lopezes, another Marrano family from Portugal, began to come here in the 1730's. All of them reverted to Judaism, the males undergoing circumcision and married couples remarrying according to the Jewish ritual. Much as Jews might oppose antagonizing Christian opinion by the conversion of Gentiles, they had no fear that the public would be aroused when Marrano refugees were converted to Judaism. Those Marranos had been Roman Catholics in Spain and Portugal, and Catholics in colonial America lived quiet and withdrawn lives; they had less status here than the Jews. Marrano abandonment of Christianity would not be resented, for Protestants too had suffered at the hands of the Inquisition. Thus when many years after his arrival in Newport, Aaron Lopez brought over from Portugal several members of his own immediate family, he did not hesitate to have them formally inducted into the Jewish fold. They dropped their Christian names and adopted Jewish ones. Michael Lopez took the name of the first Jewish proselyte, the patriarch Abraham, while his wife Joana became Abigail, whose prototype, one of the favorite women in rabbinic lore, had been the wife of the biblical David; Edward became Moses; Joseph became Samuel; and John became Jacob. (Actually, of course, names like Michael, Joseph and John were not originally Christian at all, but biblical Hebrew names.) Women converts usually took names like Sarah, Rebecca, or Abigail to signalize their espousal of Judaism. Most of these Marranos became, like Aaron Lopez himself, loyal, pious Jews, and there is every reason to believe that the Lopezes were very scrupulous in their observance of Jewish ritual, although they continued to maintain close relations with the baptized members of the family back in Portugal.

Not every refugee embraced Judaism. The Lucenas, father and son, never removed themselves from Christian ranks. Related to the Lopezes, the Lucenas may have been brought over by them. The records first locate them on these shores in the 1750's at Newport, where they appear as cousins of the Lopezes. Shortly after their arrival, however, they moved on to Savannah to become merchant-shippers and planters. While always maintaining cordial relations with their Jewish relatives, they never evinced any interest in Judaism.

In general the attitude of Jews to Marranos was one of great sympathy. Jews were exceedingly eager to be of service to those who wished to embrace the faith of their ancestors; they rejoiced in seeing them brought back to Judaism. When Aaron Lopez arrived in America during the early 1750's and submitted to circumcision, Daniel Gomez, probably a relative, congratulated him on having received "the blood of the covenant" and on having manifested his fidelity to the "Holy Law" together with his family. Years later, in November 1766 Lopez wrote to his employee Jeremiah Osborne, captain of the *Pitt*, then about to sail from London to Lisbon with a cargo of coal, "Should any of my friends in Lisbon incline to come with you, I need not recommend you to use them with the same tenderness that I might expect myself from you, being well assured of your civil and obliging disposition." In the spring of the following year Lopez entrusted to Captain Osborne a secret mission which the captain promised to conduct "with discression"—the rescue from Portugal of members of the Lopez family.

Moses, the first of the Lopez brothers to set foot in America, died in April 1767; Michael arrived a few months later in July. In a letter to Isaac Da Costa of Charleston, Aaron Lopez told of the sorrow and joy which the year 1767 had brought him:

The same Powerfull Being that deprived me of a good brother has deleiver'd from the reach of barbarous Inquiziton a younger brother of mine than the deceased, with his wife and three sons. They arrived here the 11th of July last from Lisbon in a ship I order'd there for the better conveniency of their transportation. This piece of news I take the liberty to impart to you, persuaded it will merit your aplauze, both as a Judeo and a friend.

And merit Da Costa's "aplauze" the news certainly did, for the Jews of America accepted the *refugiados* wholeheartedly. Were they not brands plucked all but literally from the burning? [12]

Social Life

The sociability of the colonial Jew was expressed somewhat informally in the synagogue, but assumed more formal expression elsewhere. Few if indeed any Jews sought relaxation in hunting or sports, but in Masonry, for instance, and in the non-Jewish eating and mutual-aid clubs which they joined, Jews often found a social life acceptable to them. There were, of course, a number of such societies which had no Jewish members, and Jews were certainly not welcome in every club. Most colonial Jews were humble immigrants, neither socially ready nor financially able to move in all social circles, while some clubs, even if they might have accepted Jews, were intended primarily for specific mercantile groups in which Jews were unrepresented. For example, the Fellowship Club of Newport, organized in 1752, was limited to men who were or had been masters of vessels. A mutual-aid society making provision for its indigent members or for their orphaned families, the Fellowship Club held meetings featuring much eating and drinking, but frowning upon cardplaying, gambling, and cursing. There were no Jewish members, since there were no Jewish ship captains in Newport.[13]

The degree to which anti-Jewish prejudices may have motivated the exclusion of Jews from various clubs is very difficult to determine. Eighteenth century Americans were still more often than not Americans "in becoming." They tended naturally enough to congregate in groups according to national origin, so that the Scots, the Irish, the English, the French, the Welsh, the Germans, and others all formed ethnic clubs meeting frequently for purposes of conviviality. The Jews were not exceptions, and like the other ethnic groups, felt more at home among their own. Newport Jewry, for instance, formed a purely social club of its own, and other Jewish communities too may have had similar societies, though no record of them has survived.[14]

The Newport club, established in 1761, met every Wednesday, in winters only. Winter was, of course, the slack season for merchant-shippers. The club's membership was limited to nine, a chairman and a secretary were elected for each month, and there was also a steward, Benjamin Myers, the beadle of the Jewish community. No one could become a member without the approval of the group as a whole, although guests were not excluded. From 5:00 to 8:00 the club regularly featured cardplaying for relatively low stakes. At 8:00 supper was served and followed by a toast of loyalty to the constituted authorities. "Conversation relating to synagogue affairs" appears to have been strictly prohibited—not an unusual provision. The Philosophical Society of Newport, whose members spent more time discussing privateering than philosophy, maintained similar strictures, and the Masons too prohibited quarreling over politics and religion. The typical colonial after all was not notable for his delicacy, and he might very well "behave unruly, curse, swear, or offer to fight," as the rules of the Newport Jewish club recognized. Nothing made for trouble more surely than discussions of religion, and club members wanted to avoid trouble. In fact, of course, all the members of the Newport Jewish club belonged to the local synagogue, whose building was under construction during the early 1760's, and disputes about the new building may have been anything but rare.[15]

However much his freedom of expression was restricted at club meetings, the Jewish businessman was subject to no such restraints during his travels. When on the road he whiled away his time in the inns by talking or arguing—even on subjects of religion and theology—with his Christian fellow travelers. To the Christian, the Jew was unfailingly an object of fascination. For the most part, however, the social life of the Jew was spent at home with his family or with groups of friends and relatives. Communities were small and internal dissension, which was hardly uncommon, did not keep people from meeting frequently at each other's homes and enjoying an active social life.

Peaks of sociability were occasioned by the holidays, most of which were celebrated with considerable merriment. Purim, for instance, provided a special opportunity for extra candles, cookies, tea, gifts, and strong drink. The holidays were good reason to drop all work and to vary the monotony of life by visits, especially to other towns or cities. Weddings and circumcisions, too, were occasions for elaborate celebration. Though some weddings are likely to have been held in one of the congregational buildings, for the most part congregants preferred to be married in their homes. Colonial hospitality was in general essentially home hospitality. When Hazzan Seixas traveled to Lancaster to officiate at a wedding there, a great deal of hospitality was certainly offered him and the Jews who came in from the countryside. Reading, Pennsylvania, may have sheltered only one or two Jewish families, but it was a great holiday for the well-to-do Jacob of Hickorytown and his daughter when they spent a week or so with Meyer Josephson in Reading. Hickorytown was a hamlet; Reading was a city of nearly a thousand souls! When the circumciser Abraham I. Abrahams of New York went to Newport to initiate a son of Aaron Lopez into the Abrahamitic covenant, the New Yorker was lavishly entertained by the grateful and generous Lopez. Even death could serve sociability. After funerals, when services were conducted at a home during the initial days of mourning, food was prepared, and the occasion was utilized to provide some social cheer. Visits from businessmen were also fillips to social life. On Moses Lopez' arrival at Charleston, South Carolina, with a cargo of goods in 1764, his fellow-Sephardi Isaac Da Costa would not hear of his staying at an inn. Da Costa insisted on taking Lopez to his home where he lodged and fed him for nearly two months.[16]

CHAPTER 59

CHANGES IN TRADITIONAL JUDAISM

In view of the sharp differences obtaining in general between European life and the American milieu, one might well ask whether there were in colonial times any intimations of the beginnings of Reform Judaism. The modern historian, influenced by concepts of religious evolution and fortified by the knowledge that hindsight has certain advantages over foresight, cannot be blamed if he is tempted to hazard the guess that the roots of ideological change in American Jewish religious life are to be found in the colonial experience. Certainly it seems logical and inevitable that "Orthodoxy," the only Jewish "denomination" of the prerevolutionary period, would have changed perceptibly on North American soil, thousands of miles away from the centers of traditional Judaism. How could Judaism have remained unaltered on the frontier of a new culture and a new civilization?

Colonial America's seven miniscule Jewish communities sustained themselves on the westernmost frontier of European Judaism, on the rim as it were of the Jewish culture-world, and America *was* different. Jews here encountered a new tongue, a different vocabulary, strange mores, and a foreign, conglomerate people. Then too, some of America's leaders in the two decades before the Revolution, men who set the tone of American thought and action, were not much interested in religion. America was simply not a religiously-oriented country like Spain and Portugal, or like the Germanies and the Slavic lands to the east where most of the Jews lived. The Jew did not stand out on these shores by virtue of a distinctive garb, and there were weaker social controls here. How many Jews in colonial America wore the traditional *peot* or earlocks?

All Jews were, to be sure, ideologically committed to observance of the laws and commandments, but there can be no question, even so, that the religious regimen tended to be less weighty here, that here the Jews more easily disregarded the traditional consensus of practice and of rigorous adherence to the "canon law," the halakah. The "rabbi" who contributed in 1711 to the building of a New York church dedicated to the worship of the Trinity never stopped to ask himself whether he was committing a sin or not. When he shipped a dozen New Testaments to the northern frontier, it certainly never occurred to Hayman Levy to ask himself whether this sale was religiously permissible or not. We know that itinerant Jewish businessmen, the younger ones especially, had no hesitation in ignoring the dietary laws, and Aaron Lopez sent a son out to board for five weeks with a Christian farmer—where the boy certainly could not have kept kosher. Would European Jews have been likely to do as the Lopezes did: maintain close ties to the Lucenas, New Christian refugees from Portugal who here on the free soil of America had voluntarily chosen to remain Christians rather than return to the Jewish faith of their fathers? It might be argued that the Lopezes retained their commercial connections with the Lucenas because they were cousins, but the Ashkenazic Naphtali Hart also did business with the Lucenas. The Gratzes, fresh though they were from the stalwart orthodoxy of Silesia and the Polish border, cultivated David Franks, who had intermarried and was rearing a family of Christians. Or witness the case of the learned Mordecai Moses Mordecai. Deeply rooted though he was in East European traditional observances, he became a member of the Freemasons. An extant portrait reveals him sparsely bearded, sporting the Masonic emblem on his chest and around his waist a lambskin apron on which was inscribed in Hebrew the biblical phrase, "Let there be light." Mordecai's orthodoxy, his belief and practice, were surely right wing, but even so, he was no obscurantist.[1]

There is, moreover, every reason to believe that while North American Jews paid lip service to the rabbinic scholarship which was with very few exceptions reverentially admired in every Old World community, they were actually little concerned with it. Jewish learning was not pursued in the slightest degree among adults, nor were there in America rabbis, rabbinical courts, rabbinical leadership, or talmudic academies. It is true that surveillance of the negligent and the belligerent was ever-present, but sanctions against the derelict were imposed only under extreme provocation. A reluctant public opinion was slow to muster its forces against the lax. Because the Jews in America looked upon themselves, unconsciously at least, as an ethnic rather than a purely religious community, they were not bent on excising those who were careless in matters of ritual. Observance here, though sincere, tended to be superficial, and in any event, compliance with the demands of tradition was not supported by the power of the State, unlike many European lands where a grant of privileges or a charter invested the Jewish community with a governmental authority in matters of religious discipline. Haym Salomon summed it up very well when he told an uncle in England that there was *vinig yidishkayt* (little Jewishness) in America.[2]

Certainly there was in America little of what Haym Salomon, with his Polish background in mind, would have called Jewishness, but does this add up to Reform Judaism? Departures from rite and custom were, after all, never deliberate, never calculated. There is no evidence at all that the Jews of colonial America ever proposed or contemplated changes in synagogal or home ritual. It must not be forgotten that they lived in a land where not only the established churches, but equally, all the Dissenters were orthodox Christians. There was simply no liberal religious pattern to follow. The American Revolution which burst forth in 1775 was essentially a conservative one, while the French Revolution and the Cult of Reason were still years away. The American Jews had no intention of breaking with the past. Europeans in origin and orientation with an old-country mind-set, they faced east, not west; they were in constant touch with the great and orthodox community across the Atlantic, and what orthodoxy they themselves had was constantly reinforced by a steady stream of immigrants from the reservoirs of transatlantic piety. The lay leaders of every American Jewish community, with the possible exception of Savannah, were foreign-born. From the vantage point of

Europe of course, the tidewater Jews were frontiersmen, but from the vantage point of America, they were urban easterners, their backs to the west, their arms eagerly stretched out to their fellow Jews abroad. In the towns and cities of British North America they made every effort to duplicate the Old World religious environment in which they had been bred.

The colonial Jew never felt the need to create a new religious denomination. Once he had adapted his dress, language, and mannerisms to the American pattern and had conformed to the superficial amenities of the Gentile world around him, he was accepted and left alone. The Judaism he knew harbored no abuses which he felt impelled to challenge. He suffered oppression from no synagogal plutocracy or oligarchy entrenched behind privilege; he encountered no unacceptable forms of congregational polity, no sacrosanct hierarchy, no untenable theology, no strain on belief and credulity. He was in any event far too busy adjusting himself to his surroundings to think of much else beyond making a livelihood and securing a minimal traditional education for his children. The typical American Jew was anything but an intellectual; there was for him no impulse to create a new faith, to reject the old because of the onslaught of modern ideas. He was virtually untouched by secularism or the beginnings of the new science with their devastating effect on traditional concepts. The new world of thought was eyed warily; it was deemed Christian, and before the older generation of Jews would open their hearts and minds to it, Christianity would have to demonstrate its good faith to the people whom it had been rejecting for sixteen hundred years. The fact is that even here in America, the Jew had to endure disabilities, and these disabilities, however minor, helped keep him loyal to traditional Judaism.

Still, in their religious life the Jews of North America were not left untouched by their Gentile neighbors. Despite American Jewry's conscious striving to remain European in its religious loyalties, despite the fact that few if any Jews here were wittingly bending their energies to acculturate themselves religiously, something did happen to the faith the immigrants had brought with them from Europe. In transitu the impulse to observe the ritual in all its detail weakened appreciably. It is true there was nothing by way of programmatic change here, but neither was there any strengthening of the older religio-cultural mode of living. Jews here remained comfortably observant, but within the prescribed framework of the life-cycle ceremonies of the home and the synagogue, the typical Jew allowed himself some latitude in his observance. His associates, he knew, were permissive; they would tolerate whatever he did, so long as he took care not to outrage the religious consensus.

Though a Reform Judaism could not have been farther from his mind, the colonial Jew actually was evolving something novel: a religion of salutary neglect. He understood that he could be observant without being overly scrupulous, that he could cut corners with impunity, and that however desultory and inadequate his practice of the faith, it would meet with indulgence from his fellow-Jews. Unless he was obstreperous, they would impose on him no harsh sanctions for his lack of meticulosity. Even had they chided him for his slack observance, he would not have denied the authority of the Torah; he would simply have excused himself on the ground of expediency, and they would have understood and forgiven him. He would never have been forgiven, however, had he dared to exculpate himself by rationalizing his neglect as a principled denial of halakic authority.

What American Jews very probably did not understand was that America was creeping up on them. Thus, when they felt and satisfied a need for intelligible private devotions by translating the liturgy into English, they never thought to dilute the tradition. Prayers in the vernacular were, after all, only a minor concession to the demands of the environment; they were scarcely uncommon in any European land. And yet the slightest deviation from tradition and authority *was* a blow at orthodoxy.

To some extent the very structure of the colonial Jewish community, its unitary character, jeopardized the tradition. The old way of life was threatened by virtue of the fact that there was but one basic religious institution in the Jewish community: the synagogue. The American synagogue became almost comparable to the Protestant church, which was primarily a one-day-a-week influence. Back in Europe a host of pious associations of every type and description completely enveloped nearly every Jew; giving play and opportunity to his every need and interest, these *hebrot* guaranteed he would remain in the Jewish ambit, a Jewish context, twenty-four hours of every day. It was not that way in America.

America's political stirrings, too, had their impact on Jewish life. As far back as 1739 Abigail Franks had written a letter venturing the opinion that Judaism was "clogged" with superstitions and that she would welcome the rise of a Jewish Luther or Calvin. (Yet in her personal life and conduct she observed the traditional ritual meticulously and urged her children not to deviate from orthodox practice.) Beginning no later than the 1760's many Americans, even those who would later support the Loyalist cause, were overt in their rebellion against traditional political authority, and political rebellion can easily spill over into the religious realm. The younger generation of Jews, rallying to the banners of the Whig autonomists, certainly reserved for themselves, if no more than tacitly, the right to freedom of thought and action in religious and ritual matters. Solomon Simson, who was already nearly forty in 1776 and would become outstanding for his political liberalism in the postrevolutionary period, may well have nursed unorthodox thoughts about religion during his first four decades. It was, in short, inevitable that for many Jews political liberalism—an emphasis on the right of both the individual and the group to work out their own destiny in a democratic manner —would eventuate ultimately in religious protest, change, and radicalism. To be sure, nothing of the sort achieved expression during the colonial period, but by the turn of the century the permissive observance of the colonial community had tended to become indifference and assimilation.[3]

Declining standards in observance and faith can be stemmed only by reform, if not within the pale of the canon law, then outside it. Reform of any sort would find no footing in colonial days. It would have to wait for its manifestation outside the Law until the generation of the 1820's and the emergence of a metropolitan, cultured, deistic spirit among the Jews of Charleston. Its manifestation within the Law would be postponed until the development of the Conservative movement at the end of the nineteenth century.

The simple fact, then, that there were no substantial modifications of Orthodoxy—indeed scarcely any intimations of change— during the colonial period is a striking evidence of the strength of

Jewish tradition and its appeal for the tidewater synagoguegoer. Prior to 1776 the typical American Jew was an orthodox religionist with American overtones and manners. He had established for himself a most satisfactory balance between the religio-cultural heritage of European Jewry and an American way of life. That this balance ever would or could be shaken is unlikely to have entered his mind as he repaired to the synagogue he had fashioned for the glory of his "holy religion."

CHAPTER 60

CHARITY

Society as the Jew conceives it, according to a rabbinic tradition which dates back more than two thousand years, rests on three pillars: on the study of God's law, on prayer, and on deeds of loving-kindness. In Jewish lore Abraham, the first Hebrew, serves as a prototype of the generous and hospitable man. His tent, Jews said, had been open on all four sides, that he might the more quickly and eagerly welcome weary travelers. And the tombstone of the biblical patriarch's latter-day namesake, Abraham Rodrigues Rivera of Newport, recalled:

> Beneficent as Abraham he constantly relieved
> The woes of poor and needy, afflicted and bereaved.

The epitaph prepared for Aaron Hart of Three Rivers, Canada, is equally revelatory of the emphasis colonial Jews laid on philanthropy:

> Here lieth the remains of Aaron Hart,
> Esquire, obit 28 Decr, 1800, AE 76:
>
> He who supported the aged and infirm, who
> alleviated the wants and lightened the miseries
> of the poor.
>
> The man possessed of these virtues requires no
> other testimony of his departed worth to be en-
> graved on this stone, placed over his tomb by
> his four sons, Moses, Ezekiel, Benjamin, and
> Alexander Hart.[1]

Although the Jew saw charity—"deeds of lovingkindness"—as a virtue important in itself, he did not practice it for its own sake only, for the succor it offered the unfortunate. There were other considerations. The pious Jew was not unmindful, of course, that the practice of charity brought rewards in heaven, but if no more than subconsciously, he was moved to benevolence by still another important concern: the typical colonial Jew was without exception native to a land which imposed disabilities on its Jewish residents; he knew only too well that a turn of the wheel of fortune might tomorrow bankrupt and impoverish *him*. He helped others so that he and his children might be helped if they should ever need the support of their fellow Jews. He accepted without demur the obligations of kinship. "It is our duty to assist the distressed," wrote a colonial Jewish congregation in an official communication. The Newporters, appealing to New York's Shearith Israel for aid in building a synagogue, were confident the New Yorkers would not be indifferent to "the extensive usefullness of a charity like this, for which we now supplicate assistance." [2]

It was also a fact not to be denied, that all Jews everywhere recognized the right of a petitioner to demand and receive help from a fellow Jew. The man at the door was a claimant, not a suppliant! And finally—this too was a weighty consideration—Jews helped one another because they feared for their own status if they deserted their poor and threw them on the mercies of the hard-pressed non-Jewish authorities.

Charity in colonial days was largely under church control. Every religious community was expected to take care of its own, and help for the poor and the suffering had for centuries been the responsibility of Protestant and Catholic churches. The West India Company was well within its rights when it insisted in the charter granted the Jews of New Netherland in February 1655 that incoming Jews "shall not become a charge upon the deaconry or the Company." Two months later, in April the company reiterated this demand: "The poor among them [the Jews] shall not become a burden to the Company or to the community, but be supported by their own [Jewish] nation." [3]

The basic categories of relief and help which seventeenth and eighteenth century European Jewish communities typically provided were food, fuel, clothing, ransoming of captives, education for the poor, dowries for impoverished girls, temporary shelter for transients, loans, provision for orphans and the widowed, care for the sick who had no means of their own, and burial of the dead. In Europe, and also in the metropolitan communities of South America and the West Indies, such welfare benefits were furnished in large measure by Jewish brotherhoods, semiautonomous religious societies specializing in specific aspects of philanthropy. If an organization of this type ever existed in colonial New York—the sources are very meager here—it may have been an education society, or possibly a pious association to attend the sick and the dying and to bury the dead. An education society would have followed the example of its London Sephardic prototype in supplying orphaned youngsters with schooling and clothes, and subsequently apprenticing them to master artisans.[4]

CONGREGATIONAL CHARITY AND THE BUDGET

Non-Jews in the colonies had a series of autonomous, ethnic mutual-aid societies as well as a number of public and semipublic relief agencies to help the poor and the unfortunate. There is no proof, however, that any colonial North American Jewish community ever established even one such association. There was simply no need for it inasmuch as the congregations, small in size and providing all types of social-welfare relief, functioned themselves in effect as mutual-aid societies.[5]

Although personal charity, the kindness and generosity one man would show another in need, was never absent, charity operated mostly on a congregational and institutional level. In Recife and London private help had been prohibited, and it may be assumed that it was frowned upon in most North American Jewish communities as well. The mass of American Jews lacked the means to duplicate philanthropic contributions.

The members of the various North American Jewish communities found it difficult indeed to keep their synagogues solvent, for a considerable part of the annual congregational expenditures went for *obras pias*, pious charitable works. In New York, for example, during the first half of the eighteenth century, a period for which budgets are available, Shearith Israel never invested less than a tenth of its income in charitable activities and not infrequently as much as a third for that purpose. In 1740–1741 Parnas Samuel Levy certified that of the £185 expended that fiscal year, £70 had gone "to the poor." Colonial Jewry would seem thus to have reflected the prevalent general pattern, for the authorities of colonial towns typically allocated anywhere from 9 to 33 percent of their budgetary resources to poor relief.[6]

How Charitable Were They?

Were Jews, in the care they gave their poor, more generous than the different Christian groups? There is no question that the Jews did succor their own, but this is not to say that the Christians, particularly the smaller sects among them, did not do equally well. The matter awaits further study.

By the standards of their time the Jews were certainly generous, but it should be borne in mind that "big giving" by the rich was not characteristic of that age. The fact that Jews were jailed as debtors suggests that their coreligionists hesitated to secure their release if large sums were involved, though such prisoners were offered a measure of relief by the Jewish community. North American Jewry had learned to give because of the help received from other Jewish communities in the islands, Surinam, and England; one-third of the costs for the building of the New York synagogue had come from abroad, particularly from those communities with which the New Yorkers maintained economic relations.[7]

If a community was to thrive, however, in the final analysis its members could not depend on the largesse of fellow-Jews in distant towns and countries. The help which came from others was material, but a community survived by virtue of its generosity to itself, by virtue of the loyalty and openhandedness with which its members supported their own local synagogue and cemetery. All Jews, even the poorest—some of whom were themselves the objects of help and charity—contributed to building campaigns. Big givers bought cornerstones; there were four to six cornerstones in every communal building and annex. The rich gave to defray the expenses of providing windows—devoid of pictorial representation—and lecterns. They donated gifts of candelabra, pentateuchal scrolls, and richly decorated cloths. The women made coverings for the Torahs and for the ark and the lectern. During the holidays when the synagogues were full, the rich, possibly not without ostentation, would outbid one another in vying for honors and offering large sums of money, though the poor gave more generously in proportion to their means than the rich.

Generosity was also exemplified in legacies, particularly from women. It should be remembered that most legacies of course, whether from men or women, were accompanied by the expectation that prayers would be recited for the deceased; the donors were concerned about the welfare of their souls after death. Some testators left money outright; others specified their bequests should be used for the purchase of a Torah scroll, for the Jewish poor, or for widows and orphans. One of the leaders of Congregation Shearith Israel at the turn of the eighteenth century left £20 "to the poor of the Jewish nation in New York." Another man, interested in religious education, bequeathed £50 to the local Jewish school on condition that it provide Hebrew instruction for the children of those who were in straitened circumstances.[8]

ADMINISTRATION OF CHARITIES

As already mentioned elsewhere, it was the parnas' duty to investigate the pleas of suppliants and to dole out money as needed. In general he had the right to give small sums without consultation, but he usually consulted with his board when the amounts involved were of any magnitude. The task of merely looking after the local poor and providing for transients must have been a very onerous one, and that is why busy and responsible tradesmen were so reluctant to accept the dubious honor of a synagogal presidency. Apparently the administration of charities was in the hands of no committee or formal organization. The one exception to this rule was the committee—usually one man—to provide for the needs of petitioning communities in the Holy Land.[9]

SOURCES FOR RAISING MONEY FOR CHARITY

Most of the money employed for alms and grants came out of the sedakah, the communal treasury, though from time to time special eleemosynary offerings were made at worship services, and funds for Palestinian needs, too, were occasionally raised in that fashion. Subscription lists for fuel made the rounds of the congregants, while charity boxes were commonly affixed to the walls of the synagogue, and portable boxes were circulated at the cemetery during funerals. The sums collected at burials were insubstantial to be sure—even when an outstanding citizen died, the amount raised never exceeded a pound or two—but it all helped. Legacies left specially for the poor were an additional source of income. All these monies were deposited in the general treasury, which in turn handed out doles as needed.[10]

COMMUNAL CHARITY IN ACTION

FREE EDUCATION, LOANS, AND PENSIONS

Customarily, Jewish children were educated at the expense of their parents, but it was a well-established tradition that no male child should go without some religious training, even if the community had to underwrite it. In colonial congregations, therefore, free instruction was provided for children without means of their own.[11]

Money was lent members on occasion, and it is quite possible that with such small sums—and also the credit extended by an enterprising and kindly fellow congregant—a man could open a modest shop in a country town. It is a matter of record that the New York synagogue gave Michael Judah of Norwalk, Connecticut, such a loan —£5—in 1744 or 1745. When Judah died over forty years later, he left a sizeable share of his estate "to the sinagouge in Newyork, and . . . to the poor widows and orphans of my own nation, living in Newyork." [12]

Pensions were provided for salaried communal officials and their widows. The congregation realized their modest incomes would not enable these synagogal employees to save much for their old age; so following retirement, some of the salaried officials were carried for years. This was true particularly of widows, who were supported until death unless relatives could assume the burden of their care. Thus pensions were granted as an act of grace, and they ceased when the pensioner found other means of support. Pensions, that is to say, were charity, not part of a system which made automatic provision for faithful servants of the community. [13]

PENSIONS FOR THE POOR

No enduring pauperism appears to have developed in the colonial Jewish community. The poor were mostly respectable middle-class people who had come down in the world. They, too, received pensions from the New York synagogue, though pension may be too dignified a term. The congregation gave such unfortunates a stipulated amount held sufficient to provide for their modest needs. Though the word pension is one the congregation itself occasionally used, it was actually a dole given regularly out of synagogal funds. Among the beneficiaries of such help in New York was David Hays, who had once served as president of Shearith Israel. Hays and his wife were carried by the congregation for at least two years.

In the same manner a number of the congregation's poor were cared for over a period of years. There was no fixed amount and each case was decided on its own merits. The sums expended were also determined by the state of the treasury; when there was less money in the sedakah, the grants were less. No distinction was made between petitioners of Iberian and Central European background, and the fact that all major recipients of aid in 1740–1741 were Spanish-Portuguese is a sufficient commentary on their reputed wealth.

In Newport, Martha Lazarus was carried on the charity rolls for the most part from about 1770 to her death in 1787. Hannah Louzada remained on the alms roster of the New York synagogue from about 1756 to 1774. The congregation, making efforts to relieve itself of her support, sent her to New Jersey and to Lancaster, no doubt to relatives. When she found herself in difficulties, probably through attempting to run her own shop, the congregation paid her debts and also saw to it that a son of hers was supported by contributions from a relative and from the sedakah. One old couple, too infirm to keep house for themselves, wished to enter a boardinghouse and petitioned the New York congregation for a supplementary grant, but their petition was refused, although such a procedure was not at all uncommon in the general community. One may be sure, however, that the chronically ill who were not ambulatory would have been provided with custodial care by the congregation. The London Jewish community had developed a system of life annuities for members on the basis of monies turned over to the congregation, and the Recife community in Brazil may also have had something similar, but so far as the minutes show, nothing of the sort ever rose in New York.[14]

It is patently very difficult to distinguish between charity to the poor and a pension. Under all circumstances, however, the genteel poor who belonged to the congregation were cared for indefinitely, sometimes till their death. The congregation would provide all types of assistance for any poor person, member, pensioner, or transient in need. A survey of the services rendered indicates that they included cash, food, wood for fuel, clothes, linen, transportation to foreign parts, fitting out to sea, board for the transient and the sick, mazzot, rent money, medicine, nursing, the ministrations of a physician, and free burial.[15]

REDEMPTION OF CAPTIVES

It was only on the rarest occasions that American congregations were asked to respond to appeals from captives, though ransoming captives persisted as a very important charity in the European lands where Barbary pirates were active into the nineteenth century. Victims of the Inquisition who emigrated were much more in evidence in this country, but they frequently received aid from their American relatives, for the most part merchant-shippers. American Jews did, of course, pray regularly for the release of imprisoned Marranos, and when some of these émigrés actually made their way to these shores, they were showered with attention. So far as we know, however, such newcomers required little or no financial help. On occasion they brought substantial means along with them, and they often had colonial relatives who kept them from dependence on congregational funds.

Imprisoned debtors may have been considered captives who merited redemption, but no systematic effort was made to release them. Those already in jail were, it is true, supplied with money, food, and religious services, such as circumcision for their children, but only in rare instances were the debts of individuals settled in order to forestall their imprisonment.[16]

SICK CARE AND THE HOSPICE

It has been repeatedly pointed out that physical and spiritual solicitude for the sick and the dying and proper provision for burial of the deceased ranked among the most important religious and social-welfare activities of the European Jewish community, which maintained such services through pious associations, holy brotherhoods, and local hospices. The responsibilities which fell to these societies and institutions in Europe were assumed in this country by the congregation itself.

The desire for kosher food, the craving for Jewish fellowship, and the low state of the workhouses and public hospitals operated for sailors and transients as well as the local sick—all these prevented Jews from looking very far beyond the congregational ambit. North American communities supported no hospices as such, but kosher boardinghouses subject to congregational supervision served that purpose. Widows took in Jewish boarders, and to augment their salaries, functionaries like the shohet and the beadle were also ready to accept lodgers. The benefits an invalid received in such a home would thus include nursing. The care accorded one ailing stranger in New

York is summed up eloquently enough in a laconic bookkeeping entry: "To cash for lodging, boarding, doctering, and burying, Solomon Solomons, £23, 8, 10." [17]

BURIAL

It was the congregation too which, without the mediation of private agencies, undertook interment of the dead. During their last moments all members of the congregation were provided with spiritual care, prayers and such like, and when death came the ritual cleansing, dressing of the body, and all cemetery needs were in the hands of the congregation. Those who had means bore the costs of their own funerals and all else that was involved, but an indigent paid nothing for precisely the same funeral, and no one was charged for the grave itself. The expenses of digging, of supplying the gravediggers with liquor, of the linen, of the coffin, and of horsehire for the hearse —all were met for the poor from the sedakah. Even good burial garments were provided if the deceased had been too poor to afford them himself. On occasion a pauper's funeral might cost as much as £9—no small sum even in local currency.[18]

OVERSEAS AND PALESTINE RELIEF

Neither European nor West Indian Jewry hesitated to invite their North American coreligionists to relieve communities which had been visited with misfortune. In 1775 for instance, London's Bevis Marks Congregation appealed to the New Yorkers on behalf of Anatolian Jews whose homes and synagogues had been gutted by fire: "As on all other occasions you have proven your zeal and fervor to help in urgent cases, we recommend the present case for your consideration." Obviously it was not the first plea for overseas relief Shearith Israel had ever received, but this time the New Yorkers did not respond, for the Revolution was about to erupt and the congregation was disturbed for its own future.[19]

Palestine was the prime beneficiary of overseas relief. European Jewries in distress could and did turn to the large metropolitan communities on their own continent, but they had no well-organized system of apostles or God's messengers (*shaddarim*) such as had been developed by the four "Holy Cities" of Palestine: Hebron, Jerusalem, Tiberias, and Safed. For centuries the Palestinian Jews had lived on the charity of the Diaspora, and their eager emissaries went to the farthest corners of the earth to garner funds. One wonders how much was left after their traveling expenses had been met, but some of the emissaries certainly provided for themselves most handsomely, and judging from past scandals, there was maladministration even of the funds that did reach Palestine. European and American Jews were well aware of all this, but they never ceased bending all efforts to help their fellow Jews in the holy cities.

Palestine was dear to the Diaspora. In Sephardic parlance she was *Terra Santa*, the Holy Land to which in God's good time all Jews everywhere would be restored. The prayer books of traditionalist Jews even today are filled with pious hopes for the speedy advent of the Messiah and Jewry's restoration in glory to the Promised Land. Those hopes were very real to the Diaspora, even to Jews who lived within the security of the Dutch and British Empires, but if a Jew could not or would not return to Palestine, he could at least support those already there, those who were studying God's word and interceding for their fellow-believers at the graves of the patriarchs in Machpelah.

The Amsterdam Jewish community evolved an elaborate apparatus to collect funds for the Holy Land, an apparatus which included an overall treasurer, several fraternities, and special days set aside for fund raising. The London Sephardim, too, appointed a special officer for *Terra Santa*, while the Jews of Recife periodically took up a collection for the land of Israel and elected a "Gabay de Terra Santa," a Holy Land treasurer, to send the Palestinians money and sugar, which was almost as good as gold. The midsummer Sabbath of Consolation, the Saturday after the synagogal rites of mourning for the Fall of Jerusalem on the Ninth of Ab, was a day set aside in Brazil to pledge funds for the needs of Palestine. During the following century Curaçao could boast of two brotherhoods devoted to the support of Hebron Jewry.[20]

Communication between Palestine and the North American colonies was usually indirect, carried on by means of correspondence through the London Sephardic community. Though there were times when the emissaries sent out by the Palestinians wrote letters directly to individual American Jews, for the most part, they worked through Bevis Marks. That is why in 1761 the London Sephardim wrote to acquaint Shearith Israel "of the wretched and deplorable condition of our poor brethren" in Safed and enclosed a Palestinian appeal for money to help that "holy and suffering Kehila" which had been ravaged by an earthquake in 1760. The synagogues and the school had been damaged, many houses had been destroyed, and 160 people lay "buried beneath the ruins." There was a "great necessity for immediate action."

More commonly, funds were solicited from colonial Jews through the dispatch of circulars, printed form letters with a blank space for the address. Such printed "general epistles" were usually sent out to America by an agent from some European city. Evidently the more responsible American Jewish merchants were known by name in Europe, and these letters were accordingly addressed to them. A Hebrew circular might be used for years, perhaps with only slight changes in wording, so that a printed appeal from Hebron, apparently first initiated in 1763, was still in use as late as 1771.

This Hebron appeal was probably typical. In bombastic, almost unintelligible phraseology, the signers, the distinguished scholars of Hebron, dwelt heartrendingly on the expulsion, devastation, and death which lay in wait for their community. Hebron Jewry had fallen heavily in debt; unless it was redeemed, the worst was to be expected. Copies of the appeal were sent to Michael Gratz of Philadelphia and Hayman Levy of New York in 1763. Daniel Gomez probably received a copy about 1770, and Isaac Hart of Rhode Island was sent one a year later. They all responded to the plea and undertook to serve as local collectors for the Hebron sufferers, unquestionably with the blessings of their respective communities. The usual procedure was to make personal solicitations or to invite offerings in the synagogue on a specified date. Apparently Gomez was the general treasurer for North America, and the sums collected from New York, Newport, and Philadelphia were forwarded to Europe for transmission to Palestine; the channels for dispatching funds abroad were no doubt well-established. The New Yorkers, one notes with interest, gave the most money, the Newport Jews subscribed somewhat less, and the Philadelphians raised a little more than one-third of what New York Jewry contributed.

During the year that Daniel Gomez served as the American agent for Hebron, the New Yorkers received a handwritten communication on behalf of Jerusalem. This Hebrew appeal had no doubt been sent from some European city, probably Constantinople, by Jerusalem emissaries empowered to collect money to help pay their community's debts and the exorbitant interest charges. In much the same spirit as the Hebron appeal of 1763, the letter asked for the "redemption of the captives" who were threatened with death by their vindictive creditors. Those who would contribute liberally were promised heavenly rewards for their generosity.[21]

Messengers of God

Much of the money with which Palestinian Jewry supported itself came most likely by way of correspondence with Diaspora communities. Funds raised by a local volunteer "Holy Land" deputy were nearly all profit, since very little expense was involved. Nevertheless, following a centuries-old tradition, the Holy Cities of the Promised Land also sent out emissaries (*shaddarim*) to collect money for the Palestinian rabbinical schools which distributed doles to their students and scholars. Often too, as has been noted, they appealed for contributions to meet a special crisis: the devastation of an earthquake or the threatened imprisonment of leaders for communal debt. The *shaddarim* must have been men of great intrepidity and endurance to make the long sea voyages from the Near East and back again; interrupting their wanderings with long recuperative rests, they kept traveling for years at a time.

They were given preferential treatment, these Palestinians on God's business. Remaining in the larger cities for stays of several months, they solicited donations, preached, gave advice in ritual matters, reawakened the colonists' latent and nostalgic respect for Jewish learning, and then moved on to the next community. All their expenses, including transportation, were borne by the host congregation. From New York they would normally leave for Newport which sheltered a well-to-do and generous group of Jews. Or if they landed in Newport, their next stop, logically, would be New York which sheltered the largest Jewry on the continent.

The first known Palestinian in America, perhaps one of the *shaddarim*, was Moses Malki, who arrived on these shores in 1759. A native of Safed and a member of a scholarly family in whose ranks well-known Palestinian apostles were to be found, Moses Malki himself was apparently an ordained rabbi. He had not come here to collect money for the victims of the Safed earthquake, but manifestly for some other purpose, since he was already in New York when that catastrophe took place. Malki spent eighteen weeks in New York, moved on then to Newport, and on leaving Rhode Island, may well have embarked for the West Indies.[22]

Samuel Ha-Cohen

Two Jews from Constantinople who landed at New York in 1768 may have been on a mission of mercy for their coreligionists in the Holy Land, but so far as the extant records indicate, the only undoubtedly authentic Palestinian messenger to come to North America in colonial days was Rabbi Samuel Ha-Cohen, who had been sent out on a fund-raising mission by the Jews of Hebron in 1772. It is beyond question that the problem which plagued them the most was the repayment of their debts. This problem had become acute in 1763, and ever since then the threat of imprisonment and the enslavement of women and children had hung over Hebron. Interest charges of twenty percent made it impossible for the community to meet its obligations to its Arab and Turkish creditors who were so demanding that the ritual silver of the synagogue had to be pawned to help make payments.

Ha-Cohen went to Amsterdam where the Spanish-Portuguese leaders sponsored his task by authorizing him to print an appeal for funds to the American Jewish communities. From Amsterdam he went to London, and there in May 1773 the Sephardim wrote a letter introducing him to the American congregations. In all probability Ha-Cohen spent part of 1773 and 1774 touring Surinam and the Caribbean in search of funds. April 1774 found him ready to sail from Barbados for North America, and by June 1775 he was in Newport as an honored guest under Isaac Hart's roof—at community expense of course. Early in September Ha-Cohen was shipped back to London; he had had to bypass America's most important city, New York, since the Americans had taken up arms against the British, and the Jews wanted him out of the war zone. New York agreed to bear half the expense of his Newport sojourn and his transportation, which totalled over £31, and he was sent on to London. His mission in this country proved a failure because of the "calamities of the times." [23]

Palestinian Transients

Hakam Ha-Cohen was unquestionably an authentic collector for Hebron; Malki may or may not have been a "messenger of God" for Safed; and there were probably other "apostles" who came west to the Americas. Carigal, the most famous Palestinian to reach these shores in prerevolutionary days, certainly had functioned in the past as an authentic *shaddar*, though there is no indication that on his arrival in North America he was representing anyone but himself. The rabbi had received a good education in rabbinic law. Ordained at the age of seventeen, Carigal was already on the road about the year 1753. He was then almost twenty-one years of age.[24]

On that first trip Carigal set out as a fund raiser for his native Hebron and traveled through the Near and Middle East and then on to Europe. By 1762 he had made his way to Curaçao where he remained till 1764 as rabbi of the community and as head of the fine talmudic academy he opened there. On Curaçao he was presumably able to collect funds for Hebron and was certainly successful in saving a considerable sum for himself. In 1764 he set out on his return to Hebron—eleven years after having left Palestine. The historian cannot help wondering how his wife fared during his long absence!

By 1768 Carigal was back on the highways and seaways. This time, he was bent on a mission for himself and in all likelihood was looking for a permanent position where he could settle down and bring his family. For two and one-half years he remained in London, where he probably learned to speak English, but he was in Jamaica by 1771 and from there was able to send substantial sums back home to his wife and two children. The following year found him in Philadelphia. After a stay of perhaps a month he went on to New York.

The New Yorkers sheltered and supported him for five and one-half months and then in 1773 dispatched him with due courtesy, one may be sure, and also with a measure of relief to Newport.

In Newport Carigal met and established a friendship with the Christian Hebraist and Orientalist Ezra Stiles. It is in the diary of the garrulous Pastor Stiles that one learns a great deal about Carigal —that "ingenious and sensible man" as he called him. After a stay of nearly five months in Newport, Carigal set sail for Surinam and later for Barbados, where he was appointed rabbi in 1774. Having finally found a resting place after all his wanderings, he was now ready to bring his wife and children from Hebron, but was stricken with disease in 1777 and buried in the island's famous cemetery. He had not yet reached his forty-fifth year.[25]

Non-Palestinian Transients

On July 5, 1783, Stiles recorded in his diary that he had met six "rabbies" at Newport. Among them were two Ashkenazim, Moses bar David and Tobiah ben Judah Loew. He also mentioned another Ashkenazi, whom he denominated "a man of sobriety" but not a rabbi, Abraham Levi of Lissa, Poland. During his Newport sojourn in the spring of 1770 Levi boarded at the shohet's house and was, incidentally, fitted for a fine garment of silk camlet. The bill—it came to nearly £19—was charged to a congregant, but one suspects that Yeshuat Israel Congregation paid for it ultimately. It may be, one writer has suggested, that Levi had quit Lissa after the conflagration which destroyed her Jewish quarter in 1767 and that he had come to America in search of a place to settle down. More probably, however, he was a transient, a respectable schnorrer, traveling all over the world, like so many other displaced Jews, at the expense of the long-suffering Jewish communities he visited. From Newport he was ready to move on to Jamaica, but before his ship sailed from New York, he wrote a thank-you note to the Newporters Aaron Lopez and Jacob R. Rivera. They had given him letters of introduction and no doubt something more substantial during his stay in town. His letters from the Rivera-Lopez clan had won him many courtesies from those to whom he presented them in New York. The thank-you letter to his Newport friends was written in Hebrew and Yiddish, and it is likely that Myers, the shohet, translated it for Levi's Sephardic benefactors.[26]

Much the same pattern is evident in the stories of the two Ashkenazic rabbis, Moses bar David from Apta, Little Poland, and Tobiah ben Judah Loew from somewhere near Cracow. Moses bar David, whom Stiles characterized a cabbalist and "a learned Jew," stayed five weeks in Newport as the guest of the Jewish community before leaving for the West Indies. Stiles reported his arrival in 1772; Tobiah ben Judah Loew came to town the following year from London. He, too, was a man of scholarly pretensions—Stiles thought him "a great cabbalist and philosopher"—and proudly boasted of his descent from two of European Jewry's greatest figures: the eleventh century French biblical and talmudic commentator Rabbi Solomon ben Isaac (Rashi) and the sixteenth century East European talmudist Rabbi Solomon Luria. Rabbi Tobiah, following his arrival in New York from London, had rested for two weeks at Mrs. Hays's kosher boardinghouse and was then given enough money by Shearith Israel to move on to Philadelphia whose Jewish community took care of his needs for about a month. He met the Gratzes there, and they gave him letters of introduction to Newport Jewry, whose guest he remained for some two months. Before leaving Newport he too sent a Yiddish bread-and-butter note to thank all who had entertained him. A letter of introduction from Lopez had brought him special courtesies from the captain of the ship that was about to hoist anchor for Jamaica. Tobiah carried with him a Hebrew and English letter from Stiles who had commissioned him to deliver it to Carigal, then in Surinam.[27]

In June 1774 Stiles reported the arrival of one "Rabbi Bosquila," a native of Smyrna. Bosquila, who had lived for many years in London, claimed to be a rabbi and showed Stiles a rabbinical ordination certificate, but admitted he had "not read the Talmud." His academic specialties, he told the Newport clergyman, were the Bible and the cabbalistic *Zohar*. Stiles realized the man was no rabbinic scholar and wrote, "He is of contracted and limited literature." Bosquila, according to Stiles, "for many years has followed traffic and laid aside his rabbinical studies." Obviously he was in America either to carry on business or to beg and is certainly identical with the Aaron

Bosqualo who arrived a month later in New York as a petitioner for charity. The North Americans treated him generously and courteously, paid his board, and then provided him with transportation to Curaçao. He was a married man, aged sixty-one, wandering from town to town and country to country.[28]

Jewish transients on these shores were not comparable to the non-Jewish vagrants who roamed North America, nor were they comparable to the Jewish beggars found in relatively large numbers in Europe. There were thousands of Jews constantly on the road in the Old World; they were victims of wars and persecutions, penniless, true paupers broken on the wheel of fortune. Fed for a night, they were housed in a *hekdesh*, a dirty hospice, and then carried by cart to the next village which sheltered a Jewish community. In America, however, there were apparently no Jewish vagrants. The local poor were kept in town and maintained there, while transients, whether of high or low degree, were supported, entertained, and finally— sometimes after months—sent on to the next Jewish community or directly abroad. That seemed to American Jews the religious, the decent thing to do. It is true that on one occasion, for reasons unknown, a stranger who had landed in Newport was lodged with Christians, but his meals were certainly taken in a Jewish home. Transients could not be maintained permanently, for the expense would have been unbearable, nor could they be put to work, for they were not immigrants who had come here to settle and sink roots. Bosquila was sixty-one, Moses bar David was fifty-two, Tobiah ben Judah Loew was forty-eight. To the eighteenth century mind these men were obviously too old to think of starting life over.[29]

Supporting transients was a heavy drain on the resources of colonial Jewry. Overseas transportation was not inexpensive. In one year (1741) three families and two individuals were dispatched by ship from New York, one for Barbados. A generation later Rivera and Lopez reached into their pockets and underwrote the provisions and transportation for two Spanish-Portuguese travelers to Barbados, that same distant island; the total cost amounted to something in excess of £67 old tenor. In the case of Surinam-bound Judah Abrahams, the departing guest received from the Newport congregation an iron pot in which to do his cooking, forty pounds of kosher beef, twenty-eight pounds of bread, a half pound of tea, two pounds of chocolate, and six pounds of sugar.

That the problem of the transient was an old one is evident in the fact that New York Jewry's constitution of 1728 made detailed provision for the care of "any poor person" who "should . . . come to this place and should want the assistance of the sinagog." An incoming stranger was allowed for his board in the city a weekly dole of eight shillings for a maximum of twelve weeks, since he might have to wait that long before a ship was ready to weigh anchor for the port of his choice. In addition, a single man was allowed forty shillings for transportation and food supplies—by 1769 this allowance would have risen to £5—while married couples in transit were allowed enough "for their maintenance whilst ashore and also for their necessarys when they depart." In the latter instance the president would consult with his associates and together they would fix on the amount to be given. How expensive it might be to send off a whole family one sees in the case of the Widow Abrams, whose husband had probably died in this country. She was determined to return home, to Europe most likely, and the New York community expected to spend as much as £50 for her and her children.[30]

Where Transients Came From

Where the transients came from during the eighteenth century is an interesting question. They appear to have made their way to North America from virtually every land which supported a sizeable Jewish community—from Palestine and Europe as we have seen, and also from the West Indies and Surinam and one or another of the mainland colonies. Curaçao and Jamaica in particular were favored islands from which transients set sail for North America. For the most part, to be sure, itinerants who arrived from the islands had not been settled inhabitants of the Caribbean communities, but were travelers on the move. Looking for relief and then moving on, they made a sort of circuit of the New World, though there is no evidence that any of these guests came back for help a second time.

Newport received from Jamaica two men named Cohen, probably brothers. They must have been professional itinerants, since the Savannah-la-Mar synagogal treasurer recommended them in his letter of introduction as worthy "objects of charity," and they had with them "credentials from the *several congregations* to the same effect." On occasion a congregation might be petitioned by a needy transient who was no schnorrer. During the 1760's, for instance, Levi Michaels of Montreal, a former New Yorker, asked Shearith Israel for "such a sum of money, upon loan," as would enable him to return to Canada. This suppliant later became well-known in Canadian Jewish history as a businessman.[31]

Where Transients Went

The two Cohens from Jamaica were supported in Newport for about a week and then sent off by ship to New York. Normally, however, incoming transients put into New York first and then went to Newport. Occasionally those who came to New York would go on from there to Philadelphia or even, though rarely, sail directly for South Carolina. From New York, too, transients who had not yet explored the West Indies would take ship for the Caribbean. The metropolis on the Hudson was also an excellent port for return to Europe via London. Thus, a London-bound man was lent money to return to England, and when Hazzan Joseph Jesurun Pinto resigned his New York post, he asked the congregation ingenuously to finance his trip back to Europe

and extend to him the same humane bounty, as has been bestowed on others that, tho strangers, and consequently never contributed to the service of the congregation, yet your humane hearts compassionated their care, and they have been relieved from their nessessite and helpt to remove from hence to some other place.

The New Yorkers accepted the hazzan's plea—to the tune of £50.[32]

The poor people sent to the islands included a schoolteacher headed for Jamaica, a "poor lad" on his way to St. Croix, a rabbi bound for St. Eustatius, and the Smyrna-born Bosquila, whose destination was Curaçao. Itinerants en route to Surinam might, if they were lucky, get a boat in New York, but most Surinam ships left from Rhode Island, whose Jews would ship the suppliants to Surinam and then ask the New Yorkers to share the expense equally. Once a Mr. Moran, an impoverished businessman from St. Eustatius, arrived in Newport and requested transportation to Surinam; Jacob R. Rivera secured passage for him from the Browns of Providence. Moron had made a detour of some 2,000 miles, but apparently there was no more direct route.

Interesting, though not unusual, is the case of Jacob de Mesquita. He too was on St. Eustatius and wanted passage to Barbados, about four hundred miles away. No vessels plied between the two islands, however, and to reach Barbados, de Mesquita, like Mr. Moron, had to go first to North America. The New Yorkers supported him and then sent him off with a note of introduction to Philadelphia, where the Gratzes were asked to raise the funds to defray his trip to Barbados. The small group in Philadelphia was assured that if there was "a dificuncy of three or four pounds," the New Yorkers would make it good "out of the sedaka here." For de Mesquita the longest way round was the shortest way home, but it seems that after all, de Mesquita did not go on to Barbados or if he did, the following year (1769) found him back at Newport, where he apparently boarded with the beadle and carried on a small business into 1770. De Mesquita was obviously no professional schnorrer, for he sought to earn his keep and was successful enough to make generous offerings to the synagogue. By extending him credit, Lopez may have helped in his rehabilitation.[33]

SOCIAL WELFARE AND REHABILITATION

At first glance there seems to have been no policy of social rehabilitation for the local poor or the transients. Every man, woman, or child who wandered into town from somewhere and turned to his fellow Jews for relief was given help—board, lodging, cash, and passage to his next destination. The records indicate no communal concern that a number of these suppliants were professional travelers who wanted money or help, but had no intention whatsoever of settling down to work. This was obviously true, in particular, of the various "rabbis" who came to town.

Apparently no complaint was ever voiced to a neighboring town or to a distant land for directing petitioners to these shores, unless of course, criminals were sent! No complaint was voiced because the North Americans gave as good as they got. If some itinerants came from the islands, others were just as promptly and expeditiously dispatched there.

Authentic Palestinian emissaries and scholars, as we have seen, were accorded special courtesies. When Rabbi Samuel Ha-Cohen of Hebron went to Dartmouth, Massachusetts, to catch a ship for England, the Newport community sent an attendant with him to the port of embarkation. People of lesser rank certainly did not receive such favored treatment. Frequently they were urged not to dally, and the records are replete with such phrases as "immediately," "as soon as possible," and "if he will not go, is to remain at his own expence."

Yet, though a superficial glance might suggest otherwise, the Jews did pursue a policy of rehabilitation in a simple unpretentious way. If a man wanted to stay and work, they would give him work. Every opportunity was accorded a stranger to enter a business of his own. De Mesquita's experience was not without parallel. A stranger would be given credit, even though it was obvious that success would make him a competitor. Thus when David Abrahams, a family man, appeared at the New York synagogue in 1747, made a modest offering or two, and applied to the Gomezes, they gave him some sundries on credit. In all likelihood he became some sort of peddler, but he did not pay his debts, and a year or two later he asked the congregation to ship him to the West Indies. He was through, and one might safely hazard the guess that the congregation was through with him.[34]

PERSONAL CHARITY

Even though congregations in this country, as in England and Brazil, probably frowned on private philanthropy, individual Jews extended personal kindnesses to suppliants. Jacob Franks had been the great Jewish merchant of mid-eighteenth century New York, and when he died the *New-York Gazette and Weekly Mercury* for January 23, 1769, carried a very laudatory necrology, written probably by a local Jew. The writer stressed the fact that Franks had been "a friend to the poor of all denominations." Franks's daughter Richa, equally noted for her benefactions, left the country for London several months after her father's death, and a fellow-passenger on the *Duchess of Gordon* described her in some pseudobiblical verses:

Moreover she was meek and charitable; her heart was soft as the bosom of compassion, tender as the eye of pity.

As the dew of the Heaven lighteth on the top of Mount Hermon, refreshing the parched ground, even so her benevolence descended in silence on the children of adversity, and her alms rejoiced the hearts of the poor.[35]

In Philadelphia, Rachel Moses, taking pity on the irresponsible Emanuel Lyons, advanced him money several times to get his clothes out of pawn. When a perfect stranger turned to Manuel Josephson for help, the New York businessman gave him £30 worth of goods at prime cost and on credit. Philip Moses arrived in Savannah from Newport and began his career as a businessman in 1771. Two years later, after he had achieved some degree of prosperity, he wrote to his patron Aaron Lopez and offered to help the impoverished Myers family in Newport.[36]

AARON LOPEZ OF NEWPORT

Charity and generosity as evidenced by an individual are nowhere better documented than in the life of Aaron Lopez. There may have been many others as kind and as sympathetic, but no records remain to document their humanity, while the numerous Lopez papers which have survived make it possible to study nearly every aspect of the life of this distinguished Newport merchant.

In 1770 an ailing transient, Moses Calonemos (Kalonimus), was well cared for by New York's Shearith Israel community; over two years later when he was in Newport preparing to set sail for Charleston, Rivera and his son-in-law Lopez paid his passage. It was an expensive gesture on their part, and also it would seem, a characteristic gesture. The generosity of which Lopez was capable remained no secret; it was widely known, and this in turn induced people to visit Newport or to write to him for favors. Hannah Louzada had been on the Shearith Israel charity roll for years, though her son-in-law Hyam Myers was a successful Canadian trader. Yet, more than once she turned to Lopez for additional help. It may well be that she was a chronic complainer, but it is also possible that she could not live comfortably on the small sums doled out to her. In a pitiful letter she wrote and told him she was over seventy, poor, and in debt for rent and doctors' bills. The Newporter's fame as "a father of the poor and a good Jew" was the core of her appeal to him.[37]

When Hayman Levy went into bankruptcy after the French and Indian War, Lopez not only wrote his former supplier to commiserate with him, but encouraged him by sending some goods on credit. Another bankrupt wrote from England to thank the Newport shipper for his helpfulness and consideration. In the trying days of July 1779 after Tory raiders had harried the Connecticut coast, Lopez sent money and supplies unsolicited to the needy New York Jewish exiles there. Recognizing the unusual character of this man, a local newspaper wrote after his untimely death by drowning, that he had embodied "the most amiable perfections and cardinal virtues that can adorn the human soul." Dozens of families could testify to his "munifecence, generosity, benevolence, and humanity." Stiles paid him this last tribute: "His beneficence to his family connexions, to his [Jewish] nation, and to all the world is almost without a parallel." [38]

CHAPTER 61

JEWISH EDUCATION

Many of the Christians who came here, such as English Pilgrims and Puritans who concentrated in New England, as well as French Huguenots and German Protestants who settled everywhere from New England to Georgia, had left Europe for the sake of conscience, but as we have indicated elsewhere, this was not true of the Jews. With the exception of the Brazilian émigrés and a few Sephardic families from the Iberian Peninsula or France, the Jews had not been denied freedom of conscience and worship in the European lands from which they came. Unlike many a Christian emigrant, they had not found it difficult to perpetuate their faith at home in Europe. Christian refugees in numerous instances had suffered attempts to suppress their beliefs and practices. As a result they were very eager to impart their religious views to their children, to teach them to read and understand the Bible and the catechism. They felt it imperative to open schools on these shores so their children would be literate. Otherwise the new generation would never understand its religious obligations or find the road to salvation—so vitally important in Christian thinking.

It is true that there was hardly a vocation which did not require some capacity in reading and reckoning, but it seems to have been religion, primarily, which prompted educational efforts. The obligation to secure instruction for their children lay chiefly on parents, who provided for teaching at home through themselves or tutors, or else sent their children to private, public, or church schools. New

England, to be sure, maintained community schools at public expense, but the instructional content was essentially denominational. In other parts of the country, particularly in Pennsylvania, there were many schools supported by churches and the tuition fees of parents. In every colony the children of the poor were able to secure some sort of an education, whether it was underwritten by public taxation or by a church, or was provided by the masters to whom they were apprenticed.[1]

The extent to which the Jews in the North American colonies were influenced by the Christian educational attitudes and institutions they found here appears to have been minimal. The Jews, it is true, did share a common point of view with their Christian neighbors in that they too were determined to educate their children religiously. However, they were concerned far less with "salvation" as such than with the continuance of their distinctive religioethnic way of life and all that it involved. Ever since pre-Christian times Jewish education had been seen and used as a religious instrumentality. The immigrant Jew who came here had had all-day religious schools in Poland, the German lands, Holland, England, Brazil, and the West Indies. With some notable exceptions—England and some of the islands of the Antilles—instruction in secular subjects was given privately, by tutors of some sort; such subjects as a rule were not taught in Jewish educational institutions. The religious schools with which the immigrants had been familiar abroad were supported or subsidized by educational societies, confraternities, and congregations, but in many instances they depended on tuition fees. Of course the Jewish community underwrote instruction for the children of the poor, and here in America some of them received their secular education, such as it was, at the expense of the synagogal members to whom they had been apprenticed.

American Jews had no thought of making rabbinical students of their youngsters. As they saw it, the prime purpose of instruction, whether private or communal, was to make observant Jews of their children who were to be conditioned emotionally to take up their religious identity. The school was only one segment of a series of activities aimed at binding Jews to the Jewish group. Much of this conditioning was, of course, carried on at home through the ceremonies of the life cycle, and the individual's Jewish identity was also fortified by an abundance of practices and prejudices acquired in the home and in the synagogue. The community sought to ensure that its children would grow up with strong Jewish sympathies, and there is reason to believe it was successful in that undertaking. Jewish education, which meant in large part the association of Jew with Jew, worked toward that end. The rote recitation of Hebrew possessed a magical formulaic quality which satisfied most congregants. There is certainly no evidence that for reasons of conscience any of the worshipers protested the reading of prayers whose language they understood most imperfectly, if at all. *Emotionally*, it would seem, they did understand their prayers well enough.

What motivated American Jews to keep their schools open was their desire to maintain a Jewish fellowship, to uphold morals, to become one with World Jewry, and to gain some knowledge of the laws, ordinances, and practices God had commanded and enjoined upon his people. Schools were, therefore, closely identified with synagogues; in Europe the two were often merged into one institution known as the bet ha-midrash, the house of study. The Christian clergyman who visited Newport in 1760 may have been annoyed to find the exterior of the synagogue marred "by a school which the Jews would have annexed to it for the education of their children." To the Newport Jews, however, it was the most natural thing in the world. Where else should their school be but hard by the synagogue?[2]

In North America as elsewhere, then, Jews maintained their ancestral traditions with respect to religious instruction and schools. Their attachment to this ancient usage was certainly not diminished—if anything it was strengthened—by the fact that a similar tradition prevailed among Christians on these shores. Determined to give their children a religious education in this frontier land and to make sure they would have the means to live Jewish lives, parents taught them Jewish practices in the home and in the synagogue, by personal example, and also created schools for them. Education was thus an essential part of the American synagogal and religious scene, as the Jews of Newport understood—and expected the New Yorkers to understand—when in 1759 they turned to the mother synagogue in New York and appealed for funds to build a sanctuary:

When we reflect on how much it is our duty to instruct children in the path of vertuous religion, and how unhappy the portions must be of those children and their parents who are through necessity educated in a place where they must remain almost totally uninstructed in our most holy and divine Law, our rites and ceremonies, and from which place they may perhaps never have it in their power to depart . . . we can entertain no doubt of your zeal to promote this good work.

It should never be thought, however, that the Jews neglected the general or secular education of their children. As an urban people engaged in some form or other of merchandising, they had to have and had to give their children some acquaintance with reading, writing, arithmetic, and elementary bookkeeping. Most Jews had such knowledge, and rare was the parent who considered it unimportant for his offspring to cultivate such skills.[3]

THE PRIVATE RELIGIOUS TEACHER

New York Jewry appears to have had private religious teachers ever since the seventeenth century; there were certainly such teachers in Recife whence the first emigrants had come. Everywhere, however, the moment a community came into being, services were held, and on reaching their thirteenth year, boys had to be confirmed into Judaism; that is, they had to be prepared to become bar mizvah. Of course a father, if he himself were competent, could train his son to read the unpointed Hebrew portions from the pentateuchal scroll and to recite the requisite Hebrew blessings, but more frequently a man's preoccupation with the task of earning a livelihood would incline him to leave the onerous bar mizvah training to a private teacher. The instructor was variously called a rebbe, ribbi, rubi, or even rabbi, though he was no rabbi as the word is understood today. These terms are all probably Ashkenazic in origin and document the impact of German and Polish Jews upon the seventeenth century Amsterdam community and its offshoots in the

Americas. One of the rubis in Recife was Samuel Frazao, and the Jewish Frazons of seventeenth century Boston were most likely his children or grandchildren.[4]

The rebbe in the American colonies was usually a poor man who also dabbled in business, or he was a beginner in commerce who needed extra income to sustain him as he commenced his mercantile career. Jerachmeel (Valentijn) Falk, who was related to Asser Levy and lived in New York during the 1680's, was referred to as a rabbi. Judah Monis, who later embraced Christianity and became a Hebrew instructor at Harvard, had very probably been a rebbe in New York about the year 1716, and there were certainly other private teachers there. By 1728 the shohet Benjamin Elias had been pensioned off by Shearith Israel, but he too had served as a Hebrew teacher. The professional hazzanim or cantors of the eighteenth century supplemented their income by teaching in the Jewish communal religious schools and also, it is likely, by tutoring the children of the well-to-do. When teaching privately the rebbes made their own financial arrangements, and unlike some of the Christian teachers, did not "board around." Teaching was only part of their activity; they might also piece together livelihoods as slaughterers, beadles, or cantors.[5]

The prerevolutionary period found teachers in all the colonies where Jews lived in large enough numbers to organize a community. The learned Joseph Simson probably taught Hebrew when he first came to these shores; he certainly needed the income to augment his meager salary as a beadle. For many years during the mid-1700's Abraham I. Abrahams functioned as the teacher and precentor of the New York Jewish community. In Newport the young Sephardi Abraham R. Rivera was given Hebrew instruction by a Dutch teacher, either Moses Calo (Calonemos) or the hazzan Touro. Various sons and daughters of Moses and Aaron Lopez were tutored by the hazzan, probably in Hebrew, from 1765 to about 1770. Aaron Lopez met Touro's tuition fees in part by supplying him with bills of exchange, yard goods, shoes, and other sundries.[6]

In Pennsylvania from the 1760's on at the latest, teachers were always available at Philadelphia where "Ribbi Moshe" supported himself in addition as a scribe; Emanuel Lyon advertised in the local press that he was prepared to give instruction in Hebrew; and finally, in 1776 Ezekiel Levy was employed as a communal teacher. Children from hinterland settlements might be sent to Philadelphia for religious training. One Pennsylvania family which had sent a son away from home, probably from a small town to Philadelphia, in order to provide him with a Jewish education, received from him a brief but beautifully written Hebrew-Yiddish note in which the child reported he was working hard at his studies and was making progress. Sometimes, however, teachers were to be found even in smaller towns which sheltered no more than one or two Jewish families. Jewish merchants who had begun to prosper often had a junior clerk who tended store, served as a shohet, and also taught the Jewish children in town. The young Savannah colony had a teacher in the 1730's, and Moses Pimenta, a South Carolina sutler, was also reported to be "learned in the law and a teacher of the Jewish youth." [7]

One thing is certain: the lot of the Hebrew teacher was far from enviable, financially or otherwise. It may not have been as wretched as that of the Christian teacher to whom the mothers of his pupils at Johnstown, New York, administered so severe a beating that he could not return to classes for a time; but the rebbe too confronted his "public relations" problems from time to time. Traditionally he was the luckless wight whose face was always slapped—metaphorically—although there is evidence that men like Benjamin Elias and Abraham I. Abrahams commanded the respect and affection of those who knew and employed them.[8]

COMMUNAL SCHOOLS

If the reader keeps in mind the fact that the colonial American Jewish community never numbered more than two or three thousand souls, he will understand why there were no private Jewish schools limited to general or secular studies, no grammar or secondary schools, or colleges. What the Jews maintained were communal religious schools—in at least two if not all of the North American Jewish communities.

No seventeenth century congregational records are extant, so it is impossible to determine the nature of communal elementary Jewish education in Dutch New Amsterdam or in early English New York. The first émigrés had come from Recife, Brazil, whose Jews had supported a fully developed educational system. Recife had had an elementary Hebrew school, three of whose teachers are known by name, as well as more advanced classes in rabbinical literature taught by the hakam, the ordained rabbi of the community. Apparently, however, no secular studies had been taught in the Brazilian Jewish schools, which were quite similar to their later counterparts at Bevis Marks, the Spanish-Portuguese synagogue in London, and on Curaçao. Both the Londoners and the Curaçaons had been providing Hebrew schools ever since the 1660's and 1670's.

In turn-of-the-century London, under the influence of the scholarly Hakam David Nieto, the commentaries of Rashi, the *Shulhan Aruk,* and the Talmud were studied by advanced students, but Hebrew had been taught at Bevis Marks since 1664 in a congregationally supported boys' charity school. That school was called Shaare Tikva (Gates of Hope). During the 1730's Bevis Marks saw some changes in its elementary educational system, for the boys' school and the privately endowed girls' charity school, the so-called Villa Real School, added English and arithmetic to their curricula that decade. The language of instruction in these schools would remain the Spanish-Portuguese Ladino into the nineteenth century, but by the 1750's the teaching of English in the boys' school had been endowed and was carried on by an Englishman who probably knew no Ladino. All this contrasted with London's Ashkenazic schools which at that time taught no secular subjects.[9]

To what extent were the Recife and London schools exemplary for North American Jewry? The question admits no easy answer. During the eighteenth century prior to the Revolution, organized Hebrew schools may have been maintained in Savannah and Charleston, though there is no clear evidence to that effect, but by 1776 Philadelphia had a school in which at least six children were taught at communal expense together with paying pupils. While lacking positive information that a formal school was in existence at Newport, we know a school annex was built onto the sanctuary and Hebrew instruction was offered by Hazzan Touro, and also in all probability by Moses V. Calo and Benjamin Myers. At Shearith Israel in Montreal, too, there may have been classes for the children, though the minutes of the Revolutionary period do not even hint at the possibility. New York very probably had had a school since the last decade or two of the seventeenth century.

The standardized curriculum sought to teach students to read the Hebrew of the prayer book and also to prepare them to celebrate their becoming bar mizvah by chanting an unvocalized portion from the Pentateuch and a chapter from the Prophets. This was the maximum goal for the average student and was attained by some. The students learned to read Hebrew mechanically and as a rule could not translate the prayers they read. They are likely to have understood their own special bar-mizvah portions, but it is much to be doubted that they could pick up the Pentateuch and translate at sight. As a matter of fact, American Jews had no interest in giving their boys an extensive Jewish education. They had no use for it in this land; it would "butter no parsnips" here.

Jewish communities which had schools naturally employed teachers, but the local rebbe was not in reality a communal official. He was essentially a private Hebrew teacher, subsidized by the community to teach the children of the poor. The Jewish school was thus a semiprivate institution for middle-class youngsters, but it was also attended by boys whose parents could not afford the tuition fees of money and fuel. In compensation for his instruction to the sons of the poor, the teacher received from the community a salary, fuel, unleavened bread for Passover, and living quarters or an allowance for rent. On occasion an impoverished widow received a grant which she paid directly to the teacher for the instruction imparted to her son. New York's Shearith Israel school was in essence no different from the Christian church schools of the Middle Atlantic provinces or some of the Connecticut public schools, for they too were partly supported by parental fees.[10]

The languages of instruction in the New York school were Portuguese and Spanish during the first half of the century, and English during the second half. Of course, if the Gomez and the Lucena children and other Sephardic boys went to a German or Polish rebbe for private instruction, as they probably did, they were at times taught in Yiddish or in broken English. The effectiveness of this type of education is best left to the reader's imagination.

The first school to be unequivocally documented was established at New York City in 1731, and if any specific pattern was followed, it was that of Bevis Marks in London. That year of 1731, as we have already had occasion to indicate, a school was built for the New York congregation by a member of London's wealthy Mendes da Costa family, perhaps in competition with the Villa Real family which endowed a girls' school in London that same year. Later that decade another Mendes da Costa established two other schools in London. The New York school was formally called the Yeshibat Minhat Areb (school of the evening sacrifice), a name derived probably from Psalm 141:2: "Let my prayer be set forth as incense before thee; the lifting of my hands as the evening sacrifice." The implication was that prayers would be offered up in the building by the pupils or on occasion by their parents, with the generous benefactor in mind. The word *areb* (evening or sunset) may have been understood as an allusion to the West, referring to the position of the New York Jewish community on the far western frontier of eighteenth century Jewish life.[11]

The New York yeshibah was a Hebrew school only, with classes held only a half day, morning or afternoon. No secular subjects were offered, and the Hebrew teaching was left to a rebbe or the hazzan, or possibly even both. Certainly, by 1737 the hazzan Machado had become the teacher. His contract required him to teach Hebrew "either the whole morning or afternoon, as he shall think most proper," and to instruct the poor without charge. As we have already pointed out, the pattern of religious instruction by the minister himself was a familiar one in the Middle Atlantic colonies where the parish school was frequently conducted by the pastor.[12]

During the decade that Machado served New York as minister and teacher, Joshua Isaacs left a legacy of £50, its income to be "for the support of a Hebrew school to teach poor children the Hebrew tongue." One might infer from Isaacs' grant that no school was then in existence at New York or that no provision was being made for class instruction of the poor, and indeed there may have been periods when for financial or other reasons the school closed down. This was certainly true of Shearith Israel's schools in the early decades of the nineteenth century. During most of his incumbency Hazzan Machado taught only in the morning from nine to twelve, but in 1747, his last year, he also held classes on Thursday afternoons from two to five. The tuition for each child was eight shillings a quarter plus a load of wood, and the congregation followed the London pattern by supervising the school through periodic visitations by inspectors.[13]

A decided curricular change was inaugurated at New York in 1755 when secular studies were introduced. By then, to be sure, schools combining religious and secular studies were no longer uncommon in the country. The Jews had been in New York for just about a century and were fast sinking their roots in American society—a process hastened by the French and Indian War, which involved Jews and Christians alike more substantially in the commercial life of the country and impressed them more strongly than ever with the need for secular education. For Jewish schools to give instruction in the vernacular of the country and in other secular disciplines was rare in the eighteenth century. Certainly nothing comparable had arisen in the ghettos of Central and Eastern Europe. Intellectually, the introduction of such studies implied a rejection of the past and of the cultural separatism which had been the norm; it connoted a recognition and affirmation of the new modern world of tolerance and acceptance in which the American Jew found himself. What Hazzan Pereira taught in the mid-1750's at the New York school was the three R's and Spanish, but the language of instruction was English. The hazzan had probably come from Jamaica and knew English well. For a time he conducted the school in his own home. His health may have made that arrangement more convenient for him, and it would also save Shearith Israel the expense of heating the school building in the winter. The congregation added £20 to the hazzan's salary and required him during the summer to teach mornings and afternoons from nine to twelve and from two to five; in the winter he taught only till four, Sundays included of course. No classes were held on holidays or because of the approaching Sabbath, on Friday afternoon. The poor were to be given free instruction, and inspections were to be made monthly by the congregational officers.

This type of school was conducted intermittently in New York until the Revolution.[14]

Shearith Israel had difficulties enough with its school. Pereira's "want of health" toward the end of his tour of duty led him to be excused from teaching on Sunday and finally disabled him altogether from officiating. In 1757 after the hazzan left, the congregation turned to the American-born Moses Franks, by then a prominent merchant in London, and asked him to find a young hazzan-teacher, someone "strictly religious," of good morals, and possessing a command of both Spanish and English. Despite the growing secularization of the curriculum, the religious content remained very important, as in all the Jewish and Christian schools in the colonies. Hazzan Pinto was finally secured, but his work as a teacher proved unsatisfactory. The New Yorkers had trouble with him—or he had trouble with them—and it was decided at length to relieve Pinto of teaching responsibilities.

In 1760 the synagogue leaders besought Pereira, then on Jamaica, "to engage a suitable master capable to teach our children the Hebrew language." "A single, modest, sober person" who knew English, Spanish, and Hebrew was what they wanted, but they were ready to settle for a teacher unversed in Spanish: "He will not suit unless he understands Hebrew and English at least." The process of Americanization was proceeding apace! One notes also that a candidate's good character weighed at least as much as his competence, in which respect the congregation followed the prevailing colonial pattern of assessing a teacher's qualifications. The new teacher was to receive £40 annually in New York currency, not sterling, as compensation for teaching the children of the needy; all others were to pay him a tuition fee, thereby augmenting his salary. Pinto was bitter at the appointment of a teacher—and understandably so, because his salary was to be cut by £20 which, together with an additional £20 "to be paid out of the sedaka," would be the new rebbe's allowance. The hazzan appealed to his London sponsors to intervene in his favor, but all they did was send him a copy of his contract with the bland assurance that they would be praying for him! [15]

In the end Shearith Israel was unable to secure a man from

abroad and the position was offered to Abraham I. Abrahams who, obviously owing to the postwar depression, found himself in severe straits. The congregation used its advantage to strike a hard bargain with him; he had to agree to a basic salary of a mere £20, but was granted in addition the "liberty of having offerings made him" by his friends during worship services. A month later, however, his salary was raised to the £40 which had originally been stipulated for the job a couple of years earlier. Most of Abrahams' income for teaching came, in any case, from the fees of paying pupils whom he taught either in his classes or at their homes. One of the Judah Hays receipt books bears witness that Abrahams taught Judah's daughter Malco (Reyna) until the family dropped him for a Christian woman teacher who charged five shillings a quarter less. Had the widowed Mrs. Hays thought it necessary to sacrifice the Hebrew and religious part of her daughter's education in order to save money? At all events Malco survived Jewishly, for eight years later she married Hazzan Touro of Newport. Abrahams further augmented his income by performing circumcisions and by serving as a part-time hazzan and beadle. One may be quite sure, also, that he nibbled at business whenever he had a chance to do so. Apparently a native Englishman, he may have known no Spanish, for he was expected to teach none, but only English, the three R's, and Hebrew. Abrahams remained in charge of the New York school at least until the Revolution when it probably had to close.

ACCOMPLISHMENTS OF THE SCHOOLS

Measured against a good school in the eighteenth century Polish ghetto or against a well-conducted Hebrew school in twentieth century New York, the Jewish elementary schools of colonial North America accomplished very little. They barely limped along and there was, of course, no advanced Jewish education to be had here. Not even one child is recorded as ever having been sent abroad for more intensive training, and the instruction available here, whether under private or communal auspices, in all likelihood was not of the highest order. Very little, moreover, was done to educate girls Jewishly, although some of them were at least taught to read the Hebrew prayers mechanically.

Bearing in mind, however, that American Jewry was a small group living on the outskirts of world culture, one concludes that the schools here were not so bad. Indeed, when it came to teaching secular subjects like reading, writing, and arithmetic, the mid-eighteenth century American Jewish school had nothing to be ashamed of by contemporary American standards. The Christian community schools of the day were scarcely better and frequently less adequate. After all, in addition to acquiring a passable knowledge of the three R's and the ability to write a tolerable letter in English, most Jewish children learned to *read* Hebrew. Very few of them, it is true, knew what they were reading, but even in London Hebrew instruction and accomplishment left much to be desired. A critical eighteenth century observer in the English capital reported that children there had no sympathy for their Yiddish-speaking teachers and that most of them barely learned to read Hebrew and could not even translate the Pentateuch, let alone find their way in the Talmud.[16]

Even from an objective standpoint, the colonial Jew might on occasion have had reason to be proud of his educational achievement. Consider, for instance, David Franks, son of the great American Jewish merchant; he had a Hebrew tutor, and when he became bar mizvah he was able to read his entire pentateuchal portion unvocalized, which would be considered a feat even today. The fifth-generation American Gershom Seixas, later to become the hazzan of Shearith Israel, knew his Bible, could read the Pentateuch unvocalized, and had the ability to consult the elementary Hebrew codes. In Newport, too, boys became bar mizvah and read their portions; some were even able to chant the services publicly. Young Jacob Mordecai, reared in Philadelphia, became a good student of the Hebrew Bible and probably had some knowledge of rabbinic Hebrew as well. How many students in present-day America can boast of more? [17]

CHAPTER 62

JEWISH CULTURE AND KNOWLEDGE

THE NATURE OF JEWISH CULTURE
IN THE COLONIES

It was, as we have seen, characteristic of colonial Jewry to create elementary schools and to provide private instruction, even in some of the towns on the frontier, and certainly this was Jewish culture of a sort. To what extent, however, can it be said that Jewish culture developed on this continent?

England sheltered a few Jews who were well-versed in rabbinic lore, and there were many in Central, Southern, and Eastern Europe. It was otherwise in America; obviously the colonies of the eighteenth century were not great intellectual nurseries, and culture for both Jews and Christians was centered in Europe. The American colonies were cultural as well as political dependencies of Europe; a European Jew would feel at home in any American synagogue. Most Jews lived in the larger towns of the tidewater, and their culture was urban, oriented to the countries and provinces whence they had come as immigrants. Even the Jews on the frontier—in Reading and Lancaster for instance—clung tenaciously to their European ways and conformed ritually as much as they could. The recent Jewish arrival might be annoyed to find slight ritual deviations; he might even question the competence of the hazzan who led the service, but he would certainly feel at home.[1]

The fate and the development of "Jewishness" on American soil cannot be grasped unless one has some notion of the nature and scope of Jewish culture as it was then known and cultivated in Europe. Jewish culture meant, in the first place, a knowledge of the

[1069]

Jewish way of life and thought, a familiarity with Jewish worship, with the rituals, observances, practices, and holidays of Judaism. A knowledge of Judaism also implied familiarity with Jewish demands in matters of food, conduct, morals, customs, and the whole cere- monial life cycle. It involved a knowledge of the Hebrew and Aramaic languages, a capacity to read and understand the Hebrew Bible and rabbinic literature. Inseparable from Jewishness as it had been shaped in the Old World, was the ability to read intelligently the basic rabbinic law codes which governed Jewish life.

On a different but not necessarily higher level, a cultured Jew was expected to have some knowledge of the philosophic and ethical works of the great leaders of the past. The prime interest, however, lay in the area of rabbinic law, an area which touched directly on the daily life of the Jew as a religionist and as a businessman. The cultured Jew, it may be said, was one who could read a simple rab- binic code with ease. Traditional Judaism is essentially a nomistic faith, and all the vast variations of ritual, practice, theology, and ethics are embraced in the scope of Law or Torah. Jews, it is true, neither emphasized nor cultivated theology to the extent Christians did, but it should not be thought they were unconcerned with the existence and nature of God or with man's relation to Him. They did write and speak about the divine origin and immutability of the revelation vouchsafed to the Jew, and they took no small notice of concepts like reward and punishment, resurrection, and the after life, though they rarely stopped to spell these concepts out or to systematize them, as did their Christian neighbors. The afterlife was, of course, linked to the glowing messianic world to be ushered in by a Messiah of the House of David. This was vital, for it meant a place in the sun and the end of all discrimination. No Jew any- where in the eighteenth century world was completely enfranchised as a Jew, but in the messianic age which might come any day, the bottom rail would be on top!

Where this Jewish culture flourished, there was not only study of it, and appreciation; there was also literary expression. Europe was the center of such life and thought and expression, but to what extent was there a transplanting and flowering of Jewish culture on these shores? How much of this cultural baggage did the newcomers bring with them?

The constant trickle of immigrants into America's small Jewish community served to keep alive the influence of European ways of thinking. Certainly up to the American Revolution, if not beyond that time, European immigrants dominated the culture of American Jewry and kept that culture strongly Old World. To a very great degree the leading American Jews—the power structure, we might say—had come to the colonies during the French and Indian War as young entrepreneurs. By the dawn of the Revolution they had reached maturity and dominated the American Jewish community. In many respects, to be sure, they had become thoroughly Americanized, but their experience here had not appreciably modified their religion or their religious attitudes. Religiously, they continued following in the footsteps of their European fathers.

Notwithstanding their remoteness from the Old World centers of Jewish life, the Jews of the New World never lost their European ties. Some of the men who began coming to these shores no later than the 1750's were itinerants whose sole purpose was to secure funds and then to continue on their way. Most of them had some Hebraic knowledge, and a few were even rabbinic scholars of some capacity. In 1774, for instance, we know of three men in New York, transients very probably, whose cultural background was considerable. These rebbes, as they must have been, were always available and for the most part apparently capable of answering simple halakic (legal) questions. They brought with them knowledge and respect for Jewish traditions; they carried reports, even gossip of other communities and their notables, and thus they served to bind the Jews of these distant American outposts to the Jews at the European hub of affairs.[2]

Among those who stalked across the tiny colonial American Jewish stage was Rabbi Carigal, clearly something of a rover, but for all that a man of good character, truly beloved wherever he wandered. Infinitely better educated than all his fellow transients, he was scarcely typical of those who came here, but he did exercise a cultural influence. This exotic adventurer from Hebron spent nearly a year all told, living and preaching in Philadelphia, New York, and Newport. Men like Carigal—there were others who came to these shores—helped maintain the respect and reverence for Jewish learning that characterized almost every Jew of that generation. He was in himself a spiritual link to the teachings and ideals of World Jewry.[3]

In view of the Jewish knowledge that learned and less learned immigrants brought with them, and in view of the training given children born and educated here, what was the face of Jewish culture in this land? What did the Jews here know of Hebrew, of rabbinic law, of classical Judaism? What was their attitude towards the importance of rabbinic study? What was the nature of Jewish and Hebraic culture in this country?

In 1773 when Carigal preached at the Pentecost service in Newport, he made very clear the classical attitude of the Jew of his day towards study and education. Jewish sufferings, he declared, were not "casualties or accidents." Jews were in exile for their sins and "the loss of Jerusalem" centuries before "was owing to the contempt and ignominy" with which her dwellers had "treated every one who applied himself to the *divine study*," the study of the Law. The Jew had to attend the synagogue and study at the rabbinical academies so he could hear God's word, the Pentateuch, and learn to understand His requirements and observe His commands. No doubt the Newport Jews who heard Carigal preach that Spanish sermon—if they understood him and many certainly did not— nodded their heads in complete assent—and did absolutely nothing about it. They and their fellows in every other American Jewish community would have done nothing, because rabbinical studies and academies had no place in their everyday lives. American Jews simply had no time for such concerns; there was in America no community which saw proficiency in rabbinic law, practice, and interpretation as a vital matter.[4]

Now this is not to imply that American Jews had no respect for the ideals and traditions of their faith. Unquestionably, in Newport and elsewhere in the land there were former Marranos, members of the Lopez clan for instance, who had once risked their lives to observe the precepts of Judaism. Unquestionably, by virtue of their historical memories and the experience of some of their individual families, most Jews were moved to revere Jewish learning. Saul Brown of Newport and New York belonged to a highly distinguished and scholarly family, while the Gratz brothers of Philadelphia were surely aware of their descent from some of the outstanding Central and East European rabbinical scholars of the seventeenth century. Manuel Myers, a president of Shearith Israel, was the brother-in-law of a Bavarian dayyan (religious judge), and another of his brothers-in-law was the son of a judge descended from one of seventeenth century Europe's most famous scholars, Rabbi Lipmann Heller. Learning meant something to a man like Myers.[5]

It was not respect for Jewish scholarship that colonial Jewry lacked; it was learned Jewish religious leaders. Certainly in the Christian sense of the learned clergy of New England who wrote books, taught in the schools and colleges, commanded attention, and profoundly influenced the thinking of the people in their communities—certainly in that sense Jewish leaders were totally absent from the American scene. There were no ordained rabbinical officiants in this country, no learned Jewish ministry, no positive expression of interest in higher Jewish education. And there was no possibility of such. Even if an American Jewish lad had returned from a European academy with a rabbinical degree, no community—not even New York—could or would have employed him unless he were willing to serve also as hazzan—at a hazzan's salary.

The American Jewish clergyman, the hazzan or precentor, knew more than the typical congregant, but probably very little more. The hazzanim were not intellectuals. Still, to declare that most of the cantors were not scholars is not to maintain that no scholarly men were to be found among the congregational employees. Some of the rebbes were men of learning. For example, Moses Lyon of New York, a native Pole, was referred to in the death records as a man well-versed in Hebraic lore. There can be no question that almost every town had at least one or two men who had received a better than average Jewish education, Hebraists and students of rabbinic law. To be sure, European scholars would never have recognized them as authoritative voices, but judged even by the best European standards, they evidenced a degree of competence in Jewish learning.[6]

Most of the immigrants who remained to set the tone of Jewish life in America possessed a practical if somewhat vague knowledge of Judaism. There were some exceptions, but in general the Jewish or Hebrew education of the immigrants had stopped at the age of thirteen when they became bar mizvah. The broker Haym Salomon exemplifies those few who came here with a below average Jewish education. It is probable that Salomon could read Hebrew mechanically, knew the Hebrew alphabet, and was able to write Yiddish phonetically, but writing a good Yiddish letter was beyond him. Yet he too had a profound respect for Judaism, for Jewish learning, for Jewish practices. As the Revolution drew to a close he asked that his father in Europe be informed: "Should any of my brothers' children have a good head to learn Hebrew, [I] would contribute towards his being instructed." [7]

BOOKS AND LIBRARIES OWNED BY JEWS

Among the early Christian settlers of Virginia and New England during the seventeenth and eighteenth centuries were men who possessed extensive libraries—hundreds of books in some instances. John Winthrop Jr. was said to have had a library of over a thousand volumes, and the collection of William Byrd of Westover, Virginia, was three times as large. There was nothing like this among the Jews of North America. Individuals among the Jews of England had large libraries, and one of them gave the British Museum some 200 Hebrew books, accompanied by a letter in florid Hebrew, but the colonial Jews were no "People of the Book" in the literal sense. The few "learned Jews" to be found here did have libraries, but they were probably never very extensive. At best they numbered their Jewish books by the dozen rather than by the hundreds, and libraries —if that term is deserved—were dismissed in the inventories with the curt phrase, "one lott Hebrew books." [8]

During the seventeenth century Samuel Sewall reported that

Samuel Frazon of Boston owned a Spanish-Jewish Bible. In the course of the next century Naphtali Hart Myers gave Newport's Redwood Library a copy of the *Matteh Dan*, a Hebrew philosophical work by Rabbi David Nieto of London. Myers also bought some books for Aaron Lopez, but the latter's total library, excluding his music scores, totaled only about sixty volumes. Ezra Stiles and Hazzan Isaac Touro once examined a Hebrew commentary to Genesis, a volume which probably came from Touro's library, and Stiles also had occasion to see a multivolume copy of Maimonides' law code, the *Mishneh Torah*, which Isaac Da Costa, onetime hazzan of Charleston, brought along with him on a trip to Newport. The Newport synagogue itself owned a volume containing a Spanish translation of the biblical Song of Songs together with a translation of the Aramaic version of the same book. The fact that a "learned Jew," Isaac Mark, possessed a picture of a famous seventeenth century Jewish scholar suggests that he too had respect for Jewish studies, and it is known that some Newport Jews contributed to help buy a copy of Montanus' *Biblia Sacra Polyglotta* for the Redwood Library.[9]

Regrettably little is known about the personal lives of the Newport Jews, but the fuller sources available for their Pennsylvania coreligionists indicate that even those in the backcountry had some Jewish and Hebrew books: liturgies, prayer books, Hebrew Bibles, and a *Tikkun Soferim*, a guide to the writing and correcting of a Scroll of the Law. Of course none of these works are particularly exceptional and do not necessarily imply much learning.[10]

More significant is the fact that one of the earliest known Jewish settlers in Pennsylvania, the apostate Isaac Miranda, owned a copy of Hayyim Vital's *Sefer Ha-gilgulim*, a mystical work dealing with the transmigration of souls. Miranda's copy had been published at Frankfort on the Main in 1683–1684, and if the Pennsylvanian could understand Vital's cabalistic work, he must have been a man of considerable learning. Miranda also owned a manuscript containing several works in Spanish and Portuguese, two of them polemics concerning the differences between Judaism and Christianity and a third dealing in prose and poetry with Isaac de Castro Tartas' martyrdom at Lisbon in 1647.[11]

Nathan Levy, the founder of the Philadelphia Jewish community, possessed what was for his day an extensive Hebrew and Jewish library, though whether he had the training to use it is difficult to determine. He was the owner of a polyglot Bible with a Hebrew text, and of a Hebrew and Latin dictionary. His library also contained twenty-two other Hebrew volumes and eight Spanish-Hebrew volumes, the latter probably liturgical books of the Spanish rite. Other Jews of the late colonial period whose estates were probated in Philadelphia owned very small libraries or no books at all; at least none were listed in their inventories.[12]

Another Pennsylvanian who possessed a relatively extensive Hebrew library was Manuel Josephson, about whose competence in Hebraic and rabbinic literature there can be no question. Josephson, a German Jew, had come to this country as a young businessman during the French and Indian War, settled in New York, and by the time of the Revolution moved on to Philadelphia. His will indicates that he left a library of general and Hebrew books, and after his death his Hebrew books were sent to a brother in Germany. From a responsum or legal opinion which he wrote in English, it would appear that he owned a number of the standard Hebrew codes —the *Tur* of Jacob ben Asher, the *Shulhan Aruk* of Joseph Caro, the *Orhot Hayyim* of the Provençal scholar Aaron ben Jacob, and probably a number of other legal works, including the Maimonidean code. When he wrote on matters rabbinic, he quoted his sources like a present-day scholar, and his Hebrew was correct and beautifully indited.[13]

In New York there were always some Jews who had Hebrew and Jewish books, if only because no worship service could be held without the standard Hebrew prayer books for the daily, Sabbath, festival, and High Holy Day devotions. Individuals owned libraries of varying size. The estate of Judah Samuel, who in all probability had come to the city in the seventeenth century, included a Hebrew Bible and five other Hebrew works. The early eighteenth century rebbe Benjamin Elias was a man of considerable learning. His library contained a manuscript of the talmudic tractate *Makkot*, either in whole or in part, as well as an edition of some books of the Bible with the commentary of Rashi, and also a copy of Jacob ben Isaac's

Ha-maggid, a Yiddish translation of the Prophets and the Hagiographa, published at Prague in 1692. He probably had other Hebrew books too.

Hazzan Machado, who followed Elias as one of the congregation's functionaries, owned a copy of Aaron Mendoza's *Dinim de Sehita y Bedica,* a Spanish epitome of the laws of slaughter published at London in 1733. Machado had secured the book almost immediately after its publication, and his copy later came into the possession of Isaac Nunes Henriques, a Spanish-Portuguese Marrano émigré who added his own manuscript notes. The shohet Jonas Phillips, later a well-known Philadelphia merchant, owned a Hebrew work on ritual slaughter.

There is no direct evidence that Hazzan Joseph J. Pinto owned a library, but there is good reason to believe he did. His learning was reflected in a well-written Hebrew letter which he sent the congregation and in which he quoted from rabbinic literature. He may have relied on his memory, of course, but it is far more likely that he made use of works at his disposal.

Ezra Stiles reported in 1772 that a New York Jew had sent him an English translation of Abraham Jagel's catechistic *Lekah Tob* (Good Doctrine). Since no such version of Jagel's work is extant, Stiles may have been referring to an unpublished manuscript translation, not perhaps of the Hebrew original, but of the Latin translation which the Lorrainese convert to Christianity Louis de Veil had published at London in 1670. Stiles also reported that the New York merchant Solomon Simson once showed him a manuscript Hebrew Bible owned by his father Joseph Simson and said to have been copied in the year 860 C.E. If so, it was the oldest complete manuscript Hebrew Bible in existence, and Stiles quite properly doubted its antiquity. The elder Simson corresponded with Dr. Benjamin Kennicott, the famous Oxford Hebraist, to whom he described his fine vocalized Old Testament manuscript, and he was also in touch with Dr. Myles Cooper, the president of King's College, on matters of Hebraic scholarship. The English translation of Jagel which Stiles saw might have been made by the scholarly and learned interpreter Isaac Pinto of New York. Pinto, who corresponded with Stiles and Rabbi Isaac Carigal, wrote Hebrew and had some knowledge of rabbinic Hebrew, particularly the Bible commentators. As an amateur philologist, he was interested in Arabic too.[14]

DIVERSE MANIFESTATIONS OF THE KNOWLEDGE OF HEBREW

Quite a number of the European-trained Jews were apparently more comfortable with the Hebrew script than with the Latin, or it may be that they preferred signing their names in Hebrew, employing their Hebrew signatures as a cryptogram. At any rate Moses Mordecai, one of the signatories to Pennsylvania's nonimportation statement in 1765, signed himself *Mosheh* (Moses) in Hebrew, while Frances Sheftall and Abigail Minis signed their wills in Hebrew. It is hard to believe that these two women, who had lived in America for decades, could not employ the Latin script. English letters from both of them are extant, but it is possible of course that they had been written for them by others. Cushman Polock of Savannah, Aaron N. Cardozo of Virginia, and Aaron Levy, the Pennsylvania land agent, sometimes used Hebrew initials as their signatures. Levy, more than any other colonial Jew, endorsed his personal papers and business documents in English, but used Hebrew letters to do so. Mathias Bush, in the flourish under his English signature, included the Hebrew for "from b'sh," no doubt the abbreviation of the European town from which he hailed. Similar devices were employed by colonial Jews living in New York, Connecticut, and Massachusetts Bay.[15]

Samuel Jacobs of Canada, who wrote English, almost invariably signed his first name with a concluding loop in which he wrote *Shemuel* (Samuel). During the autumn and winter of 1775 when the American general Richard Montgomery invaded Canada, Jacobs kept a Hebrew-script diary of a sort. Believing as a Loyalist that a day of reckoning would come for those of his neighbors in St. Denis who were pro-American, he determined to keep a record of their disloyalty. Employing the Hebrew script, he jotted down his impressions in English, but since his English was spelled phonetically and pronounced with a strong French brogue, the resultant account is nearly unintelligible. If Jacobs used Hebrew characters to protect his diary from prying eyes, he was eminently successful, for it is practically impossible today, almost two centuries later, to decipher what he wrote. Of course the employment of this Semitic script is no indication of extensive learning in the Hebrew language or its literature. Of those who made use of it, some probably knew no other script, others employed it as an affectation, some resorted to it to preserve privacy, others simply because they were more familiar with it.[16]

Another but somewhat problematic index to Hebraic knowledge is furnished by the inscriptions on the tombstones of colonial Jewry. Practically all the Newport and New York stones bear some Hebrew, and a study of epitaphs in Charleston, Newport, and New York—communities in which a number of the stones are still extant—indicates a strong desire to retain the sacred tongue.

Inasmuch as most of the phrases graven on the stones are traditional, they may well have been used and repeated mechanically. In all cemeteries, however, there are longer original inscriptions, some in rhymed verse and others, as in New York, in the form of acrostics which display considerable ingenuity and familiarity with the language. A long epitaph in Newport includes a poem punning in Hebrew on the Portuguese name Rivera, while a Hebrew elegiac epitaph written to lament the passing of Nathan Levy of Philadelphia is still extant in manuscript. All of these longer inscriptions manifest a considerable command of Hebrew, but it is not known whether they were composed here or abroad. One cannot even be sure the fulsome epitaphs were contemporary, since some of them may have been prepared in a later generation by filiopietist and wealthy descendants. It is by no means improbable that most of them were written on these shores, but certainly, American Jews sufficiently adept in Hebrew to write poetry in that language were few and far between.[17]

An additional index to American Jewry's knowledge of Hebrew is reflected in the religio-legal documents prepared in this country. It is true, of course, that such documents were frequently no more than blank certificates to be filled in by the officiant, or else were simply copied verbatim from standard formularies like the *Nahalat*

Shibah, the first edition of which appeared at Amsterdam in 1668. One New York hazzan had at his disposal a blank marriage certificate complete with instructions about the standard and traditional Aramaic phrases to be inserted. It is also true, however, that a need for particular provisions or conditions in the marriage contract might require a scribe or officiant to have considerable legal knowledge. One can see from some of these still extant ketubot that those who drew them up, as early as 1718 in New York and in the first years of the Charleston Jewish community, were not without skill in the field of Jewish law.

The Knowledge of Hebrew in the Different Communities

There is a growing body of evidence indicating the existence in every community of one or two individuals who possessed some facility in Hebrew and some respectable knowledge of Jewish lore. These, as one would expect, were the men who owned Hebrew books, composed epitaphs, prepared legal documents, wrote Hebrew letters, and settled questions of rabbinic law and custom. With very few exceptions they were all immigrants. Such persons were to be found in the South as well as the North.

In colonial Savannah the only Hebraist of quality thus far identifiable by name was Ottolenghe, the well-known convert to Christianity, but there is no evidence that Savannah's small Jewish community ever had anything to do with him. An early tradition in the Sheftall family has it that Benjamin, the first of his clan in Georgia, kept a Hebrew notebook on communal data and later translated it into English. The English manuscript is still extant, and the original may have been in Hebrew or perhaps in Yiddish, which was the mother tongue of the German Jewish Sheftalls. Both Hebrew and Yiddish, of course, use the same Hebraic alphabet.

At Charleston, Moses Cohen, one of the pillars of the town's newly-formed congregation, was a competent Hebraist if we are to judge from an extant marriage contract which he prepared. Isaac Da Costa, another founding father of Charleston Jewry, had studied under Hakam Isaac Nieto in London and was able to consult the Hebrew codes. During the Revolution, indeed, his legal advice was sought by the Philadelphia Jews about the right of a *kohen* (priest) to marry a proselyte.[18]

Charleston Jewry's nearest northern neighbor was Philadelphia where, as well as in the Pennsylvania villages west to York, one found Jews who had been given a Hebrew education. Barnard Jacobs, for example, the well-known eastern Pennsylvania shohet and circumciser, was regarded as the "Jewish rabbi" by his German Christian customers and neighbors. Still extant is a Hebrew certificate prepared by him, not without some mistakes, granting the right to perform ritual slaughtering, and he and one of his friends evidenced, too, that they could check an unvocalized Hebrew pentateuchal manuscript for errors. Mordecai Moses Mordecai and Lovi Lyons—or Judah Leib'n Seligman as he also called himself—were able to write fluent Hebrew letters.[19]

Pastor Henry Melchior Muhlenberg, the learned Lutheran divine at Philadelphia, noted in his *Journals* for July 1765 that he had held discussions with a Surinamese Jew knowledgeable about the New as well as Old Testament. According to Muhlenberg, himself something of a Hebraist, his interlocutor was well-versed in Talmud and cabala. The letters of Meyer Josephson of Reading also suggest some knowledge of Hebrew—though egregious errors do occur. Josephson's neighbor Nachman ben Moses, however, handled Hebrew phrases intelligently in his Yiddish letters, while Josephson's close Philadelphia friends and business associates, the Gratz brothers, frequently employed Hebrew expressions in their Yiddish correspondence. They were able to quote the Bible and even the Talmud. When Mikveh Israel congregation's new building was consecrated at Philadelphia in 1782, respectable if not flawless Hebrew dedicatory blessings were prepared by someone for that occasion.[20]

New England, too, was not lacking in Jews, however few they may have been, who possessed some Hebrew learning. As early as the latter part of the seventeenth century Joseph Frazon of Boston was known as a man of Judaic culture. He had studied in London under the Bevis Marks teacher Joshua de Sylva who gave only advanced students instruction in Hebrew literature. In 1728 the conversion of a reputedly learned Jew—Mordecai Marks in all likelihood —was reported in one of the Connecticut towns, Norwalk, Stratford, or Fairfield. It was said that the convert had studied in a yeshibah (rabbinical academy), and was well-versed not only in Hebrew but also in Oriental tongues and Greek.[21]

Ezra Stiles of Newport reported in his diary in 1771 that his fellow townsman Isaac Hart had asked him to read a "letter in Hebrew"—actually a printed broadside appeal—sent out by the Jews of Palestine. Stiles implied there was no one among the Newport Jews who could decipher the letter from Hebron, but he was probably exaggerating, since in another entry he recorded that he and Hazzan Touro had together examined a Hebrew biblical commentary. If Touro could read a medieval Hebrew commentary, he surely could have made out a formal communication like the one from Palestine. When the Revolution broke out Touro left Newport to serve New York's Shearith Israel, whose records designate him *maskil wenabon*—a scholarly person. We know also that departing itinerants who had been entertained by Newport Jewry would write back Yiddish thank-you letters, replete with extensive Hebrew phrases, and these notes were undoubtedly read by the shohet Myers, something of a linguist and apparently a competent Hebraist. Myers and his Newport contemporary Moses V. Calo were both referred to in 1773 by a visiting savant as *mufla* (distinguished) in their Hebraic scholarship. Even allowing for the usual exaggeration, they must have been men of respectable Hebraic knowledge. Another learned Jew to spend some time in Newport and also in New York was the shohet Isaac Mark or Marcus whom Stiles mentioned in his diary.[22]

It was in the mother community of New York that the outstanding exponents or possessors of Hebraic and Jewish lore were to be found. There one could meet Jews who owned Jewish books— prayer books, Bibles, manuscript Scrolls of the Law, manuals on ritual slaughtering, and other rabbinic works. To be sure, possession of a book, especially one written in a foreign tongue, says nothing about the owner's capacity to read or understand it, and it is often difficult to determine the extent to which most of those Jewish book-owners could do more than read their Hebrew prayer books mechanically. Did the Marranos who came to these shores, the Gomezes and the Lopezes, possess enough knowledge to translate the Hebrew of the prayers they chanted?

Still, there can be no question that almost from its earliest days, the New York Jewish community had functionaries who were people of some knowledge. Saul Brown was in the city during the 1680's, and early eighteenth century professionals like Benjamin Elias (Ribbi Benjamin he was called) and Moses Lopez de Fonseca were referred to respectfully as men of learning. In 1713 Chaplain John Sharpe reported the presence in New York of many Jews who were adept at the Hebrew language. The learned Judah Monis lived and taught in the city about 1715, and succeeding decades, too, always saw new functionaries and ribbis with a store of Hebraic knowledge. Hazzan Pinto was one of them; he understood the intricacies of Hebrew calendation, and seems also to have possessed sufficient legal competence to prepare rabbinic documents. All the teachers, shohatim, and cantors who served New York in the decade before the Revolution could claim some knowledge of Jewish law and lore.[23]

The learned New Yorkers we have named thus far were all "professionals," communal employees, but there were always "laymen" too, at home to some extent in rabbinic lore. The quotation marks should be noted, since historically the distinction between professionals and laymen has not been nearly so sharp in Judaism as in Christianity.

The New-York Weekly Journal for December 24, 1733, reported the presence in the city of "an old gentleman well-skilled in Hebrew and a great proficient in cabalistic learning." A generation later a local newspaper advertised for the whereabouts of Mordecai Hart, a runaway servant who claimed to be a great scholar able to converse in French, Spanish, Greek, and Hebrew. Before Hart entered into bond servitude, he had been a peddler in the province of New York.[24]

The outstanding Jewish merchant in all North America during the mid-1700's was the German-born English-trained Jacob Franks. He was said to have had rabbinic training and is likely to have functioned once as a rebbe. The congregational death lists refer to him as "Ribbi," though there is no record he had ever served the New Yorkers in such a capacity. It is not improbable that when Franks first arrived as a young beginner, he augmented his income by giving Hebrew instruction. In a letter to his son Naphtali in London, he used a Hebrew word in Hebrew script, scant evidence of Hebrew knowledge of course, but there is better evidence, as we shall see. Naphtali himself, born and educated in New York, also had Hebrew books in his library, though again, that cannot be taken per se as an indication of Hebraic learning. Naphtali owned a copy of the pentateuchal homilies written in Hebrew by Jacob di Alba; certainly he would have had to possess considerable skill to read such a book. Perhaps he had purchased it from an impecunious or importunate suppliant, or he may have received it as a gift from a grateful petitioner, for Naphtali Franks was one of London's leading merchants. His Philadelphia brother David owned a Hebrew Bible, but even though David might on rare occasions employ a Hebrew word in his letters, how much could he have understood of a Hebrew text? [25]

Of undoubted scholarly calibre, however, was German-born Manuel Josephson, of all colonial Jews probably the most learned in Hebraic literature. In 1761, together with Joseph Simson and Jacob Franks, he sat as a rabbinical court to authorize Hazzan Pinto's proxy marriage to Rebecca de la Torre of London. Clearly, the community respected the learning of this trio. Another immigrant who, having made his way to New York during the years of the French and Indian War, would achieve economic success in later decades was Dutch-born English-educated Uriah Hendricks. He, too, had some Hebrew training and employed Hebrew phrases and sentences intelligently in his English letters.[26]

It would seem, then, that the typical colonial Jew could at the least read Hebrew, and quite a number appear to have been capable of translating easy portions of the prayer book and the Pentateuch. The professional functionaries and a limited number of laymen could consult the standard legal works in rabbinic Hebrew, and an exceptional few were genuinely at home in Hebrew sources.

One must always maintain a proper perspective with respect to American Jewry. Though the loyalties of most of the Jews on this western frontier outpost of Europe may have left little to be desired, their religious educational goals were not high. It is not so hard to understand this. Solid citizens, those who had means and culture, had remained in Europe; the Jews who came here tended to be the more adventurous who often lacked real culture as well as means and primarily were out to make a stake for themselves. This Jewry was to make no headway religiously or culturally until the middle of the nineteenth century. During the 1700's America had no Jewish "public" libraries, no press, no bookstores for Jewish publications —there were only struggling elementary schools.

Prerevolutionary American Jews, moreover, produced little or no responsa literature. Few American Jews sought rulings from European authorities on matters of Jewish canon law. That age never saw a halakic luminary or even one ordained officiating rabbi settle permanently in the mainland colonies. Hebrew had retained its importance in most European Jewish communities, for the ghetto needed it as the language of a rabbinic law which was still authoritative in economic matters, but British North America ignored Hebrew commercial law. There was, therefore, very little incentive to study Hebrew and the postbiblical codes. The first Hebrew Bible was not printed in this land until 1814—and even that enterprise was carried out by Gentiles, primarily to produce Hebrew Bibles for Christian use. During the early 1770's when the authorities of newly established Rhode Island College voted to admit Jewish students and offered Jews the opportunity not only to "have a tutor of their own religion," but even to underwrite a chair "of the Hebrew, and Oriental languages"—in short, a department of Jewish studies staffed by a Jew—the Jews were flattered but did little to abet the matter. It is doubtful they had ever thought of giving their sons any education of that type. How would such training, they might muse, have equipped a young man for a business career? [27]

Ignorance of proper Hebrew usage abounded on all sides. Tombstone inscriptions betray errors in grammar and spelling. Letter-writers quoting Hebrew phrases made the most elementary mistakes. Congregational minutes repeatedly pluralized the term *yehidim* (members) as "yehidims"; the secretary was apparently unaware that by virtue of the suffix *im* the word already had the plural form. Of course Aaron Lopez may be excused for misspelling a simple Hebrew word. After all, he had been reared a Christian in Portugal and had probably learned no Hebrew until his arrival in the

American colonies as a man of about twenty. Nor is it strange, though Miriam Gratz knew Yiddish, that she could not read or understand Hebrew written in the same script. Women were not supposed to know Hebrew!

Haym Salomon, businessman and linguist, was probably not a typical immigrant in his almost complete lack of learning, a lack he made no attempt to conceal. Even so, as we have said, he was willing to support the religious studies of his relatives in Europe if they showed any intellectual promise—and it was understood of course, *if they remained in Europe!* Academic credentials meant nothing here, he pointed out to an uncle who had threatened to descend on him. The implication in his letter is very definite: America was no place for a Jew who wanted to immerse himself in Jewish lore; his relatives were to stay where they were. Still, Salomon scarcely exaggerated the situation. In an unsigned letter dating from about the time of the Revolution, though it could just as well have dated from the French and Indian War, a man wrote that he was going back to England: this was no place for a pious Jew, business was bad, religion weak, and only money well-regarded. And yet, despite this gloomy and essentially truthful picture, a native New Yorker like Gershom Mendes Seixas *did* manage to secure some Hebrew training, enough indeed to enable him from the 1760's on to serve with dignity and respect as a hazzan of Shearith Israel.[28]

WHAT AMERICAN JEWRY ACTUALLY PRODUCED IN THE AREA OF JEWISH LITERATURE

Not much, it is clear, should be expected from a frontier community as far as cultural enterprise is concerned. The largest Jewish community in colonial America never exceeded 400 souls, if that. The Jewish householders of New York, and of other communities as well, invested their energies, not in cultural pursuits, but in the exigencies of making a living and meeting the financial requirements of their modest synagogues, cemeteries, and charities. They were a small group, isolated from Europe and from her cultural traditions and demands. As a rule peripheral frontier groups are not culturally creative, and the colonial Jews were certainly no exception. Still, did American Jewry accomplish nothing at all in the realm of Jewish culture? A colonial Jew with a sense of humor might have answered wryly that after all he *had* survived and Judaism had survived with him. Maybe that was no mean accomplishment. The Jew did establish and maintain the basic institutions of worship, education, and social welfare, all within the ambit of the synagogue, and he transmitted them to the next generation.

For purposes of comparison, one may ask, what had the larger body of Americans accomplished by the end of the seventeenth century? The Americans numbered close to 250,000 souls by then. The first settlers, it is true, had been too busy conquering the wilderness to keep in touch with the other isolated settlements, much less to nurture and develop their common cultural interests. Even so, by the end of the 1600's they had written some poetry and a few historical works, had made some biblical translations, and had produced a number of religious works. William Bradford, Roger Williams, Captain John Smith, Edward Winslow, John Winthrop, and John Cotton were all notable men of letters; some of them had attended college in England, and they were able to function as the cultural leaders of a group of many thousands. Some eight decades later, by 1776 the country numbered about 2,500,000 people, and by then the colonists had the writings of the Mathers, the New York historian William Smith II, Jonathan Edwards, and Benjamin Franklin. Americans had written numerous church-related works—including some Hebrew grammars—some interesting books on travel, a fine study of the Iroquois Indians, and a number of very important political pamphlets. On the whole their literary production was far from negligible. A host of newspapers, books, and broadsides appeared in America—in 1774 alone about 700 separate publications. Certainly, in the light of what their neighbors produced, the Jews—an urban, literate group, be it remembered—scarcely make a good showing.[29]

The American Jewish record is not much better even when measured, not by the achievements of the large American community of 2,500,000, but by those of the smaller English Jewish community. English Jewry was probably not much larger in numbers than American Jewry, though the English Jews had certain advantages of course. Practically all of them were concentrated in one city, London, and London was part of Europe—part, that is to say, of the heartland of eighteenth century World Jewish learning. London's cultured Anglo-Sephardic Jewry was polylingual and composed poetry in English, Latin, Portuguese, and Spanish. English Jewry had slowly begun to produce a modest literature in Hebrew and in English, including liturgical works, statutes of communal organizations, reports on intracommunal battles, polemics with Christianity, and political writings on civil liberties. In addition London Jewry could boast of a small body of sermonic writings, some theology and exegesis, some pedagogical literature, Hebrew grammars, a Hebrew vocabulary, some poetry in the sacred tongue, and even some talmudic comments. None of it, to be sure, was particularly significant, but it *was* a literature. Nothing comparable emerged in the American Jewish community.[30]

Any Jewish culture that might develop in this land would be found for the most part in New York, the prime American Jewish center, such as it was. We have already noted that the New Yorkers had inscribed some Hebrew poetry on their tombstones—if it had been written by them—and they had prepared some religiolegal documents, two services of thanksgiving for British military victories, and two English translations of prayer books. The Jews of Newport had seen to the publication of a Spanish sermon in English translation. This is the extant total—pitifully little. Aside from numerous business or personal letters and some fragments of original prayers, there exists not a single book or pamphlet or literary remain that would enable us to study the mind of colonial Jewry. In short, that community left no literary heritage to mankind.[31]

CHAPTER 63

THE TEACHING OF HEBREW TO NON-JEWS

HEBRAISM, JEWISH HISTORY, AND THE AMERICAN COLONISTS

It is obvious from what we have said thus far that the Jews of colonial North America were not distinguished for their knowledge and cultivation of biblical and rabbinical literature. Still, the historian must ask whether it is not possible that in their attachment —even a mechanical attachment—to the Hebrew language and in their loyalty to Judaism, they did somehow influence their Christian neighbors. Surely, it would seem, the Jews as unitarians and Sabbatarians *could* have influenced their Christian associates religiously, and culturally too as exponents of a Hebraic tradition or orientation; they *could* have exercised some influence. In fact, however, they did not—not perceptibly at least.

The Sabbatarianism which certain American Protestant sectaries advocated had been derived not from the model of American Jewry and its religious practices, but from non-Jewish European traditions embodying a belief in the literal interpretation of the Old Testament. Christian Sabbatarianism has never needed a Jewish model; it reflects a tradition going back to apostolic times. It must be said, too, that none of the extant sources indicate any direct Jewish influence on Christian trinitarians in their interpretation of monotheism. Yet who can doubt that the very existence of the Jew and of what he stood for theologically could have served as anything but a challenge to every thinking Christian? Certainly, the constant emphasis in Christian apologetics on the validity of the Trinity must strike the observer as defensive, and suggests that trinitarian apologists were arguing against a unitarianism of which their Jewish neighbors were mute, but eloquent advocates. The point, however, is that the Jews were mute.[1]

During the colonial period many non-Jews, particularly in New England, took much interest in Hebraic and biblical studies. But were the Jews their teachers? Let it be clear at the outset that Hebraic studies were strongest in precisely those colonies like Massachusetts where Jews were fewest. Hebraic studies were vigorously pursued in Puritan Massachusetts during the 1600's, a century which found less than half a dozen Jews in all of Boston. In short, Hebrew would have been studied in New England, and no doubt in every other colony too, had there not been a single Jew in all America. With certain exceptions to be discussed below, there is no direct link between American Jewry and the Christian interest in Hebrew, biblical, and rabbinic studies. The close relation of Judaism and the Jew to Hebraic lore does make it advisable nonetheless to describe, however briefly, some aspects of the impact of the ancient Hebrew culture on the American colonies.[2]

Since Christianity had originated as a Jewish sect, Hebraic and Jewish components were of primary importance in the early days of the faith. The retention of the Old Testament in the Christian canon meant that the Hebraic element would remain constant, but a renewed interest in the language and culture of the Hebrew Bible developed in the early modern centuries under the stimulus of the Renaissance and the Protestant Reformation. During the seventeenth century, then, this renewed—rather than new—interest in Hebraism was part of the intellectual baggage brought to the colonies by some of the immigrants, especially those from England. As children of the Renaissance, many of the Puritan leaders had studied Hebrew, which seemed to them a great classical culture comparable to the Greek and the Latin. Thus, even a century later when Ezra Stiles Jr. went to Yale in 1774, he carried with him a number of books—what he considered to be a "gentleman's library." Along with the Greek and Latin classics, and a few English and French works, went a Hebrew psalter and a Hebrew dictionary.[3]

Some of the Pilgrims, Puritans, and other Protestants who had studied at Cambridge and Oxford came to America with relatively good training in classical, that is biblical Hebrew. Their children born in this country knew rather less, though there was no province where the study of the Hebrew Bible was not carried on, even if but modestly. It cannot be said that many of the Christians in eighteenth century North America could have claimed genuine competence in the field of biblical Hebrew. The English Bible was, of course, widely read and exerted a profound influence on the culture of the settlers, so that John Adams for example could write of the ancient Hebrews: "They are the most glorious nation that ever inhabited this earth. The Romans and their empire were but a bauble in comparison of the Jews. They have given religion to three quarters of the globe and have influenced the affairs of mankind more, and more happily than any other nation, ancient or modern." And he could "insist that the Hebrews have done more to civilize men than any other nation. If I were an atheist, and believed in blind eternal fate, I should still believe that fate ordained the Jews to be the most essential instrument for civilizing the nations." [4]

The Pilgrims and Puritans, owing to their intensive interest in the Bible, of which the Old Testament was physically the major part, delighted in identifying themselves with ancient Israel. Projecting their own experience into the stories of the Old Testament, they saw their flight from England as an Exodus, and they looked on America as both the wilderness and the Promised Land which was yet to become Zion. In their own hearts they knew that they were the true Israel, the Chosen People of God. But they turned to the Hebrew Bible for more than a romantic, soul-satisfying imagery. In a more direct sense, they looked to the Old Testament for a holiday like Thanksgiving, which was influenced undoubtedly by the biblical Sukkot or Feast of Booths. True, a Thanksgiving holiday had long been celebrated in Europe by Catholics and Protestants alike, but the American Puritans found a sanction for it in the Old Testament. They also followed the biblical and even the rabbinic concept of the Sabbath as a day of almost complete cessation from labor, and they gave their children Hebrew names to a degree equalled only by the Jews themselves in postbiblical times. No American Jew, however, would have gone as far as Polycarpus Nelson, who called his eldest son Mahur Shalal Hash Baz ("Make Speed to the Spoil, He Hasteneth to the Prey")![5]

Because of their Old Testament beliefs, and quite likely too because of their hostility to their Anglican oppressors, the Pilgrim and Puritan founders of New England attempted to institute commonwealths founded on the Bible and its legislation. They assumed they had been profoundly influenced by the Old Testament in setting up their polity, though the resemblance was more verbal than real. This identification with Hebrew antiquity may have become attenuated in the course of the colonial experience, but it never died out entirely. During the American Revolution the prejudice against England reasserted itself to such a degree that some individuals—how seriously?—proposed Hebrew as the national language of the new republic. The effort of the early settlers to adapt Mosaic legislation for their purposes was not very successful, but that fact never prevented them from nursing an exaggerated notion of its utility and its adaptability for their own needs. Even as late as the mid-1700's the young John Adams gave voice to this conviction when he wrote: "Suppose a nation in some distant region should take the Bible for their only law-book and every member should regulate his conduct by the precepts there exhibited! . . . What a Utopia, what a Paradise would this region be!"[6]

The chief architect of the New England attempt to take over the laws of the Hebrew Bible was John Cotton, who was following in the footsteps of contemporary English radicals. *Moses His Judicials*, the code Cotton proposed in 1636, was actually dependent only in small part on the Old Testament, but it did stress Mosaic ordinances like the need of two witnesses for a conviction, and it prohibited usury. Some of the laws Cotton set forth were borrowed from biblical regulations on the conduct of war, on trespass, pledges, deposits, seduction, theft, burglary, and inheritance. In addition to the catalogue of capital crimes taken over from English law, Cotton included several the Old Testament had denounced—idolatry, blasphemy, Sabbathbreaking, rebellion against parents, adultery, and bearing false witness. While marking the height of New England's reliance on Mosaic legislation, Cotton's legal work was adopted as a whole in no colony except New Haven. It was influential enough, of course, since some of its provisions, especially those dealing with capital crimes, found their way into the legislative codes of New Plymouth, the Massachusetts Bay Colony, Connecticut, Southampton (Long Island), New Hampshire, New York, Pennsylvania, and New Jersey. In reality, however, only a very few laws in force in colonial times stemmed directly from the pentateuchal legislation, for it was primarily to English law, not to the Bible, that the Puritans and all British North Americans looked for legislative models.[7]

There can be no question that the Hebraic tradition did play some part in the American Revolution. As they made ready to break with the British Empire, with its monarchical and aristocratic form of government, Americans required warrant for so bold an undertaking. They could, of course, have found ample precedents in the historical experience of nearly every people, but history had *divine* sanction in one book alone—the Bible. All that the Bible contained was deemed authoritative, for it represented the word of God. Those who believed in Scripture turned to it in search of moral sanction for the ordinarily immoral act of treason and rebellion. Even those who admitted doubts about the Bible were fully aware of its hold on many and so had recourse to it, if only verbally and homiletically, as a powerful instrument of propaganda. It is quite clear, therefore, why the Old Testament should have played a special role during the Revolution. Did it not, after all, rehearse the struggle of the twelve tribes of Israel—read the thirteen colonies of America—to create an independent state? The Whigs scoured it for antimonarchical passages as they moved slowly toward rebellion. In the experiences of the ancient Israelites, in Samuel's denunciations of kingship, in the revolt against Rehoboam, they found their justification for defying the "tyranny" of George III. What is interesting in this connection, and deserving of some emphasis, is the fact that the non-Jews were far more sensitive than the Jews to these biblical implications. Though most of them were Whigs, the Jews had little to say about the anti-royalist tendencies of their Old Testament forebears. The leaders of the revolt were not intimate with Jews, and some of them, like John Adams, knew the Old Testament better than the Jews did. Unlike the Jews, few of whom were students of the Bible, they had read it carefully and often.[8]

The Bible, it is worth noting, was not the only Jewish book to exercise some degree of influence in that generation of revolt. The writings of Flavius Josephus too appealed to the revolutionary imagination, and considerable interest was manifested in that well-known postbiblical Jewish historian whose work reflected or could be read as reflecting a heroic opposition to foreign tyranny. Josephus' *War of the Jews*, a classic account of the epic first-century Jewish struggle against Roman oppression, had been printed in Boston as early as 1719, but even earlier during the preceding century his works had been imported from London to be read in New England. Throughout the eighteenth century American booksellers continued to import copies of Josephus from London, where they were frequently reprinted, but significantly, it was not until 1773–1775 that his *complete* works were published in North America. Included in this four-volume publication were two appendices reflecting postbiblical Jewish history: the story of the Maccabean martyrs who died for political and religious freedom, and the account of Philo's embassy from the Jews of Alexandria to the mad emperor Caius Caligula. Both of these addenda portrayed in dramatic fashion the heroism of a small group pitted against the tyrannical ruler of a great empire. Other editions of Josephus also appeared—in 1773 alone, three different and incomplete editions, two of which, despite their American imprints, may actually have been printed at Glasgow.

It is hardly to be doubted that these volumes were prepared for the American market in order to encourage colonial resistance to arbitrary government, and how effective they proved as instruments of Revolutionary propaganda one can see quite vividly in the remark of the Whig leader Dr. Benjamin Rush, "What shining examples of patriotism do we behold in Joshua, Samuel, Maccabeus, and all the illustrious princes, captains, and prophets among the Jews!" None of the editions of Josephus, however, were published by Jews. There were no Jewish publishers in this country, and Josephus' popularity had no connection at all with the presence of Jews in the colonies.[9]

The Hebraism which recommended itself to the North American colonists was the essence of the teachings to be found both in the Old and the New Testaments and in their Jewishly influenced commentators throughout the ages. This Hebraism reflected what might be termed a Judaeo-Christian cultural force which posited a belief in a merciful God, the Father of all men and concerned as such with the social and spiritual betterment of the individual in an organized society. But to what extent can this Hebraism be attributed to the cultural impingement of the American Jew on his Gentile neighbor? Clearly, it was to no perceptible degree furthered by Jews; it was a creation of Christian émigrés who had cultivated Hebrew abroad, brought their modest Hebrew libraries with them to America, and continued their studies on these shores. Hebrew and Aramaic, it bears repeating, would have been studied in the colonies by non-Jews, had there not been a single Jew here. The persistence of the ancient Hebrew tongue in the New World of North America was completely independent of contemporary Jews.[10]

American Jews Teaching Hebrew to Christians

We have stated categorically that Hebraism in this country was in no sense dependent on or reflective of the presence and teaching of the American Jew, so a detailed analysis of its nature and impact, which were quite extensive, lies quite outside the study of American Jewish history. Still, it is a fact that there were American Jews who taught Hebrew, both classical and rabbinic, to non-Jews. Some Christians, interested in the Bible and its rabbinic interpretations, turned to Jewish teachers for information and instruction, and the work of those teachers in this connection does fall within the province of the present historical study.

As early as 1713 an English clergyman in New York had written that there were in the city learned Jews from Poland, Germany, and Hungary, Jews capable of teaching Hebrew. Those immigrants were primarily versed in rabbinic Hebrew, for in Eastern and Central Europe the Bible—more precisely the Pentateuch—was not taught as a formal subject except to children. There is no indication what-soever that the "ingenious men" of whom the Englishman spoke were ever called upon to display their ingenuity in teaching, but it is difficult to believe that the numerous Hebraists of New England took no advantage of their occasional encounters with Jews to seek enlightenment on the Hebrew language and the Jewish way of life. Pious and learned Christians were profoundly attentive to rabbinic interpretations of the Bible, and rabbinic Bibles with their numerous commentaries were available in America from Harvard College in Massachusetts all the way to the Salzburgers' library in Georgia. On the whole, however, standard rabbinical works were very rare in this country, and in any case only the exceptional Christian—or for that matter Jewish—Hebraist could make use of them. For their knowl-edge of the ancient rabbis, most Christians relied on the Christian commentaries which had already absorbed the interpretations of the major medieval and early modern Jewish commentators.[11]

JUDAH MONIS

The first Jew in this country to be known as a teacher of Chris-tians was Judah Monis, a convert to Protestantism. Monis was also the first Jew in North America to receive an academic degree—an honorary one in this instance—from an American college. The first specialist in Hebrew to be appointed by Harvard, he was also the author of the first Hebrew grammar published in British North America.

This man, who transmitted his Jewish heritage to nearly two generations of Harvard students, had been born of a Marrano family in 1683 either at Algiers or as is more probable at Venice. In all likeli-hood he had pursued his Hebraic studies in the cities of Venice, Leghorn, and Amsterdam. Although he received a good Jewish edu-cation, it is doubtful that he was a rabbi, as his Christian associates assumed and as his epitaph claims. Actually, it would seem, he had been a scribe and a rebbe, a teacher in Jewish communities. Leav-ing Italy, probably for Amsterdam, he seems then to have moved to London, to Jamaica, and at length to New York where he arrived about 1715. By February 1716 he had been accepted as a freeman in New York, and remained there for at least four years. He was designated a merchant, but also taught Hebrew to Gentiles, and probably to Jews as well. Since no congregational minutes have survived from those years, it is impossible to determine the degree of Monis' affiliation with the local Jewish community. Although he took his abjuration oath "upon the true faith of a Christian" when he applied for freemanship at New York, he seems to have still been at that time a fervent if not a belligerent Jew, and in a Hebrew letter to Samuel Johnson, later president of King's College, stressed the unitarian character of Israel's God, "the living God and there is no other, blessed be He and blessed be His name."

Not long after his arrival in New York, Monis is known to have corresponded on matters of scholarly interest with New Englanders, among them in all probability representatives of Harvard College, and by 1720 he had come to Boston where he communicated in formal fashion with the Harvard Corporation. He had submitted to the Harvard authorities a rough draft of a Hebrew grammar he hoped they would publish, and there is no doubt he wanted to teach Hebrew at Harvard and have the students use his grammar. Negotiating for some two years with the college authorities about a teaching position and other matters, he supported himself most probably by opening a shop in Boston or Cambridge. In 1721 he lent money to a tutor at Harvard, and around that time Monis began studying Christianity with a number of clergymen. Finally, on March 27, 1722, in the presence of a throng so large that some people had to stand outside, he underwent an imposing ceremony of conversion in College Hall. Benjamin Colman, preacher of the Brattle Street Church and a very important personage at the college, delivered the *Discourse* at the one-time rebbe's baptism.

One can only speculate, of course, as to the motivations which induced Monis to take this step. He had been a student of the cabala, so the concept of the Trinity could not have been altogether novel to him. With its philosophy of emanation, cabala lends itself to a rapprochement with a trinitarian concept of the Godhead, and it is rather interesting to note that an exposure to cabala typifies the three most eminent Jewish converts to Christianity to appear on the colonial American scene. Isaac Miranda of Pennsylvania, Joseph

Ottolenghe of Savannah, and Judah Monis of Cambridge, Massachusetts, seem all to have been Italian Jews who had studied cabala or sat at the feet of cabalistic teachers. Aside from that, however, the fact that Harvard College appointed Monis instructor of the Hebrew tongue several weeks after his conversion certainly suggests that such employment had been promised him. It is not improbable that Colman had even pledged himself to make Monis a full professor—tempting bait to a man who had wandered about in at least four countries, was then thirty-nine years of age, and had thus far achieved no success in his life. It is probable too that by 1722 Monis already had an understanding with the local girl whom he was to marry in 1724.

Was Monis sincere in his conversion? He may well have been. To be sure, though he did teach Hebrew on Saturday, he persisted in observing the seventh day of the week as the Sabbath, but certainly after his conversion he never gave his sponsors any reason to doubt his sincerity. He enjoyed a good reputation as a respectable citizen and seems to have been a zealous convert. Some of his sponsors, knowing full well the checkered history of proselytes, were suspicious of him at first, and even Colman implied in his *Discourse* that mundane considerations may have influenced Monis to convert. A letter to Colman from Bishop White Kennett of London questioned the integrity of all Jewish converts, by implication Monis' too of course, while Increase Mather's preface to a work by Monis also bore a trace of such wariness: "There have been some of that nation [the Jews] brought home to Christ, who have proved blessings to the world." Presumably Mather thought there were *others* who had *not* "proved blessings." Monis knew how apprehensive his sponsors were, and he assured them and the Christian world he had accepted baptism in order to be "saved"; they were not to doubt his belief in the Trinity and in Jesus Christ.

At the ceremony of conversion in College Hall, Colman spoke first, and then Monis followed with an address, *The Truth*, in which he professed Christianity and offered evidence that the promised Messiah had already come. Later that same year Monis produced two more addresses—it is not known that they were ever delivered —which he called *The Whole Truth* and *Nothing But the Truth*.

In *The Whole Truth* the neophyte discussed the divinity of Christ and the reasons why the Jews had not yet been converted to Christianity; in *Nothing But the Truth* he sought to prove to his own satisfaction at least, "and with the authority of the cabalistical rabbies," that the doctrine of the Trinity was "not a novelty . . . but as ancient as the Bible it self." These three essays, together with Colman's *Discourse* and a preface by Increase Mather, were published as one book in 1722. The fact that Mather, a former president of Harvard and one of the most influential men in all New England, had consented to write the Preface indicates the importance the church of that day attached to Monis' conversion.

The volume's title page insisted the convert's three discourses had been "written by Mr. Monis himself," but there can hardly be any question that Monis did not write them. Formulated in good English and manifesting a thorough knowledge of Christology and of Protestant theological terminology, they were surely ghostwritten for him. The strongly anti-Catholic tone of these writings is another reason to doubt Monis' authorship. Jews of that day had no love for the Roman Catholic Church, but anti-Catholic invective was simply uncharacteristic of them. Or are we to assume that in embracing the Protestantism of eighteenth century New England, Monis had also made himself an outspoken anti-Catholic?

When Monis began to teach at Harvard, he used his manuscript Hebrew grammar as a textbook, and his students had to copy his dictation laboriously into their notebooks. By 1723 he had already taught thirty students. Though the M. A. degree was conferred on him that year, it soon became rather obvious that he was not a successful teacher and that his course was something less than captivating. The title page of a later copy bescribbled by a doodler testifies all too eloquently just how much appreciated Monis' pedagogy was. The poor student victim, aggrieved by rules which meant little or nothing to him, amended his copy of the grammar so that its title page, instead of reading "Composed and accurately corrected by Judah Monis, M.A.," now read "Confuted and accurately corrupted by Judah Monis, M.(aker of) A.(sses)." All of it was not necessarily Monis' fault of course, for there is ample evidence that courses in Hebrew grammar, even those offered in Jewish schools, have frequently been anything but popular. Almost a century before Monis tried to teach Hebrew at Harvard, one of his predecessors, Michael Wigglesworth, had been driven to tears by student indifference to the sacred tongue, and years after Monis' time, President Ezra Stiles found his students at Yale so unresponsive that he was compelled to abandon Hebrew as a required course for freshmen and to make it an elective instead. Some of the boys in the course even tried to bribe him—with due gentility, to be sure.

Hebrew *is* a difficult subject and if, as he is supposed to have done, Monis taught it unvocalized, the students confronted a formidable task. To "confute" matters even more, there is reason to believe that he enjoyed no surfeit of personal popularity. Not only was he mistreated by the faculty, but some of his students, we are told, bombarded the door of his room with brickbats and even broke it open, though all this may have indicated nothing more than student prankishness. At all events, the undergraduate work was taken away from him for a time at least, and he limited himself to the teaching of graduates. Apparently, too, his courses were made optional. Monis never received much of a salary, never had tenure, never rose beyond the rank of instructor, and was always dependent on annual reelection. He frequently complained about his meager pay and finally petitioned the Massachusetts authorities for a supplementary grant-in-aid and for exemption from local taxation, privileges not uncommon among the teachers at the college. He could not live on his salary alone and on occasion made a little extra money as a Spanish interpreter. In order to supplement his modest income as a teacher he opened a shop where he sold hardware and tobacco, but even here ill luck dogged his footsteps. Some of his customers refused to pay him and he had to take them to court.

After some negotiations the Harvard authorities finally decided to help Monis publish his manuscript grammar and lent him money for that purpose. The work had by then been in use at the college as a textbook for over a decade and perhaps had proved itself. Certainly, instruction would benefit from a printed text in the hands of the students. Type was secured from London, and the font used to publish Monis' *Grammar of the Hebrew Tongue*—the book appeared at Boston in 1735—was probably the first complete Hebrew font in all of North America. Monis' *Grammar* was certainly the first Hebrew book to be printed in British North America.

The Harvard students who took Monis' course were compelled to buy his textbook. Although it contained typographical errors, as Monis was ready to admit, he insisted that it was more accurately printed than most grammars, that its rules were better, and that the examples he gave were more familiar. Actually it was by no means an easily understandable book, though it may well have been an improvement on its predecessors and probably was a good grammar for its time.

In later years Monis was appointed a justice of the peace, but for unknown reasons the appointment was not confirmed. After his wife's death in 1760 he resigned from Harvard where he had been teaching for thirty-eight years. Already seventy-seven years old at that time, he retired to Worcester County, Massachusetts, to live with relatives of his deceased wife, participated actively in the local church life, and was given a seat of honor in the church. Monis presented the congregation with two silver communion cups, and one wonders whether those cups had originally been kiddush cups, used for the Friday and holiday ritual in Jewish homes and synagogues.

Despite the fact that he constantly pleaded poverty, his estate when probated was not a modest one. Among the legacies he left at his death in 1764 was one for the relief of the poor widows of Massachusetts clergymen, a bequest still in existence today and administered by the American Unitarian Association. It is to be hoped that the shades of Monis, who had so vigorously defended the Trinity in the essay *Nothing But the Truth*, are not disturbed by the fact that a portion of his estate is now controlled by a group whose members deny the triune nature of the Deity.

That Monis had scholarly capacities is evident in the fact that he built his grammar on the Hebrew works of the Provençal grammarian David Kimhi and of the Italians Samuel Archevolti and Solomon Raphael Judah Leon Templo. It requires considerable learning to understand grammars written in Hebrew and to translate them into English. Cotton Mather, himself a Hebraist, considered Monis "a great master of the Hebrew language," and Monis certainly evinced academic if not scholarly interests. He used the library at Harvard and read works on theology, law, church history, and the New Testament. There is, unfortunately, no catalogue of his own library, though it is known to have included Hebrew books. The chief subject Monis taught at Harvard was biblical Hebrew grammar, although he may also have taught a Bible text like the Psalms. His ability to handle Hebrew may be seen in his translation of the Lord's Prayer and the Creed. His promised translations of the thirty-nine articles of the Church of England and of the Westminster Assembly's *Shorter Catechism*, if he ever made them, are not extant. Monis also proposed translating the *Larger Catechism*.

Was he competent to teach rabbinics? There can be no question that he had some knowledge of the talmudic and later rabbinic literature, especially of the classical medieval commentators. In his writings he referred to medieval rabbinic works, though he never quoted directly from them. There is every reason to believe, however, that he could find his way in the rabbinic sources and in cabala. Harvard College still possesses a manuscript of his dealing with cabala, a part of which he himself had copied. Some of the material in it is from the *Zohar*, the classical work of Jewish mysticism, but most of the manuscript concerned itself with the later sixteenth century Lurianic cabala. Monis also knew some of the writings of early moderns like Isaac Abravanel and Manasseh ben Israel. The latter's *El Conciliador*, written in Spanish, used rabbinic materials to reconcile contradictions in the Old Testament.

It is somewhat doubtful that Monis ever taught rabbinics, though he had begun compiling a vocabulary which would have been helpful to the student interested in postbiblical Hebrew. Among the manuscripts he left behind is a Hebrew-English vocabulary, a "Nomenclator," prepared by him so his students might have a basic vocabulary permitting them to use any Jewish author, even the postclassical ones. Errors in this vocalized vocabulary make it clear that Monis was no meticulous scholar.

There is no evidence that Monis ever made use of his "Nomenclator" to introduce his students to the study of rabbinic literature, nor is there any evidence that he possessed an adequate rabbinic library of his own. He could, of course, have supplemented his rabbinic needs by using some of the books housed in the college library, and there is reason to believe that he did have a working knowledge of rabbinics, some of which may have rubbed off on his students.

It is difficult to gauge the influence of this man on his pupils. From all indications Monis was not an inviting personality, and at least one of his students, his successor Stephen Sewall, despised him. Sewall, who was to become the Thomas Hancock Professor of Hebrew and Other Oriental Languages, occupying the first chair in an American school to be endowed by an American, questioned his teacher's knowledge of grammar, though Monis had probably been a better grammarian than Sewall was prepared to admit. It may be, indeed, that Monis, through his knowledge of the medieval Jewish commentators, supplied a more accurate interpretation of the Bible than did his colleagues who were dependent on Christologically-oriented interpreters.[12]

OTHER JEWISH TEACHERS

Monis was not the only man of Jewish background to offer Hebrew instruction to non-Jews during the colonial period. The 1760's saw the New York hazzan Joseph Jesurun Pinto and Emanuel Lyon of Philadelphia both advertise their willingness to teach Hebrew, as Lyon put it, "in its purity." In all probability their advertisements were designed to attract Christians interested in learning to read the Hebrew Bible, though it is hardly to be doubted that they could have given instruction in the elements of rabbinics too, had anyone turned to them for such. Around that same time Jewish settlers like Joseph Simson and Manuel Josephson as well as the hazzanim of the various congregations, the rebbes to be found in different communities, and the numerous itinerant "scholars" who were constantly coming and going, all possessed at least the knowledge if not the capacity to teach Hebrew to beginners. There is, however, little evidence that these businessmen and rebbes were called upon to give formal instruction in the Bible or rabbinics to non-Jews, although they were on occasion consulted by Christian Hebraists.[13]

Ezra Stiles as Hebraist

Nevertheless, there is reason to believe there were Christians who from time to time studied biblical Hebrew, the original text of the Old Testament, with Jews. One eighteenth century Christian student seems not only to have interested himself in rabbinics, but even to have succeeded in learning how to read a rabbinical text, though the extent to which he acquired his knowledge from Jews is not easily determined. This was Ezra Stiles, the pastor of the Second Congregational Church in Newport. One of the most scholarly men in North America, Stiles had inherited some and bought others of the indispensable books which would serve him as an introduction to classical Hebrew. Within a relatively few years his general library of over 400 volumes came to include copies of the Hebrew Bible, including a complete rabbinic Bible with the usual medieval commentaries, Hebrew grammars, a copy of the *Zohar*, a Sephardic prayer book, tractates or possibly even a complete set of the Talmud, Maimonides' *Guide to the Perplexed*, and of course, the standard lexicographical works of the seventeenth century scholar Johannes Buxtorf the Elder.[14]

Stiles had not begun studying the holy language until his fortieth year. It was then in 1767 that Isaac Touro, the hazzan of Newport, taught him how to pronounce the consonants and the vowels and also to write—or more precisely perhaps to print—the classical and rabbinic script. Stiles was avid to learn Hebrew, and with the start given him by Touro and his own considerable apparatus for the study of classical and rabbinic Hebrew, he set to work. He never had a regular teacher, and what he learned for the most part he taught himself. Though like all autodidacts he frequently erred, there is very little doubt that Stiles became uncommonly proficient as a biblical Hebraist. One can see this, for instance, in his well-known Connecticut election sermon delivered in 1783; he quoted from Daniel in the original and when he turned to address Governor Jonathan Trumbull, played with the meaning of the governor's given name *Yonatan* (God hath given [us]). Stiles's interests, however, did not stop at Hebrew but included other Near Eastern languages as well: Aramaic, Arabic, Syriac, and Coptic. He also devoted himself to Palestinian and biblical archaeology, to the geography, paleography, and antiquities of the Holy Land.

In his eagerness to learn Hebrew, especially of the rabbinic variety, Stiles went to the synagogue in Newport, tried to follow the worship services, and sought to further his knowledge of Jewish life and culture by cultivating every learned Jew who came to Newport. Through the hazzan Touro and other Jews in town, he is likely to have met most of the "messengers" and rabbis from Palestine and Europe. From each of them he learned something, and with nearly all of them he avidly discussed such mystical Jewish literature as could be read to lend support to a nonunitarian concept of the Deity. He and the visiting cabalistic adept Moses bar David conversed about talmudic and later rabbinic literature, particularly the cabalistic *Zohar*, and "Rabbi Moses" lent him three important mystical works, which Stiles spent several days reading, apparently with comprehension.

With Carigal, who was to become his friend, Stiles surveyed the whole range of Jewish lore. The two spoke of the Lost Ten Tribes, of levirate marriage, biblical archaeology, resurrection, witchcraft, "biblical criticism," paleography, and Semitic languages. He assiduously questioned Carigal—and all the other Jews he met—on the Jewish concept of the Messiah and the date of his expected advent. With Tobiah ben Judah Loew, who arrived in Newport several months after Carigal's departure for the West Indies, Stiles went over much the same ground he had covered with Carigal. He was always eager to discuss Jewish customs and ritual and ceremonial. When the South Carolina merchant Isaac Da Costa came to town, the subject under discussion was Jewish law, for Da Costa had brought along a copy of Maimonides' *Mishneh Torah*. The summer after the skirmishes at Lexington and Concord, the Palestinian Samuel Ha-Cohen landed in Newport, and Stiles had the opportunity once more to talk with a Jew of some learning. And when there was no visiting "rabbi" to edify him, he could always write to the scholarly Isaac Pinto of New York.

Stiles learned a great deal from books written by European

Christians on Jewish life; he gained much also from observing the life of the Jews in Newport and from his discussions with them. It may be said, then, that this Congregationalist minister, who was in 1778 to become president of Yale College, had many Jewish teachers. To some extent they certainly helped him to achieve proficiency as a biblical and rabbinic scholar. Curiously enough, however, Stiles's prime motivation seems never to have been scholarship as such. What he hoped to find in the ancient Jewish literature was proof of the Trinity and of Jesus' messianic character. And he was convinced his quest had met with success.

What did Stiles ultimately learn about Jewish history, literature, and religion? How much Hebrew did he know? He had read the French historian Jacques Basnage de Beauval's *History of the Jews*, in addition no doubt to other works dealing with the unfolding of Jewish history, and he had managed to scrape together a large body of knowledge on Jewish life and customs. No other American Christian of his generation could claim a greater familiarity with the details of Jewish religious practice. As we have indicated, he knew the Hebrew Bible, and his correspondence with Carigal testifies to his ability to write a rather acceptable if simple biblical Hebrew. The script he employed was the Assyrian, the square printed Hebrew, not the cursive. The history of the Bible, of the Aramaic translations and the great commentators, of the Talmud, of the Maimonidean works, of the medieval cabala—he knew something of all this literature. An academician who read widely and understood what he read, Stiles was unquestionably better acquainted with Jewish history and literature than nine out of every ten Jews he met.[15]

His was a brilliant mind. It took him scarcely four years to acquire the facility to read difficult rabbinic texts. From his diary one gains the impression that he had dipped into the Talmud, the *Zohar*, biblical commentators like Rashi and David Kimhi, and Maimonides' code, the *Mishneh Torah*. When Isaac Hart showed him a letter from Hebron Jewry, Stiles was able not only to read it but even to translate it properly. To be sure, this most learned of eighteenth century American Christian Hebraists was not adept in rabbinic lore, but it would seem that with the aid of dictionaries, he could read almost any passage in the Hebrew and Aramaic postbiblical literature. This was the extent of his rabbinic knowledge, and it was no mean achievement.[16]

JUDAIZING SECTARIANS

Since eastern Pennsylvania witnessed the rise of a Judaizing sect, one wonders whether the Jews in that area had influenced their neighbors. In 1720 Johann Conrad Beissel, the founder of this group, came to Lancaster County from Germany where he had already been exposed to Old Testament literalism and to Jewish dietary practices. On his landing in North America the master baker Beissel was already a mystic and a Judaizer who refused to use pork fat in baking bread, but it was only in this country, probably under the influence of Welsh and English Christian sectarians, that Beissel became a Sabbatarian. A few of his associates were extremist enough to circumcise themselves, and one of his followers, who was frequently demented, once made an effort to preach to the Jews in the New York synagogue.[17]

In 1732 Beissel founded the Ephrata Society, a semimonastic pacifist and communistic group of Sabbatarians, but Judaistic practices represented only one phase, and a minor one, in this establishment of the German Seventh Day Baptist Church. Beissel's was an eclectic, mystical, pietistic, orthodox type of Christianity, and Jews had no connection with it, for the Camp or Community of the Solitary was fully developed before the first Jews are known to have come to that part of Pennsylvania. Though Ephrata's Sabbatarianism was influenced by the Christian Sabbatarians of this country, it stemmed most probably from a literal interpretation of the Old Testament and looked back to the chain of Sabbatarian Christianity which had begun with the original Jewish-Christians of the Gospels. Jews in the British North American provinces apparently played no part in the rise of the Ephrata commune or in the formulation of its ideology.

During the 1740's, it is true, Jews began to penetrate into Lancaster County, and it is not improbable that individual Jews had relations with the mystics at Ephrata Cloister. Those sectarians and their neighbors, also German Christians, used Hebrew phrases as exorcisms against fire; for example, the verse from Numbers 11:2: "And the people cried unto Moses; and Moses prayed unto the Lord, and the fire abated." They were also fond of amulets which they believed protected them against fire. *Feuerzettel* or *Feuersegen* they called these paper or parchment inscriptions with the star of David and Hebrew phrases, or the initial letters of Hebrew words, or even the four Latin initials for the Hebrew *atta gibbor leolam adonay* ("Thou art mighty forever, O Lord"), a passage from the Jewish prayer book.

Some of the Germans also tacked amulet-like plates on their houses or built them into the four corners of their stone foundations in order to secure protection against fire and other disasters. These naive farmers and craftsmen may have learned the use of such Hebraic protective devices from the *Dorfjuden*, the village Jews they had known in the old country, for there is no evidence that American Jews, stemming from the same regions in Europe, continued to employ amulets here. Still, it is possible that as the Jews penetrated into Lancaster County during the 1740's and thereafter, their rustic neighbors turned to them for aid in preparing Hebrew-tinctured amulets. Beissel's successor, John Peter Miller, a student of Oriental languages, very probably knew some biblical Hebrew. Miller, however, despite his Sabbatarianism, was a fundamentalist Christian who had no sympathy for Jews, Turks, pagans, deists, and atheists. Ultimately in any case, this obscure conventicle of German Baptist Judaizers would have little if indeed any influence on the mainstream of American culture.[18]

SUMMARY

One can see that there were some Hebraic cultural influences which American Jews exerted on their non-Jewish contemporaries. They did on occasion teach biblical Hebrew to non-Jews, and they did discuss the Bible with them, naturally from the Jewish point of view since, unlike Christians, no observant Jew ever saw Christ in the prophecies of the Old Testament. Christian students of rabbinic literature generally depended on secondary sources like the writings of European Christian scholars, but there were rare occasions in this country when some turned to Jews for guidance, while inquisitive and intelligent Christians did not hesitate to discuss Judaism with their Jewish neighbors. All of this did make for intercultural knowledge and intellectual understanding between Jews and Christians, and there can be no doubt that mutual influences were operative through this cultural interplay, however difficult it may be to document them.

Did the study of the Old Testament and the later rabbinic literature perceptibly influence or promote good personal relations between Christians and Jews? The Christian who was fascinated by the Old Testament narrative and profoundly influenced by its ethic undoubtedly interested himself in the Jew, the child after the flesh of Abraham, Isaac, and Jacob. The truly religious and zealous follower of Christ desired nothing so much as to convert the Jew, the living witness to the authenticity of Christian origins. Even so, there was no far-reaching transfer of concern from the Hebrew tongue of the ancient Hebrew people to the Jews who lived in colonial America. Love of the Hebrew language did not necessarily signify love for one's latter-day "Hebrew" neighbor. The brilliant eighteenth century jurist, politician, and orator William Smith I was a good Hebraist, but that did not stop him from rising on the floor of the New York Provincial Assembly to mount a bitter attack on the Jews. The fact that Jews were the descendants of the prophets brought them no special respect or affection. If individual Jews were respected by Christians, it was because they had earned that respect, not because they were the children of biblical antiquity. The Jew of the colonies was deemed an infidel, and he had to struggle for whatever recognition he achieved socially, economically, or politically.[19]

Yet Christians and Jews did share ten-thirteenths of the Christian Bible; that is to say, they had in common an attachment to the Old Testament and thus to what the twentieth century would call the Judaeo-Christian tradition. Neither Jews nor Christians were as yet generally conscious of a shared heritage, but certainly it was to that heritage that the Jew owed some part of his limited acceptance by what was predominantly a Christian world and culture. The more the Christian read his Bible in Hebrew and in English, the more prepared he was to accept the Jew in the American body politic, not as one of his own to be sure, but still as one who had some connection with him. To some degree, then, a common Old Testament strengthened toleration of the Jew, and Hebraism furthered the integration of the Jew into American life.[20]